Hitler's
Spanish Legion

The Blue Division in Russia

GERALD R. KLEINFELD

and

LEWIS A. TAMBS

Southern Illinois University Press

CARBONDALE AND EDWARDSVILLE

Feffer & Simons, Inc.

LONDON AND AMSTERDAM

Copyright © 1979 by Southern Illinois University Press
All rights reserved
Printed in the United States of America
Designed by Guy Fleming

Library of Congress Cataloging in Publication Data

Kleinfeld, Gerald R   1936–
   Hitler's Spanish Legion.

   Bibliography: p.
   Includes index.
   1. World War, 1939–1945—Campaigns—Russia. 2. World War, 1939–
1945—Regimental histories—Germany—250. Infanteriedivision.   3. Germany. Heer. 250. Infanteriedivision (1941–1943)—History.   4. Russia—
History—German occupation—1941–1944. I. Tambs, Lewis A., 1927–
joint author. II. Title.
D764.K525   940.54′21   78-15677
ISBN 0-8093-0865-7

CONTENTS

List of Maps and Illustrations

Maps

Illustrations
(between pages 90–91)

Ramón Serrano Suñer delivering his "Russia Is Guilty" speech
Guripas of the Blue Division in transit to Grafenwöhr
Capt. Günther Collatz of the German Liaison Staff
Spanish volunteers passing through Novgorod
Gen. Friedrich Herrlein and Gen. Muñoz Grandes
Gen. Franz von Roques and Muñoz Grandes
Elements of 262 Regiment entering the kremlin at Novgorod
Surveying the enemy's former field of fire
Lt. José Escobedo

PREFACE

THE BLUE DIVISION, Spain's contribution to the Russo-German war, 1941–45, is a microcosm of the Eastern Campaign. Joining Army Group North as the 250 Infantry Division in the German order of battle, this Spanish expeditionary force served continuously in the line for two years in the siege of Leningrad. Participating in efforts to envelop the city and repelling Red Army attempts to liberate the besieged metropolis, the *División Española de Voluntarios* experienced some of the most bitter fighting on the Eastern Front. These Spanish volunteers give an entirely different perspective to the siege of Leningrad which is neither Communist nor Nazi, but Mediterranean. In culture, command structure, and tactics, the Blue Division was worlds apart from the other elements of the Wehrmacht. Their story is not merely of units and battles, but of human beings and of a great diplomatic struggle of World War II—Adolf Hitler's efforts to draw Spain into the conflict.

For many of the young Spaniards who volunteered, the Russo-German war was a continuation of their own Civil War of 1936–39—a crusade against communism. They, along with thousands of Belgians, Danes, Dutch, French, Norwegians, and Swedes, felt themselves part of an assault generation destined to revitalize Europe. Fascism had an appeal. The defense of Christendom against atheistic communism, incongruous as an alliance with Nazi Germany might be, attracted many more.

Francisco Franco, Caudillo and dictator of Spain, was as much repelled by national socialism as bolshevism. Nevertheless, he believed that the Axis might win and sought to aggrandize Spain by assuring his country a place in the New Order. For the sake of Gibraltar and North Africa, he was willing to risk war with the Allies, but only at the "hour of the last cartridge." When Hitler invaded the Soviet Union in 1941, Franco saw an opportunity to continue his anti-Communist crusade, repay the debt to the Axis for aid during the Civil War, and rid the country of the more ardent members of the Falange. He dispatched the

Blue Division and an air squadron. Since the Blue Squadron fought in a different theatre than the division, its story is not covered in this work. The Blue Division became a vehicle for diplomatic intrigue. Hitler conspired with pro-Axis Falangists and Spanish generals to topple Franco. The cautious Caudillo would be shunted aside and replaced with an amenable quisling. But Franco survived and achieved his ultimate objective—keeping his battered and starving country at peace and incidentally preserving his own regime. With the passing of the Caudillo in 1975, the veterans of the Blue Division—civilian and military alike— hold high positions under the monarchy. The bonds formed at the front continue to hold.

THIS STUDY OF THE SPANISH DIVISION OF VOLUNTEERS would not have been possible without the splendid cooperation of the *Servicio Histórico Militar* in Madrid. Brig. Gen. José Caruana y Gómez de Barreda, Director of the *Servicio Histórico Militar*, was most generous in allowing the authors full and free access to all the documents in the *Archivo de la Guerra de Liberación* relating to the Blue Division. Brigadier Caruana's staff, especially Lt. Col. José María Gárate Córdova, Lt. Col. José Sánchez Díaz, Maj. José Fournier Pérez, and Capt. Jesús Fernández González were particularly helpful.

The kindness of Brigadier Caruana in allowing us to microfilm the documents and Maj. José Julio de Valcarcel de las Casas in skillfully carrying out this task is worthy of special mention.

We are also deeply indebted to Don Manuel Guijarro y Agüero and his family for their hospitality as well as his tireless efforts in arranging interviews with numerous veterans of the Russian Campaign. Don Manuel Guijarro as an officer and active member of the *Hermandad Nacional de Ex-Combatientes de la División Azul* did everything in his power to aid the authors in contacting former *divisionarios* of all ranks and social classes.

Don Ramón Serrano Suñer not only provided us with keen insights and invaluable information, but also showed us every kindness and cordiality. We are especially grateful to Don Ramón Serrano Suñer for his frankness and willingness to grant us multiple interviews in 1971 and 1974.

Special mention must be made of Fernando Vadillo, who shared with us his vast knowledge of the Blue Division and who was always most willing to be of service. Lt. Col. Norberto Aragón, former Spanish Military Attaché in Washington, D.C., cooperated in making many contacts for us in Spain.

Biographical, organizational, and technical materials were supplied by the *Bundesarchiv-Militärarchiv*, Freiburg, and Bürgermeister i. R. Ottomar Krug; documents of the German Embassy, Madrid, by the Political Archives of the German Foreign Ministry, Bonn, through the assistance of Dr. Hans Guenther Sasse. Microfilms of *Hoja de Campaña* were provided by the *Ibero-Amerikanisches Institut*, Berlin. Embassy Councillor First Class Dr. Jürgen Kalkbrenner of the Embassy of the Federal Republic and Col. Gustav von Detten, Military Attaché, were also helpful. The *Bibliothek für Zeitgeschichte*, Stuttgart, under the auspices of Dr. Jürgen Rohwer, offered assistance; and Deputy Director Werner Haupt was particularly helpful. Dr. Robert Dorn of the firm of Otto Harrassowitz and others were instrumental in locating a number of veterans. In particular, Karl Vitus Schneider, President of the *Kameraden des ehemaligen Verbindungsstabes zur spanischen (250.) Division* offered suggestions and contact with other veterans of the Liaison Staff. Officers and soldiers of the Liaison Staff and of neighboring German divisions, were most generous in sharing their recollections. Lt. Col. (ret.) Konrad Zeller, President of the Veterans Association of the 215 Infantry Division, Col. (ret.) Heinrich Nolte, President of the Veterans Association of the 18 Motorized Infantry Division, and Maj. (ret.) Werner Bruch, President of the Veterans Association of the 126 Infantry Division, were invaluable in providing assistance.

The authors wish to acknowledge the assistance of the Archivist of the United States, Dr. James Rhoads. The Director of the Modern Military Records Section of the National Archives, Dr. Robert Wolfe, and his staff, including Mr. George Wagner and Dr. Mendelssohn were untiring in their aid.

Lt. Gen. P. A. Zhilin, Director of the Institute of Military History of the USSR, and Anatoly M. Dyuzhev, First Secretary, Cultural Section, of the Embassy of the USSR, Washington, D.C., offered assistance.

Arizona State University has been most generous in supporting this project. The authors have received Faculty Research Grants for travel to Spain, Germany, the Soviet Union, the United Kingdom, and the National Archives in Washington, D.C. Former Vice President William J. Burke and former Dean of the College of Liberal Arts George A. Peek, Jr., provided additional assistance. The History Department Associates and Chairmen Paul G. Hubbard and Wallace E. Adams were also most helpful.

Numerous typists have labored over the manuscript. In particular we should like to thank Grace Skinaway, Norma Rhodes, Mary Lou Roach, Patricia Williams, Vicky Jarvie, Meredith Snapp, Mary Payne, and Mary Frances Knox.

Our research has been aided by the efforts of the following former students: Richard Super, Craig Bills, and Donald Steuter. Special thanks go to Alexander Birkos of Mount Shasta, California, and Ellen Kaufmann of Arizona State University for translating Russian language materials.

We appreciate the initial encouragement of Professor Charles B. Burdick of San José State University and Professor Donald Detwiler of Southern Illinois University. José Gibernau of Scottsdale, Arizona and Barcelona, Spain was also most helpful.

Any errors are the sole responsibility of the authors.

GERALD R. KLEINFELD
LEWIS A. TAMBS

Arizona State University
Tempe, Arizona
15 April 1978

Hitler's

Spanish Legion

NOTE *on Abbreviations, Titles, and German and Spanish Words Used in the Text*

HKL   *Hauptkampflinie*, main line of resistance (MLR)
OKW   *Oberkommando der Wehrmacht*, High Command of the Armed Forces
OKH   *Oberkommando des Heeres*, High Command of the Army
AOK   *Armeeoberkommando*, Army High Command
OKL   *Oberkommando der Luftwaffe*, High Command of the Air Force
OKM   *Oberkommando der Kriegsmarine*, High Command of the Navy
         Rollbahn, motor highway, especially Novgorod-Chudovo highway
         The various ranks of general officers are abbreviated to "General."

FORMATION TITLES *are capitalized and given in the following form in the text:*

ARMY

Army Group North
18 Army
XXXVIII Army Corps
250 Division, for German infantry divisions
288 Rifle Division, for Russian rifle divisions
18 Motorized, for German motorized divisions
12 Panzer, for German armored divisions
3 Armored, for Russian armored divisions
269 Regiment
269 Grenadiers, for German grenadier regiments
Second of 269, for Second Battalion of 269 Regiment
1 Antitanks, for First Company of Antitanks

AIR FORCE

Air Fleet 2
VIII Air Corps

ARTILLERY

Second Artillery, for Second Artillery Group
12 Battery

Guripa and *Landser* are words for Spanish and German GIs.
Panienka was the Spanish reference, picked up along the march in Poland and applied to any peasant girl.

1

"Russia Is Guilty"

GERMAN FOREIGN MINISTER JOACHIM VON RIBBEN-
trop was a confident man. On Sunday, 22 June 1941, as the Wehrmacht
sliced through unsuspecting Russian defenses, he expected that the war
just begun would soon be over. After Russia was destroyed, the Germans could turn once more to England and Gibraltar. That was why
the foreign minister was so interested in the dispatch from Madrid.

The Spanish capital was exploding with joy, Ambassador Eberhard
von Stohrer wrote to his chief, as he described a conversation with
Spain's foreign minister, Ramón Serrano Suñer. Serrano Suñer had just
come from a conference with the Caudillo and chief of state, his brother-
in-law, Francisco Franco Bahamonde. Spain wanted to participate in
the war against communism. Spain would help. Spain offered volunteers. Would the Germans accept the assistance of armed units of the
Falange, the dominant political movement in Spain?[1]

Ribbentrop informed the Führer of the Spanish offer at once. Adolf
Hitler immediately grasped the propaganda value of foreign volunteers
in a war against Communist Russia, but he viewed a Spanish expeditionary force as something more. A volunteer legion of Spaniards, he
told Army Chief of Staff Gen. Franz Halder on the afternoon of 24
June, would bind Franco to the Reich. He directed Ribbentrop to press
Serrano Suñer for a formal declaration of war against the USSR.[2] As for
the volunteers, Ribbentrop cabled Stohrer in Madrid that same day:
"All right, but tell them to hurry."[3]

Serrano Suñer was a dedicated anti-Communist, but he had not lost his head. He knew what problems Spain would have to face if there were an official participation in the war against Soviet Russia. Franco was also a confirmed anti-Communist. Two years earlier, just after Spain had joined the Anti-Comintern Pact, Germany had betrayed that agreement by signing an alliance with the Soviet Union to carve up Catholic Poland. Then, with German acquiescence, the USSR had attacked Finland. Enraged, Franco had shipped arms to the hapless Finns and even considered sending volunteers to aid them, but dropped the plan because it was impractical and dangerous. The chief of state was, after all, a hard realist, to whom the interests of Spain were paramount.

With the invasion of Communist Russia by Germany, Great Britain and the USSR became allies. Neither foreign minister nor Caudillo wished to risk war with Britain. The Royal Navy controlled the seas over which passed grain and petroleum, vital to the Spanish economy. If Spain moved officially against Soviet Russia, Britain would retaliate. But, with the German Wehrmacht seemingly dominant on the European continent, no amount of British sympathy for Russia could dampen the public joy of the Spaniards.[4]

In the forty-eight hours after the Spanish foreign minister called on the German Embassy, it became quite evident that Serrano Suñer had not misread his people. The peninsula erupted with enthusiasm for Hitler's new war. The military, already impressed by the Nazi blitzkrieg against France, was eager to see the Wehrmacht destroy the Red Army. Since Serrano Suñer was chief of the *Junta Política* of the Falange as well as foreign minister, he had offered Falangist volunteers to the Germans. But the Spanish Army wanted to go as well. The generals were ready to send an entire corps! Their offer contained more than a hint of the traditional rivalry between army and Falange that dated from the Civil War (1936–39).[5]

The excitement in Spain did not abate. Serrano Suñer received Ribbentrop's acceptance of the Spanish offer of volunteers on Tuesday morning, 24 June. He was preparing to see the chief of the Falangist Militia, General Moscardó, the hero of the Alcázar of Civil War fame, in order to initiate recruitment, when he learned that crowds had spontaneously gathered in the center of Madrid. They were marching down the Avenida de José Antonio toward the confluence of that important artery with the broad Calle de Alcalá where the headquarters of the Falange was located.[6]

Party Minister Arrese and Secretary of Agriculture Miguel Primo de Rivera were in the massive gray building which housed the offices of secretary general of the *Falange de las JONS* (the official name of the movement, meaning Spanish Phalanx of the Committees of National Syndicalist Action). They heard the rumble of the approaching masses and rushed to the double doors that opened on to the second-floor balcony, which jutted out from the facade of the building. Above the balcony, commanding an excellent view of both José Antonio and the Alcalá, loomed an enormous red metal sculpture of the yoke and arrows, symbol of the Falange. Biting his moustache, Arrese stood behind the double doors and peered through the panes at the oncoming wave which rolled down José Antonio toward Falangist headquarters.

A crest of color rippled down the street. Falangist blue mingled with the black of the SEU (University Student Syndicate). This, and the absence of red, reassured Arrese. After all, the Civil War had ended only a few years earlier and "Red Madrid" had not accepted the Nationalist Government with unmitigated joy. The crowds were pro-Falangist, at least. But what did they want? Nervously, the short, slight, pale-faced Arrese reached for the telephone and called Serrano Suñer at the Foreign Ministry on the nearby Plaza de Santa Cruz.[7]

Serrano Suñer grasped the situation at once. He raced to Falange headquarters and passed quickly inside, almost unobserved. Scarcely pausing to speak with Arrese, he made directly for the balcony and stepped outside to receive a thunderous ovation. Smiling, Serrano Suñer accepted the deafening acclamation and surveyed the scene below. The crowd was largely, though perhaps not predominantly, youthful. There were obviously many students from the university, but women and working men were also evident.

The Calle de Alcalá was jammed. The throng overflowed into the Plaza de la Cibeles. People pressed against the great doors of the Church of San José directly across the street, hung from the massive iron fence surrounding the War Ministry on the opposite corner, and clung to the heavy columns of the Bank of Spain next door. Others, more agile or adventurous, dangled from the branches of the acacia trees which lined the Calle de Alcalá, while a few perched precariously on the narrow marquee of the Cafe La Elipa.

The warm June sun beat down through a cloudless azure sky on the tumultuous and perspiring masses. The slender young foreign minister, his prematurely silver hair glistening in the sunlight, waved his arms and

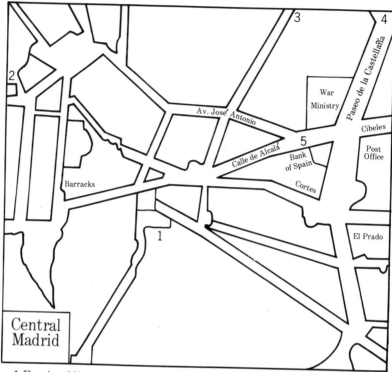

1 Foreign Ministry
2 Estación del Norte
3 to British Embassy
4 to German Embassy
5 Secretariat of the Falange

Central Madrid

drank in the enthusiasm of the moment. Then, he gave his people what they wanted—a bold, passionate speech.

"Comrades. It is not the time for speeches. But it is the moment for the Falange to dictate its sentence of condemnation: Russia is guilty!"

The throng thundered its agreement. "*Arriba España! Viva Franco!*" the excited *madrileños* shouted. Having struck the proper chord, Serrano Suñer forged ahead.

"Russia is guilty! Guilty of our Civil War. Guilty of the murder of José Antonio [Primo de Rivera], our founder [of the Falange]."[8]

But the crowd would not let him continue. People wept and screamed with a pent-up fury founded in years of bitter civil war. Here and there total strangers grabbed one another by the arm and shouted at the tops of their lungs in unison: "Russia is guilty! *Arriba España! Viva Franco!*" Joy mixed with hatred and anger. Feeling at one with his audience, Serrano Suñer summed up his credo: "Guilty of the murder of so many comrades—and so many soldiers who fell in that war brought on by the aggression of Russian Communism. The destruction of Communism is a necessary condition for the survival of a free and civilized Europe."[9]

Shouts of *Arriba España* and *Viva Franco, Viva Alemania* from everywhere in the crowd. Then came a deafening roar: "Death to Soviet Russia!" No one in the War Ministry, or for miles around for that matter, could escape the knowledge that this was a powerful and spontaneous outflowing of genuine sympathy for the new German war.

Knots of Falangist youths detached themselves from the dispersing throng and raced past the War Ministry heading toward the British Embassy on Fernando El Santo. The youths, although the crowd had been cautioned by Serrano Suñer to disperse and keep the peace, were in a fighting mood. Most of them were followers of the Anglophobe Arrese. They gathered at the British Embassy, shouting "Gibraltar is ours" and stoned the compound.[10]

The recovery of Gibraltar indeed was a primary objective of the Falange. It had also been a lynchpin of Spanish foreign policy for over 200 years. Moreover, control of that crucial rock and the western access to the Mediterranean was a goal of Nazi Germany since the fall of France in 1940. Acquisition of Gibraltar by the Axis would cut the British lifeline through Suez. Thus, the rock was uppermost in the minds of both Hitler and Franco when they had met at Hendaye after the French collapse in 1940. Franco had already moved from neutrality to the ambiguous state of "nonbelligerency" after the impressive German victory over Spain's northern neighbor. Führer and Caudillo discussed possible Spanish entry into the war and a joint campaign against Gibraltar, Operation Felix. However, Franco wanted no war in 1940, least of all against Great Britain, whose naval power he feared. He made too many conditions and the idea was shelved.

Despite the initial enthusiasm among the general population, in the government, the army, and the Falange, the Caudillo and his advisers had no intention of sending more than a token force. An infantry division would suffice. The volunteer unit would not be composed exclusively of Falangists, as Serrano Suñer had originally proposed to Stohrer, for the army intervened.[11]

The Spanish General Staff insisted that the officers and technicians of the volunteer division be selected from regular army volunteers. This demand was not a matter of vanity; it was a necessity. These professionals would unify the division, give it order and discipline under fire, and guarantee that the unit would be a credit to the Spanish military tradition. Drawing men from various occupations, educational levels, and grades of military experience, and shipping them to the Russian front with a minimum of training might provide opportunity for glamorous cases of individual heroism, but a collective slaughter might ensue if the division were not guided and led by trained professionals. Moreover, the General Staff had no desire to allow the Falange, its chief rival in domestic politics, to garner the glory for victories on the battlefields of Soviet Russia. The recruitment orders of 27 June emphasized the desire of the Franco regime to dispatch a truly national force under expert and loyal leadership. Military and Falange would join in the projected 18,000-man expeditionary force.

Announcement of recruitment for the volunteer division brought ecstatic response. Eager German consular officials reported case after case of excited Spaniards rushing to enlist. Their dispatches, from Córdoba and Pamplona, from Madrid and Morocco, gloried in the "unanimous" approval of the Spanish press and the encouraging crowds of volunteers anxiously hoping for a chance to fight the Bolsheviks. Within a few days, Ambassador von Stohrer was able to telegraph Berlin that more than forty times the required number had rushed to enlist.[12]

Despite the crush of volunteers, the General Staff directives were most precise about the composition of the division. In a directive of 28 June to the commanders of the various military regions in Spain and Morocco, the military chiefs laid down the terms for recruitment. The volunteers were to enlist for the duration of the campaign. The unit was to be termed "Spanish Division of Volunteers" (*División Española de Voluntarios*—DEV). All officers above the rank of second lieutenant were to be regulars.

The command of the DEV would be fully in the hands of the military hierarchy. Mixing between the Nationalist army and the Falangist militia would occur at lower levels, although some officers were also active Falangists. Two-thirds of the second lieutenants and sergeants were to be regulars, one-third militia. All specialists and technicians, however, were to be members of the regular army. The rank and file of the DEV was to be raised among the civil population, recruited by local Falangist militia chiefs in cooperation with the regional army staffs. If there were not enough recruits, regular soldiers would be permitted to volunteer.

Falangist, regular, or civilian volunteer, all soldiers in the division were to be approved for "political and social solvency." The Franco government, so recently a victor in a long and bloody civil war against Republicans and Communists, could not risk desertions under fire to the Russians. The DEV, which was raised in all the military regions of Spain, led by professionals drawn from all arms, and composed of soldiers from every segment of society, was to be a truly national force.

On both political and professional grounds, Franco had to be very judicious in selecting a commanding general. He wanted a battle-tested commander who would be acceptable both to the Falange and to the army, but who would also be loyal to him personally. Although of the army, Franco had never been a prisoner of the generals. He knew how to balance forces.

The Falange, determined to control the expedition, was pressing its own nomination for commanding general. Some prominent Falangists urged Franco to select Labor Minister Girón. The army, on the other hand, wanted one of their own heroes to command. For a time Franco considered Generals Moscardó, García Valiño, and Carlos Asensio Cabanillas, chief of the Army General Staff. But, urged on by Serrano Suñer and Falangist student and intellectual leaders such as Enrique Sotomayor and Dionisio Ridruejo who sensed the military's opposition to Girón and who wanted at least a general with Falangist identification, Franco returned to his own first choice. He picked an old comrade from the Moroccan campaigns, General Agustín Muñoz Grandes.

A lean, lanky *madrileño*, Muñoz Grandes was an officer's officer. Born in Madrid's working-class district of Carabanchel Bajo in 1896— he still rolled his own cigarettes—he began his military career at the Infantry Academy at Toledo. Upon graduation in 1913 he volunteered for duty in Morocco where he won rapid promotion during the protracted campaign. As a commander of native forces (*regulares*) he formed an elite unit (*harka*) which bore his name. With the establishment of the Republic in 1931, the new government chose Muñoz Grandes to head the Assault Guards, a paramilitary force designed to counterbalance the traditionalist, and therefore suspect, *Guardia Civil* (National Police).

Dismissed from command of the Assault Guards after the victory of the leftist Popular Front in the 1936 election, Muñoz Grandes found himself in Madrid at the outbreak of the Civil War on 18 July. Caught up in the massacre by the mob and militia, Muñoz Grandes was saved by his former comrades in the Assault Guards and by Republican

General Rojo. The Republican government imprisoned him, but he escaped and fled to the Nationalist lines.[13]

Commander of a rebel army corps during the Civil War, Muñoz Grandes also served briefly in the postwar Franco cabinet as general secretary of the movement and chief of the Falangist militia. During his eight months in office from August 1939 to March 1940, Muñoz Grandes distinguished himself by bombarding provincial Falangist chiefs with directives calling for the elimination of corruption, a more equitable distribution of the limited food supply, and enforcement of regulations on working conditions and minimum wage rates for laborers. Thus, Muñoz Grandes, unlike most career officers, was regarded as close to the social revolutionary element in the Falange.

Muñoz Grandes was one of the foremost soldiers of Spain. Bearing scars of nine battle wounds, he was known for exemplary courage and bravery. An English volunteer who had served under him during the Civil War recalled that Muñoz Grandes was "a magnificent soldier—and incidentally a man of great charm."[14] British Military Intelligence considered Muñoz Grandes "one of their best and most resolute generals."[15] He was also well known to the Germans, having been consulted by Admiral Wilhelm Canaris in connection with the planning for Operation Felix—the joint assault on Gibraltar.

Muñoz Grandes, however, was not eager for the post. Although Franco's first preference, the swarthy, chain-smoking general declined two invitations to consider commanding the volunteers. He was well aware that Serrano Suñer had initiated the project and that the foreign minister wanted the expedition to be a Falangist militia performance. The general's reluctance to accept the command was due to the personal enmity and political rivalry between himself and Serrano Suñer. Muñoz Grandes hated Serrano Suñer and "regarded him as an intriguer who lacked a genuinely nationalist spirit."[16] Muñoz Grandes wanted a new Spain, free of injustice and dedicated to social action. He felt that the generalissimo's brother-in-law had used his position for personal aggrandizement and that in doing so he had blunted the reformist thrust of the movement.[17]

Serrano Suñer, aware that the military hierarchy would not allow Minister of Agriculture Girón to lead the expedition, saw an opportunity to rid himself of a rival. He seconded Franco's choice and pushed the appointment of Muñoz Grandes. On 28 June, Muñoz Grandes was in Madrid. He lunched that afternoon with von Stohrer at the German Embassy on the Paseo de la Castellana. They discussed the volunteer unit and Muñoz Grandes told the Führer's envoy that he "envied with all his heart the general who would command that division."[18]

After lunch, Muñoz Grandes returned home. An urgent message awaited him. He was to call the War Ministry immediately. He rushed to the telephone, and was told that the Caudillo had relieved him of command of the sensitive military district of Gibraltar and appointed him to lead the Division of Volunteers.[19]

Muñoz Grandes knew that his division would be an amalgam, with volunteers drawn from all over Spain. The initial call, issued by the Army General Staff, projected raising roughly 18,000 officers and men from the eight military regions and Morocco. Like his brother officers, the seasoned campaigner wanted a strong stiffening of careerists in the expedition for he privately confided "that if he had to go he did not want to have toy soldiers with him."[20]

The division was structured according to the traditional Spanish model with four infantry regiments, each bearing the name of the officer commanding, and one artillery regiment. The four infantry regiments were: Regiment Rodrigo (Col. Miguel Rodrigo Martínez), Regiment Pimentel (Col. Pedro Pimentel Zayas), Regiment Vierna (Col. José Vierna Trábaga), Regiment Esparza (Col. José Martínez Esparza). Each regiment was composed of units from different military regions. (See Appendix.)

The first general order of the division confirmed the raising of these four regiments, but this was merely a provisional arrangement. Since a typical German infantry division had only three regiments, the Spaniards foresaw a reduction to three regiments by amalgamation. One of the regimental colonels was slated to become second in command of the division. The General Staff, however, fearing disruption of the recruitment effort, kept this information secret. Not even the regimental colonels were informed.[21]

Recruitment for the Regiment Rodrigo centered in the capital city. Outside the recruiting office at 62 Paseo del Generalissimo, long lines of eager volunteers filed past the posters proclaiming "Once again Spain discovers its universal mission," "We pay the Russians a return visit," "The Falange will fight Communism in its lair." Throngs of men of various ages, from fuzzy-cheeked youths to gray-haired old anti-Communists, pressed toward the tables set up in the patio of the hotel, which served as a recruiting office. Some, dressed in sporty white shoes, looked as if they were ready for a promenade in the fashionable Park El Retiro. Others were in blue mechanics' coveralls, dark business suits,

Military Regions of Spain
1941

Coruña
VIII

Burgos
VI

Barcelona
IV

Valladolid
VII

Saragossa
V

Madrid
I

Valencia
III

Seville
II

Morocco, the Balearics, and the Canaries form two additional
regions, but have no official numbers.

and a variety of other outfits, all of which served to emphasize the
broad popularity of the "crusade," as it was beginning to be called.
One enthusiastic recruit was a square set, middle-aged academician—
Fernando María Castiella, professor of international law at the University of Madrid, a member of the Permanent Tribunal of International
Arbitration at The Hague, and author (with José Maria Areilza y Martínez Rodas) of the prizewinning work, *Reivindicaciones de España*
calling for the restoration of Spain's African empire. Despite his age
and authority, Castiella signed on as a common soldier.

Friends and relatives came together, hoping to serve in the same
unit. The volunteers were registered, given a cursory physical examination and, if accepted, were directed to report to the barracks—Infante Don Juan, Amaniel, or El Pardo. The recruiting officers worked

frantically, weeding out the obviously unfit and making a special effort to select chauffeurs and motor vehicle mechanics. Their own experience in the Civil War, the vaunted mechanization of the Wehrmacht, and initial communications from the Germans had seemed to urge the Spaniards to prepare for a motorized campaign. On the last day of regular recruiting, 2 July, the office remained open until 10:00 P.M. There was also a crush of officers hoping to enlist. When all posts had been filled, forty regular army officers enlisted in the Regiment Rodrigo as common soldiers.

Falangist militiamen were reporting directly to Infante Don Juan. Many ardent young members of the official movement responded with an eagerness that all but eclipsed their more mundane lives. Like Juan Eugenio Blanco, who boarded street car number forty-nine for the barracks, they were caught up in the glory of their mission. As Blanco's tram rattled along, the young man was so carried away by his imagination that he completely overlooked another volunteer, Enrique Sotomayor, only a few feet away. Sotomayor, a university student and noted old-guard Falangist, who had been named by his friend Muñoz Grandes editor of the Seville periodical *FE*, was also on his way to Infante Don Juan.

Upon alighting, they had to slip through the press of parents, wives and sweethearts who jammed the street and sidewalk outside the barracks. Both Blanco and Sotomayor were assigned to the antitank company of the Regiment Rodrigo. A number of prestigious Falangists were enrolled in this unit. Among them was Agustín Aznar, a member of the Falangist National Council and general director for health, and Vicente Gaceo del Pino, editor of *Arriba* and an intimate of José Antonio. Also in the Regiment Rodrigo was Dionisio Ridruejo, a member of both the National and Political Council of the Falange, general director of Falangist propaganda, and one of Spain's most distinguished neoclassical poets.[22]

Since the Regiment Rodrigo was raised in Madrid it enrolled an unusually large number of university students. Some 3,000 members of the *Sindicato Español Universitario* (SEU) clamored for admission. One of the first in line was José Manuel Guitarte, an "old shirt" who had been appointed by José Antonio himself as national secretary of the incipient SEU. Apprehended in the Republican zone in 1936, Guitarte survived three years incarceration. After his liberation in 1939, he was appointed *Inspector Nacional* of the Falange's Youth Organizations. Like many Falangists who had passed the Civil War in Republican prisons he seized the opportunity to prove his loyalty to Franco and pay the Soviets a return visit in 1941. Thus, although he was a national councilor of the Falange and the national chief of the SEU, Guitarte enlisted as a private.[23]

Like Guitarte, many of the Falangists conceived of themselves as members of an assault generation and recognized that their ranking in the new Spain and in the New Order in Europe could only be bought and paid for in blood. Their commitment would be tested on the battlefields of Russia.

Although quite a few of the prominent Falangists who rushed to enlist had fought in the Civil War, as had many of the other volunteers, these recruits lacked specialized training. Instruction began immediately. The antitank company then joined the rest of the Regiment Rodrigo in the first general muster of the regiment on Friday, 4 July.

The ruins of the University City echoed to roll call as masses of volunteers joined their formations on the esplanade of the new Faculty of Medicine. Already, at 7:00 A.M., the bright summer sun beat down from a clear sky. Most of the soldiers wore their new uniforms—the red beret of the Carlists, the blue shirt of the Falange, the khaki trousers of the Spanish Foreign Legion, and black boots. The officers' attire consisted of the red beret, a khaki tunic with blue collar and cuffs, a leather harness belt, khaki trousers, and high black boots. The predominance of Falangist blue, so evident on the sunny esplanade, had already prompted citizens and politicians alike to dub this volunteer division the "Blue Division."

After roll call and close order drill, the Regiment Rodrigo moved out for the first of a series of training marches. Invoking the spirit of José Antonio, the soldiers broke into song as they tramped across the dry Castillian countryside. They sang "Cara al Sol," the hymn of the Falange.

Face to the sun with my new blue shirt which you embroidered yesterday in red. Death will find me if it seeks me and I will never see you again. I will fall in with my other comrades who stand guard among the eternal stars, but whose posture, even in death, proclaims courage.

If they tell you that I have fallen, I have gone to my post which awaits me there. Victorious banners emblazoned with the yoke and arrows will return to the joyful cadence of peace. Smiling spring will return to the awaiting sky, earth, and sea. Forward squadrons to conquer! A new day dawns for Spain![24]

The antitankers struck up a brighter note, improvising "Russia is only a question of a day for our infantry. Thanks to the antitankers, it will all be over even sooner." [25] While the brash antitankers of Madrid thus reduced the immense task ahead to an adventurous promenade, the other regiments were assembling in the provinces.

The Regiment Pimentel was raised in Valladolid, Burgos, La Coruña, and Valencia. In Valladolid, where the headquarters company, the Second Infantry Battalion, and one section of 150 mm. artillery were assembled, great numbers of volunteers crowded the Provincial Falange Office on Santiago Street. There, as in Madrid, the local officials were hard pressed to expedite enlistment. After enrollment, recruits reported to the barracks San Quentín where they trained under the practiced eye of Lt. Col. Mariano Gómez Zamalloa, who was charged with training and organizing the regiment.

At the military academy of Saragossa where numerous provisional second lieutenants from the Civil War were completing cadet infantry training prior to receiving regular commissions, the call for volunteers evoked a unanimous response. The class of 1941, an entire battalion, stepped forward.[26] Clearly, not all could go. Only the graduates with highest marks in tactics and topography were posted to the Blue Division.

There were professional as well as ideological reasons for volunteering. Although promotion in the peacetime Spanish Army was based on length of service and time in grade, combat duty was credited as double time. Giving official status to the Blue Division, the Ministry of War decreed that it would recognize the Russian front as a combat zone. Thus one month with the Blue Division was worth two months garrison duty in Spain. Medals were worth even more. A *Cruz Laureada de San Fernando* or a *Medalla Militar Individual* would raise an officer's ranking in his class of the military academy and allow him, through recognized meritorious service, to advance ahead of his classmates on the promotion list. Ambitious young officers, particularly provisional second lieutenants who had only recently decided to make the service their career, reached anxiously for the opportunity and adventure of a new campaign.

The officers of Barcelona volunteered to a man. No one was more pleased than their chief, General Kindelán, commander of IV Military Region. Kindelán had engineered Franco's nomination in 1936 as chief of state and, as Nationalist air commander during the Civil War, had formed close connections with the Caudillo and Germans of the Nazi

Spain 1941

Atlantic Ocean

France

San Sebastián

Bilbao

Burgos

Catalonia

Gerona

Lerida

Barcelona

Avila

Madrid

Murcia

Portugal

Córdoba

Andalucia

Murcia

Seville

Malaga

Cádiz

Gibraltar

Mediterranean Sea

Algeria

Morocco

Condor Legion, such as Col. (later Gen.) Wolfram von Richthofen. Although a monarchist, Kindelán was considered one of the most pro-German of Spanish generals. He had written Ambassador von Stohrer supporting the attack on the Soviet Union as soon as the news broke.

Kindelán was more than pleased that the Regiment Vierna, which was being raised principally in the military regions of Barcelona and Valencia, would have an ample supply of trained leaders. More officers volunteered than needed. Although active regulars were being brought into the Blue Division at rank, some reserve officers were obliged to accept positions as noncommissioned officers (NCOs) or as common soldiers. But even officers who had already been selected found their positions in jeopardy as political pressure from the Falange mounted. Changes were even forced at the higher levels. Major Santos García, who had been designated commander of Vierna's Second Battalion, mustering in Gerona, was suddenly replaced. The Falangist provincial militia chief in Gerona took over the battalion himself.

The Catalan Falange played a heavy role in recruitment. Not only did the movement seek to place its men in command positions, but it tried also to keep non-Falangists out of the ranks. When Carlists in the towns of Manresa and Lerida began to volunteer for the Blue Division against the wishes of their own leaders, they found themselves rejected by the Falange![27]

The Falangist recruitment chief in Barcelona, Lieutenant Colonel de Montys, required that all volunteers submit documents attesting to their political solvency. De Montys demanded either papers in the Falange or certificates of discharge from Nationalist forces in the Civil War. De Montys' restrictive practices, and the efforts of the Falange to secure a stranglehold on Second and Third Battalions of the Regiment Vierna, produced a crisis in recruitment. Separatist Catalonia, which had sided with the Republic during the Civil War, was naturally reluctant to support any enterprise of the Nationalist government in Madrid. Recruitment policies which seemed reasonable to Falangist leaders only tended to dry up still further the sources of volunteers.

Enthusiasm in the Catalan capital for Hitler's war against Soviet Russia was undeniably mixed. In the working-class districts, talk of a Spanish expeditionary force was met by unfriendly expressions. Sneering laborers muttered: "Why should we send our sons to Russia? The Germans sitting here in Spain should go!"[28] Those sentiments were reflected in the workers' absence from the recruiting lines. Most of the Barcelona volunteers came from the middle class. Younger sons of military families were especially evident.

In the rush to fill the Barcelona quota, medical officers pushed volunteers through the superficial physical examination with unusual haste. One particularly eager young man went through without any difficulty. He was able to conceal the fact that he had only one foot. At the last moment, he was extricated through the tearful intervention of his parents. When they could not get enough civilian volunteers, Falange leaders looked to the military. But the rank and file remained unmoved by the example of their officers. They declined to step forward. The situation was becoming embarrassing. Finally, after some delay, 1,200 soldiers of the Barcelona Military Region declared their willingness to go. In Gerona, the entire garrison was induced to volunteer. However, even Jaeger, the ever-vigilant German consul general, doubted whether they were "authentic" volunteers. Barcelona failed to meet its quota. The shortage was made up by shipments of volunteers from Valencia.[29]

Unlike the lukewarm attitude which prevailed in Barcelona, Spaniards in Cartagena, Valencia, and elsewhere in the districts from which Vierna drew his recruits were rushing to enlist. In Castellón, enrollment opened on 3 July and closed on 4 July. The quota was filled on the first day. While the volunteers in Barcelona marched down nearly empty streets, with only the cheers of a few passersby to wish them well, joyful crowds clogged avenues and railroad stations in Murcia and Cartagena. Trains carrying the soldiers to Valencia were forced to inch their way slowly forward through the excited multitude which blocked the tracks.[30]

Colonel Vierna knew the task before him as the recruits streamed into the depot. It would be difficult to mold them quickly into a fighting force ready for the rigors of the Russian front. But Vierna was no desk officer. He was an officer of the Third *Tercio* (Regiment) of the Spanish Foreign Legion and a combat-hardened veteran of both the Moroccan and Civil Wars. Another *africanista*, Lieutenant Colonel Canillas, was second in command. Canillas left the Caliph's Guard— the *Fuerzas Jalifianas*—to join the Vierna Regiment.[31]

Another *africanista*, Colonel Esparza, commanded an infantry regiment of 22 Division at Algeciras, in the shadow of Gibraltar. Esparza did not believe the first reports that Spaniards were going to be enlisted for war "against Communism." He thought that this was just another of the many rumors that had been circulating in the week since the Nazi attack. He remained skeptical until the provincial headquarters on the Falange advised him early on 29 June that recruitment had begun. Esparza informed the regiment at once, and offered himself as one of the first volunteers.[32]

The response was electric. Volunteers besieged the Falangist headquarters in Algeciras. Among the civilians, veterans of the Civil War and former Republican captives predominated. The surplus prompted many anxious young men to bury the recruiting officers in sheaves of recommendations, which, the colonel mused, were actually petitions to face death.

Death was no stranger to Esparza. An experienced campaigner, the short, chubby colonel was known for a volatile temperament which froze into icy calm in the face of battle. The energetic Esparza longed for the opportunity to test his skill against the Russians. But there would be few openings for regimental commanders in the Blue Division. Nevertheless, the colonel's heart skipped a beat when *Radio Macuto*—the army grapevine—brought word that his own general, Muñoz Grandes, the commander of 22 Division, had been appointed to lead the Spanish expeditionary force. Seeking confirmation, Esparza contacted the general's adjutant, Lieutenant Colonel Cárcer, who was with Muñoz Grandes in Madrid. Cárcer was noncommittal, but his manner seemed affirmative. Further evidence that something was afoot came from hasty preparations—obviously for a long journey—that could be observed at the absent general's residence.

On the evening of 29 June, after having assured his family how unlikely it would be that he might be accepted, even if Muñoz Grandes were in fact to command the Blue Division, Esparza went off to a party at the *Jardín del General*. The brilliant lights of Algeciras illuminated the bay as the officers gathered in knots to discuss the Russian war. Across the harbor, they could barely see the blacked-out British outpost of Gibraltar. The party had just begun when a messenger arrived. Esparza was ordered at once to Seville to organize a regiment of the Blue Division. He raced home to break the news to his wife and, while she packed, started to pull together a staff.

It was only natural that the colonel would look to former comrades-in-arms. For Second Battalion, he chose Maj. Miguel Román Garrido. He knew Román from the African campaigns and also from the Civil War, where they had served together in the 122 Division. Román's battalion, though organized in Seville, was raised mostly in the province of Jaen, and was consequently thoroughly Andalusian. While Second Battalion assembled in the barracks of La Puerta de la Carne, Esparza sought a commander for Third Battalion. He remembered Maj. Pérez Pérez from the colonial campaigns in the *Tercio*. He was another good campaigner and was tapped to lead Third Battalion from Ceuta in Morocco.[33]

The Spanish high commissioner in Morocco, General Orgaz, had already volunteered all the forces at his command. As he explained to

Richter, the German Consul at Tetuan, this was an *acto simbolico*. The general's gesture did, however, reflect the prevailing attitude among the Spanish troops—the Legion, the *regulares* (native forces under Spanish officers), and the *Flechas* Regiment which garrisoned the Protectorate. A flood of volunteers came forth from these elite units of the regular army. However, in spite of the fact that such prominent Falangists as the mayor of Ceuta volunteered, relatively few members of the official movement stepped forward.

The Third Battalion sailed for Algeciras on Tuesday, 8 July. As the freighter steamed out of the harbor of Ceuta, a large crowd cheered the 2,000 volunteers, who were already wearing the colorful uniform of the Blue Division—red beret of the Carlists, blue shirt of the Falange, and khaki trousers of the Foreign Legion. A jubilant High Commissioner Orgaz headed the official party. Consul Richter provided the German presence, and wished goodbye to his friends, among them Ochoa, the mayor of Ceuta. The ceremony was powerfully impressive, thought Richter, as he looked out across the shimmering waters of the Mediterranean to the massive grey hulk of Gibraltar, which rose straight out of the sea.[34] British eyes followed the ship to Spain. When Third Battalion reached Algeciras, it was joined by Divisional Mobile Reserve Battalion under Major Osés. Osés, who wore the prestigious *Medalla Militar*, was an officer of the *regulares*. He, too, was an old comrade of Esparza. They had served together in the Third Battalion of Volunteers from Ceuta during the Civil War. The Mobile Reserve Battalion had also been raised in Morocco and was composed entirely of officers and men from the *regulares* in Melilla.[35]

Once in Algeciras, both battalions entrained immediately for Seville and were quartered in the barracks of the Pineda and the Falange. The men dropped their equipment and headed straight for the cantinas. All Seville loved the heroes-to-be and scarcely a volunteer had to pay for his own drink. The carousing went on for days, interrupted only by close order drill and route marches. It all has a purpose, the officers reasoned. Even the drinking together helped to develop unit cohesion for a force destined for the rigors of the Russian campaign.

On 10 July, the troops marched to the chapel of the Virgin of the Kings in the cathedral, where the archbishop of Seville celebrated a farewell mass. A delegation of women from the Falange presented the regiment with colors, which were to be carried to the steppes of Russia. Every effort was made to demonstrate popular and government support. At 1500 hours on 15 July, the Esparza Regiment boarded trains in the railroad station at the Plaza de Armas for the trip to Hendaye, on the French frontier. The first leg of a long journey had begun.[36]

Almost from the outset of the war against Russia, the German High Command had prepared for the participation of foreign volunteers. In a war against Bolshevism, tens of thousands of anti-Communist volunteers from neutral and German-occupied countries could be expected. In order to establish guidelines, a secret meeting was held on 30 June in Berlin in the Foreign Office on the Wilhelmstrasse. The committee decided that, in general, foreign volunteers would be enrolled in national units. Germanic and Scandinavian recruits—Danes, Finns, Flemings, Netherlanders, Norwegians and Swedes—would serve in the Waffen-SS. Non-Germanic volunteers—Croats, Portuguese and Spaniards—would be incorporated into the Wehrmacht.[37] Czechs and Russians, except for selected specialists, were to be rejected.

Since the raising of a Spanish expeditionary force was already underway, it was necessary to clear up any questions concerning the integration of the Blue Division into the German armed forces. It had already been agreed that the Spaniards would serve in the Wehrmacht as a unit under Spanish officers. Details relating to organization, equipment, payment, and the like were to be worked out between the OKW and a Spanish Army Commission which was scheduled to arrive in Berlin within a week.

At 7:30 A.M. on 5 July, a regular Iberian Airlines flight carrying the seven-member Spanish Military Commission lifted off the runway at Barajas Airport, outside of Madrid. On board, Lieutenant Colonel Mazariegos, chief of the commission, settled down uncomfortably for the long trip. Major Barrera, chief of communications for the Blue Division, and Major Baldrich, chief of supply, chatted with their colleagues about the war and the prospects of German victory. After a short hop to Barcelona, Iberia's Berlin flight headed north to Marseilles, winged north again to Lyons, and then east to Munich. There was a short holdover, and the aircraft took off at last for the German capital, touching down at Tempelhof Airport at 8:00 P.M. The passengers alighted into the cool breeze of evening.[38]

Waiting anxiously, the Spanish military attaché, Lieutenant Colonel Roca de Togores, Conde de Roca-Mora, strode forward to greet Mazariegos with a bright smile. He introduced a protocol officer of the German High Command and, after a quick exchange of pleasantries, the party set out toward the Potsdam Station and the Tiergarten where they were lodged in luxury at the glamorous Hotel Esplanade on the Bellevuestrasse.

The next morning, although it was Sunday, the commission motored down the Bendlerstrasse to the General Headquarters of the Reserve Army (*Ersatzheer*) of the Reich which was housed in the former War Ministry. They were received by the chief of staff and discussed the organization and structure of a German infantry division on war footing. Everything relating to services, supply, transportation, order, and police was detailed. Mazariegos listened with growing consternation. The differences between German and Spanish Tables of Organization and Equipment (TO&E) were even more marked than the Spaniards had anticipated. Although the Spanish General Staff knew that they were going to be required to adapt their standard square division of four regiments to the German triangular model of three regiments, this structural change would necessitate fewer troops than had been raised. Madrid, Mazariegos recalled, had never received any precise information from the Germans about the strength of the Blue Division. Consequently, the Spanish High Command had advised the Germans that they were recruiting a division of 640 officers, 2,272 NCOs, and 15,780 troops. It was only now, in the Headquarters of the Reserve Army, that the Spaniards discovered that the Germans wanted 526 officers, 2,813 NCOs, and 14,397 men. The DEV, then, was overstaffed with officers, short of NCOs, and had an excess of over twelve hundred enlisted men. These troops had already been assembled for a week. Some were even moving towards the border.[39]

The Spaniards were confronted with the embarrassing possibility of being obliged to discharge surplus personnel, most of whom would be Falangist militia. Moreover, while the OKW had originally requested that the Spaniards bring along only communications equipment and informed the commission that the antitank guns would be horse drawn, the Germans now demanded from Mazariegos that the Spanish expeditionary force be accompanied by 300 trucks and 400 motorcycles. The members of the commission were flabbergasted! How could Spain possibly comply?

In a very depressed mood, the commission left Reserve Army Headquarters to lunch with the Spanish ambassador, General Espinosa de los Monteros. Later they returned to the Hotel Esplanade. At 6:30 P.M., after the rates had dropped, Mazariegos telephoned Colonel Troncoso, chief of staff of the Blue Division, in Madrid. Only sketching the results of the morning's conversations, because he feared that the line was tapped, Mazariegos then dispatched a coded telegram to General Muñoz Grandes, detailing the German demands.[40]

Madrid was aghast. To send so many men home would exacerbate the rivalry between the army and the Falange, endanger the prestige of Serrano Suñer, engender ill feeling against the Germans in Spain, and play into the hands of British propaganda. It was a political impossibility. As for the trucks and motorcycles, motor vehicles of all kinds had been in short supply ever since the Civil War. Moreover, none could be purchased either in Spain or in Portugal. Appalled, the German Embassy in Madrid wired the Foreign Office that insistence upon these two points would mean the collapse of the entire project to send a Spanish expeditionary force. "This must be avoided at all costs."[41]

While Colonel Troncoso and the army staff in Madrid tried to digest the unpalatable results of the first day's discussions in Berlin, and the German Embassy in Madrid received the first rumbles of Spanish displeasure, Mazariegos went to bed hoping that there would be no new surprises on the morrow.

Right after breakfast on the morning of 7 July 1941, Lieutenant Colonel Roca de Togores escorted the commission to the office of Gen. Fritz Fromm, commander-in-chief of the Reserve Army and chief of armaments of the Reich. After this courtesy call, they resumed their conversations with the chief of staff. The Spanish were informed that the Reich would bear all the costs of the Blue Division. The troops would be paid from the day they crossed the Pyrenees. There would also be combat pay, dependents' allowance, hospitalization, and postage franking to the Spanish border. The Wehrmacht would provide all arms, equipment, munitions, and supplies.[42] Military justice within the division would be applied according to the Spanish military code, although German military justice would prevail when Spanish soldiers were detached under temporary German command. The uniform of the Blue Division would be standard German issue, but with a shoulder shield in Spanish national colors—red and gold—bearing the legend *ESPAÑA*.

Officers and men would wear the same uniform, with only collar tabs, chevrons, or epaulettes to distinguish them. They would also be issued identical rations. For the egalitarian Wehrmacht this was standard procedure, whereas the Spanish Army still retained a strict caste system. Mazariegos, his sense of military hierarchy offended, but aware that his brother officers were ready to make any sacrifice to participate in the crusade against communism, emphasized in his evening report to Madrid that "This is the same for the entire army!"[43]

After a break for lunch at the home of Roca de Togores, the commission returned to the headquarters of the German Reserve Army and worked the remainder of the day. At 8:30 P.M., Mazariegos again called Troncoso in Madrid and, in a conversation lasting forty minutes, itemized the results of the day's discussion. Toward the end, the punctilious Mazariegos gently informed Troncoso that the Berlin-Madrid long distance calls were costing 15 marks per minute. A half-hour amounted to 450 Reichsmarks, or as much as 2,000 pesetas. That was quite a sum of money, equivalent to several weeks' pay for a Spanish officer. The commission wanted to know who was going to pay for all of the telephone calls. Mazariegos was told not to worry about it.

Meanwhile, the German Embassy in Madrid was doing everything possible to convince Berlin that the excess personnel recruited for the Blue Division should be retained and that the demand for motor vehicles should be dropped at once. OKW finally relented, agreeing to forget about the motor vehicles and, while accepting the surplus recruits, hoped that the Spaniards would keep them in reserve at home—very probably because the Germans would have to pay them should they be shipped to the Reich. However, if the Spaniards insisted upon sending all of the personnel raised, OKW would accept them, and keep the surplus as a divisional reserve in Germany or Poland. The Spanish Military Commission was told of the German decision, and Mazariegos could continue his negotiations with a lighter heart.

All was practically in readiness for the arrival of the Blue Division in Germany. The Spanish Billeting Commission crossed the frontier on 9 July on its way to Grafenwöhr, the training camp in Bavaria, and the Military Commission in Berlin had only the matter of rations to settle. On 10 July, Mazariegos took up the differences between Spanish and German diets. He pressed the point that Spaniards were accustomed to more meat and less sausage, fresh vegetables and not sauerkraut, and tough-crusted thin loaves of bread rather than the bulky and doughy German product. The Germans took note of his remarks and, realizing the impossibility of providing various national dishes within the limited capacity of the Wehrmacht, did nothing. The agenda completed, Roca de Togores invited the German officers and the commission to his home for a farewell luncheon. Ambassador Espinosa de los Monteros spoke glowingly of German-Spanish cooperation, and the officers said their goodbyes.[44]

On Friday afternoon, 11 July, as Colonel Mazariegos and his party neared Grafenwöhr, Colonel Rodrigo and his staff were sitting in the press box at the Plaza de Toros in Madrid. The colonel, his medal of the *Laureada de San Fernando* glistening in the sunlight, looked over the teeming arena. The bright blue shirts and red berets of the Blue Division were everywhere. The *corrida* was about to be dedicated to the Blue Division and no less than General Varela, minister of war, was honoring the volunteers by his presence. As the trumpets blared, announcing the parade of the *toreros*, the crowd broke into a thunderous ovation. Varela and Rodrigo rose to acknowledge the cheers. They saluted the matadors. The famous Belmonte and Gallito stepped forward, doffed their caps, and returned the salute. They began a duel of titans, each seeking to impress the soldiers by their prowess. Never were Belmonte and Gallito more magnificent as they demonstrated artistry and courage before a crowd whose passions were aroused by the deadly *mano a mano*. The pride, the glory, the passion were all there. This was the memory that the soldiers would take with them. In only a matter of hours, the troop trains would roll.[45] By 10:00 P.M. on 12 July, all was in readiness for the division to move to Germany. Transport orders had been issued for nineteen convoys. Altogether, 17,924 officers and men were preparing to set out for the great adventure.[46]

Cheering crowds packed Madrid's huge Estación del Norte on the afternoon of Sunday, 13 July. They spilled over into the plaza outside and the streets beyond. The cavernous railroad station echoed with shouts of "Viva Franco" and "Death to Russia" as thousands of excited *madrileños* pressed toward a line of wooden passenger cars of the Spanish National Railroad. Every window of the old coaches was filled with smiling young men of the Regiment Rodrigo. Tearful goodbyes mingled with brave laughter as friends and relatives reached for a last touch. Knots of people jostled each other for a chance to speak a few words to the departing troops.[47]

General Muñoz Grandes was on the platform, surrounded by a galaxy of ministers of state and high military officers. An army band, struggling to be heard above the noise, was infected by the general enthusiasm and played with desperate vigor. Suddenly, there was a visible stir. A figure in a splendid white uniform entered the station. The band struck up the Falangist hymn, "Cara al Sol," and a forest of arms rose in the fascist salute. It was Serrano Suñer.

The foreign minister was conscious of the impression made by his arrival. He greeted various members of the diplomatic corps, with a special word for the representatives of Germany and Italy, and dramatically climbed aboard the military train. As the huge crowd hushed, he spoke.

Comrades! Soldiers! In the moment of your departure, we come to say farewell with joy and with envy, because you go to avenge the deaths of our brothers; because you go to defend the destiny of a civilization which cannot die; because you go to destroy the inhuman, barbarous, and criminal system of Russian Communism.

You go to contribute to the foundation of European unity and also to repay blood for blood, friendship for friendship, to the great countries [of Germany and Italy] which helped us in our Civil War. Fix well in your memory what this means. You are going to fight alongside the best troops in the world, but we are sure that you will conquer for Spain the glory to equal them in spirit and valor.

The heroism of this Blue Division will cause the five roses [of the Falange] to flower in the tortured fields of Russia; a hope that trembles in the funeral sepulchre of our founder [José Antonio Primo de Rivera]. . . . Arriba España! Viva Franco![48]

The cheers that followed were broken by a sharp warning whistle from the engine and, as the train jerked forward, thousands of voices once again intoned the haunting and tender "Cara al Sol." The Blue Division began its journey north—to Russia.

2

Grafenwöhr

A LIGHT RAIN DAMPENED THE RUNWAY OF MADRID'S
Barajas Airport as dawn broke on the morning of 14 July. As his car
approached the terminal, General Muñoz Grandes paid little heed to the
weather. His thoughts were on his family and the campaign. His sad
face, often impassive under the greatest stress, showed no sign of emotion. When he alighted from the car and walked into the terminal, he
knew that all eyes had turned to him.

Tall for a Spaniard, standing five feet eight, Muñoz Grandes looked
every inch a commander. The general's uniform, replete with the decorations won in many engagements, fit comfortably on his wiry frame.
His bright eyes had a penetrating glance that seemed to take in all they
saw, digest it, and dissect it. They revealed an inner toughness a tenac-
ity that had made Muñoz Grandes known as a leader who held a tight
rein on his troops, as on himself, made hard decisions, and expected
them to be carried out.

Muñoz Grandes had no illusions about his task. The Blue Division
had to be whipped quickly into shape and dispatched to the front where
it must be a credit to Spain and the army. He was determined to cut the
ordinary training period by at least one-half or, if possible, even by two-
thirds. This he intended to do in spite of all obstacles.[1] There was no
doubt that the Caudillo himself desired that the division should be
rushed to the front.

Once in the terminal, Muñoz Grandes comforted his ailing wife,
María. He bid her and his young son farewell and, turning to the nurs-

ing sisters who had accompanied them to the airport, urged the nuns to take good care of his family. Having said his goodbyes, the general strode toward the waiting line of dignitaries. Serrano Suñer was not among them. The foreign minister's impulse to rid himself of a rival by sending Muñoz Grandes to Russia had misfired. He was now "alarmed at the possibility of Muñoz Grandes returning an even bigger figure than when he went. He knew that Muñoz Grandes hated him and was only too ready to attack him at any opportunity."[2]

In spite of the early hour and the weather, all of Madrid's military hierarchy was there. Their names were a roll call of the Spanish High Command. Wending his way through the line, Muñoz Grandes firmly pressed the hand of General Varela, minister of war. He reached toward General Vigón, air minister, and General Vega, sub-secretary of the army. Then, he grabbed the outstretched arm of the "able pro-Fascist" General Asensio, chief of the Army General Staff.[3] Shaking hands with General Saliquet, commander of the Madrid military district, Muñoz Grandes greeted all the assembled heroes of the Civil War. Among them he saw Millán Astray, founder of the Spanish Foreign Legion. The former legionnaire and now commander of the Blue Division walked quickly toward the shattered figure of his old chief, who had lost an eye and an arm in the Moroccan campaigns. For him, there was a warm *embrazo*. Then it was time to go.[4]

The four motors of the Focke-Wulf 200 Condor *Baden*, sputtered and roared as Muñoz Grandes and his staff approached the boarding ramp. The general's adjutant, Cárcer, carried a splendid new leather valise, a gift of War Minister Varela to the commander of the Division of Volunteers. Before entering the plane, Muñoz Grandes paused and waved at the knot of well-wishers who shouted "*Arriba España*" and "Long live the Army!" The door slammed and at 7:30 A.M. Lufthansa Flight 42 lifted off.

On 16 July 1941, Fromm hosted a luncheon for Muñoz Grandes at the Hotel Esplanade and the Spaniards passed some time in obligatory visits and formal calls. While Muñoz Grandes was being briefed in Berlin, his soldiers were moving out to join him. From Valencia, Valladolid, Vitoria, Madrid, and other points in the peninsula trains rumbled toward Irún and Hendaye on the French frontier.

The Spanish people bid a fond farewell. As the sixth expedition, comprising elements of the Regiment Vierna, passed through Avila, the authorities of the town and many citizens turned out to greet them. Lt. Col. Canillas, commander of the expedition, noted in his report to the

General Staff that he and his twelve hundred men were similarly received in Arevelo and Medina del Campo. Moving northward, the long train crossed the flat Castillian high lands. The fields of yellow wheat stood out against a clear blue sky. Millions of bright red poppies bent their heads between the golden stalks. One volunteer, dazzled by the bright landscape, imagined the poppies as red berets, bowing in the wind to the departing volunteers. In return, he doffed his beret.[5]

In Valladolid, the expedition was presented with guidons and banners. The train pulled out slowly, gained speed across the plain, and chugged into the lush green foothills of the Basque country. Winding into San Sebastián, the transport convoy paused again. The commanding general of the Sixth Military Region came himself to honor the blue-shirted soldiers. Then the train moved on. As the boxcars crammed with troops neared Irún, canteens of wine, a gift of the people, were passed around. The perspiring soldiers of the Blue Division opened the doors to let in the hot wind. Spain was melting into the distance behind them. Irún was the last town in their homeland, and then they would enter France, heading towards the front. With a touch of nostalgia, the troops broke into song.

> Adiós España,
> España de mi querer, mi querer
> Adiós España,
>   cuando te volveré a ver?
>
> [Farewell Spain
> Spain of my love, my love
> Farewell Spain,
> When will I ever see thee again?][6]

In contrast to the enthusiasm and joy displayed toward most of the units of the Division of Volunteers, the departure of another expedition of the Regiment Vierna was unmistakably cold. As the tenth expedition prepared to leave Barcelona, the well-wishers at the railroad station were mostly relatives and officers from the local garrison. The early hour only partly explained the absence of a larger crowd. The Catalan capital had not received the recruitment with enthusiasm. Maj. Mariano del Prado O'Neill, commander of the thousand-man transport, reported to the General Staff that some mothers of recruits appeared at the station and tried to have their sons released at the last moment. Two claimed that their boys were under age; another that her son was unfit for service. Furthermore, the list of volunteers was changed at the last moment.

A frustrated Prado O'Neill blamed the state of affairs on lack of smooth organization and deficient recruitment procedures of the local Falange.

Major Prado O'Neill's convoy traveled through deserted railroad stations in Catalonia and Aragón until it reached Pamplona, where the atmosphere abruptly changed. Then these troops also began to encounter crowds bidding *adiós*. In some Basque towns, exuberant peasants set off rockets in their honor and bands came out to play. Once in San Sebastián, the formal greeting by the commander of the military region marked their official departure from Spain. The train lumbered down the short coastal strip to Irún on the French border, rolled slowly across the iron trestle which spans the Bidasoa River, and ground to a halt in the railroad station at Hendaye, in occupied France.[7]

A brass band, standing amidst a forest of red and white banners emblazoned with black swastikas, struck up the rousing anthem "Deutschland über alles." The soldiers detrained and were herded into the basement of an old hotel where they stripped and took hot showers while the Germans deloused their uniforms. The men were quickly checked for venereal disease. Prado O'Neill had to turn one of his soldiers over to Spanish authorities for repatriation. Apologetically, he noted in his report that the disease had apparently been acquired in Barcelona after enlistment. Meanwhile, the Germans issued a supply of French money to the Spanish paymaster—eighty francs for each officer and twenty francs per soldier—to be distributed for use en route. The volunteers returned to the railroad station, where they were served coffee by ladies of the German Red Cross.

The third-class coaches of the French National Railway were more comfortable than boxcars, but the journey through occupied France was not smooth. The attitude of the civil population was openly hostile. Each expedition, from the first to the last, encountered unpleasant incidents. At Biarritz, Bordeaux, Poitiers, Tours, Orleans, Nancy, Lunéville, and along the entire route, Frenchmen and exiled Spanish Republicans stoned the trains and shouted insults against Spain and the Spanish Army. In several stations, volunteers leapt from the trains and attacked their tormentors. The situation became so critical that the Germans were obliged to strengthen their security forces. The French continued to shout their insults, and the troops responded with salvos of empty wine bottles.[8]

The first expeditions had traveled through France in the warm summer sun that had followed them from Spain. By 19 July, however, when the fifth expedition passed through Orleans, the skies turned gray and a

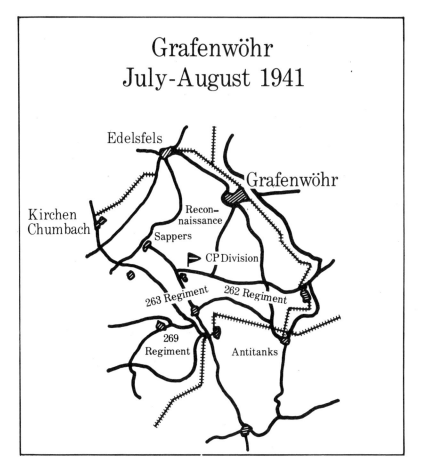

Grafenwöhr
July-August 1941

Edelsfels

Grafenwöhr

Kirchen
Chumbach

Recon-
naissance

Sappers

CP Division

263 Regiment   262 Regiment

269
Regiment   Antitanks

soft, steady rain began to fall. It continued for five weeks. The Andalusians watched the clouds close in and knew that they were far from home. When the train slid into the station at Lunéville, the cars dripping and the skies still oozing a light drizzle, a German band was there. The musicians struck up a chord, and played the Spanish national hymn, the stately "March of the Grenadiers"—but at a gallop. The troops, whose spirits were already low, were more saddened than amused.[9]

The reception changed as soon as the trains crossed the Rhine into prewar German territory. At Karlsruhe, the Spaniards were literally overwhelmed with affection. Crowds numbering 8,000 to 12,000 mobbed the *Bahnhof* (railroad station). German authorities were hard pressed to keep the people back. They prohibited the further sale of platform passes when, after thousands had been sold, it appeared that the crush of welcomers would be so great that some might fall onto the tracks and be injured. The joy of the citizens was electric and spontaneous.[10]

Meanwhile, Mazariegos and the Spanish Military Commission had arrived at Grafenwöhr from Berlin. At 1600 hours on Wednesday, 16 July, Mazariegos went to the camp railroad station to welcome the first contingent of officers: the four regimental commanders—colonels Rodrigo, Pimentel, Vierna, and Esparza—accompanied by Chief of Artillery Colonel Badillo, who had traveled by express train from Madrid by way of Paris and Frankfurt to Grafenwöhr. Mazariegos had some unpleasant news for the arriving infantry chiefs. He was instructed to inform them that a German infantry division had three regiments, not four. One of the regiments would be disbanded. Although the Spanish General Staff in Madrid and Muñoz Grandes in Berlin were aware of this, the colonels had not been told. The news struck them like a thunderbolt. Each colonel immediately feared for his own regiment. Which would be dissolved?[11]

Rodrigo, senior regimental commander, quickly called the other three colonels together at the chalet assigned to Muñoz Grandes. Pimentel and Esparza, second and third in seniority, hoped that their time in grade would protect their regiments. Therefore, they thought that Vierna, as the junior of the four infantry colonels, would find his regiment eliminated. But none of them could be certain that seniority would prevail. Too anxious to await the general's decision, they telephoned Muñoz Grandes at the Hotel Esplanade in Berlin. The general was unavailable. Until Muñoz Grandes chose to advise them, the four colonels would remain in the dark and the command and organization of the division would remain in flux. Then, the colonels separated and went to their quarters. Esparza temporarily shared chalet number thirty-three with Mazariegos, his old comrade from the Asturian campaign. The colonels stowed their gear and strolled over to the base canteen for dinner.

Sitting at his table, the diminutive Esparza did not look very military. His short thick frame was carried on stubby legs which seemed just to reach the floor. His rotund figure indicated an appreciation of *haute cuisine*. The fact that he was a diabetic did not prevent him from being a gourmet. Gout worried him more than insulin because that surely would have cut him out of active service. As long as he had his syringe, he refused to be bothered. Only trifles perturbed the colonel. Serious crises were confronted with icy calm. After dinner, Esparza walked back to the chalet and went to bed. The summer chill, the dampness, and his anxiety combined to keep him awake for a long time.

The first trainloads of troops arrived on Thursday, 17 July. Expedition thirteen from Valladolid pulled in precisely on time. The train slid to a halt adjacent to the long platform which was bedecked with Spanish, Falangist, and German banners floating from high masts. A German military band, at the end of the platform, struck up a martial air. The waiting Spanish officers, still dressed in the khaki uniforms of the Spanish Army, proudly stood at attention.

Lieutenant Colonel Gómez Zamalloa, chief of the expedition and second in command of the Regiment Pimentel, stepped smartly from the train. He saluted, and turned to greet colonels Pimentel and Mazariegos. Then he signaled a bugler, who blew a sharp note. Almost at once, the eleven hundred officers and men fell out on the platform and formed a column of threes. The men carried their bedrolls, slung diagonally across their chests and shoulders. From their right shoulders hung kit bags. The doors of the train slammed shut, the sea of blue snapped to attention, and the music abruptly ceased. The train then pulled out, and the band burst forth with "Deutschland über alles," followed by the "March of the Grenadiers" and "Cara al Sol." At a command, the troops faced the end of the platform, and then marched off under grey skies while the band played German military music. The column stumbled through the first steps, then picked up the strange beat, which was noticeably slower than Spanish cadence, and swung down the road toward the barracks of the camp.[12]

That Friday afternoon, Colonel Troncoso, chief of the divisional general staff, arrived from Berlin. He immediately took over command from Mazariegos. Troncoso carried the Tables of Organization and Equipment (TO&E), which had been translated in Berlin. There were only three sets, for three regiments. He distributed them to Rodrigo, Pimentel, and Vierna, and announced that Muñoz Grandes would arrive on the next day. A shaken Esparza was able to obtain a partial set from friends on the general staff in the chalet. It was only through the kindness of Pimentel that he was permitted to copy the missing pages.[13]

Almost as soon as the TO&Es had been distributed, the regimental commanders were advised by Troncoso that there had been a last minute change. Although the documents called for motor transport for artillery and supply, which was what the Spaniards had expected, this was not to be the case. For three reasons, the Spaniards had been convinced that they would be partially motorized. First, trucks had been extensively used in their own Civil War. Second, the German Army was reputed to be heavily dependent upon motor vehicles. Third, the German High Command had originally asked the Spaniards to bring trucks and motorcycles. Later, however, upon the insistence of the Reich Foreign Ministry, this request had been withdrawn. Now, it dawned on the Spaniards why the Wehrmacht had asked for vehicles. The Germans had none to give. The columns of the Blue Division were to be horse-drawn. Thus, the TO&Es would have to be revised.

The readjustment from motorized to horse-drawn units required a reshuffling of the division. For every single chauffeur, three horse handlers would have to be substituted. Moreover, although the divisional cavalry had recruited horsemen, these were now to be issued motorcycles. The artillery, which had only drivers, was now to be suppplied horses. The reconnaissance group, which was prepared to use horses, was to be mounted on bicycles.

On Saturday evening, 19 July, the general's car pulled up in front of divisional headquarters at 17 Kressstrasse. The assembled officers greeted him, and he was whisked away to a dinner hosted by Gen. Friedrich von Cochenhausen, commander of the military region, and General Heberlein, Grafenwöhr commandant. Immediately after the formal dinner, Muñoz Grandes summoned the leadership of the Blue Division to his chalet.[14] The general sketched his conversations with General Fromm in Berlin. The Reserve Army had promised that the Blue Division would receive the most rapid and intensive instruction possible. However, Fromm had emphasized that a German division required a minimum of three months of such training. Muñoz Grandes was unwilling to accept this. He had pointed out to Fromm that 70 percent of the volunteers were veterans, and pressed the commander of the Reserve Army for a reduction in the training period. He wanted his soldiers at the front as quickly as possible. Fromm refused to commit himself. Nevertheless, if the Red Army should suddenly collapse, the Blue Division would be rushed to the front in trucks, in order to participate in the final triumph. "What do you think," Muñoz Grandes demanded of his infantry colonels, "would be the minimum training period necessary?"[15] The most optimistic response projected a period of six weeks to two months. The general was not pleased. "We will be ready to leave for the front within fifteen to twenty days," he told the astonished officers.[16] He then dismissed them.

Next morning, the Spanish officers attended Sunday mass in the casino. The realization that they were in a Catholic area, Bavaria, helped mute the strangeness of the geography, and some of the men of the Blue Division began to feel less homesick. After mass, tailors measured the officers for their new German uniforms. The crisp, field grey tunics were set off by bright splotches of color. Highlights of crimson gleamed on the shoulder straps and collar tabs of general staff officers. Infantry officers sported white, while artillerymen wore red. Black signified sappers (engineers), and lemon yellow the signal corps. Lunch was next, followed by a meeting with the general.

Muñoz Grandes announced that he was going to break up Regiment Rodrigo. Colonel Rodrigo would serve as chief of infantry and deputy commander of the division. Pimentel, Vierna, and Esparza breathed a sigh of relief. Rodrigo's battalions were to remain intact, however, and were to be distributed among the other three regiments. Castiella, the law professor who had enlisted in Madrid, for instance, was reassigned to the assault section of Regiment Pimentel.

Each regiment now had three battalions. Each battalion had four companies, three rifle and one machine gun company, known also as a heavy weapons company, since it included a heavy mortar section. Companies in a regiment were numbered consecutively, beginning with those in First Battalion. Thus, First Battalion had companies 1–4; Second had companies 5–8; and Third Battalion had companies 9–12. The fourth, eighth, and twelfth companies of a regiment were, therefore, machine gun, or heavy weapons companies. In addition, each regiment had a bicycle company (11), close support company of artillery (13) antitank company (14), and a headquarters company with an assault (sappers) section (15).

That same Sunday, the Wehrmacht assigned to the Spanish Division of Volunteers a number in the German order of battle. Henceforth, the Blue Division would be officially designated 250 Infantry Division. The individual infantry regiments were also given numbers. Regiment Pimentel became 262, Regiment Vierna became 263, and Regiment Esparza became 269. In practice, the volunteers always pronounced each number individually. Thus, Regiment Pimentel was never the "two hundred sixty-second" regiment, but always the "two-six-two." The artillery regiment received the same number as the division, 250, as did all other independent units, such as the Mobile Reserve Battalion.[17]

From the beginning, the General Staff of the Blue Division had been structured according to standard Spanish practice, which followed the French model. This was similar to the pattern used by the United States

Army, but different from the Wehrmacht. The General Staff was not reorganized at Grafenwöhr, but was retained in the structure and function which were traditional in the Spanish Army. The table below illustrates the divisional General Staff.

However, the changes which were introduced in the division as a whole generally had the purpose of adapting to German practice. The division was, in effect, a Spanish expeditionary force. The divisional TO&E, therefore, was not exactly the same as that of a German infantry division. Although the Spanish scaled down the number of regiments from four to three, their organization was unique. Perhaps the most striking divergence was the appointment of a second-in-command of the division (Rodrigo) who was also chief of infantry. Moreover, since the Spaniards would not have a ready supply of replacements at the front, they organized a mobile reserve battalion consisting of three rifle companies. This Mobile Reserve Battalion 250 was to prove very useful in the combat ahead.

The Blue Division, as an expeditionary force in miniature, also established a base camp in Bavaria, at Hof, for the duration of the campaign. Rear services, which included hospital units staffed by Spanish medical officers, nurses, and surgeons, as well as military police composed of the *Guardia Civil*, were to be strung out along the route from Spain to the front.

DIVISIONAL GENERAL STAFF

SPANISH		GERMAN	U.S.
Chief of Staff	Colonel Troncoso	Ia*	Chief of Staff
2d Chief of Staff	Lieutenant Colonel Zanón Aldalur	IIa*	Assistant Chief of Staff
1st Section (Personnel)	Major Ollero Morente	IIa (officers) IIc (enlisted men)	G-1
2d Section (Intelligence)	Lieutenant Colonel Ruíz de la Serna	Ic	G-2
3d Section (Operations)	Lieutenant Colonel Mazariegos	Ia	G-3
4th Section (Services)	Major López Barrón	Ib	G-4

* The German division Ia, Chief of Operations, functions as a divisional chief of staff. His adjutant (IIa) serves as the assistant chief of staff.

On Tuesday, 22 July, while the transports continued to roll in from Spain, the distribution of uniforms and matériel began. The Spaniards were issued the regulation Wehrmacht uniform to replace the travel attire received in Spain. The latter was stored for use during the future journey home. The field-grey uniform was indistinguishable from that worn by German soldiers except for a right arm shield. This shield, stitched on the sleeve between the elbow and shoulder, bore bars of red, gold, and red—representing the Spanish flag—and, above them, the legend *ESPAÑA*.

The steel helmets also bore a decal of the Spanish flag on the right temple. The left side carried the German eagle. These shoulder and temple shields were, however, inadequate identification for the Falangists. Many continued to wear their blue shirts, with the yoke and arrows embroidered over the heart, under their German tunics.[18] The arms and matériel supplied to the Spaniards were general issue. The three rifle companies of Major Román's Second of 269 were issued the 7.92 mm (8 mm) Model 98K, a basic, bolt-operated Mauser. The battalion heavy mortar section received six 81 mm mortars (8 cm *schwerer Granatenwerfer*). The twelfth company drew the light model 34 machine gun with the 7.92 mm caliber.

Each of the first three sections of the 13 company, regimental close artillery support, was supplied with two 75 mm light infantry guns (*leichte Infanterie Geschütz*—le.I.G.18). The fourth section was provided with two 150 mm heavy infantry guns (*schwerer Infanterie Geschütz*—s.I.G.33). The 14 company, regimental antitank, consisted of four sections of three 37 mm antitank guns (*Panzerabwehrkanone*—3.7 cm Pak).[19]

Although this new equipment was not entirely unfamiliar to the officers and men of the Blue Division, the reorganization of the division had shaken the tenuous cohesion of the various units. Moreover, many of the men were little more than raw recruits with hardly a knowledge of close order drill. Faced with the iron determination of Muñoz Grandes to rush his troops to the front, the officers had their task cut out. In a few short weeks, they would have to do what they could to prepare the division for combat.

On Wednesday, 23 July, the last troop train from Spain pulled into the railway station at Grafenwöhr. The Division was now complete. Since many of the Spaniards had little or no military training and the distribution of uniforms and weapons had barely commenced, the first week was devoted almost entirely to close order drill and military courtesy. Training ended at 1730 with supper served at 1800. After retreat and vespers at 1845 the men were given passes to the village. The young *guripas* (Spanish GIs) wearing their red berets at a rakish angle and with their blue shirts showing through their unbuttoned Wehrmacht tunics flocked to the Rathskeller. They drank German beer and wine— mostly beer, because the wine was more expensive—and ogled the local girls. As they drank, they sang German and Spanish songs, translating the melancholy "I Had a Comrade" into their mother tongue. "Lili Marlene" and "Sole, Sole, Sole" rang through old walls in Spanish accents. The *Mädchen* of Grafenwöhr took well to the romantic Mediterranean youths who seemed determined to uphold the famous traditions of their homeland. Pairs strolled arm in arm through the twilight of the long summer evenings.

The training schedule was not harsh. There were, however, sound reasons for the emphasis on parade formation. Muñoz Grandes had to impress the Germans, especially General Fromm, who was coming to Grafenwöhr himself for the formal swearing in ceremony on Thursday, 31 July. The personal appearance of Fromm was another indication of the importance which the Germans attached to the military participation of Spain. Franco's bellicose speech of 18 July 1941, on the fifth anniversary of the outbreak of the Civil War, had aroused high hopes in the German capital that Spain would soon declare war on both the Soviet Union and Great Britain.[20] In the German view, Franco's address was "the most open declaration of his position on the side of the Axis Powers against Communism and democracy and his confidence in the final victory of the Axis."[21] The Spaniards gave further evidence that they were moving closer to the Rome-Berlin Axis when they replaced their ambassador in Berlin. Espinosa de los Monteros, a professional soldier and "a personal enemy of Spanish Foreign Minister Serrano Suñer," was replaced by a dedicated Falangist.[22] The new envoy, Count Mayalde, had been an intimate of José Antonio. As an old-shirt Falangist (*camisa vieja*) and a member of the *Junta Política*, he personified the close relationship between the official movement and the Nationalist state.[23]

Spanish willingness to sacrifice in defense of "civilization" against Russian communism did not extend, however, to eating German food. The standard Wehrmacht fare provided in the mess halls provoked a like reaction from every Spaniard—revulsion. They could not abide the fat sausages, the superabundance of potatoes and cabbage, and the strange bread. The breakfast was unsettling and the coffee unpalatable.

But the cold evening meal with tinned meat was the ultimate culture shock. The soldiers of the Blue Division longed for their garbanzos (chick peas), wine, and black tobacco. German soldiers drank beer, but the Spaniards wanted the wine of their homeland. As for German tobacco, it was pale yellow and the volunteers thought that it looked and smoked like straw. Besides, six cigarettes or two cigars a day were far from enough for the chain-smoking Iberians, the extra ration for officers notwithstanding. Prompted by the general distress, Muñoz Grandes wired the War Ministry in Madrid on 26 July for succor. He requested a trainload of supplies, enough to set up a provisioning depot in Germany, so that his men might savor Spanish food at least two or three times a week.[24]

On that same Saturday evening, 26 July, as the general's telegram requesting garbanzos sped to Spain, Adolf Hitler belabored his generals in the elaborate Führer headquarters—the Wolf's Lair at Rastenburg in East Prussia. Releasing a pent-up fury, Hitler delivered himself of a two hour and fifteen minute harangue before Field Marshal Walther von Brauchitsch, commander in chief of the Army, Gen. Franz Halder, chief of the Army General Staff, and Gen. Alfred Jodl, chief of the *Wehrmachtführungsstab* (WFSt—Wehrmacht Command). The excited Führer recognized that the invasion of the Soviet Union had reached a crucial stage and he lectured his generals on the next phase. Hitler's Führer Directive 33 of 19 July had slowed the Wehrmacht's thrust on Moscow by stripping Field Marshal Fedor von Bock's Army Group Center of its armored formations. They had been shifted to Army Group South (Field Marshal Gerd von Rundstedt) and Army Group North (Field Marshal Wilhelm Ritter von Leeb).[25] The flanking army groups were directed to move on Kiev and encircle Leningrad, while Moscow became a secondary objective. On 23 July, Halder and von Brauchitsch had urged the Führer to reverse his decision, but Hitler merely issued a supplement to the directive, 33a, which confirmed his orders. Halder reopened his arguments on 26 July, and the enraged dictator responded with the extended harangue. It was a bitter experience for the uncomfortable generals, and Halder, who was losing confidence in Hitler's judgment, was on the verge of resigning.[26]

The Blue Division was still back in Grafenwöhr, preparing for the formal ceremony of incorporation into the Wehrmacht. The morning of 31 July opened on an ominous note. The skies were gray and threatened rain. The parade ground at Kramerberg was on an open plain surrounded by pines. At 0930 the gray-green columns spilled out of the woods and began to form a gigantic U. Thousands of marching feet trampled the clumps of grass into the damp yellow earth. A podium stood atop a small elevation almost equidistant from each leg of the U. The little dais, festooned in red and gold, was flanked by cannon and tall masts bearing the national flags. Behind, a row of guidons alternated German and Spanish banners—black swastikas mixed with the yoke and arrows and the red Burgundian cross of the Carlists.[27]

The wind, which had been gusting all morning, whipped the banners. Drops of rain pelted the soldiers and bounced off their steel helmets. Finally, the intermittent showers slackened and the civilian guests began to search for patches of blue in the sky. There were representatives from the Falange in Berlin and several news correspondents. Among the reporters were Celia Jiménez of Radio Berlin and *Informaciones*'s own Alfredo Marguerie. The German military authorities and Spanish staff officers atop the mound snapped to attention as a bugle blared. Below, on the plain, the massed regiments followed. A Wehrmacht honor company preceded by a military band goose-stepped onto the field, halted in front of the reviewing stand, faced right, and stood at attention. The band struck up the national anthem and "Die Fahne hoch" [the Horst Wessel song]. General Muñoz Grandes and his staff marched out in front of the podium and faced General von Cochenhausen, commander of the 13 *Wehrkreis*. At that moment, a staff car pulled up and General Fromm emerged. The tall, corpulent commander of the Reserve Army strode briskly to the dais while the band rendered honors.

With the reviewing contingent complete, the chaplain celebrated mass. A Spanish flag, sent by the Caudillo, was blessed.[28] Muñoz Grandes then drew his sword and held it out before him. As he placed his hand on the naked blade, Troncoso approached the microphone. Troncoso's voice rang over the loudspeakers. "Do you swear before God and on your honor as Spaniards absolute obedience to the Supreme Commander of the German Army, Adolf Hitler, in the fight against Communism and do you swear to fight as valiant soldiers, ready at any time to sacrifice your lives in fulfillment of this oath?"[29] The soldiers of Spain, their right arms raised in the Fascist salute, shouted, "Yes, I swear." The roar echoed across the plain and through the dense woods. As the silence settled the sun broke through the clouds.[30]

General von Cochenhausen then welcomed 250 Division into the Wehrmacht and into his army corps. Muñoz Grandes, his habitually impassive face becoming alive with emotion, replied:

Spanish volunteers! Soldiers of honor of my motherland! . . . Before the glorious flags of Germany and Spain, you have sworn to die
before allowing barbarous Bolshevism to continue its work of hatred
and destruction which has [already] bloodied our motherland and
which today criminally attempts to impose itself on all of Europe.

Before this materialistic and brutal system which the heroic might
of the German Army is destroying in the greatest battle yet known to
history, you Spanish volunteers have gallantly risen. . . . You only
wish to destroy this monster—this lash of humanity—in its own lair.
There, in the Siberian steppes, at the side of the Germans, some modest Spanish tombs sprinkled with young blood, . . . will proclaim to
the . . . entire world the brotherhood of our peoples and the virility
of our race. . . .

Tell the Führer that we are ready and at his orders. Tell him that
we have sworn the oath and tell him that my people fulfills what it
swears.[31]

Fromm now spoke and showed his recognition of Spanish pride. The
Reserve Army commander told the soldiers of the Blue Division that
only the pressure of duty had prevented the Führer himself from being
there. He said nothing about moving the division to the front. With the
bright sun now shining, 250 Division marched off, singing "Cara al
Sol." The Falangists had worn their blue shirts under their tunics. The
troops were ready for training in earnest, and anxious to begin the
fight.[32]

The very next morning, the infantry units turned out for firing practice. The skies were gray again. There had been no mail from home.
Not even the arrival of accordions, gramophones, harmonicas, dice, and
dominoes—a personal gift of Reich Propaganda Minister Dr. Joseph
Goebbels—could compensate for this absence of contact with their families and friends.[33] The *guripas* drew closer together with the publication of their own divisional newspapers, *Nuestro Boletín* (a daily) and
Adelante (a weekly). Used mostly for political indoctrination, these
mimeographed sheets, edited by SEU leader Guitarte, were put out by
Falangist volunteers and were the predecessors of the front-line weekly,
Hoja de Campaña.[34]

Only the initiation of combat training lessened the volunteers' home-
sickness. The German instructors were generally pleased with the ac-
curacy of their charges, and even taken aback by the skill with which
the Spaniards disassembled and reassembled their weapons. Contrary
to orders, the *guripas* had been breaking down their rifles at night. This
dedication to their new arms, however, did not always extend to care

and maintenance. In this they fulfilled the worst fears of the Wehrmacht. One instructor spent days trying to impress upon the infantrymen of 269 a favorite phrase—"You can go seven days without washing, but not one without cleaning your rifle."[35] Somehow, not everyone got the message.

The cavalier attitude displayed by many Spaniards toward regulations, weapons, and the care of their uniforms, not to mention their romantic escapades in the village, led to some strained scenes with the German military. Wehrmacht drill instructors took to berating volunteers whose uniforms were more disheveled than usual. This, in fact, proved to be a sore point. While off duty, Spaniards very often failed to button their tunics properly, fasten their *Gott mit ns* belt buckles, or display military courtesy. Many *guripas*, disdaining regulation issue, also sported red berets and blue shirts. Individual efforts by German soldiers to correct these deficiencies provoked fist fights in the local taverns. When Spanish military police intervened they were often assaulted by German soldiers. The language barrier only exacerbated the situation. However, one Spanish-speaking German sergeant-major made himself very clear when he directed an innkeeper not to serve a group of NCOs from the Blue Division "since they had entered the war without having been invited!"[1]

These incidents, while jarring, were generally brushed off by the volunteers who assumed the Germans lacked Latin imagination and individuality. The Germans on the other hand, tended to take Spanish slovenliness as an indication of unreliability in battle. The Germans thought that the Spaniards were very temperamental. Both peoples had a lot to learn.

Spanish admiration for German efficiency and mechanization had already been shaken. The divisional and regimental (14 company) antitank crews—most of whom were Falangists—were galled by the late arrival of their transport vehicles. Consequently, they were initially obliged to manhandle their 37 mm. pieces through the mud of Grafenwöhr. When the transport was finally delivered, it was discovered that they were not all-terrain vehicles. The antitankers were issued luxurious limousines with radios and heaters, requisitioned in France. Late model Peugeots, Packards, Hudson Terraplanes, and other touring cars, fitted with hauling hitches, were a ludicrous sight pulling the antitank guns.[37]

Colonel Esparza of 269 Regiment received an elegant Studebaker President as his command car. His HQ staff was allotted a diminutive 7 horsepower Ford as well as three motorcycles. This motley assortment was complemented by one motorcycle and two supply trucks per battalion. The colonel's magnificent American automobile had the most modern equipment available from South Bend, Indiana: plush upholstered seats, a dashboard resembling an airplane cockpit as well as fancy hub caps and sparkling chrome plated bumpers. Like a dashing hidalgo Esparza could not wait to try it out on the Führer's new *Autobahns*. Alas, as a seasoned campaigner, he feared that the roadless expanse of Russia would swallow up the shiny phaeton.

While the raw mortar and antitank crews learned quickly, the majority of the artillerymen merely had to apply their professional skills to the familiar German pieces. Artillery Regiment 250 was divided into four artillery groups each consisting of three batteries. Batteries were numbered consecutively from one to twelve. The officers and many of the men of the three medium artillery groups—First, Second, and Third, batteries 1 through 9—knew the 105 mm. F.H. 18 field howitzer (105/ 28) and the personnel of heavy artillery Fourth Group—batteries 10, 11 and 12—were no strangers to the 150 mm. F.H. 18s (150/30). Each group drew twelve field howitzers, a total of thirty-six 105s and twelve 150s. Therefore, each battery had four guns. Colonel Badillo, chief of artillery, even transferred some of his experts to the regimental artillery companies (13). Here, transport was again a problem.

The 5,610 horses supplied to the 250 Division were definitely substandard. The animals had been hurriedly rounded up in the Balkans and shipped to Germany for military use. They arrived at Grafenwöhr suffering from malnutrition and visibly showing the effects of the long journey. The Spaniards discovered that their horses were not trained as draft animals and many were neither broken nor shod. Even had the division not lacked experienced horse handlers, the condition of the animals would have presented grave difficulties.[38]

The inexperience of the Spaniards, combined with the wretched state of the Serbian horses, contributed to wide-ranging confusion in the supply columns. The inability of the drivers to control their teams led to frequent rear-end collisions. Carts were overturned, limbers shattered, and contents strewn in the mud. Curses abounded, especially when columns from different units arrived simultaneously at a crossroads. Spanish honor would not allow one to give way before the other. Only the direct intervention of superior officers could untangle the mess. Discipline in the motor convoys was not noticeably superior. Skinned bark on trees, smashed headlights, and bent rear bumpers on the trucks paid mute tribute to the elan of the Spanish chauffeurs.

Crucial to the success of the division in the Russian campaign would be the effectiveness of the sappers. These tough combat engineers underwent rigorous training. The insignia of the 700-man sapper battalion, a rifle crossed with a spade, was an accurate description of their function. Each regiment also had its section of combat engineers. ("Section" is here used in the European sense. The United States Army equivalent is "column.") The regimental sappers served as storm, or assault, troops. These combat engineers were trained to force rivers in rubber boats, construct foot bridges, seize strong points, and destroy pillboxes with satchel charges. It was considered a great honor to belong to what was a truly elite group, the cutting edge of the infantry in battle.[39]

Spanish Ambassador Count Mayalde visited the camp on 4 August. He was already pressuring the German Foreign Office to dispatch the Blue Division to the front. Fromm reluctantly gave his consent, and on 11 August the German transport section began cutting orders.[40] That very afternoon the division commenced loading exercises at the railroad station.[41]

Just as the division was readying its departure from Grafenwöhr, a freight car bearing tons of garbanzos and casks of olive oil crossed the Pyrenees.[42] Like the garbanzos, 17,909 volunteers, 5,610 horses, and 765 vehicles were being packed into freight cars. Combat loading of the division into 128 trains began on 21 August and continued for six days.[43]

The *guripas* had been in Grafenwöhr barely a month. Many had been under arms less than three weeks. Their experience with horses was limited and superficial—some regimental artillery companies received their animals only the day before departure. Nevertheless, they and their officers were eager to be on their way for many feared that the war would be over before they arrived in the combat zone.[44]

With the division moving toward the front, Lieutenant Colonel Zanón took over as chief of staff from Colonel Troncoso, who returned to Spain.[45] A German Liaison Staff, hastily recruited under Major von Oertzen from the camp cadre, shipped out with the Spaniards.[46] The *guripas* and their German comrades looked forward to a speedy conclusion to the campaign and to a triumphal march through Red Square in Moscow.

3

The Long March

THE HEAVILY LADEN TRAINS SPED EASTWARD. GRAF-

enwöhr lay behind. Ahead beckoned adventure and destiny. After two days and two night's travel, units of the division passed through Treuburg, the last station in East Prussia, almost within sight of the former Polish frontier. Rolling through the little town of Reuss, the trains came to a halt near Raczki in Poland, where the troops piled out and offloaded the animals and the equipment. Heavy artillery Group Four and 262 Regiment however, continued by rail as far as Grodno, a major terminus. Thus, between 27 and 31 August, the division assembled in a staging area spread out over the 100 km. stretch between Reuss and Grodno, for the march to Field Marshal von Bock's Army Group Center.[1]

In an effort to alleviate severe transportation problems in reinforcing and supplying Army Group Center, the Germans had doubletracked a direct rail route to Smolensk and regauged the Russian tracks to that terminus. Nevertheless, the Spaniards had been moved only to Grodno, several hundred kilometers from the front, either because of transport problems or for other reasons which were not clear to them. There was some speculation that Fromm was still unconvinced that 250 Division was ready for combat. The men were eager but relatively untrained. The officers were unfamiliar with their commands and the new equipment. Thus, a long march could develop unit cohesion and allow the division to emerge as a fighting force. Muñoz Grandes would have to prove his bold assertions to Fromm before his men entered the line.[2]

With his division underway, Muñoz Grandes left Grafenwöhr. The general motored eastward over Berlin to Treuburg. There, he consulted with an advance party of the divisional staff, now commanded by Zanón, which had set up a temporary headquarters on 24 August. He then drove to the Wolf's Lair at Rastenburg where he had an appointment with the Führer on 1 September.[3] Hitler had just returned to his headquarters from Uman in the Ukraine. He was directing the war personally. It had been his decision to launch Army Group South against Kiev. Now that the Ukranian capital had fallen and his legions were pressing across the Dnieper toward the Don, it matttered little to him that the generals were chafing at his order to hold Army Group Center back from the thrust on the Red capital.

Ever since July, von Brauchitsch and Halder had been urging him to unleash von Bock's forces, spread out from the Ukraine to the Valdai Hills, for an assault on Moscow. Hitler had rejected their blandishments and, on 15 August, had ordered von Bock to stand fast. Meanwhile, in the north, Field Marshal von Leeb had taken Novgorod on 19 August, and was encircling Leningrad. With the capture on 20 August of Chudovo, the vital October Railroad was cut between the northern metropolis and Moscow. While Halder became increasingly pessimistic about the chances for success of Hitler's strategy, the Führer continued to strengthen the flanking offensives of Army Groups South and North and held von Bock on the defensive.[4]

The war was Hitler's to command—at a distance. Spain mattered to him. Franco's Iberian homeland fitted into his chessboard. Ever since the fateful meeting at Hendaye between Hitler and Franco in October 1940, where the Führer's plans for Operation Felix (the drive through Spain to Gibraltar) had been frustrated and he had "met his master,"[5] the German dictator had never trusted his Spanish colleague. Spain was friendly but unreliable. He wanted a quisling, but found only a Franco.

While the Blue Division had been training in Germany and Muñoz Grandes readying his men for the Russian Front, Hitler ordered a revival of Felix. On 28 July he had alerted the commander of the Western Theater to be aware that Felix could be undertaken during 1941 provided that the war in the the east would be brought to a successful conclusion in time.[6] Within a week British military intelligence reported that the Germans were "starting to accumulate bridging material at Hendaye."[7] But Franco had not approved Felix in 1940, and he was unlikely to accept it now in 1941. A month had passed since that order to reactivate Felix, and the war had not progressed that favorably. Now, as Muñoz Grandes was preparing to visit the Wolf's Lair, Hitler was annoyed at Franco's independence. Spain was an ally of sorts, but not a satellite.

Serrano Suñer, moreover, had not turned out to be a willing tool. The wily lawyer dreamed of a place in the New European Order for a Fascist Spain—a Spain which he envisaged as philosophically closer to Mussolini's Italy than Hitler's Reich. The racism of the Nazis particularly appalled him, and their crude brutality repelled him. Moreover, however much he hoped to become Spain's new strongman, he would not bind his country to a Germany which had refused to make prior concessions to Spanish aspirations in North Africa and had even preempted them. Nonbelligerency was as far as Franco or Serrano Suñer would go. They both agreed on this. They would only enter the conflict "at the hour of the last cartridge." [8]

The Spanish general's Mercedes approached the Wolfsschanze through what seemed an endless series of pine and birch forests. The blue-gray pine needles glistened in the September sun. Splashes of bright green were reflected in the cool lake water. The war seemed distant. At the first checkpoint, the general's special pass was carefully examined by men of the RSD (*Reichssicherheitsdienst*—Reich Secret Service). The car resumed its journey. A second checkpoint. Then a third. Everywhere he could see the field-gray uniforms of the RSD or the SS bodyguard of the Führer. Finally, Muñoz Grandes reached the inner cordon, known as Compound I. There were several wooden huts and a number of men were scurrying around.

Muñoz Grandes reported to the Führer what he had already told the commander of the Reserve Army, General Fromm. The Blue Division was ready for combat. From the oldest officer to the youngest soldier, the men were imbued with a fervent desire to destroy Bolshevism. [9] The Führer was prepared to grant the Spaniard's wish. The 250 Division was scheduled to join Army Group Center, which was awaiting his command to leap toward Moscow.

Hitler used the brief meeting to size up the Spanish general. Angry with Franco and disappointed with Serrano Suñer, Hitler eyed the battle-tested legionnaire as a possible collaborator and future caudillo. Muñoz Grandes would figure prominently in the Führer's plans. [10]

Meanwhile, the hastily organized German Liaison Staff had also arrived in the Blue Division's assembly area between Treuburg and Grodno. Major von Oertzen headed a comprehensive command, equivalent to an infantry divisional staff, including staff officers, a veterinarian, and enlisted personnel. The function of the Liaison Staff was to act as coordination and communication center between 250 Division and the Wehrmacht, and to supply translation services and combat liaison. The staff would also transmit instructional materials or offer advice to the division if solicited. In addition, they were to keep the Supreme Command informed about morale, fighting capabilities, discipline, and general behavior of the Blue Division.

As the division began to assemble, von Oertzen established his headquarters in Grodno, conducted some small arms practice for his men and took up contact with Chief of Staff Zanón. Von Oertzen had some complaints. The *guripas* had been misbehaving and some of the local population had protested to German authorities. Since von Oertzen had looked forward to a thoroughly trained division fully imbued with the traditional discipline of the German Army, he was dismayed to find that the Blue Division, as a volunteer unit, was not composed exclusively of careerists, and that the junior officers did not appear to have their men under firm control.

The German Military Command at Grodno complained cautiously to the Spanish Staff which had moved up from Treuburg about misconduct among the personnel of the Blue Division in the city. The *Kommandantur* reiterated the prohibition of trading supplies, especially tobacco, for foodstuffs. Soldiers should keep their tunics buttoned, their hats on, their belts buckled, and not neglect to salute officers. Fraternization with Jewish women, who were easily identified by the required yellow Star of David on their clothing, was absolutely forbidden.[11]

The German authorities were so concerned about fraternization that they authorized the *guripas* to patronize Wehrmacht brothels. Condoms were issued. Rumors that antierotic pills had also been distributed to the 250 Division abounded. The Germans then reinforced the prohibition of fraternization with Polish women (*panienkas*). The Spaniards were, however, reluctant to relinquish their *panienkas*. Indignant at the order, the *guripas* retaliated. Ten Company of 262 (Captain Portolés) showed its displeasure by marching in review before German officers flaunting inflated condoms flying from the muzzles of their rifles.[12]

These incidents, coupled with alarming reports of persistent Spanish intimacy with "persons of the Jewish race" prompted the chief of Rear Services of Army Group Center at Mogilev to dispatch a liaison officer to observe 250 Division during its march toward the front and to report daily.[13] Also, on 1 September, Lieutenant Colonel Raelke arrived from OKH. Major von Oertzen greeted Raelke with a litany of accusations against the Blue Division. Von Oertzen charged the Spaniards with theft of chickens, associating with Jews, threatening civilians, lack of discipline, and indifference toward the care and maintenance of horses, weapons, and matériel.

None of these incidents were serious, although von Oertzen was greatly agitated by them. As a line officer, he failed to appreciate the delicate problems of integrating a foreign volunteer unit into the Wehrmacht. Moreover, the political ramifications of the role of the Blue Division in the Eastern Campaign seemed to escape him. His mind fastened on difficulties and deficiencies, von Oertzen drove to Vitebsk on 6 September and reported to Gen. Adolf Strauss, Commander of 9 Army.

Von Oertzen expected to receive orders relating to the deployment of 250 Division, which had been assigned to 9 Army. Strauss, who held the northern wing of Army Group Center, listened to von Oertzen's criticism of the Spaniards, but had a surprise for the major. A new order had just arrived from OKH. The 250 Division had been transferred to 4 Army of Field Marshal Günther von Kluge, just to his south.[14] Getting back in his car, von Oertzen drove to Smolensk, headquarters of 4 Army, and reported to the army chief of staff.

That same day, 6 September, Adolf Hitler issued Führer Directive 35 from his citadel at Rastenburg. This directive called for a continuation of the offensives of Army Groups South and North, but anticipated that Army Group Center would soon be permitted to launch "a decisive operation against the [Marshal S. K.] Timoshenko Army Group [shielding Moscow]. This Army Group must be defeated and annihilated in the limited time which remains before the onset of winter weather. For this purpose it is necessary to concentrate all the forces of the Army and Air Force which can be spared on the flanks and which can be brought up in time."[15] Thus, the Spanish soldiers would have their wish. They were scheduled to join in the attack on Moscow, the capital of world communism. They would parade into Red Square under the personal command of von Kluge, a field marshal in the vaunted Wehrmacht.

The Blue Division was already moving out of the staging area toward the front. In spite of the fact that the campaign was due to begin by the end of September, Army Group Center instructed the Spaniards to proceed via a circuitous route toward the jumping-off point of Smolensk. This route was chosen, partly because of the poor conditions of the roads on the direct route, but also because of the need to firm up the division by marching.[16]

During the first days of September, the division began to fall in for the long trek eastward. As the heavily laden infantry columns—thirty-two kilos per man—lumbered across the Polish plain and approached Grodno, the men saw signs of battle. Until now, only scant evidence of combat—a few burnt out villages, a handful of shattered frontier posts and abandoned trucks and equipment—had borne mute testimony of the passage of the blitzkrieg. Now, however, scattered along the hills west of the wide river Niemen lay the debris of battle. Fifty charred Red Army tanks stood immobile among twisted trucks, overturned carts, and cold field kitchens. This site of savage fighting impressed the wide-eyed *guripas*. The officers, as trained professionals, viewed the tank graveyard as a sign of something more. Esparza observed that the German victory had been hard fought and dearly bought. The Soviets had not melted away. The Red Army had been beaten by superior tactics and command, not by superior courage.[17] With this grim glimpse of the battle to come, the columns trudged across the still unrepaired bridge that spanned the Niemen and tramped into Grodno.

A panorama of destruction confronted the volunteers. A third of Grodno lay in ruins. Hardly a house was standing in the outskirts, but the city center, dominated by the burnt out shell of the towers of St. Michael the Archangel, was still largely intact. Instead of the wooden huts they had so far encountered in Poland, the Spaniards noticed that the surviving buildings of Grodno were constructed of masonry. Some of the more modern ones, built recently by the Soviets, were in the massive Stalin style.[18] The population of the city, which had dwindled from the prewar 60,000 to 5,000 or 6,000, comprised three distinct groups—Poles, Russians, and Jews. The latter were easily distinguishable by a distinctive arm band, bearing a yellow Star of David.

The Spaniards observed the Jews gathering at 0600 each morning at the synagogues, where they were formed into work parties under the watchful eyes of German noncoms. These details were then assigned to clearing the streets of rubble, cleaning the barracks for the occupation forces, and repairing the roads. For this, they received a bit of bread and a plate of food.[19] This was the first instance in which the volunteers could observe the operation of Nazi racial policies. The remaining Jews of Grodno had then no idea of their ultimate fate, nor did the Spaniards know to what lengths the Nazis would carry their persecutions. Struggling to keep the Jews apart, the Germans reminded the Spaniards time and again not to have contact with Jewish women.

The occupation forces were also composed of three groups—Germans, Lithuanians, and Spaniards. Thus, the city had a multinational aspect, with a wide variety of languages being spoken, including Yiddish. The war began to have a more international flavor to the volunteers, who started at once to fraternize. An old hotel, the Commercial, served as a casino. The *lingua franca* in the casino was French, but even English could be heard.

After funneling through Grodno, the Blue Division split into three groups for the march northeast to Vilna. The motorized units sped ahead, while the limited road capacity of the region necessitated the use of two columns for the nonmotorized elements. Muñoz Grandes wanted to accelerate the march. He feared that the battle for Moscow would begin without his division, the symbolic presence of Spain in the fight against communism. Since the Wehrmacht had turned a deaf ear to his pleas for rail or truck transport, he now knew that his inexperienced troops would have to carry everything to the front themselves. And this would be along a roundabout route over bad roads.

No sooner had the Spaniards left Grodno than it began to rain; intermittent rain continued for three days, following them all the way to Vilna. Major Prado O'Neill and his Second Artillery Group lumbered out of Grodno at 0600 on Thursday, 4 September, over the wet roadway. A tough but considerate commander, the major with the peculiar Spanish-Irish name viewed the war from the perspective of a professional soldier and an aristocrat who bore a list of titles that could span a paragraph or cause a Communist to gasp. Among others, he was ninth Marquis of Acapulco, tenth Marquis of Caicedo, third of los Ogijares, and was married to the daughter of the Duke of Sueca. Prado O'Neill observed that, in spite of the rain and the high crown, the cobblestone highway was one of the better roads they had traveled thus far. Up to then, there had been sandpits and chuckholes, requiring much pushing and pulling. Before, it had taken twelve hours for Second Group's three batteries to cover twenty kilometers. The major looked forward to a more rapid passage on the leg to Vilna.

Second Group set up their camouflaged tents and horse lines and bivouaced in an abandoned orchard near Lida. After Sunday mass in the field, the artillerymen cleaned their equipment, while the veterinarians scurried about applying first aid to the harness and saddle sores of the exhausted horses. Some of the junior officers, however, slipped off to the town.

Predominantly a community of wooden dwellings, Lida had been harder hit by the war than Grodno. Many houses lay in ruins, and only stone chimneys poked out from the charred timbers. As the Spaniards walked along the unpaved streets in the dim light of a rainy sky, the sense of being at war among a conquered people pressed in on them.

Lieutenant Victor Jiménez, Second Artillery's interpreter, was strolling along with his friend Paco.[20] They spied two *panienkas* on a balcony. Surmounting the language barrier by means of gestures and a few Polish words picked up en route, the Spaniards wangled an invitation into the house. The girls were blondes, and very attractive. Time passed quickly and darkness soon fell. It was the hour when the partisans emerged, an unsafe time for occupation forces to be on the streets. Suddenly, a group of surly Russians burst in, and the girls spoke Russian to them. The mounting tension was broken when the green-eyed Laura brought out some *pierogi* (potato dumplings). The Russians ate, and left. Laura turned to Victor and managed to communicate the idea that these men were dangerous Communists, probably snipers, and that one of them was her uncle.

Jiménez had the gnawing feeling that he should have gone while it was still light, but there seemed no point to leaving just then. Therefore, he stayed a little longer—long enough to make love. After a while, three of the Russians returned and Jiménez began to think that it was now a good time to make his exit. Paco had already disappeared with his girl. As Laura showed him to the door, Victor looked out into the night, "as black as a wolf's mouth." Suddenly, Laura shoved him aside, and a bullet whizzed past his ear. Summoning a bit of Spanish bravado, Victor leaned against the door frame and casually took out a cigarette. As he struck a match, Laura dashed it to the floor. Grabbing him by the arm, Laura pulled Victor into the darkness of the street. They moved swiftly through the night as shots crossed their path. Victor's heart was in his throat as he placed his trust in the green-eyed Russian *panienka*.

They turned a corner, and knocked on a door. Paco and his girl appeared, and Victor caught his breath. The Russian girls exchanged a few words, and Laura indicated to Victor the direction of the Spanish camp. The girls offered to go along, but the Spaniards said that they would set out alone. The goodbyes, however, were prolonged. By the time they were ready to depart, the moon had come out and Victor and Paco had changed their minds.

The town was still. A large white moon illuminated the unpaved streets and silhouetted the chimneys of the ruined houses. Hand in hand, the couples strolled back to the bivouac. On the way, Laura told Victor her sad story. She was born in Borisov, in White Russia, where her father was an ardent Communist. He was so wedded to the party that she considered herself an orphan. Nevertheless, she had accompanied him into Russian-occupied Poland. Her father took her to his brother's house in Lida. It was the first time she had seen western "civilization." When the Germans invaded, she and her aunt remained at home, while the two men went underground.

At the Spanish camp, the young lieutenants said farewell and Victor promised Laura that he would see her the next day. But he knew that he would not. Reveille was set for 0430 the next morning, and Second Group would march at 0530 hours.

Lieutenant Jiménez walked on the cobblestone highway toward Vilna, leading his horse. It was better for both of them than riding, he reasoned. The horse was not used to the saddle, which was new and stiff. Nor was he used to the saddle, and he was also stiff and sore besides. As they walked along, he and his comrades debated the direction.

"I tell you, we're going to St. Petersburg."

"You'll see. We'll take another road and end up in Smolensk."

"The direction we're taking is exactly south to north."

"Really, it's more to the northeast."

"Well, in that case, by the time we arrive in Leningrad it will all be over and we won't have anything to do."

"Do you really believe that all this will be over in a few days?"[21]

The conversation continued in this vein until the bugler called a halt. The volunteers had lunch, the main meal of the day. A short *siesta* followed and, at 1530 the horses were cleaned and groomed. As dusk fell, sentries were posted. Each two gun section lit their own campfire and sat around toasting bread, roasting potatoes, and singing songs of their homeland. Just before turning in, they said their beads. Then, the troops crawled into their tents and wrapped their blankets tightly around them while a cold wind blew from the north and reminded them that summer was over and the Russian autumn had come.

The next day, Second Group moved out of the Polish plains and climbed into the low hills of the Baltic massif. By early afternoon,

Vilna, with its two winding rivers, lay below and before them. The delights of the ancient capital of Lithuania beckoned as 250 Division streamed by. The German Liaison Staff and the General Staff of the division had already arrived.

Major von Oertzen had not accompanied his men to Vilna. After reporting to the chief of staff of 4 Army in Smolensk on 6 September, he had stayed on another day in order to meet with the army commander, Field Marshal Günther von Kluge. By this time, von Oertzen had conveyed his criticisms of the Spanish volunteer division to the German High Command, to General Strauss of 9 Army, and to von Kluge's staff. In his explanations to the field marshal, Major von Oertzen went into exhaustive detail. Von Kluge, preparing to lead his troops into the battle for Moscow, could not fail to have been impressed—negatively. Having done what he thought to be his duty, von Oertzen motored to Vilna, arriving later in the day on 7 September.[22]

The Spaniards had been attempting to correct deficiencies on the march. As staff headquarters were being set up in Vilna, 269 Regiment was coming up. Esparza, conscious of the need to move his men along rapidly, had experimented with alternating battalions in the line of march and had tried to seek out passable parallel roads. But this was not enough for Muñoz Grandes. The general drove up to Esparza's staff car and had a brief chat with the colonel. After the general left, Esparza found himself on foot, his stubby legs pumping to keep up, alongside the horse-drawn batteries of the regimental support artillery. The cannoneers, instead of riding on the caissons, now took turns. Half of them trudged along with their colonel, while the other half rode. Every six kilometers a five-minute rest was called. The growing fall-out rate among the animals had alarmed Muñoz Grandes, and it was hoped that two purposes could be served by having half the cannoneers walk. First, the burden of weight to be pulled would be reduced. Second, those on foot could keep a watchful eye on the condition of the horses.

The Spaniards were conscious of being in an historic region. Napoleon had also crossed here, leading his Grand Army to Moscow and defeat. In World War I, German armies had tramped here, and the Spaniards observed that the Army High Command had kept meticulous notes of the location of World War I cemeteries. In 1941, as the Wehrmacht surged forward, the Germans had rushed in to restore the burial grounds of their fallen comrades. New markers and fresh flowers could be seen as the Spanish troops trudged by.[23]

By 8 September, Esparza and 269 were within twenty-four kilometers of historic Vilna. Although they had covered a grueling fifty-five kilometers that day, many in his command looked forward to visiting the city. The Germans had told them that Vilna was the last outpost of civilization. They would see nothing like it in Soviet Russia. The colonel bivouacked his regiment and authorized a number of passes.

Summoning his staff car, the well-worn Studebaker President, Esparza sped off toward Vilna. The luxurious black limousine was not what it used to be. Polish roads had taken their toll. The tires were worn and no spares were available. The shock absorbers had long ago given out. The final humiliation had come on the highway from Grodno when the steering column, jolted beyond endurance, had broken. A handy Polish mechanic had salvaged the situation with rubber bands, comforting the disheartened colonel with assurances that the rubber bands would last as long as the rest of the car.

The limousine ran more smoothly on the broad asphalted streets of Vilna. This was a large city—some 200,000 inhabitants. Splendid baroque buildings greeted the Spanish colonel and the panorama reminded him of Madrid. The thoroughfares were thronged with people. Not only were there Lithuanians, Poles, Jews, and Russians, but a German division was just passing through. His eager eyes noted that food was plentiful and that ration coupons were not required in the restaurants. He paid his respects to Muñoz Grandes and discussed the march itinerary. The division was not to enter Vilna. Instead, it would swing sharply southeastward and proceed to Minsk via Ozmiana and Molodeczno.

The next day, 9 September, Major Reinhard arrived from Army Group Center. The build-up for the attack on Moscow was underway. The rate of march of 250 Division had to be accelerated. After a conference with Muñoz Grandes, it was agreed that the division would arrive in Ozmiana by 12 September and reach Minsk by the seventeenth.[24]

The Blue Division headed out at once. The scattered units swung eastward from the Grodno-Vilna axis toward the highway that led into the heart of Russia. By 11 September, one day ahead of schedule, Second Artillery Group had reached the convergence point of Ozmiana. Here, the General Staff had set up a march control point. Since the division was scheduled to rest the following day, the young officers of Second Group badgered Major Prado O'Neill into letting them have a light truck for a last fling at civilization in Vilna.

Early Friday morning, Lieutenant Jiménez and his comrades barreled out of Ozmiana for the two and a half hour drive to Vilna. Upon arriving, they split into three groups—the gastronomic section, the cultural section, and the sex section. The latter group was the most numerous. Jiménez had not been in the city long when a friend told him that a green-eyed Russian *panienka* had been asking for him. He found Laura and they embraced. She had hitch-hiked from Lida to find him.

The day was long and sweet, and a weeping Laura implored Victor to take her along. He knew that this was impossible, and he was not sure that he wanted to. There were other *panienkas*, and girls in Spain as well. He suggested that she return to her home in Borisov, confident that the division would never pass there. During the long ride back to Ozmiana, however, he wondered if he had made the right decision and pictured himself strolling down the Calle de Alcalá with a green-eyed blond wife. But how could he, a Spanish Catholic, marry a schismatic Russian? Somewhat saddened, he bent an ear to his friends, who were chattering about their amorous adventures which always seemed to have been followed by visits to numerous churches.

Not all units were as fortunate as Second Artillery. In spite of the difficult march conditions, morale had remained high under the genial, half-Irish Major Prado O'Neill. In 263, however, things were different. Colonel Vierna was an ex-legionnaire who was accustomed to correcting minor infractions with a swift slash from his *fusta*—a pliant switch made from a bull's pizzle—and punishing insubordination with summary execution. Neither did he take kindly to the continued prodding from the general to tighten discipline and hurry along the march. Vierna bore down hard and vented his wrath on First Battalion, which he had personally raised from among Falangists of Valencia. He kicked soldiers, berated officers publicly for their inability to enforce discipline on the student volunteers, and chided the troops with the delicately derisive term *señoritos* (fops).[25]

There was not a man in the division, however, who did not notice his heart race when the big black Mercedes of another ex-legionnaire, General Muñoz Grandes, came into view. During a rest, the general would suddenly appear, step out of his touring car, and walk quickly up to a nearby knot of soldiers. His leathery face, creased with wrinkles, seemed naturally sad and worn with cares. But, on these occasions, he broke out in a broad grin and every wrinkle would smile. His whole face would come alive with an infectious good cheer and the deep-set black eyes took on a sparkle that was welcome to every *guripa*. Scorning the traditional aristocratic gulf that separated officer from common soldier, and ignoring the protests of the cooks, Muñoz Grandes demanded an ordinary ration, sat down and ate with the men. He spoke individually to many of them, asking of one about his family, of another about his sweetheart or his conquests in Germany or Russia, and of another his opinion on the war. To each the general listened attentively. Then, he would ask their opinion of their officers. To this reply, he listened very carefully. The men adored him; the junior officers venerated him; the senior officers feared him.[26]

The column of Spanish soldiers making a tired effort to gather speed before the offensive got under way was a curious sight on the dusty roads of White Russia. The infantry, heart of the division, tramped along with open tunics, weapons slung every which way, and helmets on or off. Chickens and dogs rode on the carts. Cows and horses were herded along. The pace took its toll of men and draft animals. Exhausted *guripas* collapsed along the roadside, where they were joined by equally tired horses, which had been turned loose by their drivers when they could pull no more. This debris of the march was swept up by mobile units. Ambulances carried men to the next bivouac area while trucks hauled the horses to veterinary stations. The high dropout rate of draft animals increased the work load of the remaining horses and men, especially those volunteers in the heavy weapons sections who were obliged either to carry their machine guns and mortars or pull the carts themselves.[27]

Interspersed among the foot soldiers, caissons, and carts, were the bicycle companies. These units resembled accordions, because they kept opening and closing as avid pedalers put on a burst of speed while others lagged behind. This was the scene which confronted a shocked German general on 13 September. He called for his driver to halt as they came abreast of the Spanish column. Stepping from his command car, he began to shout orders. The men trudged on. No one saluted, no one heeded his bellowing. Heads down, their thoughts were on the coming battle. Besides, this staff car was just one of many which had thrown either mud or dust in their faces for the last 700 kilometers. Enraged, he sped off, muttering to himself. The High Command would hear of this.[28]

On 14 September, Major von Oertzen reported to Field Marshal von Bock at the headquarters of Army Group Center in Borisov. He was informed that Field Marshal von Kluge had declined to accept 250 Division into his 4 Army. The haughty von Kluge, who was well informed on the progress of the Blue Division, had quipped: "Are these soldiers or gypsies?"[29] The Spaniards were reassigned to General Strauss's 9 Army. Field Marshal von Bock further instructed von Oertzen to provide Muñoz Grandes with copies of his critical reports to OKH. Two days later, Capt. Günther Collatz joined the Liaison Staff from the Führer Reserve. Unknown to von Oertzen, his replacement had arrived.

The thirty-five year old Collatz wore the coveted crimson stripes of the General Staff on his jodhpurs. He was a Silesian, from Breslau, who had joined the Reichswehr in 1928 as a cadet in an artillery regiment. Commissioned a lieutenant in 1931, he rose to battery chief within six years. In 1938, the slim, handsome young captain attended the *Kriegsakademie* in Berlin. After serving on the staff of AOK4 during the Polish campaign, he was transferred to the staff of Artillery Command, 3 Army, for the dash through France. During the first months of Operation Barbarossa, Collatz had moved forward with Security Division 444 as chief of staff (Ia). Now, he had been suddenly pulled out and sent north to join the Liaison Staff with the Spanish Volunteer Division. Collatz reported in at the new headquarters of the Liaison Staff in Minsk.[30]

Minsk struck the Spaniards as "an open-air museum of Soviet architecture," whose massive buildings, dumped on the yellow earth, looked like an unhappy marriage of "Babylon and municipal construction."[31] Many of the buildings were destroyed, almost as much as Grodno. The population, unlike the countryside, where beards, babushkas and boots prevailed, was clean-shaven, hatless, and oxford–shod; signs of the new Socialist society—the industrial proletariat. The main attraction of the city was the fact that it was the terminus of the Minsk-Moscow superhighway. This immense project, constructed by slave labor, ran due east to the Kremlin.

The great highway could be heard before it was seen. From over the rise came the roar of engines, the sounds of tires on the road, and the rush of air in heavy traffic. When the Spaniards drew near, they were given an opportunity to rest for a day. The tantalizing marvel of Soviet engineering stretched out before them as far as the horizon and beyond. The traffic was heavy in both directions. Tanks of all sizes, trucks carrying all manner of matériel, personnel carriers, motorcycles, touring cars, bicycles passed before the eyes of the gaping Spaniards. This gray mass of men and machines, broken occasionally by little knots of Russian civilians, and long columns of mud-brown-clad prisoners, streamed on like an invincible torrent. Suddenly the volunteers were stunned to see a German division clad in khaki—trucks, tanks, and uniforms. It could only have been destined for the African campaign. Something had gone wrong, and it had been rerouted to the Eastern Front. A chilling thought gripped the men of the Blue Division. For the first time, a wave of apprehension, which they struggled at once to suppress, spread among them. Looking out across Napoleon's route to Moscow, they wondered if the Wehrmacht was so invincible after all.[32]

The men's spirits lifted as they swung down the broad, smooth superhighway. Most of the volunteers were walking now. It was too cold to remain either seated on the caissons or in the carts or to stay in the saddle of the Serbian horses. Only the staff officers still rode in their touring cars, but even these vehicles now had their radiators covered against the cold. The bright sun sparkled through the crisp blue sky, but it was not enough to ward off the chill of early autumn.[33]

The Germans had no trouble picking out the Spanish division as it moved eastward along the autobahn. They did not have to squint to read the shoulder patches. The 250 Division marched with banners flying. Flag bearers led each infantry unit, while the first caisson or cart of the horse sections also carried the brilliant red and gold of Spain. The artillery pieces were particularly distinguishable. Each piece, of standard German issue, was now emblazoned with a medal of the Virgin of Pilar or the Virgin of the Kings, or La Paloma, or Covadonga. The Falangist yoke and arrows, in gleaming red, adorned many of the caissons and trucks. The luxurious motorcars of the antitankers, faded splendor on the highway, towed their little 37 mm Paks, each now baptized with its own name—*La Parrala* (a popular song about a street walker), *La Peli* (short hair), *La Chata* (pug-nose), *Yola* (a girl's name). Here and there, a bullfighter or a guitar artfully drawn on the tailgate of a truck in white chalk proclaimed Spain's contribution to the war.[34]

Even when they made camp there was no mistaking that this was a Spanish division. In garrison, on the march or at the front, bugle calls regulated the routine. Cooks in their native blue coveralls prepared a second warm meal of the day. As their German comrades gathered for the traditional cold sausage, the pungent smells of gazpacho and garbanzos wafted across the Russian steppe. Franco had come through; the garbanzo express had arrived from the homeland. The Caudillo had even begun collecting woollen clothing for the division as early as 5 September.[35] Unlike Hitler, Franco had not forgotten Napoleon.

As the artillery regiment, bringing up the rear, marched into Borisov, Jiménez noticed some new road signs on the highway. Moscow, 561 km; Warsaw, 670 km; Berlin, 1,326 km. He calculated that Madrid lay 3,196 km by air, and much further on foot. But, here he was in Laura's home town, Borisov on the banks of the Berezina. There was nothing to do but greet her family and see if his blonde Russian sweetheart had returned. She had!

The young lovers took up where they had left off and the amorous Spaniard spent hours in Laura's home. She now wore high-heeled shoes, silk stockings, and a fashionable new blouse and skirt instead of the peasant outfit he remembered. Jiménez had the uncomfortable feeling that her father, the partisan, was still alive, and nearby, and that the family was not at all glad to see him. However, Laura's sister Nina took an instant liking to Paco. Laura did the best she could, but the memory of snipers at Lida haunted him. Only a day or so before an unarmed foraging party from a neighboring unit had stopped at a village dance. On the way back to the autobahn, one of the men disappeared in the darkness. His body was found the next morning. Victor left as soon as he could and rejoined his unit.[36]

The pace of the division slowed as the lead elements moved forward from Orsha. The splendid stretches of asphalt on the Minsk-Moscow highway gave way to unfinished sections of gravel and cobblestone. Once again the toll of exhausted men and horses rose. By 25 September the motorized units led by the sappers had crossed the Dnieper at Gusino and bivouaced at Svetitsy some 40 kilometers from Smolensk. Artillery Regiment 250 brought up the rear at Orsha.

Friday, 26 September 1941, the entire division rested. The whole region was swampy, and a damp cold hung over the road. Swarms of mosquitos fed on the horses. The volunteers built their campfires bigger than before, and clustered around the warmth, not minding the thick gray smoke which warded off the mosquitos. *Radio Macuto*, the Spanish grapevine, carried the news of the day. Rumor had it that the division would never reach Smolensk, but would return to Orsha and then move north. The possibility of a change in orders did not surprise them. They were Spaniards, and the Spanish Army was accustomed to foul-ups.

That afternoon, the rumors were reinforced. Orders were passed down to turn around, countermarch to Orsha, and move northward to Vitebsk. It was a great mystery. Only Muñoz Grandes and the General Staff knew that the Blue Division had been reassigned from Army Group Center's 9 Army to Army Group North's 16 Army on orders from the highest authority.[37]

4

Novgorod the Golden

ON 24 SEPTEMBER 1941, ADOLF HITLER FLEW TO
Smolensk. He had to reconcile the final preparations for the assault
on Moscow—code name Typhoon—with a developing crisis in Army
Group North caused by Red Army efforts to relieve Leningrad. The
original mission of Army Group North had been to seize Leningrad.
To this end, Field Marshal von Leeb had been given two armies (16
and 18), one panzer group (4), and a strong air fleet (2, including
VIII Air Corps of Manfred von Richthofen). With this force, von Leeb
had driven to the outskirts of Leningrad by early September, isolating
on the way remnants of Soviet 8 Army in a pocket along the Gulf of
Finland around Oranienbaum and cutting the city's direct rail communication to the east by taking Mga on the Northern (Kirov) Railroad. His troops had cut a wide swath, seizing the western shore of
Lake Il'men, the city of Novgorod, and the upper Volkhov River. By
early September, Leningrad might have been within his grasp, but
Hitler had been troubled by the deadly street fighting for Kiev and his
mind was now on other things. The vacillating Führer, who had already changed his plans several times, was about to do so again.

On 4 September, von Brauchitsch and Halder visited von Leeb
at Army Group North headquarters in Pskov (Pleskau). Von Brauchitsch advised von Leeb that the Führer had decided not to take
Leningrad by storm. The city was to be encircled and starved out. The
troops released by this operation would then strike eastward through
the Valdai Hills where they would link up with Operation Typhoon.

Another force would tighten the siege lines around Leningrad in conjunction with the Finnish Army under Marshal Carl Gustav Mannerheim.[1]

The Führer's decision to mount other offensives before taking Leningrad appalled von Leeb on both professional and religious grounds. The sixty-five year old Leeb was in his forty-sixth year of military service. A veteran of the Boxer Rebellion in China and World War I, he had commanded Army Group C during the invasion of France in 1940. One of Germany's most distinguished soldiers, the tall, balding field marshal was considered by his peers as being more capable than von Brauchitsch and an equal to the renowned Field Marshal Gerd von Rundstedt. He rankled at the thought of taking up siege lines just when the capture of Leningrad seemed certain. Nor could the staunch Bavarian Catholic stomach the thought of starving the civilian population until death and disease spread through the isolated city.[2] Von Leeb, whose motto was "The best defense is an offense,"[3] preferred either to storm the city of Lenin or to allow the one and a half million civilians to escape eastward through the still open Schlüsselburg corridor. He told Halder that both he and his soldiers would disobey the Führer's command to mow down the populace if they tried to flee. The failure to occupy Leningrad would be a great mistake, von Leeb believed, on psychological, political, and military grounds. "Psychologically, because his soldiers had been told that Leningrad was their objective. Now, at the last moment this goal was denied them. Politically, because it would make a great impression [on the German and Russian peoples] if Leningrad fell. Militarily, one hardly needs to say."[4]

Von Brauchitsch and Halder advised Hitler of von Leeb's position when they returned to the *Führerhauptquartier*. On 5 September Hitler ordered Army Group North to: 1) encircle Leningrad, 2) push to the south shore of Lake Ladoga, take Schlüsselburg, and join the Finns across the Neva River, and 3) drive eastward across the Volkhov River and link up with Marshal Mannerheim's Finns along the eastern shore of Lake Ladoga near the River Svir.[5] Mannerheim, however, who had "assumed the Chief Command [of the Finnish Army] on the express condition that there would be no [Finnish] offensive against Leningrad,"[6] while declining to attack the metropolis, did agree to mount an attack in East Karelia.

Finnish forces reached the Svir on 7 September. After hard fighting they cleaned up the north bank between Lake Ladoga and Lake

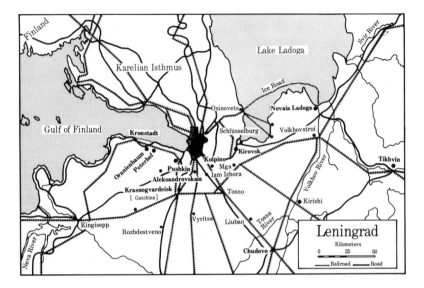

Onega. This successful advance cut the main rail link between Leningrad and the Arctic port of Murmansk. "The Russians, however, with foresight had built a loop-line which connected the Murmansk railway with the Archangel railway along the coast of the White Sea."[7] Thus, British war matériel, which was pouring into Murmansk, could still be funneled to the Red Army by way of Vologda and the now crucial rail center of Tikhvin.

The day after Mannerheim reached the Svir, German forces occupied Schlüsselburg on the southern shore of Lake Ladoga, thus isolating Leningrad. Von Leeb wanted to tighten the ring. But the Führer delayed giving permission. Then, the Russians counterattacked. Marshal K. E. Voroshilov struck out from the city, while Marshal S. K. Timoshenko attempted to punch a hole from the outside by thrusting along the Northern Railroad from the Volkhov. They also sought to succor the besieged city by establishing a lifeline across the waters of Lake Ladoga. Provisions were shipped by rail through Vologda and Tikhvin on to the Volkhov at Volkhovstroi, the junction of the Northern and Murmansk railroads, then went by barge down the river to its mouth at Novaia Ladoga, where they were reloaded and ferried across to Osinovets, a port facility within the Leningrad defense lines.[8] Thus, the city, though isolated from the land side, was not completely cut off. Von Leeb wanted to strike for Volkhovstroi and Novaia Ladoga as soon as possible.

The Führer finally agreed! Army Group North could close on Leningrad, but still had to halt in the suburbs. An assault could be mounted on the lower Volkhov. However, with Operation Typhoon fixed in his mind, Hitler issued Führer Directive 35 on 6 September. For the drive to Moscow, Army Group Center would have to be strengthened. Army Group North would have to surrender Panzer Group 4 and Richthofen's air corps. Von Leeb could have armor for only two days. But the Red Army was fighting fiercely for the lifeline.

The Soviets, led now by Gen. Georgii Zhukov, counterattacked. Zhukov, an officer of great capacity and remarkable coolness in emergency situations, came to be known as Joseph Stalin's "fireman." Thus, Zhukov replaced Voroshilov on 12 September, but was recalled to defend Moscow against Operation Typhoon on 7 October. In the meantime, his hard-driving thrusts had pressed von Leeb so severely that Army Group North was forced to appeal for more troops.[9]

In the strategy session on 24 September in Smolensk, Hitler reluctantly turned to von Leeb's plight. The immediate airlift of a parachute regiment and 20,000 mines would hold off the attacking Russians. The Führer further commanded that 250 Division be diverted from Army Group Center. Once in Army Group North, the paratroopers and the *guripas* would take up positions in a defensive sector, thus relieving battle-tested *Landser* for the threatened zone south of Lake Ladoga. Despite the fact that the Spaniards were at a rail junction at Orsha, they could not be moved quickly. Orsha lay on an east-west trunk line, which the Germans had regauged to western European standards. Over 25,000 kilometers of track had been regauged, more than the entire rail network of Spain.[10] However, many north-south lines continued to rely on Russian track, thus effectively hindering lateral movement between the Army Groups.

Hitler also gave von Leeb 227 Division from the occupation forces in France. By utilizing the regauged east-west track at the rate of seventy-two trains per day, this unit would arrive in Army Group North on the same day as the Spaniards! He hoped that these units would enable the aging field marshal to regain the initiative and, thereby, to support Operation Typhoon.[11] Von Leeb was not overwhelmed by the Führer's generosity.

The very day the Führer opened the Smolensk conference, Muñoz Grandes reported to 9 Army headquarters in Army Group Center at Velish. Strauss advised Muñoz Grandes and Captain Günther Collatz of the Liaison Staff that he had assigned 250 Division to the extreme right wing of 9 Army. This position of honor would form the hinge with Field Marshal von Kluge's Fourth Army immediately to the south.

The next morning, Thursday, 25 September, the disappointing counterorder from OKH came over the teletype. The Blue Division was not to participate in the grand offensive against Moscow. The 250 Division was to assume a defensive role in Army Group North. This was crushing news! There would be no victory parade in Red Square. For political as well as professional reasons, Muñoz Grandes had wanted much more than a symbolic role for the Blue Division. He was now obliged to return to his troops, who were approaching Smolensk, and lead them out of Operation Typhoon. On the morning of 27 September, the division faced about and marched off toward Vitebsk. The Regimental Artillery, which had bivouaced at Orsha the day before, headed the column. The cannoneers moved off the Minsk-Moscow Highway for the 100 kilometer march to Vitebsk.[12]

Vitebsk did not impress the Spaniards as being far behind the lines. The rail yards and airport were being hit daily by the Red Air Force. Hidden in the gray overcast that hung low over the city's spires, the Martin bombers suddenly dropped down and rained bombs on the crucial transport facilities. Luftwaffe antiaircraft replied at once. Spent shrapnel showered the ruined city. Many buildings had been destroyed. At night, the glow from burning grain silos illuminated the skeleton of Vitebsk.[13]

The Spanish General Staff established headquarters in an industrial section of the city and, at a council of war presided over by Colonels Rodrigo and Zanón, the unit commanders were given their embarcation schedules. Anxious for the long-awaited battle, the Spaniards christened this last leg of their journey Operation *Arriba* (Onward).

Unknown to Rodrigo and Zanón, as they issued the travel orders for *Arriba*, the head of the division would be in the line and taking casualties before the tail had departed Vitebsk. General Muñoz Grandes was already reconnoitering the combat sector. On 30 September Muñoz Grandes drove to Pskov. He was accompanied by Collatz. The next day, they were introduced to von Leeb, Gen. Kurt Brennecke, chief of staff, and the staff.

Since the Blue Division had been assigned to 16 Army of Gen. Ernst Busch, Muñoz Grandes was given an opportunity to examine the situation maps. 16 Army held the right flank of Army Group North

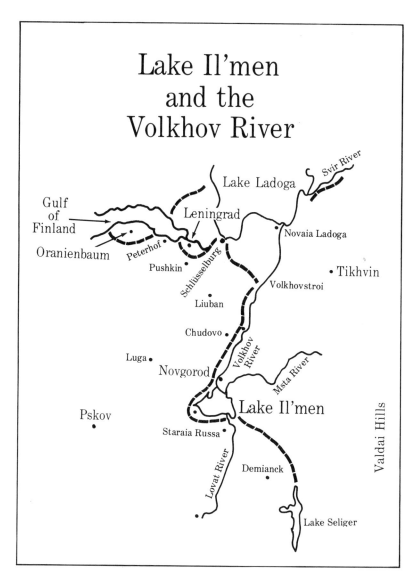

Lake Il'men
and the
Volkhov River

from Lake Seliger in the south to Lake Ladoga in the north.[14] In the
south, the front grazed the strategic Valdai Hills and swept along the
Lovat' River to its mouth at Lake Il'men. Running along the swampy
southern and western shores of the lake, the line of 16 Army bent to
include the fabled city of Novgorod at the source of the Volkhov
River, and then followed the left bank of that river northward, to the

rail crossing at Kirishi. The *Hauptkampflinie* (main line of fighting), or HKL, then swerved westward toward Leningrad and jagged suddenly north to meet Lake Ladoga near Lipki on Schlüsselburg Bay.

With this long front, facing east, Busch beat back Russian attempts to relieve Leningrad and prepared further thrusts into the hinterland. But he had another front, facing westward! The Germant salient along Lake Ladoga was only eighteen kilometers wide, extending from Lipki to Schlüsselburg; 16 Army manned the entire salient, facing east and west, including the west front along the Neva River which linked up with Gen. Georg von Küchler's 18 Army, holding the southern and western siege lines around Leningrad.

After poring over the maps in the massive, four-story headquarters in Pskov, Muñoz Grandes and Collatz motored to 16 Army HQ at Korosten on the southwestern shore of Lake Il'men. Contact between 250 Division and 16 Army had already been made. On 30 September Lieutenant Colonel Ruíz de la Serna, chief of intelligence (G-2) had arrived in Korosten for a briefing. Ruíz learned that General Busch had assigned 250 Division to I Corps, which was deployed along the western shore of Lake Il'men and the left bank of the Volkhov River. After discussing the state of the Blue Division's horses and vehicles, Ruíz had flown off at midday for I Corps HQ at Podberez'e, north of Novgorod.[15]

I Corps was one of four army corps in Busch's 16 Army—II, X, I, and XXXIX. Gen. Kuno Hans von Both, I Corps Commander, had assigned 250 Division to a sector north of Novgorod. The Blue Division was to replace two regiments of 126 Division—which regiments held the Volkhov shore from Podberez'e north to Chudovo, where the blown bridge of the October Railroad (Leningrad-Moscow) lay rusting in the deep, rushing waters of the river. The division's third regiment (Hoppe's) was still in the Leningrad sector. Von Both had reasoned that, since 250 Division was at full strength, the divisional sector could be extended further northward beyond Chudovo to Grusino, thereby relieving a regiment of 21 Division for corps reserve. The two regiments of 126 Division would be collected along the Novgorod-Chudovo road (which paralleled the Volkhov), where it would be held at 16 Army's disposal.[16]

Muñoz Grandes and Collatz were informed of these dispositions upon their arrival at 16 Army headquarters at Korosten on 2 October. After a conference with General Busch and another round of introductions, they listened to Radio Berlin which carried Hitler's speech from the *Sportpalast*. The Führer described in glowing terms the contribution of Germany's allies in the crusade against communism. When he announced that the Spaniards were just entering the firing line, the crowd broke into stormy applause. Muñoz Grandes and Collatz lifted off the next morning in a Fi 156 *Storch* to survey the front and report in to their corps commander.[17]

It was beautiful flying weather. The rain and overcast of the last few days had cleared. The bright sun sparkled off the blue waters of Lake Il'men. As the *Storch* dipped toward the northern shore, Muñoz Grandes could see the banks funnel into the source of the Volkhov River. On the left, a few meters of graying swamp quickly gave way to a slight rise that led to cultivated fields beyond. The white-walled compound of the picturesque monastery of St. George broke the monotony of the landscape. To the right, the swamp was all-pervasive.[18]

They flew down the Volkhov. From the east, the Siversov barge canal sliced through the marsh, linking the Volkhov with the Msta River. Parallel and adjacent, a raised railroad embankment ran to the river and suddenly halted before three concrete piers of an uncompleted railroad bridge. The embankment did not continue on the west side. Then several kilometers of flat, open country were cut short by the north-south trunk line, which ran from Dno to Novgorod to Chudovo.

The river narrowed to about 300 meters. Ahead, four kilometers from the point where the Volkhov issued from Lake Il'men, a cap of high ground, crowned by the kremlin of Novgorod, was split by the murky waters. Here the main stream cut due north. A branch, the Little Volkhov, flowed eastward and around the base of the rise. Ancient earthworks surrounded Russia's oldest capital. For centuries they had formed an outer defensive ring that shielded the citadel within.

The kremlin, on the west bank, was enclosed by an ellipse of red brick battlements. Through the great West Gate, past the Russian Millennial Monument of 1862, swept the Luga-Moscow highway. On, through the Water Gate, the road tumbled down the Volkhov banks to the huge iron bridge that spanned the wide river. The bridge had been heavily damaged, but German pioneers had repaired it. Now, as before, it led to the Viking trade center, Iaroslav's Yard. Further, across the Little Volkhov and beyond the marshes, rose a low range of bare hills. From this dominant position, Red artillery observers kept close watch on the west bank and the city below.

Novgorod was a shell. In their retreat, the Soviets had fired the

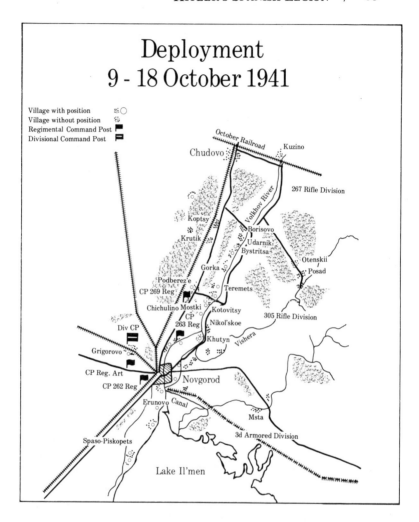

Deployment
9 - 18 October 1941

Village with position
Village without position
Regimental Command Post
Divisional Command Post

October Railroad
Chudovo
Kuzino
267 Rifle Division
Volkhov River
Koptsy
Borisovo
Krutik
Udarnik
Bystritsa
Otenskii
Posad
Gorka
Podberez'e
CP 269 Reg
Teremets
Chichulino Mostki
Kotovitsy
CP
Nikol'skoe
305 Rifle Division
263 Reg
Div CP
Khutyn
Vishera
Grigorovo
CP Reg. Art
Novgorod
CP 262 Reg
Erunovo Canal
Msta
3d Armored Division
Spaso-Piskopets
Lake Il'men

"golden city." Storming parties of 21 Division had found the city in flames on 14 August. Five days of hard fighting and numerous Stuka attacks had reduced the city almost to ashes. From the air, Muñoz Grandes and Collatz observed that, except for the kremlin, Novgorod was almost fully burned out. Many of the few stone buildings were roofless.[19] There were few traces of the prewar population of 34,000.

The *Storch* flew on. The helmetlike cupolas of the cathedral of St. Sophia lay behind. The mainstream of the Volkhov bent eastward to receive the waters of the Little Volkhov which swelled as the Vishera flowed in from the east. Looking down, Muñoz Grandes observed the shell-pocked ruins of the Monastery of Khutyn at the northern tip of the island. The flat, open, exposed ground of the island formed by the mighty Volkhov would be a difficult staging area for any offensive against the bare hills to the east. But, that was not Muñoz Grandes' problem. The 18 Motorized Infantry Division held the Novgorod sector. The 126 Division, which the Blue Division was to replace, lay to the north.

Both banks were wooded now. The west bank dropped off about two meters to a swampy strip along the water. The drop was more precipitous on the east, where the bank itself was markedly higher. It was almost a low cliff. Thus, the higher east bank was cut by more gullies, which ran back into the forest about a kilometer from the riverside. The woods continued, covering a series of rolling hills, whose ridges ran parallel to the river. This again differentiated it from the west, where stands of birch and pine tended to hug the edge of the bank. Beyond, the woods gave way to flat open fields, which lined the asphalted Novgorod-Chudovo highway (*Rollbahn*) and continued on to the railroad a kilometer away. Cultivated fields also lay between the road and the trunk line to Chudovo. Here, as in the area around Novgorod itself, the enemy held the high ground, this time under cover of woods.

Muñoz Grandes was pleased to see, as the *Storch* glided towards the sector of 126 Division and circled for a landing at Podberez'e, that the fields and open ground on the west gradually gave way and were swallowed up by a dense forest, offering plenty of cover. As the plane dipped toward the small airfield south of Podberez'e, the general noted the remains of a ferry landing which provided access to a cluster of villages on the east side.[20]

The *Storch* touched down and taxied up the muddy landing strip to a waiting line of dignitaries. Muñoz Grandes and Collatz were whisked off to I Corps headquarters, in a pair of modern stone and concrete buildings just off the Dno-Novgorod-Chudovo highway. Both buildings were surrounded by a high wooden screen, which had been erected to mask entries and exits from enemy observation across the river. General von Both greeted the Spanish general and his German escort. He had his staff give them a detailed description of I Corps deployment. Motorized 18 was completing the relief of 11 Division at Novgorod; 126 Division was stretched out between Podberez'e and Chudovo; 21 Division lay north of the October Railroad (Leningrad-Chudovo-Moscow); and 11 Division was taking over the former sector of 18 Motorized at Kirishi.[21]

The next day, Sunday, 5 October, Muñoz Grandes and Collatz drove northward toward the village of Miasnoi Bor, headquarters of 126 Division. As the general's car, which had come up from Korosten, rolled along the Novgorod-Chudovo *Rollbahn* (highway) they noted that the railroad began to close toward the road from the west while the stands of birch and fir thickened on the east until the river completely disappeared from view. Hamlets hugged the roadside. Every village looked much the same—a straggly row of log cabins, *izbas*, with picket fences. Each *izba* seemed to center on a brick fireplace. The general wondered how such flimsy structures could provide protection against the fierce winter cold. At least a wood supply was near at hand. The forest was closer now. Both the railroad and highway were nearly enveloped by trees. Cover enough for his men, mused Muñoz Grandes, but also for partisans. The railroad and highway drew together as they entered Miasnoi Bor. The Mercedes rolled to a stop, and Muñoz Grandes jumped out to shake hands with his new colleague, Gen. Paul Laux, commander of 126 Division.

The 126 Division was, like 250 Division, a new division. Formed in Rhineland-Westphalia after the successful conclusion of the French campaign in 1940, 126 Division had jumped off with Army Group North on 22 June. Crossing into Russian-occupied Lithuania, the Rhineland-Westphalians had fought their way into Latvia and then pushed eastward to Lake Il'men. After participating in the conquest of Novgorod—12 to 18 August—one of the division's regiments, 424 under Lt. Col. Harry Hoppe, had been sent westward from Chudovo to the Ladoga sector. Hoppe, in a brilliant *coup de main*, had stormed Schlüsselburg on 8 September, closing the ring around Leningrad. The other two regiments, 426 and 422, had taken up positions along the Volkhov. General Laux had been holding the line from Podberez'e to Chudovo since 26 August with these two regiments. He was anxious to reopen the offensive and looked forward to the arrival of a fresh division to bolster 16 Army's *Drang nach Osten*.[22]

Laux explained that his had been an active sector. The Ukrainians of 267 Rifle Division, although a weak unit, probed constantly across the Volkhov, sometimes in considerable strength. The conversation immediately turned to the role of the two divisions in the coming offensive. Redeployment of 126 Division depended upon the speedy arrival of 250 Division.[23]

Advance echelons, including interpreters, divisional general staff officers and liaison staff personnel, were already at Miasnoi Bor. They, as well as the motorized and horse-drawn units still in transit, drove from Dno by way of Sol'tsy, Mshaga, Shimsk, and Novgorod. Chief of Staff Zanón, and other officers, came up on 7 October. That afternoon, headquarters battery of Artillery Regiment 250 drove into Koptsy, midway between Podberez'e and Miasnoi Bor, and began to take over from Headquarters Battery of 126 Artillery Regiment. Meanwhile the divisional antitankers took up positions along the river bank immediately east of Podberez'e at Teremets.[24]

First Group, which was plodding along in the open area north of Novgorod, came under artillery fire from Russian guns on the dominant east bank. Caught without cover, they took twelve casualties. Meanwhile, Major Prado O'Neill and his command were resting just south of Novgorod, along the shore of Lake Il'men. It was Tuesday. Mass (postponed from Sunday because of march orders), inspection, and review were the order of the day. The next morning, 8 October, the caissons rumbled northward through a double line of chimneys into the Golden City, past the fallen plaster statue of Lenin in Stalin Square. Red batteries opened up. "It's the brothers of *La Pasionaria*" (Dolores Ibarruri, Communist leader of Civil War fame and post-Franco parliament), quipped a *guripa*.[25] But Second Artillery came through the fire zone between Navolok, Stipenka, and Motorovo unscathed.

The relief of 126 Division was fully under way, and parts of the Blue Division were in the line. After a continent-wide journey by rail and foot, the volunteers had arrived at the front. Eager *guripas* peered through their sights at the Bolsheviks across the 300-meter-wide Volkhov. As they settled into the foxholes and trenches dug by the *Landser* of 126 Division, they waited for Hitler's orders for the offensive to open.[26] The rest of the division, however, was still under way. While some units were entering the firing line along the Volkhov, others were boarding trains 450 kilometers away in Vitebsk. The punctilious Esparza was at the station supervising the loading of his remaining battalions. With loving attention, Esparza observed the loading of the grand, decaying Studebaker President, rescued from a repair shop. However, Esparza was dismayed to see that Russian cattle cars, without stoves, were to be used for this shuttle through the autumn cold. Surprisingly, there were no coaches for the officers, and no special treatment. Major Pérez Pérez of Third Battalion, complained to the German transport officer in charge. The terse reply, "We're not in Germany."[27]

Esparza accepted the German explanations about the lack of availability of special Russian coaches. Nevertheless, when the Germans suddenly scrounged up a modern coach for him, he did not object but quickly settled in. "Soft class," the Communist equivalent of first class, proved most acceptable to a Spanish *hidalgo*. But it, too, had neither heater nor latrine. The problem of stoves was resolved for officers and men alike at Nevel. Taking advantage of a breakfast stop, the shivering volunteers poured out of the cars and comandeered coal, wood, and anything that could be used to jury-rig a stove. The Spaniards laid the metal on the wooden floor of the cars, piled the fuel on top, and lit fires. As the smoke curled up toward the frigid sky, it met the first snowflakes of winter. It was five degrees below zero Celsius.

The trains chugged on. Guarded bridges testified to the presence of partisans, but all precautions were inadequate. Blown tracks, a shortage of captured Russian locomotives, and the lack of off-loading facilities at Dno, necessitated a two-day layover in Novo Sokol'niki from 9–11 October. And it snowed again. Convoys kept piling up in the railroad yard of the little town. Food and fuel ran short. As a result, a "Spanish fury" descended upon the townspeople. Foraging parties streamed out of the stranded trains and combed the countryside.[28]

The *Feldgendarmerie* (Military Police) in Novo Sokol'niki was appalled at the sight of hordes of Spaniards. Efforts of the *Kommandatur* to confine the Spaniards to the freight yard failed. Even personal contact between German occupation officials and battalion commanders on the troop trains only brought rejoinders of "It's due to [our troops'] attitude against the Soviet regime."[29] This anti-Bolshevik attitude did not, however, explain the sequestering of *ikons* from private homes. A printed command order presented for countersigning to each convoy chief calling for the confinement of the men to the freight yards failed to remedy the situation. Finally, under heavy German pressure, Spanish sentries were posted around the perimeter of the freight yard. The guards, however, leaned their weapons against the wall and sat down and smoked as they hailed their comrades streaming toward the town and country. Only the appearance of a Wehrmacht officer prodded them into a vertical position.[30] "Thousands thronged the freight yard. The Spanish, in addition to throwing their dead and dying horses off the flat cars and littering the tracks with the carcasses, also tore down all sheds, shacks and fences in the vicinity and used the material for fire wood."[31] Not even the station was spared. Wooden doors and window frames were pulled off and carried away for fuel. At night the scene resembled a gypsy camp, as the men gathered round the roasting pits and cut their rations from the turning carcasses. Their open fires defied the Red Air Force. Their songs of Andalusia and Seville baited the partisans.

Esparza took the long view. After stoically observing the carnival atmosphere from the window of his private railroad car, he ordered his interpreter to seek out shelter where a proper meal could be prepared. A simple hut sufficed, and afforded two days of seclusion. On 11 October, he and his men resumed their journey. The train came to a blown bridge, where crews were still clearing the tracks, and passed over a temporary pontoon bridge at slow speed.

The transports continued slowly northward through little villages with strange names. As they rolled through one small station, elderly German railroad employees shouted the latest news, "Kiev Kaput! Leningrad besieged! Moscow about to fall!"[32] The *guripas* wished for more speed, lest they arrive too late for the final victory. But arrive where? Although some volunteers were already in the line, those on the trains had no idea where they were going. Dno was the next stop. Here, the transports were off-loaded and the infantry reloaded onto German-gauge trains while usable horses and vehicles moved out on the Novgorod highway.

Critical German eyes observed the unloading. I Corps had dispatched a special detail under Captain Wessel to scrutinize and report on the Blue Division and the German Liaison Staff.[33] Wessel reported to I Corps that: "The 250 Division is structured like any other German division, and with few exceptions, armed like one (for example, they were not issued 50 mm Pak)."[34] This was the first time General von Both had any concrete information about the Blue Division. Neither he nor his staff had any idea about what to expect. Even information about the German Liaison Staff was lacking. Wessel explained that Major von Oertzen led the Liaison Staff. "A newly arrived general staff officer, a certain Captain Kollatz [*sic*] served as Ia."[35]

During their two months with the Blue Division, the Liaison Staff had learned a lot about Spanish *modus operandi*. Improvisation ruled. Even the manner of issuing orders was radically different from the German. Rather than use a command tone, senior Spanish officers gave orders to subordinates over a friendly cup of coffee in a casual manner. The rank of the person giving the orders, not his position or function, counted. Junior officers, Wessel believed, were unwilling to assume responsibility for making decisions or initiating orders on their own. Wessel also erroneously assumed that the senior officers acted likewise and that the entire officer corps was so in awe of Muñoz Grandes that they deferred to him and followed his orders blindly.

General Muñoz Grandes and his staff listened courteously to all suggestions made by the German Liaison Staff, Wessel reported, and then proceeded to do what they thought best. It mattered little when the Germans drew the Spaniards' attention to OKH directives. And, if a German should presume to use other than an amiable manner, passive resistance immediately appeared.

Unknown to Captain Wessel, Spanish passive resistance had been provoked by Major von Oertzen who seldom missed an opportunity to denigrate his comrades-in-arms. Wessel's observations, however, clashed with those of Captain Collatz who, only three days before, had written that discipline within the division was improving and that the Liaison Staff and Divisional Staff were working well together. Both Wessel and Collatz agreed that, since 700 horses were lacking, the division's mobility was seriously impaired. It was left to Corps, Army, and Army Group to evaluate Wessel's and Collatz's reports, to reconcile the more optimistic Collatz with the apprehensive Wessel, and to absorb the significance of the noted Spanish-German temperament and character differences.[36]

Army Group North was not slow to react. On 10 October, Chief of Staff Brennecke ordered Major von Gersdorff to investigate the question of leadership in the Liaison Staff. Perhaps von Oertzen was at fault, and the division would function better if he were replaced. Three days later, von Oertzen was dismissed and returned to XXXVIII Corps. Collatz was appointed to lead the Liaison Staff. The diplomatic and astute Collatz was expected to work better with the Spaniards. The young captain, who continually drew attention to the fighting spirit of the volunteers, also had a healthy respect for Muñoz Grandes. They were already developing a good working relationship as they struggled together to coordinate the shipment of the division from Vitebsk to Dno, and into the firing line.[37]

At Dno, rigid occupation measures were in force. A macabre spectacle stunned the *guripas*. The frail body of an old woman was dangling from a tall green post in the center of the town square. They inquired about the corpse. An officer from the *Kommandantur* explained: "It is difficult, comrade, to judge things by their first impression."[38]

The occupation commandant had worked in Russia during the

1920s and 1930s as an engineer and knew the language and the people. A fifty-two-year-old reservist and a decorated hero of the First World War, he had resolved to direct a humane administration. The population responded but the partisans planned his assassination. One day, as his staff car punctually returned to the *Kommandantur*, the old woman, acting upon instructions from the partisan commissar, placed two mines in the road. He and his driver were blown to bits. She was caught, tried, and hanged.[39]

Confronted by the brutality of war, a grim reminder of the strife that had battered Spain for three years, the depressed volunteers returned to their trains. They were not even cheered by the announcement from divisional headquarters that they would now receive combat pay—one mark extra per day plus 30 percent of their base pay.[40]

Upon detraining in Dno, Esparza reported in at the rear echelon of divisional headquarters. It was Sunday, 12 October—*El Día de la Raza*. After mass with the sappers in the town square, Esparza prepared to push off for Miasnoi Bor. For security, he travelled in convoy with his old friend Mazariegos, (G-3). Mazariegos told Esparza that he had just been informed that Divisional GHQ had been moved from Miasnoi Bor to some place called Grigorovo. He didn't know for certain where Grigorovo was except that it was near Novgorod. They would have to find it together.

The two colonels climbed into their limousines and, escorted by two light trucks carrying personnel of the headquarters guard, bounced over a wretched road northeastward to Soltsy. There, the Studebaker President again ran into trouble. The battery began to fail. Esparza directed a futile search through ten repair shops for battery acid. Finally, he was able to exchange the battery for a used one in good condition. Only a few miles behind the front, and no battery acid! Since Vitebsk, German organization and supply had deteriorated. The vast expanse of Russia and partisan activities were taking their toll. After Shimsk, the convoy followed a corduroy road along the western shore of Lake Il'men. They could move faster now, but the tree-trunk massage overheated the tires and one by one the patches on the tubes peeled off. Esparza began to compare the modern Wehrmacht with his Studebaker President—a finely tuned and excellent machine, humbled and brought to grief by the primitiveness of Russia.

Not far from Novgorod, they drove onto a paved road, which paralleled the railroad tracks and took them into the city and beyond. Although it was only 1700, it was pitch dark. Motoring through the ruined town was treacherous. Even the masked headlights had to be extinguished. Soviet artillery observers called down fire on any light that glimmered. Three kilometers north of Novgorod, they found the Grigorovo turnoff. Driving westward down the narrow, level road, the two colonels stopped at the Spanish Field Hospital to inquire about the location of GHQ. The pharmaceutical chief informed them that it was about five kilometers further on in a former Red Army munitions depot. Armed with the map provided by the pharmacist, they drove through increasingly heavy woods across the tracks of the Novgorod-Chudovo railroad, and entered the forest-shrouded camp. A sentry directed them to one of the low, one story buildings. There, an aide ushered them into the presence of Muñoz Grandes. The angular *madrileño* rose from his chair and greeted his old comrades. There was little time for pleasantries. The general ordered Esparza to reconnoiter his sector immediately. He called for Zanón, who took Esparza to the maps and explained the situation. His eyes sparkling, the gaunt Zanón was always a welcome sight. His tall, spare frame made him seem ascetic, like a knight-errant in a crusade, or a Jesuit on campaign. Esparza bent forward to follow his boney finger as it spread rapidly over the German *Lagekarten*.[41]

On 10 October, while Esparza was still in transit, the orders to relieve 126 Division between Podberez'e and Chudovo were suddenly canceled. Instead, Army Group North had instructed 16 Army and I Corps to shift 250 Division southward to Novgorod. The Spaniards would now replace the southern units of 126 Division, in the Podberez'e sector, and the entire 18 Motorized. The Podberez'e sector was originally to be the southern limit of the division. It was now to be the northern.

The deployment of the division extended from the northern tip of Lake Il'men to just south of Miasnoi Bor at Zmeisko. Lake Il'men would be covered, at least temporarily by the Silesians of 18 Motorized as they withdrew southward from Novgorod for reassignment.[42] Zanón told Esparza that he had been very busy reshuffling 262, the artillery regiment, and the antitankers which had already entered the line of 126 Division. He complained that he had just got the General Staff to set up in Miasnoi Bor when the order arrived, and he had had to rush down to Grigorovo in order to redeploy the division and receive the units coming up. All of this with no advance notice. He might have been prepared to accept this in the Spanish Army, but he thought that the Wehrmacht was more efficient.[43]

The chief of staff lamented that the roads immediately behind the front were clogged with German divisions rushing hither and yon—all to no point, as far as he could see. What a waste of precious fuel, and wear on the men, horses, and vehicles. He consoled himself that it was all part of a massive reorganization preparatory for an offensive, which according to the corps commander, would annihilate the enemy. Unknown to the Spaniards, they had been caught up in a command decision in the *Führerhauptquartier* and a series of squabbles between Army Group, Army, and Corps.

The Führer had ordered von Leeb to prepare a twin offensive to combine the destruction of Leningrad with the leap towards Moscow. This double attack was based upon a drive by 16 Army in two separate directions. One drive was a double envelopment of Lake Il'men, on the south and north, which was to speed 200 kilometers southeastward across the Valdai Hills toward Borovichi. From there it would push another 250 kilometers along the October Railway on to Kalinin (Tver), where it would meet the north wing of Army Group Center as Operation Typhoon struck towards Moscow. The second drive, based on Chudovo, would strike some 100 kilometers eastward across the Volkhov to capture the rail junction and bauxite center of Tikhvin. Then, completely outflanking Lake Ladoga, Busch was to press northward from Tikhvin to join the Finns at the Svir. Leningrad would be isolated, and its strangulation could begin.[44]

OKW assured von Leeb that the Red Army was at the end of its reserves. But his own intelligence reports indicated that the Soviet forces facing 16 Army were formidable. General P. A. Kurochkin, who had assumed command of the Northwest Front on 23 August had five armies—27, 34, 52, 4, and 54 with a total of thirty infantry, two cavalry, and three armored divisions. In addition, Soviet Independent 7 Army under General K. A. Meretskov lay close at hand along the quiescent Svir River front. Fifty-second and 4 Red Armies held the Volkhov, while 54 Army lay west of the river's mouth, guarding the Leningrad lifeline around Volkhovstroi.

General Busch had only four army corps (II, X, I, and XXXIX) with fifteen infantry, two motorized, and two Panzer divisions. Many of his units, however, were tied down on the Leningrad front. He had no reserves. In addition, the Red Air Force flew practically unopposed through the skies of Army Group North. However, Operation Typhoon was moving well. The northern wing of Army Group Center was approaching Kalinin, and many in the High Command were convinced

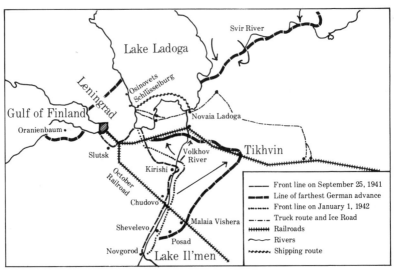

German Strike for Tikhvin

Front line on September 25, 1941
Line of farthest German advance
Front line on January 1, 1942
Truck route and Ice Road
Railroads
Rivers
Shipping route

that the enemy, faced with a threat to his capital and the isolation of his forces in the northwest, would have to withdraw. Red units facing 16 Army in the Valdai and along the Volkhov were expected to fade away into the Russian hinterland. Nevertheless, von Leeb requested more reinforcements, since 227 Division was not up to hard fighting after eighteen months of occupation duty in France, and 250 Division was practically immobile due to the lack of horses and the attrition of motor vehicles.[45]

A confusing reshuffling accompanied Army Group North's preparation for this offensive. Von Leeb suggested to Busch that 16 Army switch the commanders and staffs of I and XXXIX Corps. Busch complied. On 12 October, General von Both and his I Corps staff were to exchange with Gen. Rudolf Schmidt and his XXXIX Corps headquarters group. Busch recommended that 126 Division, a battle-tested unit, open the assault across the Volkhov for 12 Panzer and 18 Motorized at Kuzino. Von Leeb concurred. This meant that the Rhineland-Westphalians would merely be shifted slightly northward, to the down-river crossing point of XXXIX Corps at Kuzino.[46]

But the Spaniards were already moving in to replace 126 Division! No matter, the two generals agreed. The 250 Division would continue to take over the southern sector of 126 Division. However, since 18 Motorized was now to be pulled out as well, 250 Division would relieve them at Novgorod, giving the Blue Division a front comprising the entire former sector of 18 Motorized plus the former southern sector of 126 Division. Small wonder that Zanón saw German divisions scurrying back and forth, just as the Spaniards were doing![47] The attack of XXXIX and I Corps was to be reinforced by a special task force. A new group, slated to include 250 Division, 126 Division, and 18 Motorized, would be formed under Army Group North's rear area commander, Gen. Franz von Roques. Group von Roques was to break out between Novgorod and Chudovo and strike eastward.

Army Order 24 confirmed these decisions. However, Group von Roques lost both 18 Motorized and 126 Division to Schmidt's XXXIX Corps. The new group was now to consist essentially of 250 Division, which was to concentrate in Novgorod. There, the Blue Division would feint across the Little Volkhov and draw the Russians toward them, while 126 Division crossed downriver at Kuzino. As 126 Division moved southeastward toward Bronnitsy on the lower Msta, the Soviets were expected to fall back. This would give the Spaniards an easy crossing over the Little Volkhov and enable them to occupy the bare hills dominating their staging area on the island between the Volkhov and Little Volkhov. Once 250 and 126 divisions were across and united on the east bank, 126 Division would also come under General von Roques and the two would drive in tandem from Bronnitsy along the road to Krestsy and the Valdai Hills.

Army Order 24 sent the units behind the German lines along the Volkhov rushing into position. No date was set for the attack, but it was obvious that the offensive was imminent. The order activated Group von Roques at 1800 on 11 October. General von Roques established his Group GHQ at Grigorovo where he immediately took up contact with the commander of the heart of his group—General Muñoz Grandes.

The amiable sixty-four-year-old Hessian informed the Spanish commander of his mission. When Muñoz Grandes inquired about air cover for the operation, von Roques explained that Gen. Alfred Keller, an "old eagle" from World War I, had few aircraft to spare from Air Fleet I. These would concentrate on the river crossings at Kuzino and Grusino. The Spaniard was surprised to learn that even at the front, antiaircraft units remained under Luftwaffe control. Only a few 88 mm Flak 36s and 37 mm Flak 18s could be spared to protect the rail yard and bridge at Novgorod from the Red Air Force.[48]

Turning to the intelligence reports, von Roques indicated that Gen.

N. K. Klykov, commander of Soviet 52 Army, had deployed approximately two and a third divisions opposite the sector now being taken over by the Blue Division. Third Armored Division (Tank Regiments 5, 6, 7, 55, and Artillery Regiment 3) was concentrated across from Novgorod, between the northern shore of Lake Il'men and the Valdai-Moscow highway. The *guripas* ought not to be concerned about the power and mobility of this unit, von Roques went on, because it was mainly on foot, having lost all of its tanks earlier in the campaign. It had only a few light tanks now. Downriver, 305 Rifle Division (Regiments 1000, 1002, 1004, and Artillery Regiment 1004) clung to the Volkhov shore as far north as Dubrovka; 267 Rifle Division held the stretch from Dubrovka to Kuzino, but only Regiment 848 was in the Spanish sector.[49]

General Muñoz Grandes, reflecting on his flight across Lake Il'men and down the Volkhov, recalled the open ground of the island of Novgorod. Now, Novgorod was his, and his *guripas* would have to feint an attack without air cover and charge across the broad river against the bare hills beyond. And where were the assault boats? More important, when were the rest of his troops coming up?

He and Zanón discussed these matters with Gen. Friedrich Herrlein, commander of 18 Motorized and his Ia, Maj. Heinrich Nolte. The two staffs conferred daily at the forest camp of Grigorovo. The Germans briefed the Spaniards on their experiences on the Eastern front. Muñoz Grandes and Zanón were eager to learn. The Germans were impressed by the Spaniards' modest and unassuming attitude. Muñoz Grandes, in spite of his high position and long combat experience, was remarkably free of any "know-it-all attitude."

Nolte, who worked closely with Muñoz Grandes and Zanón during the transfer, considered them *gute Kamaraden*. His respect for the Spanish general grew every day. Determination was Muñoz Grandes's chief characteristic. He was able to impose his will on his volunteers whose attitude was marked by high spirits, personal bravery, and a sort of freebooter mentality. Muñoz Grandes seemed to know just when to intervene. And when he gave an order, it was blindly and unquestioningly obeyed.[50]

Esparza had just received such an order. Having driven the whole day of 12 October from Dno, nursed his Studebaker over corduroy roads and through a new battery, gotten lost in Novgorod, found Grigorovo through the grace of a pharmacist, and been briefed on a complex deployment of his regiment by the chief of staff, the exhausted colonel was now ordered to reconnoiter his sector and report back the next evening. Buoyed by the knowledge that he was at the front at last, the ex-legionnaire set out in the frigid Sunday night and promptly got lost again. The cold night of 12 October masked the relief of 18 Motorized. Second and third Battalions of 262 relieved two battalions of Col. Werner von Erdmannsdorff's 30 Regiment on the island at Novgorod.[51]

The *Landser* were glad to leave their exposed position. Third Armored had been probing across the Little Volkhov all day, but the Germans had held. It was pitch black now, and the relief operation was going well. Except that the Spaniards couldn't see where they were supposed to go. Finally, here and there, little glimmers of light pierced the darkness. The *guripas* lit matches and candles so that they could assemble their mortars! The reaction of the *Landser* was swift. "Extinguish those lights!" But nothing fazed the volunteers. After a march of 1,000 kilometers they had finally reached the war and they were going to enjoy it. As they joked and kept up constant chatter, it seemed to the veterans of 18 Motorized that the newcomers failed to appreciate the seriousness of the occasion. There was, in the words of Manuel Guijarro y Agüero, a "cosmic gap between the temperament of the Germans and the Spaniards."[52]

Meanwhile, Colonel Badillo and the artillery headquarters battery moved through snow flurries from Koptsy to Grigorovo, where they were temporarily placed under the fire control command of Herrlein until the sector transfer was completed. The next morning, when the Germans awoke at 0700, they found the Spaniards warming themselves and toasting their bread by campfires. The *guripas* greeted the *Landser* of 18 Motorized Artillery Regiment with a lighthearted "Mucho frio, amigo!" Capt. Arno Pentzien, who observed the relief, commented: "The Spaniards trumpet the whole day through. To eat, and also to pray. The bugler is a small youth of about 15 years of age. An altar is set up. The priest arrives, and the Spaniards are already there—kneeling, praying, and singing, as if the war were not raging around them. It is like a (scene from a) painting."[53]

An ebullient Victor Jiménez warmed himself at an open bonfire, built by his comrades to ward off the cold. A runner dashed up. "A message from the Major," he gasped. The lieutenant took the envelope, broke the seal, and read:

Lieutenant Jiménez:

With a special squad of men, you will carry out at sunset the sentence of execution on two Communist partisan chiefs, who were caught last night, 11 October.

You will find the prisoners in the *Ortskommandantur* at Novgorod. Having carried out your orders you will report to me.

Received from higher authorities and transmitted at 1530 hours, 12 October 1941, on campaign.

Prado O'Neill[54]

The young interpreter blanched. Picking up his men, twelve soldiers and a noncom, he started for the *Ortskommandantur*. On the way, his nervous hands checked his pistol. Then he instructed the squad in the procedure to be followed in the execution.

Outside of the building, a small crowd had gathered. "My God, was that Laura?" It was! He knew intuitively what had happened. Without a word, Jiménez rushed inside, afraid to let the girl see him. He was more nervous now. As the partisan leaders were brought before him, the young man broke into a cold sweat. One was her father, he knew it. His fingernails pressed deep into his palms and he could feel a trickle of blood. Pulling himself together he led the squad outside and out of the ruined city.

The last golden rays of sunset broke upon the small clearing. Jiménez fastened the blindfolds himself. The two partisans muttered a few words and defiantly raised clenched fists in the Communist salute. Rejoining the firing squad Victor called out *"Carquen! Apunten!"* A soul-rending scream shattered the twilight—*"Fuego!"* The twelve shots sounded as one. "Sergeant, give them the *coup de grace!*"[55]

He turned to Laura. She was frozen in an aspect of horror. Her green eyes were opened wide, her hand held against silent, open lips. Walking up to her, Jiménez stopped. The two figures remained motionless. Suddenly, with a clarity and calmness he could never explain, he drew his pistol. Grasping the Luger by the barrel, he offered it to Laura. Another cry of horror rent the night. She turned and ran, a dark silhouette against the white snow. She disappeared forever.

5

Across the Volkhov

JIMENEZ RETURNED TO THE ORTSKOMMANDANTUR IN
Novgorod. The major instructed him to proceed at once to the island,
to join headquarters battery of Second Artillery at the monastery of
Khutyn.

The *Landser* of 126 Division had taken Khutyn in August at great
cost. Dominating the northern tip of the island at the confluence of
the Volkhov, the cloister had instantly been turned into a German
bastion. Meanwhile, south at Kirillovskoe on the Little Volkhov, was
another cloister. It, too, had become a focal point of enemy fire. Time
and again the Reds tried to retrieve it, but the German defense held.
Oberleutnant Richter, of 424 Regiment, proud of the steadfastness of
his men, claimed that the monastery was being defended like the Alcázar of Toledo. The name stuck. When the *guripas* of Pimentel's
regiment arrived, they found a ready-made symbol of their own Civil
War.

Second Group made Khutyn its headquarters. The shattered towers
served as observation posts. Telephone lines stretched back across the
river to the batteries. Jiménez arrived at 2200 on 12 October and reviewed the posts. If he had planned to get some sleep, he was in error.
Heavy firing broke out a few minutes before midnight. Muñoz Grandes
suddenly appeared, even more vigilant at the front than he had been in
the march.

"How is it going?"

"Stupendous, my general!"

83

"Are the Reds firing?"

"A little bit, my general."

"Don't forget for a moment that we are Spaniards, and that we have come here to demonstrate to Europe the worth of the Spanish people."

Suddenly three grenade explosions rent the night. One of the *guripas* was hit.

"It's nothing. The Reds are as cowardly here as they were in Spain."

Satisfied, the general went on to check 262, on the rest of the island.[1]

That morning, 13 October, Esparza's trusty Studebaker pulled up just outside Podberez'e. At former I Corps headquarters he met Major Rodríguez. The commander of First Group laid out his plans for covering the sector of 269. Since Lt. Col. Hemmann of 426 Regiment was absent, the colonel reconnoitered the area and returned later. The young Hemmann, with the Knight's Cross dangling from his collar, impressed the ex-legionnaire. They agreed that the relief would take place that very night. Esparza briefed Majors Luque and Pérez Pérez whose first and third battalions were in the act of detraining under artillery fire in the station at Podberez'e. The Red Air Force flew overhead. With no time to lose, the colonel hastened back to Grigorovo. But the general was out dining with Laux of 126 Division.

On the afternoon of 14 October Esparza assumed command of the Podberez'e sector. The 269 held a sixteen-kilometer front. Third Battalion (Pérez) covered the south, along the river bank near Kotovitsy. First Battalion (Luque) occupied the shore from Germanovo to Petrovskoe, and Major Román's Second Battalion from Gorka north to Lobkovo, near Miasnoi Bor. The defensive positions followed the military crest along the river bank. They consisted of individual strong points, some 1,200 meters apart, composed of bunkers surrounded by slit trenches and foxholes. There was no continual line. Since the area between the riverbank and the Novgorod-Chudovo highway was filled by thick forest, the Spaniards also had to be on their guard against partisans who operated to the rear in bands up to 1,500 strong.

The lack of secondary roads hindered lateral movement between battalions and obliged almost total dependence on the Novgorod-Chudovo highway, which the Germans referred to as "the artery of 16 Army." In the northernmost sector, garrisoned by Second Battalion, direct contact even between strong points was impeded by gullies.

Deeper than trenches, the gullies cut through the high ground and ran down the sloping bank to the water, providing ample concealment for enemy infiltration.[2]

Zanón's map board now showed 269 in the line. The peripatetic chief of staff, who did not at all like the delays and shifting around of his troops, noted with satisfaction that Pimentel and 262 were also dug in. In accordance with his orders the division was laid out along a sixty kilometer front extending from the middle of Lake Il'men in the south to Lubkovo in the north.[3] (South, 262; center, 263; north, 269.)

The steady, roughhewn Pimentel of 262 was regarded by the Germans of 18 Motorized whom he relieved as an "unshakable 'broad sword,' a reliable veteran."[4] And not without reason. Pimentel had led a *bandera* (battalion) of the Legion in the march to Madrid during the opening days of the Civil War. When the International Brigades checked Franco's drive on the capital, Pimentel took command of 17 Division. For his leadership and courage he was awarded the *Medalla Militar Individual*. Now, like many of the volunteers, he was paying the Russians a return visit.

Pimentel's Regiment and Reconnaisance Group 250 covered the southern sector from Erunovo at the mouth of the Veriazha River on Lake Il'men to Grigorovo. The extensive lakeshore frontage was lightly held, garrisoned only by a reconnaisance group. Colonel Pimentel set up his regimental command post just off Stalin Square, in the Kremlin.[5]

According to Zanón's map, Vierna's 263, only partially in the line as yet, would be moving in to the central sector. Thus, Vierna's regiment would hold the area between Grigorovo and Chichulino. Here, they would relieve 51 Motorized Regiment of 18 Motorized, and Vierna would establish his command post at Derevenitsy.[6]

Each regiment was supported by a group of medium howitzers, with Third Artillery Group covering the southern divisional sector (262), Second Group in the center (263), and First Group in the north (269). The 150s of Fourth Artillery were emplaced on the island, where they could support the focal point of the planned attack from central and southern sectors.

Divisional reserves for the offensive were First of 262 at Leshino (in the suburbs of Novgorod), Sappers 250 in the Kremlin, Divisional Antitanks and Mobile Reserve Battalion 250. The massing of divisional reserves in and around Novgorod was in accord with the new Führer

Directive of 13 October. Adolf Hitler ordered von Leeb to hurl 16 Army at Tikhvin. Borovichi was now a secondary objective. Panzer Group 3 had already cut the October Railroad near Kalinin. It seemed that the Soviets in the Valdai and on the Volkhov would have to fall back.

On 14 October Busch issued Army Order 25. "The enemy in front of Army Group Center is beaten and to a large part destroyed," he confidently proclaimed.[7] He called upon the southern wing of 16 Army to finish off the retreating Reds. The northern wing of the army was to open the Tikhvin offensive on 16 October. Group von Roques would simulate an attack out of Novgorod while infantry units of XXXIX Corps crossed down river at Kuzino and Grusino. Once across, the panzers would roll on to Tikhvin and then wheel northward to join the Finns on the Svir. Meanwhile, 126 Division would turn south from Kuzino, and take Shevelevo on the river bank and Otenskii and Posad inland. Thrusting forward, the Rhinelanders and Westphalians would drive toward the Msta River, thus allowing 250 Division to cross the Volkhov at Novgorod. The two divisions, now both under von Roques, would force the Msta near Bronnitsy and continue to pursue the fleeing Russians in a southeastward direction toward Borovichi.[8]

Thursday, 16 October, was clear and cold. Due to the frost, the roads were passable. The Tikhvin offensive opened as the *Landser* of 126 Division moved across the Volkhov at Kuzino. Russian defense was bitter. The Spaniards began probing repeatedly in strength, trying to draw the Reds toward them and mask the true direction of XXXIX Corps.

Dawn broke. Muñoz Grandes intensified his deception. Badillo's artillery unleashed a barrage that could have covered a full-scale assault. Nervously, the Russians replied, concentrating their fire on the Kremlin, where any attack force would have to mass.[9] None of the regimental commanders was more eager to impress the general than the ebullient Esparza. He received the order to send a raiding party across the Volkhov. Time and place were left to his discretion. After personally inspecting his northernmost Second Battalion, he granted the same freedom to Major Román.

From prisoner of war interrogations, the colonel knew that he faced the 848 Regiment of 267 Rifle Division. This division, under the command of General Selenkov, was composed largely of Ukrainians, with Russian officers and Russian political commissars. Since the

Soviets doubted the reliability of the Ukrainians, who were wont to desert, they had added Tartars to the division as "corset stays." But the Tartars were themselves restive under Russian command, and were gradually filtering across to surrender.[10] Zero hour was set for 1300 on 16 October. Lieutenant Galiana would lead the regimental assault section. The colonel anxiously waited at a large mansion on the riverbank near Novaia Bystritsa, known as the *Casa del Señor*. Nothing from the opposite bank indicated that the patrol had crossed. But, heavy firing broke out to the north on his own side of the river. Esparza hastily returned to the CP of Second of 269 at Novaia Bystritsa. What had happened?

A battalion of 267 Rifle Division had stormed across the river, right into the waiting guns of the Spanish raiding party. Román's Andalusians had sprung into action. The first light of dawn caught the bodies of forty Russians on the Spanish shore. The eastern bank was littered with corpses and the shattered hulls of Soviet skiffs. Proudly, Esparza reported the capture of twenty-seven prisoners.[11]

The Red artillery fire which saturated Román's sector also pounded First of 269. One of the first to fall was Cpl. Javier García Noblejas, a Falangist "old shirt," and recipient of the *Palma de Plata*, the highest decoration of the movement. García Noblejas had enlisted in the Regiment Rodrigo during the warm heady days of June when the war was new. Now, he lay cold and still in the Russian mud.[12]

Javier's brother, Ramón, the sole male survivor of a family which had been virtually wiped out in the Civil War, took the body to Grigorovo for interment. The fallen leader was given a Falangist farewell. Corvette Captain Manuel Mora Figueroa, a hero of the Civil War, and national councillor of the *Junta Política*, represented Muñoz Grandes, whom he served as an aide. Dionisio Ridruejo delivered a eulogy over the crude wooden coffin. Then, in Falangist fashion, Agustín Aznar called the role of the fallen. "Javier García Noblejas." The serried ranks shouted "Present."[13] As the comrades filed by the open pit and dropped in a handful of Russian earth, they recalled the words of Serrano Suñer at the *Estación del Norte*—"The five roses of the Falange will flower in the tortured fields of Russia."[14]

A few hours later on Friday morning, 17 October, Busch telephoned von Roques. Sixteenth Army wanted to know if 269 could cross the Volkhov, build a bridgehead, and drive south on the east bank to open the Novgorod crossing. The 126 Division was held up at the Kuzino bridgehead. Von Roques ordered 250 Division to support 126 Division with artillery from the northern sector on 17 and 18 October. Regiment 269 was also to force the Volkhov. Once across, Esparza would assist 126 Division and then drive south to open the Novgorod bridgehead.[15] Meanwhile the Spanish artillery, in conformance with the attack plan, was ordered to shift strength to the island of Novgorod. Third Group of German Artillery Regiment 207 was also transferred to the Novgorod area. Here, Muñoz Grandes had concentrated the strength of the division.[16]

The attack out of Novgorod would encompass three waves. First, 262 would assault between Sholochevo and Volotovo, without artillery preparation. Simultaneously, and also in a surprise attack, 263 would move on Radionovo and Schendorf. Both would be supported by Sappers 250. The attack was tentatively set for the next day.[17]

On 18 October Muñoz Grandes ordered Esparza to extend his sector four kilometers northward, to Udarnik and Borisovo, replacing units of 126 Division, which was being funneled across at Kuzino. Intermittent snow punctuated 18 October. A thin white blanket covered the ground. That afternoon Esparza launched his first effort to establish a bridgehead. It failed. A thirty-man strike from Udarnik gained the opposite shore, beat off a counterattack and captured twenty-seven prisoners. But, misdirected artillery fire from the neighboring 18 Motorized rained on their position, killing two *guripas* and wounding seven, forcing the section to withdraw. Four soldiers drowned on the way back when some overloaded boats capsized. More would have been swept away if it had not been for the efforts of the POWs who astonishingly spared no effort to rescue their new captors.[18]

Another effort to open the Novgorod bridgehead from the north was set for 0800 the next day, Sunday, 19 October.[19] But the rubber boats were late. A break in the frost combined with rain turned the road from Miasnoi Bor to Udarnik into a quagmire and the entire area into slush and swamp. The dejected colonel was finally forced to abandon his grand Studebaker. Only the regiment's plebian seven-horsepower Ford was light enough to slide forward. Boats and skiffs were manhandled through the trees to the waterside. At 1500 hours Lt. José Escobedo pushed off without artillery preparation. The surprise was complete.

Escobedo led his thirty-six man section through the minefields and fell on the Russians who were dug in on a small rise on the topographical crest east of the road. They fled leaving behind booty and forty-two prisoners. Emplacing his two machine guns in readiness for

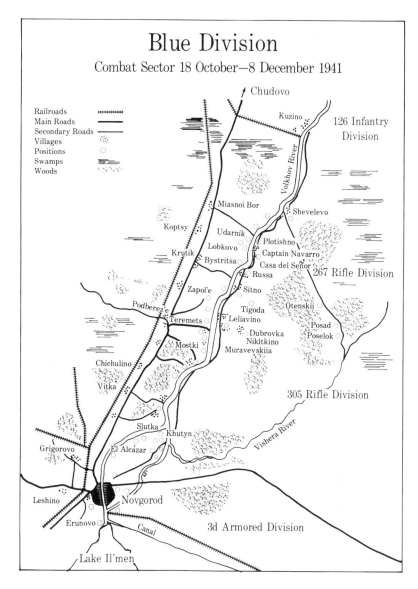

Blue Division
Combat Sector 18 October—8 December 1941

Railroads
Main Roads
Secondary Roads
Villages
Positions
Swamps
Woods

Chudovo

Kuzino

126 Infantry
Division

Volkhov River

Miasnoi Bor

Shevelevo

Koptsy

Udarnik

Plotishno

Lobkovo

Captain Navarro

Krutik

Casa del Señor

Bystritsa

Russa

267 Rifle Division

Zapol'e

Sitno

Podberez'e

Tigoda

Otenskii

Teremets

Leliavino

Posad

Dubrovka

Poselok

Mostki

Nikltkino

Muravevskiia

Chichulino

Vitka

305 Rifle Division

Slutka

Khutyn

Vishera River

Grigorovo

El Alcázar

Leshino

Novgorod

Erunovo

Canal

3d Armored Division

Lake Il'men

the expected counterattack, Escobedo evacuated his wounded. The POWs were put to work unloading the munitions and supplies which were being ferried across the 250-meter-wide river. The ammunition would be needed.

Second battalion of 848 Regiment attacked at 1900 hours. They were driven back into the darkness. Reinforced from Third of 848 Regiment, ear flaps on their pointed Mongolian hats flying, the Reds came on again within an hour. They broke into Escobedo's position, but after a brief hand to hand struggle, fell back. Smarting from their casualties, the Russians rested. Their assault of 2300 hours lacked the earlier ferocity. Pulling themselves together, they unleashed a new attack at midnight. Supported by artillery, they rolled on in waves shouting the blood curdling battle cry of *"Urrah! Urrah!"* They swamped the Spanish line. All seemed lost. But Escobedo had held two squads of 6 Company in reserve. The *guripas* attacked with all the fury of four centuries of Spanish infantry tradition. Stunned, the Russians hesitated, then scattered for the woods. The bridgehead of Second of 269 was secure. Dawn revealed the extent of the carnage. The knoll was surrounded by Soviet dead and wounded. Escobedo allowed the Russians to drag off their bleeding comrades. From Udarnik the colonel surveyed the scene. In honor of a fallen friend he christened the height Captain Navarro.

The exploits of Escobedo and his successful establishment of a Spanish bridgehead at Captain Navarro were unknown to 16 Army and Army Group North. By the morning of 20 October both Busch and von Leeb were troubled about the failure of the enemy to pull back. The two bridgeheads at Kuzino and Grusino were isolated. After more than four days of fighting they only averaged twenty kilometers by twenty kilometers. Russian resistance and unbelievable mud, characteristic of the season known as *rasputitsa*, had slowed the advance. The few roads had disintegrated. Movement and provisioning caused greater difficulties than the Reds. Hitler inquired about the effectiveness of Army Group North's panzers east of the Volkhov. Were weather and lack of roads endangering the entire operation?

Oblivious to the hesitations and doubts of the high command, Esparza and Román began to feed reinforcements across the river. Two companies of Second of 269 passed over under heavy, but inaccurate, artillery fire, climbed the bank, and moved forward 1,200 meters to the south-north road. That afternoon Esparza threw over his regimental reserve—11 Bicycle Company. These dismounted cyclists were followed by 11 Company of Major Suárez Rosello's Third of 263. Muñoz Grandes rushed up more reserves and reinforcements—Ninth and Tenth Companies of Third of 263 as well as Second Company of the Divisional Antitanks. The antitankers confidently looked forward to pitting their 37 mm Paks against the T-26s of 3 Armored. A pontoon bridge company from Sappers 514 arrived at Udarnik. Even Third Group of 207 Artillery Regiment, which was more mobile than

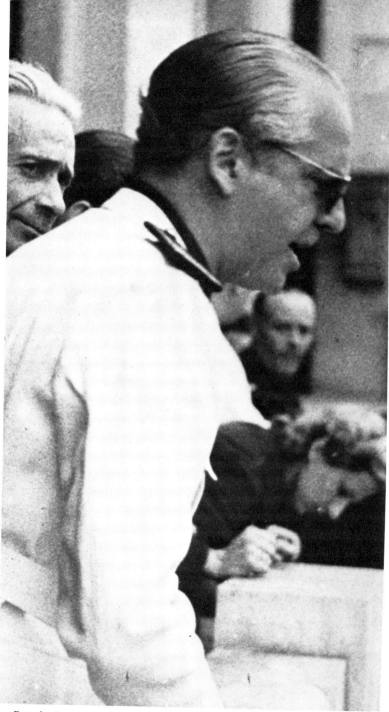

Ramón Serrano Suñer, Spanish foreign minister, dressed in the white uniform of the Falange, delivering his "Russia Is Guilty" speech to the tumultuous throng from the balcony of the Secretary General of the Falange, 24 June 1941.—Photograph courtesy of Ramón Serrano Suñer

Once across the German border, enthusiastic crowds greeted the troop trains and pressed flowers and other gifts on the guripas of the Blue Division traveling to the training camp of Grafenwöhr, Bavaria.—Photograph from the authors' collection

Diplomatic and astute, and with a keen perception of the fighting spirit of the Spanish volunteers and a healthy respect for Gen. Agustín Muñoz Grandes, Capt. Günther Collatz, here depicted in the winter of 1941–42, was appointed to lead the German Liaison Staff attached to the Blue Division on October 13, 1941.—Photograph courtesy of Lt. Col. Günther Collatz, GS (ret.)

Spanish volunteers passing through Novgorod. Contrary to popular myth, the Wehrmacht was far from completely mechanized. The Spanish Volunteer Division was furnished extensively with horses and in fact had been originally requested to bring trucks from Spain.—Photograph from the authors' collection

Gen. Friedrich Herrlein (left), commander of 18 Motorized, and Gen. Muñoz Grandes (right), commander of the Blue Division, conferring in the forest camp of Grigorovo, October 1941.—Photograph courtesy of Col. Heinrich Nolte, GS (ret.)

Gen. Franz von Roques (right) outlines the offensive across the Volkhov to Muñoz Grandes (left), October 1941.—Photograph from the authors' collection

Elements of 262 Regiment, one of three of 250 Division (as the Blue Division was designated by the Germans), entering the kremlin at Novgorod, October 1941.—Photograph from the authors' collection

Lt. José Escobedo, achieving complete surprise, crossed the Volkhov with a force at 1500 hours on Sunday, 19 October 1941, and, after capturing forty-two prisoners and defeating two ferocious counterattacks, established a bridgehead. For his gallantry in action, the wounded lieutenant, as shown here, was awarded the Iron Cross and the Medalla Militar Individual *while at the Grigorovo field hospital, 25 October 1941.—Photograph from the authors' collection*

Muñoz Grandes (right) chats with a wounded guripa *in the field hospital at Novgorod, November 1941. Of working-class background, the commanding general of the Blue Division had a lively sympathy for and understanding of his enlisted men.—Photograph from the authors' collection*

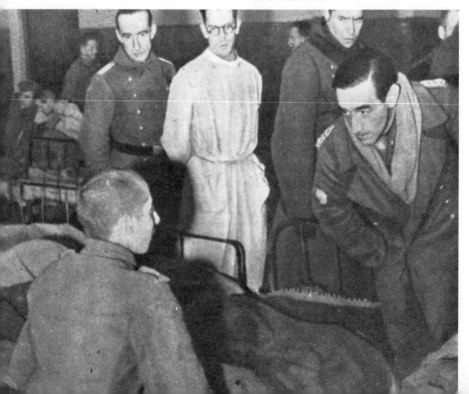

Surveying the enemy's former field of fire from a captured Maxim machine gun during the Volkhov offensive, October 1941.—Photograph from the authors' collection

Feldpost (field post office). The man on the left is a Russian POW. While the Soviets fought with a dogged fatalism in total disregard of their lives, once captured they became docile and proved excellent workers willing even to defend their Spanish captors.—Photograph from the authors' collection

By November 1941, when these 75 mm support artillery pieces were being moved up by sled to support the vulnerable Volkhov bridgehead, winter had thoroughly set in.—Photograph from the authors' collection

[OPPOSITE] *Fire mission for the 105s, winter 1941–42.—Photograph from the authors' collection*

An all-too-typical scene of warfare in the Russian winter, January 1942. Not only did vehicles have difficulty negotiating the primitive roads, but they and any mechanical equipment often froze up.—Photograph from the authors' collection

Whenever the Spaniards could, they took shelter from the howling Russian winter in izbas, *wooden cabins which, when overheated, tended to catch fire. Here* divisionarios *are celebrating Christmas 1941.—Photograph from the authors' collection*

Hitler wished to size up the replaced first commander of the Blue Division as a possible alternative to the stubborn Franco who was not about to become the Führer's puppet. Muñoz Grandes (left) met Hitler (right) at the Wolf's Lair, Rastenburg, 11 July 1942, and was captivated, gaining the impression that the Führer loved and respected Spain.—Photograph courtesy of the United States Army

Members of the ski patrol, Captain Ordás commanding, setting out across the ice at Lake Il'men to relieve their embattled German comrades at Vsvad on the southern shore of the lake. When the force set out on 10 January 1942, the thermometer read −32 degrees Celsius.—Photograph from the authors' collection

Gen. Philipp Kleffel (left) and Brigadier Emilio Esteban Infantes (right, wearing hat), second commander of the Blue Division, review the 22 March Battalion upon its arrival at Viarlevo, 1943.—Photograph from the authors' collection

Esteban Infantes (left) receiving the scroll conferring the award of the Knights Cross from Hitler (right). Sonderführer Hans Hoffmann (center) translates. At the Wolf's Lair, 8 November 1943.—Photograph from the authors' collection

its Spanish counterparts, was shifted from Novgorod to Bystritsa to lend support.[20]

Meanwhile, Román pushed southward from Captain Navarro through minefields towards Zmeisko. Brushing aside enemy resistance, the *guripas* occupied the village. Weak counterattacks were beaten back, and 848 Regiment retired to the cover of the forest. Captain Barbudo of 13 Company (close support artillery) bolstered the bridgehead by manhandling four 75 mm howitzers across the pontoon ferry which the Germans had quickly thrown up. Unfortunately, ramps were lacking at each end and only the agile infantry could pass without difficulty. The regimental seven-horsepower Ford was wrestled toward the west bank, but it stuck in the mud. Efforts to drag it nearer the pontoon using the teams from the 75s failed. Finally, a motorcycle with a sidecar was carried over. This was the only motor vehicle in the bridgehead. To the north the situation was the same. The tankers of 8 Panzer had abandoned both their tracked and four-wheel drive vehicles and slogged ahead on foot.[21]

Román sought to improve the supply situation by employing Russians. Numerous prisoners, ear flaps on their pointed Budennyi caps drooping, shoved provisions and munitions up the slippery bank and aided the evacuation of the few Spanish casualties. The POWs were practically indistinguishable from the mud in their brown uniforms. The glutenous muck had long since sucked the boots from their feet, which now were wrapped in rags. Many smiled as the Spaniards slogged by. Some, apparently unable to understand that not all Spaniards were some form of Communist, shouted "Pasionaria, gut."[22]

Meanwhile the men of 11 Company of 263, having abandoned their clogged bicycles on the west bank, plodded four kilometers northward from Captain Navarro. Just outside Shevelevo they met a mounted reconnaissance unit of 126 Division. The Spanish and German bridgeheads were joined.[23] That night, under cover of thick fog, more units shuffled over. As the *guripas* clambered up the muddy bank, they could see the cheery glow of campfires built by their comrades. To the south glimmered flashes of Soviet shells falling on Zmeisko.[24]

Rather than widening his toehold by moving eastward into the woods, Esparza sought to thrust toward Novgorod as soon as possible. His objective was the Muravevskiia Barracks opposite Podberez'e. General von Roques had just charged him with a dual mission. Two-six-nine was both to protect the south flank of XXXIX Corps along the general line Muravevskiia-Posad and to draw 305 Rifle and 3 Armored divisions away from the gates of Novgorod.[25]

Esparza directed Román to jump off at 1030 on 21 October. Pressing southward into Russa, Román ran into a fierce fire fight. Elements of 305 Rifle Division held the hamlet. Román forced them out, but the Reds rallied and the advance stopped.[26] The Spaniards now held a narrow strip three to five kilometers wide and ten kilometers long between the river and the woods. Supply was a greater problem than the Soviets. The pontoons at Udarnik could not handle vehicles. Mines and burned bridges limited the use of the road running parallel to the east bank. Moreover, munitions had priority. The men were living off raw cabbage precariously plucked from the minefields. The battalion field kitchens were enroute, but by the roundabout way of Kuzino and Shevelevo. Captured Russians were hauling supplies and constructing detours through the gullies at the burned bridges. Nevertheless, Esparza appealed to division for engineers from Sappers 250.

That Tuesday evening Esparza telephoned Muñoz Grandes. The general instructed Esparza to widen and lengthen the bridgehead in order to shield the southern flank of XXXIX Corps. A patrol was to cut eastward through the woods toward the Russian-held monastery of Otenskii. Midway, they would contact a German party from 30 Regiment of 18 Motorized which had reportedly advanced down the Shevelevo road. This road thrust through the Otenskii March to the Vishera and the Msta. Lieutenant Colonel von Erdmannsdorff's 30 Motorized Regiment had been shoved in between 250 and 126 Divisions. Advancing on a one-road front, they had been checked a kilometer and half outside of Otenskii. Not until 27 October did von Erdsmannsdorff extend his narrow salient through Otenskii, Posad, and Poselok to reach his objective, the Vishera. Consequently, the Spanish reconnaissance was canceled.[27]

Major Suárez Roselló arrived at Esparza's provisional Command Post (CP) at Borisovo at 0200 on Wednesday, 22 October. With Third of 263, he would hold the northern area from Zmeisko to Shevelevo. Wiry, balding, dynamic Román and Second of 269, spearheaded by Galiana and the assault section, would drive south. They would pierce the woods which reached the riverbank below Russa and occupy Sitno and Tigoda.

The attack jumped off at high noon. The Russians were dug in on the edge of the dark woods. Facing north, the machine gunners of 848 Regiment had a clear field of fire against Second of 269 which advanced through the open fields along the river. Artillery from the west bank was only partially effective against the well constructed machine gun nests and the riflemen concealed in the trees.

Román, his coal-black eyes flashing, commanded "Forward!" Galiana stormed ahead with his thirty-man section in open order. Men dropped under Russian fire. The rest halted. Suddenly two figures burst toward the chattering guns. Grenades hit the nest, killing and wounding the two crews. Galiana and his corporal jumped in and turned the smoking pit over to the onrushing section.

One machine gun still stuttered. Galiana and the corporal rushed along the fringe of the forest. A burst caught the pair in full battle cry "Arriba España!" Galiana stumbled a few steps forward and fell inertly into the damp grass. At that very instant the Soviet machine gunner twitched and sprawled quietly over the barrel of his Maxim. Stunned, the Russians broke. For this action Galiana was recommended for the *Laureada*. Back home, on the Plaza Castelar in Alicante, his tearful mother María received the news of her son's gallant death.

Second Battalion secured Sitno by 1600. After collecting prisoners and plunder—four Maxims in working order and numerous rifles and machine pistols—they settled in for a quiet night. Román had been ordered to hold up the advance on Tigoda. The colonel was busy reorganizing the bridgehead.

Earlier that Wednesday morning, Esparza had decided to relocate the pontoon ferry. He directed Pontoon Company 514 to move the ferry upriver to the *Casa del Señor*. The evacuation of casualties was still in progress. Aided by POWs, stretcher bearers carried officers and men through the sloppy snow from Sitno to the new crossing and then on to the first aid station at Udarnik. There were not enough stretchers so the men made slings out of blankets and carried them at the corners. Neither modern ambulances nor horse-drawn hospital wagons could negotiate the muck from Udarnik to Miasnoi Bor on the paved Novgorod-Chudovo highway. The suffering wounded were finally rescued by the pontooners of 514 who towed the ambulances to the main road with their all-terrain vehicles. The half-tracks were replaced the next day with wagons pulled by small *panje* (ponies), which could go where neither Mercedes nor Panzer dared.[28]

At the munitions lager near Grigorovo, von Roques pondered the situation. Since the attack out of Novgorod had been delayed but not canceled, von Roques ordered Muñoz Grandes on 22 October to cease weakening the strike force by reinforcing Esparza. However, the group commander was beginning to question the entire operation. Consequently, he saw no purpose in sending Esparza more men.[29] Reserve Battalion 250 had been alerted for transfer prior to von Roques' hold order of 22 October. Third Company was already motoring northward. The remaining legionnaires stood around Stalin Square awaiting transport. Then the stand down order arrived. Esparza would have to make do with what he had.[30]

Heavy firing awakened the colonel at 0500 on Thursday, 23 October. A barrage bracketed the crossing at the *Casa del Señor*. To the south at Sitno grenade blasts punctuated the rattle of machine guns and the snap of rifle fire. Upon ringing up Román's CP in Sitno, Esparza learned that the major was not available. Román had gone out to direct the defense. The wiry major was always the first to fight. Three battalions—First and Second of 1002 Regiment and First of 848—had infiltrated the positions of Second of 269 and First and Third Companies of First of 269. Working their way out of the woods and across the road under the cover of darkness, riflemen of 1002 Regiment slipped down the gullies which led to the water's edge. Then they sprang on the surprised Spaniards while 848 Regiment launched a frontal attack from Tigoda in the south.

Confident that Román had enough strength to ride out any storm, Esparza was only slightly taken aback when Muñoz Grandes suddenly rang. The fiery colonel was never more calm than when the general staff began to worry. Now, he was like ice. Assuring his commander that all would be well, he quickly paddled across the river. Upon disembarking, Esparza collided with a group of wounded *guripas*. Rather than complaining about their plight, they enthusiastically regaled him with accounts of the action. After a few *abrazos* and handshakes, the chubby colonel trudged toward Sitno, passing platoons of prisoners carrying Spanish and Russian casualties. His short legs could hardly maneuver through the slush and mud. Approaching the arroyo immediately north of Sitno, the colonel came upon Barbudo's 75s which, with barrels depressed, were firing shrapnel at clouds of shadowy figures a bare 100 meters away.

The firing slacked. As Esparza made his way down the main street, he could hear faint cheers from the other end of the hamlet. He met the gallant major. Román reported "All quiet, my colonel."[31] They spontaneously embraced and the small knot of officers and men —the chaplain, medical officers, aides, and orderlies—gathered around the pair broke into song! "Face to the sun with my new blue shirt which you embroidered yesterday in red. Death will find me if it seeks me and I will never see you again. I will fall in with my comrades who stand guard among the eternal stars, but whose posture, even in death proclaims courage." Spanish losses had indeed been heavy in the confused hand-to-hand fighting: nine officers, including Escobedo, and seventy-one men. But, First and Second of 1002 Regiment, trapped in the gulches north of Sitno, lost 250 dead and 400 prisoners. The fleeing Russians had tossed their weapons away and headed for the woods as fast as their legs could carry them. The commissars, as before, led the way.[32] Papers recovered from the corpse of a Russian major confirmed that the objective of the attack was to liquidate the bridgehead.

The scene was like a picture postcard. The snow covered everything—*izbas*, trees, fields, and even hid the mud below. The *feldgrau* uniforms of the hard working sappers stood out clearly against the whiteness, like so many sitting ducks in a shooting gallery. Esparza observed, however, that the combat units, in Spanish fashion, had improvised. The men were wearing the recently issued white long johns over their uniforms. This reversal of roles—outside instead of inside— provided camouflage without sacrifice of warmth.[33]

Muñoz Grandes, in spite of direct orders from Group, continued to feed in reserves. The divisional commander would not allow Esparza's 4,000 men to be overrun and cut to pieces on the isolated east bank. Third Company of Reserve Battalion 250 was already at hand. First Company was on the way. Battalion commander Osés reported in at the *Casa del Señor*. He advised Esparza that the remainder of his unit should arrive on the morrow.[34] Tall, handsome, ambitious Osés was an old friend of Esparza's. They had served together in Third Battalion of Ceuta Volunteers during the Civil War. Osés, already a holder of the *Medalla Militar Individual* was, like most of his men, from the *Regulares de Tetuán*.

Reserve Battalion 250—nicknamed *Tía Bernarda* or Aunt Bernardine or "the Bugger"—was one of the finest units in the Blue Division. Although carried on the TO&E as a Depot Battalion, *Tía Bernarda* served as a shock force. From their experiences in the Civil War, these tough professionals knew well the quality of Russian weapons. Upon crossing the Volkhov, the *africanistas* acted like vacuum cleaners. Captured mortars, heavy and light machine guns, automatic rifles, and machine pistols were sucked in until *Tía Bernarda* became the heaviest armed unit in the Division. The Russian machine pistols were called *rusos* in the Civil War. Now they began calling them *naranjeros* after cannon firing balls the size of oranges. Unfortunately, they were not yet completely reequipped when they took the vanguard.

Confirmation of both the general's and colonel's fears about a Soviet counterblow came that Thursday evening. An intercepted teletype message ordered the colonel commanding 848 Regiment and Third of 1004 to attack at all costs.[35] This warning from the German High Command was followed by a congratulatory message. For the first time, the Wehrmacht mentioned the Blue Division in dispatches. The OKW communique of 24 October announced: "Defending against a Soviet counterattack, the Spanish Blue Division on the northern sector of the Eastern Front has thrown the enemy back with heavy losses and has taken several hundred prisoners."[36] The Spanish back home were grateful for the news. They had received precious little information since the division had entrained for the east way back in August. In the interim, British propaganda had manufactured frightening stories which the BBC broadcast to the world about the fate of the volunteers.[37]

On 4 October, acting on express orders from the Caudillo and Serrano Suñer, the Spanish ambassador to Berlin, Count Mayalde, called at the *Wilhelmstrasse*. He told State Secretary Weizsäcker that he had been ordered to take up personal contact with the division. He insisted on going to the front himself. The Germans finally agreed. Accompanied by Roca de Togores and Victor de la Serna, editor of the Falangist daily *Informaciones*, Mayalde departed Berlin for Riga on Tuesday, 21 October. Since further travel was only safe during daylight hours due to partisans, they had to wait until Thursday morning to continue the journey. Driving eastwards towards Pskov, they passed long columns of ill-clad, famished prisoners. Appalled at the sight, they observed that apparently only those POWs repairing the roads received rations.

Upon arriving at Army Group North Headquarters, they called on Field Marshal von Leeb. Von Leeb told Mayalde that he had not intended to put the Blue Division immediately into an active sector. He would have preferred that the Spaniards could have a chance to accustom themselves gradually to the climate and the enemy. This had not been possible. Initial Spanish losses from Soviet attacks were rather high. However, once blooded, the division responded well. This confirmed his confidence in the Spaniards, which had led him to assign them to the crucial Novgorod sector in the first place.[38]

Later that day, the delegation motored on to Korosten. General

Busch had already received the news of the successful repulse early that morning of the Russian counterattack at Sitno. Therefore, he could greet the ambassador with word of a Spanish victory. Busch proclaimed that he had awarded Muñoz Grandes and some of his officers and men the Iron Cross, Second Class. At the close of their meeting, the army commander acceded to Roca de Togores's request for a daily telegram describing the activities of the Blue Division. This would be in addition to the daily killed in action report.[39]

It took four hours Friday morning to drive the forty-six kilometers along the snow-covered corduroy road from Korosten to the forest camp at Grigorovo. Smiling broadly, Muñoz Grandes emerged from his log cabin headquarters. After an *abrazo* for the Caudillo's emissaries, the general briefed them on the deployment of the division. A keen observer in spite of his reputation as a playboy, the military attaché went right to work. Shelter was more than adequate, Roca de Togores noted. Although Novgorod was destroyed, the surrounding villages provided solid protection against the −15 degree Celsius weather. Long underwear had arrived. Supply was in the act of issuing a second blanket and, for sentries only, a limited number of sheepskin-lined overcoats. These, along with the warm clothing which the Caudillo had begun to collect on 5 September, would certainly suffice for the autumn. About winter, he was not so sure. German rations were being supplemented by food sent from Spain. The traditional three hot meals a day, so different from German practice, were being served. He recommended more liquor from the motherland—with a high alcohol content so that the bottles would not shatter in the cold. Coffee, too, should be sent in order to replace the weak tea.

Deftly rolling a cigarette, Muñoz Grandes told his visitors that the division lacked remounts and motor vehicles. The general suggested that the Germans could not or would not supply either. Sixteenth Army had, however, offered fifty German fodderers and instructions on motor vehicle maintenance. Muñoz Grandes rejected this proffered assistance as incompatible with Spanish honor. Muñoz Grandes explained that the mobility of the division would be improved by the immediate dispatch of forty or fifty heavy trucks from Spain. They could be loaded, he suggested, with Franco's Christmas gift—*aguinaldo del Caudillo*.

The briefing completed, Muñoz Grandes accompanied his guests to the CP of Pimentel. The bull-like regimental commander beamed an enthusiastic welcome. Gómez Zamalloa, his *Laureada* gleaming on his tunic, came up and boomed out a greeting. Victor de la Serna thought that surely, here were men born to command. His romantic heart was already composing poems about the brave Spanish heroes writing a new chapter for Western Civilization in the snow-covered fields of the frozen Russian north. How he would write the story when he returned! His overcoat buttoned tightly and a black homburg pressed on his head, the heavy-set editor tramped around, chatting with the *guripas*. A civilian at the front, he stood out like a sore thumb.

The party continued on to the divisional field hospital in the former veterinary college at the Grigorovo turnoff, where von Roques awaited. They went into the salon, where the wounded officers lay on iron cots. With the Caudillo's ambassador and military attaché looking on, the corps commander pinned the Iron Cross, Second Class, on Muñoz Grandes's breast. Then turning to Escobedo, Muñoz Grandes described the young man's exploits.

"I award you, in the name of the Caudillo, the *Medalla Militar*, and in the name of the Führer—Chancellor of Germany—the Iron Cross."[40] He pinned the Iron Cross to Escobedo's arm sling, but had no *Medalla Militar*. Mayalde unfastened his own *Medalla Militar* from his dark blue Falangist uniform. He had won it in the Civil War. He handed it to the general, who pinned it on Escobedo's bandages. Loosening his cape, Muñoz Grandes walked into the amphitheater, where the wounded enlisted men awaited transport to the Spanish base hospital at Porkhov. With his Iron Cross dangling from his buttonhole, the divisional chief declared: "They have told me that I wear this medal in the name of all of you. In decorating me, they recognize your valor."[41] The representatives of the Caudillo had crammed as much as they could into the short, four-hour visit. Now they began their journey back to the capital of the Reich.

A few days later, a trainload of clothing and tobacco crossed the Pyrenees. The military attaché urged the Germans to speed the transit to the front, where the temperatures had fallen again.[42] The weather, however, was not yet cold enough for a hard freeze. The roads were still slush and mud. The Volkhov, though icy, still flowed swiftly. The frozen inlets along the shore hindered the launching of rubber rafts, but with the removal of the pontoon bridge to the *Casa del Señor* their employment was no longer so critical.

Esparza now commanded a thirty-kilometer front running from Kotovitsy in the south to Shevelevo in the north. He divided the fifteen-kilometer-long Sitno-Shevelevo bridgehead into three subsectors

—south (Osés), center (Román), and north (Suárez Roselló). Scattered outposts held the area northward from Zmeisko to Shevelevo. Daily patrols combed this strip, but as the colonel noted, at night this sector was really "guarded only by Providence and the stupidity of the enemy."[43]

The tactical situation did not favor the Spaniards. Squeezed into the three-to-five kilometer-wide clearing between river and forest, their line could be chopped into pieces by any attack out of the woods. The edge of the forest lay a scant kilometer from the topographical crest which, however, shielded the Sitno-Shevelevo road from Soviet small arms fire. The *guripas* occupied the Russian earthworks along this crest and from this cover commanded a clear field of fire. The ridge was only lightly held, since Esparza had concentrated in the South. The bulk of his forces could be cut off from the *Casa del Señor* crossing. Moreover, the fields along the river were ideal for armor. If the T-26s of 3 Armored ever rolled northward, it was doubtful whether the 37mm Paks could stop them.

Shaken, but not destroyed, Regiments 848 and 1002 began pulling together. Both battered units had almost distintegrated. Groups of Russians plodded along the forest trails living like hoboes. Only second lieutenants remained; the senior officers and commisars had fled. Morale was down and the Spaniards' tough fighting had driven it lower. But it was the bugles, the campfires, and the cheery singing of the *guripas* which testified to an elan that rattled the Ivans. Nevertheless, the Soviets rounded up enough forces to rush the bridgehead. Fragments of Regiments 848 and 1002 joined to form three battalions. This attack force struck at 0600 on Monday, 27 October.[44]

Advancing through the cold, predawn darkness two battalions charged out of the forest at the Spanish garrison in Sitno. Alerted by intelligence reports and awakened by intense artillery and mortar preparation, Román was ready. The Soviets got a hot reception. Tracer bullets stabbed the black sky. Shells bursts greeted the dawn. Soviet 122s and 152s blanketed the village and the opposite shore. First Artillery replied. But Spanish submachine guns were frozen. When the Soviets drew off and went to ground at 1900 they tried to dig in about 300 meters from the Spanish lines, but were driven into the forest by accurate artillery fire and a rapid counterattack. The assault then tapered off.

Tigoda and Dubrovka were Esparza's objectives. Ordering down the fresh Third of 263 from Zmeisko to Sitno on the night of 27–28

October, the colonel hoped to use them along with newly arrived Second Sapper Company in a pincers. Osés would hit Dubrovka while Suárez Roselló fell on Tigoda. Zero hour was set for 0800, 28 October, but the delay in moving Third of 263 forced a postponement until noon. When still nothing happened, Esparza left his CP at Bystritsa and crossed over to Sitno. Osés had already jumped off at 1400 with *Tía Bernarda*, but Suárez Roselló was nowhere to be seen. Searching from *izba* to *izba*, the colonel found the robust major finishing his midday meal. It was to be expected. The heavy-set *commandante* carried his love of food and drink into every campaign. But diplomacy, not anger, was the Spanish style. And besides, Esparza would never explode in a crisis. He reserved that for trifles.

"Are you ready to open the assault?" Calmly wiping his mouth with a napkin, Suárez replied:

"Yes, we are ready to attack immediately."

"Well then, I suggest you do so. Osés has already begun and is meeting heavy resistance. It would be convenient if you would attack simultaneously."[45]

Suárez Roselló rose from the table, went out, and stormed Tigoda.

Osés was already pushing south toward Dubrovka. After a fifteen minute artillery barrage, the major led off. First company of Mobile Reserve 250 formed the vanguard in the fields between the river and the road. To the left, 3 Company of *Tía Bernarda* and Second of Sappers 250 lined up between the road and the gully; 3 Company of 269 brought up the rear.

Supported closely by Barbudo's 75s and 37s from First Company Divisional Antitanks, the line surged forward. Heavy machine gun fire checked the advance on the left. Within three minutes 2 Sappers lost three dead, and thirteen wounded. But they slipped down the gully and made for Dubrovka. On the right along the river, 3 Company of *Tía Bernarda* outflanked Dubrovka's defenders, and reformed south of the hamlet. But, as the legionnaires leaped toward the enemy's rear, a hail of artillery showered their sector. Grenading forward through the shellfire, they became enmeshed in a minefield. Shattered bodies were strewn in a path toward the Soviet positions. Then the legionnaires closed. Fighting fiercely in the no quarter style learned in the Moroccan campaign, the "Bridegrooms of Death" (so-called from the hymn of the Legion, "Los Novios de la Muerte") cut, thrust, shoved and smashed with knives, bayonets, entrenching tools and rifle butts through the Russian ranks. The 100 Red survivors surrendered.[46]

Wheeling, Osés set off southward again. Ahead across the mine-field, lay the immense brick and concrete pile of the Muravevskiia Barracks. Major Osés, his battle lust aroused, wanted to storm this strong point immediately, but had already passed his assigned objective and his left flank hung open. He ordered *Tía Bernarda* and the Sappers to dig in. Still the Muravevskiia Barracks or *Los Cuarteles* drew him like a magnet. "Maybe," he thought, "I could slip in there tonight before the enemy recovers."[47] Musing over the day's battle, he wondered about the minefield that his men had run into behind the Russian lines at Dubrovka. Could it be true that the POWs were correct? Were the Reds so unsure of their own troops that they mined the line of retreat for a depth of five kilometers? ¡*Que barbaridad!*

Suárez Roselló also ran into mines on the way to Tigoda. Due to his late start, the hamlet was not occupied until 1600. The large number of Reds in the pines to the east had prevented Third of 263 from moving on to Nikltkino. The action had cost one officer and forty men, but an entire Russian battalion had been dispersed and two hundred prisoners bagged.[48]

At the most forward position in Dubrovka, the impetuous Osés peered through binoculars at the Muravevskiia Barracks. He could just make out the square, three-story concrete main structure some two kilometers distant. There were no signs of movement. They seemed to have been abandoned. He decided to give an elastic interpretation to the colonel's instruction that he "improve his position." At midnight, *Tía Bernarda* pounced. *Mala Suerte!* There were Russians all over. Rifle Regiment 1000 was holed up there with automatic weapons. Cursing, Osés withdrew. The Russians retaliated by hitting Dubrovka with artillery and heavy mortars the whole night through.[49]

Scarcely had midnight passed, when the sharp ring of the telephone jarred Esparza awake at his CP in Bystritsa. The general's voice crackled over the line. "Did you order an attack on the barracks? I overheard a telephone conversation between Osés and First Group."[50] Not quite awake, the harried commander of 269 paused, and then shot back: "Yes, my general." He hadn't, of course, but it was quite apparent that Osés had "improved his position." Shades of the march! The general was like a spider, sitting in the center of the web and monitoring radio dispatches and telephone messages. He knew everything, even, probably, that the order had not been given. Without another word, the general rang off. "Well," thought Esparza, "We'd better take the barracks."[51]

Dawn had hardly broken on 29 October when he left Bystritsa and headed for Leliavino opposite Dubrovka, where he planned to observe the attack on the *Cuarteles*. Passing through Krutik, Esparza chanced on the group commander. There was no way he could escape the eye of one or another general. With Muñoz Grandes covering the ether and von Roques attaching himself to the colonel's side, the journey was resumed.

As Esparza and von Roques approached Leliavino, they could hear the artillery barrage. The 105s were already pounding the concrete bastion. The shells were bouncing off. There followed a scene which could have been transported from the sand dunes of Morocco as the Legion stormed an enemy fort. *Tía Bernarda* advanced in a line across the snowdrifts toward the minefields, officers leading the way. First company, its right flank resting on the river, slipped southward down the bank. Second company, left flank on the road, moved right as mines and machine guns deflected them towards the Volkhov.

Mine explosions broke up the advancing ranks, while automatic weapons in the upper stories mowed down the dogged *guripas*. The wounded called " *a mi la Legión*" (to me the Legion) as on the sands of Morocco. Their comrades hurried to drag them to safety. Isolated knots of the still-living pressed forward led by Captains Echevarría and Escalera. They reached the walls of the compound, only to be driven back. Across the river, Esparza and von Roques could see the survivors standing at ease in the shelter of the bank. The men were calmly smoking and chatting while they passed around canteens filled with Russian vodka. It was so cold that the vodka had frozen in some of the canteens, which had to be banged on the hard ground to loosen some fragments of the precious elixir.

Osés ordered them on again. The companies zigzagged through the mine fields, the white snow splattered with mud and blood, and again reached the walls. Groups of twos and threes managed to penetrate some of the outbuildings, but were overwhelmed. A second fruitless assault. The Legion struck again and again. It was midafternoon now. The captains, and most of their lieutenants were down.[52] Gathering themselves together for one last effort, a handful charged the hulk of the Muravevskiia Barracks once more. Led by the last officer, Second Lieutenant Leston, these few remnants of two companies threw themselves vainly on the walls as the day faded.[53]

Emotionally exhausted after watching six hours of carnage, Esparza called a halt at 1515. "It is a work of titans, my general." Von

Roques was transfixed. "Could you take the barracks with Stukas and heavy artillery," he asked? "Without a doubt, my general."[54] They parted, and von Roques went off to call Busch. But the Stukas never came. General Keller's First Air Fleet was having enough trouble trying to support the main assault on Tikhvin.

Furious and frustrated, Osés fell back and reestablished a line on a low hill south of Dubrovka. In the tradition of the Legion, his men carried off their dead and wounded. Both captains were wounded. All five lieutenants were dead; two second lieutenants were wounded. Two sergeants dead, six wounded. Twenty-one soldiers were dead, eighty-two wounded.[55]

While the legionnaires beat vainly on the Muravevskiia Barracks, Suárez Roselló slogged through the pine woods toward Nikltkino. Fighting Indian-style, the Russians of 1002 Regiment picked off the oncoming Spaniards. Progress was held up for five hours. Meanwhile, Siberian reinforcements slipped in behind and reoccupied Tigoda. Third of 263 had to fight on two fronts. By nightfall, both villages were in Spanish hands.

The Russian strength at the Muravevskiia Barracks and the counter-attack against Suárez Roselló drew Esparza's attention to the necessity of fortifying his positions and reorganizing once more the command of his sector. Muñoz Grandes strongly urged this and, pointing out that 269 Regiment lacked a lieutenant colonel, offered to send Vierna's deputy, Lieutenant Colonel Canillas up from 263 Regiment.

At 2200, Canillas reported in at Esparza's new CP at Zapol'e. He was told that his CP would be at Tigoda. He would command a sector comprising Dubrovka, Nikltkino, Sitno, Tigoda, and Russa. His force, to be called the Eastern Group, would consist of Second of 269 and Third of 263. Román would relieve Osés the next day, *Tía Bernarda* being drawn off to reserve at Sitno. The sappers were also withdrawn to Sitno.[56]

The pulling back of the assault forces on 30 October signalled the end of the drive to open the Novgorod bridgehead. In the absence of Stukas and heavy artillery, further assaults against the *Cuarteles* seemed futile. Red Army Division 305 had been heavily reinforced with Siberians, and nine Russian battalions, albeit most not up to strength, now faced four Spanish. Nor were the battalions of the Blue Division up to strength. After scarcely ten days in the bridgehead, Second of 269 and Third of 263 were down by 50 percent. Even by weakening Novgorod, 250 Division could not reinforce Esparza enough to carry on the offensive. The last intact company of *Tía Bernarda* was being shifted from the Kremlin to the bridgehead. Orders were issued to stamp out rifle companies from the horse-drawn transport columns, now that the fallout of horses could release men for combat. The division was consuming itself.[57]

In spite of these portents and his own misgivings, von Roques held to his original mission—breach the Msta. Busch promised bridging equipment, heavy French 155s, a section of 88s, pioneers, and the reinforced Motorized Regiment 30 of Lieutenant Colonel von Erdmannsdorff. Von Roques' Order 8 of 1 November noted the anticipated assignment of these additional units to the Group and fixed the attack date for 6 November. Regiment 262 and the remainder of Regiment 263 had been poised since mid-October for the push to the Msta. Probes and counterprobes along the shore of Lake Il'men and across the Volkhov had given them the taste but not the substance of battle. Bombardments and counterbombardments pushed up the daily casualty list.

Lt. Enrique Errando Vilar frequently drove his ambulance to Pimentel's CP in the Kremlin, where the wounded from the island were collected. One day, as he looked past the Millennial Monument and across the great iron bridge, he hailed a *guripa* driving a sled. "Where does this road lead," he asked, gesturing eastward? "To glory," the young chap replied.[58]

Back on the bridgehead all was calm. In spite of von Roques's order of 1 November, Esparza felt in his bones that the attack was over. The veteran campaigner spent the days after the futile lunge at the *Cuarteles* trying to dig in. The enduring freeze, which had hardened the mud and softened the supply and transportation problems, also hindered the construction of field fortifications and dugouts for shelter. The earth was like a diamond. Explosives had to be used. Only the Soviets, "with a fatalism worthy of a better cause," seemed capable of penetrating with picks and shovels the frozen soil of Mother Russia.[59]

The Spaniards set the POWs to work. There were hundreds, and groups were assigned to each unit. This bred a kind of familiarity and the jocular good spirits of the Spaniards soon won over many a prisoner's heart. Companies used the Russians to dig shelters. Alternatively, they were employed as cooks, orderlies, and stretcher bearers. The Spaniards had their own domestics. Often, many units lent prisoners to a larger force for heavier work. The Russians and Ukrainians willingly went along. Stories abounded. One luckless *guripa* fell victim to the cold. Assigned to guard a group of prisoners, he succumbed to the frigid weather and passed out. His solicitous POWs responded instantly by building a fire and warming him until he recovered. When he did, they returned his rifle and he continued to guard them.

It was too cold for the Spaniards to make much headway with shelters, no matter what the urging of Esparza, the general, or the anxious Germans of the Liaison Staff. Even setting the Russians to work was not enough. When possible, the shivering volunteers holed up in the wooden *izbas* and built the largest possible fire in the hearth. The local peasants had to share their homes with these sudden, sometimes unwelcome guests. The icy wind made these log cabins tinder dry and any spark, or even the radiated heat from a roaring fire, could set them ablaze. And burn they would, with the rapidity of a matchbox. A heavy sleeper would be consumed before he could be awakened. Only the fortunate, and the already awake, could save themselves by jumping out of windows. A still winter scene, as if out of a Russian Currier and Ives, would greet the passerby. Suddenly, an *izba* aflame, with *guripas* and Russians popping out every window. Great consternation and then stillness again.[60]

While Esparza awaited an opportunity to move forward, the Russians received orders to drive him out. At 0600 on 2 November, 305 Rifle Division opened a counterblast. Two battalions, supported by artillery and heavy mortars, fell on Nikltkino. The lonely village was a brown island in a sea of white. Constant Soviet shelling had churned over the frozen earth that lay under its pristine blanket of snow.

Suárez Roselló galvanized his volunteers of Murcia. With the first light of day piercing the trees and shimmering across the white snow, the Spaniards squinted through their sights and let go with everything they had. The cries of *"Urrah!"* and *"ispanskii kaput!"* grew louder as Third of 1002, up to then unbloodied, came on.

Tomás Salvador and his machine gun crew were inside one of the *izbas*. The Spaniards had discovered that the MG 34s froze up in the bitter cold and had resorted to keeping them warm by the hearth. From his vantage point at the window, young Salvador saw the Russians pour out of the woods. His comrades were still asleep, so exhausted from all night sentry duty that even the bombardment had failed to awaken them. Quickly rousing the crew, he threw open the door. The smell of cordite hung in the air. The drowsy men rushed the heavy tripod into the doorway and mounted their gun. Other *guripas* were pouring out of nearby *izbas* into half-dug trenches. The machine gun chattered over their heads.

The Reds came on. They had already crossed into the muddy circle surrounding the village. Salvador was puzzled at the way they fought. The *"Russkis"* remained erect, waiting for a whistle from an officer. None dared crouch without the signal, even while they were being mowed down by his rapid fire. And, if the officer was late or had been killed, they would not crouch at all! They would either stand and die or surrender. For an Iberian individualist, such a bovine attitude was incomprehensible. Nevertheless, he admired their stolid insensitivity to death in defense of their homeland.

The Russians were only fifty meters away now. One group, avoiding his field of fire, rushed a neighboring *izba* housing the headquarters staff of Twelfth Company. The runners and dispatch riders beat them off in hand-to-hand fighting. Back in the line, the ardent Murcians rose from their shallow foxholes and closed. The wave broke. It was all over by 1100. Defiantly, the volunteers stared at the retreating Russians and shouted *"Otro toro! Otro toro!"* (Send in another bull!).[61]

Two hundred twenty-one Russian bodies sprawled grotesquely thirty meters from the line of Third of 263. The Spaniards lost fifteen dead and fifty wounded, including five officers. Nikltkino held and the morale of Third of 1002 was shattered.

The Spanish campfires, however, attracted the Red Air Force. One solitary plane made the first of what were to become nightly appearances over the sector of 250 Division. The light aircraft appeared over Sitno, dropped a few bombs, and then flew westward to the Novgorod-Chudovo highway. There, it stalked any moving thing—man, beast, or vehicle. Sounding to those on the ground like a motorcycle, *El Moto* would sneak up from behind and riddle the unwary with green tracers. Larger prey were surprised by a hand grenade or light bomb thrown from the cockpit. This nocturnal patrol along the highway reminded the *guripas* of a streetwalker. Hence, some of them dubbed her *La Parrala*. Like a persistent prostitute, she forced her attentions on the sleeping soldiers.[62]

Reeling from their losses of 2 November, the Russians withdrew into the woods. The lull was marked more by freezing than firing. Temperatures which had hovered around 0 degrees Celsius since mid-October began to plunge. By 6 November the thermometer registered −5 degrees Celsius maximum and −17 degree Celsius minimum. As early as 3 November, 13 frost bite cases reported in. Most of the men had frozen feet, brought on by standing still on sentry duty in the snow while wearing thin leather boots. This *Wehrmacht* issue fitted so snugly that they impeded circulation.

Winter clothing arrived piecemeal. The volunteers draped blankets over their heads like *babushkas* or *mantillas*, and some looked the part of old women, going to early mass. Although there was a surplus of greatcoats, some items such as woolen gloves and fleece-lined or felt boots were never issued in sufficient quantity. During the winter of 1941–42, less than 40 percent received warm boots. Like many of their German comrades, the *guripas* stripped Russian corpses for their prized felt boots, fur coats, and quilted jackets and trousers. As of 3 November, however, grave robbing was still far from the minds of the Spaniards.

General von Roques watched the sappers practicing paddling from his advanced CP in the Kremlin. He observed that it was harder now to maneuver the boats through the blocks of ice. Von Roques knew that he had been personally selected by von Leeb to lead an offensive. The repeated postponements, however, worried him. Already on 1 November OKH had ordered the field marshal to suspend the fruitless attacks of the southern wing of 16 Army.

To the north, General Schmidt's men, after battering out of the bridgeheads opposite Kuzino and Grusino on 21 October, had slogged forward on one tank front through the narrow forest trails. The slow progress prompted OKH to express its displeasure. OKH was "not optimistic about taking Tikhvin."[63] Nevertheless, the Führer, after receiving assurances from von Leeb on 20 October and again on 23 and 26 October, continued to grant the army group commander a free hand.[64]

The Russians had changed their tactics. In addition to tenacious defense and counterattacks, they repeatedly raided German supply lines. Convoys were ambushed. Roads were mined. The Germans had no response to the new, partisan-type methods adopted by regular Red Army forces other than sending out patrols. The woods were full of Russians, who unlike the Germans, could remain out in the open for days on end. Grasping at straws, the commander of 16 Army threw everything into the effort to isolate Leningrad. Either Tikhvin or Volkhovstroi had to be taken. In order to bolster Schmidt, Busch pulled out 30 Motorized Regiment from its narrow salient between 250 and 126 Divisions and ordered von Erdmannsdorff up to the Tikhvin spearhead.

To consolidate the defense of Schmidt's exposed southern flank, Busch transferred Laux's 126 Division to the Group von Roques. Together, 250 Division and two-thirds of 126 Division would have the sole mission of shielding the southern flank of XXXIX Corps. The advance to the Msta, let alone Borovichi, was postponed until reinforcements arrived.[65] Someone had to plug the yawning gap between 250 and 126 Divisions which ran from Shevelevo on the Volkhov through Otenskii and Posad and on to Poselok at the Vishera. Laux had no men to spare. Busch turned to Muñoz Grandes and threw the Spanish infantry into the breach.

6

"Share the Glory and the Danger"

A BATTALION OF GURIPAS WOULD REPLACE THE BULK
of a reinforced German motorized regiment at Otenskii and Posad.
However, while 30 Motorized Regiment had been massed at this lonely
outpost for the attack towards Bronnitsy, 250 Division was posted for
defense.

General von Roques, in a series of orders beginning on 6 November, laid out his new plans. Although expressing the faint hope that the
Msta offensive could be revived, his directive was definitely defensive.
Von Roques' one and two-thirds divisions (250 and two-thirds of 126)
would steel themselves to withstand the ever-increasing Soviet attacks
on the right flank of XXXIX Corps. Still drawn by the spectral drive
on the Msta, the doughty Hessian refused to permit Muñoz Grandes to
shift his center of gravity from Novgorod, where the Little Volkhov
had now frozen.[1]

The passing of the *rasputitsa* heralded the arrival of General Winter. Mother Russia's powerful weapon against an invader had both advantages and disadvantages. Though the Little Volkhov had frozen, the
mainstream still flowed, albeit haltingly. Ice shards threatened to break
up the pontoons at the *Casa del Señor* and Kuzino. The loss of these
supply routes would endanger the provisioning of the entire Group
until the Volkhov froze solid. Then, at last, there would be multiple

crossings. This would be a magnificent advantage for an attacker, but von Roques was now on the defensive.

The swamps on the east bank had also frozen. A grateful Schmidt could now deploy his armor on more than a one-tank front. His Panzers were no longer confined to the narrow roads. Tikhvin lay within his grasp! But his southern shield, with depleted companies manning scattered strong points, lacked the strength to extend into the great swamps. The vast open marshes, whcih had been obstacles during the advance, were now huge holes in the line through which the Red Army could flood. There were plenty of Russians to spare. New units were coming up from the Valdai, and reserves were pouring in from Siberia.

Faced with this threat, and ordered to extend his lines to a total active front of over 60 kilometers without weakening Novgorod, Muñoz Grandes decided to reconnoiter the situation personally. On Thursday afternoon, 6 November, the spider came out of his nest. He crossed the Volkhov to meet with the peripatetic colonel of 269.

Esparza was, as always, respectful but not awed. Lunch provided him an opportunity to satisfy his palate while "exchanging impressions" with his commander in the informal Spanish fashion. They discussed the state of the bridgehead and probable Russian moves. The Blue Division would be charged with defending the slim eighteen-kilometer salient running through the frozen swamps and snow-laden primeval forest from Shevelevo to Ostenskii and Posad and on to the Vishera. Esparza, pointing out that the Spaniards would be replacing the bulk of a regiment with only a battalion, recommended First of 269. They, he reasoned, had suffered the least casualties and the ardent Falangists of Madrid would fight as well as the Germans. His other battalions, Second and Third of 269, and Third of 263, were down to half strength. Satisfied, the general agreed. Lunch over, they left Sitno to inspect the bridgehead.

The battered Murcians greeted the general at Nikltkino. After being briefed by Suárez Roselló, Muñoz Grandes went out to see the men. Encouraged by his familiarity, the emboldened *guripas* regaled him with their latest jokes.

"We are reported to be an exact division, my general," ventured one mustachioed young man.

Unaccustomed to playing a straight man, the general queried "Really?"

"Yes sir, because at the rate our numbers are dwindling there will be nothing left over."[2]

While some officers frowned, the general managed a painful smile and moved on. Their cheerful attitude masked the fact that only 42 remained out of a company of 200. Moved, Muñoz Grandes smiled, and said nothing.

On the way back to Sitno and the river crossing the general and his colonel discussed the transfer of forces to Otenskii and Posad. The monastery and the village were virtually isolated from the division. Although there would be a tenuous connection with 126 Division at Radosha, a vast expanse of snow-covered forest and frozen swamp separated the two positions from the Spanish bridgehead. There was only one road, a pockmarked lane running eastward from Shevelevo. Provisioning would be a problem. Until the Volkhov froze solid, supplies would have to come across at the *Casa del Señor* or Kuzino and then be transported to Shevelevo. Here a stockpile would be built up, which could feed the garrisons.

The narrow lifeline from the supply dump was vulnerable to partisan attacks. Trees pressed right to the roadside, offering perfect cover for guerillas. In the event of a sustained Russian counteroffensive, the positions were untenable. They could be cut off at will. The Reds had already tried. The attack on Suárez Roselló at Nikltkino the previous Sunday, 2 November, by 1002 Regiment had been accompanied by an assault on von Erdmannsdorff at Posad by 1004 Regiment. Chances were that 305 Rifle Division would coordinate a succession of one-two punches on the bridgehead and the outposts.[3]

Pondering this grim prognosis, Esparza watched the general climb into his rubber boat. The crew pushed off for the opposite shore. A narrow path through the ice floes had been blasted by the sappers. The colonel observed that the blocks were beginning to form a solid sheet. Downstream, where the Volkhov broadened and shelved, the sappers had already laid a crude plank pathway. The boards distributed a person's weight over the still unstable ice. The trick was to keep proper distance and not to lose one's footing. An attempt to bring across a horse had failed. The skittish bay had broken through and could not be rescued. He froze there, half in and half out, a grotesque ice sculpture along the path to Sitno. The head bore a tragic expression of impotence and terror; its lifeless eyes catching every passing soldier's glance.

The colonel turned and walked toward the village. He passed the cemetery. Ahead stood one of Sitno's few substantial buildings. It even had a basement. Here the Spanish dead lay awaiting burial. The men had frozen as they fell, some still clutching their weapons. How grim it was for their comrades to shape the bodies into a position of repose. Sometimes it was necessary to break the arms, and even the fingers, to free the rifles.

Trudging back to his command post, Esparza passed a work party of 2 Company of regimental antitanks. The men were busily engaged in throwing up fortifications. In one of the parties, Juan Eugenio Blanco—a brash antitanker from Madrid—ruefully noted that officers always kept the men busy. Anxiously, he looked toward the forest. The dense, stunted pines bore a heavy mantle of snow. During the daylight hours, it was peaceful and picturesque. But, when darkness descended, the wood was a sinister cover for Russian raids.[4]

Night sentry duty was fearful. Although his post was only some two hundred meters north of Sitno, Blanco had to walk an eerie route. Frozen Russian dead littered the way. There had been neither time nor men to collect and bury them. These macabre figures were now used as signposts. He remembered how, when he had first arrived and had asked directions, the sergeant had told him: "Follow the road until you come to the ditch with the three Russians. One of them is still holding his rifle. Then, follow the path to the house which has two dead Ivans inside. From there, you can see to the right the big building where our own dead are in the basement."[5] A little further was his post, on a bridge across one of the gullies. The sudden cracking of ice in the arroyo always sent shivers up his spine. The rustle of wind in the forest could be the felt boots of the enemy. He was grateful that the bitter cold had forced a reduction of sentry duty from two hours to one.

Even one hour was too much in the frigid wind. Lack of winter clothing had forced his comrades to strip the Russian dead. Quilted jackets and felt boots were highly prized. But first, there was the matter of the lice. In a primitive method of delousing, the *guripas* buried the garments in the snow for three days. Unfortunately, this didn't always work. Sometimes the eternal vermin survived.

Group Order 10, calling for the Spaniards to relieve von Erdmannsdorff at Otenskii and Posad, came down the next day. Mazariegos, G-3, immediately began to organize the operation, which was to take place on the night of 8–9 November. Mazariegos cut orders for First of 269, commanded by Major Luque. Close support for Luque would be provided by two of Barbudo's 75s and four 37 mm antitank guns from 14 Company of 269. In addition, he would have Captain Pérez Bajo's Second Battery of 105s which had to take the long way around, via the bridge at Kuzino.[6]

The rest of divisional artillery began to pull back into defensive positions and 16 Army suddenly transferred out 9 Battery of Artillery Regiment 207. But Badillo was more than compensated. On 7 November he reported that the two batteries (13 and 14) of French 155s were ready to open fire. The heavy Schneiders, which had arrived a week earlier to provide the opening barrage of the Msta offensive, had been delivered without transport. Transport was now considered unnecessary, since the offensive had been suspended. The French howitzers would provide substantial support for Esparza's bridgehead. However, none of Badillo's artillery on the west bank had the range to reach Otenskii and Posad. Luque would have to rely on Pérez Bajo's *madrileños* and Barbudo's *sevillanos*.

On 8 November, as First of 269 was moving up toward Posad, the exciting news arrived that 18 Motorized and 12 Panzer had penetrated the outskirts of Tikhvin. Von Erdmannsdorff was anxious to join the rest of his division and had already begun pulling out. Luque's men began dribbling into the salient on schedule.[7]

First Company, under Captain Vallespín, relieved the Germans at the Otenskii Monastery. The huge, stone structure was a welcome sight. An onion dome crowned each corner of the quadrangular cloister, while a fifth, higher, bulb reared from the central patio. Scattered like so much refuse around the walls were a handful of ramshackle *izbas*. Twelve hundred meters beyond rose a tight ring of trees, broken only by two small slits, one narrow road coming from the Volkhov, and the other leading on to the Vishera.[8]

Luque, with 2 and 3 Companies, the two 75s and the antitanks, pushed on to Posad and Poselok. Fourth Company, heavy weapons, was late coming up. Von Erdmannsdorff could not wait. As morning broke on Sunday, 9 November, the half-tracks of 30 Motorized Regiment rumbled towards Shevelevo. A few kilometers down the road, Major Günter Engelhardt saw "the awaited Spanish machine gun company, resting in a forest clearing."[9] Engelhardt had great respect for the Spaniards. Though they were not "model soldiers in the Prussian sense, they proved themselves brave, reliable, and tough troopers, in attack as well as in defense."[10] For a German officer, commander of a crack motorized infantry battalion, this was high praise indeed! As his command car bounced along to Shevelevo and on to Tikhvin, he felt confident that the right flank of XXXIX Corps would be secure.

At 1725 hours, Field Marshal von Leeb jubilantly proclaimed that 18 Motorized and 12 Panzer had Tikhvin "fest in der Hand." Now, "the sea route over Lake Ladoga is also cut."[11] That same day, the Soviets prepared their counterblow. On 9 November, *Stavka*—Stalin's Supreme War Staff—called upon General K. A. Meretskov to save the situation. The heavy-set Meretskov, born to a peasant family in 1897, had joined the Communist party in May 1917. He was a member of the Red Guard, and served as a political commissar during the Russian Civil War. After attending training courses at the General Staff, Meretskov rose rapidly through the military hierarchy. He served as an adviser to the Republican Army in Spain from 1936 to 1937 and, upon his return to Russia, assumed the post of deputy chief of the General Staff. During the Winter War of 1939–40 with Finland, Meretskov led 7 Army—the main attack force—against the Karelian Isthmus. After the Soviet victory, Stalin appointed him chief of the General Staff, but he fell into disfavor and was dismissed in January 1941. The disastrous Soviet defeats during the summer of 1941 prompted Stalin to call Meretskov from the obscurity of a training command and post him to the Karelian Front. Here, Meretskov and his Seventh Independent Army again faced the Finns—this time along the Svir.[12]

Meretskov had watched Schmidt's advance with growing apprehension. The retreat of 4 Army threatened to pin his 7 Army between XXXIX Corps and the Finns. Now, on 9 November, as Radio Berlin boasted "*Achtung, Achtung,* Tikhvin has fallen," *Stavka* ordered Meretskov to take temporary command of 4 Army.[13]

Rushing southward, Meretskov began establishing collecting points for the scattered 4 Army and tactical training centers for new units. Although he could receive reinforcements and supplies by railroad from Moscow over Vologda and Zabor'e, Volkhovstroi and Leningrad were isolated.

Rations within Leningrad were down to the lowest level of the war. Front line troops received 600 grams of bread a day, rear units 400, factory workers 300, dependents and children 150. A fortunate few were drinking soup made from carpenter's glue. Meanwhile, Meretskov prepared his counterattack on Tikhvin. Ready or not, he would have to strike within forty-eight hours.[14]

His urgency was prompted not only by the serious situation in the metropolis, but also by the danger to Moscow posed by the advancing legions of Operation Typhoon. *Leningradskaia pravda* proudly proclaimed: "The best assistance to Moscow is the defeat and destruction of the Hitlerite bands before Leningrad."[15] Soviet leadership believed that each "enemy division tied down at Leningrad was one less available for use against Moscow."[16]

After a brilliant initial success, Operation Typhoon had come to a standstill at the end of October along the line Mtsensk-Kaluga-Kalinin. Mud and heavy fighting had taken their toll. Frost finally came on the night of 6–7 November. The armored vehicles could move forward again. On that day, the anniversary of the Communist Revolution, Stalin, despite the gravity of the situation, maintained a bold show. He reviewed a military parade in Red Square. As fresh troops, equipped for battle, marched past Lenin's Tomb in the snowy, early morning haze, the dictator saluted. They continued on straight to the front.[17]

Stalin was counting on his northern commanders—Klykov of 52 Army, Meretskov, and I. I. Fediuninskii of 54 Army—to relieve the pressure on Moscow. The defense of the capital took precedence over all other considerations. The Volkhov front would have been better served if 52, 4, and 54 Armies would have been given time to regroup and prepare for a major counteroffensive in conjunction with the new forces coming up. But they had no time. Meretskov would have to leap off at once.

Only two days after the loss of Tikhvin, he threw 44 Tank Brigade and 191 Rifle Division against the city. Strongly supported by the Red Air Force, the Russians came on. Surprised by the sudden counterblow, Schmidt's forces reeled and dropped back a few kilometers, but did not crack. German reinforcements were hurried up and the Russians were stopped before they reached Tikhvin. But the roles were now reversed. Sixteenth Army could no longer advance. The initiative had passed to the Soviets.[18]

Muñoz Grandes knew that the Russians were desperate. But Busch had strained the resources of 16 Army to take Tikhvin and had no reserves. The volunteers of the Blue Division covered an ever longer front, now including Otenskii and Posad. Lacking strength to advance, they awaited Red countermoves. On 8 November, Communist loudspeakers blared in Spanish, urging the *guripas* to defect. The enemy propaganda had almost no effect; only one deserter crossed over, bucking a flood of Russians fleeing towards the Spanish lines.

Meanwhile, the Red buildup continued. On 10 November, a patrol of Third of 269 reconnoitered over the ice of the Volkhov near Kotovitsy, just north of the island. At Khutyn, in the shadow of the great cap of Novgorod, Major Prado O'Neill anxiously peered through field glasses from his forward observation post. The Reds had moved in heavy artillery. The High Command expected an attack across the Little Volkhov at any moment. Second Artillery was ready.

General von Roques had been charged with leading an offensive. This mission had now been aborted. Defense was the order of the day. Accordingly, he was relieved. His Group was notified that Gen. Friedrich-Wilhelm von Chappuis and the staff of XXXVIII Corps would take over his command on 14 November at 0800 hours.

Esparza, who had a special fondness for the departing corps commander, hosted von Roques to a lavish lunch on Tuesday, 11 November, at his CP in Sitno. The feast featured decorated menus, Burgundy, and Hennessey cognac. Chatting easily in French, the party sipped champagne contributed by the general. Von Roques informed the Spaniards that he was resuming his post as chief of Security Units and Rear Areas of Army Group North.[19] The cordial lunch was indicative of the warm relations between 250 Division and their first group commander. Upon the recommendation of Muñoz Grandes, von Roques was later decorated with the Spanish Grand Cross of War. Relations between 250 Division and XXXVIII Corps would be radically different, for von Chappuis not only lacked the warmth and understanding of von Roques, he arrived prejudiced against the Spaniards. Major von Oertzen was on his staff.

As night fell, the Red Air Force came out in strength. *La Parrala* had escorts. They were releasing flares, strafing, and dropping incendiary bombs. It was to be another sleepless night for Esparza. The hyperactive colonel, although a diabetic, drew his energy from calories. He never seemed to sleep nor even doze. Headquarters staff was exhausted, but Esparza bounced happily on. At 2200, heavy firing erupted at Russa. Captain Temprano of Fifth Company of 269 reported that the enemy had penetrated the north end of the village and was burning the houses. This was not merely a raid, but the first full-scale night attack. Esparza ordered Temprano to launch an immediate counterassault. By 0130 Wednesday the situation was secure. Meanwhile, the Soviets jabbed at the CP of Canillas in Tigoda trying to cut Third of 263 off from Sitno. They were repulsed, but did not retreat. Now came the other half of the one-two punch; bridgehead followed by salient. At 0210, while Esparza was still on the line with Canillas, a radio dispatch arrived from Luque. "Otenskii, Posad, and Poselok under attack. Thrown back. Few casualties."[20] It looked like a black Wednesday.

What the colonel did not know was that Poselok had been under attack since midnight. A hail of heavy artillery rained out of a silent sky. The village burst into flames as clods of frozen earth, hard as steel, pelted the *guripas*. In the outposts along the Vishera, the men were deafened by drumfire. Their faces cracked in the cold as flying snow blinded their eyes. Orders had to be shouted into their ears. Nevertheless, they could still see the human wave roll across the river and hear the awesome roar, "*Urrah! Urrah!*" Within moments, the perimeter was swamped and the surviving volunteers dragged their casualties and weapons toward the burning village. The frigid cold hung about them like a shroud. As warm blood spurted from open wounds it vaporized, and a gruesome mist rose into the air.

At 0310 Luque radioed regimental HQ from Posad that the Otenskii road was blocked; he could not evacuate his casualties. Esparza alerted regimental reserve at Petrovskoe. Captain Garzón immediately roused his cyclists of 11 Company of 269 Regiment and got them moving across the river and on the road to Shevelevo and Otenskii. Help was on the way. But the Soviets continued to press on Posad and Poselok. Then, at 0430, Luque's voice crackled over the receiver at Sitno. "Attacks increasing. Second Company has sustained heavy losses. Impossible. . . ."[21] The radio went dead. Covering his fears, Esparza "put the best face on the matter."[22] He announced to his staff that transmission had been interrupted by the nervousness of the radio operators. He ordered the operators to broadcast: "I count on the magnificent spirit of this battalion to resist like the best. I have ordered 1 Company from Otenskii which will be garrisoned by Pérez Bajo until 11 Company arrives with other reinforcements. *Arriba España!*"[23]

While the colonel's attention was focused on Posad, the Russians again struck at Russa, seizing the northern half of the village. Temprano pulled back and held on. Another signal from Luque at 0559. "Situation Poselok irresistible. Many enemy. Have authorized retire upon Posad. Urge send reinforcements. POWs say they aim at attacking in depth on Posad."[24] Temprano again called. The Reds had finally been driven off into the woods, leaving dead and booty behind. Well, this was the best news of the night.

More news. Tigoda now encircled. Dubrovka, and Nikltkino under attack. The entire line in flames![25] But Esparza was convinced that the most serious situation was at Posad. Helpless, he decided to send a phantom battalion. He broadcast to Luque in clear: "I expect that the Falangist honor of your battalion will be demonstrated by the energetic defense of Posad. I expect a counterattack will permit reoccupation

Poselok. I am leaving with a battalion and a battery to reinforce Posad. *Arriba España!*[26] With the bridgehead under attack, Esparza hoped that he would not have to strip those positions to reinforce the salient. However, if worse came to worse, he would send Major Román, whom he was holding in reserve at Sitno. Hoping that his bombastic radio message would help stabilize Posad for a while, he sent Román to open up the road to Tigoda.

The Russians were deploying the entire 305 Rifle Division as well as elements of 3 Armored against his bridgehead and salient. As dawn broke, at 0800, peppery Román set out with 7 Company. Placing himself at the head of two sections, he blasted his way through two Russian companies into Tigoda and linked up with Canillas and the sappers. The Reds cut and ran for the woods, leaving forty dead, eighty prisoners, and three machine guns. During the rush, one of the Ivans had Román in the sights of his submachine gun, but his aide, Lieutenant Morajón, ran to his side. Morajón fired point blank and the Russian fell dead. The PPSH-M41 submachine gun became the agile lieutenant's trophy. For his heroism, when Román returned at 1000 to Sitno, he received a friendly reprimand from the colonel. Majors simply did not charge two Russian companies while leading only sections.[27]

During Román's absence, Muñoz Grandes came on the line. The general determined to reinforce Otenskii and Posad immediately. Since Garzón's dismounted cyclists would be some time in getting to the monastery, he ordered up 2 Company of divisional antitanks. They could speed from Sitno to the spot in their magnificent touring cars. Notwithstanding, he had some disquieting news for the commander of the 269.

The Russians had been hammering at Tikhvin without interruption since yesterday. Now, in a coordinated air and artillery attack, they had begun hitting 126 Division at 0730 this morning, 12 November. At 0800, three Russian divisions—259, 267, and 111—had flung themselves on the Rhineland-Westphalians at Krassnaia Visherka, Glutno, and Malaia Vishera. Glutno, like Posad, was surrounded and isolated and Laux was already throwing in transport and service personnel. In abandoning Pusstaia Visherka, 126 Division had been forced to leave vehicles behind. The onslaught was continuing.[28]

This was an attack on the entire Tikhvin bulge. In desperation, and without the time to coordinate a formal counteroffensive, the Russians threw in everything they could lay their hands on. Klykov, with 52 Army, smashed at the southern flank, while Meretskov, with the reinforced 4 Army, beat at the tip. Meretskov's T-26s had pushed Schmidt back fifteen kilometers. Lamenting that "the enemy is attacking everywhere," von Leeb noted that the entire front of the Group von Roques was under heavy pressure.[29] "Army Group North has no reserves. . . . The enemy believes that he can succeed everywhere and all at once."[30]

The Soviets had been pressing Posad the entire day. Luque had a five-kilometer perimeter, into which the Reds rained mortar, antitank, and artillery shells—mainly 122s. The concentration of fire cut down everything raised above the earth—trees, *izbas*, and sheds. The *guripas* had only shallow trenches and a few bunkers for shelter. Ammunition was running low. The iron rations were gone. The men were eating frozen potatoes scrounged from the cellars of the *izbas* and hacking chunks of ice-hard flesh from the flanks of the dead horses. And all the while the maimed and frostbitten lay groaning in the shallow shelters. It was a living hell!

Luque had been reinforced by Vallespín, who had rushed up from Otenskii as soon as the first limousines of Captain España's antitankers pulled into the monastery. He hadn't waited for Garzón and his cyclists. Vallespín's 1 Company literally had to fight for every meter of the four kilometers to get there. All the while, he was pounded with shells from the heavy 210s. Like a reluctant horde, parting angrily at his forward thrust, the Soviets closed in behind and cut him off. Luque's wounded could still not be evacuated. The sorely beset major watched his men fall around him. His officers fought like demons, heading flying squads which rushed from position to position, ignoring the deadly hail. Arredondo of 2 Company, and Captain Muñoz of 3 Company, along with Sergeant Nieto, *naranjeros* in hand, seemed to be everywhere.[31] The telephones were still out. But the radios were working. From Posad the forward observers called down the 105s and 75s of Pérez Bajo and Barbudo. They concentrated on the edge of the encircling woods, where the Reds nerved themselves for another rush.

During this brief respite, Esparza and Rodrigo arrived at Shevelevo, while Román rushed to Otenskii. If tireless Esparza had not slept at all on Tuesday night, he was not to have much rest on Wednesday night either. At 0100 on Thursday morning, the thirteenth, the Russians charged out of the woods toward the stone walls of Otenskii monastery. There was a fierce fight. The defenders used everything they had and drove 1004 Regiment off. Taking advantage of his success, Garzón sent a patrol groping toward Posad. There was still no way to evacuate the wounded.

At first light, Posad erupted again. Luque was hit. He radioed Shevelevo requesting evacuation and inquired to whom he might turn over command. Colonel Rodrigo replied bitterly, "to the senior captain, of course."[32] Neither Rodrigo nor Esparza were impressed with Luque's performance. His officers seemed to show more dash. The Spanish Army traditionally appreciated boldness and individual flair.

Soviet cannon and mortars continued to blast at Posad while Esparza assembled the supply column. At 0900, the Ivans jumped off but were beaten back. At 1000 the rest of Second of 269 marched out of Shevelevo to join Román, who was now in command at Otenskii. Vallespín had taken over in the crucible. Russian shells crashed down everywhere, but morale seemed to rise, rather than fall, as casualties mounted. At one point in the perimeter, originally held by a section, only a sergeant and two *guripas* were left. Back to back, they fired in all directions. Their grenades gave out. The enemy rushed their position, twenty riflemen charging right at them. The three Spaniards knew that they were dead. Rising from the bloody trench, they closed. "*Arriba España!*" A few Russians fell. The others, convinced that this was the start of a counterattack, halted, and raised their arms, shouting "*Niet Kommunist.*" Amazed, the exhausted volunteers took ten prisoners. One man conducted them to the rear, while the other two nervously settled back into their trench. Reluctant to leave his partners in such a dangerous state, the lonely *guripa* pointed his POWs toward the CP and motioned them to go on alone! They not only did, but managed to indicate to Vallespín the plight of his brave men and the captain was able to send two more *madrileños* as a reinforcement. Bodies with the young faces of university students were stacked like cordwood at the CP. This had been Rodrigo's second battalion, full of members of the Falangist SEU. Posad put an end to their academic careers.

The edge of the encircling forest was studded with Soviet 76 mm guns (M-1939). Crouching behind the low silhouetted shields, the gunners fired the flat trajectory shells at anyone who stirred. One by one the 76 mm's picked off the defenders. Of the four Spanish antitank guns, only one was left. The lonely 37 mm piece was employed as if it were a rifle. Until Román arrived with munitions, the 75s were mute. Most of the machine guns were also silent. For every three Spanish defenders, one Russian cannon belched fire. Flights of three "Martins" (SB-2 Katiusha), red stars gleaming on their silver wings, swooped down over the treetops to add to the destruction. Posad was a volcano. The defenders, their perimeter penetrated, called down fire on their own positions. Then, singing "Cara al Sol," they rose from the wreckage of their bunkers and met the Russians steel to steel. The Reds recoiled, but clung desperately to the three easternmost *izbas*.[33]

By midday, 5 and 7 Companies of 269 had fought their way through. Just in time! A new Russian assault opened at 1310 from both east and west—artillery, infantry, and this time, tanks! It was the first of three set-piece attacks. Fifth Armored Regiment rolled up the narrow lane from Poselok. This was the chance the antitankers were waiting for. A direct hit on the lead T-26! Flames; an explosion! The road was blocked. The remainder of the light tank column could not pass. The smoke and flames were visible from the cupolas of Otenskii. The deafening roar of artillery and small arms fire from Posad reached a crescendo at 1410, then slowly decreased until 1530 when it steadied into a drum roll of cannon.[34]

The guns were shifting fire. Also at 1530, they began to pound *Tía Bernarda* at Dubrovka. Four companies of Russian infantry tried to move up the road from the *Cuarteles*. Advancing in two lines over open ground they threw themselves at 2 Company, positioned between the river and the road. The cries of *"Urrah"* broke as well-directed fire tore huge gaps in the enemy ranks. The wide-eyed Russians, heavily fortified with vodka, dispersed and ran pellmell toward the comforting walls of the barracks.[35] Now as night closed in the Russians regrouped and charged. Lieutenant Malla and Sergeant Cabezas leapt up and led the legionnaires forward. Closing with grenades and bayonets, friend and foe merged. A blast felled Cabezas. Pulling up his shattered trunk, he continued to shout war cries until he died. Beaten, the Russians broke for the safety of the woods, killing their own wounded as they retired.[36] While the Soviets beat in vain at Dubrovka, the supply column trudged into Otenskii. It had taken eight hours. At almost every gulley, each truck had had to be unloaded and then reloaded at the other side. Sometimes it had been necessary to cut down trees and build bridges.

At 0800 on 14 November, General von Chappuis and the staff of XXXVIII Corps took command of the units formerly comprising the Group von Roques. Friedrich-Wilhelm von Chappuis had been born in 1886 in Schubin, in the Prussian province of Posen. He had risen through the Grenadiers to the rank of captain in World War I and had been posted to the staff of 206 Division. During the Weimar Republic, he alternated between company command and staff responsibilities, rising to the rank of major. In 1938, the aspiring von Chappuis was transferred to OKH. He was raised to general, serving in the staff of XIV Corps during the French Campaign. In April 1941, he received the rank of general of infantry.

The paunchy, bespectacled von Chappuis was appalled at the condition of his front. He saw isolated strongpoints, inadequately manned and under constant attack by a numerically superior army. The Reds were flooding across his outposts cutting telephone lines, laying mines, and interdicting supplies. The relief columns of 126 Division, convoyed by tanks of the Führer Escort Battalion, were not always getting through. The Red Air Force dominated the skies. Two divisions—3 Armored and 305 Rifle Division—faced his 250 Division, while four Russian divisions—25 Cavalry, 267 Rifle, 111 Rifle, and 259 Rifle—faced his two-thirds of 126 Division. With this mixed Spanish-German force, and against such overwhelming Soviet power, von Chappuis had to defend the southern flank of XXXIX Corps. The prospect depressed him, and his first thought was for reinforcements. In Grigorovo, corps headquarters, he came face to face with the command of the Spanish volunteer division and its German liaison staff. Perturbed at the political implications raised by Spanish participation in the war which he believed clouded the urgent military issues he faced, von Chappuis found it difficult to understand the Iberian character. Von Chappuis, in his first entry in the War Diary of XXXVIII Corps at Grigorovo, observed that the situation at Otenskii and Posad was unclear. The enemy was apparently redeploying in preparation for another attack.[37]

Rodrigo and Esparza resolved to relieve Posad at once. Evacuation of the wounded would await nightfall when darkness could cover them. But Esparza counseled the divisional chief of infantry that Posad and Otenskii could only be held at exorbitant cost. It might be wise, he told Muñoz Grandes's deputy, to pull back and avoid further unnecessary losses. They began to move out the wounded at 1600. Lieutenant Errando Vilar had brought his motor ambulance section up to within 500 meters of Posad, where they waited under cover of the woods. Stretcher bearers hustled into the dugouts. The sight horrified and sickened them. Every third man was dead. Gangrene was eating at the flesh of the living. The stench was overpowering. It was exacerbated by the diarrhea of the men. Consuming frozen rations and swallowing ice shards had wreaked havoc on their intestines. Their bowels ran continuously and uncontrollably, filling their trousers. Some medics could not restrain the urge to retch. They worked swiftly, trundling the wounded to the ambulances. Shells burst around them, and the stretchers pitched while the bearers jogged along. Pained cries and groans of their comrades gnawed at their vitals. Now loaded with their precious cargo, the ambulances crept rearward toward Shevelevo.[38]

A new face greeted Colonel Esparza—Luque's replacement, Major García Rebull. Still wearing the uniform of a captain, García Rebull had been promoted a few days earlier in recognition of his valor during the Civil War. Another *africanista*, he was, in the words of Esparza, "the classical officer of the *harka* in the best sense of the word—modest, valiant, without needs, who could live in any manner."[39] García Rebull was a quiet man, who said little—partly because he stuttered. But this in no sense implied lack of decisiveness. He had all the dash of the *tercios*. In fact, he looked a bit like a husky Douglas Fairbanks, trim moustache and all. The colonel briefed García Rebull on the deployment in the salient. Román garrisoned Otenskii. He, García Rebull, would hold Posad. Effectives were limited. Both First and Second Battalions were down to less than half strength. Second Battalion alone had lost 127 men since Wednesday. And it was only Friday.[40]

Muñoz Grandes wrung the division for reinforcements. Faced with holding a line now 110 kilometers long and strengthening the besieged salient, he began to pull battle tested units out of the Novgorod bridgehead and replace them with service and transport troops. Laux was also desperately short of men, and explained his critical situation over the telephone to von Chappuis. The new corps commander immediately arranged to meet him at Orelje, just across the river from Kuzino, early on the fifteenth. In a mood of deep gloom, the two generals discussed the possibility of pulling 126 Division back to a more defensible line which would still cover the flank of XXXIX Corps. While they spoke, the enemy surrounded and cut off Krassnaia Visherka.

That same Saturday, Esparza transferred his CP to Otenskii. This move had been prompted by a personal visit of Muñoz Grandes to Shevelevo. The general gave no such order, but his veteran colonel had much experience in interpreting subtle conversation. Accordingly, after a full meal, he had set off for the monastery with his staff and the assault section—totally oblivious, as usual, to the danger of stomach wounds. Installed in Otenskii, Esparza called Grigorovo. Muñoz Grandes informed him that he had decided to relieve all the forces in Posad. The men had fought well, he said, and it was time to share the glory and the danger. Neither officer thought that such a phrase, dripping with romanticism, was anything out of the ordinary in military conversation. The *guripas*, who picked it up at once and spread it around the division did, not because it seemed Quixotic, but because it seemed natural. Meanwhile, the forces in Posad were at last relieved. García Rebull retained command. Seven companies had been replaced by three. The manpower remained the same![41]

The relative quiet of Monday, the seventeenth, was punctuated only by occasional shellfire and sporadic strafing. At 0900 the telephone announced that the general was on his way from Shevelevo to Otenskii. Incredibly, it took two hours for Muñoz Grandes's staff car to negotiate the fourteen kilometers to the monastery. The remnants of First Battalion formed up to meet their commanding general. Their ranks hardly crowded the courtyard. Out of an original 800, only 7 officers and 180 men remained. Vallespín was the sole surviving captain. Garzón's cyclists were in even worse shape. They were down to one sergeant and fifteen men. Garzón himself was mutilated for life.

As the general paced down the thin ranks, he paused for a word with the haggard *guripas*. A smile, a nod, a pat on the shoulder warmed them. They knew he cared and they shared his pride. Addressing them, Muñoz Grandes praised their valor and then confided that the Red Army colonel commanding the forces at Posad had committed suicide. He had promised his superiors victory, and in spite of overwhelming superiority, failed. Then the general stood silent for a moment. He looked them hard in the eye. "With soldiers such as you, one could go anywhere."[42]

After the men fell out, Muñoz Grandes and Esparza went off for dinner and a chat. Suddenly smiling, Esparza began to relate a curious incident. Though wounded, Captain Muñoz had remained at his post in Posad. The only comfort he had allowed himself was to have a Russian POW assigned as his batman. During one of the attacks, the man had disappeared. Muñoz suspected that he had defected. The next day, a *guripa* was climbing around in the loft of one of the intact *izbas* and discovered his body. His hand still clasped a rifle. Peering through the transom, the soldier saw a semicircle of dead Ivans. It was a good firing position. Muñoz Grandes replied that other POWs were serving as more than cooks and stretcher bearers in the Blue Division. He hoped that they would fight as well as Muñoz's orderly. Lunch over, the general returned to Shevelevo. While the Spanish commanders were dining in Otenskii, von Chappuis was fuming back in Grigorovo.

Yesterday, the sixteenth, Busch had come up from Korosten. After a few pat words of praise for 126 Division, the corps commander had launched into a lengthy tirade on the Blue Division. For one who had been in command for only forty-eight hours and who had not yet had his first formal discussion with Muñoz Grandes, von Chappuis had had much to stay to Busch. "The 250 Division was the great problem child of the corps," he declared.[43] "In the case of a new Russian attack, the positions cannot be held by these forces."[44]

Once Busch was on the road von Chappuis requested the presence of Muñoz Grandes. A long and stormy interview ensued. Von Chappuis had opened with his principal complaint—the catastrophic fallout of horses and motor vehicles. He then tendered German officers and troops to advise and instruct the Spaniards in the care of their transport. These would also assist the Spanish quartermasters in the receiving and distribution of fodder and spare parts. Muñoz Grandes once again rejected this offer out of hand as being "inconsistent with the honor of the division."[45] Von Chappuis then "spared no words" in reviewing the causes of the situation. Stung, Muñoz Grandes replied that "the Division had been supplied with inferior horses and vehicles in Grafenwöhr. He had complained about them then, but had been put off with promises of being reequipped with Russian booty. Not only had the Germans failed to deliver, but on the contrary there was neither sufficient fodder nor adequate remounts, neither automotive supplies nor replacement vehicles."[46] His black eyes blazing, Muñoz Grandes icily observed that "the Germans seemed to regard his division—whose only goal was to fight and die alongside their ally—more as an albatross than an aid."[47] Flustered, von Chappuis inquired how the Spaniard had arrived at this conclusion. Like a machine gun, the former legionnaire spat out more than a half dozen examples.

It was unlikely that von Chappuis had ever been spoken to in such a manner by a general under his command. What he had totally failed to comprehend was that this general was not merely a divisional commander. Muñoz Grandes headed a Spanish expeditionary force within the Wehrmacht. He was the representative of the Spanish chief of state. He, not von Chappuis, had been personally briefed on his mission by the Führer at Rastenburg. He had been on active service since 1913, had been himself a corps commander and a minister of state. Von Chappuis had no understanding whatever of the sensitivity of the Spanish character, of the caliber of the man he faced, or of the intricate international issues involved.

After stewing all Sunday night over the interview, von Chappuis pulled himself together on Monday morning. He dictated a report to Busch—and, unknowingly, also to OKH. Reviewing the conversation of the previous day, he concluded with his evaluation.

The Spanish troops have up to now fought bravely but, I have the impression that under the influence of cold weather, poor shelter, . . . their valor will decline. Concerning their organization and training, the Spanish division is completely unusable for greater responsibilities. I have also the impression that the divisional commander himself knows this and seeks, as soon as possible, an honorable excuse to extricate himself personally before he himself suffers a breakdown. He seems to me ready to sustain any number of casualties, so that his force will be pulled out. . . . I therefore suggest that the Spanish division be removed from the front as soon as possible.[48]

That same Monday afternoon, Collatz sent his regular report to 16 Army. While pointing out the same deficiencies as von Chappuis, the tone of the leader of the Liaison Staff was much more optimistic and revealed considerable understanding and appreciation for the divisional commander and his men. His own position was not that secure. With the arrival of von Chappuis and von Oertzen the question had arisen as to whether a mere captain should command a liaison staff equivalent to a divisional staff.

Busch reviewed both reports the next day. He weighed the corps commander against the captain and recommended to von Leeb that the Blue Division be withdrawn and replaced with a fresh German division.[49] Poor von Leeb had other problems besides. Tikhvin was under armored attack. The I Corps drive on Volkhovstroi was stalled. Two divisions—223 and 227—fresh from France, had not performed as expected. Moreover, the Russians were reinforcing their Tikhvin attack and were resupplying Leningrad over the ice of Lake Ladoga through the gap between XXXIX Corps and the Finns.[50]

More bad news arrived at Pskov on the nineteenth. The stout 126 Division evacuated Malaia Vishera. Von Leeb was uneasy about the pullback and indeed, about the entire Tikhvin bulge. He asked von Brauchitsch for five more divisions. Von Leeb was deeply worried. He was prepared to think the unthinkable—giving up Tikhvin.

Busch, commander of 16 Army, was still sanguine. He assured his chief that the Tikhvin salient could be held with only three additional divisions. The motorized units would be replaced by infantry. Two divisions, 61 and 215, were already rolling eastward and relief could begin within a week. A third division would enable him to shift 250 Division southward to the quiescent Lake Il'men shore, taking its place at Novgorod. The freezing of Lake Il'men on 18 November had formed a vast ice plain capable of supporting heavy vehicles. Although an attack out of the Valdai across the lake was expected, it was not believed to be imminent. Thus, the Spaniards would have a chance to rest at no cost to their honor.[51]

Busch did not know Muñoz Grandes. The iron-willed *madrileño* would never accept a diminution of the role of the Spanish Volunteer Division. Muñoz Grandes was ordering his *guripas* to "defend Posad as if it were Spain." Not only Spanish honor but, perhaps, Spanish sovereignty was involved. The Blue Division had a dual mission. The first, and most obvious, was to participate in the defeat of Soviet Russia. The second, and more subtle, was to demonstrate to Hitler that the Spanish would fight and accept any casualties. Operation Felix was still in the wings, and the Führer must be convinced that any invader would pay dearly for every inch of Spanish soil. The commander of the Volunteer Division was faced with a dilemma. No matter what it cost, he had to hold Posad. Retreat was out of the question, because the Germans would take it as a sign of weakness. On the other hand, it tore at his vitals to see his men sacrificed in holding what he knew was an untenable position. The division might consume itself and his front could disintegrate. The division would have to stand by his sheer will power. He would make the *guripas* better than they were.

Muñoz Grandes was also lucky. The Russians were throwing more units against 126 Division and, after beating at the bastion in vain, gave Posad a respite. Spain, too, was lucky. Tenacious Russian resistance had obliged the Germans to transfer from France divisions which might have participated in Operation Felix. The plans revived the previous summer were once again postponed.

During the last weeks of November, as the pressure on the Pyrenees temporarily eased, the diplomatic chessboard was awash with complicated maneuvers. Franco dispatched General Moscardó to Germany and Russia. His public mission was to improve German-Spanish sports relations and to deliver the *aguinaldo del Caudillo*, the Christmas gift of Franco to the Blue Division. As Franco's chief of military household and thus the generalissimo's liaison with the armed forces he carried confidential messages to Muñoz Grandes. Almost simultaneously, Adm. Wilhelm Canaris, Chief of *Abwehr* (German Military Intelligence) left for Spain. His overt mission concerned the establishment of observation posts opposite Gibraltar. He, too, had another function. Just as Canaris was arriving in Madrid, Serrano Suñer boarded a special train for Berlin, where he was to represent Spain at a conference called by Hitler to reaffirm the Anti-Comintern Pact.[52]

The aging hero of the Alcázar made his official rounds in Germany, then on 27 November departed for Novgorod. Upon his return, Moscardó was scheduled to have an audience with the Führer. Canaris, meanwhile, was enjoying the hospitality of his friends in Madrid. He loved Spain and liked Franco. The *Abwehr* chief also "took a lively interest in . . . the Blue Division . . . and did his best to see that the various difficulties which inevitably arose between the Spanish and German Services were amicably settled."[53] Canaris's chief conduit to the Caudillo was Air Minister General Vigón, an intimate personal friend. Such close contacts with the cabinet enabled the anti-Nazi admiral to frustrate the Führer's intentions. While Hitler expected Canaris to smooth the way for Spanish entry into the war, the admiral repeatedly betrayed him. He confidentially urged his Spanish friends to keep Spain out of the conflict.[54] The admiral's formal mission was a success. He received permission to set up the observation posts, and returned to Germany on the first of December. These minor concessions by Franco were meant to reassure Hitler that Spain stood at his side.

Spain was indeed part of the anti-Communist coalition. Serrano Suñer's purpose in Berlin was to join twelve other nations in formal adhesion to the Anti-Comintern Pact. The pact was originally negotiated in 1936 between Germany and Japan. Italy joined a few months later, followed in 1939 by Hungary, Spain, and the Japanese puppet regime of Manchukuo. When the five-year agreement came up for renewal on 25 November 1941, seven additional nations signified their intention to adhere to the useless document. Many of them were either German-occupied or satellite regimes—Denmark, Romania, Bulgaria, Slovakia, Croatia, Nanking China, and Finland.

Reich Foreign Minister von Ribbentrop played host. He met with Serrano Suñer on 25 November. Count Galeazzo Ciano, son-in-law of the Duce and foreign minister of Italy, was also present. Ribbentrop was being very cordial to Ciano and invited him in order to emphasize "that everything concerning the Mediterranean comes into Italy's direct sphere of influence."[55] The conversation with Ribbentrop was followed on 29 November by a meeting with the Führer in the Reich Chancellery. Again, Ciano was present. Yet, the German dictator would scarcely have invited him if he expected hard bargaining with Serrano Suñer.

Ribbentrop had words of praise for the Blue Division. Hitler, too, was complimentary. Nevertheless, Ciano felt that conviction was lacking in their voices and had the impression that the Germans were irritated by reports of lack of discipline. The Germans did not bring up the matter of Spain's entry into the war, partly because Serrano Suñer kept stressing his country's lack of preparedness and partly because he kept asking embarrassing questions. Among the most pointed was when would Moscow be taken.[56] Eyes bulging, Ciano noted that Serrano Suñer "has not yet discovered the proper tone for speaking to the Germans, and does not seem very anxious to find it."[57] When Hitler discussed the military situation, Serrano Suñer commented that "the Führer was absolutely right when he said that there was no power in the world that could conquer the European continent militarily."[58] Gasping at the audacity of the double meaning, Ciano virtually jumped out of his chair.

Hitler returned to the Gibraltar issue. He regretted that Spanish reluctance had prevented the implementation of Operation Felix. This gave Serrano Suñer his cue. He launched into a litany of all the difficulties which beset the Franco regime. "He ended by saying that Spain will intervene because she cannot do otherwise, but that the work of moral and material preparation is very far from being complete."[59] Serrano Suñer then proposed that certain Falangist activists, currently enrolled in the Blue Division, should be returned to Spain, "particularly in regard to promoting friendship for Germany and strengthening the Government."[60] Hitler agreed. Taking his leave, the Spanish foreign minister requested permission to visit the Blue Division, perhaps at the beginning of January. Ribbentrop said that he saw no objection.[61]

The Berlin conversations were friendly, but only in a diplomatic sense. Hitler and Ribbentrop were still annoyed with Franco and Serrano Suñer, and had been ever since Hendaye in 1940. The Spaniards were simply not forthcoming and refused to be cogs in the New Order. Serrano Suñer, who needed German support for domestic reasons, came away with a minor concession. Perhaps the return of prominent Falangists from the Blue Division would placate the Old Shirts at home and prop him up against the machinations of Arrese and the hostility of the army. Hitler was still looking for a quisling, however, and was more than ever convinced that Serrano Suñer was not his man. On the other hand, General Muñoz Grandes fought loyally in the Wehrmacht.

Franco did not trust Serrano Suñer entirely either. He controlled Spain and intended to share that control with no one. In his usual fashion, and with Serrano Suñer in Berlin, the Caudillo had just privately negotiated an arrangement with Canaris. And this contact came through the military, not the Falange. Also through the military was another contact. Franco's aide-de-camp, Frigate Captain Fontán quietly dropped a hint to Germans in Madrid that his master was interested in meeting Hitler in Germany. The cover for the conference would be a visit to the Blue Division. Travelling as generalissimo, not as chief of state, he would leave Serrano Suñer at home. This Byzantine maneuvering served to recall the old expression—Castillians are single-minded; Basques can keep their minds on two things at once; a Galician, Franco, could think of three things simultaneously. At this very moment, General Moscardó was delivering the Caudillo's grand gesture of Christmas gifts to the Blue Division.

Moscardó arrived at Grigorovo on Sunday afternoon, 30 November 1941. His limousine slid to a stop on the sheet ice at Muñoz Grandes's rustic headquarters. The divisional commander stepped down from the porch and warmly embraced the bulky figure of his guest. An honor guard snapped to attention as the pair crunched over the snow and walked arm in arm into the cabin.

Moscardó's dark glasses quickly steamed as he entered the warm room. He halted to gain his bearings, unslung his camera, and doffed his military surcoat. He looked like a typical tourist. Muñoz Grandes escorted him over to Zanón's map board and laid out the situation of the division. The Germans were worried about an assault on Novgorod now that Lake Il'men had frozen. The Recon Group had already motored across the lake clear to the lighthouse at the mouth of the Lovat River, where they contacted 290 Division at Vsvad. Four days later, ten motorcyclists renewed the contact. Corps had asked 250 Division to set up a ski company.

The next morning Moscardó crossed the river to Sitno, where he was received by Esparza. Over the ever lengthening rows of crosses in the cemetery, the Falangist militia chief bared his bald head and pronounced a few words of praise. Then in unison with the assembled garrison he shouted, "*Presente!*" The call echoed three times across the Volkhov. A "*Viva Franco*" and "*Arriba España*" followed. Their emotions aroused, the *guripas* pressed around the corpulent, leather-coated figure. Moscardó would not withhold his hand from anyone. It took a quarter of an hour for the party to push through the crowd to Canillas's CP. There a steaming samovar awaited. Clusters of soldiers still hung around the hut and the three gleaming limousines awaiting Moscardó's reappearance. Beyond in the woods Soviet riflemen could hardly believe their eyes. Curiously, the Reds failed to call down artillery on the seething mob scene.[62] Tea over, the convoy sped northward. Women and children waving handkerchiefs lined the streets at Russa and Zmeisko. Three blazing *izbas* greeted Moscardó at Shevelevo. The stoves had overheated again.

A select guard, Iron Crosses gleaming on their tunics, presented arms at the entrance to the colonel's bunker. Over a map table and in between swigs of vodka, Esparza explained his dispositions. Moscardó was well satisfied, and asked his host what was next on the schedule. Dinner, of course, Esparza replied without hesitation. The menu featured "mascot cow." Bossy had been the mascot of headquarters company of 269 for many weeks, having been adopted en route to the front. She had now made the ultimate sacrifice for Spain, and graced the plate of the hero of the Alcázar. The next morning Moscardó said his goodbyes to Muñoz Grandes and left Grigorovo for Rastenburg and an audience with the Führer before returning to Spain.

The front was heating up. In the log hut at Bol. Dvor that served as his CP, Meretskov was directing his troops in the battle of the Tikhvin Bulge. On 24 November *Stavka* had ordered three armies—4, 52, and 54—to cut off XXXIX Corps at the Kuzino and Grusino crossings and to annihilate the entire Tikhvin Bulge. Fourth would jump off first, followed by 52 on 1 December and 54 on 3 December. Soviet units facing Tikhvin had achieved superiority in infantry, artillery, and mortars, but were weak in armor and lacked sufficient mortar shells to employ their beloved carpet barrages. Nevertheless, using their new tactics of interdicting German communications with air, artillery, and ground strikes the Red Army succeeded in choking Wehrmacht supplies and throttling reinforcements.[63] On 30 November Stalin had phoned Meretskov and ordered him to attack, ready or not. Three days later one of secret police chief Lavrentii Beria's dreaded enforcers arrived. G. I. Kulik left no doubt that death or slave labor camps awaited laggards. Leningrad must be relieved![64]

Von Leeb was not optimistic. His attempt to tighten the ring around Leningrad had failed. Thirty-eight Corps was in trouble and pulling back. Tikhvin was surrounded on three sides and twenty-nine train loads of Soviet troops were rolling toward what was left of the city. Volkhovstroi could absolutely not be taken. Even Schlüsselburg was in danger. Army Group North had no reserves. All front-line troops were exhausted. Moreover, the panzers were utterly useless. Their turrets could not rotate in the cold. OKH advised him that the Red Army had recaptured the city of Rostov on the Don from Army Group South. Operation Typhoon was faltering at the very gates of Moscow. With the pressure on the Russian capital easing, the "enemy will probably turn on Leningrad, because the relief of Leningrad would be a political as well as a military victory."[65]

The battle of the Tikhvin Bulge opened on 3 December, hitting the Spaniards at Nikltkino at 1400. The assault became general on 4 December and the entire Blue Division front erupted during a cold, clear, moonlit night. Silhouetted in the sky, waves of aircraft flashed down on the Spanish positions. The orange glow of Soviet artillery greeted the new day. At 0400, with temperatures thirty degrees below zero, the Reds charged across the frozen snow on Posad and Otenskii. They reached the outer ring of houses and were only thrown back after four hours of hand-to-hand fighting. Otenskii was surrounded and the Ivans clawing at the walls. Five score Communist dead lay in the shadow of the bent cross on the chapel's cupola. While the outposts were still struggling, artillery, heavy weapons, and antitank guns rained death on Dubrovka, Nikltkino, and Tigoda.[66]

At 0515 two companies attacked Shevelevo. But Esparza was ready. This time no one had to wake the sentries. A deserter, taken at Tigoda, had confided that CPs would be preselected targets. When the Reds charged through the town, the *guripas* instinctively began grenading forward. A detail examined the bodies of the fallen Russians. Underneath the white outer garments were uniforms of all arms and services. Esparza asked to see the identifications. The men were from a punishment unit. Some were former officers, some had been pilots, others even medics. The Red Army had given them a chance to redeem themselves by a life or death assignment. Soviet losses in the day's fighting far exceeded those of the Spaniards. There were at least 550 Russian dead alone. Total Spanish casualties were less than 130, still a heavy drain on the depleted battalions.[67]

Von Chappuis fretted about the sinking strength of his units. That evening he anxiously discussed the matter with Busch. The corps commander's voice rose in desperation as he described the situation over the crackling telephone lines. The 126 Division was nearing its limits. The vital crossing point at Chudovo was in danger. "The men can't understand why no one helps them in their plight."[68] The Spaniards had the same problem. Theirs was particularly acute due to the 110 kilometer length of their front. As Chudovo was shielded by 126, the 250 covered Novgorod.

"I don't believe the Spaniards can hold Novgorod against a strong Russian attack. With the loss of Novgorod, the Reds will win a prestigious prize,"[69] von Chappuis continued. Busch consoled his corps chief, "the commander of the Spanish Division told me . . . that, especially on the Novgorod front, he will be able to hold his positions."[70] With this crushing remark, the army commander made it clear that he believed and trusted Muñoz Grandes. Busch, though worried about the Spaniards, was not panicking. Von Chappuis had been stampeded into a hasty and poorly conceived opinion. He was now paying for it. He had lost the full confidence of his army commander while one of his subordinates was on the way to winning it.

But Muñoz Grandes had to prove that his men could hold. Withering attacks by 305 Rifle Division were pounding Posad and Otenskii. Suddenly the weather broke. Almost unbelievable cold, down to −35 degrees Celsius, blew in and stunned his men. Zanón had visited Shevelevo on the afternoon of 4 December. The information he brought back to Grivorovo was not reassuring.[71]

The Russians opened up again on Posad early the next day. At 0630 Soviet Reserves flowed in from Poselok and began to fill in around the perimeter. The constant bombardment increased. Flights of three Martin Bombers swooped out of the rose-tinted clouds, pummeling the Spanish positions. Anxiously, even eagerly, the *guripas* awaited the cries of *ispanskii kaput!* which heralded an infantry attack. It was a relief to face the enemy in open combat after crouching for hours and days in the freezing foxholes and bunkers.

Outside, the sentries peered from their shelters. The shells and shrill wind barely masked the Soviet loudspeakers which called in perfect Castilian: "We admire your resistance as heroic, as it is useless. Don't you know you are surrounded? Kill your officers and join us. We will respect your rank. To our rear are beautiful cities, entertainment, diversions . . . you will no longer be cold."[72] Then the sweet tones of the waltz "Ramona" wafted over the battlefield. The Reds liked "Ramona." Until recently the volunteers had answered Soviet harangues with well-aimed shells from their 37s. But artillery had knocked them out. Now the *guripas* could only reply with obscene gestures and a complete vocabulary of Castilian curses.

At 0835 the enemy surged forward in waves. Converging on the village from all sides, drunken riflemen of Regiments 1002 and 1004, supported by the light tanks of 3 Battalion of 5 Armored, overran the listening posts. As the vodka-mad Russians tumbled into the forward firing pits, they finished off the wounded *guripas* with ice picks and trench spades. But, that was the limit of their advance.[73]

From his dripping, shuddering CP, García Rebull calmly called for fire support. Under stress his stutter disappeared. Incessant air and artillery strikes had smashed his heavy weapons. Munitions were low, but he asked for nothing except artillery. The Spaniards withstood the assault. To the north, however, five rifle divisions, albeit understrength, were crashing down on 126 Division. Nekrasovo fell at noon on 5 December. Nekrasovo, like Otenskii and Posad, had been one of the shields behind which von Chappuis had hoped to form his winter line.

Only that morning von Chappuis had proposed to Busch a winter defense line. Busch himself, recognizing that the offensive was over, had removed his GHQ from forward Korosten to rearward Dno. He listened intently. The new front would run from Novgorod northward along the west bank of the Volkhov to Kostylevo—two kilometers down river from Shevelevo—where it would cross the river. The proposed HKL called for the Spaniards to abandon both the bridgehead and the salient.[74]

Thus, the corps commander had come to the conclusion that the Blue Division should withdraw behind the Volkhov. However, he could not give the order until the new HKL had been approved and constructed. In the meantime, the Spaniards would continue to die at Otenskii and Posad. The next morning, 6 December 1941, Muñoz Grandes arrived at Esparza's CP at Shevelevo. The enemy had just renewed his assaults on Nikltkino and Posad. "What do you think of the situation," the general asked. The harried colonel, who had almost half of the fighting strength of the division under his command, lost no words. "I told Rodrigo two weeks ago that the salient could only be held at excessive cost and counseled withdrawal," he said. "I still think that we must pull back while we have men who can walk out."[75]

The High Command, Muñoz Grandes confided, had authorized a retreat to the line of the Volkhov. However, he was reluctant to pull back. He had told von Chappuis that the honor of the division was wrapped in the honor of Spain and had asked for a German division to be sent in so that it could be the one which retreated! But von Chappuis had no divisions available. He then ordered Esparza to prepare secretly for a speedy withdrawal. Once ready, the colonel was to stand by and wait for the general's word to pull back in haste, but in full order, even if certain heavy equipment would have to be left behind.

The corps commander had indeed proposed the retreat of 250 Division to winter positions along the west bank of the Volkhov, and he had informed Muñoz Grandes. Sixteenth Army and Army Group North had finally approved the pullback in principle, pending the construction of defensive positions. But von Chappuis had not yet issued any such orders to Muñoz Grandes. Secretly, without informing his commander, the Spanish general was preparing to evacuate his men. This was a serious breach of authority and Muñoz Grandes knew it.

On the night of the sixth Muñoz Grandes dispatched his trusted deputy, Rodrigo, to Shevelevo with verbal orders. Rodrigo told Esparza that the withdrawal was tentatively scheduled for the night of 7–8 December. Having taken the decision, Muñoz Grandes now had to pressure von Chappuis to hurry, before the *guripas* began flooding across the Volkhov and the corps commander realized what had happened. Above all, the retreat must be in full order, and the number of casualties kept to a minimum.[76]

Posad was a passport to death. The Falangist Old Guard paid for their fanaticism in blood. Enrique Sotomayor—the protégé of Muñoz Grandes—and Quiqui Vernaci were dead. Their frozen bodies sprawled grotesquely alongside their comrades of the SEU. Agustín Aznar was wounded. Dionisio Ridruejo was a physical wreck. For them, the Civil War had finally come to an end.

In Otenskii, Juan Eugenio Blanco and his comrades of 2 Antitanks followed the battle with their eyes and hearts. As Saturday night wore on, Blanco stood on sentry duty next to his beloved piece, *Yola*. The intense cold cut through his greatcoat. Though the broken walls of the monastery gave the patio some protection from the biting wind, it was not enough. At −25 degrees Celsius no amount of stamping could warm his feet. From a nearby bunker came voices and laughter. The real attraction was the stove. Blanco cautiously advanced toward the door. "Where's the sergeant of the guard?" he wondered. "Can I slip inside and warm my feet?"[77] A vision of the Articles of War and a firing squad stopped him short.

Another half hour went by. It was past four in the morning. "Where's Mariano, my relief? He's late again,"[78] Blanco muttered to himself. Throwing duty and fear of court martial aside, he made for the tower where Mariano Ferrer lay fast asleep. Picking his way down the aisle formed by the feet of the twenty men on each side of the room, he grabbed Ferrer. Ferrer, after being shaken awake, mumbled "Consider yourself relieved and go to bed."[79] Swearing, Blanco stumbled out again into the courtyard to resume his post. Cursing even louder, Ferrer appeared a few minutes later.

After warming his hands and feet and swallowing a sardine, Blanco bedded down between Sergeant Patiño and Corporal Arza. As he dozed off, Blanco heard the drone of Soviet aircraft. "So what," he mused, "they come all the time and I'm too tired to get up and go to the bomb shelter downstairs."[80] A terrified scream jolted Blanco into consciousness. Opening his eyes, he saw a hole in the ceiling where the bomb had entered. The noncom opposite him lay split in half with the unexploded bomb sticking out of his vitals. Tensing, Blanco considered rising and running, but instinct kept him flattened on the floor. He had hardly gotten "Our Father, who art . . ." out of his mouth when the bomb detonated.[81] When he came to, he could see the clear night sky through a mist of dust and jumble of timbers. Ferrer's shouts shot through the gloom. With a sense of animal joy, Blanco scrambled out from beneath the rubble. Nine other men emerged. None were wounded. The other thirty were all dead. Of one of his friends, not a trace remained.

At noon that Sunday, 7 December 1941, reports began to arrive at corps headquarters in Grigorovo that Posad was surrounded. Muñoz Grandes himself called on von Chappuis repeatedly and painted a picture of desperation. He told the corps commander that: "the four companies in Posad had effectiveness of 2, 9, 11 and 16! A command to break out would apparently not be heard . . . because shortly all the men in Posad and Otenskii would be dead, sacrificed to bombs, shells, tanks, and crushing enemy infantry attacks."[28] Muñoz Grandes appeared to von Chappuis to be cracking under the tremendous pressure.

Muñoz Grandes was indeed under much more pressure than von Chappuis knew. He had other worries besides the garrisons of Posad and Otenskii. If the salient was overrun, he might lose the entire bridgehead and with it, half his division. There would be virtually nothing, certainly nothing in corps reserve, to stop the overwhelming Red forces from crossing the frozen Volkhov, perhaps taking Novgorod, cutting the lifeline of 16 Army, and turning north to trap XXXIX Corps. The encirclement of Leningrad might be broken. Hitler might consider the Spaniards unable to hold a defensive line, perhaps even a defensive line in the Pyrenees. The division would be lost. Spain would be lost. He deliberately lied to von Chappuis about the number of effectives in Posad.

At 1630, without receiving any authorization from von Chappuis, Muñoz Grandes ordered Esparza to begin the retreat at 2100. Román and García Rebull were to be alerted at 1900. Until then only Rodrigo, Zanón, and Esparza would know. Muñoz Grandes took full responsibility. He told Rodrigo and Esparza at Shevelevo that they would be permitted to take any action necessary to ensure order and discipline. This included summary execution. Any such measures would be in his name. His subordinates would share no blame for anything connected with the unauthorized withdrawal.

Deeply disturbed, and totally unaware of what was going on under his very nose, von Chappuis telephoned Busch at 1900. He recommended that 250 Division be permitted to retire across the Volkhov. The army commander agreed. He had already issued orders to evacuate Tikhvin on the morrow. His prime concern was to protect the flank of the retreating XXXIX Corps. Stressing this, he authorized von Chappuis to pull back 250 Division. At 2214 von Chappuis issued Corps Order 73. By that time, the Posad garrison had already passed Otenskii and the men in the monastery were moving westward in full order.[83] The next day, Canillas evacuated the bridgehead. The battalions fired the villages before they pulled back across the frozen river. The last truck out of Sitno carried the crosses from the cemetery.

7

"Nailed to the Ground"

"NAILED TO THE GROUND," MUÑOZ GRANDES RE-
peated. "Not one step backward."[1] Esparza knew what the general
meant. The new line would be held. From his temporary CP in Udarnik, the colonel checked on the units as they withdrew through the
scratch forces to the west bank of the Volkhov. Von Chappuis doubted
they would hold. The Spanish had begun pulling back from Posad and
Otenskii prior to receiving his authorization. The divisional commander seemed more concerned with getting his men out—they had disengaged without a single casualty—than salvaging the supplies and
artillery. At Otenskii the provisions had been thrown open to the
troops who stuffed themselves with chocolate and cognac without pre-
senting the proper requisitions. Instead of loading the trucks with the
remaining rations, the Spaniards used the vehicles to carry out their
wounded. No place remained for supplies, which were abandoned to
the Reds. When the corps commander reproached Muñoz Grandes
about this, the Spanish general seemed singularly unperturbed.[2]

Monday afternoon, Busch called from Army headquarters at Dno,
and von Chappuis complained bitterly that 250 Division was a "hole
in the line."[3] He asked for more divisions. Busch again consoled von
Chappuis with assurances that the situation on the Spanish front was
known to higher authorities and asked for an appreciation of Muñoz
Grandes's own evaluation of his division. The army commander had
finally reached the conclusion that it would indeed be best if the weak-

ened Blue Division were replaced, but he wished to include in his recommendation to von Leeb a full report from XXXVIII Corps.

Acting under the instructions of Busch, von Chappuis summoned Muñoz Grandes for an interview. The corps commander opened with the crucial question: Can your division hold? Muñoz Grandes was unable to give a flat yes or no. He assured von Chappuis that morale was still good. However, his battalions had suffered heavy losses. First of 269 had only 250 effectives out of 800; Second only 225; Third of 263 and *Tía Bernarda* were down to 200. Von Chappuis reminded Muñoz Grandes that the old entrenchments of the previous fall were still there. Muñoz Grandes replied that these were jumping off positions, not defensive field works.

Von Chappuis returned to the attack. "Can your men hold?" Muñoz Grandes shook his head:

"Even in spite of the cold the wish is there, but the battalions are so weak . . . that it is doubtful if they can hold."

Von Chappuis shot back: "Then I shall recommend that you be pulled out for rest and resupply behind the front."

Eyes blazing, his voice hard, Muñoz Grandes quietly answered: "We will recuperate in the line. My soldiers will fight to the death."[4]

The corps commander reported the conversation in painstaking detail, concluding with the recommendation that, not only should the division be withdrawn, but also that Muñoz Grandes be replaced. The divisional chief "no longer had the necessary energy and initiative for successful leadership."[5]

Busch knew full well what von Chappuis failed to point out. Laux's 126 Division was in no better shape than 250 Division. Cases of spiritual collapse and apathy were evident. The fallout of horses was approaching that of the Spaniards. Artillery and vehicles had had to be abandoned to save the troops. Laux considered the situation of his division desperate. In XXXIX Corps, some units had ceased to exist. Whole regiments were ghosts. One battalion of 18 Motorized lost half of its combat strength, 250 men, in the frigid retreat from Tikhvin. The temperature had plummeted to -40 degrees Celsius, and many had died when the cerebral fluid suddenly froze solid under their steel helmets. Von Leeb received the reports from 16 Army with growing consternation. He recognized that the Tikhvin offensive had failed and was seeking to find a line at which his men could hold.

The entire winter campaign had reached its crisis. By the end of November, Hitler, von Brauchitsch, and Halder had still believed that success was in the offing. On 20 November, Army Group South had taken Rostov on the Don. On 23 November, Halder pronounced Russia a defeated power, whose military was "no longer a danger."[6] The advance on Moscow could be resumed when the mud froze, and Tikhvin was in German hands. The first week of December drew a different picture. The Red Army had counterattacked in the south, recapturing Rostov. The defeat was not serious, but it was the first Wehrmacht withdrawal in the east, and broke a mystique of victory. Terrified of capture, the transport troops panicked. Hitler had intervened personally, refusing to countenance retreat, and had fired the Army Group South commander in chief, Field Marshal von Rundstedt. In the end, the Führer had had no choice, and Rostov was lost. Meanwhile, von Bock's forces had run out of steam at the gates of Moscow by 4 December and could go no further. The Reds were bringing up reinforcements and Army Group Center would have to stand somewhere and hold. When it came to Tikhvin, Hitler had been as reluctant to sanction a pullback as at Rostov. On 6 December, he had told Halder, who by now was convinced that things had gone awry, that Russia had suffered eight to ten million casualties against half a million Germans. It now appears that Hitler had overestimated these Russian losses, which were closer to five million. Moreover, they were being made up. Tikhvin should be held, Hitler told the OKH chief of staff. The Spaniards should certainly remain in the line. All would stand.[7]

The next day von Leeb had telephoned Rastenburg several times and the Führer had backed down enough to evacuate Tikhvin. The dictator was now dealing directly with the army group commander, over the heads of von Brauchitsch, Halder, and OKH. On 8 December, Hitler succumbed to the inevitable and issued Führer Directive 39, announcing that the "severe winter weather which has come up surprisingly early in the East, and the consequent difficulties in bringing up supplies, compel us to abandon immediately all major offensive operations and go over to the defensive."[8] Thus did Hitler attribute defeat solely to the weather, without reference to the indecision, lack of foresight, and the resistance of Soviet troops. Army Group North was ordered to continue to deny the enemy the railroad to Volkhovstroi and to keep open the possibility of union with the Finns and the strangulation of Leningrad.

Von Leeb was at the end of his tether, and it was becoming clearer that only the Volkhov would provide a winter defense line. The Spaniards had already set themselves up there, and Busch by 9 December had thankfully observed that 250 Division could hold out for a while. But Keitel told von Leeb that the Führer was undecided over whether to sanction a general retreat of XXXVIII and XXXIX Corps to the line of the river because "when we retire, the troops come apart, as at Rostov."[9] On 10 December, Hitler authorized a minor pullback of XXXIX Corps, but von Leeb was not optimistic. "Whether we can hold here depends on the Spaniards and 126 Division," he lamented.[10]

With his men safely behind the barrier of the Volkhov, Muñoz Grandes felt relieved. Unaware that the Spaniards had withdrawn, the Red Air Force continued to pound Posad and Otenskii for hours after the evacuation. This allowed two forgotten *guripas*—one an airplane spotter, the other a heavy sleeper—to stroll unmolested down the Otenskii-Shevelevo road to freedom on the morning of 8 December. Not until midday on the ninth did 305 Rifle Division close up to the riverbank. Even then the Reds declined to attack, allowing Canillas to pull out of the bridgehead without interference.[11]

On Wednesday, 10 December, Muñoz Grandes reshuffled his meager forces to provide some depth in defense. He charitably reduced the exhausted and ailing Esparza's command to two battalions. The Blue Division had another ten days to rest. Meanwhile, 126 Division and XXXIX Corps were being battered rearward. Red commandos struck behind the German lines. Supply columns were ravaged, reinforcements cut to pieces, and communications interrupted. Sixty-first Division lost six batteries, half of its artillery.[12] Meanwhile Russian supply was getting through. A road from Vologda through the taiga to Lake Ladoga was completed. The trucks could go to the front and straight on across the ice to Leningrad. The siege was broken.

Russian successes stimulated partisan activity which took on a particularly nasty character. Dionisio Acebal, along with four other anti-tankers, went foraging to the rear. When they failed to return, Captain España dispatched a patrol. The five were found dangling from trees, their eyes gouged out, tortured and mutilated. Except for *La Parrala's* nightly visitations, air attacks were sporadic, bombardments infrequent, and Soviet probes limited and generally confined to the Lake Il'men sector.

The period of inactivity helped to revive and restore the division. Juan Eugenio Blanco joined his comrades by the warm fire in an *izba* at Arefino. The vodka tasted good, and the burning logs felt even better. Singing, the men returned to life.

On 14 December, Busch recommended to von Leeb that 16 Army

be withdrawn to the Volkhov. Von Leeb agreed and said that he would seek Hitler's approval. Hitler fumed that "pulling back behind the Volkhov means we shall lose the Schlüsselburg salient. The enemy will hold the railroad and break through to Leningrad."[13] An hour and a half later Keitel telephoned Pskov and summoned von Leeb and Busch to the *Führerhauptquartier* on the morrow.

Hitler greeted von Leeb and Busch like a tiger backed into a corner. Listening to all the arguments once more, he gave in and ordered the retreat. Watch out for Novgorod and Lake Il'men, he told the field marshal. The Spaniards had a wide front and, if that area should be lost the army group would be broken in two. Von Leeb did not need that advice. He knew that the Reds were concentrating in the Valdai and could either strike north or south of Lake Il'men. Hitler would hear no more of withdrawals. At midnight, on 16 December, he sent for Halder. There were to be no more retreats on the eastern front, he commanded. Nor were second line defenses to be constructed; if they existed the tendency would be to retire. The order was issued on 20 December.

This famous decision, commanding the Wehrmacht to stand and die, saved the army. With the experience of Rostov, Hitler knew that retreat could lead to panic. There was inadequate fuel for a pullback, ice and snow would slow the troops, and the Russians would fall upon his soldiers as they had upon Napoleon's Grand Army. Any general who withdrew would be cashiered and, many were. Rundstedt had only been the first. Three dozen others followed. Tens of thousands of *Landser* perished, but the Eastern Front held. Hitler was now convinced that he alone could master the situation. Von Brauchitsch, nominally commander in chief of the army, had long since become superfluous. On 19 December 1941, his resignation was accepted by the Führer. Henceforth, Hitler was both supreme commander of the armed forces and commander in chief of the army. Both OKW and OKH were directly responsible to him, and he would take personal charge of operations.

Novgorod was one of the danger points. On 20 December, POWs reported that masses of Russian transports were moving out of the Valdai toward the Golden City. The Russians were reorganizing their command in preparation for an assault against the vital nerve center. The divisions immediately opposite—3 Armored (now realistically renamed 125 Rifle Division) and 305 Rifle Division—had been detached from 52 Army and designated Independent Army Group Novgorod, GHQ at Proletarii on the Msta. All signs indicated an imminent attack.[14]

Busch was nervous. The winter HKL of 16 Army would be manned by exhausted troops and a concentrated enemy attack across the Volkhov could reach the *Rollbahn* and the railroad in short order. His line had three crucial foci, whose loss to the Russians might doom Army Group North. South of Lake Il'men, Staraia Russa was a vital depot and transfer point. It was one of the keys to defense from an attack out of the Valdai Heights. North, of course, was the Volkhov crossing at Chudovo, from which Red units could turn north or south, strike directly toward Leningrad and roll up his forces. In the center was Novgorod, whose defense was the task of Spanish volunteers. Although 126 Division had disengaged and withdrawn behind the Volkhov, and 18 Motorized was on its way to back up the Spaniards, he was still uneasy. He wanted 81 Division, which was due from La Rochelle on 27 December, to replace 250 Division. Von Leeb, fully aware of the politics involved, refused. He preferred to shift 250 Division southward to cover Lake Il'men, while 81 Division took over Novgorod. "Even if each Spaniard were personally brave," the field marshal agreed, "250 Division could not hold its long line. They suffer too much from the cold."[15] If the enemy attacked before 81 Division arrived, "We are in trouble. One can only hope that the Spaniards hold."[16]

Novgorod was silent. Most of the civilians had been evacuated earlier that month. Cold air hung over the city. Night was clear and the stars shimmered crisply, like diamonds studded in black velvet. A quarter moon brightened the snow-covered rubble. Furtively, human shadows darted along, while cars with masked headlamps rushed through almost empty streets. Just by the iron bridge across the Volkhov the remains of a Soviet tank, a KV-1, lay overturned, a great green hulk, burned and lifeless. December had begun so peacefully. Friday, the twelfth, Pimentel welcomed 7 Company back from Posad. One captain, two sergeants, three corporals, and twenty-five men! They were the lucky ones. One hundred and seventy were not so lucky.

Saturday night, 13 December, was *Violeta*'s turn. Hospital train *Violeta* alternated with *Lili Marlene* in evacuating the wounded: Podberez'e and Grigorovo to Porkhov and Riga. Errando Vilar delivered distinguished company—Agustín Aznar and Dionisio Ridruejo—to the advance railroad station and silently placed these survivors of Posad in their bunks. All was dark. The station lay under direct enemy observation. A flicker of light would bring down a hail of fire.[17]

Northward, near the airfield at Krechevitsy, Lieutenant Ruíz made his rounds. Ruíz returned to the bunker, a reinforced concrete electrical substation in full view of the Reds across the river. He lit his stove only at night so the telltale smoke would not draw artillery fire. Since daylight lasted a short six hours, nine in the morning until three in the afternoon, he had ample time to heat his shelter.

Snug and safe, he began sampling the Christmas candies and liquors which were arriving from Spain. The problem was, however, with the Führer's Christmas gift. Each officer had received an elegant bottle of French champagne, but his had shattered when the liquid froze in transit. Ruíz found that upon unwrapping the newspaper around the bottle he had a magnum-shaped block of ice. Picking out the shards of glass and bits of paper and straw, he proceeded to place the block in a pot on his stove. In a few minutes he was sipping champagne—flat and warm, but nevertheless champagne. Once again Spanish improvisation had triumphed over the Russian winter.

Nochebuena, Christmas eve. One by one the men of Ruíz's machine gun section knelt before the chaplain. As the priest heard their hurried confessions, the others stood about the lieutenant's bunker in animated conversation. They pushed Corella toward the stove, shouting for him to recite some poems. The dark, sloe-eyed Valencian began. "I go dreaming, along the road in the afternoon. The golden brown hills, the green pines, the dusty trails. . . ."[18]

As he spoke, scenes of Spain appeared in the minds of the men—the sun, the sparkle, and the women. Enchanted, the men listened, transported to happier times and warmer climes. The bard finished. Only the drone of the priest giving absolution broke the silence. "I hope our recital has not disturbed you, pater," queried the lieutenant. "No, don't worry. . . . Tomorrow, I'll bring you Communion."[19]

The poet Corella peered over the sights of his MG 34. Dawn was just breaking and his romantic heart was filled with the wonder of Christmas. As the sun struggled up in the eastern sky, inspiration overpowered him. There it was before his very eyes—the barbed wire, the white snow, the frozen river, and beyond the enemy and dark forest. Above all, he envisioned God, blessing his tortured world like the rising sun bringing light. "What was that?" He could not see in the half light. Corella grabbed the binoculars and feverishly focused them on the opposite shore—a Soviet soldier. Hunched, the man moved cautiously from his trench toward a ruined *izba* in no-man's land. There Ivan stopped, apparently secure in the feeling that he was still sheltered by the darkness. Then, he carefully selected a large timber from the rubble and loading it on his shoulder, turned to retrace his steps.

Corella, no longer the dreamer, slowly swung the burnished blue barrel toward the distant figure. He had him square in the cross hairs now. The Spaniard's hand rested on the firing lever. Corella no longer saw a Soviet soldier. He saw only a man who had gone out to get firewood. Corella had a sure kill at that distance. A slight pressure of the hand and it would all be over—another corpse stretched in the snow. "But, would it change the course of the war? What would the death of one man, a man engaged in a harmless task, accomplish? What difference would one man make in an army of millions? . . . In any case the Soviet soldier was a man. A man who would be killed casually and uselessly on Christmas morn."[20] The Christian in Corella triumphed over the anti-Communist. If he mowed the Russian down—a legitimate act of war—he would violate the spirit of the holy season and he would never be able to compose his poem. Still he had to do something.

A burst of machine gun fire shattered the silence. Puffs of snow erupted in front of the Russian. Terrified, the Ivan threw himself flat. Corella smiled, tracked to the rear of the prostrate figure and squeezed off a dozen rounds. A burst to the left, another to the right, bracketing the Russian. The Ivan divined the *guripa*'s intentions. He rose, picked up the log and turning his back slowly, walked toward the safety of his own position. Corella tracked his every step. Squinting through the sights, the *guripa* watched the Russian rifleman toss the timber into the trench and then climb down. Corella saluted his disappearance with a burst of fire—a farewell salute and an ominous warning. The truce was over.

Rifle Division 305 had been heavily reinforced. From far to the east, the Russians had rounded up teenagers on the pretext of evacuating them to the safety of Siberia. The brighter youths had become suspicious when they were outfitted in warm winter uniforms and loaded on trains heading westward. Concluding that they had been conscripted, they wondered to which training camp they would be sent. They were unceremoniously dumped out at Kresttsy, where the confused youngsters, along with several trainloads of middle-aged men, ex-convicts, and Tartars were herded on to trucks. The motor column passed through Plaschkino on the Msta, headquarters of 305 Rifle Division, and paused briefly at an abandoned factory near the river. There, a rifle and 120 rounds per man were issued.

A ripple of nervousness ran through the ranks. The convoy continued on to Posad where they off-loaded and formed up. The boys looked around. This was no training camp. The wreckage of war lay around them. The thud of artillery drifted from the west. Even the dullest realized that they were at the front. Their ragged ranks faced a commissar in the center of the clearing.

The Hitlerite bands have been defeated before Moscow. Now we must rescue the Heroic City of Lenin from the Fascist hordes. Novgorod is heavily defended. We will envelope it from the north and the south. You will cross the Volkhov and cut the highway and railroad north of the metropolis. Then you will turn southward and liberate this ancient city of Mother Russia from which Alexander Nevsky marched forth to destroy the Germanic invaders centuries ago. The city is defended by reactionary filth. Spanish mercenaries of Hitler's Fascist lackey, Franco. Drive these pillagers of the Soviet people from the Motherland! [21]

The conscripts saw the last of the commissar at Posad. Clouds of gung-ho *politruks*—commissar candidates—drove them down the Posad-Shevelevo road. Near the river the untrained replacements were parceled out to the 1002 at Nikltkino and the 1004 at Shevelevo.[22] Then they went across to be slaughtered.

Across the river at Koptsy, Esparza blinked himself awake. Christmas morn. The colonel lamented the absence of a Castilian creche, with its carefully constructed scene of Christ in the manger. Like most of the volunteers, he had adopted Germanic Christmas tradition and his CP was decorated with a fir tree festooned with candles, paper, and a new Spanish emendation, inflated condoms. Even the supply trucks and divisional staff cars had mounted small pines on the running boards in honor of the occasion.[23]

At 0600 the Russians arrived bearing gifts. Two rifle companies hit 7 and 8 companies of Second of 269 at Udarnik. "Damn atheists," thought Esparza, "they are profaning the Holy Season."[24] Far to the south on Lake Il'men at Erunovo, transport troops supported by a company of 18 Motorized beat off another Soviet assault. The tankers, with their eyes on future armored attacks, also tested the ice on the lake. A ten-ton Panzer II sallied forth across the surface.[25] The next morning, Friday, von Chappuis began to implement Corps Order 76. The entire northern subsector of 250 Division northward to Plotishno would be transferred to 126 Division. As Laux's men moved southward, they in turn would be replaced by 215 Division. This shortening of the Spanish line, von Chappuis hoped, would enable Muñoz Grandes to build a divisional reserve of more than a regiment. Thus, the Spaniards could hold Novgorod until relieved by 81 Division out of France.[26]

In order to facilitate the pending transfer and to ease the strain on Esparza, Muñoz Grandes dispatched Zanón. The chief of staff assumed temporary command of the sector of Third of 263 from Gorka north to Bystritsa, leaving Esparza to connect with 126 Division. Esparza, ravaged by diabetes, was still capable of bursts of energy, but he was rapidly waning. He drew himself up for a tour of his shrinking subsector. Once commander of more than half the division, the still-proud colonel had been reduced to a line encompassing three villages. His friend, Muñoz Grandes, was keeping him at the front and in a critical area, while tenderly lightening his responsibilities. Even Zanón was now technically his subordinate. Thus did the Spanish Army reward dash and daring.

Setting out by sled with two aides, Esparza took the road to Bystritsa. There, he visited the general headquarters company composed of Muñoz Grandes's musicians and typists. They were commanded by the general's office manager, an infantry captain so mutilated in the Civil War that the army had only dispatched him to Russia on the condition that he sit at a desk and command clerks in the security of divisional headquarters. But Posad had changed all that, and every officer was needed. "*Sin novedad mi coronel,*" reported Captain Purmuy, as he saluted with the stump of his hand. His one eye blinked in the cold. The diabetic colonel smiled and returned the salute.

Esparza and his escort headed north for Lobkovo, some two kilometers distant. There was no road, so they made their way along a creek, then began to climb a hill. Esparza's hyperactive eyes now searched the terrain. In the distance, he could make out an old chapel, where Lieutenant Escobedo had his platoon. At Lobkovo, Captains González and Temprano snapped to attention as the colonel appeared out of the snow. They reported that what was left of their three companies—6, 7, and 8—were in excellent shape—considering what they had gone through. Esparza raised his binoculars and swept the horizon. To the north, he noticed two bare hills, which seemed to command a series of gullies running parallel to the river. He caught the implications at once and ordered the immediate establishment of intermediate positions on the crests. Feeling a sense of satisfaction that he had not lost his touch, the colonel went on another two kilometers to Udarnik. Here, the 60 men of 5 Company and 2 Antitanks were stationed. Román was in command, a sign of little to worry about. Comforted, Esparza took a staff car back to his CP.

He dropped off to a sound sleep, but was awakened at 0230 Friday morning. Lobkovo on the phone. Temprano reported heavy firing from the north in the direction of the new intermediate position. He did not know what was going on since there had not been time to lay wire. Second Lieutenant Rubio Moscoso and his platoon had barely managed to dig a few foxholes since the colonel sent them up the day before. The colonel immediately initiated a round-robin telephone survey of the sector CPs. All the lines were intact. At Udarnik, Román had not heard anything. The wind in the woods must have masked the firing.[27]

Temprano called again. A sergeant, his white camouflage splattered with blood, had stumbled in. The intermediate position was under heavy attack. Moscoso's first thought was to warn Temprano. Lacking communications, he had sent the sergeant and two soldiers. Upon reaching the Lobkovo-Udarnik road, 300 meters to the rear, the party encountered a long column of Reds moving northward in close order towards Udarnik. The mission was now more important than ever. A break in the column gave them a chance. The three *guripas* boldly walked out of the woods and through the Russian formation. In the momentary confusion, the sergeant, though wounded, got through. His comrades perished.

Temprano reported that no Russians were in sight. "Ah," pondered the colonel, "the Ruskis are up to their favorite trick again. They must be sneaking up on Román's CP. They are probably attempting to break through at the juncture of the 250 and 126, just as they tried two days ago between the 126 and 215."[28]

The colonel contacted Román immediately.

"Do you hear anything yet?"

"No, *mi coronel*. I'll go outside and listen." There was a pause. "Nothing at all, *mi coronel*."

Román then tried to call the post nearest the intermediate position. No one answered.

"I don't like the sound of this, *mi coronel*."

"Send out the patrols."

Non-coms dashed out of the CP and began throwing open the

doors of the *izbas.* "Vamenos, Hay jaleo!" (Let's go! There's a fight on!)[29]

The sleepy *guripas* stirred. "Why us?" Why always the 269?" one moaned. Yesterday, *Radio Macuto* had rumored their relief by the Germans. Instead, the Russians were coming. Outside the sharp wind cut like a knife. Flashlights flickered on the brick walls of the former chapel as the men, hooded and bundled in the −36 degree Celsius darkness, fell in.

A squad would reconnoiter northward towards Laux's Germans at Plotishno while Lieutenant Ochoa's section would move southward towards Lobkovo. The lieutenant, known as the Alcalde—he had resigned as mayor of Ceuta to join the Blue Division—led his thirty-two men through the gap in the barbed wire. They marched down the lane in the mine field, out of the perimeter, and on to the Udarnik-Lobkovo road. It was 0330; almost six hours of darkness remained.

The trees seemed to close in as the section, hunched in the icy gale, stumbled southward. Gusts churned up the powdery snow, limiting visibility to a few meters. Orders had to be shouted. The rustling of trees and the whistle of the wind blotted out all other sounds. The *guripas* could see little and hear nothing. Neither could the Russians. The two columns met head on. The surprise was mutual. Both threw themselves in the ditches and opened fire.

"Deploy!" shouted Ochoa. The section split and bounded through the snow into the woods on each side of the road. The Russian column, which seemed to stretch kilometers southward, followed. "Fall back," yelled Ochoa as he fired his Very pistol. The red flare rose through the tunnel formed by the trees. Unslinging his machine pistol, the lieutenant knelt behind a trunk and opened fire. Crimson tracers tore at the Soviet shadows, whose *naranjeros* sprayed the retreating Spaniards. Five *guripas* were down. Ochoa was hit. Dragging their wounded, the shattered section leapfrogged back toward Udarnik. Brushing aside Siberian scouts, the *guripas* reached the first houses. Swarms of Russians closed in. Only an hour had passed. Román rang up Esparza and reported. "The situation is grave, *mi coronel.* Lieutenant Ochoa has a serious chest wound and we have lost 15 men out of 32. The enemy appears to be very numerous."[30]

Esparza told Román he had alerted Lieutenant Petenghi, with his assault section, and Vallespín at Miasnoi Bor. They would be trucked southward to Udarnik. Unfortunately, it would be several hours before they arrived. The colonel also advised the major that García Rebull was on the way northward from Vitka to Lobkovo. Once the reinforcements were in hand, they would attack down from Udarnik and up from Lobkovo, enveloping the Russians near the intermediate position.

Román hung up the receiver. He ordered Lieutenant Cuervo of 2 Antitanks to place one of two 37 mms in the door of the chapel. This would give the gunners a wide field of fire including part of the woods, and would also protect the wounded who lay groaning inside on the floor. Juan Eugenio Blanco helped roll *Yola* into the doorway. Román then asked for volunteers. Someone had to slip down and see what was going on at the intermediate position. The drowsy sentry from Otenskii, Mariano Ferrer, stepped forward. With Ferrer on his way, Román pulled in his outposts. The Russians followed, occupying the southernmost *izbas*. Still they did not attack. They contented themselves with hosing the houses with machine gun fire and plopping mortar shells into the village. The Reds had not brought over any artillery. "Artillery," thought Esparza. With the Reds stacked up along the Lobkovo-Udarnik road, they could be cut down by a carpet barrage. Rodríguez's First Group was too far south to fire effectively, but there was a German battery at Miasnoi Bor.

The colonel got the battery commander on the line, explained the situation, and gave him the map coordinates. The German refused. Esparza calculated that three Soviet Battalions from Regiments 1002 and 1004—a total of 1,500 men—had crossed over. Banging down the receiver, Esparza turned. The roar of shell fire reverberated over the gale. The Reds were pounding the road between Koptsy and Miasnoi Bor and it was being showered with shrapnel. The enemy was trying to prevent the arrival of reinforcements. Simultaneously, 305 Rifle Division hit 126 Division at Plotishno. Temprano called. Russian riflemen were pressing on his positions. Udarnik was under attack. The Soviets, having lost the advantage of surprise, had been left with two options—withdraw or press on and expand their wedge. The *politruks* chose to press on—teenagers, old men, and even Tartars were expendable.[31]

Major Román glanced at his watch—0600. Raising his eyes, he peered out the open window. An *izba* was burning, filling the air with acrid smoke. The Russians were still getting into position. Soon they would strike. *Yola* barked again and again from the chapel doorway. Firing furiously, Blanco's crew tried desperately to keep more Soviet riflemen from surging out of the forest and reinforcing their comrades already in the village. They had started the action with *Yola* pointing due south. Now she was trained almost due north. "We are completely cut off," thought Blanco. He glanced at his diminutive old friend, Vicente Gaceo del Pino, who was feverishly working his rifle a few steps away. "Theoretically, there is no hope. The waves, ever reinforced, come on in compact masses. The only thing left is for us to die in the best possible style."[32]

Zero six thirty. Román rang up Esparza.

"We are surrounded by a battalion, *mi coronel*. My 30 remaining men are holed up in the chapel and a few nearby *izbas*. I intend to counterattack."

"I think you should wait, Major Román, until Vallespín and Petenghi arrive. Then we can catch them on two fronts," counseled the colonel.

"I am attacking, *mi coronel*."[33] Shoving Yola forward, Blanco's gun crew and the remaining infantrymen charged out of the chapel. *Yola* barked again as they grenaded forward. Firing, the walking wounded stumbled along. Crouching behind the gun shield, Blanco put a shell into the window of an *izba* 200 meters away in the clearing in front of the chapel. The dozen infantrymen took it at a rush. Two *guripas* dashed out of the doorway yelling *"Arriba España!"* They had been captured by the Russians. Grabbing rifles, they joined the assault. Behind, Vicente Gaceo, the friend of José Antonio, lay mortally wounded. By 0730, Udarnik was once again in Spanish hands.

Petenghi came up within half an hour, Vallespín by 0900. Day broke, clear and cold. The 126 Division had meanwhile repulsed the Soviet attack on Plotishno and, realizing that the main Red assault had come in the Spanish sector, immediately dispatched four companies to Udarnik to assist 250 Division. But the Reds had fled by the time they arrived.

Román led the column southward past windrows of fallen Russians. García Rebull was simultaneously advancing northward from Lobkovo. A patrol broke trail through the deep snow for Román's relief column. Helmets, bodies, weapons, equipment lay scattered along the roadway and woods. The frozen body of a Spanish corporal sprawled at the encounter point of the night before. Ahead rose the hill of the intermediate position. Soviet riflemen blocked the way. Between the lines lay Mariano Ferrer. Still alive, he tried to crawl toward the Spanish scouts. Already twice wounded, he was hit again. When he was rescued, the medics saw that all of the fingers on both hands were frozen and had to be amputated. Picking their way up the slope to

Moscoso's position, the *guripas* passed scores of Russian dead. The patrol topped the crest. Silence. Then cries of rage and anguish. The *politruks* had done their work. The Spanish dead lay nailed to the ground with Soviet ice picks. The wounded had been finished off. An ice pick gleamed in the center of a fallen *guripa*'s forehead.[34]

A primeval growl of rage ran through the Spanish ranks. While Román and García Rebull's men screamed forward at the fleeing Soviets, Petenghi's Assault Section, supressing their fury, stalked the Russians in the dark forest. Caught on the open ice of the Volkhov, the riflemen of 1002 and 1004 were gleefully mowed down while Rodríguez, firing in enfilade at extreme range, tore their ranks to shreds. By noon the situation was restored. No prisoners were taken.

The *politruks* rallied their men for one more try. At 1400 the remnants of three battalions—some two companies—stormed over the ice from Russa and smashed at the Old Chapel. Lieutenant Escobedo fell wounded at the first volley. Overrunning the platoon, the Reds began their grisly work again. But before they could finish, García Rebull came panting in from Lobkovo with two companies of First of 269. Within ten minutes the Reds had been tumbled off the hill and driven out on to the ice. Not one survived.[35] The action lasted less than twelve hours. Russian losses: 1,080 dead by body count. No prisoners. Spanish casualties: officers, 3 dead, 4 wounded; other ranks, 32 dead, 61 wounded. All from 269.[36]

Word of the Red atrocities reached Enrique Errando Vilar at Borisovo. He had brought his ambulances north from Grigorovo to pick up Román's wounded and was standing about watching the Germans pry a pair of Soviet soldiers out of a nearby basement when the report came. Vilar noted the change in his men's faces when the news hit them. A certain lifting of the head, a tightening of the jaws and clenching of the mittened fists indicated an unspoken resolve.

Muñoz Grandes did not realize how prophetic he had been when he commanded his volunteers to hold as if they were nailed to the ground. He, too, felt the rage and fury that now gripped his men. To channel their released emotions, to calm them, and to show them that he shared their grief, he issued a proclamation:

> Soldiers! The action initiated on the 24th culminated yesterday the 27th with [the enemy's] maximum effort. With forces enormously superior to ours he tried to break our lines.
>
> I am fully satisfied with you and I wish to offer tribute and gratitude to those valiant ones of the Intermediate Position who complied

with the order: "It is impossible to retreat; you have to stand as if you were nailed to the ground." No one retreated. The barbaric Russians, during the brief time that they occupied the position, used it to nail our dead and wounded to the ground with picks. The order was carried out to the letter. . . .

For once, Red bestiality has served to make even more sublime the gallantry of our soldiers.

What pride to be Spaniards!

Muñoz Grandes[37]

The British had already given the Spaniards up. Triumphantly, the BBC broadcast that Novgorod had fallen to the Red Army. There was consternation in Spain, but the Wehrmacht speedily issued a denial and Muñoz Grandes penned a New Year's greeting to the Spanish people proclaiming "hard is the enemy and harder the Russian winter—even harder are my men."[38]

8

Vlasov and the
Volkhov Pocket

"RAGAMUFFINS," HITLER SAID TO SS GENERAL SEPP

Dietrich, Commander of the famous *Leibstandarte Adolf Hitler*. It was evening on 4 January 1942. The cold wind blew outside as the Führer slouched in his chair.

The Spaniards are a crew of ragamuffins. They regard a rifle as an instrument that should not be cleaned under any pretext. Their sentries exist only in principle. They don't take up their posts, or, if they do take them up, they do so in their sleep. When the Russians arrive, the natives have to wake them up. But the Spaniards have never yielded an inch of ground. One can't imagine more fearless fellows. They scarcely take cover. They flout death. I know, in any case, that our men are always glad to have Spaniards as neighbors in their sector.

. . . nothing has changed in a hundred years. Extraordinarily brave, tough against privations, but wildly undisciplined. What is lamentable with them is the difference in treatment between officers and men. The Spanish officers live in clover, and the men are reduced to the most meagre pittance.[1]

The Führer's judgment accurately reflected the reports he had received. The Spanish élan, in the establishment of the bridgehead and

154

in their dogged defense of Posad and Otenskii, had proven their valor. After the withdrawal across the Volkhov, the question had been— would the Spaniards hold? The events of 27 December answered that. By 4 January, the idea of replacing the 250 Division had been quietly dropped. Instead, von Leeb decided merely to shorten the divisional front. The Spaniards turned over their northern sector, down to Kotovitsy, to 126 Division. Mobile Reserve 250, Third of 263, and 269 were pulled out and placed in reserve.

On 6 January, a reluctant von Chappuis carried out the Führer's order and pinned the Iron Cross, First Class, on the tunic of Muñoz Grandes. The Spanish commander, recognizing that his decoration was intended as a symbol for the entire division, had no illusions about the true feelings of the corps chief. As he stood there, on the steps of his CP at Grigorovo, he winced and visibly recoiled when von Chappuis reached toward him. For Colonel José Martínez Esparza, the war was over. His physical condition was so weakened that his life was endangered. Esparza, along with Lieutenants Ochoa and Escobedo, began the long journey back to the motherland via Riga and Berlin.[2]

For the past weeks Muñoz Grandes had been engaged, contrary to the Führer's orders, in constructing a divisional second line of defense. Rodrigo laid out a series of interlocking strongpoints behind Novgorod. Muñoz Grandes was worried. Although the atrocities of 27 December had hardened the resolve of his men, he knew that they were cold and hungry. Ten minutes of sentry duty was all some could stand. Rations were meager. Some of the troops were being sent to field hospitals with preliminary diagnoses of anemia or tuberculosis. Closer examination revealed malnutrition and vitamin deficiency. Many survived on toasted bread, butter, marmalade, and wine. Others were living on vodka and cigarettes. The average *guripa* was ingesting the equivalent of 2,500 calories per day, while divisional medical officers maintained that a minimum of 4,000 was necessary. Eyes were turning to Spain for supplements—rice, cod, sardines, dried fruits, nuts, and olive oil. Casualties amounted to some 15 percent of the entire division and almost 30 percent of the combat effectives. Although a few officers had dribbled in to replace those sent home for specialized schooling, no large contingents were coming up. The division was consuming itself. Nevertheless, with dwindling forces, Muñoz Grandes had to man the line.[3]

On 7 January 1942, all hell broke loose in 16 Army's southern sector. Overnight, incredibly powerful Russian thrusts breeched the line of the Lovat River, and surged forward fifty kilometers to the outskirts of Staraia Russa, the main supply dump of X and II Corps. Four fully winter mobile Soviet armies converged on six stretched out and static German divisions. Red armor and motor driven sleds sliced the railroad between Staraia Russa and Shimsk. Busch no longer had a southern front! The stricken commander of 16 Army dispatched 18 Motorized to Staraia Russa, which was soon encircled. He also sent 81 Division to the southern shore of Lake Il'men.[4]

In this winter war without a front line, German units were cut off and surrounded. One was a small unit of 290 Division, defending Vsvad at the mouth of the Lovat. Captain Pröhl commanded the small garrison at Vsvad. His handful of North Germans from Divisional Antitank Battalion 290 were soon joined by the remnants of overrun outposts. By Thursday morning, 8 January, Pröhl had some 543 men in the isolated stronghold. Struggling to keep alive, X Corps could spare no units for relief. The call went out to 16 Army. Busch was throwing everything into the battle for Staraia Russa—police units, Letts, local Russian home guards. He cast about and, remembering the Spanish reconnaissance across the ice of Lake Il'men, ordered Chappuis to dispatch a Spanish unit for the relief of Vsvad.

At the headquarters of 250 Division in Grigorovo, a knot of figures hunched over a large wooden table spread with maps. Their eyes followed the general's hand as he drew a thin red line across the large blue splotch that indicated Lake Il'men. "Here is Vsvad, . . . not more than 30 kilometers from our bank. There is the German strongpoint that we must liberate. The command is clear. The Germans have been beaten south of the Lake. Only Vsvad holds out. The Army Corps has no more reserves. Only us."

Zanón broke in. "Excuse me, sir. But we ourselves have no usable battalions at hand. Two-six-nine is practically nonexistent; 262 is holding Novgorod, and what is left of 263 is spread out over the entire front. We have no reserves either."[5]

"The ski patrol," a timorous voice suggested. "Ah, yes," the general replied. "I was down there yesterday, visiting their CP at Samokrazha. Captain Ordás, who has recently taken command, has a mixed force of some 200 men."[6]

A howling wind encircled the ramshackle *izba* that served as radio hut for the ski company. It blew across the open expanse of Lake Il'men and swept the snow into swirls that pelted Radioman Varela as he stomped his feet in the doorway. "The division is on the phone," shouted a young man, and Varela leapt at the receiver. After a few

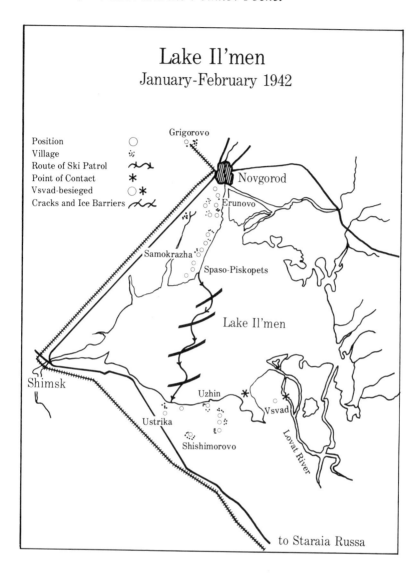

Lake Il'men
January-February 1942

Position ○
Village ⁙
Route of Ski Patrol
Point of Contact ✻
Vsvad-besieged ○✻
Cracks and Ice Barriers

Grigorovo

Novgorod

Erunovo

Samokrazha

Spaso-Piskopets

Lake Il'men

Shimsk

Uzhin

Ustrika

Vsvad

Shishimorovo

Lovat River

to Staraia Russa

words, he raced out again into the wind, returning with a slim and spare, almost little, man who bounded into the room and seized the telephone. Everyone fell into a hush until Captain Ordás had finished.

Ordering his officers to meet with him at once. Ordás began to spread out the large maps. When the five lieutenants—Ortero, Castañer, Porta, García, and Santiago—entered, he was busy plotting the route to Vsvad. The general had placed his confidence in the ski company, he told them. They must prepare to march out the next morning, diagonally across the lake, at as fast a pace as weather would permit. Although he calculated it would take eight hours to reach Vsvad, three days provisions would be carried. Nine automatic rifles would give extra fire power. The young officers understood. "Una gesta heroica."[7]

The thermometer hung steady at −32 degrees Celsius on Saturday, 10 January as 205 men of the company mustered in their winter whites before the captain. The wind, interminable and unyielding, thrust snow into their faces. It was 1000 hours, and there was no warmth from the sun.

Muñoz Grandes had dispatched his adjutant, Corvette-Captain Mora Figueroa to wish them Godspeed from their jumping-off point at Spaso-Piskopets. "You are going to liberate a battalion of German comrades," he said to them. "You will cross the lake. The march will be short, but hard. You will face Soviet forces in superior numbers. If any one of you are ill, say so now."[8]

Forward, Ordás bellowed, with all the force his small chest could supply, and he trudged ahead, taking point. Beside him strode a middle-aged heavy-set figure whose shadow almost swallowed the diminutive captain. Ordás threw a confident glance at his companion, Sergeant Willi Klein, German interpreter attached by the Liaison Staff to the ski company. They had not had time to become friends, but Klein had lived in Spain as a merchant in Bilbao before the Civil War. He had been a prisoner of the Reds until liberated by the Nationalists. Klein had much respect for Ordás, whose bearing earned him the sobriquet "the Prussian." It was not only the crisp efficiency that impressed Klein, for the little officer with the bright, active eyes was a hero. An old *africanista*, he had led his Moroccans in the Civil War, and had been awarded the *Medalla Militar*.[9]

The company swung heavily into the route of the march. Supply sleds bore the provisions and equipment. The Spaniards had wanted to commandeer the sleds and horses, but the Russian peasants had feared of ever getting them back. They volunteered to go along as drivers. Altogether, seventy *muzhiks* accompanied the Spanish relief force. After a few hours, Ordás summoned Varela to radio their progress to headquarters. But the generator had frozen. Without a flinch, he ordered Varela to march back to get another. "You know the route," he said calmly. "Catch up as soon as you can." For once in his life, the garrulous radioman was struck dumb. He turned, and headed on. A man who loved to curse, Varela had the opportunity on his lonely trek to run through his entire repertoire. Ordás sent back the first frostbite cases, on sleds, as well.[10]

The cold was unbelievable, as a bitter east wind blew in their faces. The sun rose high, but still brought no warmth. It soon fell behind, as Ordás's column followed the compass bearing weaving between or around deep crevasses and huge ice barriers, thrown up by the heaving of the lake surface. Varela and his team, struggling to catch up, took deep burning breaths.

A speck ahead. It was not moving. They came nearer and saw a figure lying face down in the snow. The frozen body was already covered with a thin sheet of crystal-clear ice. They turned him over. "It is Felipe," one said. "Now María and her child back in Bilbao are alone. . . . Pity. . . . At Posad he got the Iron Cross and now he freezes here alone, far from the motherland. The whole war is a load of *mierde*."[11] They pushed on. It was −53 degrees Celsius. The coldest winter in a hundred years.

Varela reported to Ordás in proper fashion, as "the Prussian" preferred. "I could embrace you Varela, but I dare not, or we would freeze to one another. . . . Great that you're here. Get me the division."[12]

10 January, 2130 hours. Muñoz Grandes to Ordás: "The garrison of Vsvad is holding out valiantly. . . . It is absolutely necessary to rescue them. The honor of Spain and the spirit of the fraternity of our people [with the Germans] demands it."

11 January, 0200 hours. Muñoz Grandes to Ordás: "You are the pride of our race. Trust in God and attack like Spaniards."[13]

They went on. After what seemed an endless march, in which a projected eight-hour trek had lasted twenty-two hours, the ski company reached the southern shore of the lake near Ustrika. Two sentries of 81 Division watched nervously as a column of soldiers neared their post. One of the men, from Hamburg, strained to see. He turned to his comrade, freezing in a fur coat sent by some honorable *Hausfrau* to the boys at the front, and muttered. The Reds are here! A sergeant and some men deployed. As the shadows approached through the morning light, the sergeant shouted out:

"Stoj!"

A voice queried in response, "Aleman?" Again, "Aleman?"

"Good grief, sergeant," one of his men cried, "don't shoot. They're Spaniards." Then a voice in German from the lake.

"Don't shoot! We're comrades. Spanish Blue Division. I'm Sergeant Klein, interpreter." And Klein rushed forward so that there would be no mistake.[14]

The Spaniards were taken to what seemed like a palace—a little wooden *izba* with a stove. And hot tea! Ordás, Otero, the other officers, and Sergeant Klein were told that Vsvad still held out and that they would come under the temporary command of 81 Division, which was bunched along the Il'men shore. Gen. Erich Schopper's Silesians were almost cut off and were trying to counterattack in a desperate fight to stay alive and restore the front. The Ski Company was a welcome reinforcement, weak as it was. Ordás had to evacuate 102 of his men at once due to frostbite. Eighteen were double amputees. The captain was told that they would fight alongside Lithuanians as well as Germans.[15]

Safe on the southern shore of the lake, but not yet at Vsvad, Ordás reported back to Muñoz Grandes, whose staff kept a log of the radio dispatches:

11 January 1010 hours. Ordás to Muñoz Grandes.
After climbing over six great ice barriers and crossing crevasses in the ice with water up to the waist, we have arrived at Ustrika. . . .
. . . .

1030 hours. Muñoz Grandes to Ordás.
I know of your efforts during the arduous march. . . . The garrison at Vsvad is still holding out. You must relieve it no matter what the cost—even if all of you remain frozen on the lake. You must go on, alone, if necessary, even until death. You must reach Vsvad or die with them. In the name of the Motherland, I thank you. Don't lose heart. I trust you.

14 January 1000 hours. Ordás to Zanón.
We are pushing on to liberate Vsvad.

1300 hours.
We have taken Shishimorovo. Our garrison here . . . reinforced by Germans and Letts.

17 January 2200 hours. Ordás to Muñoz Grandes.
Enemy counterattacked with two battalions accompanied by antitank guns and six medium tanks, which rapidly overran the Spanish vanguard. The surrounded detachment defended itself heroically. . . . Of the 36 Spaniards in the vanguard, 14 died. The remainder broke out and joined the company. We are digging in . . . and will

resist the forthcoming heavy attack. At 2100 hours we received order to establish an advanced outpost at Maloe Utchno.

19 January 1330 hours. Ordás to Muñoz Grandes.
At 0700 hours today the enemy launched a mass attack on Maloe Utchno smothering the garrison of 25 Spaniards and 19 Germans. The attack was supported by tanks. The company deployed and succeeded in rescuing 5 wounded Spaniards and 2 Germans. The enormous enemy concentration prevented us from retaking the outpost. The garrison did not capitulate. They died with their weapons in their hands. We observe a great mass of the enemy in the direction of Maloe Utchno. We await the attack. We know how to die as Spaniards.

19 January 2300 hours. Muñoz Grandes to Ordás.
You speak as only heroes would. This is the only way to build an empire. Courage. Your conduct is the pride of this brave Division. In spite of everything you will conquer. There is a God and he will grant you victory because you are the most valiant sons of Spain. An embrace which will not be the last.

20 January 1430 hours. Ordás to Muñoz Grandes.
Last night we were bombarded three times by Russian aircraft. At dusk, great enemy masses moved against our position. Various volunteers have gone out to ignite the enemy tanks [with Molotov cocktails]. The forward movement of the attack has been checked and the enemy is retiring. God exists.

1600 hours.
Commanding General of 81 Division congratulates us and awards medals.

21 January 0945 hours. Ordás to Muñoz Grandes.
This morning a detachment departed Maloe Utchno for Vsvad. The Vsvad garrison, which broke out last night, embraced our men [on the frozen lake] 7 kilometers east of Uzhin. Your orders have been completely carried out.

1100 hours. Ordás to Muñoz Grandes.
Our force has returned [from the lake]. The majority are frostbitten.
· ·

25 January 0140 hours. Muñoz Grandes to Ordás.
Tell me how many valiants remain.

1845 hours. Ordás to Muñoz Grandes.
We have 12 left.[16]

The saga of the ski company and its effort to relieve Vsvad is among the most heroic episodes on either side in World War II. Alone, a Spanish island in a sea of strangers, these brave Iberians fought and died, and won an immortal place in history. In contrast to the derogatory and critical comments about the Spaniards in the War Journal of XXXVIII Corps, which extended even to failure to praise the Ski Company, the War Journal of the Liaison Staff fairly sparkled with pride. Ordás's men fought "superbly" and "the little remnant battled bravely on."[17] General Schopper addressed a personal message of commendation to his comrade in Grigorovo and awarded thirty-two Iron Crosses. The Caudillo sent a special message decorating Ordás with his second *Medalla Militar Individual*. Franco also honored the Ski Company with a unit citation—*Medalla Militar Colectiva*. A furiously proud Muñoz Grandes sent a special packet of documentation to report the unit's achievement to Adolf Hitler, who read it in the warm comfort of Rastenburg while his soldiers froze for lack of winter uniforms and died holding off the Russians.

The Soviet strike south of Lake Il'men was part of a major counteroffensive launched on several sectors of the long front. Stalin had found the invaders weaker than he expected as he drove them back from Moscow in December and determined to open a series of ambitious assaults in the new year. The Red Army made gains in the area of Army Group South, and penetrated deeply into the lines of Army Group Center. Powerful units struck at the juncture with Army Group North, threatening to envelop 9 Army and seize Smolensk, Vitebsk, and Rzhev. Only the arrival of a few reinforcements and the charismatic command of Gen. Walter Model, who replaced Strauss, averted disaster. The thrust south of Lake Il'men was the northern hinge of that drive on 9 Army and it, too, had foundered. But Stalin had planned another, concurrent, assault. Strong forces were to cross the Volkhov, slicing straight through to Jamburg (Kingisepp), west of Leningrad. The siege was to be broken; 18 Army cut off and annihilated.

The Soviet dictator had set the stage on 10 December, as Typhoon crumbled at the gates of Moscow. On that day, Meretskov had been summoned to the map room in the Kremlin. Stalin stood aside while his chief of staff, Marshal Boris Shaposhnikov, laid out the plans. Meretskov, appointed commander of a newly created Volkhov Front, returned to his headquarters. Operational orders arrived from *Stavka* on 17 December. His front consisted of 4, 52, 2 Shock, and 59 Armies. The main blow was to be south to Chudovo with 2 Shock Army (formed out of 26 Army) while 52 Army was to take Novgorod and 59 Army would assist 2 Shock Army from the north. The Leningrad garrison would break out and meet them.[18]

The Germans had seen it coming. Von Leeb knew that his HKL was thinly held and reconnaissance had reported enemy build-ups. Busch, also, had been concerned as the Soviets probed the Volkhov line, identifying and placing German units. In fact, Stalin had concentrated 2 Shock Army opposite the junction of 126 and 215 Divisions near Arefino.[19] A shock, or striking, army was a special force designed for penetration. Its soldiers were given extra pay and rations, fortified with vodka, and shepherded by a high concentration of trained officers and political activists of the Communist party. Fanatical exhortations and vodka combined to produce an offensive spirit that did not stop short of barbarous brutality. Since huge quantities of artillery and other weapons were also made available, the expected result was disorder and even panic in the enemy ranks. Second Shock Army was a powerful force indeed, consisting of 327, 366, 383 Rifle Divisions, 25, 80, 87 Cavalry Divisions, 22, 23, 24, 25, 53, 57, 58, and 59 Brigades, ten ski battalions and Artillery Regiment 18. The brigades were actually mini-divisions, each composed of about 3,500 men and organized into three rifle battalions, one grenade thrower battalion, and a light artillery section. They were especially appropriate for mobile strikes.[20]

Field Marshal von Leeb was worried. South of Lake Il'men his front was in ruins. Second Corps was virtually surrounded at Demianck. He realized that Meretskov had been checked on the Volkhov, but expected 2 Shock Army to resume the attack at any moment. On 12 January, von Leeb telephoned Halder and asked the chief of staff for plenary authority to extricate II Corps, adding that "we cannot reckon that the Volkhov front will hold [either]."[21] All day, the lines between Pskov and Rastenburg burned with heated conversation. Finally, at 1650, Hitler himself came on the wire. Refusing von Leeb's request to retreat, the Führer queried: "Shall I come [to Pskov]?" The field marshal demurred. "Then, come here tomorrow," he ordered.[22]

If von Leeb thought that it was cold in Pskov, his reception at the *Führerhauptquartier* was frigid. Army Group North would stand where it was. No reinforcements could be expected. The flight back was clouded with gloom. Torn by duty to his commander in chief and loyalty to his men, the veteran of the Kaiser's army could not bring himself to order the senseless sacrifice of II Corps. Two days later he resigned. Hitler appointed von Küchler to succeed him. Eighteenth Army was taken over by Gen. Georg Lindemann, who moved up from L Corps.

On 13 January, the very day that von Leeb had faced Hitler at Rastenburg, Meretskov unleashed his strike force. A rolling artillery barrage hit the front of 126 Division at 0800, reaching as far west as the *Rollbahn* and gradually sweeping northward to 215 Division. At 0900, 52 (V. F. Yakovlev), 2 Shock (N. K. Klykov), and 59 Armies (I. V. Galanin), which were stacked up along the east bank between Dubrovka and Kuzino, burst across the Volkhov. Surging forward under a frosty, clear sky the southernmost wave swamped Third of 424 at Gorka, Lobkovo, and Udarnik—the same sector where the Spaniards had repelled the Russian assault of 27 December. Meretskov's main effort, in the center, broke through between Iamno and Arefino near the juncture of 126 and 215 Divisions. Meanwhile, the northern torrent battered Dimno.[23]

All was calm in the Spanish sector. Artillery exchanges were normal. *La Parrala* patrolled as usual and Red propaganda loudspeakers blared away. The only sign of the immense effort to the north was a sudden upsurge in Red Air Force activity, mostly dive bombers beginning their run on Gorka and Arefino.[24] Army Group North was shivering as the well-equipped Russians poured across the Volkhov.[25]

Shoveling transport troops into his battalions, Rodrigo, now in command of 269, was becoming increasingly anxious about the Russian penetration to the north. He feared that the Reds might break through to the *Rollbahn* and then turn south toward Novgorod. The depleted 126 Division was strung out between Kotovitsy and Arefino facing three Red infantry divisions and five brigades.

Col. Harry Hoppe, commanding 424 Regiment, was holding the Volkhov around Gorka and Udarnik. At 1900, Teremets fell. A call went out to the Spaniards. Rodrigo ordered out Román with the hastily assembled Second of 269. Román marched at once to join Hoppe at Podberez'e. He arrived in the middle of the night to find the town a melee of units—combat personnel rushing to the front, service troops getting out of the way. Hoppe was planning to strike the next morning to recover Teremets, only five kilometers away.

At 0600 Wednesday Second Battalion moved eastward along the road to Teremets. The attack, preceded by an artillery bombardment, was scheduled for 0730. Román, however, was late in coming up. The waist-deep snow impeded his progress. Russian artillery observers called down a barrage from the east bank. When Román finally got 5 and 6 Companies to the jump-off positions at the edge of the woods, all was quiet. The *guripas* advanced at 0755 and reached the southern row of houses. They had hardly got inside when the Russians launched a counterattack in overwhelming force. Most of the Spaniards were caught in the open by mortars and antitanks. After an hour's bloody battle, Román rescued what was left. Seven and 8 companies fired from the woods over their retreating comrades and cut down many Russians. Ruefully, Hoppe suspended the attack and observed that most of the Spanish casualties were caused by their failure to arrive in time. He determined to try again the next day. While Second Battalion holed up in the woods, the hero of Schlüsselburg beefed up his command. He brought in pioneers and motorcyclists, a platoon of 20 mm flak, and five Mark III tanks from 12 Panzers. Rodrigo reinforced Román with mortars and Petenghi's assault section. Muñoz Grandes dispatched two batteries.

The artillery hit Teremets in the early dawn. At 0715, a mixed force of Spaniards and German motorcyclists floundered forward through the deep snow. While the tankers were still trying to get their machines moving, the infantry penetrated the west rim of the village. By the time the Mark III's came rolling down the main street, there was bitter hand-to-hand fighting. Teremets was a meat grinder, with the Reds throwing in more and more men all day long. By 1500, four of the panzers were knocked out and still more Russians were coming up. Sadly, Hoppe called off the attack. Back in Podberez'e that evening, Román visited his wounded at the Spanish first-aid station. Muñoz Grandes, ever solicitous, came up the next morning. Even he was shocked to see that only fifty were left of the two hundred who had marched out to recover Teremets.[26]

Fifteenth January was a black day for Army Group North. The failure to retake Teremets proved that the Russians had solidly established their bridgehead. A six kilometer gap had opened between 126 and 215 Divisions. Fortunately, 215 Division held on to the northern shoulder at Dimno, but 126 Division gave way into islands of defense. At Senitsy, little Capt. Ernst Klossek swung his machine guns northwards and stemmed the Red tide, earning the Knight's Cross. A southern shoulder only held fast near Podberez'e. Second Shock and 52 Army flowed westward through this narrow corridor, taking Koptsy on 19 January and Miasnoi Bor on the twenty-third, cutting both the *Rollbahn* and the railroad, the artery of 16 Army.[27] While 16 Army reeled, Radio London continued to report the imminent fall of Novgorod. By the week of Muñoz Grandes's birthday, 24 January, enough patchwork units—Legion Flanders, Netherlands SS Legion, Escort Battalion Reichsführer SS, Group Jaschke—had been thrown in to channelize the Russian torrent.

Somewhat as a birthday present for Muñoz Grandes, divisional intelligence chief Ruíz de la Serna, who had just returned from Spain, reported that the Spanish sector need not fear a frontal assault. Russian commissars had been telling their men that 250 Division had so punished 305 Rifle Division in three months of combat that they preferred to seek a weaker opponent.[28] Not mentioned by the Spanish intelligence chief was a fact well known to both the Russians and Germans. The Ivans were singularly reluctant to engage the *guripas* in hand-to-hand combat. This was not merely due to Spanish excellence in this style of fighting, but also to their Moroccan habits. The legionnaires showed a disconcerting proclivity of mutilating prisoners captured in such actions and sending them back to the Russian lines minus various appendages—ears, noses, and fingers. Not mentioning the terror tactics of the *africanistas*, Military Attaché Roca de Togores was bragging to Madrid that the Blue Division was "impregnable."[29]

The Caudillo was not so certain. The map board in El Pardo revealed the full extent of the German disaster. With Busch hanging on by the skin of his teeth south of Lake Il'men, and the Reds driving a huge spearhead between him and Lindemann's 18 Army north of Novgorod, the Blue Division had become a lonely salient. Soviet shock armies flowed on both sides of the Spanish breakwater threatening to engulf it. The Führer had hundreds of divisions; he had only one. Both Falange and Army would clamor for a share of victory, but Franco alone would be the father of defeat.[30] In the undisguised hostility between the twin pillars of the Spanish dictatorship, the army was increasingly jealous of any prominence given the Falange. Even the designation "Blue Division" was eschewed by the generals, who preferred "Division of Volunteers."[31]

Foreign Minister Serrano Suñer, thoroughly hated by the military, was being pressed within the official movement by the rising star of Arrese. Struggling to hold on to his position of influence, Serrano sought the assistance of the Germans, who spurned him rather than become embroiled in the camarilla. Since meeting with Hitler in November, he had been attempting to bring leading Falangists from the division home to Spain, but he had been thwarted by Muñoz Grandes. When queried by the Germans, Muñoz Grandes had enough political acumen to try to evade the issue. Finally, confronted by a definite German request for an answer, he gave a categorical no. No Falangist, no matter how notable, would return on any conditions other than those pertaining to an ordinary *guripa*. He was a soldier first, and a politician second. Favoritism would destroy the morale of the division. It was precisely what he opposed in Spain. He dreamed of returning a hero, and cleansing his country of military cabals, Falangist intriguers, and even Franco.

The Caudillo had not risen to the top by placing complete trust in any man. Not Serrano, his brother-in-law, nor Muñoz Grandes, his comrade-in-arms. As early as November, Franco had begun dropping hints to Germans who would not route his views through the embassy that he would like to visit with Hitler again. In mid-December 1941, Ribbentrop's trusted aide Rudolf Likus traveled to Madrid to explore German-Spanish relations without going through Ambassador von Stohrer. Likus gained the distinct impression that Franco's aide-de-camp, Frigate Captain Fontán, was interested in conveying his chief's pro-German sympathies to Berlin. Further, that Franco wanted the Blue Division pulled out of the line for a rest to a place where he could review it in a formal ceremony as generalissimo of the Spanish Army and—without the presence of Serrano Suñer—speak privately to Hitler about closer relations with the Third Reich and a "reorganization" of his government.[32]

When Likus reported this to Ribbentrop, the foreign minister ordered that a Spanish go-between be found who might approach Franco with a view to arranging the Caudillo's visit. Since Fontán's wife was the former Blanca Suanzes Fernández, it was a short step to Adm. Juan Antonio Suanzes Fernández, a boyhood friend of the chief of state and former minister of economics and industry.[33]

Suanzes secured an audience with Franco on 3 January 1942 and broached the question of whether the dictator was still interested in traveling to Germany. Franco told Suanzes that he could not leave the country just then, because the domestic political situation would not permit it. Suanzes returned for a second audience on 7 January, during which Franco confided in his old friend that the political pot was indeed bubbling.

The day before, 6 January—The Feast of the Three Kings—Franco related, he had received an assemblage of generals. General Kindelán had acted as spokesman. The generals were unanimous in their opposition to Serrano Suñer. They wanted him out. Moreover, they believed that Spain stood too close to Germany, which impeded the importation of vitally needed foodstuffs from the Anglo-Saxon powers and Latin America. Finally, they thought that a combination of the posts of chief of state and prime minister was too much of a burden for any one man. Franco cut Kindelán short in mid-sentence, and the generals did not react, but the Caudillo was now more than aware that Serrano had to go. He could not drop his brother-in-law yet, though, without seeming to give in completely to the generals. The Caudillo was also considering replacing Muñoz Grandes. In the meantime, he had to balance warring factions in the army and ensure that the Blue Division survived the crisis at the front.

On 10 January 1942, Franco ordered Ambassador Mayalde to press the Germans to pull the division out of the line. Chief of Militia Moscardó had told von Stohrer that the Caudillo wanted a regular rotation of personnel. He suggested an exchange of 2,000 to 2,500 men every three to four months. Restored to its original strength, the Blue Division would be ready for the spring offensive.[34] A few trainloads of replacements, mostly regulars, were already being sent up. Nothing substantial could be done, however, until negotiations with the Germans were completed. The Caudillo and the General Staff wanted above all a regular system of rotation and replacement, such as the Condor Legion employed during the Civil War. Franco had his own reasons for wanting the division brought home piecemeal.

The divisional commander, meanwhile, had requested refurbishing with Spanish trucks. Muñoz Grandes's suggestion had been received with enthusiasm by the Army General Staff. Generals Asensio and Vega had assured Lt. Col. Ruíz de la Serna, when he visited Madrid in December, that the vehicles would soon be on the way. But, internal army politics and personal jealousies intervened. War Minister Varela, an Anglophile and an enemy of Muñoz Grandes, delayed the shipment.[35]

Asensio, in spite of the war minister's attitude, was determined to move ahead with refurbishing the division and was even to dispatch fifty-two trucks. Col. Guenther Krappe, German military attaché in Madrid, offered his full cooperation. However, although OKW was quite anxious to receive 3,000 Spanish replacements, the Germans did not want to pull the Blue Division out of the line. They had nothing to put in its place. Consequently, they kept insisting that the situation at the front was not serious and that the division had a reserve battalion at hand.

This proved to be a highly mobile reserve. Early in January, Krappe reported to Asensio that the reserve battalion was in Hof. By the end of the month OKW was claiming that it was with the division at the front. All the while the Spanish chief of staff knew that Mobile Reserve Battalion 250 had been virtually wiped out at the Muravevskiia Barracks in October.[36]

Since it appeared that nothing could be accomplished in Madrid, Asensio dispatched Franco's crony, General Martín Alonso, to Berlin. His instructions were to press for a pullback of the division and to negotiate details of replacement and rotation. Meanwhile, Mayalde returned to Madrid. The ambassador was told by Serrano Suñer that his personal first priority was rotating out the Falangists. Clearly, the army and foreign minister were working at cross purposes.

The arrival of Martín Alonso in Berlin at the end of January heightened the dilemma of the High Command. The High Command was also getting pressure from the other end. General von Küchler was demanding either reinforcements for 250 Division or a fresh German unit.

Meanwhile, Mayalde cornered Weizsäcker on 5 February. The ambassador pointed out that the Blue Division had suffered heavy losses, especially officers. The necessary replacements were ready to leave Spain. All that was needed was to relocate the division and prepare it for reorganization. Then it could participate in the great spring offensive. Moreover, it was necessary to release the Falangist student volunteers. During their absence the Communists had won over a majority of the students at Spanish universities, especially Barcelona. Rotation was absolutely necessary to restore the political balance at home.[37]

Franco shored up his international position by meeting with the Portuguese prime minister, Antonio Oliveira Salazar, in Seville on 12 February 1942. Although Serrano Suñer was present the Caudillo cunningly bypassed him by conversing with his guest in his native dialect, Galician. Salazar conveyed to Franco his apprehensions about a possible invasion of the peninsula. Franco, shunting his foreign minister aside, firmly took control of the conference. When Serrano Suñer returned to the Andalusia Palace Hotel he told his aides "I am now alone."[38] How right he was. In the future the Caudillo would not only monitor foreign policy but direct it.

Following Salazar's departure, Franco made another of his ambiguous speeches. The Blue Division, he proclaimed to the Seville garrison, was defending Western civilization in Russia. He declared that Europe must defend itself against the Communist peril. If, he bombastically asserted, the "road to Berlin lay open," not one division, but one million Spaniards would offer to go in defense.[39] While boldly speaking of one million fighters against Communism, Franco was instructing his diplomats to press for a withdrawal of the Blue Division from the line. As the Caudillo's ambassador, no less than the foreign minister's loyal servant, Mayalde harrassed Weizsäcker again on 13, 16, 21, and 26 February. Ribbentrop was finally forced to take up the question of pullback with the Führer. Hitler pronounced a definitive no.[40]

On 26 February, while Mayalde confronted Weizsäcker in Berlin, Serrano Suñer hammered at Stohrer in Madrid. The Spanish foreign minister emphasized that the "sons of the most pro-German families in Spain should be brought home."[41] Finally, the Germans decided that the charade had gone on long enough. Although OKW was not going to pull the division out, Keitel told Weizsäcker to ask Spain to send a responsible General Staff officer to discuss details of replacement and rotation.[42] General Asensio, who had been clamoring to visit the Blue Division for over a month, arrived in Berlin. His conversation with Keitel on 14 March 1942 was short and to the point. Relief battalions of 800 to 1,000 men would be sent up over a period of four to six months. Thus the division would not only be brought up to strength but replaced.[43]

Muñoz Grandes was unaware of the maneuvers in Madrid to rotate home most of his veterans. The divisional commander only expected 3,000 to 4,000 replacements, not the total exchange of his effectives. He pointedly told Asensio this at Königsberg on 22 March and also reiterated that while the Caudillo might have wished the Blue Division pulled back or placed in a quiet sector he had always wanted to stay and fight. These were good men, he said, and they had just won him the Knight's Cross. Pointing with pride to the glittering medal, Muñoz Grandes went on. Regarding the rotation there would be no favorites. Concluding, Muñoz Grandes thanked the chief of staff for sending the trucks from Spain. Although many had broken down en route, fourteen had made it to Grigorovo. The remainder were being repaired at Riga.[44]

Asensio returned to Berlin to work out the details with Fromm. In accordance with the Asensio-Fromm Agreement, Brigadier Emilio Esteban Infantes, chief of staff of the Barcelona Military Region, who had repeatedly requested a command in Russia, was relieved and posted to Madrid. He immediately began to assemble a cadre for a new—a second—division.[45]

While the lights burned late in the embassies at Madrid and Berlin, three Soviet armies had been pounding at the HKL on the Volkhov. By the end of January, they had blasted "a passage through the German defensive field with infantry, armour, cavalry units and ski battalions."[46] Their spearheads raced westward through the frozen swamps and forest, reaching Eglino, halfway to Leningrad, before 1 February.

Losing forward momentum as they outran supplies, the Reds expanded the developing Volkhov "pocket" northward, and abandoned the effort to reach Jamburg. Soviet troops threatened Liuban on the main Chudovo-Leningrad rail line, and Marshal Fediuninskii opened a full-scale drive on Pogost'e with 54 Army, to thrust down to Liuban from the north. Fediuniskii's punches were contained, however, and the Germans fought hard to keep the Soviets from encircling Chudovo and catching all of I Corps.[47]

The Red flood was so swift that little islands of *Landser* remained surrounded, but still fighting, near the Volkhov. The 215 Division had held most of its front, and 126 Division had survived to form a southern edge of the narrow channel which served as the supply line for 2 Shock Army. The little town of Mal. Zamosh'e was one of these islands, garrisoned by Waffen-SS and units of 426 Regiment. When it became apparent that they could hold out no longer, the call went out once more to the Spaniards. Naturally, it was to *La Segunda*, Second of 269.

Román's remnants had returned to Chichulino on 17 January. They rested and received reinforcements from Second Transport Company while their comrades along the river beat back a series of company-sized assaults at the unfinished railroad bridge, the Alcázar, and Krechevitsy.

The Russians had hit First of 263 north of Krechevitsy before dawn on 20 January. Slipping over the ice of the river, the Ivans of 125 Rifle Division (formerly 3 Armored) bypassed the Spanish outposts and infiltrated rearward. The service troops in the village awoke to find the Russians in the streets. Cooks, cobblers, horse-handlers, convalescents, and the usual collection of goof-offs found behind any front, jumped from their beds, rushed to the windows and opened fire.

In the warm company kitchen, Sergio threw off his blankets, grabbed a rifle and joined his comrades at an open spot at the window.

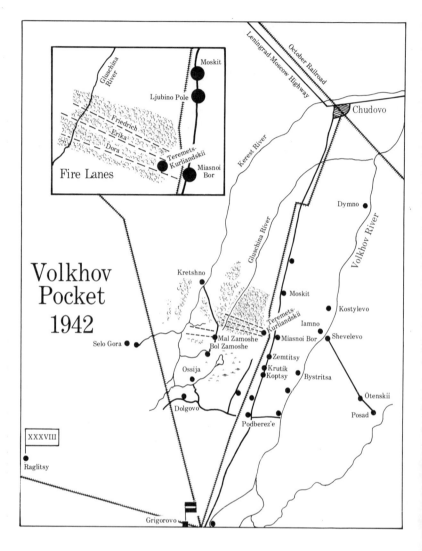

When the officers and sergeants finally established order among the wild and anarchic resistance and swept the Soviets out of the hamlet in a brisk counterattack, Sergio was in the van. Quiet restored, Sergio returned to his pots and pans. His fellows clapped him on the back and offered him cigarettes and cognac. Sergio's "muchas gracías" was heavily accented. Spanish was seldom heard on the streets of his home town, Kiev.

The young chap had been captured during the Russian assault late in December. Since Spanish soldiers traditionally disdained routine menial tasks, he was put to work. There had been some discussion about sending him to a POW camp, but by mid-January as long columns of bedraggled prisoners snaked southward from the Soviet bridgehead, this ceased. The Spaniards were well aware that sending Sergio to a stalag would be a death sentence. Even in the Novgorod camp, rations were so short that Muñoz Grandes ordered all dead horses delivered to the POWs so they would have something to eat. Sergio, however, was stuffing himself in the company kitchens. Besides, he was a good fellow and First of 263 was short of men. Moreover, 125 Rifle Division was certain to try again.

These Soviet probes were designed to hold 250 Division before Novgorod and prevent XXXVIII Corps from utilizing its only intact division as a reserve. The intelligence summary of 125 Rifle Division reported that 262 and 263 Regiments were offering stubborn resistance. Nevertheless, on 1 February, Muñoz Grandes offered to assist his close comrade Laux and dispatched another battery—the 12—to support 126 Division at Podberez'e. The offer, bypassing von Chappuis, signified Muñoz Grandes's respect for Laux and his disdain for the corps commander. Three days later, the divisional sector was extended to Vitka.[48]

The long line of trucks stretched northward along Chichulino's main thoroughfare. Motors idling under a clear, star-studded sky, they swayed as the *guripas* of Second of 269 and 9 Company of 263 clambered aboard. Their mission—to reach Mal. Zamosh'e. While the men rested, Román briefed his officers. The relief operation would be supported by the Luftwaffe which had been supplying encircled Mal. Zamosh'e for over a week. The remaining 140 defenders were too weak to break out with the wounded through the resuscitated 305 Rifle Division. Two columns, one German and one Spanish, would push northward from Bol. Zamosh'e to liberate them. *Landser* of 426 Regiment would form the right wing of the advance, *La Segunda* the left. Fortunately, the major observed, 3 Battery was at Ossia. One could better coordinate the operation with gunners who understood Spanish. Román bent over the map table. His Iron Cross, First Class, glistened in the flickering light as he traced the route.

At 0600 before dawn on 12 February, *La Segunda* was underway to join the Germans at Bol. Zamosh'e. After standing around stamping their feet in −10 degree Celsius snow flurries, the two columns pushed off at 0930. Román, circling westward across the frozen marsh, floundered forward through waist deep drifts. The progress of the some 600 white-robed Spaniards was further impeded by their heavy armament. At 1100 the pickets ran into a Soviet patrol which was soon brushed aside. By this time, however, the *Landser* of 426 Regiment were stopped at Coordinate 47. With the Luftwaffe nowhere in evidence they called down the artillery. But to no avail. It was up to Román.

The *guripas* were now struggling through a dark forest, where the snow was deeper and the drifts higher. They encountered two more enemy patrols. One fire fight cost them two killed. By 1500 the tired column was within a kilometer of Mal. Zamosh'e. But they were still trapped in the woods. It took them three hours to fight their way through the snow and heavy Russian resistance. It was pitch dark. Soviet artillery blanketed the area. Not until midnight did the exhausted Spanish infantry stumble into Mal. Zamosh'e.

The evacuation began immediately. Two companies broke trail at once, while the remainder loaded up the German survivors. A sudden blizzard hit them enroute, masking Russian patrols which snapped at their flanks. All through Friday the thirteenth the weary column dribbled into Bol. Zamosh'e. Many had been on their feet for thirty-six hours. Casualties had been incredibly light—two dead and four wounded. The next day Muñoz Grandes awarded *La Segunda* its second *Medalla Militar Colectiva*. He also proposed Román for a battlefield promotion.[49]

Second of 269 enjoyed only a brief respite. The Reds hit Liubtsy at dawn on Saturday the fourteenth and began massing for an attack on Bol. Zamosh'e. At 1500, Rifle Regiments 1000 and 1002 came on in a broad semicircle—west, north, and east—against the Bol. Zamosh'e perimeter. Luxuriously supported by artillery, antitank guns, Stalin organs, and close support cannons, the Ivans of 305 Rifle Division overran the west of the village. Since the Spaniards comprised 50 percent of the garrison, they were called upon to plug the gap. Captain Izquierdo led 6 Company and his ex-horse handlers of a section of 8 Company into the breach. Heedless of losses, the Soviets hit the perimeter again at twilight, at 2000, and at 0500 Sunday morning. They were driven back into the darkness. At first light Román dispatched a patrol to reconnoiter his sector. Russian bodies were everywhere. The defenders counted three hundred enemy dead.[50]

The vain predawn assault on Bol. Zamosh'e heralded a general Soviet attack on 126 Division. The Soviets, in an effort to expand their bridgehead southward toward Novgorod, also hit Liubtsy and Zemtitsy where railroad and *Rollbahn* converged. Laux's front was a tower of

Babel. Aside from the Spaniards and his own Rhineland-Westphalians, his command consisted of Legion Flanders at Liubtsy and the Netherlands SS Legion west of Dolgovo. These "International Brigades" formed the southern edge of the corridor which was the lifeline of 2 Shock Army. The motley force fended off a series of persistent Soviet blows throughout February.

A steady stream of wounded were trundled westward to Riga by the hospital trains, *Lili Marleen* and *Violetta*. There, two first class hospitals were provided, completely staffed by medical teams and nurses from Spain. Convalescent *guripas* enjoyed the sights and pleasures of the Latvian capital. Napoleon had termed the city a suburb of London, so full of wares and peoples from other lands it was even then. Much like the British metropolis, the fog rolled in from the wharves. The Spaniards marveled at how it shrouded the tiled roofs of the European-style buildings. This was the West, not Russia. Beautiful women wore magnificent furs or skated in short skirts on the canal or the Duna River, and were ogled by Germans, Swedes, Dutch, Belgians, French, Flemings, Finns, Norwegians, Estonians, Spaniards, and others in addition to the native Letts. A cosmopolitan town, with a flourishing opera in which elephants marched pompously through the scenes of *Aïda*. A happy town, oblivious to its burned out synagogue and the emaciated Jews sweeping the streets.

The Riga station of the Wehrmacht radio broadcast programs in Spanish bolstered by recordings from Madrid, and three-day-old Spanish newspapers were hawked on the main thoroughfares. Shopkeepers learned a few words of the Latin tongue, and the *guripas* took over the Café Luna where they sang the *canto hondo*, danced the flamenco, and avidly read *Hoja de Campaña*, which rolled off the presses in Riga every week. The establishment quickly became a little Spain, known to every soldier on leave. They learned about the wonders of Kirschwasser, a potent brandy from Königsberg. It was every *guripa*'s dream to be lightly wounded and sent to Riga. So enticing were the marvels of Riga that a few *guripas* deserted rather than return to the front. They supported themselves by organizing criminal gangs, preying upon civilians and soldiers alike, a curse to the Wehrmacht and the MPs of the Blue Division.[51]

The radio broadcasts from Riga helped to keep spirits high among the *guripas* at the front. The Russians kept battering at the shoulders of the Volkhov Pocket and stabbed heavily at Liuban on the Chudovo-Leningrad road. Von Küchler drew together his defenses. On 23 February he transferred **XXXVIII** Corps to Lindemann's 18 Army. This left Busch only the sector south of Lake Il'men where, with three corps, he could devote himself to rescuing his line. By placing the entire circumference of the Volkhov Pocket under Lindemann, Küchler made possible a closer coordination toward a future counterattack and facilitated a release of units from the relatively quiescent Leningrad sector.

On 24 February Lindemann visited von Chappuis at Raglitsy. The corps commander's GHQ, moved from Grigorovo to a safe rear area in December, was now right on top of the action. The luckless Prussian, surrounded by his staff and two of three generals in his corps—Erich Jaschke and Paul Laux—heard his new commander explain that 18 Army would be preparing a counterattack at once. The Volkhov Pocket would be cut off at its neck. According to von Küchler's plan, **XXXVIII** Corps would drive north from Bol. Zamosh'e over Mal. Zamosh'e to link up with I Corps near Kretshno. He would give von Chappuis 58 Division under Gen. Friedrich Altrichter from the Leningrad perimeter to spearhead the advance.[52]

The corps commander demurred. The reinforcements would not be enough, and it would be difficult to get through in that sector. Rather, von Chappuis proposed that the northward attack follow the railroad, highway, and riverbank. Lindemann consented to carry von Chappuis's objections to Army Group.

On Monday, 2 March 1942, von Chappuis stood silently before the Führer. The corps commander, along with his superiors von Küchler and Lindemann, had flown to Rastenburg that morning. Lindemann explained the plan for sealing off the Volkhov pocket. Hitler rejected the move from Bol. Zamosh'e to Kretshno, opting for the advance up the railroad and highway. The more open terrain, the Führer remarked, would enable the Luftwaffe and heavy artillery to provide greater support. Jump-off would be 7 March. Von Chappuis felt relieved that his project had been accepted, but he did not really want to attack at all. He feared his forces were too weak. The die was cast, however. The generals returned to the front.[53]

By 5 March only two days remained before the scheduled opening of the main offensive—Operation *Raubtier* (Beast of Prey). Altrichter's 58 Division was coming up fast. The cracking of the ice of the river heralded the arrival of *rasputitsa*. Soon the Volkhov would again be a barrier. It was now or never for 2 Shock Army. Soviet spearheads were west of Finev-Lug and approaching the Dno-Leningrad road. The Liuban attack, however, had miscarried. Three divisions and a brigade were surrounded. Fediuninskii's effort to free them from the north stalled. The battle hung in the balance.[54]

The tension was beginning to tell. The Germans were forced to put off their attack until at least 9 March. Ground fog covered the battlefield. Keller could not bring Air Fleet One to bear, and Hitler insisted that Lindemann not move without full air support. Von Chappuis could stand it no longer. On the morning of 6 March, he rang up Lindemann's mobile CP, "Lindy." As usual, Lindemann was roaming his corps. Chappuis mournfully left word that he was reluctant to attack.

The next day, Lindemann appeared at Raglitsy. "It will not succeed," von Chappuis repeated. "We cannot pinch off the pocket without further reinforcements." "Why did you not tell that to the Führer when you were at the Wolf's Lair?" Lindemann retorted. "I could not get a chance to speak," came the reply. The army commander's face betrayed impatience and displeasure. "The attack *will* succeed. A general must believe in victory and so inspire his troops." "That I cannot do," von Chappuis intoned. "Then you should report sick!" A pause, and von Chappuis mumbled that he would do what he could.[55]

Stalin was having trouble with his commanders also. After Meretskov flew in and out of the pocket and reported disorganized command and supply, the Soviet dictator ordered up "a high powered mission" including Marshal Kliment Voroshilov, Georgii Malenkov, and Nikolai Bulganin. He also dispatched Gen. Andrei A. Vlasov, a bright young star who had distinguished himself in the defense of Moscow, and named him deputy commander of the Northwest Front. While Meretskov attempted to get things moving, and Fediuninskii tried again at Pogost'e, Lindemann put his attack together.

Two jaws would close on the lifeline of 2 Shock Army. Fifty-eight Division supported by 126 and elements of 250 Divisions would snap northward between Samoshskoe Swamp and the railroad and highway toward Mostki while SS Police Division, aided by 215 Division, moved southward. Contact would be made along the line of Fire Break Friedrich, which ran from Teremets-Kurliandskii to Miasnoi Bor. Friedrich was the northernmost of three fire lanes—Dora, Erika, and Friedrich—which formed a funnel running east to west on the Soviet supply line for 2 Shock Army. Provisions flowed from Posad, Otenskii, and Shevelevo on the east bank of the Volkhov on through Iamno, Plotishno, Miasnoi Bor, Teremets-Kurliandskii to Finev-Lug and Liuban.[56]

A significant change now occurred in the Spanish order of battle.

Rodrigo took over the division's northern sector, but his command was no longer a single regiment. Instead, just as the Germans had been forced to accept fragmentation of units, Muñoz Grandes was being obliged to do the same. Rodrigo retained Third of 269 and received Third of 263, both of which remained in place. The heterogenous force was called "Combat Group Rodrigo," a patchwork agglomeration of misaligned units. Such combat groups were now all too familiar on the entire German front. They were a testimony to the inability of the Wehrmacht to maintain an adequate flow of trained replacements and to the fact that the Germans simply did not have enough men to cover the front.[57]

Some of the wounded were dribbling back every day. Agustín Aznar and Dionisio Ridruejo had returned. After recuperating in Riga, the pair rejoined 2 Divisional Antitanks on the island. As usual, the Falangists gathered during off duty hours to discuss the political situation in the homeland and to listen to the shortwave radio. RNE (Spanish National Radio) broadcast daily to the Blue Division. The *guripas* listened avidly while mothers spoke movingly to their sons at the front. "*Cara al Público*" [Face to the public] also carried news about their returned comrades. Lieutenant Escobedo, having survived his wounds, was relaxing in Jaen and some thirty-five convalescents were enjoying the newly established "Blue Division Home" at 14 Calle de Atocha in Madrid.[58]

Petite and sparkling Celia Jiménez from Radio Berlin was also very popular. Her comments usually provoked a philosophical discussion among the habitues of Lieutenant Muñoz Calero's hut—Aznar, Ridruejo, Guitarte, Carlos Pinilla Turanzas, and Errando Vilar, as well as occasional drop-ins like Castiella and Eduardo de Laiglesia. Another Spanish woman, the Communist Dolores Ibarruri—*La Pasionaria*—had also recently been the subject of spirited comment. A few weeks ago she had favored the Division with a lengthy harangue over the Russian loudspeakers. Obscene gestures and catcalls had greeted her threats and pleas.[59] The session always ended with a rosary.

Prayers were in order. Red artillery and air ceaselessly pounded the front. Podberez'e and Krutik, where 58 Division was building up, received special attention. Second of 269 reported heavy enemy air activity. On 9 March, Vallespín was wounded. The effectives of the division continued to decline; 250 Division numbered 13,766 officers and men. A similar situation prevailed in the entire army. Laux, although reinforced, still counted only 10,843.[60] Lindemann, deftly deploying these depleted divisions, became a master improviser. Patching together a melange of units and commanders, he awaited only clear weather and the Führer's signal to unleash "Beast of Prey."

On 14 March the meteorologists gave their blessing. Lindemann descended on Raglitsy. "Are you ready, von Chappuis? We jump off tomorrow. If the enemy is not cut off from his supply, then our front cannot hold. No delay is possible. The Russians have been threatening Liuban since noon." [61] Stukas screamed out of a cold, clear Sunday sunrise. The faint light glistened on the deep snow drifts piled ever higher by the cutting wind. The attack goals east of the Novgorod-Chudovo highway were limited to pushing Soviet infantry back into the woods in order to free the road from small arms fire. The bulk of 424 Regiment was to roll up the riverbank from Zapol'e, while Second of 269 cut eastward from Koptsy and Krutik.

Román was ready before dawn. *La Segunda* shoved off at 0800 and immediately ran into heavy fire from the Red dugouts. Deep snow made going slow, but by midday the *guripas* had closed and the Russians were fleeing through the woods leaving numerous dead, prisoners and automatic weapons. Having reached his objective, Román settled in the former Russian emplacements a kilometer and a half from the highway to await the inevitable Communist counter assault.

Román's advance opened up a gap between Second of 269 and 209 Regiment to the north. The Soviets were quick to take advantage of this opening and rushed in. Hoppe hurried up 6 Company of 424, which suffered heavy losses. Soviet counterthrusts continued all through the night of 15–16 March. The Germans, caught short of their attack objectives, spent a night in the open under unimaginable conditions of cold (−29 degrees Celsius) and cruel wind without shelter. Frostbite cases mounted. Many of the wounded froze where they fell.

Thirty-eight Corps's failure was more than offset by I Corps's success. Von Both managed to move south almost to Mostki. [62] The drive reopened on Monday morning, 15 March 1942. While XXXVIII Corps stalled, I Corps, led by SS Police Division, pressed on. Unnerved, von Chappuis telephoned Lindemann on 17 March and pleaded for permission to abort. "That is not a subject of discussion!" thundered the army chief. "Tomorrow the SS Police Division will advance beyond its original objective [at Firebreak Friedrich] towards you. All you have to do is attack. But you must win some ground." [63]

Two days later on 19 March Gen. Alfred Wuennenberg, having punched a narrow prong—twenty km long by three km wide—southward, led the SS through Firelane Friedrich past Firebreak Erika and into Clearing Dora. Here, four kilometers west of Miasnoi Bor, they met 58 Division. The pincers had closed.[64] Russian artillery replied in rage. Román, holding east of Krutik, saw his bunkers disintegrate around him. Stormoviks strafed the slit trenches. Then, adding to the incessant roar a new, subtle sound was heard. A drip, a trickle, and then a torrent of black, putrid, vile water running riverward—the *rasputitsa*![65]

The snapping of the Soviet supply line isolated 130,000 men. Provisioning had swelled during the week of 12–19 March. Meretskov, anticipating both the German offensive and the *rasputitsa*, sought to store sufficient supplies for a siege. Success still seemed possible. Klykov and Meretskov hurled armor, air, and artillery at Lindemann's fragile barrier. At this precarious moment Klykov suddenly took ill.

Before dawn on Saturday morning Vlasov flew into the cauldron to take over 2 Shock Army. Hurling T-34s and the entire NCO School of 2 Shock Army from the west and Siberian assault troops of 59 Army from the east, he punched a hole through Clearing Erika on 27 March. Vlasov immediately petitioned *Stavka* for permission to evacuate. Stalin refused.[66]

Von Chappuis was also having difficulty with his superiors. Lindemann had bluntly told him on the twenty-fifth that "the situation requires hard decisions and inspired leadership or else the army is lost."[67] Desperate, von Chappuis turned to Muñoz Grandes. On Thursday, 26 March, the corps commander motored to Novgorod and nervously ordered the Spanish general to ready two battalions for the Zapol'e sector. Muñoz Grandes offered one, Third of 262. The unhappy Prussian had lost again. On this note they parted, as it turned out, forever. The next day Vlasov broke through at Clearing Erika. Von Chappuis, blamed for pusillanimity characterized more by complaints and pleading for reinforcements than confident command, was summarily dismissed by von Küchler on 29 March. The disgrace proved too much to bear. He committed suicide five months later.[68]

Gen. Friedrich Haenicke, formerly commander of 61 Division, was ordered to take over XXXVIII Corps. He immediately directed Muñoz Grandes to extend his divisional sector northward. Teremets—minus the Russian-held village—came under Spanish control again. As the Germans scrambled to hold, the Russians sought to widen their corridor. On 31 March Vlasov unsuccessfully attacked Liubtsy and Zemtitsy. Simultaneously, Soviet armor began to move southward out of Firelanes Erika and Dora. Hoppe, fearing an assault on Krutik, alerted Román the next afternoon. On 2 April, Holy Thursday, a late spring blizzard hit the battle zone. Visibility was limited to two meters. Orange glows from Soviet shellbursts winked through the gloom. Román, crouching in his bombed out CP on the shoulder of the highway, awaited word from his outposts to the east on the edge of the woods.

At 0800 a frantic ringing of the field telephone heralded the arrival of Russian infantry. Supported by artillery, mortars, and rockets, the Ivans briefly pressed forward and then retired, leaving their dead in the wet snow. About 1100 two dozen T-34s debouched from the woods. Bells clanging, motors roaring, and tracks whirring, they headed for the highway. Román, realizing that he had absolutely nothing with which he could stop a twenty-eight-ton tank, passed the word, "Let the tanks go by, and wait for the infantry." [69]

The *guripas* lifted their fire. Eighth Company called in: "We're surrounded." The mortar sections were overrun. Captain Campano glanced up at the dark hulk crashing over his firing pit and calmly snapped his Kodak. Men against steel; individual officers and men managed to deflect most of the tanks with hand grenades. The crews were disoriented by the explosions. Since only the lead tank had a radio, and the pack communicated by ringing bells, all they could do was to thrash around firing wildly and clanging fiercely. Nevertheless, by 1600 eight T-34s were rolling on toward ruined Krutik where the remaining *guripas* now clung to the highway for a last stand.

At this critical juncture, Capt. Werner Bruch threw together a mixed force of couriers, telephonists, and sappers with his own cannoneers of 13 Company of 424 Regiment and rushed in to reinforce Román. Unlimbering their lone 150 mm, the Germans opened up at the T-34s at point-blank range. The Red attack faltered. Colonel Hoppe quickly threw in five Mark IIIs and an 88 mm Flak. [70] By morning of Good Friday, Román's remnants were able to counterattack under cover of the Flak and restore the line. *La Segunda* lost four officers, two sergeants, five soldiers killed and seventy-one wounded, in the two days of fighting.

The slaughter at Krutik did not interfere with more important matters. The eternal philosophical debate between the real and the unreal had been settled by the Spaniards centuries before. They had weighed the flesh and the spirit and come down heavily in favor of the soul. Consequently, as the Marxists hurled masses of men and materiél at their lines to the north, the rest of the division gathered for *Semana Santa* (Holy Week) services.

The Russians of Novgorod watched as Muñoz Grandes led his officers and men in the solemn ceremonies of Easter. Confession at 0800 was followed by high mass at the forest camp at Grigorovo. Robed in resplendent white, Father Joaquín Mur, the divisional chaplain, led Fathers Cases Santamaría and Prad Lerena across the clearing to the crude field altar. The chill wind wafted the burning incense toward the swaying trees which served as rustic ruedos. The bareheaded congregation, numb from the cold and still in their clammy greatcoats, was glad when Consecration came. Now the general and his *guripas* could kneel in the slush and snow and ease their aching limbs as the soldiers' chorus entoned the *De Angelis* accompanied by the Capuchin Conrad Simonsen playing an organ looted from only God knew where.

Soviet aircraft and artillery notwithstanding, the ceremonies continued on Maundy Thursday and Good Friday.[71] Zanón had hardly finished the *via crucis* when he had to dash back to GHQ. Lindemann had arrived. Over a cup of real coffee, Muñoz Grandes regaled his army chief with the glories of Román and *La Segunda*. "The battalion is down to a hundred men. Even these had been scrounged from service units."[72] The old cavalryman was impressed. Muñoz Grandes opined that as soon as the 3,000 replacements arrived, he would be ready to join in the closing of the Volkhov Pocket by moving northward to his former sector boundary at Shevelevo. Regarding problems, there were few. He wanted more clothing, not as special treatment, but principally to counter British propaganda in Spain. Of deserters, there were only a handful. He was executing them. Lindemann responded warmly to the aggressiveness and sangfroid of the Spaniard. After von Chappuis it was refreshing. Now he knew why the two had never hit it off. Muñoz Grandes was a man after Lindemann's own heart. The *guripas* were soon talking about *querido* Lindemann (cherished Lindemann).

Divisional GHQ immediately ordered probes in force across the Volkhov. Since the river was already running free from Lake Il'men down to the railroad bridge, the rubber boats were trotted out again. On Easter Sunday, 5 April, the wreckage of Román's battalion was ordered back to Novgorod where it would once again—the third time—be replenished. At last replacements were on hand from Spain.[73] About 1,000 reinforcements had dribbled in between September and January. In late February, however, the pace had quickened. Asensio in Madrid had responded to Krappe's suggestion that mixed battalions of 300 to 400 men be dispatched while negotiations continued. The army chief of staff faced a dwindling pool of volunteers. Returning veterans spread the word about severe temperatures and tough fighting against heavy odds. There were complaints about a superior attitude adopted by some Germans in dealing with Spaniards who had come to spill their blood in a comradely effort. Pensions promised by the Germans for widows and war wounded were late in coming. Madrid blamed Berlin and Berlin blamed Madrid. Although officers seemed as anxious to go as ever, Asensio noted that noncoms, always in short supply, were now even more reluctant. Nor were conscripts in the post–Civil War army anxious to exchange peacetime Spain for Russia in war. As for the long list of Falangists who had volunteered in July, many had had a change of heart.

Asensio concluded that the monetary rewards were insufficient and the ranks of glory seekers thinned. He recommended that all who served on the Russian front as provisional sergeants be given permanent rank; draftees who joined the Blue Division for six months would be exempted from further military service. As for the Falangists, the chief of staff suggested a subtle recruiting campaign. This would be an internal matter of the Falange, where it was well recognized that those who had proved their loyalty in blood would be the leaders of the future.[74]

There were to be two phases of recruitment—a replacement phase, February to March, and a rotation phase, April through October. The first, the Krappe-Asensio formula, designed to bring the division back up to strength, consisted of sending mixed battalions of 300 to 400 men every ten days. These were mostly regulars. The second, following the Asensio-Fromm agreement, was intended to rotate the entire division. A series of march battalions of 900 to 1,000 men were organized by Esteban Infantes and dispatched from Logroño. They were recruited by the Falange, but included a high percentage of jobless civilians who were attracted more by the monetary rewards, meager as they were, than by idealistic goals.[75]

Phase one was in full swing. On 26 March a shipment of replacements reached Novgorod.[76] The tour of duty was over for Errando Vilar. The young man did not wish to leave without saying goodbye to his general. Muñoz Grandes, who had an open-door policy for his men, received the lieutenant in his pajamas at 0700. After a brief parting word, the ardent Falangist went off to get his pass and board the train. Back through Riga, Königsberg, and Berlin. A bit of sightseeing, some shopping, and a quick interview with Celia Jiménez, a treat for the young chap. Then, on to Hof, for a quick change to red beret, blue shirt, and khakis of the Spanish volunteer uniform. By now, he was anxious to see the familiar peaks of the Pyrenees and show off his Iron Cross to friends and family. At last, the red-and-gold banner at Irún. Home, and it was warm.

Another hero was also home. Ridruejo, too ill to remain at the front, was invalided back to Berlin. Then, on 22 April, the poet of the Falange flew into Barajas airport. There to greet him were Serrano Suñer, Pilar Primo de Rivera, Victor de la Serna, and assorted "old shirts" from the days of José Antonio. He was quickly whisked into downtown Madrid. The next day, Thursday, Ridruejo attended the monthly mass for the souls of the departed volunteers at the Church of Santa Barbara. It was good to be alive and home.[77]

All over the peninsula, other Spaniards were heading out. At the Cavalry barracks in Valladolid Major Cuesta was busy organizing the new Recon 250. By early April the squadrons were rolling northward. A brief stop at San Sebastián for a review by General Esteban Infantes and formal command ceremonies. Colonel Sagrado took over March Battalion 7 for the journey to Bavaria where the eagles were gathering.[78]

On 21 April, Lieutenant Oroquieta was relaxing with his parents in Saragossa. He had managed to arrange a brief leave from his regiment —Second *Tercio* of the Legion. Suddenly the telephone rang. It was Lieutenant Apestequi calling from the railroad station. He and a group of Oroquieta's comrades were on their way to San Sebastián to join a march battalion for the Blue Division. Since they had a few hours layover, Oroquieta agreed to join them for lunch. Over a glass of *vino tinto*, they persuaded him to accompany them to the frontier for a last farewell. Boarding the train, Oroquieta saluted the convoy commander, Major LaCruz, and enquired if there were any openings. "One, just one," replied the major, "But that decision is up to Brigadier Esteban Infantes."[79]

The next day, Wednesday, after a briefing by the general, LaCruz presented the young lieutenant to the bemedaled, short, stocky figure. Mustering his courage, the legionnaire requested permission to join the expedition. A heavy silence followed. Then, the brigadier smiled. Gleefully rushing out into the streets of San Sebastián to buy a few necessities—razor, toothbrush, cigarettes, and cognac—Oroquieta paused. He had to telegraph his parents in Saragossa and tell them the news. "I am going to Russia," he wired, "Don't worry. See you soon." [80] His mother gasped as she read the message. Little did she know that it would be twelve years before she would see her son again.

Just as he was about to leave the telegraph office, Oroquieta remembered that he was an officer in the Legion. Shouldn't he ask permission to go or at least let them know he was leaving? He got back in line. The next morning the train rolled down the hill toward the iron bridge over the Bidasoa. For luck the volunteers tossed their last Spanish coins into the murky waters. Clenched fists and gray skies were part of the routine as the convoy moved through France. Warm waves and happy smiles greeted them in Germany. Detraining near Grafenwöhr at Auerbach/Saale they felt at home.

Sagrado arrived on 12 April with March Battalion 7 (Relief Transport 1). All of the officers were regulars as were one half of the noncoms who had generally been drawn from artillery and sappers. Falangist militia, mostly unmarried country boys aged twenty, comprised over two-thirds of the other ranks.[81]

All of the expeditions followed the same routine—medical examination, exchange of uniforms, issuance of personal equipment and small arms, firing practice, oath to the Führer, and embarcation. In addition to personal equipment, each march battalion also drew horses, autos, and for the journey, field kitchens. An expedition was usually ready to depart within two weeks after arrival at Auerbach. March Battalion 7, however, had to wait almost three, due to a lack of German uniforms for the troops. The brief training cycle, completely inadequate for the raw militia, was further vitiated by the shortage of munitions. Armament production was not up to the demands of the Russian front. This was driven home to the recruits when one of the two cartridge clips originally issued was recalled. The desperately needed ammunition was rushed eastward.[82]

The shortage of uniforms and clips and the abbreviated training at Auerbach in the spring of 1942 were reminiscent of Grafenwöhr during the summer of 1941. The routine, though truncated, was essentially the same. Even relations between Germans and Spaniards were almost identical. The Wehrmacht complained bitterly about Spanish Military Police who spent their guard duty armed and replete in full field equipment sitting in the village beer halls savoring the splendid lagers. By the end of April, March Battalion 7 was uniformed, rationed, and ready to go. The German populace turned out to bid them Godspeed. After all, the Führer himself had just proclaimed that the Spaniards were second in valor only to the Finns.

Addressing the Reichstag in the Kroll Opera House in Berlin on 26 April, Hitler declared "[the Spaniards] have done all that we ask of our own soldiers. . . . They and their general know the meaning of loyalty and bravery unto death."[83] Accolades ringing in their ears, March Battalion 7 rolled on. Within three days of leaving Hof they were in Riga. Two days later the recruits off-loaded in Novgorod. At noon, 5 May, Major Cuesta reported in to Muñoz Grandes at Grigorovo. Distribution of the men began immediately. Sagrado replaced Pimentel of 262 in the Kremlin. Pimentel would command Return Battalion 1.[84]

Weaponless, but loaded down with souvenirs and stolen ikons and swinging *Wolchow-stock* (carved staffs), the *guripas* gathered in Chievischtschi. Neither the mud nor the mosquitos, nor the miserable *izbas* dampened their spirits. It was spring and they were going home. The fields were lush green, wild flowers poked their heads out of the cracks between the logs in the corduroy roads. Even the children had reappeared, seemingly for the first time since December when they skimmed over the frozen river on their ice skates. A few kilometers eastward the lake sparkled and the veterans fortified their rations with fresh fish scooped out of Lake Il'men after tossing in a grenade.[85]

The short nights, 10:00 P.M. to 4:00 A.M., seemed doubly long. Sleep was almost impossible. Masses of mosquitos filled the warm darkness, penetrating nets and bed clothes. Characteristically, volunteers composed a caustic song.

> Mosquito, mosquito,
> Now you have me more than half eaten,
> Please go chew on another,
> Even if it's my brother.[86]

On Monday, 11 May, Return Battalion 1 marched to Grigorovo to board trains for the journey home. As they stood before the long line of cattle cars, Muñoz Grandes and his staff turned out to bid them farewell. The general's speech was pregnant with political import. After praising them for their valor on the battlefields of Russia, which had restored the honor of Spanish arms, he reminded them that the war was not over.

> The enemy is still on his feet, torn and defeated but still on his feet. You . . . have no right to expect a respite because you are leaving. You go to another front, where Spain, covered with glory but always

humiliated, waits while others debate about giving us a handful of wheat in exchange for the sacred treasure of our national independence. You will not stand for this!

. . . I, your general, am tired indeed—tired of seeing a foreign flag over Gibraltar.

My last order to you . . . *Arriba España! Arriba Alemania!* [87]

There were many who noticed the pointed omission of the customary cry of *"Viva Franco!"* Muñoz Grandes was fighting on two fronts— Russia and Spain. Only if Franco was with him would he be with Franco. The British must permit grain to pass and return Gibraltar to Spain. Hitler's New Order was the best guarantee of that. Moved at Muñoz Grandes's words, the returning volunteers spontaneously shouted: *"Viva España! Viva nuestro general!"* Some of the *guripas* could not contain their tears. They were leaving too many memories and too many comrades behind. Then, it was time to go. Within a few days they off-loaded at Hof; the familiar blue shirts, red berets and khaki trousers again. Then on 24 May 1942, Hendaye, then Bidasoa, Irún, and San Sebastián—home. [88]

Crowds thronged Madrid's Estación del Norte. The banner-bedecked locomotive, whistle shrieking, edged forward over the packed track toward Platform 1. A forest of arms stretched toward the train as the bands of the Eleventh Infantry Division and the Municipality of Madrid attacked the National Anthem. At high noon, the aged coaches shuddered to a stop. The hangarlike station, festooned with Spanish, Falangist, Nazi, and Italian flags, vibrated to the roar of the multitude as Pimentel stepped on to the platform and saluted.

All of Madrid was there: Serrano Suñer, Varela, Vigón, Arrese, Miguel and Pilar Primo de Rivera, Galarza, Milán Astray, Asensio, Martín Alonso, Ridruejo, Celia Jiménez, along with other high functionaries and representatives from the Axis powers. The chant of "Franco, Franco, Franco," shook the shell of the station as the volunteers filed off the train. A spontaneous shout of approval rose from the crowd as they sized up the soldiers. These ruddy, healthy youths bore no sign of privation. Rather, they reminded one of the fabled lean bronze veterans of the *Tercios* of Flanders from Spain's heroic past and Golden Age. The *guripas'* struggle to maintain a rigid line along the length of the convoy collapsed when the crowd surged toward them, broke through the honor guard and shattered their ranks in a welter of *abrazos*, handshakes, kisses, and flowers.

Into this melee of emotion rumbled the second trainload of returning volunteers. They, along with the first arrivals, pushed through the cheering crowd toward the waiting trucks and clambered aboard. Cries of "Long live the valiants of Spain," and "Long live the Blue Division," mixed with shouts of *Viva España*, and *Viva Franco*. Showers of laurel and bouquets greeted the *guripas* at the banner-laden City Hall. Crossing the crowded Puerta del Sol and entering the Calle de Alcalá the convoy crawled on toward José Antonio where thousands massed before the balcony at Falangist Headquarters. Here, the silver-haired figure of Serrano Suñer took the salute under the enormous red metal sculpture of the Yoke and Arrows as the crowd sang "Cara al Sol." That Monday evening was reminiscent of carnival. When the contingent fell out the next day for a *Te Deum* at El Retiro Park, thick tongues, bleary eyes and upset stomachs predominated. The mass at El Retiro was attended by all the cabinet. Only the Caudillo was absent. Once again, Franco declined to identify the Volunteer Division with the Spanish state by his presence.[89]

As the veterans returned to their former haunts and chatted with their friends, the conversations always drifted toward the Volkhov. On 30 May, Lindemann pulled tight the drawstring on the Volkhov Pocket. Preparations for strangling 2 Shock Army had been under way since mid-April. Von Küchler, convinced that Vlasov was not going to withdraw, but would wait out the thaw and then reopen his attack westward toward Leningrad when the ground hardened, flew to the *Führerhauptquartier* on 13 April. Hitler's optimistic evaluation that the Reds would sit in the swamps and starve to death was not shared by his army group commander.[90]

Von Küchler knew that he was getting weaker while Meretskov was getting stronger. He asked Hitler for reinforcements. The Führer, his eyes on the Caucasus and the oil fields of Baku, replied that he had no infantry to spare. Indeed he had not. By mid-April the German Army on the Eastern Front had lost 257,020 officers and men killed, 900, 241 wounded, and 57,566 missing. The Führer needed every man he had for the spring offensive.

Indicative of the shrinking manpower pool was the OKH order of 2 May. All Wehrmacht infantry divisions were cut from three regiments of three battalions down to three regiments of two battalions. This 30 percent reduction applied to all units except 250 Division.[91] As replacements began to file in from Spain and the Volkhov started to run, the Blue Division assumed an even greater role in closing the pocket.

Vlasov was desperate. So was Stalin. Leningrad was in dire straits.

Tens of thousands were starving and the ice road over Lake Ladoga was about to break up. Failure of the winter offensive was blamed on divided command—M. S. Khozin in Leningrad, and Meretskov along the Volkhov. On 23 April Stalin consolidated the two fronts under Khozin, who promised "to lift the blockade."[92]

The next day the Road of Life melted away. Leningrad was isolated again. Branded by *Stavka* as failures, Meretskov and Fediuninskii were fired.[93] On 29 April Khozin threw everything into a maximum effort. Seeking to slice through Wuennenberg's narrow salient at Mostki, he hurled four divisions from the west and seven regiments from the east. Caught between Vlasov's anvil and Galanin's hammer, the prong flattened but held. By 12 May, 2 Shock Army could do no more. Two days later Stalin gave the order to withdraw. The five brigades of 13 Cavalry Corps were the first out. Immediately realizing that Vlasov had given up and was retreating, Lindemann ordered pursuit. The pocket collapsed like a balloon. The Reds streamed through the gap at Clearing Erika. On 30 May, with Stuka support, the Germans struck. Within twenty-four hours, Vlasov was trapped once again.[94]

There was so much coming and going in the Spanish division that Lindemann thought that everyone, including Muñoz Grandes, was being replaced. Many familiar faces were disappearing. On 12 May, Major Bañuls of Third of 269 with Combat Group Vierna was wounded. López Barron (G-4) was relieved four days later by Lieutenant Colonel Goya, who was also appointed second chief of staff. With the arrival of 892 officers and men of March Battalion 8 on 25 May, Gómez Zamalloa's replacement—Lieutenant Colonel Robles—took over as second in command of 262. Major LaCruz and Lieutenant Oroquieta came up on the same transport. Both were posted to Antitanks 250. The chief of sappers, Major Enríquez, was replaced by Major Bellod. On 27 May Colonel Salazar motored in from Riga. Zanón, the gaunt chief of staff, was slated to go home as well. Soon Muñoz Grandes, except for old friends like his aide, Cárcer, would be alone.[95]

The sealing off of the pocket on 30 May required a further shifting of Spanish forces northward. In accordance with Corps Order 96, Salazar, the new Chief of Staff, moved Cuesta's Recon 250 along with a special Tank Killer Group up to Dolgovo. Here they joined 2 SS Motorized Infantry Brigade to form a corps reserve. Third of 262 under Major Cartagena was also pulled out of the line and held in readiness at Tiutitsy for instant intervention should the Russians threaten to break out.[96]

The Soviets beat in vain against the encirclement. T-34s, heavy artillery, Red aircraft, and riflemen struck at the siege lines. Major Santos Margallo of First of 263 at Tiutitsy was hit by shrapnel on 1 June. He died two days later in the hospital at Grigorovo as the Soviets cannonaded Novgorod. Concentrating their fire on the Kremlin, Red artillerymen smashed that ancient symbol of Mother Russia—the golden cupola of Saint Sophia.[97] Two hundred miles to the east in the Kremlin of Moscow, Stalin fretted. On 8 June he summoned Meretskov to Stavka. "You, Comrade Meretskov, are to take command immediately."[98]

As the Soviet blows gradually increased in intensity, the German ring softened and small units of 2 Shock Army began to seep through. On 12 June "Group Cuesta"—Recon 250 and Tank Killer Group—moved out of Dolgovo and entered the line at Bol. Zamosh'e.[99]

A patchwork unit, Task Force Hoppe, was to take Mal. Zamosh'e and assist in plugging the Soviet escape route through Firelanes Erika and Friedrich. Hoppe and his staff would command two international formations—Burk and Cuesta. *SS-Standartenführer* (Colonel) Burk headed a force composed of Battalion Valentin of 20 Motorized, Cartagena with Third of 262, Colonel Vitzthun with the Legion Flanders, and five Mark III tanks. Four columns closed in on Mal. Zamosh'e on the morn of 25 June—Cuesta from the south, Burk from the southeast, Cartagena from the northeast, and 285 Division from the north. The Russians were gone.[100]

Meretskov and Vlasov had launched their last effort at 1130 on Tuesday, 23 June. Second Shock had driven eastward while Fifty-ninth shoved westward. Toward dawn, they had punched open a narrow peephole, and the Ivans of 2 Shock began to pass through. But the flanks could not hold and the gap closed again at noon.[101] Vlasov ordered every man for himself, and organized resistance collapsed. The Battle of the Volkhov Pocket was over.

Some 16,000 Red riflemen had escaped. Another 14,000 remained within the iron ring. Mopping up began immediately. The Spanish Ski Company and 1 Company of 263 Regiment were rushed northward to join 58 Division while Cuesta and Cartagena continued the clean up.[102]

On 28 June Radio Berlin blared out the OKW announcement of the German victory. General Lindemann issued a special proclamation to the men of 18 Army.

On 13 January the enemy, with vastly superior numbers, crossed the Volkhov. . . . His goal was the liberation of Petersburg.

The remnants of 2 Shock Army and parts of 52 and 59 Armies are destroyed!

Almost all units of 18 Army fought shoulder to shoulder, men of the Army, the *Waffen-SS*, Spaniards, Dutch, and Flemings fought in this battle.

In the period 13 January–28 June we took 32,759 prisoners. . . . The enemy lost over 100,000 dead and wounded . . . 649 cannon, 645 grenade throwers, 2,259 machine guns, 171 tanks, 21 aircraft, 2,066 motor vehicles.[103]

Colonel General von Küchler was promoted to field marshal by a grateful Führer.

The Spaniards had been in the forefront from the very beginning. Grimly holding on to Novgorod while the Soviets smashed through the lines of the Lovat and the Volkhov, the Blue Division was the solid hinge of XXXVIII Corps. Units of Spaniards were lent to other divisions as the Germans struggled to recover. For a time, the Russian winter offensive threatened to envelop the volunteers; there were anxious weeks in Madrid and Grigorovo. Muñoz Grandes rushed men from support services into the ranks while Spain and Germany haggled over reinforcements. His was a two-front war. On the Volkhov and in the swamps, but also in El Pardo and Rastenburg, he held the line, for which he was admired by Hitler, and relieved by Franco. The German Führer, fuming over the Caudillo's continuing coolness, was beginning to eye the steeled commander of 250 Division as a potential paladin in Iberia. Franco saw the danger. He had already selected a replacement for Muñoz Grandes. Brigadier Esteban Infantes had arrived in Berlin on 14 June.

9

Conspiracy, Change of Front, and the Palace of Catherine the Great

EARLY IN JUNE, A CURIOUS LETTER ARRIVED AT THE
German Foreign Ministry. Addressed to Councillor Rudolf Likus, it
had been posted by a Captain Hoffmann who lived in Berlin on Neiden-
burger Allee. "My son, *Sonderführer* Hans Hoffmann," the writer
began, "is attached to the Liaison Staff of the Blue Division. General
Muñoz Grandes has asked him to get in touch with you, in order that
his thoughts might be conveyed to the appropriate personages."[1]

Likus read the documents with growing interest. On 14 June 1942,
the very day that Brigadier Emilio Esteban Infantes paused in Berlin
on his way to take command of the Blue Division, Likus passed the
confidential correspondence on to the foreign minister. As Ribbentrop
avidly read the memo, he realized that the date of Muñoz Grandes's departure was rapidly approaching. The general had suddenly become a
matter of high policy. The issues which he had raised with Hoffmann
were of such import that Muñoz Grandes could not be permitted to
leave the Third Reich before the Führer evaluated the situation. Nor
could Esteban Infantes be allowed to take over the division. Ribbentrop went directly to Hitler.

For weeks, the Führer had been eyeing Spain with rising anger. He had never trusted Franco and had always disliked Serrano Suñer. Now, as he detected in the Nationalist state growing monarchist sentiment supported by the British, his mood had turned to cold fury. Day after day, at lunch and at dinner, he treated his subordinates to a barrage of invectives about the ineffectual Spanish government, its increasing unreliability as an ally, and the danger of "priests and monarchists . . . joining together to seize power." [2] On the Führer's orders, *Sonderführer* Hoffmann was summoned to Berlin. Likus was instructed to ascertain the relief schedule.

On 16 June, Brigadier Esteban Infantes motored to Hof. Here, he inspected his rear services, donned his Wehrmacht uniform, and took the oath to the Führer. He was advised that he would depart Berlin for the front on the nineteenth. All was in readiness for the change of command. Suddenly, a hold was placed on the entire proceedings. Hitler sent Admiral Canaris to Army Group North. The *Abwehr* director met with the commander of the Blue Division at Lindemann's GHQ. They were old acquaintances. Canaris had met Muñoz Grandes in 1940 at Algeciras, while on a trip to reconnoiter for Operation Felix. After chatting privately, Canaris returned to Germany, reporting that Muñoz Grandes no longer expected to be replaced. The admiral was immediately sent on a new mission. Hitler dispatched him to Spain. Traveling under an assumed name, he arrived in Madrid on 22 June 1942 and requested an audience with the Caudillo. Without disclosing anything other than that it was the Führer's wish, he asked if Muñoz Grandes could remain in command of the Blue Division temporarily. Not a little suspicious, Franco assented. [3] The delay in force, Likus rushed to Novgorod, where he, too, had a private meeting with Muñoz Grandes. Only Hoffmann, acting as intepreter, was present. Then, Likus dashed back to Ribbentrop. No sooner had he arrived than the general was commanded to the Wolf's Lair "at the earliest possible moment." [4]

What had happened? What had *Sonderführer* Hoffmann written to his father? What had Muñoz Grandes said that could send the Third Reich into a frenzy of activity, and so excite the Führer's interest? The Hoffmann papers contained a desperate, last-ditch attempt by Muñoz Grandes to contact Hitler and pour out his thoughts about Spanish politics and German-Spanish relations. But there was much more than that.

The younger Hoffmann, who had spent many years in the peninsula, and spoke the language moderately well, had listened intently as the general related that the Nazi-Soviet alliance of 1939, which set the stage for the rape of Catholic Poland and the start of the world war, had been most unpopular in his homeland. There had been demonstrations for Finland when the USSR invaded that hapless land, Muñoz Grandes said. Moreover, reactionary circles had capitalized on the public mood of anti communism by giving a certain anti-German flavor to their spirit. The British had not been slow to pick this up and attempt to establish contact with these groups, which they had not supported in the Civil War. At that time, Muñoz Grandes had been secretary general of the movement, and had sought to counteract the reactionary forces. When Germany attacked the Soviet Union in 1941 and the Falange called for volunteers, the reactionaries were taken aback by the enormous public enthusiasm. They joined in, and tried to appear in the forefront of the fight alongside the Third Reich. However, they saw the volunteer division a threat if it were in the hands of the Falangists, and tried to capture control of it. In bitter behind-the-scenes struggles the Falangists succeeded, and the DEV was moulded of soldiers instilled with anti-Bolshevism and loyal to the spirit of the movement. But the reactionaries did not give up. They fought against an entry of Spain into the war and for a diminution of Spanish assistance to Germany. In this they were supported by the English.

There was a danger in Spain, Muñoz Grandes went on, that the "meaning of our national uprising" in the Civil War "would be brought to naught."[5] Spain's domestic difficulties "cannot be solved except simultaneously with a decision in foreign political affairs."[6] The general's remarks revealed that he counted himself a social revolutionary, against reactionaries as well as Communists. He left no doubt that he regarded Hitlerite Germany as Spain's natural ally—as a model for national socialist revolution and anti-Marxism and as a champion of anti-colonialism. He wanted the British ousted from Gibraltar and wished Spain to replace France as the arbiter of North African affairs. But the Germans had not helped their own cause. Instead of treating his *guripas* as brothers, they had acted as judges. "We do not have to be reminded of our faults," he chided Hoffmann. "I fight against them every day."[7]

"Now is the last hour," he proclaimed.[8] We must move to "the final destruction of our domestic and foreign enemies."[9] In the Führer, who had spoken so highly of the fighting qualities of the Blue Division, he placed his trust. It was this bombshell which led the Germans to delay Esteban Infantes in Berlin and hurry Likus to Novgorod.

Ribbentrop, plotting with Walter Schellenberg, Head of Section VI (Foreign Espionage) of SS Chief Heinrich Himmler's Reich Security

Main Office (RSHA), had been seeking to overthrow Franco for the past year. The Caudillo's refusal to enter the war was depriving the Germans of Gibraltar. A series of conspiracies with disgruntled Old Shirts such as Eduardo Ezquer and Geraldo Salvador Merino had proved fruitless. Muñoz Grandes seemed better placed for success.[10]

The general told Ribbentrop's emissary that he fully understood how he was being honored by the attention the Germans were showing him. It was clear to him "what responsibility I am undertaking and I am prepared to stake everything, including myself, for friendship with Germany. Next to my friendship with Germany, my driving force is hatred for England, which has oppressed my country for generations."[11]

Now, he was about to be replaced. Pulling a piece of paper from his pocket, the general explained that it was a letter from Esteban Infantes. He was later to describe it as a mincing letter, but he merely read a part of it to Likus, the part containing instructions from General Varela. The war minister had ordered Esteban Infantes to proceed at once to Novgorod and there to assume the rank of second-in-command of the division until 50 percent of the effectives had been rotated. At that time and "regardless of whether General Muñoz Grandes agreed that the time had come for himself to be replaced," Esteban Infantes was to take command.[12]

Muñoz Grandes paused, and then went on. He knew that the Germans had held Esteban Infantes in Berlin. Let him come, the iron-jawed Spaniard boasted, his Knight's Cross quivering as he spoke. "I will dominate him with the force of my own personality. He can assume temporary command so that I can take a brief furlough in the peninsula where I can have the opportunity to negotiate with the government. I am ready to take the risk."[13] He promised to lay out his plans before Hitler or von Ribbentrop, should they agree to see him.[14]

The general was most specific about his plans for Don Juan, son of the last king, Alfonso XIII, and pretender to the Spanish throne. "He has attempted to contact me. . . . I told him that . . . he is nothing to me [but] the . . . son of an English woman who has grown up in England, the country which is Spain's bitter enemy."[15] Such words were music to Hitler's ears. He had already formed his opinion of the decisive, energetic general who had held his ground during the winter campaign. Not only did his men fight, but the general urged them on against overwhelming odds to triumphs brought by force of will and bravery. A man after his own heart! And now to learn that he had political ambitions as a social revolutionary and anti-monarchist. So different from his own officers corps, which seemed steeped in the aristocratic tradition.

Contemplating the report from Likus, Hitler told Walter Hewel, an old intimate from the Munich putsch of 1923, that

we must promote as much as we can the popularity of General Muñoz Grandes, who is a man of energy, and as such the most likely one to master the situation. I am very pleased indeed that the intrigues of the Serrano Suñer clique to get the general dismissed from the command of the Blue Division were frustrated at the last moment; for the Blue Division may well once more play a decisive role, when the hour for the overthrow of the parson-ridden regime strikes.[16]

The German dictator was apprehensive about a reactionary coalition of the "clerico-monarchical muck," against which a revolutionary force embracing many of the Falange might be ready to proceed.[17] The commander of the Blue Division offered enticing possibilities. He might become the Führer's paladin.

Exuding his undoubted charm, a delighted Adolf Hitler welcomed Muñoz Grandes to Rastenburg on 11 July. Muñoz Grandes was captivated, gaining the impression that Hitler loved and respected Spain. "Basking in the Führer's glance," he told Likus afterwards, "Spain has for me ceased to be an unhappy land."[18] Passionately, the general poured out his heart. He described the leaders of his country—Varela: the ruination of the army. He was responsible, along with his comrade Serrano Suñer, for the replacement of the division, a replacement which was nothing less than "a direct sabotage against Germany."[19] The new recruits were ill-trained and of dubious military value. Some were suspected Communists who had only come to desert. The "new commanders move around as if they were puppets on a string. Like creatures, they duck out of sight as soon as . . . [I] appear."[20] Serrano Suñer: a mere mention of the name sent Muñoz Grandes into a paroxysm of rage. "When Milans del Bosch was returning . . . [wounded] to Spain, he asked in jest what message he should bring to S[errano] S[uñer] when he met him. [I] answered: Tell him that I may still not return alive . . . but if I do, I will personally shoot you and your cohorts."[21]

For more than two hours, the general explained his hopes and plans. He would stay at the front, if Hitler would allow it. But he wanted to go back to the peninsula confident of German support and ready for a thorough housecleaning. The youth of his country and uncorrupted elements of the Falange were with him. His immediate ambition was to become chief of government under a more or less figurehead Franco, who would remain chief of state. His administration would be marked by the closest possible friendship and cooperation with Germany.

Hitler cautiously accepted this new role of collaborator and they agreed to set up a permanent line of communication outside of normal channels. This was necessary because Ambassador von Stohrer and Embassy Councillor Heberlein were close to Serrano Suñer. Both believed that it would be best to keep Spain at peace, because otherwise Spain would prove more a liability than an aid to Germany. Ribbentrop had already installed his own agent, Erich Gardemann, in the embassy. Ribbentrop and Likus would be the go-betweens.[22]

Turning to military affairs, Muñoz Grandes asked the Führer if the Blue Division could not be transferred to a more active front. Hitler had been forewarned to expect this request. Army Group North was against it, if purely military considerations were taken into account. The division was not capable of significant offensive operations. But Hitler had other matters on his mind. He told Muñoz Grandes that 250 Division would be shifted. Muñoz Grandes, enthralled and enraptured, returned to the front with the blood pounding through his veins.[23]

Rumors of the Hitler-Muñoz Grandes meeting were soon pulsating through the corridors of El Pardo Palace. The Spanish Secret Service reported that Col. Günther Krappe, German military attaché, had contacted Muñoz Grandes's friend and fellow Falangist, General Yagüe, at his country estate, San Leandro in Soria. On 16 July, Stohrer, who was not in on the conspiracy and was being bypassed by Ribbentrop, acting on unofficial Spanish request, queried Berlin about the tenor of the meeting. The cryptic reply: only military matters were discussed.[24]

Barely hours afterward, on the sixth anniversary of the Nationalist uprising, Franco delivered a commemorative speech. The dignitaries of Spain and members of the diplomatic corps thronged the former Senate chambers on Calle de Bailén near the Royal Palace. The new American ambassador, Carleton J. H. Hayes, shared a box in the rear of the red-velveted, white and gold walled hall with other representatives of the Allied Powers.

As the balding, bespectacled professor leaned over the balcony, he could see in the box below the huge figure of the German ambassador, von Stohrer, wrapped in a military cloak. The six-foot-tall giant was surrounded by the Italian, Japanese, Nanking China, Manchurian, Croatian, Rumanian, Hungarian, and Vichy French representatives. Hayes's lips moved to a wry smile at what seemed to him the perfect caricature of the Greater German Reich and its satellites. His eyes then roamed idly over the glittering array of Falangists occupying the main floor and fixed on the tribune, guarded by Old Shirts and veterans of the Blue Division.[25]

At 8:15 p.m., Franco and his entourage entered the chamber and took their seats on the platform. Serrano Suñer was on the generalissimo's right, Arrese on the left. The thrust of his speech was directed toward domestic peace and reconstruction. He dwelt very little on the war, stressing only Spain's continued anti-Communist stance and the heroism of the Blue Division. Should his country be threatened, he boasted, three million men would be mobilized. The most important element of Franco's speech was an omission. Neither Germany nor Italy was mentioned.

Hayes was delighted. He felt that "after appeasing the Axis for two years, General Franco was starting to 'appease' the United States and Great Britain."[26] The Axis reaction was as negative as that of the Allies was positive. Hitler moved forward his plans to make Muñoz Grandes a hero. Events came to the Führer's aid.

Erwin Rommel's *Afrika Korps* was tearing up the sands of Egypt. Von Bock's Army Group South was driving toward the Don and the Volga and Erich von Manstein's 11 Army had just stormed the fortress city of Sevastopol. Manstein's victory proved to Hitler that a city which appeared to be impregnable could be taken by assault. His gaze turned north to Leningrad. On 23 July, Hitler issued Führer Directive 45. "Army Group North is preparing to capture Leningrad by the beginning of September. Cover name: Fire Magic [later changed to Northern Light]. For this, they will be reinforced by such other Army troops as necessary."[27] Among "such other troops" was 250 Division. Muñoz Grandes had announced to his staff the impending transfer from the Volkhov to the Neva immediately after his return from the *Führerhauptquartier*. *Radio Macuto* spread the news throughout the division.

Many of the veterans of the winter campaign were already gone. On 21 June, Rodrigo had been promoted to brigadier. He was immediately relieved as chief of infantry. A still unscathed Román followed a much thinner Rodrigo back to Madrid, leaving Captain Bonet in charge of Second of 269. It was an honor. *La Segunda* had a tradition of valor and endurance which was unequaled in the division. Even the Soviet official history of the Great Patriotic War recognized Second of 269 as the best in the division.[28]

Artillery chief Fernández Landa was next. On 2 July, Colonel Bandín assumed his command. A few old faces were, however, still around —at least for a while. García Rebull continued to command First of 269, and Petenghi held on to the Regimental Assault Section. Prado O'Neill remained emplaced on the Island, languidly observing the shell bursts of his Second Artillery Group. The fighting also went on.[29] July had opened with a series of sweeps to the west. Elements from all three regiments—262 (Colonel Sagrado), 263 (Colonel Villalba), and 269 (Lieutenant Colonel Cabrera)—beat through the thickets and swamps rounding up the fleeing remnants of 2 Shock Army. Chewing their bitter antimalaria pills, the *divisionarios* pushed through mosquitoes and underbrush. The sickly sweet odor of corrupting corpses hung heavily in the stagnant air. Starving, the Reds gave themselves up gladly. Some were so hungry they had been driven to cannibalism. Others had committed suicide. A few had managed to link up with the partisans in the woods to the west. To the north, Recon 250 (Cuesta) continued to collaborate with 58 Division collecting prisoners. Spaniards and Germans cooperated in bagging 7,000 officers and men, including the supply and sanitary chiefs of 2 Shock, 44 cannon, and numerous small arms, and masses of materiél. On 12 July, two intelligence officers of XXXVIII Corps picked up General Vlasov.[30]

On 25 July 1942, the feast of St. James, the Spaniards probed. Three assault boats piloted by Germans slid silently over the dark waters. Halfway over, the diminutive *guripa* standing in the lead craft burst into song. The other fourteen Spaniards took up the melodic strains of "Cara al Sol." The six Germans cringed at this breach of security and wondered if they would return home alive after an action with such daredevils. As the three rafts touched ground, the *divisionarios* sprang ashore and slipped inland. Whispering the password "Santiago," the three knots of soldiers regrouped near the road. No one was about. Not a shot had been fired. The Russians had pulled back to their second line. As the launches sped back over the Volkhov, one Spaniard commented, 'It's hardly worth the effort to cross the river any more."[31]

The Reds retaliated on Saturday, the twenty-ninth, raiding the monastery of Iur'evo. The cloister was garrisoned by 1 Section, 2 Company, Antitanks 250, under Oroquieta. Oroquieta, after serving as LaCruz's paymaster, had wangled a combat command. He proved himself that Saturday eve.[32]

Two days later, the Ivans struck before dawn out of Teremets. After an hour and a half of intense artillery preparation, 300 Russians

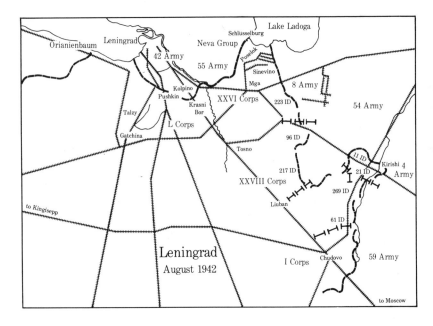

rushed Third of 263 in the Zapol'e sector, now under Lieutenant Colonel Bolumburu, who had replaced Canillas as second in command of 263. In bitter hand-to-hand struggles, he shoved the Russians back into the open. There, caught in the daylight and exposed to shrapnel and machine gun fire, the assault force was cut to pieces. One hundred dead sprawled on the soggy earth. Group Bolumburu lost nineteen killed and thirty-eight wounded.

The predawn attack of 31 July was one of a series of efforts by 52 Army to break northward from Teremets. Only the slim Zapol'e salient stood between that isolated toehold and an extensive Soviet bridgehead stretching from Bystritsa to Arefino. Here, 52 Army also faced Group Robles. Robles, second-in-command of 262, enjoyed the curious distinction of having a Dutch mortar company from SS Regiment *Nederland* attached to his combat group. His heterogeneous unit, however, successfully beat back a determined Soviet assault on 3 August. To the north, 59 Army still menaced Mostki. This elongated strip between the road and the riverbank, running from Bystritsa to Arefino, was all that remained of the enormous Volkhov Pocket. Ringed in by German steel, the Russians would cling to the hard won stretch for the next year and a half.

Eighteenth Army had intended to restore the old HKL on the Volkhov but the impending loss of 250 Division forced Lindemann to aban-

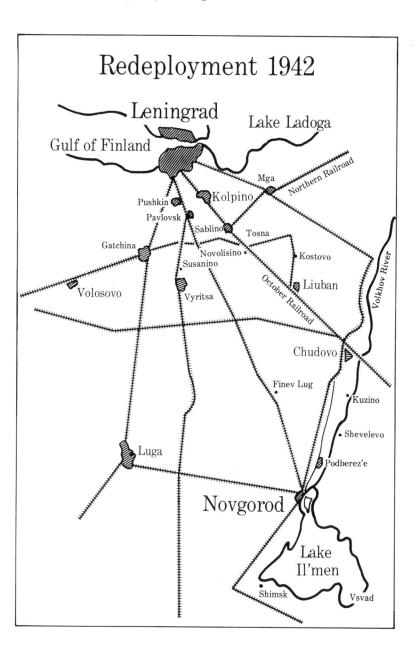

Redeployment 1942

Leningrad

Lake Ladoga

Gulf of Finland

Mga

Northern Railroad

Pushkin

Pavlovsk

Kolpino

Sablino

Tosna

Gatchina

Novolisino

Kostovo

Susanino

Volkhov River

Volosovo

Vyritsa

October Railroad

Liuban

Chudovo

Finev Lug

Kuzino

Shevelevo

Luga

Podberez'e

Novgorod

Lake
Il'men

Shimsk

Vsvad

don this plan.[33] The Blue Division was numerically the strongest
Wehrmacht division in 18 Army. It still had three battalions in each
regiment, and these continued to be maintained by replacements from

the peninsula. Thus, unaffected by the Führer's reorganization of German divisions, 250 Division retained the character of an expeditionary force.

For these reasons, it was necessary to locate a large division to replace 250 Division on the Volkhov. Lindemann frankly pointed out that removing the Spaniards from their sector was risky business.[34] Von Küchler finally had to yank the vitally needed 20 Motorized out of 16 Army at the Staraia Russa front. Last December, von Chappuis was complaining that the Spaniards were a hole in the line; but the hole was obviously much bigger when they were not there.

By Tuesday, 11 August, Recon 250 and Third of 262 from Group Robles were struggling to entrain for the Leningrad front. Cursing because they had to march down the hot, dusty, mosquito-clouded road, the men threw their packs into the waiting cattle cars and tried to tie the heavy equipment down on the flat cars. Exhausted, but elated at the prospect of embarking on a great enterprise, they sang as the trains rolled northwestward along the Novgorod-Leningrad Railway towards Susanino.

> We're leaving Novgorod,
> road to Leningrad,
> fleeing from the mosquitos
> we delightedly depart.

> On the Volkhov front,
> a thousand comrades have bought it.
> And those which have not yet been hit
> Will catch it in Leningrad.
> Will catch it in Leningrad.[35]

Due south of Susanino lay Vyritsa, designated site of the divisional CP. The two towns formed the western edge of an eliptical zone some fifty kilometers south of Leningrad, and barely southeast of Krasnogvardeisk (Gatchina). The division would concentrate here. As the units arrived, the temporary combat groups were to be dissolved and they would be returned to their original regiments. Recon 250 began training at once for an assault on a well-defended city.[36]

Back at Grigorovo, Acting Chief of Staff Goya continued to move the division out. Many of the *guripas* had formed more than temporary liaisons with the local *panienkas*. Marriages, performed with the full ceremony of the Orthodox Church, were common, particularly among the transport troops stationed along Lake Il'men. Muñoz Grandes had refused to recognize the validity of these unions, and lovers were torn apart when repatriation came. Many of the young Spaniards volunteered for another tour of duty so they could remain with their wives. Now, they had to uproot and carry them northward like camp followers.[37]

On Saturday, 15 August 1942, *Requetés* from the *Tercio* of Begoña flocked to the sanctuary of their patroness in a suburb of Bilbao. Spanish traditionalists particularly venerated the Virgin. Carlist veterans of the Civil War gathered annually in their parish churches throughout the Basque provinces on the Feast of the Assumption to attend a memorial mass for their fallen comrades. War Minister Varela, a dedicated Carlist, knelt in the front pew of the dark, packed church. Outside in the sunny plaza, a red bereted overflow crowd closely followed the ceremony. Mass over, the *Requetés*, who always displayed great enthusiasm on such occasions, burst from the small sanctuary shouting "Long Live the King, Javier de Borbón," and other Carlist slogans.

A small group of Falangists, who chanced to be in the square, reacted violently to what they took as a provocative and treasonable demonstration. The Carlists countered with taunts and then fists. Caught in the rush of the *Requetés* and fearing a beating, one of the Falangist youths pulled a hand grenade out of his pocket, yanked the pin, and tossed it into the crowd. The bomb exploded as General Varela passed through the doors of the church. The war minister was uninjured, but numerous Carlists were killed and maimed.[38]

The detonation of the grenade in Bilbao blew open the entire Spanish political situation. An investigation disclosed that the bomb throwers were intimates of José Luna, vice secretary of the Falange and a close associate of Serrano Suñer. Although the Falangists had acted in self defense and the war minister was not the target, Varela demanded satisfaction and punishment not only for the culprits, but also for the Falangist leaders accused of provoking the incident. Varela and other generals began to circulate a petition to the commanders of the military regions requesting their support in "this attack against the Army."[39]

Franco and Arrese toured the north country making conciliatory speeches and stressing that the army and the Falange were pillars of the state. Not a word about the bombing at Begoña, nor the portents of impending crisis, appeared in the heavily censored Spanish press. Nevertheless, thousands of miles away, Muñoz Grandes knew.[40] A constant stream of information reached the general at Grigorovo. He had spun a web of listening posts over the entire peninsula. Friends, sycophants, informers, contacts, veterans of the Blue Division—all dedicated either to revolutionary national syndicalism or self-serving patriotism—supplied him with news.

Esteban Infantes had been languishing in Berlin since mid-June. Hitler's hold order left him hanging in the air. War Minister Varela was urging him on, but OKW would not grant the authorization to continue to the front. Esteban Infantes had written Muñoz Grandes imploring him to intercede. The iron-willed schemer never doubted for a moment that he could dominate his supposed replacement even if he were absent on leave. Accordingly, Muñoz Grandes had written OKH on 21 July requesting the Germans to allow Esteban Infantes to report in at Grigorovo as deputy commander and chief of infantry. OKH refused.[41]

The Germans suspected Esteban Infantes of pro-English sentiments. He was, after all, an intimate of the traditionalist Varela. Whatever the doubts about his dedication to the German cause, Esteban Infantes did have a sound staff record. The fifty-year-old Castilian had entered the Infantry Academy in his home town of Toledo in 1907 at the tender age of fifteen. By twenty, he wore the three stars of a captain. After years in Morocco, where he served as an aide to General Sanjurjo, he returned to the peninsula in 1928 with the rank of lieutenant colonel. He then taught at the Military Academy, newly founded by Franco at Saragossa. With the establishment of the republic and his complicity in the attempt by Sanjurjo to overthrow the new government, he was imprisoned. After sharing the same cell with his fellow *africanista* Varela, he was cashiered. Surprised in Madrid by the uprising on 18 July 1936, Esteban Infantes went into hiding until he was able to make his way to the Nationalist lines. There, he served as a staff officer during the initial phases of the campaign. As chief of staff of the Army Corps of Castile, he performed with marked ability during the battle of Brunete in 1937. His able leadership of 5 Navarese Division of *Requetés* during the closing days of the action, and his energetic staff work at Teruel, earned him the *Medalla Militar Individual*. Promoted to brigadier in 1940, he was appointed chief of staff of the Army of Morocco and then of IV Military District in Barcelona. In March of 1942, his repeated petitions to the War Ministry for active duty on the Russian front were heeded by his friend Varela, and he was designated to succeed Muñoz Grandes. Primarily an organization man, rather than combat leader, Esteban Infantes had a reputation for hard work rather than flair and dash. Muñoz Grandes considered him "obedient and a born subordinate."[42]

It was as a subordinate that Muñoz Grandes was prepared to receive him in the division, if necessary confronting the Germans with a *fait accompli*. The means existed. Only recently, in response to Spanish pressure, the Wehrmacht had authorized a regular courier aircraft to link 250 Division with its rear services and the peninsula. The plane, a Spanish Junkers 52, began its weekly flights in July 1942. Suddenly, on the evening of 18 August, Field Marshal von Küchler learned, quite unofficially of course, that Esteban Infantes was en route and would land in Pskov on the morrow in Muñoz Grandes's own courier service.[43]

Perplexed and outraged, especially because he did not want any Anglophile Spanish generals in his command, von Küchler telephoned OKW for instructions. Keitel wired back within hours that Esteban Infantes had departed Berlin without the Führer's permission. "In no case would the Führer allow" him to replace Muñoz Grandes.[44] Esteban Infantes was to be put under observation as soon as he arrived. OKW was adamant. Esteban Infantes was not to be deputy commander, although he could take over Rodrigo's old post of chief of infantry.

After enmeshing Esteban Infantes in paperwork, Muñoz Grandes went off to bid farewell to the dead. The general was silent as he and his faithful aide Cárcer, drove down the pine covered road from GHQ to the hospital cemetery. His thoughts were on the division and on Spain, and on those who had fallen and the cause for which they had died.

The current political crisis troubled him. He knew that the Franco regime and the forces behind it had the goal of keeping Spain out of the war at any price. Therefore, they were following a passive and contradictory policy in order to mask their intentions. They saw in him, Muñoz Grandes, a danger, and were seeking to turn him aside. His own well known position toward Germany, his strong domestic views, and his clear decisiveness frightened them.

The ruling clique was already taking defensive measures. First, they were sounding out the Germans about their possible reaction to a change in Spanish domestic policy in a Falangist direction. Secondly, the impending cabinet shuffle was designed to draw Muñoz Grandes into the government and isolate him in a ministry. He would be used to insure friendship with Germany. No fundamental changes in either foreign or domestic policy would be made. Thirdly, the reactionaries would take the wind out of his sails by proclaiming his pro-German and social revolutionary policies as their own. He believed that his life was in danger. Either his enemies or the British Secret Service might strike at any moment.

The Opel Admiral ground to a halt at the cemetery. Muñoz Grandes and Cárcer alighted. The general, hatless and with his hands clasped behind his back, began to pace slowly down the rows of crosses. Names, Spanish names, familiar names, lept to his eyes—Navarro, Noblejas, Galiana, Díaz, Méndez, Sotomayor, Moscoso, Gaceo, Margallo. *No hay tierra en el mundo que no conoce tumba española.* (There is not a land on earth which does not hold a Spanish grave.) These were the good ones.

The recent arrivals were different. His First Division had been composed mostly of Falangists and friends of Germany. This Second Division was made up largely of professionals—legionnaires or soldiers. There were even some Reds. In the last two months twenty had deserted to the Russians. The new officers had been selected by Esteban Infantes from the Varela wing of the army. They were ideologically far from National Socialism.[45]

Back in Spain, the dead of Begoña cast a pall on the political situation. On 29 August, the ministers of army (Varela), air (Vigón), and interior (Galarza) tendered their resignations. Pressed to the wall, Franco had to do something. As late as 1 September 1942 Serrano Suñer still seemed secure. Varela, however, had obviously overreached himself. His circular letter to the commanders of the military districts and his subsequent resignation had challenged the authority of the generalissimo. Franco determined to fire him. Serrano Suñer was safe until Admiral Carrero Blanco queried: "Doesn't Your Excellency understand that unless Serrano Suñer also goes everyone will say that it is he who rules here and not Your Excellency?"[46] Franco fired both of them —Varela and Serrano Suñer—on 3 September. José Luna, a social revolutionary and Galarza, a monarchist, were also dismissed. Appointees followed departures. General Jordana, a monarchist and Anglophile, succeeded Serrano Suñer. General Asensio, a pro-German friend of Muñoz Grandes, took over from Varela. Mora Figueroa, an Old Shirt recently returned from Russia, followed Luna. Pérez González, an early protégé of Serrano Suñer, but a loyal *franquista*, replaced Galarza. Franco himself assumed Serrano Suñer's old post of chief of the *Junta Política* and, as such, head of the movement.[47]

Admiral Canaris, who had been rushed to Madrid to evaluate the situation, believed that "the replacement of Varela by Asensio as Minister of War signified a solidifying of pro-German sentiment within the Armed Forces."[48] Regarding German reluctance to accept Esteban Infantes, the enigmatic chief of *Abwehr* recommended that he be left with the division and kept under close observation until, if the Führer wished, Canaris could suggest to his friends in Spain that he be recalled. Like most of the German observers, Canaris suggested a wait and see attitude about the new Spanish cabinet. There seemed, after all, little urgency. Rommel stood at El Alamein. List was approaching the Caucasus. Von Paulus was in the suburbs of Stalingrad.

Likus concurred with Canaris. He advised Ribbentrop that

> the cabinet shuffle was neither a fundamental change of course, nor did it mean a final decision by Franco. It is apparent that the situation in Spain would have been definitely decided if Muñoz Grandes [had been there] to speak with Franco. . . . The entry of Spain into the war would then only have been a case of arranging with Germany the proper moment. It is certain that Muñoz Grandes would have become Minister of the Interior.[49]

Likus felt that the plan of Muñoz Grandes had lost some of its impact, however, due to the departure of Serrano Suñer.

Muñoz Grandes gave Likus his own analysis at Vyritsa on Saturday, 5 September. His first reaction was that, with Varela and Serrano Suñer out, it appeared that Franco was moving on a pro-German course and that Spain would soon enter the war. Thus, he was spared having to intervene with force. On the other hand, time would tell. If this did not turn out to be the case, he would not shrink from whatever action was necessary.

> I have personally no ambitions, but I will place myself in the service of my countrymen when I return covered with glory after the victory [at Leningrad]. I know my people, and know that they will follow when I call.
>
> The new government and my personal friend Asensio will give me a grandiose reception. I will use that moment to demand of Franco, in the name of Spain's dead in Russia, an unequivocal decision. And, he will know that the majority of all Spaniards demand such a decision.[50]

Regarding the new ministers, Muñoz Grandes believed "Jordana to be a man of second rank, a man of honor, an instrument of Franco

. . .; Asensio a friend, a supporter of Germany, [who] I expect to work in the Falangist direction. He is a step forward. Mora Figueroa is a Falangist and friend of Germany. A win for our side, especially since he will make no compromises."[51] Nevertheless, Muñoz Grandes had misgivings about the sincerity of Franco's seeming approximation to the Axis. He "did not exclude the possibility that the cabinet shuffle was merely another political maneuver."[52]

The general was correct. Franco still believed in German victory.[53] Nonetheless, Hitler's visions of grandeur were not entirely shared by the Caudillo. Franco had a better appreciation of the power of the Anglo-Americans and continued to play a double game. He allowed his new foreign minister latitude. Count Jordana was a gentleman of the old school and another of the many *africanistas* in high positions. When the generalissimo appointed his first regular cabinet in early 1938, Jordana received the portfolio for foreign affairs. He held the position until August of 1939. Now, after three years, he was back and, though loyal to Franco, determined on a policy of neutrality.

Immediately upon taking over the Foreign Ministry in the Palacio de Santa Cruz, Jordana summoned Doussinague, chief of the Technical Cabinet in the Foreign Office.[54] Jordana inquired if Doussinague would like to stay on as political director. The energetic legal expert replied that "he would accept on the condition that he would be left free to work for a modification of Spain's foreign policy."[55] As an international lawyer, he did not understand Spain's stance of "non-belligerency." He could not, he told Jordana

defend something he could not comprehend. Neutrality, on the other hand, was something which was well understood. A neutral had obligations, but it also had rights.

Jordana was in thorough agreement. However, before neutrality could be announced, two things had to be accomplished. First, the Spanish press had to cease being pro-Axis and second, the Blue Division had to be withdrawn.[56]

When Ambassador Hayes called on Jordana on Tuesday, 8 September, he was greeted cordially by the new minister. "Jordana made clear his anxiety to have better relations with the United States" and, since the Americans had "observed strict neutrality during the Spanish Civil War," he believed that "Spain should observe real neutrality in the current international conflict."[57]

Franco was not willing to go as far as his foreign minister. The

Axis still semed triumphant everywhere. Perhaps too triumphant. Mayalde, the Spanish ambassador in Berlin, had just transmitted an alarming message.

> If the Germans succeed in occupying Stalingrad, and thereby cutting off all petroleum shipments to the north of Russia, or if Rommel advances [further] into Egypt . . . Berlin will turn again towards the Iberian Peninsula, Gibraltar, and French Morocco. [This is especially critical] taking into account . . . the danger of an Allied invasion . . . and the impressive preparations underway in the United States.[58]

From Washington, Ambassador Cárdenas warned that rumors abounded of an impending Allied effort against the Azores, the Canary Islands, and/or Africa.

On 25 September, OKW resurrected the plans for the invasion of Spain. The new code name—"Gisela."[59] Whether these plans were Allied or Axis, Spain was caught in the middle. Franco tested the waters for peace.

Four days later, Hayes hosted a state dinner at the Embassy for Myron Taylor, President Franklin D. Roosevelt's personal representative to the Vatican. Jordana made his first official appearance. Taylor was returning to Washington after urgent conferences with Pope Pius XII. "Count Jordana obviously liked him personally and was greatly impressed by him, but aside from expatiating on the menace of communism, he was quite noncommittal about Spain's attitude and policy."[60]

When Hayes and Taylor arrived at Barajas Airport the next morning, they were advised that Taylor's flight had been canceled by a "high official." A note from the Caudillo awaited them on their return to the Embassy. The generalissimo wished to talk with Mr. Taylor. The two Americans went immediately to the Pardo Palace. Jordana joined them and they were all ushered into the Caudillo's private study. The room was large. Tapestries hung on the walls. Hayes and Taylor sat facing the windows, between which hung three "conspicuous autographed photographs—the Pope's in the middle, and (amazing company for him) Hitler's on the right and Mussolini's on the left."[61]

In what was obviously a prepared speech, Franco carefully laid out his three-war theory. There were, the Caudillo maintained, three wars under way simultaneously. One was a war between the United States and Japan for domination of the Pacific. In this, Spain was neutral. The second was a colonial struggle between Germany and Italy, the have-nots, and Britain and France, the imperial powers. Spain did not care who won, but wanted her share. The third, and most important, was the war of Christendom against "barbarous and oriental, communistic Russia."[62] In this, Spain was a belligerent. Franco's great fear was that the wars had become merged and that communism would be triumphant. He intimated that the Axis and the Western Allies should seek a peace of accommodation and turn their efforts to the destruction of Soviet Russia.

Within a fortnight, the Spanish ambassador in London called on Whitehall with a similar proposal. On 12 October, the duke of Alba presented Sir Alexander Cadogan, permanent under secretary of state for foreign affairs, with a series of notes which he "described as a summary of Spanish policy [and] which he had compiled on the basis of certain indications he had had from his Government."[63] After pointing out that Spain was not the instrument of any foreign power and emphasizing that his government was merely defending its own national interests, the duke of Alba called Cadogan's attention to the danger of communism. While Franco's ambassador to the Court of St. James carefully introduced the possibilities of peace and called for a united front against Bolshevism, the Blue Division was battling the Red Army at the gates of Leningrad.

Twentieth Motorized Division had begun to dribble into the Novgorod sector during the second half of August. By 27 August, most of 250 Division had been relieved and was on its way to the training area near Vyritsa. As the jumble of companies and battalions detrained at Novolisino, they tramped out toward their unit command posts. By the end of the month, most of the regimental COs, with the exception of recently arrived Colonel Rubio of 269, had their commands well in hand. *La Segunda* was still back on the Volkhov. Reintegration of regimental commands ran simultaneously with a strict training schedule. Operation Northern Light was about to begin.[64]

Field Marshal Erich von Manstein had returned to the Crimea on 12 August. Fresh from vacationing in Rumania, he eagerly looked forward to forcing the Straits of Kerch and hurling his 11 Army eastward. However, a new directive from OKH awaited the now-famous commander. His XXX and LIV Corps commands with some of their divisions were to be shifted to Leningrad for Operation Northern Light. The great guns used in the shattering of Sevastopol were already on their way. Disturbed at the change in plans because he felt that Hitler was, "as usual, chasing too many objectives at once," von Manstein diverted his flight northward to the Führer's headquarters at Vinnitsa.[65] The directives for the assault on Leningrad had already been drawn up. Von Küchler had gone over the main points with Hitler on 8 August. While agreeing that the major effort to breach the defenses would have to be made from the south, rather than the east, the Führer had insisted that house-to-house fighting must be avoided. Eleventh Army was to be employed in the thrust, but von Manstein himself was not immediately designated to take part. Not until 21 August did von Küchler learn that he was to be supplanted by the victor of Sevastopol. Hitler, of course, made the decision personally, and von Manstein was sent scurrying after his army.

Eleventh Army would take over all divisions from Oranienbaum eastward to the Neva. Lindemann's 18 Army retained the Schlüsselburg-Lipki salient and the Volkhov front. Von Manstein arrived breathless on 27 August and set out reconnoitering the front south of the metropolis, which seemed to lie "within clutching distance."[66] The city heart was only twenty kilometers away.

The field marshal's binoculars swept eastward from the Pulkovo shipyard on the Gulf of Finland, past the silhouette of St. Isaac's Cathedral, the pointed tower of the Admiralty, and the fortress of Peter and Paul, to the huge Kolpino works near the Neva, which was still turning out tanks. The siege lines stretched along high ground. Between them and the city in the distance lay a vast peat bog, curving around the southern suburbs from the gulf to the river. The flat, open pasture was crisscrossed with a whole net of field works which were distributed in depth and offered a formidable barrier. It looked far more difficult than Sevastopol.

Intelligence estimated that the Red garrison totaled nineteen rifle division, one rifle brigade, one frontier guard brigade, and one or two independent armored brigades. These could be speedily reinforced by militia from the factories. Manstein would dispose of just over thirteen divisions. However, since two divisions would have to be retained on each flank—Oranienbaum and Schlüsselburg—only about nine and a half could be employed in the assault. None too much. Still, he would have powerful support—the heaviest siege guns in the world, von Richthofen's VIII Air Corps, and several of the new Tiger tanks.[67]

The day after his arrival, von Manstein paid his respects to von Küchler at the latter's headquarters train concealed in a pine forest near Bol. Zaborov'e. Bending over the map table, von Küchler detailed the deployment. His L Corps under Gen. Phillip Kleffel was laid out in a broad arc between the Gulf of Finland and the curve of the Neva; 225 and 58 Divisions faced Oranienbaum, while 215 Division, 2 SS Infantry Brigade (Dutch, Norwegians, Reserve Police, Letts, and Flemings), 121 Division, and SS Police Division held Peterhof, Panovo, Pushkin, Pavlovsk, Krasni Bor, and Nickol'skoe. General Wodrig's XXVI Corps (227 Division, part of 12 Panzer, and 5 Mountain Division), in the Schlüsselburg-Lipki salient south of Lake Ladoga, would come under von Manstein when the attack opened. The two additional corps headquarters (XXX and LIV) and the assault divisions from the Crimea were on their way. Two divisions were available from Führer reserve: 250 and 3 Mountain.[68]

The intention was to break through from the south, advance to the suburbs, then turn eastward and cross the Neva. After cleaning up the east bank of the river to Lake Ladoga, the offensive would skirt the eastern edge of the metropolis and swing north along the lakeshore to link up with the Finnish army standing in place on the Karelian Isthmus. Leningrad would thus be completely isolated and would fall without any costly street fighting. Although Hitler and von Küchler had discussed the use of air power and artillery to create havoc in a burning city during the attack, von Manstein demurred. At Sevastopol, "we learned that the Russians are not moved by terror attacks. Only a slow, steady, and continual bombardment will gradually have an effect on them."[69]

They agreed that the initial phase of the operation—Case George —should be accompanied by maximum air and artillery support. Three corps would open the attack: L on the left, LIV in the center, and XXX on the right. Kleffel's L Corps would storm the key heights of Pulkovo and then move northward along the Pulkovo-Leningrad road while Gen. Erik Hansen's LIV Corps (28 Light, 250, and 132 Divisions) advanced astride the Pushkin-Leningrad railway. Then, Gen. Maximilian Fretter-Pico's XXX Corps would seize Kolpino and, joining LIV Corps in the suburbs, wheel eastward and force the Neva. Von Küchler pessimistically pointed out that he had requested twice as many divisions for Northern Light as were available. Von Manstein, however, believed that "though the force was none too big . . . and the success of the operation was somewhat problematical . . . still, it was up to us to prepare as best we could for the attack we were called upon to make."[70]

The Spaniards were also determined to do the best they could. The long daylight hours allowed plenty of time for drill and instruction. Spirits rose as the men drew new equipment, small arms, and animals. The sight of masses of troops and matériel moving up, the warm days, the welcome absence of mosquitoes, and the sprinkling of undamaged, teaming villages and former country estates, with their well-built houses and picket fences, combined to contribute to a sense of confidence and well-being. Of even greater import, the *panienkas* were friendly.[71]

General Hansen came over to Vyritsa from 11 Army GHQ at Rozhdestveno. Although 250 Division was still attached to L Corps for administration and supply, it was to pass to LIV Corps sometime in mid-September for the attack. Hansen wanted to get to know his divisional commanders. Hansen and Muñoz Grandes hit it off right away. Acting Chief of Staff Goya and Chief of Operations Major Andino listened as the corps commander outlined the plan. Muñoz Grandes would be given the glory he sought.[72] The Spaniards, along with 28 Light and 132 Divisions, were to drive straight out of Pushkin down the railroad line right into Leningrad. Once the outskirts were reached, 250 Division would spread out and shield the flanks of the two German divisions as they wheeled eastward and leapt the Neva. "The success of the attack depends on two factors," von Manstein had stressed in his orders for Case George.[73] These were "the silencing of enemy artillery, which is strong and well emplaced . . . [and] the greatest possible concentration of our own artillery in support of the attack."[74] In order to achieve the necessary fire control, Artillery Chief Bandín and his deputy, Lieutenant Colonel Santos would assume command of all pieces in 250 Division. Hansen pointed out that von Mainstein's experiences at Sevastopol had underscored the necessity of overwhelming firepower. The great railroad rifles, 240 mm howitzers, and mortars, including the monster 540 mm Karl, were taking up their positions. Soon, the guns would open up and smother the Russian batteries.[75] Then, the shock troops would stream forward. Hansen left Muñoz Grandes satisfied, and anxious.

But one of the assault divisions had already been diverted. On 27 August 1942, the very day von Manstein arrived, the Reds unleashed a stunning offensive to relieve Leningrad. A resuscitated 2 Shock and 8 Soviet Armies slammed at the eastern edge of the Schlüsselburg salient. Meretskov had spent all summer preparing the breakthrough. Despite German air superiority, he was able to mask his movements and gain a three to one advantage in men, four to one in tanks, and two to one in artillery south of Lake Ladoga in the Mga-Sinevino sector. A similar Soviet buildup began in the west. The eight divisions of 55 Red Army were to leap the Neva near the mouth of the little Tosna River and roll eastward along the Northern Railroad towards Mga. When the two drives met, the Leningrad and Volkhov fronts would be united and the city would be liberated.[76]

Meretskov opened up on Thursday, 27 August. General Wodrig's XXVI Corps shuddered under two hours of drum fire followed by a ten-minute rocket barrage. Waves of Russians flooded the HKL. An eight-kilometer gap yawned in the German front.[77] For two days, the Soviets streamed forward. Then, 12 Panzer arrived from the Neva and 170 Division was pulled out of XXX Corps and rushed into the hole. Meretskov's momentum slowed and finally stalled. Von Manstein's preparations also halted.

Radio Macuto quickly carried rumors of the battle of Lake Ladoga. The sounds of trucks carrying *Landser* eastward and the low rumble drifting from the Tosna reverberated throughout the bivouac. *"Hay jaleo"* (there's a fight on), whispered the veterans. Von Küchler alerted the division and, on 31 August, ordered 250 Division northward from Vyritsa to Pushkin. Here, Muñoz Grandes was to hold his men in ready reserve behind 121 Division. A Red attack was expected from either Pulkovo to the west of Pushkin or from Kolpino to the east. Since all of the main roads were clogged with German troops marching toward the endangered Schlüsselburg salient, the Spaniards were directed to slip up secondary roads on the night of 1–2 September.[78]

The bivouacs were a scene of feverish activity. Everyone had expected to remain in the training area for four to six weeks. Now, suddenly, in midmorning on Tuesday, 1 September, the order came down to move out! Since the march was to be made under cover of darkness, everything had to be ready by dusk. Rubio got I and III Battalions of 269 underway from Vyritsa at 2130. They marched over the low, rolling hills into Krasnogvardeisk (Gatchina). Gatchina was the first Russian city the *guripas* had seen unscarred by war; gardens, stores, cross-topped, bulbous churches, and even a hotel. The rumble of switch engines and boxcars drifted through the night from the marshaling yards—the supply terminal for the besiegers of Leningrad. Tramping northward, 269 passed the bustling airfield where the Junkers and Dorniers were loading for their nightly run against the City of Peter the Great. Next came the 600-room palace built by Rinaldi in 1766–81 —a West European rococo palace deep within Russia.[79]

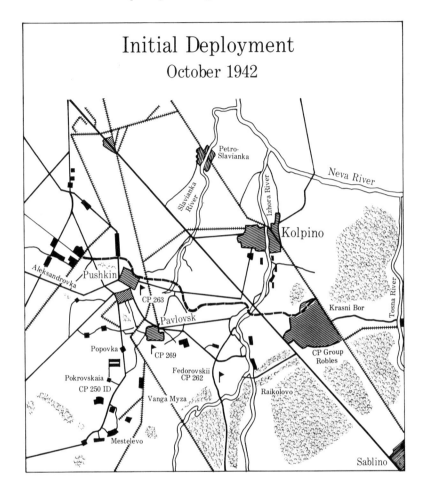

Initial Deployment
October 1942

The *guripas* began to sing as they tramped by the railroad station at Viarlevo which, as the months passed, they began to call *Villa Relevo* (return villa). By Thursday, 3 September, most of the combat units, with the exception of the artillery, had closed on Pushkin. The next morning a group of staff officers, eager to gain a view of the battle, scaled the Pushkin heights. Through the yellowing leaves of the heavy poplars, birches, and elms, they saw a towering column of smoke arising just beyond the tall chimneys of Kolpino. The SS Police were getting hit hard at the mouth of the Tosna. Simultaneously, Meretskov succeeded in breaking through near Mga.[80]

That Friday afternoon, Hitler telephoned von Manstein. He directed the field marshal to take over L and XXVI Corps at once in order to stave off disaster. There was no choice but to "attack and restore the situation" before proceeding with Northern Light.[81] In the south, the campaign was going very well. Von Paulus had entered Stalingrad. The energetic von Manstein took hold. He ordered Hansen at LIV Corps to pull out 121 Division, replace the East Prussians with the Spaniards, and slip 121 Division behind the embattled SS Police as a reserve.

Hansen, accustomed to the dynamic von Manstein, rang up Muñoz Grandes. Relaying the relief order, he explained that 121 Division had to be out and 250 Division in by the morning of the seventh. The sector of the Blue Division would run eastward from Aleksandrovka to the Izhora River. Villalba's 263 would take over Pushkin on the night of 5–6 September. Rubio's 269 and Sagrado's 262 would take over at Pavlovsk and Annalova the following evening.[82]

The general sent Villalba scurrying to the front to reconnoiter. As the colonel drove up the road from Antropshino through the tree covered hills, he realized that he was approaching what had been an imperial capital, the center of the vast dominions of the once-mighty Romanovs. Here, in the countryside around the summer palace of the tsars, the Russian aristocracy had built their villas and dachas, surrounded them with beautiful parks, and shielded them from the roads behind the dense trees.

Rolling down the hill into the vale of Pavlovsk (Slutsk), he passed the great gates leading to the palace of Paul I, son of Catherine the Great. Just beyond, a bridge crossed the Slavianka River and led on to the northern half of the little village. The quaint wooden houses had been the summer homes of the St. Petersburg bourgeoisie. Up the hill and four kilometers on lay Pushkin (Tsarskoe Selo), a town of about 30,000 with broad, straight streets and numerous villas. As the colonel motored down Cadet Street, he noted that the former Hussars Barracks and Artillery Quarters to the left and right had been hard hit by shell fire. Turning right at Admiralty Gate, he was stunned by the magnificence of the great Imperial Palace of Empress Catherine II. The immense green and white rococo building, crowned by the five golden domes of Palace Chapel, lay in an English park just across a large pond. The once manicured gardens were dotted with arbors, triumphal arches, statues, grottoes, picturesque bridges, and artificial ruins. Now, after a year of cannonading, ruins, real ruins, were everywhere. St. Catherine's Cathedral was a shambles. Shell holes yawned in the Alexander Palace. Down past the Triumphal Arch, through the Moscow Gate, and just beyond the Leningrad trolley station, lay the front line.[83]

Villalba returned to divisional GHQ at Vyritsa. Upon reporting to Muñoz Grandes, he was advised of further details about the relief. Gen. Martin Wandel's East Prussians were to leave in place some of their antitank pieces and heavy mortars. With growing satisfaction, Villalba learned that 407 Regiment would turn over two 76 mm and four Russian 45 mm Paks. Neither Villalba, nor his comrades Rubio and Sagrado had anything heavier than 37 mms in their fourteenth companies. His fellow colonels would also inherit two 76mms, but no 45mms. There was also something for Bandín: Artillery 250 received two heavy French 220 mm mortars emplaced near Pavlovsk.[84]

Villalba's battalions were already on the way. Alvaro de Laiglesia, a reporter for *Informaciones*, watched as the long columns swung up the road. With the keen eye of a veteran, he proudly observed the regularity of their formations. As a former *guripa*, he also noted that no one carried a rifle with mathematical precision and that each individual's gas mask cannister slanted at a different angle. To the right and left of the asphalted road rose formidable fortifications. Giant searchlights crouched in dugouts awaiting darkness and the advent of the Red Air Force. Ahead, camouflaged beneath the poplars, huge siege guns stood silent, their mute muzzles pointing north toward Leningrad.

Sprawled in the ditches lay an entire battalion, sipping *café con leche* and munching on bread and cheese, lunch after an early morning march. In their midst, a bubbling field kitchen. Farther on, the sweet sound of an accordion, nearer a knot of *divisionarios* singing a fandango. Their music of the homeland was almost drowned out by the clash of gears of supply and munitions trucks as they ground their way up the grade.[85]

The horses leaned forward in their harnesses as they struggled to move the heavy howitzers. Major Prado O'Neill and II Artillery Group had rolled out of Novolisino at dusk on Saturday, 5 September. All night the caissons rumbled northward. Only eleven months ago, these same cannon had trundled into Novgorod under enemy shellfire. Once again, II Group was lucky. No casualties. Even the long months on the island of the Volkhov had not been very costly. Most of his original cannoneers had been rotated home now, but he still had a third of the officers who had crossed the frontier with him at Irún.

The genial marquis would support 263. While the battery commanders positioned their pieces, Prado O'Neill inspected the observation posts. From Pushkin, the Leningrad skyline leaped to the eye—to the left, beyond Aleksandrovka, rose the Pulkovo Heights, topped by the Observatory; in front, the plain and city; to the right the Slavianka River, more open ground, the Izhora River, and then Kolpino; to the right near Pavlovsk, where 263 lay resting awaiting the cover of darkness. Villalba was ready to move in. So were Rubio and Sagrado. But there had been a last-minute change in plans.[86]

On 5 September at 2200 hours, Hansen ordered the front of the Blue Division extended to the right. SS Police Regiment 2 would withdraw from in front of Kolpino. The Spaniards would leap the Izhora River, cross the Leningrad-Moscow Highway, and close up to the embankment of the October Railroad. This move, dictated because the SS was so hard pressed on the Tosna, transferred to the Blue Division a sector which was eccentric to its main deployment and provisioning routes and directly accessible only by a corduroy road. It could be most easily reached by circumventing the Izhora and circling southward through the woods to Sablino. Once in Sablino, an approach could be made by the Leningrad-Moscow Highway, which led past the town of Krasni Bor, nestled between the road and the railroad. The addition of the Krasni Bor sector almost doubled the divisional front from twelve to twenty-two kilometers. The Krasni Bor appendage was rendered all the more dangerous by Russian possession of the village of Iam Izhora. Believing the shift to be temporary, since the area east of the Izhora would return to XXX Corps as soon as Case George began, Muñoz Grandes decided to keep his center of gravity, as originally planned, between Aleksandrovka and the Izhora. Villalba and 263 were on the left, Rubio and 269 in the center, and Sagrado with 262 on the right. He determined to garrison the additional, disjointed sector with a scratch force—Group Robles, under Lieutenant Colonel Robles, deputy commander of 262.[87]

The Blue Division was thus poised for its temporary defensive responsibilities while the enemy penetrations at the mouth of the Tosna and at Mga were being cleaned up, and ready at any moment to shift in place for the opening of Northern Light. It was much like Novgorod a year ago. Then, too, 250 Division had come into position as an offensive was about to begin, had concentrated for the push, and then seen its sector extended as success eluded the Germans. Muñoz Grandes hoped that history would not be repeated.

The greatest weight lay to the west: 263 and Second Artillery Group (CP Pushkin), First and Third of 269 (CP Pavlovsk), First and Fourth Artillery (CP Glasovo), First and Second of 263 (CP Fedorovskii), Third Artillery (CP Voiskorovo), Group Robles—Mobile Reserve 250 and Third of 262 and Ski Company (CP Krasni Bor). As usual, the Spanish tried to create their own reserves by having two units in the line and one to the rear. Spanish antitanks, divisional and regimental, were scattered throughout the sectors. Muñoz Grandes's CP was at Pokrovskaia.[88]

Villalba was hardly in the line at Pushkin when the Russians jabbed. In the dark early morning hours of Tuesday, 8 September, a mortar barrage hit a machine gun nest of 9 Company of 263 near the railroad station. A Soviet assault squad rushed forward grenading as they came. Cpl. Manuel Fuentes León picked up the bombs as they fell in the trench and tossed them back. Alert as ever, Prado O'Neill dropped 147 rounds on the Red jump-off points to dampen any inclination to push the attack. The Russians retreated. First blood to the Spanish.[89]

While Third of 263 was proving its mettle, Mobile Reserve Battalion began a forty kilometer approach march to the Krasni Bor sector. Sloshing northward in a driving rain from Vyritsa toward Fedorovskii, the legionnaires of 3 Company cursed their luck. The first autumn rains, and they had to get march orders. Captain Oroquieta had received his second pip only last month. He had been immediately transferred from Antitanks 250 to *Tía Bernarda*. By the time Reserve 250 reached Fedorovskii, it was dark. After a brief rest, they crossed the Izhora and relieved the SS Police along the Leningrad-Moscow Highway. Oroquieta's 3 Company sat astride the road embankment, which rose out of the surrounding plain like a great earth wall. In spite of the rain, Oroquieta and his *guripas* refused to take cover. The scene was spectacular. Flashes of antiaircraft guns filled the night. Slender shafts of searchlights crisscrossed the black sky. Multicolored flares floated serenely earthward. "Signs of an active front, much more active than the Volkhov," mused Oroquieta.[90]

Dawn broke, revealing the long rows of Spanish trenches. Immediately ahead, the tall smokestacks of Kolpino came into view, then the great factories and the enemy lines. Fresh earth showed where the Russians were digging two deep antitank ditches before the town. The Soviets were apparently well aware of German preparations for an offensive. Then, as the sun rose higher, Leningrad unfolded before Oroquieta.

Closer to his post on top of the highway, Oroquieta made out a row of dragon's teeth (concrete antitank obstacles) climbing up, across, and down the embankment. This line of cement blocks marked the boundary between him and the enemy in Iam Izhora. Shell holes still marked the salient, scene of bitter fighting the month before when the Reds had shoved the SS out of the village. His own firing pits were shallow and lacked communication trenches and covered approach routes to the second and third lines. As a legionnaire, he did not like the German system of continuous defensive works. He preferred the traditional Spanish device of utilizing the interlocking fire of a trinity of independent entrenchments (*islotes*). This provided defense in depth, required less manpower—one squad per *islote*—and was more immune to enemy bombardment. He resolved, with the commanding officer's permission, to begin reorganizing his sector immediately.

Muñoz Grandes did not care for the German system either. Interlocking strong points rather than a solid line were more to his liking. He surmised that Wehrmacht practice as well as German offensive spirit and plans had precluded their building a defense in depth. They would not begin to do so for months. He told engineering chief Lieutenant Colonel Palomares to get started at once. Although he could not change everything, he immediately began to do what he could to alter the fortifications. The number of listening posts was reduced. These were replaced by crossfire from the front, which was reorganized for mutual support. The economy of forces enabled Muñoz Grandes to beef up the front line, which he backed by redoubts constructed for sheltering reserves. Each field piece was to be encircled by powerful perimeter defense.

Division 250 faced parts of two Red armies—42 and 55. Forty-second Army defended the area from the Gulf of Finland to Pushkin. One regiment of its 189 Rifle Division confronted 263. Fifty-fifth Army held the low ground from Pushkin to the mouth of the Tosna. Ninetieth Rifle Division and elements of 72 Division opposed 269 and a part of 262 in the center of the Spanish line. Units of 56 Rifle Division squared off against Group Robles. Although the Leningrad garrison was better equipped and trained than the Soviet forces before Novgorod, the divisions still averaged only around 4,000 effectives. They were, however, continually reinforced from Leningrad, had ample reserves, and were backed by T-26, KV-1, and T-34 tanks.

Captain Jorreto (G-2) reported that the Soviet entrenchments were continuous and, though only a meter deep due to the marshy soil, were reinforced by logs and well sprinkled with machine gun nests. The entire line was protected by *chevaux-de-frise* (called by the Germans *spanische Reiter*, these were makeshift barriers framed in barbed wire).

Morale was poor, and desertions were frequent. Seventy-second Rifle Division was a penal unit whose troops had been rounded up from slave labor camps in Siberia.[91] The big difference between the Leningrad and the Volkhov fronts, Muñoz Grandes noted, was in the strength of the Red artillery. Three powerful concentrations defended the southern approaches to the city. The Spanish were within range of two of these—Group Pulkovo and Group Kolpino. The assemblage around Pulkovo counted thirteen batteries, while Kolpino was ringed with forty batteries. To these could be added the long-range rifles of the Baltic Fleet and thirty railway batteries in the city.

Bandín and Santos disposed of nine batteries of medium howitzers, three heavy howitzer batteries, one battery of French 155 mm howitzers, and two French 220 mm mortars. In addition, the thirteen companies of the three regiments counted a total of fifteen 75 mm and six 150 mm infantry guns.[92]

On paper, it looked as if Artillery 250 had more than a chance. However, most of the Red batteries were rifles, whereas the Spanish were equipped with howitzers and mortars. They had to sit helplessly and watch trains and trucks stream in and out of the tank manufacturing plants at Kolpino, since nothing they had would reach that far. They were simply outranged, if not outgunned. From the day 250 Division replaced 121 Division, the *divisionarios* found their munitions dumps at Antropshino and their supplies, services, and hospital at Mestelevo under precise long-range bombardment. The Spanish batteries were so effectively bracketed by Red artillerymen that, in order to avoid obliteration, the pieces were scattered.

Tough fighting by the Germans stalled the Red advance toward Mga from the eastern side of the Schlüsselburg-Lipki salient within a few days after von Manstein took over. By 21 September 1942, the Soviet spearhead was cut off. To save troops, 11 Army concentrated artillery from the Leningrad front, including the pieces intended for Northern Light, and pounded the resultant pocket. In the end, a mere 12,000 prisoners survived to surrender. It was a splendid defensive victory. But was there still a possibility for von Manstein to shift back to Leningrad and open Northern Light?

Muñoz Grandes was training his men as if Case George were imminent. *La Segunda* joined these exercises when it finally arrived at Pavlovsk on 13 September. Once again, 269 was united. And just in time. The Russians struck all along the front.[93] By 13 September, the Reds had discovered that 121 Division had been replaced by 250 Division. That Sunday, Soviet propaganda loudspeakers switched from German to Spanish and from "Heimat deine Sterne" (Homeland, thy stars) to "Ramona." The disc jockey was a recent deserter from 7 Company of 262. The Spaniards had made their presence felt by reconnoitering the front. Patrol clashes were frequent. The Reds, knowing that they had a new division facing them, decided to try it out.

A shower of Soviet shells and mortars hit First of 262 at 2200. As the fire lifted, a Russian company swarmed out of the darkness. Caught in a cross fire before they reached the wire, they melted away, leaving dead and whimpering wounded in their wake. Simultaneously, two more companies came on at Third of 262 at Krasni Bor. Group Robles had only scattered wire and mines. The Reds were on the sentries and into 9 and 10 Company trenches in one rush. A hundred Ivans began working their way through the labyrinth of 9 Company's position and 150 more wriggled forward into 10 Company's network. As usual, the Soviets paused to loot—chocolate and cognac were always their undoing. Captains Pardo and Portolés led their companies forward through the dark tunnels. Grenades, knives, and trench spades flashed in the night. Pardo was wounded but refused evacuation. Portolés, pistol in hand, pushed down the black corridors. Then it was all over. The Russians were running. As they retired, Third Artillery opened up from the Izhora and caught them in the open. Panting, Portolés counted his casualties—two dead and twelve wounded. Some of the men had been with him on the Island and in the Volkhov Pocket.

The dapper Portolés, with his pencil moustache and pomaded black hair, was a beloved commander and a genuine hero, the kind men loved to follow. Born in Saragossa, he had served in the Legion. He had returned to his native town to found the local cell of the Falange. Wounded and decorated in the Civil War, he had volunteered to continue the struggle in Russia. Tenth Company was proud of their captain, with his Iron Crosses and *Medalla Militar*, and flamboyant Volkhov *Stock*. They gave their best for him. The Russians left fourteen dead, one gravely wounded, and three heavy machine guns in the trenches. An uncounted number of wounded lay groaning in no-man's-land.[94] Trench raids and patrol clashes continued. So did the relief of the division. On 17 September, Cuesta bid farewell to Recon 250 and departed for Viarlevo (*Villa Relevo*) to lead Return Battalion 7 home. Here, he was joined by the hero of Posad, Major García Rebull.

Muñoz Grandes, already doubting that von Manstein had enough strength left for Northern Light and anxious to improve his defensive position before turning his division over to Esteban Infantes, proposed eliminating the Iam Izhora bulge. On 26 September, he petitioned LIV Corps for permission to storm Putrolovo and Iam Izhora. Hansen came over from Sablino to Pokrovskaia to discuss the plan. Confident that Case George was about to begin, the corps commander was reluctant to launch a signal which might alert the Russians to Northern Light.[95]

Unknown to Hansen, Northern Light was already flickering out. Two days later, on 30 September, von Manstein telegraphed Halder. Citing high losses and expenditure of munition and matériel, he requested delay until massive reinforcements came up. Meretskov's offensive, while failing to liberate Leningrad, had succeeded in snuffing out Northern Light. Hitler, however, was "unwilling to give up the idea, although he was not prepared to set more limited objectives by carrying out 'George' alone. . . . Discussions dragged on and one plan superseded another."[96]

Muñoz Grandes's intuition had proved correct. He would win no prestige before Leningrad. Glory may have been lacking, but death there was aplenty. The three divisional cemeteries in front of the semicircular palace of Paul I at Pavlovsk, near Fedorovskii, and at Mestelevo, were beginning to fill. The advent of the autumn rains, the gray skies, and the sodden, falling leaves made the funerals even more solemn. The trenches turned into a quagmire, the howitzers sank to their hubcaps, and the secondary roads were inundated with mud. The *rasputitsa* had returned.

It was breakfast time on Monday, 12 October. Most of Portolés's 10 Company had drifted rearward in the predawn darkness to gather around the horse-drawn field kitchen which had come down from Krasni Bor. They were cold and huddled together as they crowded around the steaming kettles seeking warmth, hot coffee, and a bit of hard bread. Why worry? Things had been relatively quiet in Group Robles since 72 Rifle Division had replaced 56 Division. Suddenly, at 0530, a hail of artillery and mortar fire burst upon the positions of 10 Company. Dropping their mess kits and canteen cups, the *guripas* dived for cover. Before they could react, the snap of rifles, the staccato of *naranjeros*, and the thud of grenades sounded from left and right. The Russkis! A battalion of Rifle Regiment 133 surged forward. Volkhov *Stock* in hand, Portolés leapt from his bunker and shouted "*Viva la decima!*" With his runner, Arredondo, at his side, the captain dashed up the icy communication trench. The cry of *Urrah, Urrah, ispanskii kaput* mingled with *Arriba España*. It was a nasty business. One *guripa* too close to an Ivan to pitch his potato masher pounded frantically on his face. His comrades pulled him off as they pushed forward. Struggling ahead, they shoved the Russians out of the trenches and followed them into no-man's-land.

By now, the howitzers along the Izhora were lobbing shells into the Russian second line. The counterattack gained momentum. Two of the pursuing *divisionarios* fell near the Soviet trenches, some 200 meters aways. Portolés and Arredondo spearheaded a small party which sped to help. They covered the frozen mud at a bound, but arrived breathless and out of munitions. Arredondo began slinging clods, simulating grenades. A Soviet officer stood up, smiled, and drew his index finger across his throat. Then, he opened up with his submachine gun. Arredondo burst ahead, yanked out his trench knife, and threw himself at the Red officer. He was cut down in midair. But, Portolés's party surged forward and rescued their wounded.[97] Safe back in his own positions, Portolés breathed a sigh of relief. A silent prayer to his own Patroness of Saragossa—the Virgin of Pilar, whose day it was—wafted skyward.

The next morning, Tuesday, 13 October, a column of staff cars sped over the wet roads toward Pokrovskaia. The drivers slowed through the village, then resumed their pace through the woods until they came into sight of the pretentious, two-storied neoclassical hunting lodge which served as divisional GHQ. An honor guard awaited in the drive. The *guripas* snapped to attention as Field Marshal von Manstein alighted. Muñoz Grandes saluted briskly, smiled, and warmly grasped the field marshal's hand. Major Collatz, chief of the Liaison Staff, translated the general's greeting. Then, the Spanish commander escorted his guest up the steps, across the arcaded porch, and into the chateau. He introduced Esteban Infantes, Chief of Staff Colonel Salazar, the recently arrived G-2, Captain Alemany and the G-3, Major Andino. The formalities over, the party strolled past the Services and Intelligence offices and mounted the broad staircase to the general's study.[98]

Muñoz Grandes invited von Manstein to sit down and offered him cognac, coffee, and Havana cigars. Delighted at the aroma of a real Havana, the field marshal leaned back in the upholstered armchair and lit up. The atmosphere was cordial as tobacco smoke filled the ornate, map-hung room. Only three people—von Manstein, Muñoz Grandes and Collatz—were present as they discussed top secret Case George. Fuming, Esteban Infantes and his personally selected staff milled around the Operations and Personnel offices outside. Precise, elegant Salazar, white dickey gleaming, clipboard in hand, stood ready to take notes, should he be needed. Inside, the field marshal and the general discussed the enemy dispositions. Von Manstein, who still had hopes for George, inquired about the training for the attack, made some recommendations, and directed Muñoz Grandes to make certain that his defense was tight. He did not want to lose any of his jumping-off points.[99] The Conference over, von Manstein complimented Muñoz Grandes on the splendid spirit of his men as exemplified by the heroic action of Portolés's company the day before. Corps had noted that there were more than a hundred Russian dead, too many for just a probe. Then, after Esteban Infantes and the rest had been called in for a ritual photograph, the victor of Sevastapol headed back toward Rozhdestveno.

The German buildup continued. Munitions and supplies were replenished. Corps rolled up 300 mm cannon and more French 220 mm mortars between Aleksandrovka and the Izhora. By 28 October, 250 Division was tense, trained, and at top combat strength with 14,626 effectives. Moreover, two march battalions were on the way. The next day, 11 Army rated the Blue Division as an attack division. They were all ready but had no place to go.[100]

Words and plans could not save Northern Light. The great offensive was canceled by the Führer on 19 October. Ten days later, Case George was also scratched. Von Manstein and 11 Army were withdrawn to lick their wounds, while LIV Corps remained and was transferred to 18 Army. German fortunes declined as events moved rapidly. In three weeks of November 1942, the Third Reich suffered a trinity of catastrophes—on 4 November the British took the offensive in Egypt, on 8 November the Anglo-Americans landed in West Africa and began to roll toward Tunis, and on 19 November the Russians cracked the flanks of the southern front, surrounding von Paulus and 250,000 men of 6 Army in Stalingrad within four days. Manstein was rushed to Rostov to try and rescue him, but failed. Hitler would not give the order for Paulus to break out. It was the beginning of the end.

On Saturday afternoon, 7 November, American and British ambassadors Carleton Hayes and Sir Samuel Hoare in Madrid received a mysterious warning telegram "Thunderbird, . . . Sunday, November 8, two a.m. Spanish time."[101] Operation Torch, the Allied invasion of French North Africa, was about to begin. The two ambassadors consulted and decided that Hayes would request an audience with Foreign

Minister Jordana shortly before two Sunday morning. Jordana and Hayes would then present to Franco President Roosevelt's communication guaranteeing Spanish neutrality and territorial integrity.

Hayes, fearing a violent Spanish reaction, prepared for immediate evacuation of the embassy and began burning his secret papers and cyphers.[102] He was worried. In spite of Count Jordana's open desire for neutrality and his dismissal of pro-Axis diplomats such as Count Mayalde, the foreign minister had just warned the ambassador about Spanish sensitivity to any Allied incursion into North Africa. That very morning, Jordana had crisply informed Hayes that "Allied occupation of French Morocco and Oran might force Spain into the war."[103] Now, Hayes was burning his papers awaiting the moment to confront Jordana with a *fait accompli.*

After rousting Jordana out of bed, Hayes returned to the embassy while the foreign minister sped towards El Pardo. The count, who had been informed of the general tenor of the American president's message, rushed in to confer with the Caudillo. As usual, Franco deliberated. He called in Asensio (minister of army), Vigón (air), and Moreno (navy). Then, he summoned Hayes for 0900. The ambassador expressed his gratitude at being received on such short notice. He handed the generalissimo the official communication. Franco had been well prepared by Jordana and Doussinague. He seemed pleased that Spain was not involved.

Allied guarantees notwithstanding, the Germans were still on the Pyrenees. Hoffmann, conspiring in Madrid, had already recommended that, in the event of an Anglo-American landing, "we must rely on our military friends, Asensio, Muñoz Grandes, and Yagüe" to influence the Caudillo toward joining the war on the German side.[104]

Hoffman had followed up Colonel Krappe's visit to Yagüe when he arrived in Spain in early October. Yagüe wanted Muñoz Grandes returned immediately, replacing Arrese as secretary general. He, Asensio, and Muñoz Grandes would form a triumvirate and, after a few months, "go to Franco and force him to make a decision . . . [thus] frustrating the Anglo-American plans in the Mediterranean and North Africa."[105] The gruff, bemedaled warrior was no politician, but he knew where he stood. He demanded that the Germans arm Spain so that it could fulfill its proper role as a Mediterranean and African power.

Arrese, whom Yagüe wished to replace with Muñoz Grandes, was also enmeshed in the German plots. Embassy Councillor Gardemann, working with Ribbentrop and his agent Hoffmann, was trying to get Arrese to Germany under a cover mission to confer with Nazi party leaders. The secretary general would rendezvous with Muñoz Grandes and thereby link up with the triumvirate.[106] Asensio agreed with this plan. Franco was more likely to be influenced by Arrese than by anyone else. The minister of war also seconded Yagüe's suggestion that Muñoz Grandes be released and returned forthwith. Hopefully, Falange and army could be reconciled by combining Arrese with the triumvirs. The Nationalist state could then be guided into the German camp.

The Allied invasion of North Africa accelerated the conspiracy. Arrese struck at the drift from nonbelligerency to neutrality by requesting and receiving Franco's permission to visit Berlin and by appointing Castiella, over the opposition of Jordana, head of the movement's Foreign Branch.[107] Events, however, overtook these efforts.

On 11 November, the Wehrmacht occupied Vichy France and Corsica. The Nazis now held the entire length of the Pyrenees. The next day, Franco prepared to call up the classes of 1941 and 1942 and, perhaps even 1938 to 1940. This would raise the strength of the armed forces to 750,000 men. Three days after that, the Spanish embassy in Berlin reported that Hitler intended to demand passage through Spain. The Caudillo called "his cabinet and, after a full discussion, it was decided that the Spanish government would refuse such a request and that partial mobilization be decreed on the following day."[108]

Hitler conferred with Grand Admiral Erich Raeder on 19 November. The possibility of an Allied strike at Spain was raised. The Führer was worried. He ordered Rundstedt, C-in-C West, to prepare to mine the passes in the Pyrenees just in case, and to build a mobile assault force based on 7 Panzer as the heart of Operation Gisela. But, what if Spain would resist a German invasion?[109]

The same Thursday that Hitler and Raeder examined Germany's deteriorating situation, Ambassador von Stohrer tried to convince the Caudillo that the Anglo-Americans were planning to seize the Balearic Islands. The generalissimo rejected the idea, but pointed out that Spain sorely lacked modern armaments with which to resist any such invasion, should it occur. Since it was clearly in the interest of the Third Reich to see the Spanish armed forces capable of resisting an attack, he would appoint a military commission to prepare a list of required armaments which Germany could then supply.

The chief of state and his foreign minister were, however, more apprehensive about an Axis than an Allied invasion. When von Stohrer called on Jordana a few days later to allay Spanish fears by offering guarantees, the foreign minister ironically replied that a "joint German-Italian declaration . . . [was] superfluous."[110]

Hitler believed that the return of Muñoz Grandes was now imperative. The general was the keystone of the pro-Axis triumvirate and Germany's last best hope for a shift in Spanish policy. Asensio and Yagüe also wanted him home. Arrese, whose visit to Germany had been delayed, was eager to see him. So was Franco. The Caudillo "wanted him out of Germany to put a stop to his intrigues there. . . . Franco . . . described Muñoz Grandes as being in open rebellion against him [and] now disliked and feared him."[111] The sentiment for his return was unanimous.

On Wednesday, 2 December 1942, Count Mayalde and his replacement Vidal journeyed eastward to the Wolf's Lair—Mayalde to pay his farewell respects, Vidal to present his credentials. Vidal also carried other charges from the Caudillo—to request the relief of Muñoz Grandes and to petition for delivery of arms, artillery, and aircraft.

Hitler responded with effusive words of praise for the Blue Division and its commander. The Spanish soldiers, he said, "stood next to our Finnish allies on the first rank of all our allies on the Eastern Front . . . [and] he was reluctant to release Muñoz Grandes, whose capacity . . . and leadership were so . . . excellent that he feared no replacement could equal him."[112] When Vidal protested that other generals in Spain were as capable, that the Caudillo wanted Muñoz Grandes at his side for important tasks, and stressed that the general's sick wife also needed him home, the Führer agreed. As for the weapons, "I will do everything possible. I only await the list which you have announced in order to know your needs. Then I can decide."[113]

With the Führer's permission the general was ready to return to Spain. He thought the time ripe for a brief trip home to get things organized. Cancellation of Northern Light had dashed his hopes for more glory, but it would be different in the spring. In the meantime, the daily drain on the division from raids, patrol clashes, and air and artillery bombardment was depressing. So was the news from Stalingrad, which he hoped could hold out until, like Demianck (Demjansk) in his own sector, the Germans could punch in and relieve it. The winter was hard on the nerves, but at least warm clothing and new equipment had arrived for his men. He was pleased and proud when his infantry regiments, like others in the Wehrmacht, had been raised to the status of grenadiers in early November. The *guripas* seemed to like the new designation, though the German *Landser* were curiously unimpressed. Still, he mused, a few days at home would be good for him. His wife, María, had written that their only son was ill with typhus. Besides, most of his own people had already gone. The relief was almost complete. Even Prado O'Neill and Petenghi had departed. Collatz, his good friend on the Liaison Staff, was also being transferred. On 8 December, citing illness in the family, he formally requested leave from LIV Corps commander Hansen.

Like the good soldier that he was, Muñoz Grandes scouted ahead. His agents not only wrote to him, but also reported in. On 10 December, Castiella came to Pokrovskaia. The general confirmed what had been rumored in Madrid. Franco had offered him a cabinet post or the ambassadorship in Berlin. He had rejected both, because he believed that the reactionaries would use him up without changing their policies.

Two days later, Muñoz Grandes received another and even more distinguished visitor—Admiral Canaris. The *Abwehr* chief had just returned from Spain, where he had discussed the Spanish request for armaments with the German military attachés. He had also visited Air Minister Vigón and General Martínez Campos, inspector general of artillery. Martínez Campos, an "intelligent officer and keen observer," had, as chief of intelligence, cooperated with Canaris during the planning for Isabella.[114] The new position made him a leading candidate to head the Spanish Armaments Commission which would soon leave for Germany. But they had discussed more than weapons. Canaris had been sent to Spain to sound out Spanish reaction to a possible German invasion under Operation Gisela.[115]

The questions raised by the admiral in Madrid had been of such a political nature that Vigón and Martínez Campos suggested he ask Franco personally, or Foreign Minister Jordana. Such a meeting could easily be arranged among friends. Campos, however, did venture his own impressions: "I think that the Caudillo, when it comes to our own national territory, will only make one concession, and only one. If the Allies attack Spain, he will permit German troops to pass through, I repeat, pass through, Spain in order to reach Morocco. . . . If you Germans invade us, we will fight to the last."[116] Martínez Campos invited Canaris to lunch the next day at his own house. He assured the admiral that Jordana would be present. Three hours prior to the meeting, Canaris surprised his aide, Col. Erwin von Lahousen, by drawing up a summary of the impending conversation with the foreign minister.

According to this text, "Spain intended to defend its frontiers against any invader . . . and would fight to the last man to defend its national independence and neutrality."[117] The possibility of Spanish intervention on the Axis side existed, Canaris pointed out, but depended on the fulfillment of seven major points: 1) stabilization of the eastern front; 2) maintenance of the Axis position in Tunis; 3) publication of German peace objectives detailing the future status of Norway, France, Belgium, the Baltic States, and the Ukraine in the New European Order; 4) approximation of the Third Reich to the Vatican and the Christian Churches; 5) assurance that National Socialism would not become a "western variant of Bolshevism"; 6) deployment of military forces for the preservation of Spanish Morocco and the reconquest of Algiers and French Morocco; 7) adequate economic guarantees.[118] Count Jordana arrived at Martínez Campos's house in time for tea. He immediately plunged into a long conversation with Canaris. When the dialogue ended, the admiral signaled Lahousen, and instructed him to code the message and wire it to Berlin. "Without changing a word?" inquired his aide. "Without changing a word," replied Canaris.[119]

The admiral had then flown to Germany and, after a brief pause in Berlin, had proceeded on to Army Group North, supposedly to inspect the *Abwehr* services. Here, he met with Muñoz Grandes. Now, thoroughly briefed by Castiella and Canaris, the general prepared to return home.

The clink of glasses and the sound of laughter filled the warm, well-lighted dining room at the palace of Pokrovskaia. Muñoz Grandes leaned back in his carved chair and smiled. This was his *despedida* (farewell party). That Saturday afternoon, 12 December 1942, 18 Army had informed him that he could fly out tomorrow, weather permitting. Up to now, the winter had been mild, and rain was forecast.

Corps commander Hansen had come over. As he looked at his long, lean host, he wondered if Muñoz Grandes would return. General Lindemann felt that he probably would not. Nevertheless, Hansen had cut orders designating Esteban Infantes as temporary divisional commander.[120] Hansen was still not sure of Esteban Infantes. Only three days before, he had sent his appraisal of Muñoz Grandes's replacement on to OKW. He had been forced into making a comparison.

Esteban Infantes is a kind of obliging aristocrat. He has been trained as a staff officer for the command of large units. He is hard working and of good will. General Muñoz Grandes considers him obedient and a born subordinate. He is not as strong a personality as the present commander, who is an outspoken, front-line fighter. [Muñoz Grandes] makes the officers uncomfortable, but the troops think him first rate. Esteban Infantes is still untested for a crisis. . . . The return of Muñoz Grandes is, however, urgently desired, since he is firmer, more soldierly, tougher spiritually and more pro-German, [as well as] strongly anti-Communist and anti-English.[121]

Hansen's impressions coincided with those of Collatz, the departing chief of the Liaison Staff. Collatz evaluated Esteban Infantes as diplomatic, polished, courteous, and fragile. Muñoz Grandes was "personally very brave," a combat leader who often went to the front in the thick of the fighting.[122] Though he kept his officers on a short rein, Collatz thought, he was open and easily approachable.

A recently arrived member of the Liaison Staff, Paul Alfons, Prince von Metternich-Winneburg, scion of one of Germany's most illustrious families, was very impressed with Muñoz Grandes—"a great personality, a real trooper who could relate to his men. He always ran around without his decorations." Muñoz Grandes's most singular feature was simplicity, Metternich believed. Moreover, when the replacements came up, Muñoz Grandes actually went down to the line and took over companies during local actions. This gave him a chance to know the new men. Esteban Infantes, on the other hand, was "a diplomat. One could not chat with him. He was very politic."[123] Hansen considered the physical and psychological profiles of the two men: one—angular, lean, sinewy; the other—smooth, rotund, soft. One, he knew, had a tough, inner fiber; of the other, he was not so sure. He resolved to keep Esteban Infantes under surveillance, as originally ordered.[124]

The general was up before dawn. Today, if the weather held, he would see the Führer. A brief farewell, a few *abrazos*, and then the Opel Admiral whisked Muñoz Grandes and Cárcer over the slushy roads to Gatchina. There, in the worsening rain a Junkers, motors sputtering, awaited. Gen. Rudolf Schmundt, Hitler's adjutant, showed Muñoz Grandes into the Führer's simple quarters at the Wolf's Lair. Hoffmann, who would serve as interpreter, followed. Hewel was there, and OKW Chief of Staff Gen. Alfred Jodl. A smiling Hitler greeted his Spanish guest effusively. The Führer expressed his appreciation and recognition of the general's leadership of the Blue Division by announcing that he was conferring upon Muñoz Grandes the Oak Leaves to the Knight's Cross of the Iron Cross. It was a signal honor, since that coveted decoration had been awarded to very few non-Germans. Nevertheless, the intention was political, since the Führer hoped thereby to elevate Muñoz Grandes's status. The Blue Division, Hitler went on, was "equal to the best German divisions."[125] Then, the two launched into a lengthy discussion ranging over both political and military questions. The future role of Spain was the main subject. Hitler wanted to know, especially in the wake of the North African landings, if Spain would fight to defend herself against the Anglo-Americans. Only in that case, of course, would he be willing to give her weapons, which were sorely needed elsewhere. France, he said, had betrayed him, and he would no longer defend her interests. Muñoz Grandes was unequivocal, confirming that his country would indeed fight if the Allies moved in, but emphasizing that Germany must reassure his people of her determination to hold Tunis at all costs. At this, the pro-German elements in Spain would take hold and swing her to intervention. As a "son to his father," Muñoz Grandes asked Hitler for advice.[126]

Flattered and oozing pleasure from every pore, Hitler explained that Muñoz Grandes was more important just then in Spain than in Russia, and that he could see that Spanish neutrality as well as intervention could offer certain advantages for their cause. Muñoz Grandes should find out from Franco what would be done with the weapons Germany could supply, and report loyally to him about Spain's attitudes and plans. Despite all the warnings from Canaris and his embassy, Hitler still appeared uncertain whether Spain would defend herself against the Allies and not at all clear whether there would be resistance if Germany moved in. The general left no doubt that he had ambitions to acquire French possessions in North Africa, and the Führer hinted broadly that he no longer had any objections. He stressed that he wanted to shield Europe from the United States and the Bolsheviks, and welcomed Spain as a confederate. But, Spain would also have to play her role, unlike France, and even defend Portugal against the Allies. Muñoz Grandes promised to move his country to the German side, to see Franco as soon as he arrived home, and to use the secret, speedy means of communication through Ribbentrop's confidants. Although neither spoke of overthrowing Franco, it was clear that they had agreed to work hand in hand.[127]

Muñoz Grandes, Cárcer, and Hoffmann arrived in Berlin on Monday morning, 14 December, 1942. They had intended to stay at the Esplanade, but switched to the Hotel Adlon, where Castiella awaited.[128] That evening, the general called on Foreign Minister Ribbentrop. Ribbentrop seconded the Führer's comments. Spain had, he suggested, a better view of the conflict now that the Anglo-Americans had brought the war closer to her frontiers in North Africa. The general replied "that he knew the situation was serious and it was necessary not to lose a moment. . . . For a long time I have wanted to bring our two countries together. . . . There is no use crying over past mistakes. . . . I know that most of the fault is ours. My Fatherland has slept."[129]

"Victory is certain," boasted Ribbentrop. "Our goals, now as before, are to save Europe from Bolshevism. . . . Germany will attack again in the summer. . . . The Slavic mentality knows how to suffer and endure, but is subject to sudden depression and collapses. . . . After that, the bulk of the Wehrmacht will be free for other offensives. We will not permit the Anglo-Saxons to maintain themselves . . . in North Africa . . . which is the sphere of influence of our friends, Italy and Spain . . . France has been relegated to a secondary role there. . . . The Führer assured Serrano Suñer that Germany was prepared to approve Spanish aspirations in North Africa after the war."[130] It was a smooth lie, and produced the desired effect. Muñoz Grandes broke in. "Serrano Suñer kept that to himself," he blurted out, visibly impressed and surprised.[131] "In the battle for the freedom and future of Europe," Ribbentrop cooed, "Spain can play a historic role." "Yes," Muñoz Grandes agreed, "the main purpose of my return is to bring this understanding to the Caudillo and my people."[132]

The next afternoon, the general visited with Jordana's new ambassador to Germany. Vidal's chief concern lay in what Muñoz Grandes and the Führer had discussed at the Wolf's Lair. The general replied— "only military matters."[133] Later that evening, Muñoz Grandes and Cárcer boarded a Wagons-Lits sleeper for Paris and Irún. Hoffmann would join them in a few days.

Muñoz Grandes returned like a king in triumph. Veterans from Russia shared the train with him, many of them wounded. As the cars clacked across the iron bridge over the Bidasoa on 16 December, newspapers all over Spain proclaimed that Franco had promoted him to lieutenant general. It was a sly move, for he was now too high in rank to command a mere division. This was the Caudillo's way of saying that he would not return to the front.

In spite of the general's wishes for a modest reception, thousands turned out even at Irún. Franco sent General Martín Alonso as his personal representative. Also there were Mora Figueroa, vice secretary of the Falange, Aznar, national councillor for health, and a host of other functionaries. A private salon car awaited too whisk him through the night to Madrid. Crowds appeared everywhere to mark his passing, especially at San Sebastián and Avila. There was a brief stop on Thursday morning one hour outside of the capital at El Escorial. Here, his wife María stood on the platform clutching a bouquet of red carnations. Beside her were Colonel Canillas, formerly of 269, now secretary to Asensio, ex–chief of engineers Lieutenant Colonel Ontanón, adjutant to the army minister, and Lieutenant Colonel Barrón, secretary general of the Security Office.

Punctually at 1100 the train rolled into the Estación del Norte. Ex-*guripas*, unable to contain themselves, rushed the still moving cars and, clinging to anything they could find, pressed their smiling faces against the windows. Shouts of *Viva la División Azul, Viva Muñoz Grandes, Viva Franco, Viva la Falange,* and *Gibraltar es español* rang out through the high ribbed vaulting. A human river had been flowing into Onésimo Redondo since early morning. Once again, all of Madrid was there, even Franco's only daughter, Carmencita Franco Polo.

Wearing the same uniform of sixteen months before—red beret, blue shirt peeking over the collar of the olive-green tunic, yoke and arrows embroidered in red below his ribbons, jodhpurs, and black boots—Muñoz Grandes stepped off the train, helped his wife to the platform, and saluted. General Saliquet, commander of the First Military District (Madrid), returned the salutation and entoned the ritual greeting, "*A sus ordenes, mi general*" (At your orders, my general).

Muñoz Grandes had hardly arrived when electrifying rumors crackled through the air. "If he is given command of the Second Military Region (Seville), he will probably attack Gibraltar. If he is named High Commissioner of Morocco, he may invade French Morocco. Either event would mean war."[134] The general was also reported to be especially anxious for the post of captain general of Madrid. Franco, however, had no immediate appointment in mind. Instead, he, like Hitler, bestowed honors.

On 19 December, the Caudillo presented Muñoz Grandes with the *Palma de Plata*, highest decoration of the Falange. It was the first such award since the death of José Antonio. In their conversations, he intimated that there would soon be a concrete answer for the Führer, and that Muñoz Grandes himself might be asked to carry it. That very day, the generalissimo addressed the War College in the presence of the highest army officers. Choosing his words carefully, he said: "The fate and the . . . future of Spain are closely bound to German victory."[135]

Muñoz Grandes was pleased and told Likus later that he believed that speech to be the first result of his discussions with the chief of state. Pressures were being brought to bear. Yagüe, recently appointed to command the Spanish forces in Morocco, had come up from Melilla. Asensio had begun to establish a good relationship with Arrese. But Franco was, as usual, playing a double game.

While Franco ringingly tied Spain's future to the Axis, his foreign minister was in Lisbon negotiating a joint neutrality pact, of which the British highly approved. Both Jordana and Salazar feared involvement on one side or the other. But, their Iberian Bloc was also something more. They foresaw the collapse of Western civilization and a Bolshevik victory. Jordana was ever more conscious of these possibilities.

Winston Churchill had summarily rejected the Spanish offer of mediation proffered by the duke of Alba. Acting under the instructions of the prime minister, Foreign Secretary Anthony Eden had informed the United States and the Soviet governments of Franco's effort. Stalin, who had always suspected the West of perfidy, was not wholly reassured and suggested that the rejection be broadcast.[136]

Muñoz Grandes had ample opportunity to chat with his colleagues during the round of ceremonies which followed his return. On 21 December, he, Asensio, and other high officers assisted the generalissimo in the graduation exercises at the Cadet School at Toledo. The same afternoon, one of the last relief expeditions of original volunteers arrived at San Sebastián. Some of these 1,400 returnees, like many who had come back earlier, immediately set off on a pilgrimage. From all over the peninsula—Seville, Salamanca, Santiago, Madrid, Valencia—little bands of veterans converged on Saragossa to pay homage to the Virgin of Pilar. As *guripas* they had made a pledge to their patroness, now they walked as pilgrims. The Virgin had seen them safely home. In return, they laid their medals at Her shrine.

Homage was also paid to Muñoz Grandes. On Wednesday, 23 December, the armed service chiefs and a galaxy of officers came to honor the new lieutenant general. The next day Muñoz Grandes officiated at the awarding of a command baton to Gómez Zamalloa. The general warmly praised his old comrade who now headed the elite War Ministry Guard, crucial post in any coup d'état.[137] Muñoz Grandes was taking care of his own and showing the veterans at home that he had not forgotten them. The *Diario Official* of the War Ministry announced the formal conferral of the *Medalla Militar Individual* on frail and failing Lieutenant Escobedo, iron Captain Ordás, stout Major Román, and light-hearted Captain Portolés. Sipping coffee in the cafes, many a volunteer felt himself suddenly transported to the Volkhov and the Izhora as he read the announcement. He could see Escobedo storming a machine gun nest or hear Portolés shouting *"Viva la Decima,"* and whisper "I, too, was there."[138]

The military triumvirate had, meanwhile, attracted another member. Asensio now boasted that he was on the best of terms with Arrese. If Muñoz Grandes, Asensio, and Yagüe could really strike a bargain with the secretary general of the Falange, the conspirators would become a junta and power could be theirs.

On New Year's Eve, Franco invited Muñoz Grandes and Asensio for dinner. After the customary concluding toasts, the Caudillo drew Muñoz Grandes aside for a lengthy discussion. The general pressed Franco for a clear decision in favor of Germany. The Caudillo appeared not to be offended. He promised to write Hitler, but he thought that Germany should supply arms so that Spain could defend herself against the Anglo-Americans. Muñoz Grandes hoped that the Caudillo would carry through and that his promises would not dissolve into a plethora of commissions and procrastinations. He really wanted to be a loyal follower and did not want to run the risk of civil war. Franco seemed reasonable. He left wishing that the Caudillo would indeed act energetically and spare him the necessity of a coup d'état.[139]

Muñoz Grandes met with Hoffmann later that very evening and told the German emissary that Franco seemed suspicious of him. The Caudillo appeared to fear his rising popularity and that his friendship with Germany might carry Spain into war. Admiral Canaris, who was secretly spending New Year's Eve at the *Abwehr* outpost in Algeciras, shared the Caudillo's sentiments and hoped that Spain could stay out of the war. He had stopped off to see Jordana on his way through Madrid.[140]

The foreign minister had emphasized that Germany had nothing to fear from the recently formed Iberian Bloc. Spanish policy would not deviate from its previous course. What had changed was the situation in North Africa. The encirclement of Spanish Morocco by Gen. George Patton's army had obliged Spain to mobilize and to initiate an extensive rearmament program. New weapons were an urgent necessity. Spain would like to look to its old friends Germany and Italy. However, Spain was desperate. "If Germany does not understand our needs and does not supply the war matériel we need, since our requests are urgent and important, we will have to look elsewhere, and we will try to obtain armaments anyway we can."[141] Jordana and Franco wanted weapons to guarantee Spanish nonbelligerency through strength. Muñoz Grandes, Asensio, and Yagüe wanted arms so Spain could fight forward and win a place in the sun of the New Europe.

Asensio's feelings were even stronger that those of Muñoz Grandes. The war minister confided to the former Blue Division commander that he was ready to move. "If [you] Muñoz Grandes, are not sent to Hitler with full powers to delineate the conditions [for Spain's entry into the war], I will resign as Minister of War and place myself at [your] . . . disposal. You can count on me and also on Yagüe."[142]

There was no doubt that Yagüe could be counted on. Prior to returning to his troops in Morocco on New Year's Eve, he, Asensio, and Muñoz Grandes had agreed to bring Spain into the war during the summer of 1943. He told Hoffmann that there were, of course, conditions. 1) The Axis must retain control of Tunis. 2) A new offensive must be launched in Russia. 3) Germany must deploy operational forces in North Africa. Assuming that these prerequisites were fulfilled, Yagüe remarked calmly, "Then, Spain will fall on the Anglo-American flank [in North Africa]."[143]

10

The Krasni Bor Crucible

ASENSIO HAD NO NEED TO TENDER HIS RESIGNATION.
Franco was apparently convinced. But without arms there could be no
foreign policy. If Spain were to cover Germany's southern flank and
threaten the Allies in Africa, he had to have the latest weapons. Accordingly, as usual, he temporized.

Epiphany, 6 January 1943, fell on a Wednesday, the chief of state,
following his annual custom, offered a banquet for the diplomatic
corps at the white stone and granite Royal Palace. The Banquet Hall,
hung with Gobelins, its ceiling adorned with the famous *Return of
Columbus from America*, echoed to the suppressed murmur of courtly
conversation. Spanish etiquette had separated the warring factions,
with the dwindling number of neutrals forming a *cordon sanitaire*.
When the dinner ended, the assembled ambassadors and ministers rose
and began to drift about the huge hall. The host, Franco, dramatically
directed his steps toward the British ambassador. Eyes turned, ears
strained. Pulling Sir Samuel Hoare aside, the chief of state launched
into a prepared monologue.[1]

Fear of the spread of communism dominated the Caudillo's
thoughts. "The Russians will not stop at the Rhine if they defeat Germany, no matter what treaties they sign or promises they make. . . .
England, given the development of the predominance of the United
States in the world, would then be isolated. . . . Would not an honorable and advantageous peace be preferable than these extremes?"[2] The
white-thatched, haughty ambassador, smiled, but said nothing. Hoare,

aware of Churchill's rejection of the Spanish offer of mediation and unwilling to disparage Britain's Russian ally, decided not to debate the issue. Instead, he determined to take up the matter later with Jordana. The Epiphany banquet was the last official function for Ambassador von Stohrer in Madrid. His failure to bring Spain into the war and his lack of influence over the new foreign minister prompted his recall. Jordana honored him with a farewell reception.[3] Muñoz Grandes attended the *despedida*, but his mind was on the military commission soon to depart for the Reich. In conversations with Canaris, the general told the *Abwehr* chief that "without arms Spain would be more of a hindrance to Germany" than a help. "We must have weapons" to enter the war.[4] The Spanish armaments commission got underway on Thursday, 7 January 1943. They carried a long initial want list. Moreover, Spain had no reserves of either petroleum or grains, since the Anglo-American blockade had prevented stockpiling. Less than two weeks' supplies were on hand. Von Stohrer had known this and had attempted to convince Berlin. He was dismissed.

The day after the armaments commission departed for the Third Reich, Muñoz Grandes met with Arrese, Mora Figueroa, Raimundo Fernández Cuesta y Merlo—a former secretary general, recently appointed Spanish ambassador to Italy, and Manuel Valdés, vice secretary for services. This gathering of the pro-German clique within the Falangist hierarchy reinforced the alliance forged between the military triumvirate and the movement led by Arrese. Franco, though seemingly slipping to the side of the Axis powers, now sensed his own position threatened.

Meanwhile, von Stohrer's replacement, Hans-Adolf von Moltke, bustled into Madrid. Franco, faced with the new ambassador from the Reich, could no longer temporize about a written answer to the Führer. On the other hand, he had no wish to entrust Muñoz Grandes with the letter. Now thoroughly suspicious of the general, the Caudillo would not dispatch him again to the Wolf's Lair. Instead, he chose to give the missive to Arrese, who was due to depart on 16 January 1943.

Arrese's mission was ambiguous. Although Jordana had informed von Moltke that the secretary general was only going to discuss relations between the movement and the National Socialist party, the foreign minister, upon being prompted, intimated that Arrese might be carrying a letter to the Führer. Muñoz Grandes knew better. There definitely was a letter. The only question was whether it was as strong as the triumvirate wished. In any event, Franco was very close to

Arrese and the former commander of the Blue Division urged the Germans to impress the secretary general with their ability to win the war.[5]

A catalog of official party ceremonies, meetings, visitations to monuments and the Brown House in Munich, bracketed Arrese's visit to the *Führerhauptquartier.* Hitler was a gracious host, beaming in the presence of von Ribbentrop and National Socialist party *Reichsleiter* Martin Bormann, his right-hand man.[6] Franco's letter was delivered with little formality. It was brief, and was far from what had been hoped. The Caudillo hailed the Führer and praised the monumental sacrifices of the German people in their campaign against Bolshevism. He appealed to Hitler as a European to defend the continent against both the Russians and the Americans. He stressed that his own recent treaty with Portugal, establishing the Iberian Bloc, strengthened anticommunism and European unity. He intimated that Germany and Great Britain had no basic differences. He subtly suggested that Germany should seek peace in the West while continuing the crusade in the East. Regarding the arming of Spain with German weapons, he emphasized that Europe itself would thus be further strengthened and shielded. The Caudillo, however, failed to promise that Spain would use these weapons to resist an Allied onslaught.[7] This was not enough for Hitler. Franco's curious omission in refusing to confirm what Jordana and everyone else had made public numerous times, namely that Spain would resist an Anglo-American landing, baffled the Germans.

In the weeks since the new year, Axis fortunes had been declining everywhere. Gen. Mark Clark was preparing a final assault on Tunis from Algeria. Gen. Bernard Montgomery's Eighth Army had occupied Tobruk and Bengazi and was approaching Tripoli. Zhukov, having ringed in von Paulus at Stalingrad, had just been ordered by Stalin to liberate Leningrad.[8]

At the siege lines, Brigadier Esteban Infantes was getting used to commanding the division. After chafing for months under the ill-disguised hostility of Muñoz Grandes, he viewed his liberation with relief and hungered to prove his mettle. Colonel Salazar, white dickey and all, had once again departed. This time for good. Major Andino replaced him as chief of staff, but continued on as chief of operations.

Prior to his departure, Muñoz Grandes had planned a series of trench raids to keep the Russians off balance. These went on throughout December. The Russian winter took hold as the slush turned to ice and the snow drifts piled higher. Everything froze but the peat bogs. Artillery and mortar exchanges were a daily occurrence. The Russians moved up rockets and antiaircraft guns. Portolés, the dapper Catalan hero, fell victim to Soviet shellfire on 20 December 1942.[9]

Replacements continued to flow into the division. Rubio's regiment typified the ebb and flow of personnel which Muñoz Grandes had so decried. Captain Merry Gordon assumed command of 9 Company of 269, while Capt. Salvador Massip and Lt. Francisco Soriano, just in from the peninsula, joined 7 Company of *La Segunda*, and Major Palazón, *La Segunda*'s CO, turned the battalion over to Capt. Manuel Patiño and returned to Spain on leave. Patiño, who had come up with the Fourth Expedition back in April, had won recognition while leading a daring raid late in November.[10]

Christmas of 1942 had dawned black and menacing. The *guripas* celebrated by roasting the few scrawny chickens they could chase down. The dinner at Pokrovskaia was more sumptuous. Esteban Infantes was in a jovial mood. He was on his own. Muñoz Grandes had continued to press Hansen to permit an assault on the right wing at Iam Izhora. Corps had finally approved the project but, at a conference on 8 December between von Küchler, Hansen, Muñoz Grandes, and Esteban Infantes, the designated divisional commander, Esteban Infantes, had recommended dropping the planned occupation of the two villages. He claimed that, since the ground was frozen, heavy casualties would be incurred in holding the newly won positions because the men could not dig in. Hansen replied: "Certainly you can reduce casualties by keeping your men in their bunkers."[11] The air was heavy with irony as Muñoz Grandes and Hansen had exchanged knowing glances. The Blue Division would soon be following a different drummer.

Within three days of the conference, the Reds were digging an elaborate system of advanced defenses in Iam Izhora.[12] Most of the Soviet earthworks were being thrown up in the peat bogs to the northeast of the "bastion"—a heavily fortified position in the center of the Krasni Bor sector. *El Bastión* spanned an old antitank ditch which formed the boundary between Mobile Reserve 250 and Second of 262. To the left of the redoubt—garrisoned mostly by the machine gunners of Captain Arozamena's 8 Company—astride the Moscow-Leningrad Highway, stood Captain Oroquieta with third of *Tía Bernarda*. To the right of the bastion, toward the October Railroad, snaked *El Trincherón* (the Great Trench). Major Payeras had his CP of Second of 262 between *El Bastión* and the October Railroad manned by SS Police.

Payeras and Lieutenant Colonel Robles, the Krasni Bor sector commander, watched with growing apprehension as the Soviet earthworks drew closer.

Esteban Infantes determined to attack. Andino and Robles planned the operation down to the last detail. Robles, a hard-bitten *africanista* who had distinguished himself both in Morocco and in the Civil War, was slated for relief shortly. But he threw himself into the project. The Germans had great respect for Robles. He was known as one of the coolest Spanish commanders. Both on the Volkhov and before Leningrad, in spite of the fact that he was only a lieutenant colonel, Muñoz Grandes had entrusted him with his own sector.

Wednesday, 29 December 1942, dawned clear and cold with a light frost. Captain Iglesia got 6 Company of 262 to the front line about 1130. Packed into the trench, the men stamped their feet, tried to keep warm, and checked and rechecked their rifles and grenades. They were quiet while Iglesia made a last-minute survey. As he slowly swept the trenchscope, he could make out little activity. The Russians should be eating lunch when they hit. Beyond the white plain sprinkled with patches of pine and spruce towered the chimneys of Kolpino. Quiet there too.

At 1325 all hell broke loose. Batteries from three sides of the bulge blasted away. Brown smoke, dirty snow, and dust closed off the horizon. Within five minutes over 500 shells hit the Soviet positions. Then, the range lengthened. *"Al Asalto!"* yelled the officers and sergeants. Stiff after two hours of standing in the cold, the men clambered awkwardly out of the trenches and stumbled forward. They were out in the open now, yelling. Second Lieutenant Mengotti was hit even before he could clear the edge, but he shrugged off the wound and burst ahead crying *"Arriba España!"* By the time 6 Company had reached the enemy wire, the sappers had cut lanes through the barbed rows and were marking passages through the minefields. Suddenly, a sickening explosion threw Lieutenant Muro into the air like a limp rag, to collapse a crumpled blood-spattered heap. His combat engineers, however, kept on, sweeping and lifting lanes through the mine-strewn bog.

The Russians reacted weakly. Many were cut down as they lurched from their bunkers. Six Company had covered the 300 meters at a leap and the blood lust was on them. The fever grew and rose to delerium as they passed their dead and wounded. A machine gun sputtered from the right. The thud of grenades strangled its staccato.

The acrid odor of cordite and the singular smell peculiar to the Russians—a curious combination of sweat and cabbage—permeated the trenches, which contained picks, shovels, broken rifles, and a few battered corpses. The sound of slab and satchel charges filled the air as the sappers began their work of demolition. Muffled whimpers seeped from the shattered shelters. Red Riflemen broke for the rear. The *guripas*, insane with fighting fury, pursued them, jabbing the fleeing figures with bayonets. Iglesia let fly a green and white flare: position occupied. The problem now was how to hold the men. They were hunting down the survivors.

The officers and noncoms frantically called the men off and began driving them rearward. Stunned, the *divisionarios* shouted "Back? We want to go on to Kolpino!"[13] Iglesia knew it was impossible, but the men didn't. He tossed an orange smoke grenade—"mission accomplished, retiring"; the artillery shortened its range, and the gray knots of *guripas* sullenly trudged back towards their own lines. Booty-laden, drained, and exhausted, they tumbled into the trenches.

The entire action had taken only forty minutes. Twelve bunkers and three machine gun nests had been destroyed. Seventy Russians had been "put to the knife."[14] Spanish losses were minimal, six dead, nineteen wounded. A neat set-piece action.[15]

Corps Commander Hansen was pleased. During a conference with General Lindemann on Friday, he observed that Esteban Infantes seemed to have "come out of the shadow of the strong personality of . . . Muñoz Grandes."[16] He seemed hard working and made a good appearance among the troops. Summing up, Hansen was confident that Esteban Infantes could do his job.

A new chief of the Liaison Staff arrived on the morrow. Lt. Col. Wilhelm Knüppel, a forty-one-year-old Pomeranian, was transferred from 268 Division. Knüppel had both staff and line experience, having served with XXXXIII Corps and commanded 483 Grenadier Regiment. He settled in right away at Pokrovskaia and took charge.[17] But German fortunes were declining, even in Army Group North.

Zhukov planned well. Preparations for Operation *Iskra* (Spark)— the liberation of Leningrad—had begun early in December 1942. A repeat of the First Battle of Lake Ladoga, the attempt to join the Neva and the Volkhov fronts, was called for. Early in January 1943, Meretskov met at the Smolny with Gen. L. A. Govorov, Leningrad front commander, to coordinate the details. Meretskov's deputy, Fediuninskii, his new chief of staff, M. N. Sharokhin, and the meddling but forceful political commissar Mekhlis, also attended.[18] General M. P. Dukanov would break the barrier of the Neva with 67 Army while

Meretskov's main striking force, 2 Shock Army (Gen. V. Z. Romanovski), pushed westward from the Volkhov. The two drives would be coordinated by Marshal K. I. Voroshilov. Zhukhov handled the relations between Leningrad and *Stavka*. Dukanov would force the Neva between Dubrovka and Schlüsselburg, annihilate the defenders, meet 2 Shock, and then wheel southward toward Mga. Romanovskii would smash through between Gaitolovo and Lipki, annihilate the defenders, and seize the dominating Sinevino Heights. Should either drive stall, the other would continue until Leningrad was relieved. Twenty-sixth Corps was to be squeezed like a sponge in the twelve-kilometer corridor separating the two Soviet armies. The tactic of annihilation would obliterate the German divisions in their path.[19]

Operation *Iskra* opened with a crushing barrage at daylight, 0930, on 12 January 1943. Govorov had been able to line up 140 cannon, rockets, and mortars per kilometer along the Neva, Meretskov, 160, for a total of 4,500 barrels. The German defenses simply disappeared under this hurricane of fire. Men went mad from the two and a half hour battering. The avalanche advanced. Lindemann threw in his thin reserves, but the Soviets still ground forward through the plowed-up swamp and forest. By 16 January, 18 Army was desperate. All Lindemann had left was a narrow corridor one kilometer wide linking Sinevino and the Lake Ladoga shore. He cast about for anything to shore up XXVI Corps.[20]

Lindemann considered pulling out the entire SS Police Division. The Spaniards would move right to cover part of their line. Hansen objected. This would give 250 Division more than a thirty-kilometer sector, depleting their reserves. "It would be too wide for them to hold in the event of a Russian attack."[21] This turned out to be his last, prophetic warning to Lindemann. Hansen resigned on 15 January.

Hansen had lost the debate with Lindemann. In view of the threatening situation facing XXVI Corps, SS Police would be pulled out to help defend the Sinevino Heights. Over the next few days, 250 Division would shift to the right, while 5 Mountain Division closed to the left. The new divisional boundary would be three kilometers east of the October Railroad at the Bol. Izhorka River. This meant that the Krasni Bor sector would be enlarged to include the entire length of the embankment of the Moscow-Leningrad Railroad and half of the low-lying swamp between the terreplein and the Tosna River, a total of five kilometers of new line.

Esteban Infantes decided to place the entire eastern sector under

Colonel Sagrado of 262. He suppressed Group Robles, since the lieutenant colonel was going home soon anyway, and assigned 262, Mobile Reserve 250, the Ski Company and 2 Company of Divisional
Antitanks the area from Iam Izhora toward the Tosna. Major Castro
and his First of 262 replaced the Germans on the October Railroad
and the peat bog to the east while 9 Battery joined Major Reinlein's
First Group. Sagrado, with his center of gravity shifted eastward, transferred his CP from Fedorovskoii to Krasni Bor.[22]

With the divisional line now thirty-four kilometers wide, Esteban
Infantes sought desperately to find something to use as reserve. Ah,
La Segunda! Captain Patiño and his battalion were resting at Pavlovsk.
After weeks in the line under daily mortar and artillery fire, Second of
269 had been pulled out from Rubio's right wing on the night of 10–11
January and sent to the hamlet.[23] Although the *guripas* were only a
mortar shot away from their previous positions—*los arbolitos* (the little trees), *la trinchera aguado* (the flooded trench), Mari, Sevilla,
Petra, and so forth—life in Pavlovsk was calm. They were glad to get
under a solid roof, sit by a warm fire in the red brick bungalows, and
pick their lice. After an unusually mild winter, the temperature had
suddenly dropped to −12 degrees Celsius during the day, and plummeted to −23 degrees Celsius at night. The distant rumble out of the
northeast had been going on for four days now. "There's something
burning," sniffed the veterans. There were still some fifty oldtimers left
in the battalion of five hundred. Recalling the days of *Caballero* Román and Posad, Otenskii, Teremets, and Bol. Zamosch'e, they muttered, "If they send anyone, it'll be us."[24]

Saturday afternoon, one day after Esteban Infantes had begun relieving the SS Police, the brigadier received another call from Corps.
"Second of 269 is assigned to Corps Reserve and will depart for Sablino immediately."[25] This left only two companies as divisional reserves. And, he now had a long front with an additional sector, an
appendage with eccentric communications. Esteban Infantes was beginning to dread calls from Corps.[26]

Some twenty trucks from the Transport Company pulled into Pavlovsk at 1900. More than five hundred *guripas* milled around in the
darkness, gathering their gear and loading the heavy weapons, radios,
and extra rations. Motors idling, the drivers peered through the windows of their snow-covered cabs. It was too cold to get down and chat.
The men of *La Segunda* worked quietly, no jokes, no singing. Not until
the column got underway at 2000 did they begin to sing.

Headlights hooded, chains whirring, the convoy slipped and skidded over the icy, windswept road to Fedorovskii, across the Izhora, and down the Moscow-Leningrad Highway. The men pitched and rolled on the hard wooden benches inside the packed canvas covered flatbeds. Occasionally, a *divisionario* would cry out that his foot, hand, or leg was frozen. The column halted from time to time as a vehicle spun off the road. Then, it was all out and push. Bruised and battered, the men stumbled off the tailgate at 0900 Sunday morning, 17 January 1943, in Sablino. It was still dark.

Flotsam from the front streamed southward through Sablino and Ul'ianovka. Ambulances, hospital trains, and wounded horses groaned down the highway. Columns of tanks, trucks, sleighs, cannon, and infantry moved northeastward toward Mga. These masses of men and matériel, however, were unable to stem the Red tide. Advance units of 67 and 2 Shock Armies met Monday morning at Poselok 1, seven kilometers south of Schlüsselburg. The blockade of Leningrad was broken![27]

Gen. Werner Hühner and his East Prussians of 61 Division struck northward from Sinevino, snapped the thin Russian ring and rescued their embattled comrades. Facing about, Hühner prepared to break out. Under the cover of all the batteries the Germans could concentrate on the Sinevino Heights, Hühner smashed out and escaped to the south. Lindemann's main objective now was to hold the heights. He hoped that his artillery there could interdict Soviet supply columns as they sought to traverse the newly won corridor to Leningrad. Zhukov was well aware of this. His attack plan called for the immediate seizure of Sinevino.

Orders came down at 0045 on Thursday, 21 January, to truck *La Segunda* to Mga and Kel'kolovo, where Patiño would report to Hühner.[28] By 1330 on Thursday afternoon, the battalion was on its way. The *divisionarios* were well rested, having spent the previous days watching the passing parade, servicing their equipment with the new winter lubricants, building bonfires, singing, and toasting their bread. Now, they were jostling northeastward under steel gray skies through jammed roads to the Sinevino hills. Darkness came at 1500 and, with it, −40 degree Celsius cold. Motors began to freeze, trucks stalled. Patiño impatiently ordered officers to mount another vehicle and push on, while he detailed Lieutenant Soriano to stay behind with the stranded section from 7 Company and the two from 5 Company. They would follow on foot.[29]

The convoy ground through the dark forest. By 2100 they had passed through what was left of Mga and Kel'kolovo. Orders awaited. Captain Aranda led the battalion toward Sinevino while Patiño searched for Hühner's CP. Combat Group Hühner, 61 Division and the remnants of 227 Division, was holding the most exposed northeastern edge of the heights. The *Landser* were strung out along the forested forward flanks of the hills along the Kornaia River. Beyond the frozen stream, the ground fell away to rolling open peat bogs which disappeared into Lake Ladoga. *La Segunda* was assigned to 162 Grenadiers, Colonel Vehrenkamp commanding. To Vehrenkamp's left, facing Poselok 5, lay the shrunken 176 Grenadiers (61 Division), to his right confronting Gontovaia Lipka, the survivors of Col. Maximilian Wengler's 366 Grenadiers (227 Division). While Patiño received his instructions, Aranda and the battalion trudged uphill to the town of Sinevino itself.

Sinevino was a shambles. Loaded with equipment and bundled up like bears, the *guripas* skirted the shattered streets and plunged into the black forest searching for 162 Grenadiers. German officers showed the Spaniards their torn and exhausted *Landser* and confessed that the Reds had crossed the Kornaia and were slipping southward. With that cheery news, they saluted and departed. Aranda checked the compass bearing and slogged on through the snow down a narrow firebreak pointing northward. Soon there were no more Germans. Aranda halted. Suddenly shells screamed in. Aranda and eight of his men fell.[30]

By now it was well past 0100 Friday morning. After locating Vehrenkamp and then thrashing around through the thickets, Patiño finally rejoined his battalion. Calling a council of war, he informed the officers that Second of 269 was smack in the center of a gap in the German lines. They were on the front. They were the front!

In spite of the darkness and the unknown terrain, Patiño deployed. He opened the battalion like a fan, seeking 176 Grenadiers on the left and 366 Grenadiers on the right. While patrols floundered toward the flanks and shells burst in the branches above, Captain Müller led 6 Company to the left, 5 Company of Lieutenant Acosta set up astride and east of the fire lane, while Captain Massip took 7 Company ahead and to the right. Captain Olmedo of 8 Company parceled out his pieces, a machine gun section to each company, the 81 mm mortars near the road between 6 and 5 Companies.[31]

There were no fieldworks. The line had been lost the day before. The *guripas* scurried around gathering logs and branches, throwing them up into parapets, and shoveling snow over them. They built their breastworks facing northwards, but soon Soviet infiltrators began sniping from the south. Patiño found a half dozen shallow bunkers along the road some 400 to 500 meters behind 5 Company. Here, the battalion chaplain and medical officers set up shop. They would be busy. The initial trickle of wounded turned into a torrent as dawn approached. Around 0600, 11 and 71 Rifle Divisions opened up with everything they had—artillery, assault guns, antitanks, rockets, and mortars. The crushing fire fell on *La Segunda* and 366 Grenadier Regiment for two and a half hours.

Patiño's improvised snow shelters gave way almost immediately. As first light flickered at 0900, Müller's and Acosta's positions along the edge of the forest came clearly into view. Massip, more forward and in the open, was exposed. Russian antitankers entrenched in a copse across the clearing began laying their sights on individual *guripas*. Crash-boom, and then death or mutilation. Müller and Acosta couldn't take it any longer. Seeking shelter in the shattered woods, they pulled back toward the CP.

Regiments of Russian riflemen rushed forward as the barrage lifted. Filtering through the stumps, they stumbled on the Spanish positions. Six and 5 Companies held. The Soviets brought up their heavy mortars, blasted away, and then tried again and again. Bombard, rush, retire, the cycle continued all day. Machine gunner Juan Ramírez stuck to his piece although three times wounded. He was hit again. As Ramírez slumped dead over the steaming barrel, his loader shoved the corpse aside and continued firing. The Russians fell in windrows but, confident and flushed with victory, they still stormed forward.

By midday, over one hundred *guripas* were down as were a half a dozen officers. After first aid, the lightly wounded either returned to their posts or pulled the serious casualties rearward on *akjas*—Finnish hand sleds. While the medical officers worked feverishly, Chaplain Freixas scrambled from post to post giving absolution to the living and ministering extreme unction to the dead and dying. Patiño's CP was now in the front line. Telephone communications with 7 Company had been cut since 0930. A few wounded had begun dribbling back all morning. The news they brought about Massip was not reassuring.

Massip had managed to link up with Wengler and his Westphalians during the predawn darkness. Wengler sent over two machine gun crews to supplement the section under Second Lieutenant Casas of 8 Company. There still were not enough to cover the sector. However, Massip did what he could, personally placing and sighting each automatic weapon. Out in the open and confronting Russians concealed in a small patch of woods, Massip had organized his defenses in the traditional Spanish trinity of strong points—*islotes*. He commanded the westernmost *islote*, Lieutenant Castro and Second Lieutenant Abraín held the others. Russian shellfire took a terrible toll. Shapnel struck the captain in the forehead, but he shrugged it off and continued scampering from foxhole to foxhole encouraging the men and helping throw up tree trunks and snow parapets.[32]

Massip was making his rounds as dawn broke on Friday morning. Flurries of movement among the spruce and fir ahead. A regiment burst into the open. *"Urrah! Urrah!"* echoed over the icy glen. Shouting, Massip opened fire. The machine guns spewed death. Corpses piled up before the fragile Spanish front. Beaten back, the Russians tried again and again. Channeling their columns toward the open left flank, they succeeded in swinging to the rear. Seventh Company was surrounded, but the *islotes* held. A machine gunner collapsed in a heap. Massip pushed the body aside, jumped astride the mount, and opened fire. A bullet slammed into his left eye. He reared back and then resumed firing as a mass of bloody pulp oozed down his cheek and froze. Then men cried out "To the rear, my captain," but he refused.[33]

A medic plastered a bandage over his face and Massip resumed his rounds. But yet another bullet smashed into the captain. He pitched to the ground. It was his right leg. The *guripas* cried out "To the rear, my captain."[34] He shook his bandaged head no! No longer able to walk, Massip crawled along the battered line. Second section was gone, blown to bits during the latest bombardment. Abraín and Casas were both dead. Five of the six German machine gunners lay stiff and still. The survivor had just received orders to retire. Massip tried to plug the gaping holes in the line by repositioning his remaining pieces.

The Russians came on slower now. Small knots of Soviets slipped into the clearing. No more mass frontal assaults. With a handful of *guripas*, Massip struggled to close up on Castro. They slid into the snow pit. The long day dimmed. The Russian storming party was only twenty meters away. A few cartridges remained, but that was all. Dragging himself painfully to his feet, Massip pulled the pin on his last grenade and died in the act of throwing. A burst caught him full, strangling his final order "Fix Bayonets!"[35]

News seeped back to Patiño's CP. Wounded survivors haltingly whispered that the Seventh still stood. Vehrenkamp sent news of another sort. They must counterattack. Forming his remaining 200 men into a wedge, Patiño led them forward at midnight. Bitter, hand to hand fighting followed and, in a confused melee, 6 and 5 Companies succeeded in regaining their positions.

By daybreak on Saturday, 23 January, contact had been reestablished with Massip's men. The Seventh still stood, but Wengler of 366 Grenadiers, hard pressed himself, ordered them out as he pulled back. Bearing their weapons, their wounded, and the blanketed body of Massip, the survivors went into ready reserve behind 366 Grenadiers.

Sunday started out as a day of rest. The Russians, however, had reinforced, bringing up 349 Rifle Division to bolster the flagging 11 and 71 Divisions. Luckily Soriano had now come up and, when Vehrenkamp requested thirty men at 0900 to plug the line, the young lieutenant led a section from 6 Company into the gap. The rest of the *guripas* wandered around looking for lost friends, singing, and toasting their bread.

The next day, Monday, it was Patiño's turn to take a section in. He fell wounded. The meat grinder went on. A section in and then an ever smaller section out. On Tuesday morning, 26 January, a shell crashed down on the shallow CP. Six officers, one sergeant, and five soldiers wounded. Three days more of the same. Finally, on Saturday, 30 January, the relief order came. At 0830 the battalion formed up and marched out of the dark woods for Sinevino. A solitary truck awaited. The survivors clambered aboard. There was room to spare. When *La Segunda* fell out on the parade ground at Pavolvsk it mustered 1 officer—Soriano—6 sergeants, and 20 men. Total casualties for the second battle of Lake Ladoga and the defense of the Sinevino Heights—124 dead, 211 wounded, 92 missing, 66 frostbitten, and 12 sick.[36]

General Phillip Kleffel, L Corps Commander, was watching the developments south of Lake Ladoga with an anxious eye. The lean, lanky Prussian saw his corps stripped of artillery and combat-ready units to shore up the Ladoga front. His mixed force on the Leningrad perimeter included 215 Division on the Gulf of Finland and a motley international combination, 2 SS Infantry Brigade, comprising Dutch, Flemings, and Norwegians, the latter on a six-month term of enlistment and yearning to go home before they were swamped by hordes of Russians. On the evening of 22 January 1943 he had inherited thirty-four more kilometers of front and the Spanish Volunteer Division from LIV Corps.

Leaving nothing to chance, Kleffel headed out the next morning at

0915 to meet with Esteban Infantes and Knüppel and obtain a first hand view of the dispositions. The snow fell in shimmering crystals through the light haze over the peat bogs as the corps commander's staff car slid over the roads to Pokrovskaia. He met with Knüppel first, and decided that this was his best link to the divisional staff. Then, he went on to see Esteban Infantes and Andino. They told him that 250 Division had indeed a long front, and that the right wing held by 262 had been broken into two subsectors because of its width. Aside from a shortage of machine pistol ammunition, munitions were in adequate supply and the HKL was well built up. The *islotes*, which the Germans called *Igel* (or hedgehogs), gave good coverage. Esteban Infantes assured him that enemy assaults could easily be shoved back to their jumping off points.

Kleffel went out to Krasni Bor on Monday to check Sagrado's 262. Things did not seem quite so rosy.[37] There was a lack of barbed wire and mines. He reckoned that Sagrado needed at least 500 rolls of wire and 4,000 mines right away. The entire regiment had only four hollow charge shells for antitank use and neither glass smoke grenades nor Molotov cocktails. Sagrado proposed to use light field howitzers against the KV-1s and the T-34s, to supplement his Paks. His Second of 262 had a pair of 75 mm antitank guns. They were the only pieces in the regiment which might be effective against Red armor. Although he did have two Russian 76 mms they were short-barreled howitzers and their shells could not penetrate Soviet steel plate. Neither First of 262 nor Mobile Reserve 250 had anything other than the almost useless 37 mm Pak of which there were a total of twenty-seven in the sector. Kleffel went on to First Artillery Group and met Major Reinlein. There seemed to be an adequate supply of shells for the howitzers for curtain fire, and the cannoneers were prepared to use their pieces against individual tanks. In that case, however, the forty-eight rounds available per battery would hardly suffice. A bit sobered, Kleffel resolved to continue his tour of inspection on Thursday.[38]

The corps commander's observations at Krasni Bor rattled Esteban Infantes. In a general order to the division the next day, 26 January, he demanded immediate counterattack with all available reserves should the Soviets move. Significantly, he decried false confidence. "There is nothing worse than the optimism expressed in the phrase 'everything is all right.' "[39] The same day, the brigadier ordered fortification work to be rushed to completion within two weeks.

Although Spanish morale was high, and both officers and men

showed confidence in their equipment, Kleffel sought out Lindemann on Friday to discuss 250 Division.[40] The army chief was worried about continued reports of an enemy buildup near Kolpino and promised to help out if he could now that things were stabilizing at Sinevino.

Driving hard, Kleffel popped in on Knüppel on Tuesday, 2 February. What was going on in Sagrado's sector, he demanded. The Krasni Bor sector still appeared dangerous. He visited the second line along the heights running eastward through the center of Krasni Bor and along the narrow-gauge railroad from Popovka toward the Tosna. The machine gun nests and light field fortifications were unoccupied due to the shortage of men. The "Spanish riders" were in place, but had not been strung with wire.

The following day, Corps ordered Esteban Infantes to beef up Sagrado with Recon 250 and to move four pieces from First Group and 9 Battery forward for antitank use. Three 75 mm Paks from the Norwegians of 2 SS Infantry Brigade were also detailed to Krasni Bor, to be under the command of German artillery in the area. With the corps commander breathing down his neck, Knüppel reported increased enemy movements near Kolpino. Esteban Infantes, however, was not as worried as Kleffel. He told corps that an attack was indeed in the offing, but that it would only be a holding attack.[41]

The Germans thought otherwise. Field Marshal von Küchler arrived at L Corps Headquarters at Taitsy on Saturday, 6 February. The army group commander was as certain as Kleffel that an attack out of Kolpino straight into the right wing of 250 Division was imminent. Kleffel was moving up all he could, including artillery, but von Küchler felt that 55 Red Army would hit the thin Spanish lines with a tremendous artillery preparation, such as had been employed south of Lake Ladoga, and then penetrate the remaining defenses with armor and infantry. Almost dripping with gloom because he had no reserves to give L Corps, von Küchler drove over to Pokrovskaia. Brigadier Esteban Infantes exuded confidence. It was not reassuring.[42]

Late that evening, in a special order to sector chiefs, Esteban Infantes commanded that as many Paks as possible, except those in the *islotes*, should be pulled out of the front line and emplaced to the immediate rear. Each company was also to send four machine guns, preferably heavies, to this support line. He and the corps commander expected the Soviet artillery preparation to concentrate on the HKL, and wanted to save whatever possible to repel the subsequent assault. Kleffel, therefore, followed up by insisting that the *islotes* in the second line along the Krasni Bor heights be manned with a platoon of Antitanks 250.[43] He instructed Esteban Infantes to send the sappers, Antitanks 250, and 11 Battery over to Sagrado's sector. Kleffel also ordered corps headquarters transferred within a few days to Novolisino, just southwest of Krasni Bor. Moreover, the SS Police would be slipping back between 250 Division and 5 Mountain that very day. Although hit hard at Sinevino, they were still strong.[44]

The buildup at Krasni Bor continued. The additional batteries called for a higher ranking officer. Bald, bespectacled, artillery chief Bandín designated his deputy, Santos. Santos assumed overall command of Reinlein's First Group and 9 and 11 Batteries. As the 150s came up, individual 105s were rolled forward to a support line for direct fire against armor. Santos joined Reinlein in his bunker near the northern edge of the Krasni Bor heights.[45]

Rumors of a Russian offensive were true. The Soviet High Command had to widen the corridor leading from the Volkhov into Leningrad.[46] The Germans still held the Sinevino Heights. Though Soviet engineers had constructed a makeshift railway running into the city, German artillery was only 500 meters distant. Leningrad's land link with the rest of Russia soon became known as the "corridor of death." Shells from the Sinevino Heights tore the tracks into a twisted mass. Nevertheless, on Sunday, 7 February—the 526th day of the blockade —Train 719 chugged out of Leningrad's Finland Station for Volkhovstroi. But the connection was too tenuous, the cost in men and matériel too heavy. *Stavka* determined to enlarge the corridor by encircling and destroying Group Hilpert on the Sinevino Heights.

Two prongs would pinch off Sinevino. Fifty-fifth Army would crash out of Kolpino in the west while Fifty-fourth Army pushed from Pogost'e in the east. The primary objective was the double envelopment of Mga and Sinevino. Should this prove impossible, 55 Army was still charged with a secondary objective—the interdiction of the Sablino-Mga Railroad and Highway, the only supply route for Group Hilpert. Eighteenth Army would then have to abandon the railroad junction of Mga and the dominant Sinevino Heights. The siege would be truly broken.[47]

Whether 55 Red Army smashed down the October Railroad to Sablino or wheeled eastward towards Nikol'skoe, through a break in the forest to the Tosna and the Sablino-Mga spur, the frail Spanish right wing at Krasni Bor was in the way of the steamroller. Stalin was enthusiastic about the plan. He allotted Govorov in Leningrad seven rifle divisions, five infantry brigades, and three armored brigades. Meretskov on the Volkhov had four rifle divisions, four infantry brigades, and two armored brigades. Artillery regiments poured into Kolpino and Pogost'e to support the twin attacks.[48]

"Kolpino is bristling with batteries and armor," Fedor Smirnoff told his Spanish captors over a glass of vodka on the night of 7–8 February.[49] "Thirty tanks are concealed in a subterranean garage . . . batteries are everywhere; the town is full of troops. . . . There is an insistent rumor that a great offensive will soon be unleashed."[50] As Smirnoff spoke, 45 Guards Division began slipping into reserve along the east side of 72 Division in front of Krasni Bor. Darkness and dense ground fog masked their movements.[51]

On Monday, 8 February 1943, Esteban Infantes drove through the light haze from Pokrovskaia to Krasni Bor. The small town between the Moscow-Leningrad Highway and the October Railroad was built on the alluvial fan of the Izhora River. Here, where the Izhora and Tosna rivers broke through the line of hills, the contours changed. Rather than an abrupt drop from the tableland to the Neva delta, the land slowly slid northward. As the Opel emerged from the pine and spruce forest west of Krasni Bor known as the Red Woods, the brigadier could make out the fold in the ground just north of the town center, where the land dropped away to the white, frozen plain beyond. Only a few scattered *izbas* and patches of trees relieved the monotony to the north.[52]

The Opel braked to a stop almost immediately upon entering the town. Sagrado and his staff awaited outside the CP on the edge of the forest. Bowing his general into the *dacha*, the colonel reviewed his deployment. The town itself was substantial. The many brick buildings offered protection for the troops and the numerous civilians who had chosen to remain in their homes. The western subsector had two battalions—Third of 263 and Mobile Reserve 250. Captain Calvo, with Third of 263, held the last of the hill line in front of Putrolovo. At the Izhora, Calvo abutted Mobile Reserve 250 under Captain Miranda, whose Second (Captain Ulzurrún) and Third (Oroquieta) Companies in turn extended eastward across the Moscow-Leningrad Highway. This Izhora sector received close support from a two-gun section of 150 mm infantry cannon from 13 Company of 262, which was dug in just south of the Highway and Iam Izhora. Two batteries of 105s—7 and 8—emplaced behind the Izhora between Samsonovka and the great meander of the river which enclosed a paper mill, provided addi-

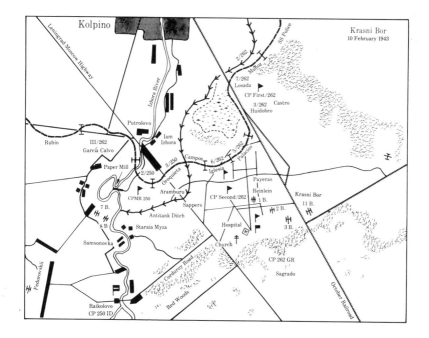

tional cover while 12 Battery (150 mm) fired from Fedorovskoii. Inside the mill's high cement walls, which encircled the log yard, stood the sector's ready reserve, First Squadron of Recon 250.[53]

Beaming with confidence, Sagrado continued. The low lying area between the Izhora and the October Railroad was protected by an elaborate system of trenches called *El Trincherón*. Anchoring on the river in the west, slicing through the highway in the center, and embedding in the embankment in the east, *El Trincherón* extended almost six kilometers. The one possible weak spot, where the line broke at an old abandoned Russian antitank ditch, was backed up by a formidable redoubt of *El Bastión*. This ditch, which swept out in a broad arc south and east of Kolpino and curved from the Izhora behind the Spanish lines, through no-man's-land and on back to the Russian rear, also formed the boundary between Mobile Reserve 250 and Second of 262. Although the snow-filled moat impeded communications, an approach road, shielded from Soviet eyes by white woven mats, snaked parallel to *El Trincherón* and a kilometer behind *El Bastión* and bridged the barrier. Should this open, unprotected trail prove impassable, Sagrado could always receive or send reinforcements or supplies by another log road running through the fringe of the forest from Raikolovo to Krasni Bor.

Sagrado had two battalions in the line, Second of 262 Regiment (Payeras)—7 (Campos), 6 (Iglesia), and 5 (Palacios) Companies; and First of 262 Regiment (Castro)—3 (Huidobro), 1 (Losada), and 2 (Muñoz) Companies; plus strong reserves—two squadrons of Recon 250 and more than two companies of combat engineers. His main disposition lay in the lowlands immediately north of the town, so close in fact that many of his front line bunkers mingled with scattered trees and *izbas* of the outskirts. Major Payeras had placed the CP of Second of 262 dead center between the highway and the railroad. To Payeras's left, near the road embankment, part of 1 Company of Major LaCruz's Divisional Antitanks garrisoned *El Bastión*. Third Company (Aramburu), of Major Bellod's Divisional Sappers backed up the redoubt at the junction of the highway and the covered approach road. Echeloned in the town behind Payeras lay the puny 37s of 3 Company of Antitanks, Reinlein's First Group of 105s and, near the hospital and the regimental CP, the Norwegians. After Kleffel's complaints, each battery of First Group had been supplied with 1,500 rounds. Behind and beyond to the left, well camouflaged by the trees, squatted Reinlein's heavy mortar section, a French 220 mm monster.

Here, in the southern suburbs near the Sablino Forest, Sagrado had concentrated his reserves. Major Bellod with the assault section of the combat engineers was stationed a block in front of the colonel's bunker, while two squadrons from Recon 250 were held in readiness to the right on either side of the October Railroad. Captain García Ciudad, who commanded Recon 250, knew his position was crucial. His dismounted cavalrymen and cyclists not only covered the FH 18s, 150s of 11 Battery by the Popovka Railroad Station, but also the junction between First and Second of 262.

Major Castro, whose First of 262 stood on Sagrado's right, held a rectangular salient rather than a front. Castro's linkage with Payeras at the October Railroad formed an acute angle, then his line ran north by northwest for two kilometers along the double-tracked, six-meter-high embankment, before veering sharply eastward into the peat bogs to join with Regiment 3 of the SS Police. Part of his forces, therefore, faced west; the rest north. Castro had placed his CP well forward in his leftward leaning rhomboid which, unlike that of the SS Police, was devoid of trees. This forest, however, in the German sector did conceal the Blue Division's 9 Battery of 105s. A divisional antitank company and a two-cannon section of 75s from 13 Company of 262 helped cover the dangerous angle, or "Panzer beak," where Castro's front crossed the tracks. Here the peat bog was so soggy that deep trenches could not be dug. Parapets were thrown up. The Spaniards did not have enough time since taking over the line in mid-January to make major improvements. For emergencies, Castro could draw on a divisional sapper company which was on standby behind his CP. The Divisional Ski Company was also reportedly on its way. Castro could use them. He had five kilometers of front. All three rifle companies were in the line. The terrain was ideal for armor and none of the Divisional Antitank Companies were equipped with anything heavier than the 37 mm "door knockers."[54]

Optimism prevailed at Sagrado's CP. After detailing his dispositions to Esteban Infantes, he offered the brigadier lunch. The battalion and group chiefs joined them—chubby Miranda of Mobile Reserve, lean, angular Payeras of Second of 262, preoccupied Castro of First Battalion, bespectacled, scholarly Reinlein of First Artillery, lighthearted La-Cruz of Divisional Antitanks, heavyset Bellod of the Sappers, and cavalryman García Ciudad of Recon 250. All crowded around the table.

Many of the captains and majors were, however, not as confident as the colonel and brigadier. The majority had been on the Russian front far longer than either Sagrado or Esteban Infantes, and were nervous about commanding so many new recruits who had just arrived in fresh march battalions. Moreover, they were well aware of the effectiveness of Soviet artillery and armor. They knew that there were only seven Paks in the regimental sector capable of even slowing a KV-1 or T-34, and three of these 75 mm antitank pieces were with the Norwegians sitting in front of Sagrado's CP. They were in the line. The staffs were in the rear. Esteban Infantes did not tour the front as often as his predecessor. Whereas Muñoz Grandes might pop up at any time, eliciting joy from the soldiers and apprehension from the officers, Esteban Infantes preferred to command through subordinates. His infrequent visits to the sector CP's were formal occasions, generally highlighted by luncheons, such as this one.[55]

Sobered, Esteban Infantes returned to Pokrovskaia. Scratching around for further forces, he ordered Lieutenant Colonel Bolumburu of 263 to alert First Battalion under Major Blanco Linares. They would begin trucking immediately from Pavlovsk to Fedorovskii. Esteban Infantes was still unwilling to abandon his thought that it would be a holding attack. Nevertheless, he now began to fear that, if the Russians should break into Krasni Bor they might wheel westward, cross the frozen Izhora, move on the supply dumps and services at Mestelevo, pin 269 and 263 against the low line of hills and annihilate the division. He directed the transport, service, and sanitary chiefs to squeeze out a couple of companies. As a last resort, he could also call on the 45 officers and 800 men of the Return Battalion under Robles gathering near Vanga Myza at *Villa Relevo*. Although unarmed and anxious to be on their way, they formed a pool of veterans which could be summoned in case of catastrophe. However, since that was unlikely, he decided not to disturb them.[56]

On Tuesday morning, 9 February, with Robles relieved and awaiting repatriation twenty kilometers away at Viarlevo, Esteban Infantes named Lieutenant Colonel Araújo as deputy commander of 262. Araújo was also given command of the regiment's western subsector along the Izhora. The lieutenant colonel posted himself to Samsonovka to set up his CP and contact his battalion chiefs, Captains Calvo and Miranda of Third of 262 and Mobile Reserve 250.[57]

Soviet air activity over Araújo's Izhora sector and the rest of 262 was heavy all morning. A half dozen Red reconnaissance planes roamed back and forth over Krasni Bor. Two fell flaming through the hazy sky. A brief but intensive barrage burst on Pushkin, Pavlovsk, and Krasni Bor. It appeared that the Reds had reinforced their artillery regiments. Esteban Infantes requested a Stuka strike, but Keller's First Air Fleet had no planes to spare. Confirmation of the Communist concentration at Kolpino came at midday.[58]

Two *guripas* threw open the door of Oroquieta's bunker. They ushered in a Ukranian deserter, Evgenii Vereshkin. He was tired and hungry. He belonged to Antitank Regiment 289. They had entered the line before Mobile Reserve 250 the previous night. While the others had been busy emplacing the 76s and 45s he had escaped. Third Company's lines were only seventy meters away so it had been a short crawl.[59]

"Kolpino is crowded with troops. Many batteries are being brought up behind the town. Like the 289, most come from 42 Army or from Schlüsselburg [67 Army]. Trucks are unloading shells everywhere."[60] Oroquieta had heard all of this before. Then, unbuttoning his tunic, the Ukrainian said, "The Reds will attack tomorrow morning."[61] Startled, Oroquieta looked up. Clean, crisp, fresh white underwear showed up against the open mud brown uniform—the Russian tradition of *gimnasterka!* Just before battle the Russians bathed and changed. If death should surprise them, they at least retained the dignity of dying clean. Convinced, Oroquieta rushed Vereshkin off to Miranda at the CP. It was coming and it would be big.

Shortly after the Ukrainian arrived, the Russian batteries began ranging. First the antitanks and divisional artillery bracketed the front. Then, the great guns of Kolpino precisely picked at Pokrovskaia, Antropshino, Mestelevo, Fedorovskii, Samsonovka, Raikolovo, and Krasni Bor. Seemingly only a few stray shells, but Bandín, Santos, and Reinlein understood.[62] At 1300, Spanish artillery observers counted 138 vehicles in a truck convoy entering Kolpino. Eight trains followed. An hour later, the Reds blew up their own mine fields in front of Krasni Bor. Small parties then slid out of the assault trenches and began lifting any remaining mines. Bandín opened fire. From 1400 to 2300 Spanish artillery harrassed Kolpino. The Reds did not even deign to reply.[63]

Night began to close at 1700. Except for the swish of Spanish shells winging towards Kolpino, the front was quiet. From the top of the Moscow-Leningrad Highway, where he had concentrated his antitank defense, Oroquieta watched the darkness lower on the plain. The cold was glacial. He would be glad to get back to his warm bunker. To his left in the flickering sunset, he could make out the positions of Captain Ulzurrún and his 2 Company of *Tía Bernarda* snaking on to the Izhora. To the right, the rest of his own 2 Company, then the old antitank ditch and 7 Company of 262 (Campos). Beyond he traced *El Trincherón* as it rambled toward the railroad. Then, the flat slash of the embankment as it cut the slate-gray sky. A last glance around, a word to the sentries, before hurrying off to his command bunker on the east side of the shoulder of the highway.[64]

Oroquieta had hardly settled down when an old friend burst into the dugout, Lieutenant Blesa. They had not seen each other since the Civil War. Blesa, a signal officer, was accompanied by four German technicians. They carried a telephone interceptor set which could monitor the Soviet communications system. They installed the listening device close to the Russian outposts and began using 2 Company radio to inform Divisional GHQ of their findings.

Back in Pokrovskaia, Alemany (G-2) kept Esteban Infantes informed. POW reports, Russian ranging, mine sweeping, and now the telephone messages all pointed toward tomorrow at Krasni Bor. The brigadier still hoped that it might be only a holding attack. Nevertheless, he instructed transmissions to install an auxiliary divisional GHQ in an *izba* at Raikolovo. Here, on the Izhora, where the log road ran from the river through the Red Woods to the Moscow-Leningrad Highway, he could observe the action and intervene if necessary. He also issued a cheery communique to the troops.

Miranda came up personally to Oroquieta's command post to deliver the message. While the officers and men crowded to listen, the Castilian captain confirmed his plans. The first line would take a beating during the barrage, but the machine guns of Captain Aranda's 4 Company in close support some 200 meters behind *El Trincherón* should survive. If the Russian riflemen broke through, he and Captain Aubá would counterattack with the battalion assault section and 1 Company, which were being held in dugouts around the battalion CP, some 500 meters to the rear. If the Reds hit them with armor, they were in trouble. The CP of 1 Company of Divisional Antitanks under Oroquieta's old friend Apestequi was in *El Bastión* to the right rear, but Apestequi's scattered unit had only 37 mm Pak. On the other hand, Captain Diez-Miranda and his two 150s of 13 Company of 262 behind Ulzurrún should be able to do something with direct fire. Youthful Miranda's usual cheerful face grew serious. The plan was clear. Let the tanks go through, close in, seal off the breach, and stop the Russian infantry.[65]

Pulling himself erect, Miranda smiled, bounded up the stairs, and made for Ulzurrún's 2 Company to the left. Oroquieta settled down again. Suddenly a sentry knocked. "Noises, my captain."[66] Darting up into the icy darkness, the captain could hear the clank of shovels, the clunk of hammers, and Russian command voices. They were digging emplacements for the new artillery. Later, a new sound, the deafening roar of tank engines in the distance. The motors would mutter all night. It was so cold, they could not be turned off for fear of freezing.

A wave of frigid air rolled into the three-meter-deep dugout of Captain Palacios as a runner threw open the door. "Close it, close it or we'll freeze solid," yelled the captain.[67] The courier, wearing white camouflage, bundled from head to toe with duffer, double-pantaloons, and felt boots, extended a heavily gloved hand bearing a blue envelope, a *soldograma*.

Palacios sent for 5 Company's three section chiefs. "Tomorrow the bulls will run," he told them. He instructed them to double the sentries and check their positions, but not to wake the men. "Let them sleep," he mused, "for many it may be their last."[68]

Casually dropping a pineapple grenade in his pocket, in case of surprise, the captain stepped out. Buttoning up until only his eyes, nose, and mouth showed, Palacios passed down *El Trincherón*. The snow-covered parapets of 5 of 262 crossed a long unused secondary road running from Krasni Bor past the frozen frog pond and on to Kolpino. On the left, 6 (Iglesia) and 7 (Campos) Companies of Second Battalion, and then *Tía Bernarda*. An abandoned trench angled rearward from the center of Palacios's line. Should the shelling get too heavy or 6 Company get into trouble it could come in handy. He ordered a squad to clear it of snow. To the right, the railroad embankment towered over 3 Section under Second Lieutenant Castillo. Castillo's section curved to connect with 3 Company of First Battalion commanded by Captain Huidobro. Facing west, Huidobro had his company strung out along two kilometers of the October Railroad and could cover the copse before Palacios with flanking fire. Behind Palacios were a few innocent *izbas*, scattered spruces, Payeras's CP, and the town itself, moving upward to the low heights.[69]

The angle formed by his 5 Company and 3 Company of Huidobro worried Palacios. He decided to move his observation post to Castillo's 3 Section, advised Payeras of the change, and requested more hand grenades and 100 antitank mines. Payeras passed the requisition to regiment, and regiment to munitions dump, at Sablino. Piles of both soon began stacking up on the damp floor of the command bunker. "We'll bring the ignitors and detonators for them next," the supply sergeant cheerfully remarked.[70]

At 2030, three trucks ground out of Mestelevo. By special order, the regular nightly supply convoy to Krasni Bor had left earlier than usual. The lumbering vehicles carried 4,200 rations, up by 700 since the day before yesterday when additional forces had joined Sagrado. For Sergeant Espiñeira this was a well-known route—Mestelevo, Novo-lisino, Sablino, Krasni Bor. He had been in charge of the convoy for weeks and it should be an easy drive tonight. The Ruskis were quiet and the new moon still had two hours before it set.

Juan Negro could clearly see the Kolpino plain. Moonlight danced in the snow. Many of his fellow *guripas* from Huidobro's 3 Company turned out to enjoy the view from the October Railroad. Rumors of a Russian attack had been bubbling for days but, except for the occasional faint sputter of motors from Iam Izhora over in front of *Tía Bernarda* some six kilometers to the west all was quiet. Even the Spanish batteries had now become silent. So still and calm, in fact, that it was unnerving after the usual blast of battle.[71]

Negro's buddy, Juan, an ebullient Andalusian, broke in, "The Russians are going to attack. . . . They're up to something. I bet this quiet won't last."[72] Negro didn't know. It seemed so peaceful. The white plain, the patch of pines a kilometer away where the Russian trenches were and "Look! Look!" whispered Juan, pointing. "The Russians are coming by the thousands." A weaving, zig-zagging ribbon of black dots worked its way behind the woods. "We'd better tell the sergeant." "Don't you think eyes more important than ours are watching?" replied the Andalusian.[73]

Corps called 250 Division at 2300. "The attack will certainly be tomorrow."[74] Ten minutes later, Kleffel followed up the telephone warning with a telegram carrying his final instructions for the coming day. They were based, he wired, on the experiences gained in the Lake Ladoga battle. Shortly before the attack, the front line was to be stripped of most of the defenders, to avoid destruction under the drumfire. As many as possible of machine guns and light Paks should be held in the second line. Better in bad positions here than directly in the HKL in the path of Soviet shells. Heavy Paks and reserves were to be behind the second line. As soon as the front was lost, a counter assault should attempt to regain it. Then, another pullback to the second line for the resumption of Soviet shellfire. Since wire and radio would go at once, coordination was to be by flares. And, of course, good luck was needed.[75]

Help was on the way. In the final hours of Tuesday, 9 February, Lindemann alerted 390 Grenadier Regiment of 215 Division, one battery from Assault Gun Section 226 with five pieces, three assault guns from III Luftwaffe Field Corps, three Flak Companies of two 88s each from III Luftwaffe Field Corps, and one light rocket section from XXVI Corps. The self-propelled guns would be powerful defense against KV-1s and T-34s, and so would the 88s. This all presumed that the Luftwaffe would release the units to the army, always a touchy problem within the Wehrmacht. The Luftwaffe Field Corps, holding the Oranienbaum pocket, could be expected to resist any weakening of its strength and make an appeal to Reich Marshal Hermann Göring's headquarters, OKL—High Command Luftwaffe, if the situation warranted. That would leave Lindemann no choice but to ask von Küchler to request OKH to negotiate with OKL.

As for 390 Grenadiers, they had been scheduled to go up to Group Hilpert, but First and Second Battalions were to be held at the Sablino junction. At 2345, corps ordered the regimental commander, Colonel

Heckel, to go into standby alert as of 0630 the next morning for immediate action in the Krasni Bor sector.[76] Lieutenant Förster, 0-1 of the German Liaison Staff, rang up Sagrado's CP. He informed his counterpart with 262, Franz Jobst, that Heckel would arrive at Krasni Bor on the morrow for a briefing. Jobst had hardly hung up and informed Sagrado at 2330 when the Red Air Force unleashed a shower of bombs over the town. The raid continued for an hour and a half.[77]

At midnight, Padre Pumarino appeared at Oroquieta's bunker. The captain crowded as many of his 196 men as he could into the shelter for Confession and Communion. Then, the *guripas* drifted off to their dugouts for some sleep. Around 0200, Wednesday, the field telephone rang. Shaking himself awake, Oroquieta picked up the receiver. It was Ulzurrún. He had just returned from patrol and had surprised a Russian party cutting wire. Ulzurrún had killed a few and captured a lieutenant. The officer was reticent. Blesa and his Germans hadn't picked up much either because the Reds were rarely using the telephone and, when they did, all conversations were coded. The tank motors were, however, still throbbing.[78]

In his CP near the western suburbs of Kolpino, V. Popov, commander of 1 Independent Armored Battalion, was concentrating on three crumpled sheets of paper. He had made careful notes that afternoon when the final attack orders were given out and wanted to be certain that he understood and memorized everything. Pen in hand, Popov checked the numbered sections of his outline against the 1:25,000 map and underlined what seemed to be the main points. The dispositions of 55 Red Army provided a heavy concentration against the sector of Sagrado's 262.

On the west, 72 Rifle Division (187, 133, 14 Regiments) and 289 Antitank Regiment faced Third of 262 and Mobile Reserve 250 on either side of the Izhora; then, 63 Guards Division (269, 270, 342 Regiments), supported by Popov's 1 Independent Armored Battalion (twenty-one tanks) opposite Second of 262 to the October Railroad. Echeloned behind Popov and 63 Guards was 45 Guards (129, 131, 134 Regiments). To the east massed 43 Rifle Division (65, 708 Regiments) and 1 Red Flag Armored Brigade (sixty tanks). Thus, more than a division would be thrown against each Spanish Battalion. Reserves included 34 and 250 Ski Brigades and 35 Motorized Ski Brigade (thirty-six tanks).

Popov went over the objectives. His unit would support 63 Guards, which was entrusted with the main thrust, between the east rim of Iam

Izhora and the October Railroad. The center of gravity would be on their right wing swinging in an arc to take Krasni Bor and the heights and rolling eastward toward Nikol'skoe. Seventy-second Rifle Division would strike south over Putrolovo and Iam Izhora to the west while 43 Division to the east of the railroad embankment smashed through First of 262 (Castro). A thick forest prevented the attackers from wheeling immediately east and enveloping SS Police, so they had to drive straight south to Stepanovka and Popovka where open ground led eastward to Nikol'skoe. Popov's battalion would reconnoiter as far south as Sablino after the initial breakthrough had been achieved. "Ah," Popov muttered as he came to item 6 on his outline. "I am with the First Tank Company."[79] All was in readiness. The code word was *Raduga* (Rainbow). The Spaniards would be crushed by the steamroller and 55 Army would do its part to eliminate Group Hilpert and liberate the Sinevino Heights, guaranteeing safe passage to Leningrad.[80]

Palacios was fuming. The igniters and detonators for the grenades and mines had still not arrived. He had doubled the lookouts but, aside from some noises of rustling and scraping, all was quiet.[81] Negro watched an army of ants crawling forward. The faint sounds of their muffled movements reached him as he stood in the foxhole between the ties on the October Railroad. Finally, his relief appeared and, stomping his feet to restore circulation, he directed his steps toward the section's shelter on the east side of the embankment. The smell of sweat and stale tobacco smoke hit him as he entered. Everybody was awake, chatting around the stove. He grabbed a sandwich and sat down at the center table. An envelope awaited. By the light of a wick smoldering in an empty sardine can filled with oil, he read the letter from his mother. Words of love and encouragement. Stumbling to his bunk, he dropped in fully clothed and slept.

"Come on! Come on! To your post! Haven't you slept enough? Let's go! Let's go! Hurry!" shouted the sergeant.[82] Negro seized his rifle and helmet, stuffed his mother's letter in his pocket, and rushed up the stairs. Dawn was just breaking. Although the sun had not risen, the first rays illuminated the white plain to the west. The sky was clear. He dashed down the rails and jumped into the machine gun nest. He was the first loader for 3 Section. Silence, and it was still. The smoke from the bunkers drifted slowly upward. The gunner told him that Captain Huidobro and a corporal had crawled out with a mining party into no-man's-land during the predawn darkness and had lain there listening. Just a few noises from the left, that was all. Maybe he had dreamed about the army of ants last night.

Out of Negro's line of sight, but showing clearly in the binoculars of the artillery observers, thirteen KV-1s and T-34s crept toward 5 and 6 Companies.[83] The sergeants and corporals ran down the line. "Everyone to the bunkers except those on duty."[84] It was Negro's turn to stand to. Glancing down the tracks where the four 37 mm Paks were dug in along the west side of the shoulder, he could see nothing out of the ordinary. At the end of the line, 1 Company under Captain Losada took over. Unknown to Negro, Losada was cooly observing forty Soviet tanks debouching from Kolpino to take up positions on either side of the October Railroad. SS Police confirmed the sighting, twenty tanks east of the embankment. By turning his head, Negro could make out the positions of 1 and 2 Companies in the Panzer beak. Here, in the peat bogs to the northeast, where First (Losada) and Second (Muñoz) Companies tied on to the Germans, it was also calm. Suddenly a hissing sound. A red flare rocketed skyward over the Russian lines.[85]

It was 0645, Wednesday, 10 February 1943. Kolpino erupted like an angry volcano. Eight hundred barrels spewed fire over Sagrado's sector. The earth shook and heaved. "Where snow had lain the fierce heat laid bare the scarred grass, and a moment later grass and topsoil as well disappeared. A landscape like the mountains of the moon was created."[86] Oroquieta had just picked up the field telephone to answer Ulzurrún when the hammer hit. They could not hear each other. Even three meters down, the roar was deafening. So many guns were firing at once that it was impossible to distinguish the individual discharges. Dust shaken loose from the shelter ceiling filtered downward choking the assault section. Oroquieta cranked the field phone. Nothing! The lines to Miranda had already gone.[87] The drumfire caught Palacios strolling down *El Trincherón* sucking on a lemon. The pines burst into flame like giant Roman candles. Shell flashes blinded him, but within seconds even they were obscured by a dirty gray cloud of peat, smoke, and ice crystals which cut visibility to less than a meter. The acrid odor of cordite strangled him. The trench collapsed. The command bunker disappeared. The telephones went. Only ten minutes had passed.[88]

Oily, black smoke shrouded the front. "Spanish riders," barbed wire dangling, galloped through the air. Beams, planks, rifles, machine guns, antitank pieces, hurtled skyward, fell down, and rose again. Stray arms and legs sailed through the fire storm. Here and there a headless torso bounced back to earth. Men went mad. Shell after shell thudded into the railroad embankment. But the well-packed barrier shrugged off the bombardment. Just before he had to put his head down for good, Negro had seen pinpoints of light winking to the rear. The Spanish batteries were replying. The men of 3 Company cheered. First Group fought back, firing as fast as it could. Third Group joined in, and so did the German batteries, but they were hopelessly outgunned. As the dust cloud raced toward him, Negro caught a glimpse of the front. The rust-red dots of the Soviet shells were concentrating on 5 and 6 Companies. "The dots expanded, devoured the smoke, clawed at the sky, rose into a steep cliff of red fire."[89] Negro flattened out in the bottom of the trench. Like the rest of the *guripas*, he was standing to awaiting imminent assault. The sergeants and corporals pushed down the passage distributing cognac and cheering the men. It was cold, −30 degrees Celsius.

Casualties were still light in 3 Company. Even when Stalin's Organs began to play, the terreplein hardly trembled. Huidobro came by from the antitank observation post. Though communication with Major Castro's CP had been cut, he still had a line back to the batteries. He had just called in artillery on the copse where the Reds were massing in front of Palacios and Iglesia.[90]

Iglesia was dead. He had been one of the first. Cannon shells ploughed in their flat trajectories toward the trenches and bunkers of 6 Company. Mortars and howitzers sent their deadly missiles arcing over the positions. Exploding charges scattered hot, screaming metal while clods of peat flew in every direction. Bodies soon littered the tortured ground while the bleeding survivors hugged the warm mud of gaping shell holes or staggered aimlessly toward nowhere, seeking shelter. There was no more 6 Company.

Sweating, in spite of the cold, the cannoneers of First Group loaded and fired at a rate beyond belief. No one thought of rest. Responding to the report of the thirteen tanks in front of 5 and 6 Companies, they shortened their range at 0730. Bursts covered the iron monsters with mud and fragments. Clumsily, the KV-1s and T-34s pivoted rearward and then, firing their 76s, fell into file paralleling the torn and heaving remnants of *El Trincherón*. Crouching over the trembling firing table in his command bunker, Reinlein strained to hear the incoming messages from the forward observers. Most of the telephone lines were gone, but some of the radios still crackled. Behind Reinlein, near the entryway, stood Lieutenant Colonel Santos and his staff. A flash of light, a deafening explosion, the crush of concussion. Santos, a captain, and three lieutenants fell, their flesh ripped and riddled by searing shrapnel.[91]

Overhead the fire storm raged on engulfing everything from the front to the forest. Some of Reinlein's guns were gone, swamped in a sea of steel. First and Second Companies on the Panzer beak were calling desperately for fire support. Losada's and Muñoz's parapets had disintegrated at the first tap of the Russian hammer. The flotsam of battle flowed back.

Huidobro scooped up the stragglers as they stumbled past. Most were wounded. Many were unarmed. All were dazed. Some bore the blank, uncomprehending look of a hurt child. Huidobro sorted them out and sent the lightly wounded into the trenches along the embankment. Some refused to stop. Raw recruits, they fled to safety. The sky was still dark with shells. It was terrifying even at Pokrovskaia.[92]

Esteban Infantes had spent a sleepless night. The blows of the barrage rolled southward, rattling the blacked out windows of the palace. A few minutes after 0645 Captain Calvo called from Third of 262 to confirm the intensity of the cannonade. He reported that 187 Regiment of 72 Division seemed exceptionally somnolent when compared with the rest of the front. The brigadier sat at his desk, listening. Time ticked by: ten minutes, twenty, a half an hour, an hour. The study still reverberated to the *redoble de tambor* (drumfire). Was this really only a holding attack?

Around 0800 the sound seemed to shift. Esteban Infantes, now convinced that the major effort was on Krasni Bor, told Bolumburu who had sent Blanco's First of 263 over two days before, to alert 9 Company. Rubio was also to rush reinforcements from 269 eastward to the Izhora. *La Segunda*, under Captain Merry Gordon—farther away from Scotland than his ancestors of the Catholic clan had ever imagined—fell out for action at 0800.[93] Pulling on his gloves, the divisional commander called for his limousine and departed for the advance observation post at Raikolovo.[94] Closely followed by an escort car, the Opel Admiral sped north toward Pavlovsk. This was the easiest route to the Izhora. Inside, Esteban Infantes fretted. His two companions, Chief of Staff Andino and the general's nephew, GHQs interpreter, were silent. The brigadier urged the driver on. Short of Pavlovsk a curtain of fire covered the road. Skidding about, the convoy made for Antropshino, where a secondary route ran to Fedorovskii and Raikolovo. Antropshino was a shambles. Burning trucks, crumbled carts, and screaming horses lay scattered along the main street. *Izbas* flamed along the way. The hurricane had hit and hurried on. Picking its way through the wreckage, the Opel took the turn to Fedorovskii. The brigadier's watch marked 0830.

The two cars bounced eastward over the rough corduroy road. The sun was up now. Light snow punctuated a hazy, gray sky. A warning shout. Aircraft! Braking to a sliding stop, the passengers threw themselves out of the doors and plunged face down in the snow along the shoulder. Esteban Infantes turned his head. Four Soviet planes streamed by, strafing. The features of the pilots were plainly visible through the glass canopies.[95]

Taitsy was a beehive. Corps was trying to keep a handle on the action. The Russian guns were pounding as far east as the Tosna, but there was no doubt that the focus was Krasni Bor. All German batteries within range were firing, concentrating on the Soviet pieces and the march routes for the masses of infantry. Heavy railroad guns were being brought up. Aerial reconnaissance had reported twelve tanks coming down the Kolpino–Iam Izhora road and another fourteen on the October Railroad. At 0720, Kleffel consolidated 390 Grenadier Regiment and the 600-man Sapper School at Kamenka as Combat Group Heckel and ordered the colonel to take his men at once to the southern edge of Krasni Bor. On 11 February they would be joined by the self-propelled guns of Antitank Section 563, which was being rushed by 18 Army from Riabogo. Lindemann also transferred four Panzer VI Tigers and an assault gun section from 10 Luftwaffe Field Division to L Corps to bolster the SS Police on Sagrado's right. Kleffel would have felt more relieved if the Luftwaffe had been able to spring into the skies, but weather had kept most of the German planes down. One fighter, hit over Kolpino, had already been lost, but Flak had brought down a Red bomber. The 88s were on their way to Sablino, and should arrive later in the day.[96]

As the artillery lifted over Sagrado's line, Red infantry moved up from the holding trenches into the assault positions. Regiment 270 of 63 Guards Division had come up from 67 Army the night before. Mortarman Fedor Terein and the rest of his comrades of 1 Company now crouched before Payeras's sector awaiting the order to spring forward. Just behind Terein's 52 mm mortar section a tank throbbed.[97]

Palacios knew what to do. As soon as the fire lifted around 0800 he hurried up the remaining automatic weapons, not into their nests, which were destroyed, but into the craters. *El Trincherón* was gone, replaced by a strip of churned mud. The men emerged like moles. One of them staggered to and fro. Infuriated, because he disliked cognac courage, Palacios grabbed the *guripa* by the shoulders and spun him around: the face disfigured, the eyes bleeding, blind. Beneath the crimson featureless mask was Lorenzo Araújo.

"To the rear immediately," shouted the captain.

"No, my captain. I can't see, but I'm still alive," the youth gasped, brandishing a bayonet.

"*Bravo, muchacho, bravo,*" cried the captain.[98]

An enemy company leapt out of the frog pond. Chorusing "*Urrah! Urrah!,*" the guardsmen drove diagonally toward the embankment. Castillo opened up. His 3 Section slashed them in the flank as they sped forward. So effective was their fire that Palacios did not even bother to call in artillery by launching a red rocket. He knew the batteries were busy. A bloody stream of stiffening corpses lay between the pond and the railroad.[99]

Negro watched as the Reds pounced forward from the pond and the patch of pines. There seemed to be thousands. He was right; 63 Guards Division had three regiments—269, 270, and 342—echeloned for assault. Convinced that the Spanish lines were destroyed, they came on confidently crying "*Urrah! Urrah!*" There was a lump in Negro's throat. So many Russians! "*Calma, calma,*" soothed the officers.[100]

Huidobro radioed back to Reinlein. "Enemy attacking in great masses. Fire at woods in front of me."[101] Shells spurted among the advancing ranks, but the edge of the avalanche reached the wire. The mines that Huidobro had placed the night before did their deadly work. Stomping on their shattered, screaming comrades, the Reds approached the barbed barrier. Stunned and surprised, Negro saw his fellow *divisionarios* jump to their feet. Shouting, laughing, jumping up and down, they unleashed volley after volley and rolled grenade after grenade on the struggling figures below. The *guripas* had gone mad. Blood lust seized them. All the tension that had coiled in their tight bodies during the hour and a half bombardment sprang like a spring. Panting, they fell back into the trench. Sixty-third Guards drew off, leaving their mutilated countrymen behind. A sepulchral silence followed. "Look to the wounded," whispered Lieutenant Alturas.[102]

Somehow, Losada and Muñoz had also survived the first attack. After a last battering by two Stalin Organs, 43 Rifle Division, supported by fourteen KV-1s and T-26s from 1 Red Flag Brigade, flooded forward on both sides of the Panzer beak. First and Second Companies struggled from their ruined trenches and shoved them back by 0830. To Muñoz's right, SS Regiment 3 also turned back their share.[103]

Major Castro was out of touch. All communications with Muñoz's 2 Company next to the Germans had been cut since the beginning of the barrage at 0645. He gathered from the retreating wounded that losses had been extremely heavy. Castro sent up a platoon from the Ski Company to assist Muñoz. The skiers, however, were caught in the treeless bog by Red aircraft and strafed and bombed to pieces. The few who escaped scanned the skies for the Luftwaffe and, cursing, spun off eastward to SS Police.[104]

Another punishing barrage on the Panzer beak, and then the infantrymen and tankers of 43 Rifle and 1 Red Flag again descended. Losada called for fire support. Castro ordered the two nearby 75s from 13 Company to open up. Shrapnel tore at the ranks of the riflemen, but they came on, overwhelming Losada. As a last gesture of defiance, the captain radioed "Fire on my position."[105] All the officers of 1 Company fell. Little bands of *divisionarios* formed knots of resistance. Gallantly, Muñoz launched a counterattack, but he, too, was crushed by the steamroller. Collecting the survivors of his 2 Company and the remaining machine gunners from 4 Company, Muñoz drew off to the east. The steamroller ground on. Castro was next. Surrounded and out of shells, he blew up the 75s and fought his way south toward 3 Squadron of Recon 250 at Popovka. Of I Battalion, only Huidobro still held.[106]

Third Company turned back a second assault, then another—this time spearheaded by flamethrowers. But the Reds flowed through the hole east of the embankment. Huidobro was surrounded on three sides. Between attacks, the Russians tried to soften him up with artillery, but the captain cooly strolled along the top of the terreplein shouting, "This is nothing men. They won't get through. We're Spaniards."[107] Looking up, the *guripas* implored him to come down. He ignored them. Finally, Lieutenants Duque and Borquez jumped up, grabbed the slight, bespectacled captain, and forced him into the trench.

To Huidobro's left, part of Palacios's 5 Company still stood. Palacios and Castillo clung to the angle by the railroad. The second infantry attack at 0845 which had been preceded by a punishing air raid on 6 Company, carried away Palacios's left. Flanked and surrounded, 1 and 2 Sections succumbed. Palacios picked up a few survivors from his own scattered sections and some from 6 Company and shook out a line angling to the rear in the secondary trench he had cleaned out a few hours before. By 0915, 5 Company was down to thirty men. A solitary light machine gun remained.[108]

Popov's tanks and 63 Guards poured through the place where 6 Company should have been. Dazed and panic-stricken Spanish stragglers fled rearward to the road and the forest. Others made their way toward the railroad or *El Bastión* to carry on. Iglesia had moved his men forward into no-man's-land prior to the artillery preparation. He had thus hoped to thwart Soviet intentions of destroying his company in *El Trincherón*. He failed. The barrage, which had concentrated on the center of the sector of Second of 262, blasted a belt so wide that his men were engulfed in a sheet of fire. The captain died with them. Enough shaky *guripas* staggered up to fend off the first rush by the Reds, but the strafing and bombing by a squadron of nine aircraft finished them off. This strike was part of a major effort by Thirteenth Red Air Army which unleashed 110 Stormoviks, I-16 Ratas, and LAGG-3s on L Corps that Wednesday morning. There was hardly anything left for the tanks and flamethrowers.[109]

Captain Campos watched the death throes of 6 Company. Like Palacios, Campos's 7 Company had beaten back the wings of infantry on each side of the Reds' flaming armored attack on 6 Company. Guardsmen from the crack 45 Division and KV-1s, T-34s, and T-26s from 1 Independent Battalion were now to his front, right, and rear.

The Russians reached *El Bastión* and the covered road. Setting up a machine gun, Campos sprayed the 200 guardsmen concealed on the covered road, cutting down about 120. Then the captain led a four-man foray. Bombing and machine pistols scattered the remainder. Muffled blasts and shots from *El Bastión* indicated that some machine gunners from 8 Company still struggled on. But Campos could not come to their aid. Twelve tanks were forming in front of him.[110]

Four KV-1s led off. Eight more, followed by infantry, lined up behind. Campos grabbed some T mines—at least his detonators had arrived—and, accompanied by a small party of volunteers, wiggled out forty meters into no-man's-land. Crouching in shell holes, they waited until the forty-eight-ton, 2.75-meter-high monsters slowly churned past over the tortured earth. Then, diving below the angle of fire of the chattering guns, they swiftly shoved the charges into the tracks. Two, tracks flopping and bogies spinning, came to a dead stop. The third lumbered on, bogging down in a crater, and was finished off by *guripas* in the front line. The fourth turned tail. The others followed. The center of 7 Company held, but losses had been heavy and the attack had succeeded on the left. Moreover, masses of men and armor were moving through the hole where 6 Company had been and fanning out toward the Izhora and Krasni Bor. Campos directed his men to break out to the rear and fall back on *El Bastión*.

Around 0945, Oroquieta's right section chief advised him of 7 Company's retreat. The exposed section requested instructions. Oroquieta ordered "Stand fast!"[111] Ulzurrún had been overrun an hour ago. Third of Mobile Reserve 250 was now surrounded. The captain had been hopping ever since Ulzurrún's call had been cut off at 0645. Luckily, the radio operated long enough for Oroquieta to advise Miranda of his incredible casualties. But the wireless soon went and he was only able to communicate with great difficulty by sending *soldogramas*. The runners had a hard time of it. Since Oroquieta's lines were so close to 72 Division, 9 Artillery Regiment tended to overshoot because they were afraid of unloading the heavies on 133 Regiment in the assault positions. This somewhat spared 3 Company from the pounding received by Ulzurrún and Campos but it turned the wounded Miranda's CP and the reserve shelter to Oroquieta's rear into a moonscape. Direct fire from the 45s and 76s of 289 Antitank Regiment made up the difference. Their steady, accurate fire, supplemented by mortars, slowly melted 3 Company's position. Moreover, these pieces continued to pound away when the artillery lifted for the infantry.[112]

Lieutenant Fedor Shusi urged the assault section of Second Battalion of 133 Regiment onward. Overhead arched the tracers from the tanks in Iam Izhora. Submachine guns blazing, First and Second of 133 Regiment raced toward Ulzurrún's line. The acrid odor of cordite hung heavily in the air as panting Second Battalion backed up the attack. Surprisingly, some Spaniards were left. Shadowy figures had risen up out of the smoking, mangled soil. A machine gun began to chatter, then another. Shusi's section passed their own dead and wounded. Third Battalion had taken heavy losses from the Moscow-Leningrad Highway. Dodging on, the lieutenant led his thirty submachine gunners into what remained of the trenches. Dead Spaniards lay everywhere. Many were locked in a last, mortal embrace with a dead or dying Russian. Others, screaming strange slogans, still clawed at the attackers as they passed. First and Third Battalions stumbled in the hand to hand fighting. When they finally slugged through the trench system, effectives were down by over 50 percent. Out of the 260 men in 6 Company, a punishment unit brought up especially for the charge, only 6 remained. Stunned by their casualties but elated by their victory, the Soviets prepared to push on to the Izhora, where the wounded Ulzurrún awaited with a scant score of men from 2 Company of *Tía Bernarda.*[113]

Sagrado's front was now pierced in three places: between the Izhora and the highway (2 of Mobile Reserve 250), between *El Bastión* and the railroad (6 Company), and between the embankment and the SS Police (First Company). The Reds were advancing on Krasni Bor and the heights.

Esteban Infantes slowly picked himself out of the snow, scanning the sky as he absently brushed his fur-collared greatcoat. Then, he looked around. No casualties. The vehicles were unscathed. The two cars sped on to Fedorovskii.[114] An agitated Captain Marzo greeted the brigadier. His men of 3 Company of 263 had been adjusting their equipment in the *izbas* when the first shells burst. At 0700 a round had hit the hut housing Lieutenant Rosaleney's 1 Section. Twenty-one men went. Now, after another hour and three quarters, Marzo had seen a score more go.[115] And the cannonade continued. Esteban Infantes was furious. He ordered Marzo to get the men out of the *izbas*, no matter how cold it was. Running down Blanco, Esteban Infantes told the major to move First of 263 into a series of newly opened emplacements edging from Fedorovskii towards Raikolovo. Raikolovo appeared to be burning. In order to lessen the chances of further losses from shellfire, Blanco was instructed to start slipping squad-sized sections eastward toward the billowing provisional divisional GHQ.[116]

Pushing his way through a stream of ambulances, walking wounded and fugitives, the brigadier reached Raikolovo. The advance field hospital was in flames. Many of the patients had received additional injuries. Esteban Infantes shooed the hospital staff southward to Ladoga and then, visibly shaken, turned toward his temporary CP. The town, though hard hit, was not the site of the holocaust. The huge column of smoke came from Krasni Bor.

Sagrado came on the line. His report was not reassuring. Krasni Bor had already received two air raids. The shelling continued. His CP was being hit with regularity. Santos was dead. Reinlein had taken his place. He had ordered each battery to conserve shells for the last resort—self-detonation. First Battery was firing at elevation zero at a half dozen Soviet tanks which had outdistanced their infantry and were milling around the northern edge of Krasni Bor. Information from the Izhora was unavailable. But, he understood that Ulzurrún had been killed leading a last futile counterattack. Miranda, though wounded, was desperately trying to stop up the hole where 2 Company had been. The CP of Second Battalion was supposedly surrounded, Payeras dying. Of Castro, little was known, but Russian armor and infantry were rolling through the Panzer beak. A few pockets in the first line still held out. Forward observers could see four *islotes*: Oroquieta on the Moscow-Leningrad Highway, Campos and elements of 6, 7, and 8 Companies along with 2 Antitanks in *El Bastión*, Aramburu with 3 Sappers and some strays on the highway behind the bastion, and Palacios and Huidobro along the embankment. Thus, everywhere the Spaniards clung to the high ground, islands of resistance in a surging Red sea.

Waves of infantry and tanks now rolled toward the second line along the heights. Would the thin dike be swamped? Sagrado was not confident. Shells had been pounding his CP since 0645—almost three hours now—in the wide swath of the incredible bombardment. Altogether 35,000 rounds had been dumped on his sector. Somewhat shocked by the enormity of it all, Sagrado, his voice quivering, communicated that the KV-1s, impregnable colossi of the battlefield, were only meters away. Virtually nothing could stop them. Projectiles merely bounced off their plates. They shrugged off the 37 mm Paks like bugs. Then, they simply squashed them.[117]

Sagrado had not yet committed his local reserves—LaCruz's headquarters staff and the four companies of sappers and cyclists under Bellod and García Ciudad. He was also trying to scrape up some more from the scattered, fleeing wretches. Some had obeyed, others had just kept on retreating.[118] Sagrado rang off. Ashen-faced, Esteban Infantes turned to Andino. Did Army and Corps know? Could they help?

Corps knew. So did Army. At 0915, Lindemann advised Army Group that this was indeed the expected pincers attack to join Kolpino and Pogost'e. There was heavy artillery fire in the Pogost'e sector and, although the Soviet infantry had not yet jumped off, they were certain to move soon. More Red tanks were concentrating south of Kolpino. Lindemann had rerouted 212 Division, on its way to Group Hilpert, to Sablino, where its 316 Grenadier Regiment would be the first to arrive. Air support for Sagrado was not possible, he lamented, due to the weather. On the other hand, the Red Air Force was flying. At least, Lindemann proclaimed, there was some immediate assistance under way. Heckel was heading out from Sablino with his two battalions of 390 Grenadiers. But he would have to push them hard through streets clogged with supplies and troops. Heckel's Third Battalion had not yet arrived, nor had any of the assault guns and heavy Paks.[119]

Sagrado needed help. By the time the brigadier got through to the colonel again around 0930, the situation had further deteriorated. Although harassing fire still flailed his CP, the barrage on the town had just lifted and, brushing aside the antitankers, Soviet armor closely followed by infantry had penetrated. They were being held at bay directly in front of the guns of First Group. Miranda was gone. Nothing now stood between the Reds and Raikolovo. Iglesia was dead, Palacios wounded. Still no news from First Battalion. Sagrado was preparing to counterattack, but offered Esteban Infantes little hope for success. Bands of *divisionarios* were making for Sablino. Others crowded the corduroy road running through the Red Woods from Krasni Bor to Raikolovo.[120]

Rattled by this discouraging news, Esteban Infantes hung up. He stared glassy-eyed at the wall. No one was more lonely or isolated at that moment than Esteban Infantes. His soldiers and officers had each other. He was the only Spanish general in Russia. There were neither superiors nor equals from among his own countrymen to whom he could turn for advice, encouragement, or words or comfort. There were only his German allies, already suspicious of his leadership ability. Before he could appeal in despair to Kleffel, he had to remember that he was the sole repository of the honor of the Spanish army in Russia.[121] What to do? Knüppel! The German colonel's harsh voice crackled over the line from the Liaison Staff's advance observation post just across the Izhora at Chernaia Rechka. "Yes, Herr General." "*¡La tropa me abandona!*" croaked Esteban Infantes. (The troops are abandoning me!)[122]

Communications between Raikolovo and Sagrado's CP were tenuous. Master Signal Sergeant Gil, in the telephone central at Krasni Bor, did what he could. The subterranean exchange near the colonel's *dacha* had shaken off the three hours of shelling. Above, buildings burned. Many of the brick shops along Sovietskii prospekt, which ran northward to Kolpino, were gutted. However, the two-story wooden schoolhouse to the west, which served as the Field Hospital, had only received a few hits. Just in front of Gil's switchboard, a street leading eastward to the Popovka Railroad Station intersected Sovietskii prospekt. Calls flickered in from the front.[123]

The news was mixed. The second line was holding, but probably not for long. Around 0930, Sagrado had instructed García Ciudad of

Recon 250 to rush up 2 Squadron under Captain Andújar from regimental CP to rescue the wounded Payeras. Then, Captain Manjón with 3 Squadron, was sent straight up the railroad tracks from Popovka to the junction of First and Second of 262. Andújar was winged almost at once, but gallantly carried on. However, these costly efforts to plug the hole between Campos and Palacios and to support Huidobro were foredoomed to failure. They did, nevertheless, inflict heavy losses and temporarily parry the Russian thrust.[124]

The line held. Three new *islotes*, manned mostly by 2 Squadron, now backed up the four remaining in the old HKL. The new resistance centers were: Major LaCruz's CP of Antitanks 250 on the left front of Reinlein's fire direction center, CP of First of 262, and the forward observation post of Captain Butler's 2 Battery between Payeras and the embankment. Even the tanks were temporarily checked. Captain Cantalapiedra had dug in his Paks before the 1 Battery of Captain Andrés. At point blank range, even Cantalapiedra and his 2 Antitank Company could do something. They knocked out four tanks.[125] Sagrado reported this momentary success to Esteban Infantes, but the nervous brigadier felt certain the horde would come on again, even stronger than before, sweeping away the defenders. Near despair, he believed that all was lost and hoped that Heckel with 390 Grenadiers would arrive in time to stem the onslaught.[126]

Fifty-fifth Army would not be denied. Just after 1100, tanks and infantry overran Payeras's CP and Butler's forward observation post and poured into the town. Skirting the strong points, they drove straight toward Sagrado's headquarters. In their advance, they surrounded two of the three Norwegian Paks. The luckless antitankers, caught up in a linguistic maelstrom, blew up all three pieces, broke out, and made for the woods. Sagrado, his back to the wall, personally led a counterattack. Jumping off from the sapper CP, some 200 meters in front of regimental headquarters, the colonel, Reinlein, and Bellod, beat the Russians back some 500 meters beyond the gun pits of 1 Battery. Their surge liberated some Spanish prisoners, but the positions rewon earlier by 2 Squadron were gone. Captain Andújar, who had fallen with his cavalrymen, lay bleeding. Russian riflemen, picking through the pockets of Spaniards sprawled on the battlefield, probed him with a bayonet and left him for dead. When the counterattack reached him, he painfully rose up and joined in.[127]

Puffing, Sagrado summoned Reinlein of First Group and Bellod of Sappers 250 for a conference. Exhausted and dazed, the colonel decided to leave the majors in direct control. Reinlein was given command of the western regimental sector from the Moscow-Leningrad Highway to Sovietskii prospekt and Bellod that from the main street eastward to Popovka. Sagrado then informed his deputy commanders that a German regiment was coming up from Sablino and, since all contact with Raikolovo had now been lost, he was going to the rear to try to phone Esteban Infantes. The colonel departed for 2 Battery of H.K.A.A. 289. Upon arriving at the French 155s in the forest camp, Sagrado found out that the German gunners had also lost all communication. He then decided to try the munitions depot deep in the forest behind Krasni Bor. Meanwhile, the defense continued—without the colonel.[128]

Reinlein and Bellod took hold at once. Pulling their advance elements back about 100 meters, they established a new line along the heights running just north of the middle of the town. On the left, Reinlein scraped together what was left of 2 Squadron, stragglers from 5 and 6 Companies, lost legionnaires from Mobile Reserve 250, and orphaned antitankers. About the only intact unit he had was Major LaCruz's assault section, but it was somewhere off to the west. While Reinlein raced around in his motorcycle and sidecar shoring up the west, Bellod, basing his defenses on what remained of 1 and 2 Sappers and assisted by Major Castro—who had finally fought his way through —Captain García Ciudad, and Lieutenant Frago threw out a line to the east. Bitter fighting raged around the railroad bridge near the Stepanovka-Chernyshevo-Nikol'skoe road, where Manjón had been hit, but a back-up was needed. Rounding up retreating elements of First of 262, 3 Squadron, and cannoneers, they pieced together a front running from Butler's 2 Battery in front of Bellod's bunker across the October Railroad and on past the train station at Popovka. Here, Captain López, whose 150s of 11 Battery still pounded away, replenished his ranks with the ragged ghosts who drifted in. An Army Artillery Unit (ARKO) 138 perimeter defense company from corps reserve under Lieutenant Loppel reinforced his command by taking over defense of the Popovka Railroad Station.[129]

The Russians continued to press, but their probes lacked the earlier push. Reinlein, having checked his new dispositions, began radioing the remaining *islotes* in the western sector. At 1100 he got through to 3 Sappers. Aramburu had just thrown back another attack. The combat engineers on the highway behind *El Bastión*, like their comrades in Krasni Bor, had seen the barrage lift at 0930. Fifteen minutes later, as

Campos gave way, two tanks and clouds of foot soldiers came up on Aramburu's flank. One KV-1 blundered into a minefield lain the previous night and blew up. The second, shepherded by its shielding infantry, drew off. Swarming past, they split and made for the Izhora and Krasni Bor. A pause followed during which Campos and Arozamena, with the remnants of 6, 7, and 8 Companies in *El Bastión*, managed to make contact with Aramburu. Taking further advantage of the respite, Aramburu ordered additional mines placed. He flung them out on the flanks. This left little for the highway. Here, he scattered the empty, wooden packing boxes, hoping to scare off the Russian armor which might ram down the road from Iam Izhora where Oroquieta still stood.[130]

The machine guns of 3 of *Tía Bernarda* had sprayed 133 Regiment as it smothered Ulzurrún. Then, as the riflemen debouched behind, 1 Section had counterattacked. Ten out of thirty returned. The captain hurried up and down what remained of his ramparts shouting *"Arriba España! Viva la muerte!"* (Up Spain! Long live death!) As he loped along, he passed shapeless, bloody blobs of flesh plastered to the sides of the trench. A bullet slammed into his shoulder. Stuffing the hand of the paralyzed arm into his pocket, he carried on. He hoped that the cold would close the wound and stop the hemorrhaging.[131]

Twenty men from sector reserve clambered in. They were all that was left of 1 Company. Miranda, though wounded, had led them in two counterattacks in a valiant effort to stop 133 Regiment followed by 14 Regiment as they flooded 2 Company. He had been killed in the second violent shock.

Staggered but not stopped, 133 and 14 Rifle Regiments swept on toward the Izhora. After stumbling before a smashing grenade attack by a platoon of sappers under Lieutenant Caraballo, the Reds lurched on to the two 150s of 13 Company. Captain Diez Miranda defended his pieces in the antitank ditch to the last. Both Caraballo and Diez Miranda bought time with their lives. The Soviet shock troops had paid a butcher's bill of 65 to 85 percent casualties, but they had reached the river, within easy striking distance of Staraia Myza and not far from Raikolovo.[132]

Oroquieta was now cut off left and rear. Most of his officers were gone. The crushed bunkers were crammed with groaning wounded which he had refused to evacuate because he would not spare any men as stretcher bearers. Two of the German radio operators had just been killed by a burst which destroyed their transmitter. This, however, relieved Lieutenant Blesa, whom Oroquieta detailed to take over 1 Section on the left where he had sent the reserves. The captain still had seventy men, one machine gun, and three automatic rifles; it was only about 0930.

Armor advanced as the artillery lifted. Vomiting fire, five T-34s, motors roaring, rumbled toward Oroquieta. Accelerating, they loomed ever larger. "They look bigger than they are," he thought. Arriving at the wire, the tanks turned, destroying what left of the *chevaux de frise*. The *guripas* began pitching grenades, which exploded harmlessly, hardly scratching the white paint. "Oh, if we only had a few bottles of gasoline," wished Oroquieta, recalling the Civil War.[133] The T-34s reformed in a file and, with a burst of speed, rolled over and through the line.

Oroquieta's heart leaped. The tanks were heading right for a minefield. But many had self-detonated during the drumfire. Four tanks passed through without incident. The fifth broke down near the old antitank ditch fifty meters behind his command bunker. There it stayed, harassing 3 Company from the south. To the north, infantry appeared. Elbow to elbow, arms at the ready, the riflemen advanced in a majestic march step. White-caped, they came on with the slow, steady, irresistible glide of a glacier. Only drunken cries of *"Urrah! Urrah!"* indicated their humanity. Oroquieta opened fire. About a battalion arrived at the crushed wire where the men fell in heaps. The legionnaires went wild. The battered Bolsheviks drew back. Minutes later, they tried again. Another failure. Changing tactics, the Soviets let fly with their antitanks and mortars, destroying Oroquieta's last automatic rifle.[134]

Meanwhile, Campos had retired, unhinging Oroquieta's right. Stoically, the captain watched the long columns of Russian infantry swing through the gap in close order. Though his *guripas* fired and fired at their long, open flank, the impassive guardsmen marched on toward Krasni Bor. A few, detaching from the host, posted themselves in the antitank ditch to the rear of 3 Company. Oroquieta was encircled. The balance of the battle, he concluded, was beginning to tip in favor of the enemy. He concentrated his remnants astride the high ground on the highway. He still had a few cards to play. It was going on 1030.[135]

Palacios was enjoying a few moments peace. Though the Soviets were sniping at him from all sides, he was still holding on. The Reds had cut in behind Huidobro's company and were now hitting him from the embankment, but it was still relatively calm. However, the bombardment began again at 1045. When it ended, the Red Air Force took over for a few passes; 43 Rifle Division brought up machine guns to the embankment, pinning him down. The ring tightened. By noon, almost out of munitions, Palacios fired his red Very pistol requesting artillery fire on his own position. No one responded. The Reds were now so close that they had to call off their guns for fear of hitting their own riflemen. As the afternoon advanced, silent desperate struggles between isolated individuals went on in the twisted trenches and broken bunkers. Almost the only sounds which reached Palacios were the gurgle of death and groans of the wounded.[136]

Huidobro had fallen just before the second artillery preparation at 1045. Hit in the throat, the captain had pitched backward, landing spread-eagled in the mud. A group of horrified *divisionarios* gathered around. Arms flung outward in the shape of a cross, Huidobro managed to murmur "Hold the position!" Alturas assumed command. When the bombardment ceased, 63 Guards hit the embankment from the west while 43 Division clawed from the east. The order was to hold. Alturas obeyed.[137]

The line officers were dying at their posts. As long as they lived, the men held. There was no lack of nerve at the front. In Raikolovo, the brigadier's hand twitched as he reached once more for the telephone. The wires to the front had almost all been severed, but not those to the rear. Pulling himself together, the general used the telephone as if it were the only weapon he had. Puffing nervously on a cigarette, he called Rubio at Pavlovsk. The colonel should come to Raikolovo at once in order to take over the division "should the worst happen."[138] By that he meant his own death or incapacity.

Rubio was an ideal man to handle the situation. He had mastered just such a crisis five years before at Gandesa when the Republican armies had smashed the Nationalist front on the Ebro River. His cool head, courage, and combat leadership had won Rubio the *Medalla Militar Individual*. Leaving his deputy, Lieutenant Colonel Cano in command of 269, Rubio raced to Raikolovo to try to restore order.[139] With Rubio on the way, Esteban Infantes breathed a little easier. His panic had passed, but he was worried about Sagrado. He also needed reinforcements. A call went through to *Villa Relevo*. Robles was summoned to "take over the most threatened sector."[140] Volunteers were requested from the Return Battalion. All of the officers and 100 men faced about and marched off to aid their comrades. Sniffing powder, Robles led the way to Raikolovo.[141]

Esteban Infantes had hardly put down the receiver at 1130 when the Corps Commander arrived. On his way from Taitsy to the new Corps headquarters at Novolisino, Kleffel had gone first to see Knüppel at Chernaia Rechka. Here, at the edge of the corduroy road, fleeing and wounded *divisionarios* were seeking refuge from the battle. The advance field hospital at Ladoga was not far away, nor the main divisional hospital at Mestelevo. Ambulances, trucks, sleighs, staff cars, and a meat wagon from the butcher company hurried off the suffering cargo. The head of the Liaison Staff gave Kleffel a quick briefing, which included a description of the state of mind of the commander of the Blue Division. Sobered, the general rushed at once to Raikolovo.

Esteban Infantes had pulled himself together. The arrival of Rubio had reassured and stiffened him. Believing Sagrado to have been crushed and anticipating that the Germans would plug the hole, his main worry was to prevent the Soviets from turning west, crossing the Izhora, and surrounding his other two regiments. He had sent Marzo north to Podolovo and intended to feed the rest of Blanco's battalion into Samsonovka. Battalion Merry of 269 was still in transit. Kleffel, on the other hand, was concerned that Esteban Infantes had lost his nerve, especially after what he had been told by Knüppel. He was counting on the Spaniards to hang on at Krasni Bor until Heckel could arrive.

Where was Heckel? That was what Esteban Infantes wanted to know. The two generals were both aware that the colonel and 390 Regiment were supposed to be coming up on the outskirts of Krasni Bor at that very moment. In fact, he was still 2.5 km outside of Sablino in a forest camp, and was again ordered at 1145 to head out. The Spaniard also wanted to know what had happened to the Luftwaffe. The Red Air Force seemed to dominate the skies. He himself had been strafed. Krasni Bor had been raided again and again. The weather had just begun to clear. What possible excuse could Keller have now? Kleffel was also anxious for answers to these questions. He phoned Lindemann. With bitter irony ringing in his voice, Kleffel offered congratulations to the Luftwaffe for its intervention in the battle.[142] Lindemann promised to do what he could, and get von Küchler to order air support.

Kleffel told Esteban Infantes that he was calling up more reinforcements all the time, and it was now apparent that the Soviet main effort was not at Pogost'e, where Meretskov's initial advance had been thrown back, but at Krasni Bor. Kleffel stressed how important it was for the Spaniards to hold the heights until the German troops he had been promised could make their way to the front. Not satisfied either with Esteban Infantes or Heckel, Kleffel sped off to SS Police, and then on to Novolisino.

At 1225, Kleffel again spoke to Lindemann. The Spaniards were still holding the heights. A pocket remained on the October Railroad. No Luftwaffe yet. The Russians were very strong. The 18 Army commander responded that he would rush two regiments of 24 Division from Chudovo to Sablino. He ordered that the entire Krasni Bor sector be turned over to General Reymann of 212 Division as soon as he could get his Bavarians to the scene.[143]

The midday situation was fluid. The Soviets had suffered heavy casualties. Fifty-fifth Army was bringing up replacements and reserves and preparing to throw its main weight eastward to achieve its objective—cutting off Group Hilpert's lifelife, the supply route from Sablino to Sinevino. Besides stumbling from losses and being stalled by the persistent *islotes*, the Reds wasted time when many of their troops, having occupied the Spanish positions, stopped to loot. The simple German fare, plus delicacies from Spain, proved irresistible to the hungry Russians. Cognac and chocolate were their favorites. Some of the riflemen drank themselves into a stupor. Without his protective shield of infantry, Popov was unwilling to press First Independent Armored Battalion on to Sablino. Thus toward noon the Russian effort diffused, precisely at the moment when the Spaniards were at their weakest. Assault squads threw away numerical advantage chasing small groups of *divisionarios*. Others hunted down individuals. Concentrated attack was replaced by infiltration. Carousing guardsmen roamed the streets of Krasni Bor. Isolated defenders successfully eluded them by seeking shelter among the inhabitants, who hid them.[144]

With the thrust of the attack blunted, Reinlein and Bellod were able to firm up their defenses. Just before noon, however, Butler, harassed and out of ammunition, had to blow up 2 Battery. Bellod's eastern sector now ran from Sovietskii prospekt to the Popovka Railroad Station. Here, 11 Battery was still in action. Farther right, Lieutenant Colonel Bock of SS Police Artillery had taken up the slack by throwing a mixed combat group along the Stepanovka-Nikol'skoe road at 1130. In covering the heights, Bock helped shield the open left flank of SS police, exposed by the Spanish retreat.[145] Glancing off Bock, Red armor overran 9 Battery at 1300. SS Police turned west to face 43 Division. To the north, Muñoz, having swung back on the Germans, fought on.

Around 1200, Liaison Lieutenant Jobst hurried to 262 CP. Capt. Walter Speer, adjutant of 390 Regiment, had finally arrived. Jobst briefed him and urged him to convince Heckel to get a move on. Speer responded with assurances that 390 Grenadiers would come up between 1400 and 1500. Since Spanish signalmen had temporarily restored communications, Jobst now called Knüppel at Chernaia Rechka. The liaison chief advised Jobst that Heckel had been ordered to take over the entire sector, including all Spanish units.[146] Reinlein believed that he could hold until Heckel got there. LaCruz had rushed out to round up some more of his antitankers. At 1240, Campos and Arozamena were able to break out of *El Bastión* and fall back on Aramburu. Up on the highway, Oroquieta fought on.[147]

From his commanding position atop the Moscow-Leningrad Highway, Oroquieta ruefully observed a column of Spanish prisoners being conducted to the Russian rear. "Who could they be," he sadly sighed.[148] Rescue was out of the question. His reduced company was ringed in and tied down. Just before noon he spotted three German aircraft flying low over the forest. He hoped that they would soon come to his aid. How was he to know that they were reconnaissance planes and had reported a further buildup of Russian armor? Then, he ducked down.

After a brief, but intense, mortar barrage, Russian infantry charged. The third mass attack. All Oroquieta had left were rifles and grenades. These sufficed, for 12 Battery opened up from Fedorovskii and inflicted frightful losses on the closely packed riflemen. As the excitement abated, the captain realized that he had been hit again. This time in the right leg. Hobbling around, he counted his men—80 percent casualties. Of his six officers, only Blesa and Second Lieutenant Navarro were left. Smarting from their recent repulse, the Reds resumed their mortar fire.[149]

The guardsmen were too close to Palacios to employ their mortars. The struggle continued in deadly silence. Even the embankment was quiet. Early in the afternoon Alturas had given 3 Company the order to break out and make for Krasni Bor, two kilometers to the rear. Palacios cursed. He turned to Castillo, his sole surviving officer. "If Huidobro were still alive, the Reds would never have taken us in the flank from the railroad."[150] Even if he were now ordered to evacuate, Palacios couldn't. Not enough men were left to carry the wounded, nor enough munitions or weapons to fight through. He would try and stick it out, cost what it may.

"The moment for heroic decisions has arrived," entoned Esteban

Infantes. Forcing a confident smile the brigadier tried to cover the sinking feeling in his stomach. Masking his emotions and apprehensions, he continued. "We must do everything we can to protect that flank on the Izhora. Since it is impossible to reinforce Krasni Bor, we will send the reserves there [to the Izhora] and leave the forces [in Krasni Bor] to hold out as best they can."[151]

Robles understood. It was up to him. The entire sector had been his for months. He knew it and the men better than anyone else. Araújo was new. Sagrado was out of touch. An old, trusted comrade in arms, Cano of 269 would take over the Izhora while he tried to salvage the rest. The G-2, Alemany, had gone over to Krasni Bor to take a look and should return soon. Robles took hold. Smiling and paternal in spite of the crisis, the tall, cool lieutenant colonel reviewed the situation from his command post at Raikolovo. Major Blanco had arrived at Podolovo at noon with First of 263. Beating back an attack, he had then pushed 3 Company (Marzo) and 2 Company (Allende-salazar) across the Izhora. Both were now moving north, Marzo on the river, Allendesalazar on the right, with 4 Company following. First Company (Urbano) remained in reserve. Battalion Merry—*La Segunda*—was coming up.[152] Captain Blanco Rodríguez of 5 Company of 269 reported to Robles at Raikolovo at 1330. Robles instructed him to cross the river, form up to the right of Allendesalazar, and advance on the encircled Oroquieta and Aramburu three kilometers to the northeast.[153]

Ever since the alert at 0800, the men of *La Segunda* wondered where they were going. *La Segunda* was a shadow. In spite of replacements and returning convalescents, only two incomplete companies, 5 and 8, fell out. A skeletal section from 7 tagged along. In order to avoid the cannonade, Merry Gordon had led *La Segunda* in a roundabout way from Pavlovsk to Annalova and then to the Izhora. A macabre welcome had awaited at Annalova. Below the wooden balcony of a *dacha* dangled the body of a partisan. As the corpse swung by the two leather service belts used to string him up, the *Gott mit uns* buckles glistened in the sun. Chatter in the column ceased as the *guripas* stared questioningly at the Wehrmacht sergeant and two Russians who stood below the swaying, stiffening body. Why, they wondered?[154]

A brief rest while Captain Blanco Rodríguez went on to Raikolovo. Bread and butter, sausage, canned spinach, all cold. Half the water in the canteens was frozen. Fifth company now moved through the snow. Their mission, Blanco Rodríguez had explained, was to link up with the Spaniards who still resisted between the Izhora and the Moscow-Leningrad Highway. The captain took point. The triangle advanced. Nobody on the left. Finally a reference point in the flat, open white plain—a fallen aircraft. Here they left the wounded. Knots of bodies, Spanish and Russian; in the pockets of the Russians, Spanish tobacco. Booty.

The Soviets were almost indistinguishable from the snow in their white capes. Resistance stiffened. Heavy fire from the front. With only a few shouts and hardly any shots, the lead platoon fell lazily into the snow. The mortar squad opened up. The captain took off his horn-rimmed glasses and blinked his ice-covered eyelids. Lieutenants Miranda and Soriano—the latter the lone survivor of Sinevino Heights—looked expectantly at Blanco: to the left, nothing; to the right, nothing; to the rear, only God knew; forty meters to the front, Sergeant Medina and his squad, dead, and beyond, the Russians.[155] Fifth Company could not advance crawling, let alone charging. The problem now was to hold.

Five hundred meters to the left there seemed to be something that looked like a gully. "Could it be the Izhora? We've got to get over there," thought the captain.[156] Now the Soviets began peppering the three hectares where 5 Company deployed. Up from the gully rose the turrets of two tanks. Rapidly, the T-34s moved toward the Spaniards, who hugged a fold in the field. "Wait for the infantry before you fire," shouted the captain.[157] The wounded didn't complain. They tried to look after each other. Cover was so scarce that the *guripas* built parapets out of the dead. Three corpses per prone rifleman—one in front, one on each side. Their clammy, frozen flesh absorbed the humming metal from the Russian mortars.

The crisis came. Almost indifferently, the Soviet infantry advanced. Slowly, in compact masses, their white camouflage blending with the gray horizon behind, they reminded one of a horizontal flurry of large snowflakes. It was a clash of arms, not voices. Only a few shouts rang out—a solitary *urrah* or a Spanish curse. The captain observed everything—a pair of horn-rimmed glasses peeking over a mound of snow. It was going well. The machine guns were singing. A mortar bomb plopped into one of the machine gun nests. The smashed barrel and tripod slowly spun upward and then tumbled to the ground. The captain saw a few rifles poke up from the hole and open fire. "Good, it was enough," he mused. Somehow, he was reminded of Suvorov's maxim, "Bullets are folly, bayonets wisdom."[158]

Casually, with "Spanish grace," the captain lit a cigarette. He had just taken a satisfying puff when a Russian soldier fell at his side. The rifleman carried half a magazine of bullets in his body from the machine pistol of Lieutenant Miranda, some six meters away. At that moment, the battle shifted. The Reds drew off. Calmly, the captain considered the price of the victory and the brief peace it had won.[159]

Ahead of Blanco Rodríguez, Oroquieta continued to cling to the highway. The afternoon wore on. Sporadic attacks were punctuated by mortar and antitank fire. During one of the breaks, when the Soviets were shifting tactics, a Russian strolled up the highway from the south straight into the Spanish positions. The drunken rifleman proudly showed the Spaniards two bottles of captured cognac and a pile of looted cigarettes. Oroquieta tried to interrogate him, but he was too incoherent. Deciding to let the Russian sleep it off, Oroquieta ordered him assisted to a side trench where he promptly dozed off, oblivious to the cold, the mortars, and the antitank guns.

The Soviet soldier had hardly begun to snore when a welcome sight greeted Oroquieta's eyes. A squadron of Stukas were striking Kolpino. Marvelling at the chilling sound of their sirens as they dove toward their targets, the captain ruefully noted that the Luftwaffe had arrived too late. Munitions were low, and the grenades were gone. It was after three.[160]

Time was also running out for Palacios. He was out of ammunition. The silent struggle went on. Palacios concentrated around the only serviceable bunker. Sounds of pain and terror drifted up from the depths. Calling Castillo, the captain went below to comfort the wounded and dying. Barely three minutes later, shouts from the sentries sent the pair scurrying back up the ladder. The Russians were all around them. Castillo fired his last half clip from the machine pistol. A few fell. They were a mixed lot—Nordic types mingled with gigantic Mongols. One of the Russians whom Castillo had hit lay moaning in the bottom of the trench. A Soviet noncom asked the man if he could stand. The rifleman shook his head, no. The sergeant raised his pistol and finished him off with a bullet in the nape of the neck.

"Prisoners," thought Palacios. "And, if they do this to their own what will they do to our wounded?" "*Daviia! Palleiali!*" (Get moving! Hurry!)[161] Night closed behind the little column of thirty-five Spanish prisoners—twenty-one of them were wounded—as they emerged from *El Trincherón* and staggered out into the open plain. Hundreds of corpses strewed their path. Hundreds of humped figures crawled away in fear like snails, leaving behind a trail of blood in the filthy, mangled snow.

Juan Negro scrambled rearward towards Krasni Bor. Out of the squad which had slid down the embankment, only he and Corporal Pedro Pérez remained. It was going on three when the pair reached the first houses. If they could just hole up in one of the huts till nightfall, they could then slip through the Soviet patrols to the Spanish lines. But the Russian armor and infantry were everywhere. Dodging behind *izbas* and trees, firing and running, they worked their way toward the southern edge of town.

"I can't go on," gasped Juan, collapsing on the ground.

"Let's go! Don't be a fool!" snapped Pérez, bending to lift him.

As the corporal leaned over a shell burst between their feet, leaving them flattened and covered with snow and ice. Stunned, they stood up. Negro couldn't feel anything, but Pérez was torn and bleeding.

"Let's go! Let's go! It's nothing!" mumbled the corporal.

"But you're hit! Let me bandage you."

"Do you think we have time for such foolishness? Leave the rifle. We're out of ammo and it's just something else to carry. You're hit too."

"Me?" queried Negro. He began to feel himself all over. Pérez passed his hand over Negro's back. It came away covered with blood. "Let's go."[162]

Stumbling through the darkening streets, the two helped each other southward. Mortar, cannon, and antitank shells flared in the twilight, killing friend and foe alike. Not a square meter lay unscarred or bare of a body. Rounding the corner of an *izba*, Juan and the corporal collided with a Soviet squad. Negro closed his eyes waiting for the blast from the leveled burp guns. They were prisoners![163]

Once again the Russians came on. They were lethargic now, Oroquieta observed. His exhausted legionnaires, however, seemed to be able to snatch a siesta between assaults and awake resuscitated, like Lazarus. Oroquieta and Blesa breathed a sigh of relief as the riflemen of 133 Regiment withdrew. Suddenly, a bullet slapped into the center of Blesa's forehead, killing him instantly. Oroquieta burned with sorrow and rage. A brief prayer for his childhood friend and then the captain turned to count his men—thirteen, five of them wounded but still on their feet. The last of Mobile Reserve 250. Another half hour and it would be dark enough to try and break out. Too late. In an instant the riflemen were upon them. Thirty muzzles pointed downward into the ditch where Oroquieta and his men lay. *"Chassi est?"* (Do you have a watch?) barked the Russians.[164]

Three of the four sparks of resistance—Alturas, Palacios, and Oroquieta—had flickered out. Aramburu's *islote* still flared. When Campos and Arozamena had fallen back from the bastion they had taken up the defense of the rear. Aramburu now had enough to hold his hedgehog atop the highway. He also had enough officers to conserve command integrity. After a few fruitless attacks the Soviets gave them a wide berth. At 1530 a Spanish signal party pushed out toward Krasni Bor in an effort to relay the wire and restore telephone communication. It got entangled with a Russian column and pulled back. A similar effort an hour later also got chopped up and returned. Disappointing, but not discouraging. Aramburu knew that Reinlein still held the city. To the east he could see fire winking along the edge of the heights.[165]

Reinlein and Bellod had had a busy Wednesday afternoon. While the Soviets paused to regroup and reinforce, the infantry looted. Shorn of the bulk of their accompanying troops, the armor hesitated until the officers and commissars could get the men back under control. After midday, they had begun to grind on again. Meanwhile, the two majors had succeeded in stabilizing the situation, although they had to blow up 11 Battery. LaCruz was on his way with what was left of his assault section. He was coming by way of the Red Woods. Here, on the corduroy road he had found a motley group of leaderless *guripas*. Honor had kept them from retreating further, the absence of officers from returning. Sorting out the wounded, he had sent them rearward to Raikolovo. Picking up a lieutenant, he shoved the others back toward *El Trincherón*. Soviet fighters had made two passes at LaCruz's party, lightly wounding four, as they neared Krasni Bor at 1330.

The weather was fine for 13 Red Air Army. First Air Fleet, however, refused to fly. Nevertheless German reconnaissance pilots dared while the old eagle, Keller, declined. Aerial observers watched 55 Army build up for the second phase of the offensive—the strike toward Sablino and Nikol'skoe. At 1230, the Luftwaffe reported six tanks trying to break into northwestern Krasni Bor. Fifteen more were forming a kilometer behind, eight were on the edge of the town to the east, and another fifteen to twenty were coming up. Half an hour later, the observer radioed that the Spaniards were holding in the middle of Krasni Bor and along the heights to Popovka. At 1325, the scout plane signaled that the six tanks had smashed into the town. Eight more were "hard before the lines," while an additional thirty, accompanied by infantry, were moving down from Iam Izhora.[166] Ten minutes later four KV-1s with infantry aboard rammed down the Stepanovka road toward Combat Group Bock and 9 Battery, which the SS Police had succeeded in rewinning.[167]

First and Third Batteries were fighting for their lives. Wild scenes filled the streets at Krasni Bor. *Guripas* fired from windows and doors at the infiltrating Russians. Others sniped from the rooftops. Sappers pitched grenades and Molotov cocktails at the iron monsters. The rations trucks under Sergeant Espiñeira, pressed into service for munitioning, charged through groups of guardsmen and *guripas* and raced to the hungry guns of First Group. Sleds and ambulances loaded up at the schoolhouse hospital and then dashed through the shellbursts for the cover of the forest. Reinlein believed that they could hold until the Germans arrived. Sagrado was not so sure. Around 1500, the two again separated.

Jumping into the sidecar of his motorcycle, Reinlein sped to the munitions depot. The radio was out, but the telephone worked. By 1515, he had Esteban Infantes on the line. The major calmly reported on the chaos at Krasni Bor. The brigadier advised him that the Luftwaffe was on its way, and that Combat Group Heckel should be arriving at any moment. Delighted, Reinlein leaped back into the sidecar and, the white hood of his reversible jacket flapping in the wind, raced down the Moscow-Leningrad Highway in search of the German point, which was approaching the junction of the corduroy road to Raikolovo.[168]

Reporting to Colonel Heckel, Reinlein briefed his new sector commander. Pointing to the map, the major proudly proclaimed that 1 and 3 Batteries were still in action. They were now the resistance centers. Morale was high, in spite of all the casualties, and would rise even higher when the *guripas* saw the German reinforcements. Should Heckel so order, he would be glad to lead a counterattack. The colonel replied that he had already one battalion on the highway and one heading northeastward through the woods, in order to close up with the Spanish defenders of Krasni Bor. Earlier, he had dispatched Lieutenant Ulrich into the town to make contact. Ulrich had not found any Spaniards, but there were Russians everywhere. The young lieutenant had encountered a tank, which had set his *Kübelwagen* (Volkswagen jeep) afire. Escaping a hail of machine gun fire, he had managed to report back to the regiment. Heckel then told Reinlein that "he was shocked to have met on the Highway Spanish soldiers who were going back to Sablino."[169] Reinlein retorted that "all of the officers of those soldiers had either been killed or wounded."[170] With this parting defense of the honor of his countrymen, the major returned to 1 Battery. He did not have to dodge flying shells nor fend off Russian infiltrators. They had been beaten back again.[171]

A kaleidoscope of units defended the gun pits. Looking rearward, Reinlein observed that the Germans had advanced another 300 meters and then dug in. Heckel was obviously not going to close up on Aramburu, himself, or Bellod. The German colonel seemed content to creep up to the edge of the forest and contemplate Krasni Bor. Once again, like it or not, Reinlein was in charge. Two colonels had failed him, one German, one Spanish.[172]

Sagrado, who had returned to Krasni Bor, again left Reinlein around 1500. He then fought his way westward with part of his staff. Before he reached the highway, he chanced upon his ordnance officer, who had stayed at the regimental CP. Sagrado announced that the day was lost, and set out southward into the Sablino Forest in search of 390 Grenadiers. After pushing a kilometer through the snow-laden trees, he was challenged by a five-man German patrol. The *Landser* led the party another two kilometers toward Sablino where their battalion had halted. Sagrado was told that this was the battalion that Heckel had sent into the woods. The German colonel was on the highway. Forcing his way through seventy-centimeter-deep snow, Sagrado tramped towards Heckel's CP. When he arrived at the highway at 1830, he was unable to locate Heckel. The colonel again turned northward to Krasni Bor. Here, he met his regimental munitions officer, Lieutenant Vega. He ordered the lieutenant to go to the intersection of the corduroy road and the Moscow-Leningrad Highway. Sagrado, "in contrast to what might logically have been expected," faced about and made for Sablino in order to confer with General Reymann of 212 Division, who had taken over the entire sector.[173]

Reymann was counting on Heckel to stop the Russians until he could swing his Bavarians into action. The German general knew that the heavy Paks and the self-propelled 75s of Antitanks 563 and Self-Propelled Gun Section 226 would eventually give Heckel powerful support. Lindemann was assuring him that the Luftwaffe would go into action on the morrow and that three more grenadier regiments—316, 366, and 374—were advancing to bolster the sectors of Krasni Bor and the SS Police. At least three Tiger tanks would join the latter to help destroy the Russian advantage in armor.

Some of this aid, however, was conditional. Lindemann could only move two regiments from 24 Division at Chudovo if he could replace them with units from the Luftwaffe field divisions. Although von Küchler had released these forces to him, Keller had complained vigorously that approval from the High Command was necessary if Luftwaffe ground troops were to be split up. Service rivalry kept the affair bubbling until late in the evening, when a treaty could be negotiated in Berlin between the two arms of the Wehrmacht.

Kleffel notified Esteban Infantes at 1630 that Reymann had assumed command of the sector from the Izhora to the October Railroad. Grenadier Regiment 316 would deploy between the river and the highway. Heckel, now attached to 212 Division, would carry on between the highway and the railroad.[174]

Kleffel seemed unaware that Aramburu, Reinlein, and Bellod were still hanging on. Esteban Infantes, although he had Alemany's eyewitness report, could not enlighten the corps commander. All he knew was that the officers from *Villa Relevo* who had tried to reach Krasni Bor by way of the corduroy road to replace casualties had been turned back by Soviet patrols and that Captain Segura, who had led a signal party down the same road, had been killed while trying to restore communications. All Esteban Infantes really knew was that the same Russian force that threatened the road was now approaching Chernaia Rechka and his own CP at Raikolovo.[175]

Robles and Cano were doing what they could. With the Reds before Raikolovo, the western escape route for the wounded and dispersed from Krasni Bor was severed. This advance also endangered the rear of Battalion Blanco of 263 and Blanco Rodríguez's 5 Company from *La Segunda* across the Izhora. Moreover, corps insisted upon the Spaniards sticking it out in Staraia Myza. When Cano had reported to Robles, the sector commander had explained that no more forces could be expected from either 263 or 269. Their lines had already been thinned out so much that a mere tap by 42 Red Army might poke through. Forty-second Army also appeared to be extending eastward, because 187 Regiment of 72 Division, which had been facing Third of 262 (Calvo), was sliding east and south through the hole where *Tía Bernarda* had been and toward Staraia Myza. Corps might be able to help with some Letts and Flemings. However, since the Germans had been hurrying up Heckel since early morning, it might not be wise to count too heavily on them.

Robles had ringed Raikolovo with the mortars and machine guns of 4 Company of 263 and 8 Company of 269 and had stiffened the perimeter with the one section from 7 of 269. Ninth of 263 should arrive around 1500. He would like to use these as subsector reserve if he could persuade the brigadier to release them from protecting the CP. Just to the north, at Podolovo, only signal, supply, and sanitary personnel were at hand. Further on, at Samsonovka, the situation was chaotic. Alemany had gone up and reported that dispersed officers and men roamed around the village to no apparent purpose. The G-2 could not get any information about Major Blanco, who was engaged across the river at Staraia Myza.[176]

Cano set out immediately from Robles' command post at Raikolovo to scout his new Izhora subsector. He knew that Third of 262 had an old, well established front but he understood that the Battalion —which had not been attacked—had suffered almost 40 percent casualties during the bombardment. He also feared that Calvo's flank on the Izhora was open. Therefore, Cano hurried northward to Moiskorovo to check on 14 of 262 and Third Artillery Group. Here, all appeared under control. He then dashed to the paper mill, where Captain Ortega with First Squadron of Recon 250 and knots of legionnaires and cannoneers from 13 of 262 held out behind the high walls. As Cano crossed the great meander of the Izhora, he got caught in a heavy artillery barrage. Ignoring this inconvenience, the lieutenant colonel continued on to 7 Battery, immediately south of the mill. He found the four 105s firing at elevation zero at a densely packed mass storming across the frozen river. Cano could hear them screaming and shouting. The shrapnel was too much for the Soviets. They streamed back. Sending a *soldograma* to First Squadron directing Ortega to open radio contact with him at Samsonovka, Cano hustled on to Araújo's former CP. Arriving breathless at 1530, he was informed that Staraia Myza had just been lost. First Battalion of 263 was hobbling back from the other side of the Izhora. Where was Major Blanco? No one knew. Without even going to his CP, Cano, assisted by Captains Urbano (1 of 263) and La Fuente and Lieutenant García, got the *guripas* into a defense line around Samsonovka. When Cano finally entered his headquarters he found Blanco. He had just arrived—the last man alive out of Staraia Myza.[177]

Three Red tanks were in Staraia Myza. More armor and infantry were coming up. If 72 Rifle Division pushed westward the entire division might be lost. Ortega radioed in from the Paper Mill, "I can hold with what I've got."[178] But the big buildup was opposite Samsonovka. Cano requested Robles to release some of the reserves at Raikolovo. Esteban Infantes concurred. Part of 9 of 263 would, however, remain at Raikolovo for defense. Another section would cover the corduroy road. Robles had already pushed a patrol accompanied by Prince Metternich along this route—no Reds, no Germans. Where was 390 Grenadiers? Above all, what had happened to Allendesalazar and Blanco Rodríguez? Allendesalazar had succeeded in driving 3 Company of 263 Regiment through to Miranda's former command bunker. All he found were Spanish dead and drunken Russians. But, he had lost all contact with Blanco Rodríguez on his right.[179]

A runner loped over the snow toward 5 of *La Segunda*. The captain listened while the *guripa* breathlessly gave his message. They needed his help on the Izhora. Blanco Rodríguez looked around. It had been half an hour since he had rolled back the Russians. He had just redeployed his company in an old antitank ditch. Good cover, especially with the minefield his men had found to the right. The *guripas* were lifting some of the mines and scattering them to the front against the ever present armor. What could he tell the runner? The boy's wounded sergeant and thirty men needed help, but he had no orders to pull back. He sent them a case of cartridges and a thermos of hot coffee. The *café con leche* was for the wounded sergeant.[180]

Fifth Company was down to fifty-two volunteers plus eleven combat-ready wounded. Miranda had a bullet in the leg. Three hours ago, 142 of them had marched past the swinging partisan in Annalova. One of his scouts returned. He had chanced on a stray Spaniard. He was from Blanco's battalion. The Soviets had stormed Staraia Myza. The captain refused to accept the idea. Staraia Myza was one of the few firm reference points he had, except for the downed aircraft.

The *guripas* uncovered more abandoned trenches. Fifth Company's position grew stronger by the minute. The antitank ditch particularly interested the captain. It must have been excavated over two years ago when an authentic siege of Leningrad existed. Now, the siege had become the most heroic masquerade of the entire Eastern Front. The ring around Leningrad was at best a skirmish line of sentries. He was one of the sentinels.

His batman had thrown up a windbreak of ammo boxes and canvas. Blanco Rodríguez and Miranda sat inside, drinking melted snow and eating bread and chocolate. The snow shook from a distant cannonade. To the left, a pillar of fire—Staraia Myza; to the right, a column of smoke—Krasni Bor.

Throwing aside the canvas, the captain and lieutenant went out. A Russian, hands in air, stood there. "*Styk na Zemle*" (My bayonet is in the ground), he repeated.[181] A knot of livid *divisionarios* clustered around the tall prisoner. Among them were the five surviving members of the assault section. One, known as Ferrol from his home town, poked a *naranjero* into the rifleman's kidneys. "*Styk na Zemle*," entoned the Russian.

"Quiet down," called the captain.

"Shall I finish him off now, my captain?" queried Madriles, the runner.

"How'd you bag him?" questioned the captain.

"He got lost. He thought we were Russians. When he realized who we were he tried to shoot, but I was on him before he could pull the trigger. I was going to knock him off, but Santemano said I should bring him to you so he could tell us where our units are."

"And Santemano?" asked Blanco Rodríguez.

"Here I am, my captain," responded a strange, weak voice. Santemano appeared around a corner of the ditch. He collapsed at the captain's feet. Blanco Rodríguez tore aside the white cape and, ripping open the tunic, spied a small hole in the blood-covered chest. Santemano looked like a wax doll. He was dead. A sepulchral silence settled over the group. Ferrol took a tighter grip on his submachine gun.

The POW understood that he was going to die. He made the sign of the cross in reverse, right to left, Russian fashion. The tension broke. He was going to live. Seated in the shelter, the Red rifleman now repeated, "*Ya nye govoriu*" (I won't talk).[182]

Juan Negro was not talking either. Numb with fear and cold, he tramped along between two files of Soviet soldiers. They were Kirghiz —short, but powerfully built, well shod, and warmly encased in furs. After being captured with Pérez in Krasni Bor, Negro had been herded at bayonet point into a corral on the edge of town with some 300 other Spanish prisoners. Most were wounded. The more able-bodied supported or carried their less fortunate comrades. Those who could no longer go on fell out and were finished off by a quick bayonet thrust.[183]

Dusk closed in as the column crawled through *El Trincherón*. Spanish corpses were scattered through the wreckage. As they struggled on, a flight of Stukas flew overhead. At last the Luftwaffe! It was after 1530. Ahead, Kolpino flared as the bombs found their mark. Another squadron of Junkers 87 approached. Suddenly, the sound of sirens split the twilight. They were diving. In the darkness, the pilots of 54 Squadron had taken them for a Russian force. Blinding blasts tore at the columns. Negro saw his fellow prisoners tear open their tunics and bare their chests. They preferred death by their German allies to imprisonment by their Russian enemies. The gull-winged dive bombers pulled away, leaving friend and foe alike dead and dying. New guards replaced the fallen. Reaching the Red lines, they were greeted by a mob of enraged, drunken Russians who pointed their rifles at the ragged band. As if by prior agreement, and in spite of efforts to restrain them, the more gravely wounded broke ranks and threw themselves at the leveled guns. A fusilade cut them down. "At least they won a glorious death and spared themselves an ignominious captivity," pondered Juan.[184]

The dwindling group of prisoners paused at the Soviet front—the same front that Negro had seen crawl like an ant hill the previous night. Half-naked, drunken female soldiers were stripping the Russian dead. Long hair flying, singing and shouting, they cursed the POWs. One of them called out and, pointing to a young Navarrese who had had his chin destroyed by an explosive bullet, jerked him from the column. Negro assumed that the woman had been moved by compassion. A crisp order and they stripped the lad. Unable to speak or cry out, he stood naked in cold darkness, his lower jaw dangling by torn tendons. The woman shoved him to the ground and, inserting a hand grenade into the bloody hole, laughingly stood back to watch. The POWs began to shout and scream in rage and protest, but their captors bayoneted them into silence. A sharp explosion, a soul-wrenching cry, the mass twitched, and was still. As a final caprice, one of the women seized a rifle and drove a bayonet through the corpse, sticking it upright through the ground. Then, with a wild laugh, they grabbed the Navarrese's helmet and placed it atop the upturned butt of the rifle in a macabre parody of the German symbol for a fallen hero.[185]

A few heroes still held out along the heights. The remaining pieces of 1 and 3 Batteries continued to fire. Reinlein had hardly returned to the bunker of Captain Andrés when the Soviets unleashed another attack. Tanks, surrounded by swarms of infantry, rumbled southward down Sovietskii prospekt. The *guripas* were defenseless against the KV-1s. Diving for cover in the rubble of the ruined brick buildings, they waited until the iron monsters passed and tried to pick off the shielding infantry.

Sapper Sergeant Palomo had just come into the crucible. He had been enrolled in a special assault course at the Army Pioneer School when the alarm sounded. When he came up to Krasni Bor with the 600 men of Battalion Kamenka, he found the front so fluid that he was unable to join his old company—3, under Aramburu. Reporting in to Bellod's CP, he threw himself into the melee.

On down the narrow street came the KV-1s and T-34s. Palomo grabbed a magnetic mine and, crouching low, jumped out of a shattered store. He attached the explosive and sped off. The tank shuddered and briefly stalled, but the reinforced armor of the KV-1 shook off the blast. The monster resumed its slow, stately pace. Palomo then leaped atop a second tank. Throwing open the hatch cover, he deftly dropped a grenade down the turret. Leaping off, he sprinted away, Russian riflemen yelling "*Urrah, Urrah*" at his heels. Behind a muffled blast. Smoke poured out of the hull. Palomo, meanwhile, his pursuers distracted and too close to fire for fear of hitting their own, escaped. Other tanks, however, ground on.[186]

Lt. Constantino Goduidionachvili was with Major Bellod when the attack started. Legionnaire Lieutenant Constantino had just returned from scouting towards *El Bastión*. Ever since the breakthrough, the former Tsarist cavalry captain and veteran of the Spanish Civil War had been scrambling to help hold the second line. He was discussing the situation with Bellod in the major's CP when, at 1615, a KV-1 rounded the corner from Sovietskii prospekt and, firing its 76 mm cannon, began clanking down the street toward the Popovka Railroad Station.

Capt. Muñoz García also saw it coming. He ordered his sappers to strew the street with T mines. But the tank commander, cautious without infantry escort, turned around toward the two-story hospital near regimental headquarters. Inside the wooden schoolhouse, Lieutenant García López watched as the KV-1 advanced, cannon booming and machine gun chattering. It was rolling right toward the main door of the field hospital. Many of the wounded, unable to move and fearing that they were going to be squashed by the tremendous treds as they lay on the floor or in their cots, began screaming. Others dived out the rear windows.

Individual *divisionarios*, gripped by the sheer horror of the scene, tried to stop the iron monster by flinging Molotov cocktails and affixing magnetic mines. Invincible, the KV-1 crunched on. Suddenly, out of the shadows, rose Bellod's runner, Sapper Antonio Ponte Anido, Seizing two T mines, he cooly slipped up to the steel sides and shoved them into the whirling tracks and bogies. A searing blast shook the street. Tracks flailing, the tank jerked to a stop like an injured dinosaur. Both Ponte and the tank were finished. Confronted with courage such as this in dark, narrow, rubble-strewn streets, the Soviets called off the attack.[187]

Major LaCruz came up with his antitankers from the corduroy road. As the small column pressed through the gathering darkness and passed the regimental CP, the *guripas* glanced at the mutilated iron monster. Reaching 1 Battery, the antitankers plopped down in a corner of the artillery bunker. Blood stains smeared the floor. The dead crowded the other corner.

Reinlein and LaCruz huddled in consultation. *Radio Macuto* reported that the regiment had been relieved but, with communications out, confirmation was impossible. Moreover, Heckel had yet to move up. By 1700 it was quiet in Krasni Bor. Little bands still clashed, but the guns were silent.[188]

Heckel still hesitated. At 1700, as darkness closed in, corps signaled 390 Regiment to jump off and restore the old HKL. Two Tigers would help Heckel in the morning. Kleffel also instructed 374 Grenadier Regiment, which was rushing into Popovka, to hold the October Railroad and close on SS Police. On the Izhora, 316 Grenadiers, still offloading in Sablino, would hurry up to attack on the morrow out of the Red Woods. Powerful forces were finally near at hand for a stunning counterblow. Meanwhile, the Spaniards waited and wondered.

Shadowy figures slipped through the night toward 3 Sappers on the Moscow-Leningrad Highway. "*Alto! Quien Vive?*" shouted the sentries. "*España!,*" the voices replied. A group of ragged legionnaires stumbled in. They were from Mobile Reserve 250, the last of Oroquieta's *islote*. They had held until 1700. Aramburu welcomed them and placed them in his perimeter. He had no orders to retire.[189]

Reinlein and LaCruz made their rounds. All was quiet. The ambulances and Sergeant Espiñeira's supply trucks were getting the wounded out as quickly as they could. Although the point of 390 Regiment had yet to come up and Heckel was reporting to corps that he was in the town and could find neither Spaniards nor Russians, the German mess sergeants seemed able to get through. Around 1800, they served hot food and coffee to the exhausted *guripas*. Over at Popovka, the sappers and cyclists clung to the narrow-gauge railroad track. But Bellod had had enough. Colonel von Below had rushed 374 Grenadiers up the October Railroad from Sablino without delay and was already forming up behind him. Von Below hurried his men into the line, taking over from von Bock and Bellod as rapidly as possible and extending eastward along the heights. Advised that 390 and 374 Regiments had assumed command, Bellod pulled out what was left of Recon 250, First of 262, and his combat engineers, and fell back toward Sablino at 1830. Lieutenant Frago, commanding a section of Second Squadron, decided he was too far forward to hear the withdraw order. He and his men stuck it out until noon the following day.

Watching Bellod go, Liaison Lieutenant Jobst worried. Combat Group Heckel should have been here hours ago. He resolved to seek out the CP and set out westward from Popovka. After an hour's walk, Jobst encountered Heckel at 1930 in the woods south of the Orthodox church. Heckel announced that his Regiment 390 was in position and had taken over the sector.[190]

Fifteen minutes later three shot-up supply trucks parked in the Motor Pool at Mestelevo. Last night's convoy had returned. The service troops gathered round as the drivers told their story. They had been in the thick of it, munitioning, hauling wounded, dodging infantry and tanks. One man was wounded, another evacuated, hit by an antitank round. Espiñeira had refused to return: he had stayed to fight. They had come back by way of Tosno where they had left a load of wounded. The German rear had been boiling. New units detraining, artillery off-loading, Panzers and assault guns rumbling northward to Krasni Bor. The transport troops were convinced that the Russians would be stopped.[191]

A new line now existed along the edge of the forest from the Moscow-Leningrad Highway eastward to the SS Police. However, at 2000, when German shells began crashing into Krasni Bor, Reinlein and LaCruz decided that the Germans had no intention of immediately advancing any further. But, they were reluctant to retire. As yet no news directly from division. Moreover, little bands and even individuals who had hid out until nightfall were still seeping back from *El Trincherón*. They would stay and scoop up these stragglers. Nor did they want to abandon Aramburu north of the Red Woods.

Robles prowled the corduroy road. When word had filtered back about Sagrado's disappearance, he had set out from Raikolovo towards Krasni Bor with a squad and a small staff. He set up his CP in a hut beside the road. Regiment 262, of course, no longer existed, but the lanky legionnaire embraced the waifs and strays and shepherded them into a shaky line along the northern fringe of the Red Woods. Here, between the Izhora and the Moscow-Leningrad Highway, a huge gap yawned. Regiment 316 was going to come up from Sablino but, until it arrived and formed a firm line, division and corps were in mortal danger.[192]

Aramburu was also endangered. Around 2200, the assault section of Antitanks 250 was routed out of the resistance center at 1 Battery and hurried off to the Highway to back up 3 Sappers, should they be able to break out. From the top of the highway, the scouts could see flares floating over the town. Below, on the black plain, thousands were grappling in darkness. When they touched, rifles snapped, knives glinted, and men died. Some shells were hitting over by the October Railroad. To the west, mortars flashed along the Izhora.

Esteban Infantes took the call at 2025. Lindemann on the line. As Metternich translated, the brigadier reported.

The situation west of the Izhora is unchanged. To the east on the other hand, it is unclear. The perimeter around Raikolovo is occupied by three companies. Northeastwards of Staraia Myza, there is no connection with 316 Regiment. I understand that 390 Grenadiers has pressed forward to the middle of Krasni Bor. . . . [We have] no contact with Krasni Bor, [but] are trying tonight. Three tanks are still near Staraia Myza.

Lindemann crisply replied: "Staraia Myza must be held unconditionally. Together with 316 Grenadiers, you will attack northward."[193]

Robles was more than willing to work with 316 Grenadiers, but he could not wait. By 2100, he had been able to scrape up enough strays to shake out a scratch company. Officers were lacking, munitions scarce, and automatic arms nonexistent. He had convinced his cannoneers without cannon, infantry without weapons, and cooks without kitchens that powerful friendly forces had closed up on each flank and that they were really in the second line. He, of course, knew otherwise. Seventy-second Rifle Division seemed certain to attack in the morning.

A confident sentry, secure in the knowledge that he was safe in the rear, calmly called. A column in close order was coming down the corduroy road. The voices were neither Spanish nor German, but the helmets appeared about right. Stepping out, the lieutenant colonel held up his hand. *Halt!* They were Estonians. the captain commanding explained in wretched German that they were two companies from Battalion-East 658, sent up to provide perimeter defense for Artillery Group 138. Several German batteries had been exposed by the breakthrough. Could Robles direct him?

The crafty lieutenant colonel, feigning not to understand, invited the captain into his *izba*. Over a map, by candlelight, Robles—who knew that the batteries were emplaced three kilometers away—pinpointed "the actual location."[194] Curiously enough, the Estonians would have to deploy along the fringe of the Red Woods between the Izhora and the Moscow-Leningrad Highway, if they were to give the proper protection to the field pieces. The Estonian captain exited, barking orders. The gap was plugged.

Palacios stood stripped naked in the center of the Soviet CP. He faced a tall intelligence officer seated behind a pine table. To the left, dozing on a pile of sacks, lay a Red Army general. A dead cigarette stub dangled from his open mouth. Between the two officers slumped a smirking, small dark man dressed in a black *rubashka* and rain coat —Ortega, a Spanish Republican.

"Your name?" Ortega queried with a superior tone.

"I won't say a single word until you allow me to dress," responded the hidalgo.[195]

This was Palacios's second interrogation. He and Castillo had been pulled out of the small POW column almost immediately after their capture. The two officers were escorted to a regimental headquarters in the southern suburbs of Kolpino. They had trod the corpse-covered plain and encountered Russian army women stringing telephone lines and collecting the dead. The first interview had been cut short by a Stuka attack. Then, they had been hustled to Kolpino and thrust into an *izba*. Inside, were Alturas and Molero, who had been taken when they tried to escape from the railroad embankment. Both had been with Palacios in the *regulares* during the Civil War and spoke Arabic.

"*Mektub*" (It was written), sighed Palacios.

"Yes, but *muymalmektub*" (badly written), quipped Molero.[196] The four laughed.

A sentry had prodded Palacios awake. Upon entering the dimly lit CP, he was instructed to empty his pockets. A first-aid kit, a handkerchief, some lemons, fell on the table. Then, a pineapple grenade appeared, forgotten by the captain and overlooked by those who had searched him. Frightened, the Russians had told him to strip.

"What battalion are you from?" questioned the Communist, Ortega.

"It is undignified for an officer to be interrogated in this manner. Let me put on my captain's uniform and I will allow myself to be questioned."[197]

The Soviet intelligence officer stood up, shouted, and pounded the table. Then the general, without even a glance in Palacios's direction, ordered Ortega to return the clothes.

"Your name?"

"Teodoro Palacios Cueto."

"Battalion?"

"Fifth Company, Second Battalion."

"Look at the map. Show us where the CP, hospital and artillery are."

"I can't."

"Where are the munitions depots?"

"I can't. I don't know how to read the map."

"Aren't you a professional soldier?"

"Yes, sir."

"And you don't know how to read a map! What do they teach you in the Academy?"[198]

On it went for almost an hour. Shouts, table pounding, but no personal violence. The Russians were really more interested in propaganda than information. The intelligence officer and Ortega were most insistent about a radio broadcast. Palacios should plead with the division to lay down its arms. He refused. More threats, more promises. The general dozed. Finally, the tall officer spat:

"The 7000 casualties inflicted on the Red Army will be avenged."[199]

Dismissed, Palacios turned to gather up his things.

"You won't need them. He that takes up arms against the Soviet Union and loses pays the price of defeat with his life."

"I know how to lose," retorted the Spanish captain, "but the USSR does not know how to win!"

As the captain made for the door, he heard the Russian shout, "Your time has come. Your officers will meet the same fate!"

"They will also know how to fulfill their duty!" Palacios shot back.[200]

For the first time, the general raised his head. With a surprised expression he looked Palacios straight in the eye. As Palacios departed, he felt certain that he was going to die.[201]

Sagrado was safe in Sablino. The disheveled colonel had arrived about 1900 and had immediately requested an interview with General

Reymann. The commander of 212 Division was not anxious to see him, and allowed him to cool his heels for over three hours. Meanwhile, Sagrado telephoned Esteban Infantes and advised the brigadier that "his CP had been destroyed by fire from Russian tanks and occupied by Red infantry"—an assertion refuted by the regimental liaison officer, Lieutenant Jobst.[202] "Lacking any means of help, the colonel continued, he had searched southward for Heckel, whose arrival had been reported and who could have advanced but did not. In fact, prompt intervention would not only have supported his Spanish troops, but also have been helpful in holding the sector."[203] Not until Bellod came in from Popovka did Sagrado learn for certain that his men were still carrying on.

When the colonel was finally ushered into Reymann's room, the reception was frigid. Jobst, who had arrived from Heckel's headquarters, interpreted. Reymann instructed Sagrado to remain in Sablino. He was not to return to Raikolovo, but stay and help collect the stragglers. Esteban Infantes, Sagrado was informed, had dispatched a staff officer, Lieutenant Fernández Cavada, to take charge. Furthermore, Reymann declined to employ the reorganized Spanish units in his sector. The interview ended. Sagrado was shattered, but he did pull himself together enough to send more munitions to Reinlein in Krasni Bor. This was his last order as colonel commanding 262.[204]

First Group had only one serviceable 105. The other cannon which had held the Red armor and infantry at bay were dismounted and destroyed. Except for an occasional Russian or German shell, it was quiet in Krasni Bor. Once in a while shots rang out from the Russian-held sector. Fleeing townspeople said that the Red Army was shooting the civilians for collaboration. What else could the inhabitants have done? The Spaniards had been their bread and butter.[205]

The German bombardment increased as midnight approached. Reinlein and LaCruz were losing more to their ally's fire than to their enemy's. No strays had stumbled in for hours. Still no news from division. But it was now certain that the Germans had taken over. It was time to go.

Blowing the last piece, Major Reinlein and Captain Andrés pulled out of the *islote* around 1 Battery. They had about half a hundred cannoneers. Major LaCruz and Captain Apestegui followed with almost a hundred antitankers and infantry. The small column passed the riddled hospital, their battered regimental CP, the ruined Orthodox church, and was approaching the entrance to the corduroy road near the

Moscow-Leningrad Highway when a German lieutenant appeared out of the shadows. He wanted to talk to the officer in charge. Reinlein and LaCruz went over. The translator had trouble. While the interpreter was doing his best, the Spaniards noticed bright red collar tabs peeking above the white reversible coat worn by the young lieutenant. He was an artilleryman, and obviously wanted them to stay. His battery of 155s was emplaced to the south in the Sablino Forest and, if Reinlein and LaCruz left, his pieces would be fully exposed to Soviet infantry assault. He would have to blow them.

LaCruz declined. Reinlein, having felt the agony of defending his own guns all day and finally destroying them, hesitated. Here was a fellow artilleryman in a desperate situation. Besides, Aramburu might still be alive. Finally, he assented. LaCruz tried to dissuade him. No use. The antitankers went southward towards Sablino, while Reinlein, Andrés, and their half a hundred cannoneers entrenched in front of the German battery. It was just after midnight. Black Wednesday, 10 February 1943, had passed.[206]

"Bury the dead," ordered Aramburu.[207] The three captains— Aramburu, Campos, and Arozamena—had decided to try and break out. Krasni Bor was still. The Izhora had flared for a while around 2300. But that was almost two hours ago. They feared that the Red Army had engulfed all and gone on to Sablino. Destroying everything they could not carry and loading up the wounded on hand sleds, stretchers, and blankets, they pulled them down the highway. Big, quiet, Aramburu concluded that this was the quickest and most direct route to the rear. The ditches also offered some protection. Preceded by patrols, some 200 men—the survivors of four companies: 3 Sappers, 7 and 8 of 262, and 3 of *Tía Bernarda*—struck southward. They were discovered. Soviet submachine guns opened up from the flanks, but were brushed aside. After what seemed like hours, they ran into the antitank assault section near the corduroy road four kilometers from their starting point. Slowly, dragging their wounded, they made for Sablino. After another kilometer or so, they began to meet the *Landser* of 390 Regiment. Aramburu requested the whereabouts of the colonel commanding. Reporting to Heckel, he quickly became aware that the lieutenant colonel was not pleased. Rather, he was surprised. There were not supposed to be any Spaniards in Krasni Bor.[208]

When Reinlein and Aramburu withdrew, 55 Red Army followed up and finally achieved its immediate attack goal—the southern edge of Krasni Bor. On the west, 72 Rifle Division had gained the Izhora.

To the east, 43 Rifle Division was moving on Nikol'skoe. After succeeding in breaking through—72 Rifle Division against Ulzurrún, 63 Guards against Iglesia, and 43 Rifle Division against Losada—the Russian attack had bogged down. This occurred in spite of the flight of large numbers of raw Spanish recruits, who panicked under the shelling and the death of their officers. The surviving units on the high ground—Oroquieta, Aramburu, *El Bastión*, Palacios-Huidobro—and the new *islotes* established by the midmorning counterattack—CP Antitanks 250, CP Second of 262, OP 2 Battery—disoriented the Soviet thrust. The Red Army generals were astounded that anyone at all was left alive after the tremendous artillery preparation, and had not been ready to accept the staggering casualties inflicted by the *islotes* and Spanish and German artillery. They had only been willing to waste the punishment units.

Moreover, the Russian officers lost control of their riflemen through looting and losses and, when command integrity was restored, made the significant error of throwing away their initial advantage by frittering away time on the hedgehogs and other isolated bands rather than concentrating and continuing the advance. Shorn of their infantry escort, the overcautious tank commanders hesitated to press on through Krasni Bor to Sablino and Nikol'skoe. This allowed Reinlein, Bellod, and von Bock to establish a line based on the artillery emplacements along the heights.

Sagrado's departure had, therefore, little effect on the outcome. Von Below's prompt arrival ensured that Bellod's and von Bock's efforts were not in vain. This permitted SS Police to change fronts and dig in. Had Heckel moved with the decisiveness of von Below, there would have been a better chance to save the Krasni Bor Heights. The afternoon assaults by Battalions Blanco and Merry and the decisive efforts of Robles and Cano succeeded in screening the open right flank of 250 Division and further diffusing the Red effort.

Dogged Spanish resistance and Russian errors combined to gain time for 18 Army and L Corps to rush powerful forces to this vital sector. Each minute was dearly bought. Almost 2,200 Spanish casualties paid for the precious hours. The battle of Krasni Bor was over, but 55 Red Army had only stumbled. It had not been stopped.

11

Sin Novedad
and Neutrality

"OUR ORDERS ARE TO ATTACK," REPEATED MASTER

Sergeant Aleksandr Vinogradov.[1] Savoring a bit of vodka, the sergeant further informed his Spanish captors that 72 Rifle Division would soon press on as reinforcements arrived. Forty-fifth Guards from the Kolpino reserves had already been committed. During the night of 10–11 February, a trainload of 1,500 replacements from Kronstadt rattled into Kolpino.

Early Thursday morning, Esteban Infantes, who had returned to Pokrovskaia, sent his daily dispatch to the Spanish military attaché in Berlin. Since neither the general nor his staff really knew what was happening, the telegram was abbreviated and confusing. "The division finds itself locked in hard fighting in Krasni Bor. Spirit of the division excellent. Our casualties: 3 killed, 10 wounded."[2]

The wire did not get through to Berlin until Friday, 12 February. Although alarmed, Roca de Togores decided to wait for further news before informing Madrid. Somehow, the small number of casualties did not seem to tally with the report of a major engagement. A few hours later, a second telegram arrived. After briefly describing the Soviet attack, Esteban Infantes listed losses of three infantry battalions, two antitank companies, two sapper companies, and one squadron, but only two batteries. Obviously, the general still did not have a complete grasp of the situation. Nevertheless, he urged the immediate dispatch of two march battalions—a total of over 2,000 men—as well as replacements for six infantry, one sapper, and one cavalry majors. In addition, Esteban Infantes asked for the immediate sending up of an additional general staff officer.

Stunned by a plea to rush replacements for obviously enormous losses, Roca de Togores telephoned Madrid. Unable to reach the chief of staff, García Valiño, he asked that the call be put through to the minister of war, Asensio. The general listened patiently while the colonel explained that Esteban Infantes's fragmentary report had been partially confirmed by Tass and the BBC. He had already alerted 20 March Battalion at Hof, Roca de Togores continued. This would cover about half of the casualties, including some of the line officers requested by division.[3] Asensio approved. Ringing off, he ordered the march battalion then concentrating in Logroño to accelerate its preparation for departure. He instructed his G-4 to collect additional supplies for immediate shipment to the front. He also cast about for a general staff officer.[4]

A bugle echoed through the corridors of the Superior War College. Class was over. An orderly awaited Lieutenant Colonel Villegas. He was to report to the War Ministry immediately. Dashing down to Buena Vista Palace, Villegas was advised that his petition to join the Volunteer Division had been granted. General Kindelán, director of the Superior War College, tried to dissuade Villegas from abandoning the classroom for the front. But Villegas, who had served in Morocco with Esteban Infantes, was determined to go. Villegas's decision was a disappointment for the general, who continued to oppose Spain's policy of approximation to the Axis.[5]

Franco's policy contained as much ambiguity as approximation. Early in January 1943, he had singularly favored the British ambassador and had suggested a negotiated peace. Then, the Caudillo had sent a leaderless armaments commission to Germany and dispatched Arrese with a noncommittal letter to the Führer. January droned on. The low-level armaments commission languished in Germany. Hitler, fretting about the Casablanca Conference between Roosevelt and Churchill (14–24 January), feared an Anglo-American invasion of Iberia.

Preparations for launching Gisela had surged with von Moltke's arrival in Madrid on 11 January 1943 and convening of the Casablanca Conference in French Morocco. In spite of the fact that the Franco-Spanish frontier was hermetically sealed, von Rundstedt's activities in southern France were immediately observed by Spanish Intelligence. The concentration of Spanish-speaking Wehrmacht personnel at Pau, the upswing in radio and telephonic communication between the five divisions near Perpignan, and the requisitioning of 2,000 rooms for billeting at Montpellier alarmed Madrid. Jordana had initially dismissed these reports as rumor, but it was difficult to keep doing so.[6]

By 20 January, the day after Arrese's visit to the *Führerhauptquartier*, it was evident that preparations for Gisela were mounting. With the Caudillo's concurrence, Jordana instructed Ambassador Vidal in Berlin to request an immediate audience with Hitler or, failing that, Ribbentrop, and to inform them with absolute decisiveness and energy that "Spain will oppose with force of arms any invasion of its territory."[7] Doussinague spent the day in his office at Santa Cruz Palace awaiting Vidal's wire from Berlin. An old friend entered. Waving his arm toward a stack of dispatches on his desk, Doussinague said, "You have come to see me on the day which could be the last day of Spanish independence."[8] One of the reports on the pile fixed 0500 the following morning as zero hour for the German invasion. The vigil went on. Still no news from Vidal.

At 0600 the next morning, the telephone rang in the Foreign Ministry. The sleepy watch officer snapped awake when he was informed that the German Embassy was on the line. Von Moltke insisted upon seeing Jordana. The duty officer refused. It was too early, the minister was not yet awake. Two hours later, an agitated German diplomat arrived at Santa Cruz Palace demanding an immediate audience for his ambassador. Since it was well after 0800, the duty officer agreed and advised Jordana, who consented. Von Moltke carried a message from the Führer. Lies, all lies, insisted Hitler. All rumors relating to German troop movements toward the Spanish frontier were false. The Third Reich had no intention of invading Spain.[9]

After this rocky beginning to his term as ambassador, von Moltke prepared to present his credentials to the chief of state on 23 January at Oriente Palace. As von Moltke made the customary speech, the Caudillo replied with a few polite words of his own. Soothing the German impatience with his attitude of late, he trotted out the usual mention of the Blue Division as the clear indication of Spain's loyalty to the anti-Bolshevik cause, shedding blood alongside Germany against the "barbarous . . . claws of communist bestiality."[10]

Then, he drew the ambassador into an adjoining room. He urged von Moltke to impress upon Hitler that the war had gone on long enough, and that all of Europe would lose if it continued. "The longer a war lasts," he lamented, "the more problematical is victory."[11] He hoped that Hitler would accept the help of Germany's friends in finding the road to peace. The ambassador was not so pessimistic. Germany will end the war by force of arms, he declared. They left it at that.

German fears would not be allayed until the arms issue was settled. The two dictators were in fundamental disagreement. Hitler wanted a defensive alliance in exchange for weapons. If Spain were invaded, German troops would automatically enter Iberia. Failing a formal alliance, the Führer would settle for a firm Spanish guarantee to resist what he regarded as an imminent Allied invasion and, hopefully, for an invitation to enter. Franco, on the other hand, wanted to strengthen Spanish neutrality. He did not want any foreign armies—Allied or Axis—in Iberia. Hitler was still suspicious that Franco might use the arms against the Wehrmacht if he invaded first, and kept stressing how Spanish soldiers must be trained in modern weaponry before delivery. Franco, for the same reason, wanted delivery first, training later. The situation remained unsettled, the Germans suspicious, the Spaniards wary.

Acting upon instructions from Berlin, von Moltke presented a *demarche* on Friday, 20 January. Meeting with the chief of state and the foreign minister, the ambassador told them that the Reich demanded a written guarantee that Spain would resist any Anglo-American invasion. Von Moltke stressed that the delivery of arms was predicated on the condition that these weapons would only be employed against Germany's enemies. Franco replied that he did not understand why a written declaration was necessary, since he had already taken defensive measures. He had nine divisions in Morocco. The Caudillo continued "If anyone tries to attack us, we will fight as one man, with arms or without them. It has already been proven during our Civil War, when the Republicans held Madrid, and controlled the Treasury, the Army and the Navy, that we could win, thanks to our courage and our faith in victory."[12] In the course of the conversation, Franco came to understand that further procrastination might provoke the Germans into invading Spain. He instructed Jordana to continue the conversations on Monday.[13]

When the foreign minister and the ambassador met, each had a draft ready for the other. Jordana's memorandum, in the form of a personal letter which could be disavowed by the chief of state at any time, stated that Spain would promise to defend itself only after the arms arrived. Moreover, the note did not specify the Allies as the presumptive aggressors. Since this was unacceptable, von Moltke produced his own draft. The agreement would be a secret protocol in which Spain obligated itself to defend Iberia, the islands, and Morocco against the Anglo-Americans with all the forces at its disposal. Jordana agreed, and said that the ambassador's draft could certainly be the basis for further discussion.

The Casablanca Conference had made Hitler jittery about Allied intentions. His uneasiness increased when Churchill flew from Casablanca to Cairo and then, reportedly, went on to Lisbon, where he was supposed to visit Salazar. Well aware of the close relations between the two peninsular leaders, as expressed in their Iberian Bloc, the Führer became anxious about Churchill's journey.

Doussinague arrived home late on Saturday evening, 6 February. The political director was tired and immediately went to bed. He had hardly dozed off when, at 2330, the telephone buzzed. It was Hans Lazar, press attaché at the German Embassy. Lazar, a stout swarthy Armenian, had shown himself a solid friend of Spain in the past and once again was proving his attachment. The embassy was boiling, he informed Doussinague. He had been summoned at 2300 and found von Moltke, the new first secretary, Andor Hencke, who had replaced Heberlein, and the military attachés fuming.

A group within the embassy, led by Colonel Krappe, who was beginning to despair of bringing Spain into the war under the triumvirate —Muñoz Grandes, Asensio, and Yagüe—had engineered a plot to convince the new ambassador that Spain had entered the British orbit. They told Lazar that Franco had motored to Lisbon to confer with Churchill. Swiss radio, fed false information by Mussolini who still hoped to drag Spain into the war, had confirmed the meeting. Von Moltke had his hand on the telephone as if he were going to call Berlin. Von Rundstedt's legions would certainly follow. Lazar had tried to reason with the ambassador and did succeed in delaying until he could check around. Could Doussinague help? He could! He was able to convince von Moltke that there had been no trip, no conference, and that Franco was asleep in El Pardo. The immediate crisis passed, but the Spaniards finally realized that they had to do something to reassure the Germans once and for all. Franco and Jordana decided to sign the secret protocol.[14]

On Tuesday, 9 February, von Moltke wired Berlin that "the Spanish Government is prepared to sign a secret protocol promising to defend the Iberian Peninsula against any Allied invasion" as soon as the Germans "realized their intention to provide Spain with modern arms."[15] The Spanish action was none too soon. That same day, Hitler "issued further decrees concerning 'Gisela.'"[16] With the *Afrika Korps* boxed in in Tunisia, "the Führer believes it possible," an OKW memorandum cooly reported, "that the next operation of the Anglo-Saxons will be directed against the Iberian Peninsula. . . . [He] has decided that, in order to protect the [German] U-boat bases [in France], as soon as the Allies land . . . he will order the implementation of Gisela."[17]

The urgency of the situation as Hitler saw it was emphasized by the prompt dispatch of Admiral Canaris to Spain. On Wednesday, Intelligence in the German Madrid Embassy was alerted to the imminent arrival of the *Abwehr* director, who was covertly coming to ascertain the firmness of Spanish resolve. He would interview two of his oldest contacts, Air Minister Vigón and former intelligence chief Martínez Campos. Moreover, he had been instructed not to see Franco, Jordana, or Muñoz Grandes, lest the government learn the purpose of his trip. Hitler, as usual, was playing a triple game. Now, after months of procrastination, although he did not have a defensive alliance, at least he had his guarantee. He was willing to bargain with Franco over the arms.

Only a few days later, Roca de Togores was startled to learn from OKW that the Führer was anxious to receive a top level armaments commission preparatory to fulfilling Spanish wishes in a most generous manner. Delighted and relieved, the Caudillo appointed Martínez Campos to head the commission. The general would leave in mid-March. An expert at double-dealing himself, Franco gave Martínez Campos another mission. He was to make a detailed and close inspection of the Third Reich and evaluate Germany's chances of winning the war now that Stalingrad had fallen, the blockade of Leningrad had been broken, and Tunis was about to give way.[18]

Franco was not certain who was going to win, but he did fear Soviet Russia. And yet, Franco could not really be certain that Germany would lose. Martínez Campos would find out. The lean, sinewy general with a hawklike face regarded by the German military attaché as "clever, well-informed, and able" was preparing for his journey to Berlin.[19] Fiftyish and somewhat hard of hearing, Martínez Campos spoke fluent English and French, and enough German to get along. Pro-German in spite of his monarchist sentiments, he was distrusted by Foreign Minister Jordana, who succeeded in circumscribing the general's power to negotiate. The struggle between Foreign Ministry and War Ministry was only a part of the Byzantine conflict that permeated Spanish domestic politics and hopelessly entangled them with international complications.[20]

The balance of power in the Mediterranean had clearly shifted toward the Allies. A glance at the map was sufficient to convince even the most casual observer, and Muñoz Grandes was much more than that. By March 1943, it was obvious that the Germans would be unable to fulfill the three preconditions—Axis control of Tunis, a new offensive in Russia, and deployment of an operational army in North Africa—that the triumvirate had required for Spanish entry into the war.

After a flurry of receptions and a shower of honors immediately following his return in December, Muñoz Grandes had submerged. Placed at the disposal of the minister of war in January, the general continued his contacts with his confederates, but the course of the war, the threat of a German invasion, the waning danger of an Anglo-American landing in Iberia, and the distance between him and the hypnotic charm of the Führer cooled his ardor. Muñoz Grandes was still pro-German and would continue to communicate with Berlin by cypher, but his patriotism precluded his pushing Spain into a losing struggle. He was also co-opted by the Caudillo. On Monday, 3 March, the generalissimo announced the appointment of Muñoz Grandes as chief of his Military Household—a post of influence but not of power. The Allied ambassadors breathed a sigh of relief. They had feared that the general would be posted either to Morocco or Gibraltar.

Martínez Campos arrived in Berlin on 13 March. He carried an urgent shopping list designed to help push the Allies back into the sea should they land. Air and coastal defense needs came first. Keitel, of course, kept Germany's inability to fill the order to himself when he met Martínez Campos on 16 March. While Martínez Campos was exchanging impressions with Keitel, Reich Propaganda Minister Dr. Joseph Goebbels wrote in his diary: "Neither Spain nor Portugal wants the enemies of the Axis to march through their territory. . . . Spain has an appetite for Algiers, but for the present there seems to be no practical way of gaining possession of Algiers except by entering the war. But that is exactly what the Spaniards do not want to do."[21] Two days later Keitel and Martínez Campos went on from Berlin to the Wolf's Lair. Hitler welcomed his guest, and remarked that Germany really did not demand that Spain become an ally in order to receive arms. In fact, the only precondition was that Spain agree to defend itself.

The Führer tried to convince Martínez Campos that Spain should begin small, with a few weapons which were easy to introduce and not technically beyond the capacity of its armed forces. The tempo and complexity would increase in time. The Spanish general politely stuck to his instructions, suggesting that as much as possible should be delivered as soon as possible.

The interview over, Martínez Campos was whisked off to visit the armaments industry. The Germans made a special effort to impress the general with their organization, technology, and production facilities. Above all, his hosts sought to dazzle him with stories about new secret weapons which would strike terror into the Allies, turn the tables, and win the war. Martínez Campos, clever and cool as he was, was overwhelmed by the efficiency and technical superiority of the Nazi war machine. The tour, which went on for ten days, had only one sad note. News arrived that Ambassador von Moltke had suddenly died on Monday morning, 22 March.[22]

The ambassador lay in state in the chapel of his private palace at 3 Hermanos Béquer. The Caudillo sent his condolences. Jordana, Muñoz Grandes, Moscardó, Arrese, and other high dignitaries crowded in to pay their respects. During the wake, General Muñoz Grandes and Colonel Wilhelmi, the German army attaché, drew aside.[23] "It will be difficult to replace the ambassador, because in a short time he had won great sympathy here. He will be difficult to replace," murmured the general.

I doubt more and more that there will ever be a real understanding between Germany and Spain. That is most regrettable, since the defeat of Germany means the downfall of Spain. Both parties are guilty. Both nations have their strengths and their weaknesses, their cares and their needs.

One thing is clear. That is, Spain will defend Spanish territory against *anyone* who comes uninvited.[24]

When Wilhelmi reported to Hencke what had been said, the first secretary was struck by the note of pessimism in Muñoz Grandes's words. Embassy Councillor Gardemann was not so certain that the death of von Moltke alone was the cause of Muñoz Grandes's pessimism. Writing to Berlin, he opined that "the time is past when Spain could be brought into the war. October [1942] was the last opportunity."[25]

Manuel Valdés confirmed Gardemann's analysis a few days later. In a conversation with the vice secretary, the councillor learned that over six weeks ago "Muñoz Grandes had convinced the Caudillo to steer a clear course towards Germany, but the failure of the weapons to arrive allowed the opposition to undermine the decision. . . . Germany failed to seize the opportune moment."[26] The Anglophiles were gaining control, Valdés emphasized. Friends of Germany such as Guitarte and Castiella had already lost their posts as heads of the SEU and the Falange Exterior. Franco himself was increasingly taking over the direction of all policy—domestic and foreign. Those around him urged different foreign policies. Jordana favored neutrality. Muñoz Grandes, Asensio, and Yagüe still were partial to Germany, but were drawing back. Varela, Kindelán, and Alba preferred the Allies. Spain seemed to be slipping from nonbelligerency toward neutrality.

The plot of the triumvirate had collapsed. As Muñoz Grandes had said, all shared responsibility—Spain, Germany, the Allies. The fortunes of war had turned against the Axis. Spanish generals, their eyes heretofore dazzled by the blitzkrieg of the Wehrmacht, had begun to see—but, not Martínez Campos.[27]

"The German war machine is invincible," Martínez Campos told the Caudillo.[28] Franco, who trusted his former intelligence chief, was startled. Wonder weapons were not only on the drawing boards, but in production. The general succeeded in convincing Franco that the Germans could yet win the war. According to Serrano Suñer, who was out of power but not out of touch, Martínez Campos's visit to the Third Reich and interview with Hitler was one of the most important of the war. If what the general said were true, Spain would have to be more cautious than ever.

Happily, Martínez Campos could advise the generalissimo that the prevailing opinion in the Reich capital seemed to be that Spanish entry into the war would at this point be detrimental to the Axis cause. Moreover, the Germans appeared to be convinced finally that Spain would resist any attack, Italo-German or Anglo-American. Meanwhile the western Allies and the Russians were still advancing.[29]

Some ten days before Martínez Campos returned from the Third Reich, Lt. Col. José Villegas bid *adíos* to his wife and daughters. A swarm of well-wishers crowded around his coach in the Madrid Railroad Station of Principe Pio. It was his Saint's Day—St. Joseph—19 March.[30]

That very Friday morning, the Soviets launched their last maximum effort to exploit their hard-won gains of 10 February at Krasni Bor. Beginning at 0515, Russian artillery blanketed the Spanish line along the Izhora and the German positions near Nikol'skoe. Fifty-fifth Red Army had been trying to break out of the Krasni Bor box for the last five weeks. Their main weight had been eastward toward Nikol'skoe, where open ground led to the Sablino-Mga railroad and highway—the supply route of Group Hilpert. But the Soviets also sought to slice westward across the Izhora.[31]

Savage fighting had raged around Staraia Myza. In spite of a series of onslaughts by 72 Rifle Division, the Spaniards had somehow managed to hold. On Thursday, 11 February, Robles and Cano had ordered 5 Company of 269 to attack Staraia Myza. Captain Blanco Rodríguez led his men southward out of the Paper Mill, only to be beaten back. Lieutenant Soriano, however, managed to cling to the eastern edge of the Izhora. Urbano and Marzo, with 1 and 3 Companies of 263, moved up to help. Blanco Rodríguez joined in. Though the town was taken and three tanks knocked out by artillery and two captured, 72 Rifle Division launched an armor-tipped counterattack. Blanco Rodríguez fell wounded. Staraia Myza was again lost, or what was left of it.[32] Nevertheless, by nightfall the Izhora sector had been stabilized.

When Robles was pulled out to take over the reorganization of 262, Colonel Rubio assumed overall command of Cano's Izhora subsector. At the request of Corps, Esteban Infantes instituted an investigation of the conduct of Sagrado at Krasni Bor. Kleffel began his own of Heckel. Sagrado was relieved and sent home. Heckel, already in disfavor with his divisional commander, took his regular furlough on 3 May, but was relieved and transferred to *Führerreserve* before he could return.

Most of Robles's men were unarmed. His regiment—he officially took command later in the month—was a skeleton. As Robles whipped the remnants of 262 into shape, shattered sappers and cyclists, as well as Letts, Estonians, and Flemings, drifted in to stiffen the line of the Izhora. The officers who had served so well during the crucial hours of 10 and 11 February—Urbano, Marzo, Allendesalazar, and Soriano —fell one by one. But the Izhora held.[33]

While Rubio and Cano clung to the Izhora and Robles resuscitated 262, Esteban Infantes tried to restore Spanish prestige. The day after the battle of Krasni Bor, he met with Kleffel and Reymann at Pokrovskaia. Putting on a bold face and praising the conduct of his men, he proposed the reconquest of the Moscow-Leningrad Highway up to *El Bastión*. Kleffel considered counterattacking, but the Izhora was still shaky. Moreover, the confidence of the corps commander in Esteban Infantes's judgment had suffered considerably, and he declined.[34]

Lindemann concurred. Two days after the battle, the army commander told Army Group, "I don't trust the Spaniards any longer. We must transfer them to another sector."[35] The same day, Lindemann and Kleffel discussed 10 February. Kleffel was full of praise for the Spanish officers, who had fought very bravely, he said. The leadership of the regiment, on the other hand, was not sufficiently energetic. The two generals agreed that while the officers lived, the *guripas* had fought well, but the German command had long appreciated that the constant turnover in the ranks, with untrained troops coming up from the peninsula, increased the possibility of panic under artillery fire and armored attack once command integrity was broken. Lindemann praised the Spanish officers to Army Group the following day, reserving special commendation for the artillery.

That same Saturday, Reinlein returned from Krasni Bor. He, Captain Andrés, and the cannoneers had succeeded in saving the German battery. Now, three days after the sector had been turned over to 212 Division and forty-eight hours after they had been ordered out, they were finally relieved. As the gallant band gathered on the parade ground at Pokrovskaia, fatigue and hunger showed in their strained faces. Disdain crept over the countenances of Reinlein and Andrés as they stood at ease while the brigadier's fulsome praise washed over them. Their expressions seemed to say, "Where were you, my general?" Seeking to gain stature by association, Esteban Infantes awarded Reinlein a well deserved *Medalla Militar Individual* and appointed the major his personal adjutant.[36]

But the German generals were not deceived. They knew that it was the line officers and not the leadership of the division that had come through. All of Kleffel's apprehensions when Muñoz Grandes had left were revived. Von Küchler and Lindemann discussed pulling the division out of the line and sending it back to Novgorod. Esteban Infantes traveled around accompanied by his new adjutant, forlornly hoping that respect would be transferred to him. Instead the Germans shoved 170 Division behind his line, almost, but not quite, as "corset stays."[37]

On 20 February, Esteban Infantes appointed another one of his heroes, Robles, to official command of 262. That same afternoon, the military attaché in Berlin received the butcher's bill for Wednesday and Thursday, 10–11 February. Roca de Togores read the following figures as shown in the table opposite.[38] Thus, out of the 4,200 officers and men engaged at Krasni Bor, 53 percent fell. Soviet losses were between 7,000 to 9,000 for a gain of three to five kilometers, an average cost per kilometer of 2,500.[39]

The arrival of 20 March Battalion enabled Esteban Infantes to make up about half of his losses. The front settled down to routine patrol clashes, raids, and bombardments. Soviet air activity and vehicle traffic out of Kolpino continued heavy. The weather was warm for March. Daily thaws and nightly freezes signaled the early arrival of the *rasputitsa*.

With the coming of spring, the roles would again shift, for the last time. The Russian offensives lost steam, and the Wehrmacht again began to plan for attack. The winter campaign had resulted in huge losses for the Germans. After Stalingrad, they had pulled back from the Caucasus toward the Crimea, and the Soviets had advanced from the Don to the Donetz. In March 1943 the Vyazma and Demianck salients were evacuated. With the recapture by the Germans of Kharkov and Belgorod, an enormous bulge around Kursk projected into the gut of Army Group Center. Hitler considered the opportunities open to him and prepared his counterstroke—Operation Citadel, the amputation of the bulge. Moreover, he still intended to use the Spaniards in an assault on Leningrad.

On 14 March, von Küchler transmitted to Lindemann an OKH directive for Operation Leningrad, later to be called *Parkplatz*. The High Command envisioned a defensive phase for Army Group North, in which divisions released from Demianck would be refurbished and built up as attack divisions. Another outfit was to be prepared as an attack division—250. All was to be ready for July, when the operation would be launched. *Parkplatz* involved two steps—an advance to Lake Ladoga would reestablish the siege, then the city would be stormed.[40]

Two days later, Lindemann drove over to Pokrovskaia to alert Esteban Infantes. He stopped first to see Knüppel. The liaison staff chief advised him that, if any difficult orders were involved, it would be best if the army commander signed them himself. The implication was that Kleffel was not getting along with the Spanish brigadier, undoubt-

SPANISH CASUALTIES AT KRASNI BOR

	KILLED IN ACTION	WOUNDED IN ACTION	MISSING IN ACTION	TOTAL CASUALTIES
Officers	48	55	5	108
NCO's	130	95	19	244
Other Ranks	949	885	67	1,901
	1,127	1,035	91	2,253

edly a result of the Krasni Bor battle. Putting on his best face, Lindemann drove on.[41]

"Yours will become an attack division," the army commander confided. "One regiment will be trained at a time, beginning with 262." "My division will be back up to 15,000 within weeks," Esteban Infantes boasted. "We are well in position now, but still lack some weapons. However, there is no sign of an impending attack."[42]

For a few minutes on Friday morning, 19 March, it looked like a repeat of Krasni Bor—drumfire, air attacks, roaring tank motors in Iam Izhora, and the immediate destruction of all communications. But the shelling did not last long and it concentrated on the Spanish artillery rather than on the front line. The Soviets had learned the lesson of Krasni Bor. However, they failed to suppress the Spanish guns. When the Red infantry charged Robles at Podolovo and Putrolovo, they were engulfed in a hail of shrapnel. Again and again, they charged First and Third of 262 under Major Castro and Captain Calvo. Desperate because they had to open the Moscow-Leningrad Highway before the *rasputitsa* melted the surrounding bog into a sea of mud, the Soviets succeeded in briefly overrunning the advance outpost flanking the road. Third Battalion countered and, in hand to hand fighting, shoved 72 Rifle Division back. Captain Merry Gordon fell wounded, but by mid-afternoon hundreds of riflemen hung on the wire and the Izhora was secure. Under Robles's able leadership, 262 was once again a fighting force. Fifty-fifth Red Army also failed in its major effort to move eastward and slice the Sablino-Mga Road.[43] Robles, Bellod, and Castro had done their duty. They departed early in April with Return Battalion 11.

Lieutenant Colonel Villegas was in Hof awaiting his new uniform. Hof, and the Hotel Strauss, he found very pleasant. Villegas made his obligatory visits to the Spanish Hospital, where he attended evening prayers, and the camp on the outskirts of the town, where he inspected the warehouses crammed with cartons of Spanish uniforms. He also purchased his personal equipment—pistol, binoculars, boots, wool socks, and undershirts of such extraordinary length that he could fold them triple against the expected cold. While he waited for his new uniform to arrive from the tailor in Berlin he shared his delicacies from Spain with Capt. Georg Lotter, contact man for the permanent Spanish staff. After dinner, the lieutenant colonel retired to his room. Martial music still blared from the radio as he dropped off to sleep. Tomorrow he was off early to Nürnberg to take the oath to the Führer, then on to the front.

For once, Villegas was up before the German guard tramped through the cobblestone streets singing stout-hearted war songs. The new uniform fitted perfectly on his short, stocky frame. It was magnificent, much more impressive than he had imagined. Buckling on his pistol belt and fixing his helmet square on his gray close cropped hair, Villegas strutted proudly out into the hotel hall and down the stairs. Pushing open the glass doors, he triumphantly entered the dining room where Lotter and two other German officers awaited. Clicking his heels in imitation Prussian fashion and stiffly saluting, the lieutenant colonel, his round impish face beaming, stood before the trio in all his glory.

Something was wrong, terribly wrong. Their faces showed consternation, surprise. They said nothing. Finally, Lotter spoke. He almost strangled on his words. The uniform was that of a general in the General Staff.[44] The golden collar patches and shoulder straps would have to go, along with the shiny buttons and flaming crimson pants stripe. But how, at 0600 in Hof? Muffling Villegas in a cape and cautioning him not to remove it, Lotter hustled the lieutenant colonel into a waiting car before anyone else could observe this desecration.

The military vehicle sped down the autobahn, through the dark pine forests with the early morning sun just beginning to glint between the heavy branches, on to Nürnberg. Suddenly, ahead on the empty road a brown uniformed figure appeared waving a red flag. The driver stopped. A few phrases were exchanged. Then, the staff car crossed the median and drove on in the opposite lane. Villegas was alarmed. He soon understood. A submarine—or, better said, half of one—proceeded in a stately fashion down the autobahn. Villegas was stunned. Arriving in Nürnberg, Lotter rushed Villegas to a tailor. Within forty-five minutes, Villegas was demoted from general back to lieutenant colonel again.

The oath over, Villegas continued on to the front. Königsberg, Tilsit, and finally, Riga. The forest was overpowering. Even Riga seemed to emerge from the trees where partisans lurked. The weather was cold and gray. He felt the presence of the front. The trimotors roared as the Junkers 52 lifted off at Riga for the 600-kilometer flight to Gatchina. Below, the ever-present forest flowed by. Then, immense Lake Peipus, white and frozen. Again the trees. Villegas was impressed, and slightly overwhelmed by the monotony and expanse of the Russian landscape. He felt as if he were flying off into eternity. Here, he mused, "man is a slave of the environment, not its master."[45] He also pondered on the absence of rock and stone. "Russia could never create a great architectural style," he concluded. "The people lack the tradition of ideas transformed into stone. . . . The lack of stone had [therefore] deprived the Russian peasant of a sense of continuity and sustained effort."[46] Villegas's suspicions about Russian architecture were confirmed at Gatchina. Even Rinaldi's splendid palace was of lath, stucco, and plaster of Paris—a facade masquerading as a monument.

The palace at Pokrovskaia was little better—pretentious, but without substance. As chief of staff, he was assigned a working and sleeping room on the second floor—a table, a typewriter, a cot, a telephone, a radio, and many maps. Sanitary facilities were nonexistent. Andino, whom he replaced on 10 April, but who still ran Third Section (Operations), and Alemany (G-2) reported that things were quiet. The tobacco ration had again been cut. Daylight saving time had been introduced on 29 March. March Battalions 20 and 21 had brought divisional strength back up to 15,025. The artillery was not yet up to strength. The Germans were short of guns. Second SS Infantry Brigade still lay to the left at Aleksandrovka, while 254 Division held the Red Woods to the right. The Reds had sent up fifty-eight barrage balloons during the afternoon, but they only stayed aloft half an hour. Last year when the division entered the siege lines, these balloons were only along the Neva. Now they told him, they were also at Leningrad and Kolpino. Enemy traffic was normal, and the usual Soviet shells pasted Pushkin, Pavlovsk, and Modolovo.[47]

All was quiet in Madrid, but not necessarily serene. The silent struggle for Spanish allegiance went on. Hoare was bullying Jordana with the assertion that Britain would be the great European postwar power. Neither Communist Russia nor the United States would be the arbiter of European destiny. The ambassador also cautioned the foreign minister against hoping for "any premature peace, or any separate peace between one section of the Allies and the Axis."[48]

The Foreign Office backed up His Britannic Majesty's ambassador. On 2 April, J. K. Roberts, writing from Whitehall, suggested to Hoare that he remind Jordana about Prime Minister Churchill's rejection of the Spanish proposal of mediation and that if Franco wished to ingratiate himself into the Allied dominated postwar community, "the latter will be inevitably influenced by the policy and attitude shown during the war, and in particular between now and the end of the war, by individual neutrals such as Spain. The Ambassador might at this point be able to work in a warning about the continued presence of the Blue Division on the Eastern Front."[49] Foreign Secretary Anthony Eden followed up with a confidential memorandum to Hoare on 8 April 1943. The duke of Alba had just told Cadogan, he related, that he had recently had a long talk with the Caudillo, whose attitude had changed greatly. The Allies, Franco now admitted, were unbeatable. But it would still take them a long time to conquer Germany. The Germans were assuring him that they had new weapons to redress the balance in the air, but he was skeptical.[50]

While Allied and Axis agents maneuvered in Madrid, Hitler and Mussolini met at Klessheim Castle in Salzburg. The Duce, terrified at the imminent collapse in Tunisia, pleaded with the Führer to seek a compromise peace in the East and then slash through Spain at the Anglo-American rear in North Africa. Hitler declined. "A march through the Iberian Peninsula without Spanish approval was clearly impossible; the Spaniards would fight for their country."[51]

Hitler was convinced. So was Brigadier W. W. T. Torr, His Britannic Majesty's military attaché in Madrid. On 21 April 1943, Torr reported to London:

> After the long and uphill fight of nearly the last three years, during which it looked as if *Spain* would join up with the Germans or be invaded by them, I now feel for the first time some confidence in prophesying, firstly, that *Spain* will not now enter the war on the side of the Axis, and secondly, that if *Germany* decided to invade *Spain*, that *Spain* will resist this and her Army will fight them.[52]

Jordana, unaware of Hitler's decision and Torr's assessment, still worried about the Wehrmacht. He was also preoccupied with the possibility of Communist domination of Europe. On 16 April, in a speech in

Barcelona, the foreign minister made the first public call for a compromise peace. It was hailed by neutrals and rejected by belligerents.[53]

The duke of Alba had come home on leave. He gave a gala ball at his country estate in Andalusia in honor of his daughter's debut. Hayes attended, along with the monarchist elite. Two weeks later, Franco toured the province. During a visit to the ambassador's town house in Seville, the Caudillo told Alba that he was "convinced that the war would drag on so long that both sides would eventually welcome a negotiated peace."[54] On 7 May, Hoare flashed this information to London. Two days later in Almeria, the chief of state issued a general call for peace, because without peace between Christian peoples, he said, barbaric anti-European communism would triumph. Perhaps, however, armistice negotiations were already under way. If so, they might not be to Franco's liking.[55]

The phone rang at 0715 in Villegas's office. It was hot and sticky. The drowsy chief of staff shook himself awake. What could be the matter? Office hours did not start until 0900. Villegas, who had already adjusted to the *sin novedad* (nothing new) situation on the front, had posted Spanish-style summer office hours for GHQ last 28 April, 0900 to 1300, and 1600 to 2030.[56] Reaching over, Villegas lifted the receiver. Lieutenant Förster of the Liaison Staff on the line. "There is an order for divisional artillery. Neither division, corps, nor army artillery will fire tomorrow [17 May] from 0800 to 1700 hours. . . ." "That's all?" thought Villegas. "Military or political reasons? A truce?"[57]

Monday morning, 17 May, came. The German guns were silent. So were the Russian. What was going on? Were the Nazis and the Communists once again drawing together as they had in Poland? Rumors of negotiations had been emanating from Sweden for over a year. May 1943 was an opportune time for both Hitler and Stalin. The balance of power in the East was equal. Both Wehrmacht and Red Army were nerving themselves for a titanic struggle at Kursk. The Axis had lost Tunis on 12 May, but the Anglo-Americans were unable to assure the Soviet Union that they could open a second front this year. Stalin was furious. He wanted a cross-channel invasion, not the occupation of Sicily and southern Italy. The scales of war hung, poised for a decision.

May 17 might have indicated the opening of peace negotiations. Years later, unconfirmed reports indicated that Soviet Foreign Minister Vyacheslav Molotov had disappeared from the Kremlin in June and traveled 330 kilometers behind German lines for a secret rendezvous with von Ribbentrop at Kirovograd in the southern Ukraine. Both sides were to have wanted peace but Hitler supposedly insisted that the Dnieper form the future frontier of the USSR and Stalin would not consider anything less than the prewar boundaries. It was said that the gulf was too great to bridge with negotiations and the discussions collapsed.[58] Villegas never did find out what 17 May 1943 was all about. Nevertheless, in the light of the unsubstantiated hearsay evidence later revealed by Sir Basil Liddell Hart, one cannot help speculating that this might have had something to do with the cease-fire.

By the end of May, all of the units of the Blue Division were about up to full strength, although most of the new arrivals had only three weeks' training. March Battalion 23, led by Major Gueda, was made up mostly of Falangist militia. About 15 percent were, however, former *divisionarios* who, in spite of the shrinking pool of volunteers and the decline of German fortunes, had signed on for another one year tour of duty. Another 3 percent—all recruits, mostly Marxists—had come to try and desert. About one out of ten succeeded. All of the noncoms were regulars.[59]

The month ended on a festive note. The Caudillo promoted Esteban Infantes to major general. Martínez Campos visited the division. Swinging his cane, he stepped off the train and embraced Esteban Infantes. His mission in Berlin had been moderately successful. The Germans had suddenly become very amenable. Unknown to the Spaniards, Hitler had abandoned all plans of forcing Spain into the war.

The evening of 1 June, von Küchler returned to Army Group Headquarters at Pskov from the Wolf's Lair. The field marshal had had an exhausting but exhilarating day. He had discussed *Parkplatz* with Army Chief of Staff Kurt Zeitzler. It would be difficult, von Küchler had said. At least seven additional divisions would be necessary and these would only suffice if the Russians did not also bring up reinforcements. Zeitzler had agreed, and suggested that the attack on the Lower Volkhov to reestablish a foothold on Lake Ladoga be launched simultaneously with the assault on Leningrad itself. This would prevent the enemy from shifting his forces from one sector to the other. However, the Führer had yet to make up his mind whether to go through with *Parkplatz* after all. That would depend upon the success of Operation Citadel, the amputation of the Kursk bulge, and what forces could be spared. The build-up for Citadel and *Parkplatz* was underway.

The Spanish Blue Division was girding for the attack. More officers arrived from Spain. On 14 June, stout, moustachioed, Colonel Navarro and tall, ascetic Colonel Amado took over as chieff of staff and as commander of 263 respectively. With the appointment of Navarro, Villegas became deputy chief of staff. Amado had hardly settled down at his CP in Pushkin when 56 Rifle Division struck.[60]

After months of quiescence, the Soviets sprang into action. Taking advantage of the few hours of darkness and further covering their formation with smoke, five rifle companies leaped forward at 0230 on Thursday, 17 June. An intense half hour artillery, antitank, and mortar barrage on the positions of *El Dedo* (the Finger) of 262 and *El Alcázar* of 263 preceded the infantry attack. Spanish cannon immediately began blasting the Communist concentrations. The Reds stormed forward under a stream of fire, and briefly broke into the trenches. But it was all over by 0330. The major effort had been directed against *El Dedo*. The punishment company spearheading this assault was annihilated. Only two men were captured. Dawn revealed one hundred and thirty bodies spreadeagled on the ground or dangling from the Spanish riders. With morning, Soviet loudspeakers blared across the battlefield. The entire punishment company was accused of deserting. Not a man had returned.[61]

At night, the great guns growled. Around 2200, just as the Spanish program from Radio Pleskau (Pskov) signed off, the evening concert began to tune up. Shell flashes and bomb bursts illuminated the Leningrad backdrop—the dome of St. Isaac's Cathedral, the Admiralty spire, the towers of SS. Peter and Paul, and the smokestacks of Kolpino. The *guripas* loved to watch the show—the multicolored tracers reaching toward the Junkers in the yellow sky, the crimson flashes of the antiaircraft guns, the silhouettes of sausage-shaped barrage balloons, and the red winking pompons—hypnotized the gallery. Peering down from the Pushkin Heights at the spectacle below, some of the men mused on their mission. Why didn't the Russians accept that they had come, not to conquer, but to liberate—not as invaders, but as missionaries? Their purpose was to return Russia to Europe. But even the people below in the city of Peter the Great, founded specifically to integrate East and West, stubbornly refused to understand. Maybe, after nearly two years of fighting on the Russian front it was the Spanish volunteers who failed to grasp the situation: Hitler's racial policies and the Nazi world view aimed at carving a German *Lebensraum* in the Soviet Union and enslaving the population. This was not the spearhead of Western civilization returning Christianity to an unfortunate people. And, many of their German comrades realized that only too well and had already reduced the war to a basic question—either Germany or Russia would conquer; one would rule, the other would be crushed.

Suddenly, a great orange flash followed by a deafening muzzle blast cut short their speculation. *El cañon del coronel* (The colonel's cannon)! The legendary railroad rifle was one of a pair which 18 Army Artillery slipped up into the Spanish sector under the cover of darkness. A special train consisting of munition, sleeping, kitchen, and command cars was pulled by a diesel locomotive. It sneaked in for a few shots and then retired, leaving the *guripas* to face the fury of the Russian reply. Heavy-caliber shells pounded Pushkin during the night of 1 July.[62]

From the beginning, Operation Citadel ran into tough resistance from Red forces which had had months to dig in and knew an attack was coming. On 19 July 1943 the Allies landed in Sicily and gave the Reich a two-front war in Europe. Hitler believed that he now had to divert troops west and called off the offensive. Although von Manstein wanted to go on, German losses had already been terrifying—70,000 men killed and 2,900 armored vehicles destroyed—and von Küchler had been rationing three or four Tigers in February! He would get no reinforcements for *Parkplatz* now. Rather, he would have to surrender infantry to block the Soviet summer offensive that followed.[63]

It was a hot, sticky July day at Pokrovskaia. Esteban Infantes had been preparing for weeks. The eighteenth marked the seventh anniversary of the Nationalist uprising and the general had been collecting delicacies, coffee, and fine wines to celebrate the occasion. Even a German dance troupe was scheduled to perform for the distinguished guests: Generals Lindemann, Kleffel, Eberhard Kinzel (chief of staff of Army Group North), Hans Speth (18 Army chief of staff), Walther Krause of 170 Division, and Friedrich Köchling of 254 Division. The Spanish staff, along with Knüppel and Förster, danced attendance on the glittering galaxy.

Esteban Infantes beamed as he led the brilliant array to the palace park, where white linens and bouquets graced the rustic tables. The clink of glasses and happy chatter filled the air. All was quiet. It was cool under the trees as they took their places. Promptly at 1400, white-coated waiters began to serve the head table where the generals sat. The first course over, Esteban Infantes rose and praised the Germans with appropriate words. Tall, angular Lindemann had just stood up to reply when the sky fell. Scores of Soviet 122s pounded Pokrovskaia. General Kinzel's monocle almost, but not quite, dropped out of his eye. Esteban Infantes sat transfixed as clouds of dust, waves of concussion, and shards of shrapnel rolled over the picnic tables. Everyone looked at each other. Seconds passed. Who would be the first to run? Finally, Esteban Infantes looked at Lindemann. Their eyes met, an imperceptible nod and, decorations jangling, the generals dashed for the palace basement or jumped into the zigzag trenches Villegas had opened last April. The guard of honor—front line fighters all—had not waited for an order. They had dived for shelter immediately. Several of the staff had been wounded, Alemany mortally.[64] Alemany became another statistic in the bloodiest seven months in the history of the division. Between 19 December 1942, when Esteban Infantes took command, and 23 July 1943, casualties totalled 2,151 dead, 3,456 wounded, and 1,950 sick.[65]

The banquet had not been a success. Kleffel was not pleased. He drew the conclusion that the Russians had pinpointed all CPs and that, prior to their next attack they would attempt to wipe out the entire leadership of the Corps. He ordered the immediate construction of well-protected alternate GHQs.[66] Russian might was growing. Kursk had tipped the balance. The Allies had begun squeezing tighter their petroleum embargo on Spain. Wonder weapons notwithstanding, Franco began to consider withdrawing the Blue Division.

Jordana and Doussinague had been urging this move for months. Determined to steer Spain away from non-belligerency toward neutrality, they had also sought to ensure balanced press coverage of the war. By July, their efforts had almost met with success, although some Falangist and Germanophile newspapers still published only Axis communiques. Circulation and advertising for such dailies were declining. Victor de la Serna, publisher of *Informaciones*, who had covered Operation Citadel, found himself near bankruptcy. He was 500,000 pesetas in debt to Juan March, the pro-Allied tobacco king, for the building which housed his press and offices. In order to keep *Informaciones* afloat, he turned to the Germans for a loan.

Governmental and financial pressures aside, it was Kursk, culminating with the fall of Mussolini on 25 July, which tended to push the Spanish press toward a neutralist position. Doussinague claimed that "the battle of the press was won in July."[67]

What was left of nonbelligerency was the Blue Division. Moreover, Franco was worried about the possibility of another Nazi-Communist alliance. News of the supposed armistice of 17 May had been passed on to El Pardo. A month later, the Caudillo inquired of the new German ambassador, Hans Heinrich Dieckhoff, about the military situation. Dieckhoff replied that "we will fight until the Russians are exhausted."[68] "This calmed and strengthened the Caudillo," reported the ambassador. "Apparently, recent rumors of German inclinations to negotiate with the Bolsheviks had reached him and had not failed to impress him."[69]

Franco was even more impressed by the United States ambassador who, on 29 July, called on him and suggested the speedy withdrawal of the Blue Division. Hayes also recommended an early and unequivocal declaration of neutrality and the immediate institution of an impartial policy in the press and governmental agencies. Franco calmly reviewed the historical background of the present situation, and again reminded Hayes of his three-war theory, which the professor once more refused to accept. Satisfied and hopeful nonetheless, Hayes departed El Pardo. Within a few days, the ambassador could see tangible results. The Spanish press, radio, and newsreel services swung decisively toward neutrality. But all really important decisions would have to wait. After all, it was summer. Franco went north to his high, cool, hunting lodge in Galicia. The foreign minister and his staff entrained for a six weeks' stay on the beaches of the Bay of Biscay at San Sebastián.[70]

Not everyone went away for the August holiday. Major Román had important things to do. He made a pilgrimage to his local parish church in Jaen, where he offered his Iron Cross at the shrine of the Good Shepherdess in gratitude for having been permitted to return home alive and unscathed. He also called on the Military Hospital, where Lieutenant Escobedo, who had never recovered from his wounds, underwent periodic treatment.[71]

Early in August, Hayes departed on a different kind of pilgrimage, northward to San Sebastián. In his first conversation with Jordana on 7 August, he learned that Franco had already cautioned the news media and that a declaration of neutrality could be expected at the first auspicious moment. Regarding the Blue Division, "Jordana had long believed that the sending of it to the Eastern Front was a mistake and that it should be withdrawn."[72] The Caudillo had just consulted with the service ministers and they had agreed to gradual retirement. Negotiations with the Germans, however, must precede any such action. Moreover, the "proposal had met objection from a certain general who had been associated with the Blue Division."[73]

Muñoz Grandes met Sir Samuel Hoare at the door of Franco's hunting lodge on Friday evening, 20 August. His Britannic Majesty's ambassador was shown to the Caudillo's second floor sitting room overlooking the wooded slopes of Galicia. The chief of state and his foreign minister awaited. Hoare concentrated on three points—the Falange, nonbelligerency, and the Blue Division. Unperturbed, the generalissimo listened, and complacently commented about war, weather, crops, and politics. Disconcerted at his inability to bait Franco, Hoare flew back to Madrid and then home. Upon landing in London, the ambassador granted an explosive interview to the BBC and Allied correspondents. Sir Samuel proclaimed that he had demanded the withdrawal of the Blue Division.[74]

The Spaniards were furious. Jordana called Hayes in on 26 August 1943. The foreign minister told the American that Dieckhoff was protesting vigorously, that Hoare had complicated extricating the division, and that the gesture of withdrawal would have little advantage for Spain unless it appeared voluntary. "The British Ambassador, probably unwittingly, was now making it appear as forced. Hence, there would be added difficulty and delay."[75] Delay, not only in withdrawing the Blue Division, but also in ending the war.

On 23 August, Father Conrad Simonsen called on Field Marshal von Leeb at his country estate in Bavaria. He had come on a mission from the Caudillo. Franco had concluded that the Allies had rejected his peace plan because they would not negotiate with the Nazis. Still seeking to save Europe from the Communists, he had decided to try to overthrow Hitler. Following the recent Italian example, where Marshal Pietro Badoglio had seized power from Mussolini and then sued for peace, the Spanish dictator urged von Leeb to do the same. The field marshal did not blink an eyelash. "Under such circumstances, I stand available," he told the Capuchin, but he doubted that the Nazis would freely step aside, even to save their country. The plan came to naught.[76]

Thursday, 9 September 1943, slowly dawned. Soviet loudspeakers manned by Spanish deserters broadcast the latest Allied communiques. Darkness lifted, revealing a cloudy day and, in front of the position of 10 Company of 262 at Aleksandrovka, an immense, red-lettered poster. *Españoles, Italia se ha capitulado! Pasaros a nosotros!* (Spaniards, Italy has surrendered! Join us!) Enraged at this equating of Spaniards and Italians, Colonel Valcarcel's *guripas* slipped out to the Soviet wire and tore down the offending sign. A few hours later, another announcement appeared, this time in the Spanish trenches. It proudly boasted— *No somos Italianos!* (We're not Italians!)

Von Küchler was not so sure. That Thursday, 401 Grenadiers from General Krause's 170 Division rolled up behind the Spanish sector as reserve, just in case.[77] The Germans were jittery. Kharkov had fallen. Smolensk was endangered. The Allies had invaded the Italian mainland and Italy had capitulated unconditionally. In spite of all these reverses, however, Spanish replacements continued to flow to the Russian front. That same day, March Battalion 25 arrived and Return Battalion 14 gathered at *Villa Relevo.*

Across the Baltic at Stockholm, Swedish newspapers were reporting the imminent recall of the Blue Division. Similar rumors circulated throughout Spain. The new German military attaché, Col. E. M. Doerr, who had visited 250 Division in mid-August before taking up his post in Madrid, sought reassurance from his Spanish colleagues. They quickly pointed out that march battalions were still gathering at Logroño. Further promises came from Lieutenant Colonel Ruíz de la Serna of the Attaché Section. On 10 September in San Sebastián, he confided in Doerr that retirement of the Spanish Volunteer Division had neither been demanded by the Allies nor contemplated by the generalissimo.[78]

The next day, Doerr advised Berlin that the Falange was experiencing mounting difficulty in assembling recruits for the Blue Division. He related this to a marked upswing in what he termed "an anti-German trend in the Spanish press."[79] The military attaché was particularly disconcerted by a speech delivered at Burgos by Arrese on 11 September.

Party Minister Arrese told the hierarchy of Castile and Léon that the Falange was an indigenous movement, not a foreign import. The objective of the movement was not the establishment of a totalitarian state, but the integration of mankind into a universal community. This has been Spain's mission throughout history, he proclaimed. The presence of the Blue Division on the Russian front was part of this mission. "Some people [mistakenly] believe that [the Blue Division was sent] to help a friendly nation or repay with human flesh a debt of gratitude."[80] The Blue Division was a continuation of our destiny, Arrese continued. "If in this war Communism is not defeated . . . we will have to consider [the dispatch of the Blue Division] as a romantic gesture."[81] Arrese was obviously attempting to disassociate the Falange from Nazism and

Fascism. He also inferred that the presence of the Blue Division in Hitler's Wehrmacht was incidental to its main purpose. Was Arrese signaling that the time has come to disengage? Doerr thought so.

Despite a cloud of denials, the mustering of another march battalion, and the purchase of large supplies of brandy for winter issue, the rumors persisted. Acting Army Chief of Staff Barroso advised Brigadier Torr that the Spanish General Staff was now convinced that "Germany could not win the war . . . that morale in Germany was very low indeed."[82] Nevertheless, it was not easy for Franco to withdraw the Blue Division, declare neutrality, or dismantle the Falange "in a day or at the stroke of a pen."[83]

The decision came on 24 September. Now that everyone had returned refreshed from the mountains and seashore, weighty matters could be considered. At a secret meeting of the Council of Ministers, the Caudillo announced his intention of transforming the division into a legion. No discussion was permitted. A "reliable source" carried the news to Dieckhoff.

Muñoz Grandes, when queried about the decision by the Germans, advised that he had not been consulted because the Caudillo knew his position in advance. Allied pressure was growing, he complained. As if to cushion the blow, the former conspirator allowed that, if the pressure were to become unendurable, Germany's friends in Spain might still want to know if the Reich would be able to help his country resist. Could the Reich move strong forces quickly, he wanted to know? It was a rhetorical question.[84]

Still nothing concrete from Franco—not until 1 October—when he declared neutrality. The next day Vidal received instructions to inform Germany of Spain's intention to withdraw the Blue Division, but to leave a smaller "legion" at the front. The reasons for the decision, Vidal was to emphasize, were: lack of volunteers, fear of sinking fighting spirit owing to the "difficult" situation on the Eastern Front, and lastly, pressure by the Allies.[85]

Ambassador Dieckhoff, unofficially aware of the decision for days, had an audience with Jordana that evening. Only at the conclusion of their conversation did the nervous foreign minister inform the German emissary of the telegram to Vidal. The withdrawal was to be undertaken "with the greatest regret" but, recruiting had stagnated a long time ago and it had become necessary to employ "unpleasant compulsive measures" to ensure that the march battalions were filled.[86] A second reason was just as significant, Jordana continued. The division had fought hard and well, he maintained. But, under the present circumstances, with the declining fighting spirit among the *guripas*, there was a danger of a loss of prestige for Spain. "Only tangentially," did the minister mention Anglo-American pressure, which would evaporate once a legion was formed of "real volunteers."[87] The measure had been discussed carefully, even among "those generals who were among the most vigorous defenders of the concept of the Blue Division," and they had agreed.[88] Sarcastically, Dieckhoff asked how one could have volunteers for a legion when there were none for a division. Well, Jordana replied, we are thinking about a unit the size of a regiment.

Jordana was justifiably nervous. Neither he nor Franco could guess what the German reaction would be. Hitler, who had never liked the Caudillo, might do something rash. The Blue Division was at the front, facing the Red Army but surrounded by the Wehrmacht. At one word from the Führer, Esteban Infantes and his men would become hostages. "The Spaniards have demanded the Blue Division back," Hitler exclaimed. "Yes, I've heard," replied Zeitzler.[89] "We will handle the people very decently," Hitler added. "But the weapons stay here," Jodl warned.[90]

Morale in the Division was high. Everyone seemed secretly pleased at the defeat of Italy. One officer laconically commented to Knüppel that "if you had given all those weapons to us rather than the Italians, the Anglo-Americans wouldn't be where they are today."[91] There was, however, great elation over the rescue of Mussolini in mid-September. "The Spaniards thought the feat much more impressive than had the Germans won a battle," remarked the chief of the Liaison Staff.[92]

Late Monday evening, 4 October 1943, Army suddenly advised Division that General Lindemann would arrive the next morning to award the Knight's Cross to Esteban Infantes. Stunned at this precipitous presentation, the staff wondered what it was all about.

Querido Lindemann appeared promptly at 1015 with the new corps commander, Gen. Wilhelm Wegener who had replaced the ailing Kleffel. As Esteban Infantes beamed, Knüppel and the Spanish staff watched the decoration hung around the general's neck. The ceremony over, Lindemann inquired about the morale of the division. A week ago, Knüppel had reported that Villegas had confided to him that, without a good deal of propaganda, 250 Division could not be brought through another Russian winter. The Spaniards had been reserved of late, officers talking about going home. A German indoctrination unit had been allowed only restricted access to the regimental sectors.[93]

"Morale is good, my general," replied Esteban Infantes, "and losses have been small, only 300 in the past three months." Knüppel listened avidly. He knew that Esteban Infantes had not yet been told. Army had called him the night before to explain that the Blue Division was to be pulled out of the line for "further training."[94] How was he to guess that he had been deliberately deceived, for Lindemann had already been informed by OKH that 250 Division was going home. The voice of Esteban Infantes broke into his thoughts. The Russians had tried another probe and failed.

Captain Morón had just come up with March Battalion 26. G-1 had sent him over to Cano at 269, who in turn assigned him to 9 Company of Major Sabater's Third Battalion. Morón barely had time to acquaint himself with the positions at Pushinskii-Central east of the Slavianka. The weather was cold. The mud in the trenches froze if not trodden for two hours. Each day, dawn came later and darker.[95]

Artillery, mortars, and antitanks began hitting Morón's positions at 0445. After drubbing the company's one kilometer front for an hour and a quarter, 72 Rifle Division shifted the barrage rearward to concentrate on Sabater's CP. Two companies of Third Battalion of 213 Rifle Regiment emerged out of the smoke-filled predawn darkness. Long capes flowing, the riflemen streamed forward through the lanes cut in the Spanish wire. The *guripas* eyed Morón. How would the new captain react? Morón tried to ring up battalion. The line was gone. Grabbing a machine pistol, he opened up on the shadowy figures flapping forward in no-man's-land. The veterans on the firing step looked pleased. They felt better now. Although new, Morón was one of them.

The captain was fortunate. His section leaders were old hands. Aware of the proclivity of their *divisionarios* to rush to close, they led them out to clean up. Sabater also sent up the assault section. They counted twenty-five Russian dead. Among them lay a major who had refused to surrender. He was the commander of Third Battalion. As the haze lifted, the *guripas* could make out forty pairs of Soviet stretcher bearers carrying off the wounded. Spanish casualties amounted to a dozen and a half. By the time Lindemann had arrived to decorate Esteban Infantes, the front was back to normal—*sin novedad*.[96]

As Esteban Infantes enthusiastically described the repulse, he noticed that Lindemann seemed somewhat reserved. When the commander finished, the colonel general advised him that 250 Division would be pulled out for rest and instruction. Esteban Infantes was pleased. His unit had been in the line for two years. He had long been requesting training for his recruits. Moreover, rumors of an impending offensive against the Oranienbaum pocket were in the air. With his men rested and fully trained, he hoped to end his term as commander with an offensive victory.[97]

Within twenty-four hours, his hopes were seemingly satisfied. The Spaniards were to move westward beyond Gatchina to the area of Volosovo-Nikolaevka, immediately south of Oranienbaum.[98] Group, Army, and Corps scrambled to find a replacement division. At first, 28 Light was to be rushed into the breach, but it was so busy that General Schopper and his 81 Division were alerted. Schopper remembered the Spaniards from January and February 1942, when his *Landser* fought shoulder to shoulder with Captain Ordás and the Ski Company on the way to relieve Vzvad. Finally, however, it was decided to move 215 Division in to replace the Spaniards. Veterans of the winter campaign of 1941–42 on the Volkhov remembered that 215 Division had held the northern pillar of the pocket while 126 and 250 Divisions held the southern.

The pullout began on the night of 7–8 October. The five battalions in reserve—First and Third of 262, Second of 263, and First and Second of 269—began their long march westward over muddy, half-frozen roads to Volosovo and Nikolaevka. Their route led through the rear area of 126 Division, their old friends from the Volkhov. The Rhineland-Westphalians, now commanded by Gen. Harry Hoppe, had shared the glory and the danger with the Spaniards during the Tikhvin campaign and the Volkhov Pocket.

The battalions in the line tarried until 170 Division could move east and 215 Division come up. On 12 October, *el Día de la Raza*, the artillery began to roll and 189 Rifle Division hit the railroad finger still held by Second of 262. The Reds were driven back into the predawn darkness, abandoning casualties and weapons. Just two years before, 262 had been moving into the line of the Island of Novgorod. That same Tuesday afternoon, Esteban Infantes, still officially unaware of the withdrawal of the division, turned over the sector.[99] No courier plane had come from Berlin.

Lindemann finally enlightened him at 1500 that afternoon. Scarcely hours after receiving the word to inform the Spaniards from OKH via Army Group, the 18 Army commander motored to Nikolaevka to brief the Spanish commander personally. He had been instructed to use the utmost tact and to show appreciation and gratitude for the comradely fashion in which the Volunteer Division had fought in the

Wehrmacht. With Reinlein, Knüppel, and Metternich looking on, Lindemann gave the news to Esteban Infantes. The general, and everyone else, was shocked. He had received a veiled hint from Madrid some ten days before, but nothing definite. Esteban Infantes found himself unable to answer Lindemann's questions about the strength and composition of the proposed legion, when it would be likely to be ready, or how long it would be expected to stay at the front. The army commander knew more than he did. Embarrassed, and perplexed, Esteban Infantes asked for time to contact the military attaché in Berlin. Confused himself, Lindemann returned to his headquarters and reported to von Küchler that he had high hopes that the legion would be a large unit.[100]

By 17 October, movement of 250 Division from the Leningrad front to reserve behind Oranienbaum was complete. Alertness was needed. Partisans were active. Moreover, the men had to be kept busy. Three hours a day were devoted to training and care of equipment, another one and a half to physical exercise, and half an hour to propaganda and theoretical instruction. But the *guripas* were being disarmed. Moreover, they felt they were being treated like Italians. Depressed, the *divisionarios* sat in their *izbas* and toasted their bread. Most of them just wanted to go home.[101] With or without instructions from Madrid, Esteban Infantes issued orders for repatriation. He based his commands on his own assessment of what Lindemann had told him that the German military attaché in Madrid had picked up from a conversation with García Valiño, army chief of staff.

Officers and men with the longest service would return first. On 17 October, members of 6 and 7 March Battalions, plus NCOs from the First Division were ordered to begin concentrating at Gatchina. In order to build up a *Legion Española de Voluntarios* (LEV), all *divisionarios* up through 21 March Battalion were to be polled about remaining. Men with less than six months active duty—22 March Battalion on—were to stay. The recruiting campaign among the veterans failed completely. Doubts about the composition of the legion, length of service, leadership, rotation, and employment dampened the *guripas'* enthusiasm for the German cause. Without information from Madrid, it was impossible to answer these questions. Moreover, the men did not have to be told that Russian confidence was growing, the enemy's power mounting, while the Wehrmacht no longer seemed as mighty as before. Moreover, many would have preferred to stay in Spain rather than enlist in the division.[102]

The courier plane finally arrived on 20 October. It bore the new military attaché, Lieutenant Colonel Bernardos, and dispatches from both the Ministry of War and the Foreign Ministry. No sooner had he broken the seals than was it evident to Esteban Infantes that Asensio and Jordana shared radically different views on the strength, composition, and role of the legion. If these matters were not resolved quickly, the pool of possible volunteers would continue to evaporate. Lindemann told Esteban Infantes to get the matter straightened out.

A TO&E for the legion awaited Esteban Infantes in Berlin. The Army General Staff proposed an infantry force of five battalions, plus a depot unit, a total of 4,500 officers and men. This proposal was almost immediately revised downward. During the following ten days' tug of war with Asensio and Muñoz Grandes on the one side and Jordana and Doussinague on the other, interspersed with frantic telephone calls from Esteban Infantes in Berlin and a couple of flights by Bernardos back to Madrid, the Caudillo deliberated.

The chief of state's "Minister of War and other Generals were still convinced that Germany could not lose the war and represented a danger to Spain."[103] Therefore, some Spanish presence on the Eastern Front was necessary. The question was, how much? In addition, Franco himself "wished to spread repatriation [of the Division] over a period of time in order to avoid many thousands of young Spanish adventurers arriving at the same time and becoming the centre of Falangist and German demonstrations."[104] Meanwhile, the exasperated Germans had reached the conclusion that the Spaniards were not serious about a legion and that all this delay was a cover for duplicity.[105]

The Caudillo decided on All Saint's Day, 1 November. Deputy Chief of Staff Villegas spent the following morning visiting the Spanish batteries deployed south of the Oranienbaum pocket. He was worried about the withdrawal, which was not by organic units, but by march battalions. Batches of 500 to 600 from 6, 7, 8, and 9 had already left, taking with them valuable veterans, technicians, noncoms, and such Russians as they could smuggle along. Unit structure and command integrity were crumbling. What if the Reds should break through the thin line of Luftwaffe field divisions around Oranienbaum? The division was almost leaderless and practically unarmed. The men barely had enough weapons to fend off the partisans. That very Tuesday, a band had attacked a sapper detachment near the Leningrad-Jamburg road. Of course, if instructions had arrived for a legion, that would be some armed protection while the remainder were shipped home.[106]

An urgent order awaited Villegas at Nikolaevka. He was to report immediately to Madrid. Early Thursday morning, he was ushered into the presence of the generalissimo. A brief, precise report by the lieutenant colonel, a few short, sharp questions from Franco, then clear, definite verbal instructions, and the audience was over.[107] The division would be repatriated piecemeal. A legion of 1,000 to 1,500 men would continue the campaign. Villegas returned to carry out the Caudillo's orders.[108] Now, he knew about the legion, but Esteban Infantes, still in Berlin, did not.

A staff car slid to a stop before the Hotel Eden in the dark of the morning on Sunday, 7 November. A major alighted, strode into the lobby, and rang up Esteban Infantes. The general bustled down the stairs and the auto sped off to the railroad station. The train rattled on toward East Prussia. By 1600, it had reached the area of the Masurian Lakes. A brief stop so that Esteban Infantes could tour the monument to the great victory of Field Marshal von Hindenburg over the Russians in 1914 at Tannenberg, and then the locomotive chugged on. The train ground to a halt. Thick forest lay along both sides of the tracks. Here, hidden in the woods, steam up, they would spend the night.

Esteban Infantes joined Gen. Walter Buhle for supper in the dining car. The Spaniard disliked the chief of the Army Staff at OKW. He had asked too many questions about the legion that Esteban Infantes could not answer. The conversation was diplomatic, not cordial. At midnight, Buhle rose and informed the general that Hitler would receive him soon. They were at the Wolf's Lair.[109]

An armed escort accompanied Esteban Infantes and Hoffmann through a series of concentric fences. Just before 1600, they strode into the inner compound—a square surrounded by wooden barracks. An officer led the pair toward one, somewhat isolated from the rest. They entered a small room where a lieutenant colonel received them cordially. He stepped back, opened the door, and there stood the Führer. Esteban Infantes was stunned at the lack of ceremony. He advanced nervously, and grasped Hitler's outstretched hand. Surreptitiously, he glanced leftward—a simple, even austere, room with a rustic map-covered table and four rough-hewn chairs of pine. Here, the great decisions of the campaign were made!

Hitler smiled. It was not an easy, natural smile. The Führer presented Esteban Infantes with a parchment confirming his award of the Knight's Cross, then invited him to sit down. Keitel joined them. Hitler and Keitel sat silent, motionless, observing the Spanish general. Esteban Infantes broke into a cold sweat. Minutes passed. Dark pouches bulged below Hitler's pale, expressionless eyes. His whole posture was one of fatigue. As the clock ticked, Esteban Infantes turned away from the icy gaze and sneaked a look through a glass door into what seemed to be a monk's cell—a small cot, a simple table, and a plain wooden chair. Hitler's quarters lacked only a crucifix to complete the monastic scene, he thought.

Without any preamble, Hitler suddenly began to speak. Starting slowly, he discoursed on the Herculean efforts of the German Army. The voice gradually increased in speed and intensity. The gray face took on color. The hunched back straightened. The listless arms and hands became animated and flailed the air. The man became alive, transformed. He seemed to rise out of the chair, fill the room, and dominate the world!

The genie had been let out of the bottle. Esteban Infantes sat transfixed, hypnotized. The figure before him became a giant—the words lucid, the judgments certain, the decisions confident. Choosing his words carefully although not seeming to do so, Hitler sought to impress Esteban Infantes's master in Madrid. Convincing and inflaming the conduit to Franco, he spoke about the sacrifices of the "German soldier, fighting from the North Pole to the African desert, from the Volga to the Atlantic, without being able to concentrate his efforts against the Russians."[110] Again and again, Hitler cried out: "The Anglo-Americans are blind! The danger is to the east and they will not let me fight it! All Europe will suffer the consequences of this error. The enemy is not I; the enemy is Stalin!"[111]

Fixed in the Führer's gaze, Esteban Infantes felt himself carried away. Then, just as suddenly as he had begun, Hitler stopped. He collapsed back into his crumpled, gray shell. But the spell stayed. Esteban Infantes came away a believer.[112] The Führer had not even mentioned the withdrawal of the division or the formation of the legion. Such details were left to Keitel. That evening, Esteban Infantes flew back to the front.[113]

The reception for the returning veterans in Spain was cold. Since neither Franco nor Jordana wished to publicize the pullout, official ceremonies were furtive and subdued. By 16 November, 3,347 had been quietly repatriated.[114] The next day, Wednesday, Esteban Infantes issued General Order of the Division 69 establishing the legion. The *Legion Española de Voluntarios* (LEV) would be modeled on the *Ter-*

cio of the Spanish Foreign Legion. Of regimental size, it would consist of three battalions—two infantry and one mixed (artillery, antitanks, sappers, and recon). There would be a total theoretical strength of 2,133 (103 officers, 530 NCOs, and 1,500 men). Colonel Navarro assumed command. Villegas replaced him as divisional chief of staff.[115]

Navarro overcame the recruiting problem with direct action. He had an adequate pool of officers and NCOs. In Knüppel's judgment, the officers were among the best in the division. *Guripas* were in short supply. By mid-November almost half of the division was already on the way home. Few had volunteered before departing. Prospects were dim. He might have to draw heavily on March Battalion 27, which had come up just in time to be repatriated. Many of these men had been press-ganged and were unreliable. The weather was foul and German fortunes were declining. The enemy was expected to attack soon in great strength. Navarro decided on a dramatic gesture.[116]

The ring of hoofbeats echoed over the frozen Leningrad-Jamburg highway. The men in the skeletal companies strung out along the roadside craned their heads. A group of horsemen appeared, at full gallop. Reining in, mount steaming, the lead rider pivoted. The speech was short. He offered nothing except death and glory, no relief and probable annihilation at the front. It was the kind of offer to appeal to the romantic and adventurous among the veterans. Esteban Infantes proudly wired Madrid "[we] have 1,500 authentic volunteers selected from an even larger number."[117] Navarro had his legion. They immediately began concentrating at Jamburg. With that headache out of the way, Esteban Infantes flew off, leaving Villegas to watch over the dwindling division.

The first snow fell on Nikolaevka on 4 December—the day of Santa Barbara, Patroness of the Artillery. The next day it thawed, followed by another freeze and snow on the eighth. That evening, in honor of the Immaculate Conception, Patroness of the Infantry, Villegas dined with Knüppel and some of L Corps staff. Talk turned toward the war, past victories and the dark future. Fifteen divisions had been pulled out of Army Group North since summer to shore up the remainder of the Russian front. The Soviets were preparing a full-scale offensive to destroy 18 Army. Lindemann and von Küchler were considering withdrawal to the half-completed Panther Line shielding the Baltic states. The mood was somber. It was a farewell party for Knüppel. The next morning, he left to escort a return battalion to Irún. Villegas stayed on another week to supervise the delivery of the last cannon, horses, and vehicles. All remaining weapons, except for 200 rifles for the defense of the train between Volosovo and Riga, were turned in by 12 December. Finally, on 13 December, the last supply, transport, and general staff troops of Return Battalion 31 headed out. Villegas could relax. Aside from the fact that it was almost Christmas and he missed *turrón*, wine, and nuts—there would be no *aguinaldo* this Advent—his only worry was his cook. The perplexed chef was trying to figure out a way to smuggle his *panienka* home. Villegas made a quick pilgrimage to pray at Alemany's tomb, and was ready to go. His Junkers lifted off the icy airstrip at Gatchina at 0900 on Tuesday, 14 December. Only the legion, the wounded, and the dead remained.[118]

Brigadier Pimentel greeted General Esteban Infantes at Irún on Friday, 17 December. The reception was subdued as it had been for the officers and men who had preceded him. In spite of local newspaper announcements, the public failed to turn out for Esteban Infantes. Only provincial authorities attended. Accompanied by Reinlein, Knüppel, and a handful of other liaison officers, Esteban Infantes boarded the night train for Madrid.[119]

The express slid into an empty *Estación del Norte*. Only a small knot of officials awaited on the platform of the cavernous, steel-vaulted station. Muñoz Grandes, Saliquet, and Arrese, along with a few Falangists and former officers of the Blue Division forced smiles as Esteban Infantes stepped off the sleeping car. The German delegation, led by Embassy Councillor von Bibra, and comprising General Krahmer and the service attachés, stood respectfully by. Neither Dieckhoff nor any cabinet ministers, except Arrese, appeared. There were no *vivas*. No newspapers, not even *Informaciones*, had announced the arrival of Esteban Infantes in Madrid. A limousine whisked him away through empty streets to his hotel. There, a warmer atmosphere prevailed. The lobby was crowded with Falangists attending the First National Council of Provincial Chiefs. Still dominated by the spell of the Führer, Esteban Infantes delivered an impromptu speech forecasting the ultimate victory of the Third Reich.[120]

Arrese had opened the First National Council of Provincial Chiefs on 14 December 1943. One of the movement's most illustrious Old Shirts was missing—José Guitarte. He had died after a long illness three weeks before on 21 November, the tenth anniversary of the founding of the SEU and one day after the seventh anniversary of the execution of José Antonio. Muñoz Grandes had attended the funeral mass for his former *guripa*.[121] Guitarte's death was a fitting prologue

to the *Primero Consejo Nacional de Jefes Provinciales.* Upon closing
the conference, Franco and Arrese, with Muñoz Grandes standing behind, urged the black-uniformed Falangists massed in the Old Senate
on Calle Bailén to subordinate their will to Spanish interests and to
channel their revolutionary militia spirit into more peaceful and pro-
ductive pursuits. Moreover, all Spaniards were urged to live and work
together in harmony.[122] Doussinague later told United States Embassy
Councillor Willard L. Beaulac that Franco's and Arrese's speeches
closing the council

> indicated that the post-civil war period was ended in Spain. Franco
> had forced Arrese to make his speech. Arrese had not wanted to
> make it. But Franco knew that only the Chief Minister of the Fa-
> lange, himself, could say effectively what Arrese said, and Arrese
> had had to say it.
>   . . . Franco's and Arrese's speeches, together with other recent
> developments, indicate that the Falange is on its way out, at least
> as a dominant political force in Spain.[123]

Only a year ago, the triumvirate had been ready to seize power. Now
the conspiracy lay in ruins. Jordana's and Doussinague's policies had
triumphed. The press battle had been won in July, neutrality declared
in October, the Blue Division withdrawn in November, and the Falange
tamed in December. But there remained the legion.

Mass on Sunday morning, 28 November, officially inaugurated the
Legion Española de Voluntarios. The *Tercio* (regiment) had been
concentrating near Narva at Jamburg for over a week. Navarro and his
adjutant, Captain Urbano—a veteran of the Izhora campaign—had
watched as Major Ibarra led his First *Bandera* (1, 2, and 3 Rifle Companies and 4 Heavy Weapons) into the splendid two-story barracks of
the former Red Army camp. Major Lena, commanding Second *Bandera* (5, 6, 7, and 8 Companies), with his men from Second of 263,
had already arrived. The sappers, cyclists, antitankers, cannoneers, and
signalmen of Major Quintanillas's Third *Bandera* were on their way
from Volosovo.[124]

Navarro and most of the officers were worried. They had only two
weeks to whip the legion into shape and weld it into a cohesive fighting force. Moreover, many of the men were from 27 March Battalion,
which had been filled by press gangs back in Spain.[125] There was much
indoctrination to do. The officers immediately began to impose discipline and instruct the recruits in the basics of combat. The men had to
learn to think and act as a unit. Navarro's well-chosen officers and

veterans did their best. Still, within the first two weeks, seven legionnaires deserted and six sought to escape service by self-mutilation. Navarro, in spite of the fact that his authority to call a general court martial and impose the death penalty had not yet been confirmed by the War Ministry in Madrid, summarily hanged one man caught attempting to desert.

The training schedule, though brief, was tough. The Germans concluded that "under the quiet, professional, and decisive leadership of Colonel Navarro, the Legion . . . will further purge itself of uncertain elements and be able to hold a quiet place in the front."[126] Navarro culled out seventy-five unreliables during the training period and shipped them home forthwith. He had no wish to jeopardize his own reputation or that of the Blue Division. The legion asked for, and was granted, an additional week to set its house in order.

On 13 December, the legion was alerted, winter clothing was issued, and by 15 December 1943, had entrained for Liuban, headquarters of XXVIII Corps. It was assigned to 121 Division under Helmut Priess, which was holding a forty-kilometer front on the Liuban-Mga Road. The legion marched to Kostovo, relieved 405 Grenadiers and deployed over an eleven-kilometer line. In spite of the fact that Army Group North had held this region for over two years, the road was narrow and in dreadful condition. When they arrived, Navarro and his men found that 405 Regiment had not had time to clear a field of fire and had been spread especially thin because the swampy area had not frozen solid in the mild winter and no major attack was expected locally. Another immediate problem was typhus. Fortunately, the Russians were relatively quiet. This allowed the Spaniards to set up showers and saunas to clean up. There was the usual enemy assault to test the new unit and harrassing artillery fire.[127]

Christmas passed without incident, enlivened only by distribution of the *aguinaldo del Führer*. Navarro welcomed his old friend *Rittmeister* Dr. Edwin Haxel to his command post "Westphalia." Haxel had joined the Liaison Staff as an interpreter in March of 1942 on the Volkhov. An old cavalryman, he had trotted to within thirty kilometers of Moscow in the initial advance of Army Group Center. He had missed the battle of Krasni Bor while attending General Staff School in Paris. Now, he was assigned to replace Knüppel.[128]

For over two months, *Stavka* had been preparing for the final liberation of Leningrad. A greater concentration of firepower than had been present at Stalingrad confronted Army Group North—21,600 cannon, 600 antiaircraft pieces, 1,500 Stalin organs, 1,475 tanks and self-propelled guns, and 1,500 planes. The Leningrad and Volkhov fronts counted 1,241,000 officers and men. Von Küchler's 741,000 troops had 10,000 guns, 385 tanks, and 370 planes and were divided into two armies, 16 and 18. But most of the mighty Soviet force was poised opposite Lindemann alone. The Red Army envisaged a dual attack. Meretskov would strike westward across the Volkhov at Novgorod with 50 and 54 Armies, while Govorov would smash out of Oranienbaum and Leningrad with Fediuninskii's 2 Shock and 42 Army. By overturning the two pillars of 18 Army—Novgorod and Pushkin— the Soviets hoped to entrap Lindemann's entire command and annihilate Army Group North. Only holding attacks were planned on XXVIII Corps, where the legion lay.

The steamroller surged forward on 14 January 1944, crushing everything in its path. The Germans—10 and 9 Luftwaffe Field Divisions, 126, 170, and 215 Divisions—gave way or were overrun between Oranienbaum and Pushkin. Catherine the Great's palace was pounded into rubble. Unable to penetrate the defenses of Novgorod by leaping out of Teremets, Meretskov launched motor sleds across frozen Lake Il'men, landing at Samokrazha, from which Ordás had once set out to liberate Vzvad. The garrison of the Golden City, 28 Light Division of XXXVIII Corps, was encircled. Hitler refused them permission to withdraw until 19 January. The Spanish Legion was caught between the two pincers of the Russian advance.[129]

The Soviets launched their holding attack on XXVIII Corps on the night of 14–15 January. By 19 January, the Reds succeeded in infiltrating as far west as Liuban and a general German retreat was under way. The legion was ordered back to cover the vital Liuban rail and supply center. Surprised at the sudden evacuation order, Captain Morón led his legionnaires of 2 Company through the dense woods and half-frozen swamps. After an all-night march, the Spaniards arrived late in the afternoon of 20 January. They were greeted with news of the fall of Novgorod and Pushkin and rumors even more frightening.

The hub was a shambles. Overturned sleighs, abandoned vehicles, burning supply dumps, and retreating service troops revealed the extent of the disaster. Soviet artillery bracketed the city and organized partisans haunted the ruins and the roads, blowing tracks. The legion was shaken out to the east of the town as a screen. A *bandera* fended off thrusts at the railroad station. There was no line. Only the inexperience and poor coordination of the Ivans, combined with the stubborn resistance of isolated hedgehogs and spontaneous combat groups such as at Liuban, prevented the annihilation of Army Group North.

On 26 January, after the fall of Tosno, the legion was ordered further southward to defend Luga. Rail transportation proved unavailable. The next day, the Soviets proclaimed the official end of the 900 day siege of Leningrad. The *Tercio* began a 140-kilometer retreat over crumbling roads by forced march. The soggy weather and terrain destroyed their felt boots. They had been fighting and moving since 15 January without rest or hot food. Trucks might have carried them, but the highway was one way—west. No traffic was permitted in the opposite direction, and thus vehicles could not make round trips. There were not enough to ferry soldiers and, once loaded with equipment at Liuban, they disappeared westward.

The legion fought its way through bands of partisans, passing through Oredesh just in time to rescue a hospital and a munitions depot. Exhausted, they stumbled into Luga, under command of XXVI Corps. General Grasser came out to see them and was shocked and startled at their condition. Grasser, whose own retreat from the Ladoga front had found the Soviets hard on his heels, was almost surrounded at Vyritsa, south of Gatchina, and his staff had been forced to burn much of XXVI Corps's papers. He was hoping to make a stand here at Luga. However, Grasser was forced to conclude that the Spaniards were in such bad shape that, desperate as he was, he could not employ them in the shield he was attempting to piece together.[130] Haxel and Grasser agreed that the legion was in danger of wholesale collapse and disintegration, and that reentry into the line would likely incite mass desertions. The men needed rest.[131]

Grasser instructed the Spaniards to turn over most of their heavy weapons, supplies, wagons, and horses to the defenders of Luga and to entrain for Estonia. It took ten days to cover the short stretch to Taps, midway between Narva and Reval. The chaotic rail situation was due to partisans, air raids, and the confusion and disorder of the general retreat. They found themselves in a caravan of trains creeping west, seeking the shelter of the Panther Line. One of the casualties of the disaster was Field Marshal von Küchler. Hitler dismissed him on 29 January and appointed his famous fireman, Gen. Walter Model, as commander in chief of Army Group North just in time to see his forces expelled from Russia and take up positions along a front defending the Baltic states. Here, the retreat was temporarily stopped.[132]

After a few days rest at Taps, the *Tercio* was rearmed and regrouped. Imposing iron discipline, Navarro and his officers strained to re-create a fighting force. Model, impatient and scrounging for every regiment he could find, alerted the legion for coastal defense in spite of the fact that they were not yet ready. The irascible dynamo would not wait. Vitebsk and Pskov were already under attack. Known for his personal heroism, his disdain for pessimistic evaluations of his staffs, and his belief that will power could compel little knots of men to work miracles, Model wanted them in the front line. He planned to throw the legion straight into the path of the Russian steamroller. Haxel, fully aware of the political repercussions if the *Tercio* were slaughtered, summoned all the diplomatic skill he could and convinced the general that the political risks were greater than the potential military gain. When the commander in chief relented, the cavalryman sighed quietly in relief. As he turned in that night, Haxel thought to himself that surely this conversation with Model had been his greatest service to Germany and Spain in the war.[133]

The liquidation of the legion had already been decreed. On 11 February 1944, Jordana told Dieckhoff that Anglo-American pressure was focusing on the withdrawal of the *Tercio*. He also expressed concern that the performance of the LEV was less than exemplary and might tarnish the glory won by the Blue Division.[134]

Allied pressure was indeed intense. Two weeks before, the United States and Great Britain had embargoed petroleum and food shipments to Spain. Their press was engaged in a bitter campaign against the Franco régime. The media was seconded by W. Averell Harriman, United States ambassador to Moscow, who wired Washington that Spaniards had been "captured on the Volkhov front and it has been established beyond shadow of doubt that the Spanish accomplices of Hitler are continuing secretly to support the German Fascist invaders."[135] Worried and fearing an invasion, Franco redeployed the army which he had concentrated along the Pyrenees and posted the troops along the Atlantic and Mediterranean coasts. He then sought to placate the Allies as best he could.

Hitler decided to act before the Spaniards had been obliged to ask. On 20 February, the Führer notified Franco that the legion would be repatriated to strengthen Spain's hand against the Allies. Bernardos flew to Reval to advise Navarro. The two Spanish colonels called on

Model in his GHQ at Segewold on 3 March. They informed the army group commander that Franco was withdrawing the legion so that he could have his *matadores* around him in this time of peril.[136]

Two days later, Navarro returned to Taps. Keeping mum, he ordered the *Tercio* out for what seemed to be another routine march to Lechts. The legionnaires fell out, grumbling, under a chill, but bright, blue sky. By 0800 on Monday, 6 March 1944, they were converging from their different cantonments on Lechts.[137] By 1130, the LEV had fallen in before stout, gray-coated Navarro and his staff. His voice filled with emotion, the colonel addressed them:

And now, my legionnaires, on this day whose sunshine and beaming heaven remind us of our Spanish homeland, I want to speak of you and for you—for this day . . . is a day of sorrow for our Motherland. A day of sorrow, because certain dangerous and temporary events of this war compel us to yield before our enemies. . . .

The legionnaires shuffled and strained to hear the Colonel's words.

Spain must consent . . . to the painful and tragic necessity of our withdrawal. This is a bitter moment. . . .
The Legion must return to Spain!" . . .

There was muttering in the ranks. The officers seemed struck dumb, while the men exchanged furtive glances.

England and the United States, which stop at nothing, compel us to return home. But these countries will shortly themselves fall victim to their own actions. . . . England and the United States know very well . . . that they cannot avoid war against Communism. . . .
Return home with the proud feeling that you have done your duty.
Today, on this day of sorrow, you will carry your rifles barrels down, as in a funeral or in Holy Week. . . .
Long live the Legion! Long live the Legion!
Franco! Franco! Franco![138]

12

Tattoo

THE FIRST CONTINGENT OF RETURNING LEGIONNAIRES

rolled into Irún on 31 March 1944. Within a fortnight, the last transport had arrived and, with it, Colonel Navarro.[1]

Many of the volunteers of both legion and division were die-hard anti-Communists or irrepressible adventurers who wished to get back into the fray. Some had even refused to return despite Spain's proclamation of neutrality and the official declaration that "all persons performing military service for belligerent governments are subject to loss of Spanish citizenship."[2]

The Caudillo's wishes notwithstanding, the German embassy in Madrid was bombarded with petitions from veterans wishing to head back to the front. The diplomats were cautious and wary, but the Wehrmacht responded enthusiastically. Haxel was posted to Madrid to organize recruitment and establish an underground network to smuggle the Spanish volunteers across the Pyrenees into southern France. At Lourdes, Special Staff F under Captain Karl Taegert collected the eager recruits. Unlike their predecessors in the Blue Division and legion, who had served in the Wehrmacht, these men were eventually incorporated into the Waffen-SS.[3] During April and May 1945, the Spanish SS Battalion, under Captain Miguel Ezguera Sánchez, defended Berlin to the last along with other foreign forces—Frenchmen, Italians, Latvians, Lithuanians, and Rumanians.[4]

The returned volunteers watched the *Götterdammerung* from the sidewalk cafes of Madrid, Barcelona, and Seville. As the Allied armies smashed the New Order and pulverized the Third Reich, they wondered whether their efforts and the sacrifices of their comrades had been in vain. Their 4,500 dead were now in Soviet hands. The Red flag flew over the cemeteries at Sitno, Grigorovo, Pavlovsk, Mestelevo, Riga, Königsberg, and Berlin. Three hundred Spanish prisoners had disappeared into the maw of Soviet Siberia and were not to see their homes again until 1954. Spanish military hospitals continued to treat some of the 8,000 wounded, 7,800 sick, and 1,600 frostbitten from the campaign. Out of a total of 47,000 officers and men who fought on the Eastern Front, 22,000 were either killed, wounded, injured, ill, or missing. Although some men were wounded on several occasions and were counted as casualties each time, thus pushing the total upward, many *guripas* signed on for a second or third tour, magnifying the number who served. When both of these factors are considered, however, there was still a casualty rate of 47 percent, or almost half of those engaged.[5]

Estimated losses inflicted on the Red Army during the two years 250 Division was in the line totalled 49,300. The *guripas* were proud that they had traded two for one with the Ivans. Nevertheless, they had great respect for the Soviet soldier.[6] The Russians, they believed, were solid fighters, displaying great patience and fortitude. They were able to endure bitterly cold weather and could live out in the open during the winter with minimum shelter and supplies. The Red Army man was extremely resourceful in living off the land and turning the forest to his advantage. Each man was his own combat engineer, building roads, fortifications, and camps with comparative ease.

On the attack, the Soviets tended to lack spirit and enthusiasm. They advanced slowly, mechanically, in compact masses, and they hesitated to close. During a final assault, they generally held back, went to ground, and pitched grenades rather than rush forward with bayonets. Having gained the Spanish trenches, Red riflemen paused to loot, thus losing their initial advantage. Vascillating and seizing anything alcoholic he could find, the Soviet soldier was easily surprised and scattered by Spanish counterattacks. Mass Russian attacks supported by splendid armor, excellent artillery, and air cover, were nonetheless formidable.

The puny 37 mm German antitank pieces were worthless. Since the Reds had tactical air superiority and the Spaniards controlled no flak, Soviet planes struck at will. Soviet mass infantry tactics were necessitated by lack of training and education and by centralized command structure. *Stavka* was willing to waste punishment units, Ukrainians, other minorities, and raw recruits. The compact masses were an ideal target for Spanish artillery and automatic arms fire. Once broken and scattered, individual riflemen either made easy prey or surrendered. The Russian soldier lacked individual initiative and, isolated, he suffered moral disintegration.

At night, the Soviets almost reigned supreme. Russian patrols were always dangerous. Probes and attacks out of the predawn darkness were a constant threat. Due to the laxness of Spanish sentries, the Reds were almost certain to gain the Spanish lines. Here, however, the assaults broke down because of looting and the ability of the individual *guripa*, once aroused, to react quickly.

On the defense, the Russians were tenacious and withstood artillery bombardment with stolid fortitude. Once again, however, they tended to give way under an impetuous advance and surrender rather than fight to the death. They made ideal prisoners. Captured, they immediately became meek, mild, and cooperative, exhibiting the bovine attitude of exchanging one master for another—commissar for captor.

The artillery was undoubtedly the senior Soviet service. Russian cannon were well served, accurate, and overpowering. The range and precision of Red artillery improved as the war progressed. The Spaniards were amazed at the difference between the bombardments on the Volkhov and Leningrad fronts, and they had the greatest respect for Soviet firepower. The well-trained and professional Spanish artillerymen, hunching over their howitzers, wished they had something to match the long-range rifles of the Reds.

Technically and numerically, Russian armor was superior. Only the lack of skill of the crews and the timidity of the tank commanders, Spanish officers believed, prevented the Red Army from exploiting its superiority. Communication between vehicles was also deficient. Moreover, the Russian tactic of utilizing their marvelous tanks as infantry support rather than armored flying cavalry, combined with the overcaution of the tank commanders, caused them to throw away most of this advantage.

In spite of these deficiencies, the Soviets stressed overwhelming strength. Crushing artillery bombardment, masses of troops, and great numbers of tanks combined to give the Red Army assault the overpowering aspect of an irresistible steamroller. The unique Soviet military doctrine of annihilation, not merely of defeating or crushing an enemy, but of literal annihilation, was applied to the Spaniards at Posad and Krasni Bor.

The individual *guripa* considered himself second to none—Russian or German. The *guripas* thought of themselves as warriors, whereas the Germans were soldiers. Although Wehrmacht line officers displayed initiative and even dash, the Spaniards believed the *Landser* to be overcontrolled and overspecialized. They were convinced that the Germans were excessively dependent upon their military organization and supply system and, when these broke down, tended to come apart. Once on the Volkhov, when incorrect ammunition arrived, the Spaniards accepted this as the way things were in a war. The Germans, however, became upset.

Spanish and German tactics were worlds apart. While the Wehrmacht, in the tradition of the western front in World War I, still preferred continuous defensive lines on a static front, the Spaniards drew on their experiences in Morocco and the Civil War and constructed isolated strong points. These *islotes* provided defense in depth, and permitted interlocking fire, and enabled an economy of forces.

The Spaniards believed themselves to be masters of improvisation. They would try to make do with what they had. Like the Russians, they preferred to live off the country, cost what it may to the civilian population. Spanish conduct behind the lines was unruly but, unlike Nazis, they considered the Russians to be human beings, not *Untermenschen* (subhumans). This attitude, in spite of the requisitioning, enabled the *guripas* to form firm bonds with the peasants. Both on the Volkhov and at Krasni Bor, the civilians protected the Spaniards from partisans and the Red Army. Along Lake Il'men, the *panienkas* alerted the sleeping sentries when danger threatened.

In the line, the Spaniards exhibited great courage and élan. Though their hopes for driving toward Moscow with Operation Typhoon were soon dashed they entered the line in time to participate in Operation Tikhvin—the great effort to seal off Leningrad and link up with the Finns. Concentrating in Novgorod the *guripas* forced the Volkhov and sought desperately to open the road to Msta, Borovichi, and the Valdai Hills. But Russian resistance and the *rasputitsa* compelled them to accept a defensive role shielding the southern flank of the Tithvin salient. Tempered by the grim reality of the Volkhov at Otenskii and Posad, the *divisionarios* were finally forged into a professional fighting force by the crisis of 27 December 1941. From that date on, they displayed a stoic willingness to undertake any assignment—Like Il'men, Teremets, the Volkhov Pocket—no matter what the cost. The Blue Division was the solid pivot of XXXVIII Corps during the Russian attempt to liberate Leningrad during the winter of 1941–42 and fought shoulder-to-shoulder with German and international units in the destruction of the Soviet forces.

As the First Division was rotated home in mid-1942, and the students, poets, intellectuals, and *africanistas* were replaced by mechanics, field hands, and clerks, the Blue Division's hopes for offensive action were again raised. Operation Northern Light on the Leningrad front under Field Marshal von Manstein offered the men that opportunity, but once again they were assigned a defensive role at Pushkin. This phase reached a climax at Krasni Bor in February 1943. During their two years in the line 250 Division was entrusted by Army Group North with two crucial pillars of the Leningrad siege—Novgorod and Pushkin. Both on the Volkhov and before Leningrad, in spite of the doubts of the German High Command, these unorthodox but plucky soldiers won the admiration of their comrades. Hitler proclaimed the Spaniards the only virile Latin race.

Although tending to disdain the drudgery of cleaning weapons or digging trenches—such manual labor, they believed, was for Germans and POWs—the *divisionarios* were dashing in the attack and firm on the defense. To take cover was considered almost cowardly. Their forte was to close—hand-to-hand combat their element. Thus, without much training, they were often wildly undisciplined in assault, rushing forward with high spirits and even abandon. It was sometimes difficult for the officers to get them back under control. The line officers, while they clung to the caste system, led. Unlike their German counterparts, who directed their sections and companies from the rear, they went first. This, along with the shortage of NCOs, accounts for the high number of officer casualties.

The officers and men of the First and Second Division were of relatively equal caliber. The difference in tone of the divisions, often thought to be a reflection of the quality of the personnel, was really more a matter of leadership. Even though the First Division contained a high percentage of students and idealists, the troops were essentially the same, untrained and spirited Spaniards. Muñoz Grandes and his men had been tested the day they entered the line. None of them was, as yet, experienced in the Russian campaign. Therefore, the rotation of personnel cannot entirely explain the difference in reputation of the

First and Second Divisions. The craggy *Frontschwein* created the division in his own image. Aggressive, dynamic, hard, Muñoz Grandes galvanized the division by force of his own will. His commands at Posad—"Share the glory and the danger"; to the intermediate position on the Volkhov—"You will stand as if nailed to the ground"; and to Ordás on the ice of Lake Il'men—"You will go on, alone if necessary," poured his own steel into the division and made the men better than they were.

Simplicity and justice marked Muñoz Grandes's style. Although always ready to listen to his soldiers and ever available to the lowliest *guripa*, he would not tolerate cowardice. When confronted with cases of self-mutilation or desertion, he promptly shot the offenders. Often at the front, he was adored by line officers and combat troops, and feared by staff and service personnel. He tended to neglect logistics and supply, which were first brought into order by Esteban Infantes.

Esteban Infantes, as a staff officer, succeeded in improving services and communications, which his predecessor had had little time for. The division ran more smoothly, but it lacked the panache of the earlier days. The tautness of the First Division became plastic. Both commanders allowed their line officers considerable latitude, but the colonels felt themselves always in the shadow of the *Frontschwein*, while his successor seemed far away at headquarters. The First Division, therefore, fought as a unit, the Second as individual regiments. Muñoz Grandes led the men, then, while Esteban Infantes sought to be their father. Faced with numerous instances of self-inflicted wounds and desertion, he tried to understand and preferred to impose prison sentences, rather than the death penalty. He showed mercy, Muñoz Grandes justice. Discipline and morale suffered.

Both men were fully conscious of their mission. The Blue Division was a Spanish expeditionary force with political, as well as military, purpose. The division had to prove to Hitler that the Spaniards would and could fight, that they were willing to accept losses. The command, "You will defend Posad as if it were Spain," had a double meaning. As long as the Wehrmacht stood on the Pyrenees, Posad was Spain. The Spanish Army had no illusions that it could stop a German invasion. The best that could be done was to convince the Führer that the cost would be prohibitive.

On the other hand, anti-communism was not a façade, neither for the volunteers or their commanders. The Soviet Union had intervened in their Civil War, and they viewed Stalin's empire as the heart of an atheistic, barbarous system which had as its goal the destruction of Christendom. Some of them were idealists, who saw themselves as crusaders. Throughout Europe, many young men, whether on the right or the left, viewed one another as part of an assault generation. They could not sit still in a tortured world. Rather, they rose up and battled, offered their lives to turn society around. Little wonder that, while a few of their comrades had become ardent Communists, others were fervent fascists. They looked for, and found, leaders.

Muñoz Grandes and the Falange, fearing both Russian and Anglo-American domination of Europe, sought a place for Spain in Hitler's New Order. Like Asensio and Yagüe, they were prepared to risk all to bring Spain into the war on the side of the Axis. Social revolutionaries, and fascists, they sought in Hitler and Mussolini kindred spirits.

Franco was also an anti-Communist and a European, but he trusted no one. Because of this, he would never place the destiny of Spain in the hands of anyone else. Drawn to Germany, especially by Axis aid in the Civil War, he remembered the Ribbentrop-Molotov Pact, the depredation of Poland, and the sacrifice of Finland. Aware that his shaky government and broken nation could hardly fight a new war, he resolved to stay at peace until the last moment, and the Blue Division became part of his maneuvering to keep the conflict away from Iberia. The division was also a convenient dumping ground for ardent Falangists who advocated social revolution and were impatient with the temporizing of the Caudillo. Many of them died in Russia and, if they returned like Muñoz Grandes still burning for action, he co-opted them.

The cost was high. As the veterans sat in the sidewalk cafes, they asked themselves, "Was it all worthwhile?" By April 1944, the legion was home with tales of disaster. The Falange was a hollow shell, subject to the will of Franco. The Army, even Muñoz Grandes, Asensio, and Yagüe, was the instrument of the chief of state. The Allies were advancing everywhere.

The newspapers of 27 April 1944 announced the passing of another hero.[7] As he stood at the bedside of the dying Lieutenant Escobedo in the Military Hospital at Jaen, Major Román stared at the frail youth whose wound had never healed and must have wondered if so many had not fallen in vain. *Una gesta heroica!* More than the *guripas* knew, they had helped keep foreign armies from their homeland.

Heroic gesture, fascist fanaticism, Christian crusade, the Blue Division was all of this and more. The volunteers, and those who had to be impressed to serve, became pawns in a diplomatic chess game and counters in a plot to bring Spain into the war. The Blue Division was an expeditionary force reflecting Franco's position as Hitler's most independent ally. The division helped the Caudillo assess the relative strength of the Third Reich and the Soviet Union. Frightened by what he learned of Russian power, he drew closer to the western allies and strove to bring the Anglo-Americans to make peace with Germany.

The Blue Division was a microcosm of the Eastern Front. The human tragedy of the conflict is often obscured in accounts of the gigantic clash of armies of millions. The story of this one unit, of Mediterraneans locked in the siege of Leningrad, lends dimension and perspective to the struggle for the metropolis of the North.

APPENDIX

NOTES

SELECTED BIBLIOGRAPHY

INDEX

Appendix

Initial Call of the Blue Division, July 1941

Military Region	Officers	Non-Commissioned Officers and Technicians	Men
1st Region (Madrid)	89	273	2,299
2nd Region (Seville)	90	249	2,160
3rd Region (Valencia)	72	201	1,598
4th Region (Barcelona)	70	193	1,758
5th Region (Saragossa)	45	180	1,347
6th Region (Burgos)	55	169	1,293
7th Region (Valladolid)	69	183	1,549
8th Region (Coruña)	48	123	1,154
Morocco	63	177	1,682
Communications	15	66	99
Motor Transport	7	64	862
Guardia Civil (Military Police)	1	2	28
GHQ-Div.	17	7	89
Subtotal	641	1,887	15,918
		Grand Total	18,446

Regiment Rodrigo
(*Col. Miguel Rodrigo Martínez*)

Military Region	Unit
I-Madrid	Regimental Headquarters Company
I-Madrid	1st Infantry Battalion
I-Madrid	2d Infantry Battalion

355

V-Saragossa	3d Infantry Battalion
I-Madrid	2 Sections 75 mm Close Support Artillery
II-Seville (Algeciras)	1 Section 75 mm Close Support Artillery
II-Seville (Algeciras)	1 Section 150 mm Close Support Artillery
I-Madrid	Regimental Antitank Company

REGIMENT PIMENTEL
(*Col. Pedro Pimentel Zayas*)

MILITARY REGION	UNIT
VII-Valladolid	Regimental Headquarters Company
VI-Burgos	1st Infantry Battalion
VII-Valladolid	2d Infantry Battalion
VIII-La Coruña	3d Infantry Battalion
VI-Burgos	1 Section 75 mm Close Support Artillery
VIII-La Coruña	2 Sections 75 mm Close Support Artillery
VII-Valladolid	1 Section 150 mm Close Support Artillery
III-Valencia	Regimental Antitank Company

REGIMENT VIERNA
(*Col. José Vierna Trábaga*)

MILITARY REGION	UNIT
III-Valencia	Regimental Headquarters Company
III-Valencia	1st Infantry Battalion
IV-Barcelona (Gerona)	2d Infantry Battalion
IV-Barcelona (Lerida)	3d Infantry Battalion
V-Saragossa	1 Section 75 mm Close Support Artillery
IV-Barcelona	1 Section 150 mm Close Support Artillery
III-Valencia (Paterna)	2 Sections 75 mm Close Support Artillery
III-Valencia	Regimental Antitank Company

REGIMENT ESPARZA*
(*Col. José Martínez Esparza*)†

MILITARY REGION	UNIT
II-Seville	Regimental Headquarters Company
II-Seville	1st Infantry Battalion

II-Seville	2d Infantry Battalion
Morocco (Ceuta)	3d Infantry Battalion
II-Seville	1 Section 75 mm Close Support Artillery
Morocco	2 Sections 75 mm Close Support Artillery
II-Seville	1 Section 150 mm Close Support Artillery
II-Seville	Regimental Antitank Company

---

*It would have been logical to call this regiment the Martínez Regiment. However, because Martínez was such a common name, it was always termed the Esparza Regiment.
†DOPS, Reg. Vierna, July 1941, DEV 28/33/1, pp. 36–38; DOPS, Reg. 269, July 1941, DEV 28/33/2, p. 26.
Source: General Staff, First Section, General Order of the Division 1 July 1941, *Archivo de la Guerra de Liberación, División Española de Voluntarios, División Azul,* 28/1/1/2, p. 2.

NOTES

CHAPTER 1. *"Russia Is Guilty"*

1. Stohrer to Foreign Ministry (Auswärtiges Amt, hereinafter AA), 22 June 1941, German Embassy Madrid Papers, Politisches Archiv–Auswärtiges Amt Bonn (hereinafter *Madrid Akten* or United States National Archives File T120/Roll 269/Frames 234669–70).

2. Andreas Hillgruber, *Hitler's Strategie: Politik und Kriegführung 1940–1941* (Frankfurt: Bernard & Graefe, 1965), p. 500; Generaloberst Halder, *Kriegstagebuch* (KTB), ed. Hans-Adolf Jacobsen (Stuttgart: W. Kohlhammer, 1964), 3:10; Ribbentrop to Stohrer, 24 June 1941, T120/275/234678.

3. Stohrer to AA, 23 June 1941, *Madrid Akten*, 234672; *New York Times* (hereinafter NYT), 23 June 1941, p. 10, 24 June 1941, p. 5.

4. Interview of the authors with Don Ramón Serrano Suñer, Madrid, December 1971; Stanley G. Payne, *Politics and the Military in Modern Spain* (Stanford: Stanford University Press, 1967), p. 430; Donald S. Detwiler, "Spain and the Axis During World War II," *Review of Politics* 33, no. 1 (1971): 49.

5. Stohrer to AA, 24 June 1941, *Madrid Akten*, 234680–81.

6. Serrano Suñer interview, December 1971; Ramón Serrano Suñer, *Entre Hendaya y Gibraltar* (Madrid: Ediciones y Publicaciones Españolas, 1947), p. 295.

7. Serrano Suñer interview, December 1971; Ambassador Alexander W. Weddell to Secretary of State, Madrid, 30 June 1941, United States National Archives (USNA), Department of State File 740.0011/13372; NYT, 25 June 1941, p. 6; Charles Foltz, *Masquerade in Spain* (New York: Houghton Mifflin, 1948), pp. 161–62.

8. Vicesecretaría de Educación Popular, *1er Cuaderno, División Azul* (Madrid: 1942); José M. Doussinague, *España tenía razón* (Madrid: Espasa-Calpe, 1949), pp. 53–54.

9. Serrano Suñer interview, December 1971; Arthur Loveday, *Spain: 1923–1948* (London, 1939), pp. 183–84; Sir Samuel Hoare, Viscount Templewood, *Ambassador on Special Mission* (London: Collins, 1946), pp. 114–16.

10. Stohrer to Ribbentrop, 22 June 1941, *Madrid Akten*, 234669–70; Donald S. Detwiler, *Hitler, Franco und Gibraltar* (Wiesbaden: Franz Steiner, 1962), pp. 95–104.

11. Stohrer to AA, 27 June 1941, *Madrid Akten*, 234703 and 28 June

1941, *Madrid Akten*, 234709; NYT, 27 June 1941; Galeazzo Ciano, *Ciano Diaries: 1939–1943*, ed. H. Gibson (New York: Doubleday, 1946), p. 370; Weddell to State, Madrid, 27 June 1941, USNA, State 740.0011/12554; Weddell to State, Madrid, 28 June 1941, USNA, State 740.0011/1260; Edgar O'Ballance, "The Spanish Blue Division in the Second World War," *Royal United Service Institution Journal* 109, no. 635 (August 1964): 240.

12. Units being organized for the fight against communism, Estado Mayor Central del Ejército, Servicio Histórico Militar, Madrid, *Archivo de la Guerra de Liberación, División Española de Voluntarios, División Azul* (hereinafter DEV), Armario 28/Legajo 1/Carpeta 1/Documento 2 (hereinafter 28/1/1/2).

13. Stohrer to AA, 27 June 1941, *Madrid Akten*, 234707–8; June 1941, *Madrid Akten*, 234710; Ramón Serrano Suñer, *Entre Hendaya y Gibraltar*, rev. ed. (Barcelona: Ed. Nauta, 1973), p. 210; Interview of the authors with Serrano Suñer, Madrid, June 1974; Sir Samuel Hoare to Foreign Office, Telegram 1019, Madrid, 4 July 1941, Public Record Office (PRO), Foreign Office (FO) 371/26940/7798/ p. 31; Maj. Alan Lubbock to M. I. 3 Colonel, No. 415, Madrid, 2 July 1941, PRO, FO/341/26940/8058, p. 34; As related to the authors by Harold Milks, former AP correspondent in Madrid; Interview of the authors with José Miguel Ortí Bordas, Tempe, Arizona, September 1974.

14. Peter Kemp, *Mine Were of Trouble* (London: Cassell, 1957), p. 96.

15. Spanish Volunteers to Fight Against the Soviet, FO, 6 July 1941, PRO, FO 371/26940/7798, p. 30.

16. Payne, *Politics*, p. 427.

17. *Ibid.*; Charles B. Burdick, *Germany's Military Strategy in Spain During World War II* (Syracuse: Syracuse University Press, 1968), p. 80; NYT, 6 July 1941, p. 15.

18. Likus Memoranda, 18 June 1942, T120/82/62772–74.

19. Muñoz Grandes to Jacinto Miguelarena, *Informaciones*, 9 August 1941, p. 7.

20. Hoare to FO, Telegram 989, Madrid, 4 July 1941, PRO, FO 371/26940/7798, p. 31.

21. Diary of Operations (hereinafter DOPS), Regiment Rodrigo, July 1941, DEV 28/33/1, pp. 41–42; DOPS, Regiment 262, July 1941, DEV 28/33/1, p. 35; General Staff (GS), 1st Section, General Order No. 1 of the Division (DGO-1), July 1941, 28/1/1/2, p. 2; Heberlein to AA, 4 July 1941, T120/295/234719–20; DOPS, Regiment Vierna, July 1941, DEV 28/33/1, pp. 36–38; DOPS, Regiment 269, July 1941, DEV 28/33/2, p. 26.

22. *Informaciones*, 2 July 1941, p. 3; NYT, 28 July 1941, p. 4, 6 July 1941, p. 15; Heberlein to AA, 5 July 1941, T120/295/234722; Interview of the authors with Col. García Albea, Isidoro Palomo Yagüe, Manuel Lascano, Lt. Antonio de Zurbiaurre, Lt. Col. Trigo, Manuel Guijarro y Agüerro, and Basilio Guijarro Olmedo at *La Vieja Guardia*, Madrid, De-

cember 1971 (hereinafter *Vieja Guardia* interview); Heberlein to AA, 11 July 1941, T120/295/234758–60; Juan Eugenio Blanco, *Rusia no es cuestión de un día* (Madrid: Publicaciones Españolas, 1954), pp. 6–7; *Informaciones*, 10 July 1941, p. 3, 11 July 1941, p. 4; Enrique Errando Vilar, *Campaña de invierno* (Madrid: Rehyma, 1943), p. 42; Serrano Suñer, *Hendaya*, rev. ed., p. 308; *Hoja de Campaña*, 28 November 1943, p. 1; Interview of the authors with Manuel Guijarro y Agüero, Madrid, December 1971.

23. *Informaciones*, 4 July 1941, pp. 1, 3; Stanley G. Payne, *Falange: A History of Spanish Fascism* (Stanford: Stanford University Press, 1961), pp. 233–34; Victor José Jiménez y Malo, *De España a Rusia* (Madrid: Imp. de Madrid, 1943), p. 26.

24. "Cara al Sol," Himno de la Falange Española, by Juan Telleria, 1936.

25. Blanco, *Rusia*, p. 8.

26. DOPS, 262, July 1941, DEV 28/33/1/2, pp. 33–34; General Staff, 2d Section (Intelligence), 7 July 1941, DEV 28/28/2/3, p. 48; Interview of the authors with Lt. Col. Norberto Aragón, Spanish military attaché. Washington, D.C., June 1971.

27. George Hills, *Franco* (New York: Macmillan, 1967), pp. 55–57; Kindelán to Stohrer, 23 June 1941, T120/295/234673; Jaeger to Stohrer, 2 July 1941, T120/295/234747–48; DOPS, Regiment Vierna, July 1941, DEV 28/33/1/4, pp. 36–37; Jaeger to Stohrer, 19 July 1941, T120/295/234754–57.

28. Jaeger to Stohrer, 10 July 1941, T120/295/234754–57.

29. Jaeger to Stohrer, 2 July 1941, T120/295/234747–48; Hoare to FO, No. 268, Madrid, 8 July 1941, PRO, FO, 371/26940/7798, p. 43.

30. *Informaciones*, 3 July 1941, p. 7, 4 July 1941, p. 3.

31. DOPS, Regiment Vierna, July 1941, DEV 28/33/1/4, pp. 36–37.

32. José Martínez Esparza, *Con la División Azul en Rusia* (Madrid, Ed. Ejército, 1943), pp. 9–12.

33. DOPS, 269, Report, DEV 28/33/2, pp. 25–26; *Informaciones*, 4 July 1941, p. 3, 5 July 1941, p. 3; Martínez Esparza, *División Azul*, p. 21.

34. Richter to AA, 10 July 1941, *Madrid Akten*, 234752.

35. Martínez Esparza, *División Azul*, p. 14; DOPS, Mobile Reserve Battalion 250, July 1941, DEV 28/33/2, pp. 3–4.

36. DOPS, 269 Report, July 1941, DEV 28/33/2, pp. 25–26; Martínez Esparza, *División Azul*, pp. 20–22; *Informaciones*, 11 July 1941, p. 4.

37. AA Memoranda, Bureau of State Secretary, 2 July 1941, T120/295/234734–41; OKW/WFST, Directive concerning the employment of foreign volunteers in the struggle against the Soviet Union, 6 July 1941, T77/554/173078–119.

38. Division 250 (DIV), DOPS, July 1941, DEV 28/33/1, p. 2.

39. Heberlein to AA, 4 July 1941, T120/295/234719–20.

40. DIV, DOPS, July 1941, DEV 28/33/1/2; Report of billeting commission from Berlin, Madrid, 7 July 1941, DEV 28/28/3/1, pp. 1–4.

41. Heberlein to AA, 9 July 1941, T120/295/234729–31.

42. Ritter to Madrid, 11 July 1941, T120/295/234745–46; Billeting commission, Madrid, 7 July 1941, DEV 28/28/3/1, pp. 1–4; OKW/WF St, Directive concerning military justice for Spanish volunteers, 28 August 1941, T77/554/1730699–701.

43. Billeting commission, Madrid, 7 July 1941, DEV 28/28/3/1, pp. 1–4.

44. Eisenlohr to Madrid, 11 July 1941, T120/295/234743–44; Diary of the commission, Madrid, July 1941, DEV 28/33/2/2, p. 22.

45. *Informaciones*, 11 July 1941, p. 3.

46. General Staff, State of the Forces, 2200, 12 July 1941, DEV 28/26/4/4, p. 9.

47. *Informaciones*, 12 July 1941, p. 1, 14 July 1941, pp. 1, 8; NYT, 15 July 1941, p. 5; Robert Hodgson, *Spain Resurgent* (London: Hutchinson, 1953), pp. 117–18; Thomas J. Hamilton, *Appeasement's Child: The Franco Regime in Spain* (New York: Knopf, 1943), pp. 237–38; Martínez Esparza, *División Azul*, pp. 25–26.

48. *Informaciones*, 14 July 1941, p. 1.

CHAPTER 2. *Grafenwöhr*

1. Muñoz Grandes to Jacinto Miguelarena, *Informaciones*, 9 August 1941, p. 1.

2. Hoare to FO, Telegram 1019, Madrid, 4 July 1941, PRO, FO 371/26940/8058, p. 31.

3. Payne, *Politics*, p. 430.

4. *Informaciones*, 14 July 1941, p. 3; Martínez Esparza, *División Azul*, pp. 26–27; DIV, DOPS, July 1941, DEV 28/33/1/2, p. 9.

5. Jiménez y Malo, *España*, p. 17.

6. DIV, DOPS, July 1941, DEV 28/33/1/2, p. 9; GS, 2d Section, Expedition 6, 21 July 1941, DEV 28/28/2/2, p. 27; Blanco, *Rusia*, pp. 9–10.

7. GS, 2d Section, Expedition 10, Relation of Incidents, 21 July 1941, DEV 28/28/2/2, p. 31; DOPS, Second Artillery Group, July–August 1941, DEV 28/33/2/1, pp. 11–12; DOPS, 12 Company, Third of 262, July 1941, DEV 29/39/3, pp. 1–2.

8. GS, 2d Section, Incidents, 19 July 1941, DEV 28/28/2/2, p. 16; GS, 2d Section, Informative note, 20 and 21 July 1941, DEV 28/28/2/2, pp. 20, 21, 26; GS, 2d Section, Expedition 13, 22 July 1941, DEV 28/28/2/2, p. 41.

9. Jiménez y Malo, *España*, pp. 18–19; GS, 2d Section, Incidents, 21 July 1941, DEV 28/28/2/2, p. 25.

10. GS, 2d Section, Expedition 10, 21 July 1941, DEV 28/28/2/2, p. 33; GS, 2d Section, Expedition from La Coruña, 21 July 1941, DEV 28/28/2/2, p. 35; GS, 2d Section, Expedition 6, 21 July 1941, DEV 28/28/2/2, p. 26; GS, 2d Section, Incidents, 19 July 1941, DEV 28/28/2/2, p.

16; GS, 2d Section, Expedition 14, 22 July 1941, DEV 28/28/2/2, p. 36; *Informaciones*, 18 July 1941, p. 6; *Völkischer Beobachter*, 19 July 1941, p. 1.

11. Emilio Esteban Infantes, *La División Azul* (Barcelona: Ed. AHR, 1956), pp. 19–20; GS, Diary of the Commission, July 1941, DEV 28/33/2/2, pp. 17–26; Martínez Esparza, *División Azul*, pp. 46–47.

12. DIV, DOPS, July 1941, DEV 28/33/1/2, pp. 8, 11; GS, Gómez Zamalloa to 2d Section, 22 July 1941, DEV 28/28/2/2, p. 41; GS, 2d Section, 19 July 1941, DEV 28/28/2/2, p. 16; DOPS, 262, July 1941, 31 July 1941, DEV 28/22/1/2, p. 35; Martínez Esparza, *División Azul*, pp. 53–54; Personal observation of the authors, Grafenwöhr, June 1974.

13. Martínez Esparza, *División Azul*, pp. 52–55.

14. DIV, DOPS, July 1941, DEV 28/33/1/2, p. 12.

15. Martínez Esparza, *División Azul*, p. 56.

16. Ibid., p. 58.

17. José Díaz de Villegas, *La División Azul en Línea* (Barcelona: Ed. Acervo, 1967), p. 146; DIV, DOPS, July 1941, DEV 28/33/1/2, p. 13.

18. GS, no date, DEV 28/27/3/1, p. 1; Díaz de Villegas, *Línea*, pp. 137, 157, 161, 174, 183; War Department, *Handbook on German Military Forces*, TM-E 30-451 (Washington: War Department, 1945), pp. II–2; GS, DGO-13, 29 July 1941, DEV 28/1/1/7, p. 106.

19. GS, TO & E Infantry Regiment, July 1941, DEV 28/27/4/1, p. 74.

20. GS, 3d Section (Operations), Daily Instruction Schedule, 23 July 1941, DEV 28/1/1/12, p. 38; *Informaciones*, 18 July 1941, pp. 1–3; Heberlein to AA, 18 July 1941, T120/95/106955–56; Stohrer to AA, 27 July 1941, T120/95/106966–68.

21. Heberlein to AA, 18 July 1941, T120/95/106956.

22. Bismarck to AA, Rome, 26 August 1941, T120/95/107045.

23. *Informaciones*, 14 July 1941, p. 8; Strack to Ribbentrop, Memorandum, 23 July 1941, T120/95/106959.

24. Roca de Togores to Madrid, 26 July 1941, DEV 29/44/1/5, p. 60; General Instruction 4, 10 July 1941, DEV 29/44/1/5, pp. 34–36.

25. H. R. Trevor-Roper, ed., *Hitler's War Directives* (London: Sidgwick and Jackson, 1964), pp. 85–88; KTB, Halder, 3: 103–120; *Kriegstagebuch des Oberkommandos der Wehrmacht*, Hans-Adolf Jacobsen, ed. (Frankfurt: Bernard and Graefe, 1965), 1: 440–42; Hillgruber, *Hitler's Strategie*, p. 693.

26. Trevor-Roper, *Hitler's War Directives*, pp. 89–90; Albert Seaton, *Russo-German War 1941–1945* (London: Arthur Barker, 1971), p. 143.

27. Jiménez y Malo, *España*, p. 34; Vicesecretariá de Educación Popular, *Ier Cuaderno*, p. 5.

28. GS, 3d Section, Oath, 30 July 1941, DEV 28/1/1/7, p. 126; Errando Vilar, *Campaña*, p. 16.

29. DIV, DOPS, July 1941, DEV 28/33/1/2, p. 15.

30. Martínez Esparza, *División Azul*, p. 74; Jiménez y Malo, *España*, pp. 33–34; *Informaciones*, 1 August 1941, p. 1, 3; GS, 3d Section, DGO,

Organization of units for the Oath, 28 July 1941, DEV 28/1/1/3, pp. 96–99; GS, DGO-13, 29 July 1941, DEV 28/1/1/2, p. 106; GS, 3d Section, Addition to DGO-13, 29 July 1941, DEV 28/1/1/3, pp. 107–8.

31. Martínez Esparza, *División Azul*, p. 75.

32. *Völkischer Beobachter*, 5 August 1941, p. 3; Martínez Esparza, *División Azul*, pp. 73–77; Jiménez y Malo, *España*, pp. 33–35; Blanco, *Rusia*, pp. 13–14; DOPS, 262, July 1941, DEV 28/31/1/2, p. 33.

33. GS, 2d Section, 2 August 1941, DEV 28/28/4/3, p. 17; GS, 2d Section, Distribution of Donation, 8 August 1941, DEV 28/28/4/4, p. 35.

34. GS, 2d Section, General Instructions 2004, 2 August 1941, DEV 28/28/4/4, p. 31; *Informaciones*, 4 August 1941, p. 3; "Cien números de 'Hoja de Campaña,' " *Hoja de Campaña*, 10 January 1944, p. 4.

35. Martínez Esparza, *División Azul*, pp. 78–79.

36. GS, 2d Section, Informative Note, 17 August 1941, DEV 28/28/4/3, p. 24; GS, 2d Section, Informative Note, 26 August 1941, DEV 28/28/4/3, p. 26.

37. Blanco, *Rusia*, p. 13; Martínez Esparza, *División Azul*, p. 97.

38. Interview of the authors with Lt. Col. Günther Collatz, chief of Liaison Staff, GS (ret.), Bad Aibling, August 1971; Martínez Esparza, *División Azul*, pp. 82–84; XXXVIII Corps, Summary of Weapons, 22 December 1941, T314/898/127.

39. DOPS, Sappers 250, July-August 1941, DEV 28/33/12/1, pp. 26–30.

40. *Informaciones*, 4 August 1941, p. 3; GS, 2d Section, 11 August 1941, DEV 28/28/4/3, p. 22.

41. DOPS, Second of 262, August 1941, DEV 29/36/12/1, pp. 9–10.

42. Military Attaché to Muñoz Grandes, Berlin, 11 August 1941, DEV 29/52/1/1, p. 1; Military Attaché, Berlin, to War Ministry, Madrid, 20 August 1941, DEV 29/52/1/1, p. 3; GS, 2d Section, Effectives of the Division to 20 September 1941, DEV 28/1/16/3, pp. 52–53.

43. Jiménez y Malo, *España*, p. 34.

44. Interview of the authors with the Conde de Lemos, Spanish Consul in Cologne, 1940–44, Madrid, December 1971.

45. GS, 1st Section, Order of the Day 35, 20 August 1941, and Order of the Day 36, 21 August 1941, DEV 28/7/10/2, pp. 84, 88.

46. Interview of the authors with Karl Vitus Schneider, president, *Kameradschaft ehem. Angehöriger des Deutschen Verbindungstabes der blauen Division*, Nurnberg, June 1974.

CHAPTER 3. *The Long March*

1. Tomás Salvador, *División 250* (Barcelona: Ed. Destino, 1962), pp. 63–65; KTB, Liaison Staff, T315/1726/48 and 314–15; Jiménez y Malo, *España*, pp. 38–39.

2. Collatz interview, August 1971; Esteban Infantes, *Azul*, p. 50.

3. Hillgruber, *Hitler's Strategie*, p. 694; *Informaciones*, 1 September

1941, p. 1; *Völkischer Beobachter*, 2 September 1941, p. 3; Martínez Esparza, *División Azul*, pp. 102, 135, 148; Military Attaché to Heberlein, Madrid, 10 September 1941, T120/295/234784; GS, 1st Section, Effectives of the Division to 20 September 1941, DEV 28/1/16/3, p. 52.

4. KTB, Halder, 11 August 1941 and 22 August 1941, 3: 170, 193.

5. Detwiler, "Spain and the Axis," p. 45.

6. OKW, KTB, 1:446 and Burdick, *Germany's Military Strategy*, p. 128.

7. Brigadier W. W. T. Torr to FO, Madrid, 6 August 1941, PRO, FO, 371/26940/7798, p. 86.

8. Serrano Suñer interview, December 1971.

9. *Völkischer Beobachter*, 2 September 1941, p. 2; *Informaciones*, 1 September 1941, p. 1.

10. Serrano Suñer interview, June 1974.

11. GS, 1st Section, Local Commandant, Grodno, 26 August 1941, DEV 28/7/7/1, p. 6.

12. Ciano, *Ciano Diaries*, pp. 411–12; *Vieja Guardia* interview, December 1971.

13. KTB, Liaison Staff, 1 September 1941, T315/1726/00091.

14. KTB, Liaison Staff, 6 September 1941, T315/1726/94. The assertion made by Raymond L. Proctor in *Agony of a Neutral: La División Azul* (Moscow: Idaho Research Foundation, 1974), p. 151, that the Blue Division was assigned to Col. Gen. Hermann von Hoth's 19 Army is incorrect on several counts: 1) there was no 19 Army; 2) Hoth did not have a "von"; 3) Hoth commanded 3 Panzer Group; 4) 250 Division was assigned to von Kluge's 4 Army.

15. Trevor-Roper, *Hitler's War Directives*, p. 96.

16. DIV, DOPS, September 1941, DEV 28/33/7/2, p. 7; DOPS, 269, August–September 1941, DEV 28/34/3, pp. 5–17; DOPS, 263, September 1941, DEV 28/33/7, p. 22; DOPS, Second of 262, August–September 1941, DEV 29/36/12, pp. 5–14; José Alvarez Esteban, *Agonia de Europa* (Madrid: 1947), pp. 243–45.

17. Martínez Esparza, *División Azul*, pp. 145–46; Alvarez, *Agonia*, pp. 249–50.

18. J. L. Gómez Tello, *Canción del invierno en el este* (Barcelona: Caralt, 1945), pp. 42–43.

19. Jiménez y Malo, *España*, pp. 44–45; Martínez Esparza, *División Azul*, pp. 145–46.

20. GS, 2d Section, Unit interpreters, DEV 28/28/3, p. 27.

21. Jiménez y Malo, *España*, pp. 63–64.

22. KTB, Liaison Staff, 7 September 1941, T315/1726/94–95.

23. Martínez Esparza, *División Azul*, pp. 149–58.

24. KTB, Liaison Staff, 9 September 1941, T315/1726/95.

25. Kemp, *Trouble*, p. 117; GS, 2d Section, Informative Note, 10 September 1941, DEV 28/28/5, p. 13.

26. Jiménez y Malo, *España*, pp. 82–84.

27. Guijarro interview, December 1971; Interview of the authors with Fernando Vadillo Ortiz de Guzmán, Madrid, December 1971.

28. GS, 2d Section, Informative Note, 15 September 1941, DEV 28/ 28/5, pp. 14–15.

29. Privately reported to the authors; KTB, Liaison Staff, 14 September 1941, T315/1726/96.

30. Personal communication of Lt. Col. Günther Collatz to the authors, 9 June 1975.

31. Gómez Tello, *Canción*, p. 44.

32. Angel Ruíz Ayucar, *La Rusia que conoci* (Madrid: Ed. del Movimiento, 1954), pp. 36–38.

33. Martínez Esparza, *División Azul*, pp. 169–70; KTB, Liaison Staff, 19 September 1941, T315/17/26/98; Jiménez y Malo, *España*, p. 123.

34. Jiménez y Malo, *España*, pp. 121–22.

35. Ibid., pp. 83–84; Heberlein to Berlin, 10 September 1941, Madrid, T120/295/234784.

36. Jiménez y Malo, *España*, pp. 121–42.

37. DIV, DOPS, September 1941, DEV 28/33/7/2, pp. 14–15; Martínez Esparza, *División Azul*, pp. 177–78; Jiménez y Malo, *España*, pp. 139–43.

CHAPTER 4. *Novgorod the Golden*

1. KTB, Halder, 3:213; KTB, Nord, 5 September 1941, T311/53/ 7065252.

2. Erich von Manstein, *Lost Victories*, trans. and ed. Anthony G. Powell (Chicago: Henry Regnery, 1958), p. 75; Office of United States Chief of Counsel for War Crimes, Evidence Division, Interrogation Branch, Interrogation Summary 3718, Kurt Brennecke, 9 October 1947, United States National Archives; Bernhard von Lossberg, *Im Wehrmachtführungsstab* (Hamburg: Nolke, 1949), pp. 133–34.

3. Office of United States Chief of Counsel for War Crimes, Evidence Division, Interrogation Branch, Interrogation Summary 3550, Wilhelm Leeb, 25 September 1947, United States National Archives.

4. Ibid.; Interrogation Summary 3719, 8 October 1947, p. 3, United States National Archives.

5. KTB, Nord, 5–7 September 1941, T311/53/7065251–63; KTB, Halder, 3:213–16.

6. Carl Gustav Mannerheim, *The Memoirs of Marshal Mannerheim*, trans. Eric Lewenhaupt. (New York: Dutton, 1954), p. 427.

7. Ibid., p. 431.

8. Dimitri V. Pavlov, *Leningrad 1941: The Blockade*, trans. J. C. Adams (Chicago: University of Chicago Press, 1965), pp. 18, 96–101; Leon Gouré, *The Siege of Leningrad* (Stanford: Stanford University Press, 1962), p. 109.

9. Otto P. Chaney, Jr., *Zhukov* (Norman: University of Oklahoma Press, 1971), pp. 104–5.

10. Military Attaché to Minister of War, Berlin, 30 October 1941, DEV 29/52/3, p. 19.

11. KTB, Halder, 24, 25 September 1941, 3: 248–49; KTB, Nord, 25 September 1941, T311/53/7065364; Harrison E. Salisbury, *The 900 Days: The Siege of Leningrad* (New York: Harper & Row, 1969), p. 293; Von Leeb to OKH, 24 September 1941, OKH, *Chefsache*, T78/335/6291812–14.

12. KTB, Liaison Staff, 24–25 September 1941, T315/1726/99; DIV, DOPS, September 1941, DEV 28/33/7/2, pp. 15–16; DOPS, Artillery Regiment 250, September 1941, DEV 28/33/7, p. 32.

13. Martínez Esparza, *División Azul*, pp. 183–84.

14. KTB, Nord, T311/53/7065376–402.

15. 16 Army to I Corps, Outgoing Orders, 16 Army, 28 September 1941, T312/545/8152567–69; KTB, 16 Army, 30 September 1941, T312/544/8151310.

16. KTB, I Corps, Appendix, 28 September 1941, T314/40/1160.

17. *Völkischer Beobachter*, 5 October 1941, p. 3; Vicesecretariá de Educación Popular, *Ier Cuaderno*, p. 25; KTB, 16 Army, 1230, 2 October 1941, T312/544/8151439; KTB, Liaison Staff, 2–4 October 1941, T315/1726/100.

18. Collatz interview, August 1971.

19. KTB, Halder, 19 August 1941, 3: 188; Werner Buxa, *Weg und Schicksal der ll. Infanterie-Division* (Bad Nauheim: Podzun, 1963), p. 34.

20. Personal observation of the authors, June 1974.

21. KTB, Nord, 5 October 1941, T311/53/7065411; Nord, Dispositions, 24 September 1941, T311/136/7181565; KTB, 16 Army, 5 October 1941, T312/544/8151455; KTB, Liaison Staff, 4 October 1941, T315/1726/101; KTB, I Corps, Appendix, 5 October 1941, T314/40/001181.

22. KTB, 126 Division, 5 October 1941, T315/1350/626; Gerhart Lohse, *Geschichte der rheinisch-westphälischen 126. Infanterie-Division, 1940–1945* (Bad Nauheim: Podzun, 1957), pp. 7–50; I Corps, Commands, Reports, 1941, T314/40/1174; KTB, Liaison Staff, 5 October 1941, T315/1726/101.

23. I Corps, Orders Received, T314/40/1181/86; KTB, Halder, 3: 263–68.

24. GS, 3d Section, General Order of Operations, 4 October 1941, DEV 28/33/13/4, p. 26; KTB, Liaison Staff, 5 October 1941, T315/1726/101; DIV, DOPS, October 1941, DEV 28/33/11/3, pp. 20–21; DOPS, Artillery Regiment 250, October 1941, DEV 28/33/12/1, p. 50; I Corps, Incoming Orders, Report to I Corps, 6 October 1941, T314/40/1173–75.

25. GS, 3d Section, General Order of Operations, 4 October 1941, DEV 28/33/13/4, p. 26; Alvarez, *Agonia*, pp. 283–84.

26. DOPS, 262, October 1941, DEV 28/33/12/1, pp. 2–4; DOPS, 269, October 1941, DEV 28/33/12/1, p. 12.

27. Martínez Esparza, *División Azul*, p. 187.

28. Nord, Incoming Reports, Final Report on Operation Arriba, 16 October 1941, T311/72/7093723; Martínez Esparza, *División Azul*, pp. 187–90; Nord, Incoming Reports, 20 October 1941, T311/72/7093734–36.

29. Nord, Incoming Reports, 21 October 1941, T311/72/7093737.

30. Ibid.; Martínez Esparza, *División Azul*, p. 192.

31. Nord, Incoming Reports, Final Report on Operation Arriba, Transport Office Novo Sokolniki, 16 October 1941, T311/72/709372324–25.

32. Ruíz Ayucar, *La Rusia*, p. 80.

33. I Corps, Incoming Reports, Report on 250 Division, 6 October 1941, T314/40/1173.

34. Ibid., 2 October 1941, T314/40/1168.

35. Ibid., 1168–69.

36. I Corps, Incoming Reports, Collatz to I Corps, 29 September 1941, T314/40/1165–66.

37. KTB, Nord, 10 October 1941, T311/53/7065433; KTB, Liaison Staff, 13 October 1941, T315/1726/101; Collatz interview, August 1971.

38. Ruíz Azucar, *La Rusia*, p. 85.

39. Ibid., pp. 80–90.

40. Jiménez y Malo, *España*, p. 146.

41. DIV, DOPS, October 1941, DEV 28/33/11/3, p. 25; Martínez Esparza, *División Azul*, pp. 195–99; DOPS, 269, October 1941, DEV 28/33/12/2, p. 12.

42. GS, 3d Section, I Corps Order 120, 10 October 1941, DEV 28/33/13/3, p. 48.

43. General Order of Operations, Grigorovo, 15 October 1941, DEV 28/33/13/3, pp. 29–31.

44. KTB, Nord, 9 October 1941, T311/53/7065432–39.

45. XXXVIII Corps, Situation Maps, 2 November 1941, T314/900/662; 16 Army, Situation Map 45, 24 September 1941, T312/548/856728; KTB, 16 Army, 10 October 1941, T312/544/8151459; Memorandum on a conversation between Busch and von Brauchitsch, 19 September 1941, T312/548/8157268–71; KTB, 16 Army, 5 October 1941, T312/544/8151445; KTB, Nord, 6 and 10 October 1941, T311/53/7065414 and 433; GS, 3d Section, I Corps Order 120, 10 October 1941, DEV 28/33/13/3, p. 48.

46. I Corps, Orders Received, 9 October 1941, T314/40/1193; I Corps Appendix to KTB, T314/40/1192–93.

47. I Corps, Orders Received, 9 October 1941, T314/40/1192–94; KTB, 16 Army, 9 October 1941, T312/544/8151455–56.

48. Hermann Plocher, *The German Air Force versus Russia, 1941* (New York: Arno Press, 1965), pp. 153–56, 291; I Corps, Orders Received, 10 October 1941, T314/40/1195–97, 1209–11; 16 Army, Orders and Reports, 20 October 1941, T312/546/8153791.

49. 16 Army, Situation Map 45, 24 September 1941, T312/548/8156728; Gómez Tello, *Canción*, p. 84.

50. Personal communication of Col. H. Nolte (GS) Ret., to the authors, 20 February 1975.

51. DOPS, 262, 1 October 1941, DEV 28/33/12/1, pp. 4–5.

52. Guijarro interview, December 1971.

53. Arno Pentzien, Artillery Regiment 18, Kriegstagebuch, ms., as cited by Col. H. Nolte (GS) Ret., personal communication to authors, 20 February 1975.

54. DOPS, Artillery Regiment 250, October 1941, DEV 28/33/12/1, p. 50; DOPS, Second Artillery Group, October 1941, DEV 28/33/12/1, p. 53; Jiménez y Malo, *España*, p. 197.

55. Jiménez y Malo, *España*, pp. 187–99.

Chapter 5. *Across the Volkhov*

1. DOPS, Second Artillery Group, October 1941, DEV 28/33/12, pp. 56–57; DOPS, 262, October 1941, DEV 28/33/12/1, pp. 4–5; Jiménez y Malo, *España*, pp. 200–201.

2. DOPS, 269, October 1941, DEV 28/33/12/1, pp. 12–13.

3. GS, 3d Section, General Order of Operations, 16 October 1941, DEV 28/33/13, pp. 29–31; I Corps, Order 120, 10 October 1941, T315/1350/1086–90.

4. Personal communication to the authors by Col. H. Nolte (GS) Ret., 20 February 1975.

5. DIV, DOPS, October 1941, DEV 28/33/11/3, p. 28; DOPS, Reconnaissance 250, October 1941, DEV 28/33/12/1, pp. 46–49; DOPS, 262, October 1941, DEV 28/33/12/1, pp. 4–5; GS, 3d Section, Order of Operations, 15 October 1941, DEV 28/33/13/3, pp. 29–30.

6. Military Attaché to War Ministry, Report 65, Berlin, 30 October 1941, DEV 29/52/3, p. 8.

7. 16 Army, Army Order 25, 14 October 1941, T314/40/1224.

8. Ibid., 1224–29; Group von Roques, 15 October 1941, DEV 28/33/13/3, pp. 55–56.

9. DOPS, Artillery Regiment 250, October 1941, DEV 28/33/12/1, p. 51.

10. GS, 2d Section, POW Interrogations, 15–19 October 1941, DEV 28/28/6, pp. 9–40; 126 Divsion, Report of Enemy Units, 12 October 1941, T315/1356/662–66.

11. Martínez Esparza, *División Azul*, pp. 215–23; DOPS, 269, October 1941, DEV 28/33/12/1, p. 14.

12. GS, Section IIa, 250 Division, List of Important Individuals Killed in First Actions, 11 November 1941, T311/72/7093745; *Informaciones*, 25 October 1941, p. 3.

13. *Informaciones*, 27 October 1941, p. 1.

14. Errando Vilar, *Campaña*, pp. 30–31; Serrano Suñer to Stohrer, Madrid, 14 January 1942, T120/295/234813–14.

15. KTB, 126 Division, 16 October 1941, T315/1350/637; KTB, 16

Army, 17 October 1941, T312/544/8151559; Group von Roques, Order 3, 17 October 1941, DEV 28/33/13, pp. 61–62.

16. DIV, DOPS, October 1941, DEV 28/33/11, pp. 29–30.

17. GS, 3d Section, General Order of Operations, 18 October 1941, DEV 28/33/13/4, pp. 38–40; 16 Army, TO & E, 10 October 1941, T314/40/1214.

18. DIV, DOPS, October 1941, DEV 28/33/11, p. 30.

19. KTB, 16 Army, 19 October 1941, T312/544/8151479; Martínez Esparza, *División Azul*, pp. 228–33; DOPS, 269, October 1941, DEV 28/33/12/1, pp. 14–16.

20. DIV, DOPS, October 1941, DEV 28/33/11/3, p. 31; Group von Roques, Order 5, 14 October 1941, DEV 28/33/11, p. 67.

21. KTB, Nord, 21 October 1941, T311/53/7065476; Gómez Tello, *Canción*, p. 116.

22. Alvarez, *Agonia*, p. 299.

23. AA 126 to 126 Division, 20 October 1941, T315/1353/786; Martínez Esparza, *División Azul*, pp. 232–40; KTB, 126 Division, 20 October 1941, T315/1350/644; DOPS, Third of 263, October 1941, DEV 29/36/12/1, pp. 18–19.

24. DOPS, 269, October 1941, DEV 28/33/12, p. 15.

25. Busch to von Roques, 19 October 1941, T314/40/1251; Von Roques to Busch, 20 October 1941, T312/548/8157218–19.

26. GS, 2d Section, POW Interrogation Reports, 21-25 October 1941, DEV 28/28/6, pp. 45–56 and DEV 28/28/7, p. 22; DOPS, 269, October 1941, DEV 28/33/12, p. 15.

27. 16 Army to Group von Roques, 22 October 1941, T314/40/1254; Group von Roques, Order 5, 19 October 1941, T315/353/802.

28. 126 Division, Operation Tikhvin Report, 16 October–11 November 1941, T315/1350/393; Martínez Esparza, *División Azul*, pp. 254–55; DOPS, 1st Sanitary Company, October 1941, DEV 28/33/12/1, pp. 59–63; Errando Vilar, *Campaña*, pp. 32–33.

29. KTB, 16 Army, 20 October 1941, T312/544/8151482–84; Group von Roques, Order 6, 22 October 1941, T315/1354/225–26; 126 Division, Daily Reports, 18 and 20 October 1941, T315/1353/777, 812, 870; Report of General von Roques to 16 Army on Use of 250 Division, 20 October 1941, T312/548/8157218.

30. DOPS, Reserve Battalion 250, October 1941, DEV 28/33/12/1, p. 43.

31. Martínez Esparza, *División Azul*, p. 260.

32. GS, 2d Section, Information Bulletin 13, 25 October 1941, DEV 28/28/5/4, pp. 22–23.

33. *Informaciones*, 29 October 1941, p. 8.

34. Martínez Esparza, *División Azul*, pp. 257, 264.

35. GS to 269, 1955, 23 October 1941 in Martínez Esparza, *División Azul*, p. 265.

36. *Völkischer Beobachter*, 25 October 1941, p. 1.

37. Embassy Memorandum, Madrid, 29 September 1941, T120/295/234792–93.

38. Roca de Togores to Madrid, Report 65, 30 October 1941, DEV 29/52/3/1, pp. 18–20.

39. KTB 16 Army, 23 October 1941, T312/544/8151490; *Informaciones*, 27 October 1941, p. 1.

40. Errando Vilar, *Campaña*, p. 35.

41. Ibid.

42. Roca de Togores to Muñoz Grandes, 1 November 1941, DEV 29/52/4, p. 1; GS, 250 Division, Winter Campaign Report, 1941–42, 10 May 1942, T314/903/889–91.

43. Martínez Esparza, *División Azul*, p. 269.

44. GS, 2d Section, POW Interrogation, 30 October 1941, DEV 28/28/6, pp. 82–83; GS, 2d Section, Information Bulletin 18, 30 October 1941, DEV 28/28/5, p. 27.

45. Martínez Esparza, *División Azul*, pp. 271–72.

46. DOPS, Sappers 250, October 1941, DEV 28/33/12/1, pp. 40–41; DOPS, Reserve Battalion 250, October 1941, DEV 28/33/12/1, pp. 43–44; DOPS, 269, October 1941, DEV 28/33/12/1, p. 16; 16 Army, Daily Report, 28 October 1941, T312/546/8154556.

47. Martínez Esparza, *División Azul*, p. 272.

48. DOPS, 269, October 1941, DEV 28/33/12, p. 16; DIV, DOPS, October 1941, DEV 28/33/11/3, p. 34; DOPS, 12 Company, Third of 263, October 1941, DEV 29/39/3, pp. 45–48.

49. GS, 2d Section, Appreciation of the Enemy 3, 4 November 1941, DEV 28/28/7/2, p. 7.

50. Martínez Esparza, *División Azul*, p. 273.

51. Ibid.

52. Gómez Tello, *Canción*, pp. 128–29.

53. DOPS, Reserve Battalion 250, October 1941, DEV 28/33/12, pp. 44–45.

54. Martínez Esparza, *División Azul*, p. 274.

55. DIV, DOPS, October 1941, DEV 28/33/11/3, p. 34.

56. DOPS, 269, October 1941, DEV 28/33/12/1, p. 17; DOPS, Reserve Battalion 250, October 1941, DEV 28/33/12/1, p. 45.

57. DIV, DOPS, November 1941, DEV 28/34/1/1, p. 2; DOPS, Reserve Battalion 250, DEV 28/34/1/1, p. 42; Salvador, *250*, p. 118.

58. Errando Vilar, *Campaña*, p. 49.

59. Martínez Esparza, *División Azul*, p. 278.

60. Ibid., pp. 278–80; Günther Collatz to Nord, 23 October 1941, T311/72/7093714; Collatz to Nord, 5 November 1941, T311/72/7093290.

61. DOPS, 269, November 1941, DEV 28/33/12/1, p. 19; Salvador, *250*, pp. 120–21; DOPS, 12 Company, Third of 263, November 1941, DEV 29/39/3, pp. 56–58; A. García Pérez, *Héroes de España en campos de Rusia 1941–1942* (Madrid: Camarasa, 1942), p. 12; DOPS, Third of 263, November 1941, DEV 29/36/12/1, p. 21.

62. Errando Vilar, *Campaña*, pp. 47–48; Ruíz Ayucar, *La Rusia*, p. 162; DOPS, 269, November 1941, DEV 28/33/12/1, p. 19; Martínez Esparza, *División Azul*, p. 280; DIV, DOPS, November 1941, DEV 28/34/1/1, p. 2; DOPS, Reserve Battalion 250, November 1941, DEV 28/34/1/1, p. 42; DOPS, 263, November 1941, DEV 28/34/1/1, p. 40.

63. KTB, 16 Army, 27 October 1941, T312/544/8151586.

64. Conversation of von Leeb with the Führer, 26 October 1941, T311/51/7004485–88.

65. I. I. Fediuninskii, *Podniatye po trevoge*, 2d rev. ed. (Moscow: Voennoe izd-vo Min-va Oborony SSSR, 1964), pp. 66–70; KTB, 16 Army, 2 November 1941, T312/544/8151620; KTB, Nord, 1–5 November 1941, T311/54/7066377–94.

CHAPTER 6. *"Share the Glory and the Danger"*

1. Group von Roques, Orders 9–11, 6–8 November 1941, T315/1350/1119–24; DIV, DOPS, November 1941, DEV 28/34/21/1, p. 3.

2. Martínez Esparza, *División Azul*, p. 280.

3. GS, 2d Section, Intelligence Bulletin 20, 3 November 1941, DEV 28/28/7/1, p. 2.

4. Martínez Esparza, *División Azul*, pp. 282–83; GS, 250 Division Winter Campaign Report, 1941–42, 10 May 1942, T314/903/889–902; Blanco, *Rusia*, pp. 20–22; Salvador, *250*, p. 123.

5. Blanco, *Rusia*, p. 22; Alvarez, *Agonia*, p. 319.

6. Group von Roques, Order 10, 7 November 1941, T315/1350/1123; DOPS, 269, November 1941, DEV 33/12/28/1, p. 19; DIV, DOPS, November 1941, DEV 28/34/1/1, pp. 3–4; Chief of Infantry (CI), November 1941, DEV 28/34/1/2, p. 29.

7. Col. Günter Engelhardt, Ret., former commander Third of 30, as cited by Col. H. Nolte, personal communication to the authors, February 1975.

8. Gómez Tello, *Canción*, pp. 129–30; Errando Vilar, *Campaña*, pp. 66–67.

9. Engelhardt, as cited by Nolte in personal communication.

10. Ibid.

11. KTB, Nord, 9 November 1941, T311/54/7066415.

12. Paul Carell, *Hitler Moves East, 1941–1943*, Evald Osers, trans. (Boston: Little, Brown, 1964), p. 269; Mannerheim, *Memoirs*, p. 330; Seweryn Bialer, ed., *Stalin and His Generals* (New York: Pegasus, 1969), pp. 634–35; Kiril A. Meretskov, *Na sluzhbe narodu* (Moscow: Izd-vo polit. lit.-ry, 1970), pp. 214–15, 236.

13. Salisbury, *900 Days*, p. 397; Pavlov, *Leningrad*, p. 114.

14. KTB, XXXIX Corps, 11–12 November 1941, T314/925/1232; Pavlov, *Leningrad*, pp. 114–15, 121–22.

15. 6 November 1941.

16. Gouré, *Siege*, p. 144.

17. Carell, *Hitler*, p. 162; Carl Wagener, *Moskau 1941* (Bad Nauheim: Podzun, 1966), pp. 107–13; Chaney, *Zhukov*, pp. 154–55.

18. Meretskov, *Na sluzhbe narodu*, pp. 236–37; KTB, Nord, 10–11 November 1941, T311/54/7066417–18.

19. DIV, DOPS, 8–10 November 1941, DEV 28/34/1, p. 3; DOPS, 269, 8–10 November 1941, DEV 28/33/12/1, p. 19; DOPS, Second Artillery Group, November 1941, DEV 28/34/1/1/1, pp. 50–55; Office of United States Chief of Counsel for War Crimes, Evidence Division, Interrogation Branch, Interrogation Summary 3764, Franz von Roques, 14 October 1947, United States National Archives; Martínez Esparza, *División Azul*, p. 284; Esteban Infantes, *Azul*, p. 67.

20. DOPS, 269, November 1941, DEV 28/33/12/1, p. 20.

21. Martínez Esparza, *División Azul*, p. 288.

22. Ibid.

23. Ibid., p. 289.

24. Ibid.

25. DOPS, 269, November 1941, DEV 28/33/12/1, p. 20; DOPS, 12 Company, Third of 263, November 1941, DEV 29/39/3, pp. 66–68; DOPS, Third of 263, November 1941, DEV 29/36/12/1, pp. 22–23.

26. Martínez Esparza, *División Azul*, p. 289.

27. DOPS, Second of 269, November 1941, DEV 29/38/2/4, p. 31; DOPS, Sappers 250, November 1941, DEV 28/34/1, p. 58; DOPS, CI, November 1941, DEV 28/34/1/2, pp. 29–30; DOPS, 269, November 1941, DEV 28/33/12/1, pp. 19–20.

28. KTB, 126 Division, 12 November 1941, T315/1350/674.

29. KTB, Nord, 12 November 1941, T311/54/7066419.

30. Ibid.

31. DOPS, 269, November 1941, DEV 28/33/12/1, p. 20; Esteban Infantes, *Azul*, pp. 72–73; Errando Vilar, *Campaña*, p. 68.

32. Martínez Esparza, *División Azul*, p. 296.

33. Gómez Tello, *Canción*, p. 131.

34. DOPS, Second of 269, November 1941, DEV 29/38/2/4, pp. 31–32; DIV, DOPS, November 1941, DEV 28/34/1/1, pp. 5–6; DOPS, 269, November 1941, DEV 28/33/12/1, p. 20; DOPS, CI, November 1941, DEV 28/34/1/2, pp. 29–30; Martínez Esparza, *División Azul*, pp. 296–98; Gómez Tello, *Canción*, pp. 130–31.

35. Interview of the authors with Manuel Guijarro y Agüero and Roberto de San Román y de la Fuente, Madrid, June 1974.

36. DOPS, Reserve Battalion 250, November 1941, DEV 28/34/1, pp. 43–45; DOPS, CI, November 1941, DEV 28/34/1/2, pp. 29–30.

37. KTB, XXXVIII Corps, 13–15 November 1941, T314/898/763–66; Lohse, *126.ID*, p. 75.

38. Martínez Esparza, *División Azul*, p. 340; Errando Vilar, *Campaña*, pp. 65–76; DOPS, 269, November 1941, DEV 28/33/12/1, p. 20.

39. Martínez Esparza, *División Azul*, p 304.

40. Vadillo interview, December 1971; DOPS, CI, November 1941, DEV 28/34/1/2, pp. 29–30; Errando Vilar, *Campaña*, p. 70; DIV, DOPS,

November 1941, DEV 28/34/1/1, p. 5; DOPS, Second of 269, November 1941, DEV 29/38/2/4, pp. 31–33.

41. DIV, DOPS, November 1941, DEV 28/34/1/1, p. 7; DOPS, 269, November 1941, DEV 28/33/12/1, pp. 20–21; DOPS, 262, November 1941, DEV 28/34/1/2, p. 37; DOPS, CI, November 1941, DEV 28/34/1/2, p. 30; GS, 1st Section, Order to 269, 18 November 1941, DEV 28/34/2/3, pp. 33–35.

42. Martínez Esparza, *División Azul*, p. 318.

43. 16 Army, Memorandum on Visit to the Commander of XXXVIII Corps, 16 November 1941, T312/548/8157260.

44. Ibid.

45. XXXVIII Corps, Report to AOK 16 on 250 Division, 17 November 1941, T311/72/7093766.

46. Ibid., 7093766–67.

47. Ibid.

48. Ibid., 7093768–69.

49. Report of Liaison Staff, 17 November 1941, T311/72/7093756–58; XXXVIII Corps, Memorandum of Chief of Staff, 17 November 1941, T311/72/7093765; 16 Army, Situation Report to Nord, 18 November 1941, T321/548/8156610–13.

50. KTB, XXXVIII Corps, 18 November 1941, T314/898/771; KTB, Nord, 16–18 November 1941, T311/54/7066432–40.

51. KTB, Nord, 22 November 1941, T311/54/7066442–49; KTB, Nord, 19 November 1941, T314/898/770; KTB, 16 Army, 18 November 1941, T312/544/8151681.

52. Burdick, *Germany's Military Strategy*, pp. 144–51; Foreign Office, Eden to Hoare, 17 September 1941, PRO, FO 371/26940/8058; Foreign Office, Military Attaché, Madrid, to M. I. 3, 20 December 1941, PRO, FO, 371/31234/8037; *Informaciones*, 17 November 1941, p. 1; *Informaciones*, 18 November 1941, p. 1; Heberlein to Berlin, 12 November 1941, T120/95/107178; Kramarz to Ritter, 19 November 1941, T120/95/107191.

53. Paul Leverkuehn, *German Military Intelligence*, trans. R. H. Stevens and Constantine Fitzgibbon (London: Weidenfeld and Nicolson, 1954), p. 131.

54. André Brissaud, *Canaris: La Guerra Española y La II Guerra Mundial*, 2d ed. (Barcelona: Ed. Nóguer, 1972), pp. 318–21; Erich Zimmermann and Hans-Adolf Jacobsen, *Germans Against Hitler*, 3d ed. (Bonn: Press and Information Office, 1969), p. 235; Detwiler, "Spain and the Axis," pp. 47–48.

55. Galeazzo Ciano, *Ciano's Diplomatic Papers*, trans. Stuart Hood, ed. Malcolm Muggeridge (London: Odhams, 1948), p. 461.

56. *Informaciones*, 25 November 1941, p. 1; *Informaciones*, 26 November 1941, pp. 1, 6; *Informaciones*, 29 November 1941, p. 1; Ribbentrop-Serrano Suñer Conversation, 25 November 1941, Document 501, *Documents on German Foreign Policy 1918–1945* (DGFP), ser. D, vol. 13 (Washington, D.C.: U. S. Department of State, 1964), p. 831.

57. Ciano, *Papers*, p. 461.

58. Hitler-Serrano Suñer Conversation, 29 November 1941, Document 523, *DGFP*, D/13, p. 905; Ciano, *Papers*, pp. 461–62.

59. Ciano, *Papers*, p. 461.

60. Hitler-Serrano Suñer Conversation, 29 November 1941, Document 523, *DGFP*, D/13, p. 906.

61. Stohrer to Weizsäcker, 3 December 1941, T120/95/107192.

62. Martínez Esparza, *División Azul*, p. 324; DOPS, 269, December 1941, DEV 28/34/3/1, p. 17.

63. Meretskov, *Na sluzhbe narodu*, pp. 241–44; Fediuninskii, *Podniatye po trevoge*, pp. 79–85; Pavlov, *Leningrad*, p. 139; Salisbury, *900 Days*, pp. 402–3.

64. Salisbury, *900 Days*, pp. 403–4.

65. KTB, Nord, 2 December 1941, T311/54/7066482.

66. DOPS, Second of 269, December 1941, DEV 29/38/2/4, pp. 32–33.

67. DOPS, DIV, December 1941, DEV 28/34/3/3, pp. 26–27; DOPS, 269, December 1941, DEV 28/34/3/1, pp. 17–18.

68. KTB, XXXVIII Corps, 4 December 1941, T314/898/797.

69. Ibid.

70. Ibid., 798.

71. DIV, DOPS, December 1941, DEV 29/34/3/3, p. 28; Martínez Esparza, *División Azul*, pp. 331–37; KTB, 16 Army, Conversation between Busch and von Leeb, 8 December 1941, T312/544/815/1826.

72. Blanco, *Rusia*, pp. 27–28.

73. Errando Vilar, *Campaña*, pp. 93–98; Gómez Tello, *Canción*, pp. 131–32; Blanco, *Rusia*, pp. 26–32; DIV, DOPS, December 1941, DEV 28/34/3/3, p. 28; DOPS, 269, December 1941, DEV 28/34/3/1, pp. 18–19.

74. KTB, XXXVIII Corps, 5 December 1941, T314/898/799; XXXVIII Corps, Plan for a Winter Line, 5 December 1941, T314/898/1480–86; KTB, XXXVIII Corps, 6 December 1941, T314/898/802.

75. Martínez Esparza, *División Azul*, p. 340; DIV, DOPS, December 1941, DEV 28/34/3/3, pp. 28–29; DOPS, 269, December 1941, DEV 28/34/3/1, pp. 18–19; Military Attaché to Madrid, Report 73, Berlin, 9 December 1941, DEV 29/52/5/2, p. 14.

76. DIV, DOPS, December 1941, DEV 28/34/3/3, pp. 28–29; Martínez Esparza, *División Azul*, p. 243; KTB XXXVIII Corps, 5–6 December 1941, T314/898/798–802; Col. García Albea, *Vieja Guardia* interview, December 1971.

77. Blanco, *Rusia*, p. 33.

78. Ibid.

79. Ibid., p. 35.

80. Ibid.

81. Ibid., p. 36.

82. KTB, XXXVIII Corps, 7 December 1941, T314/898/803–4.

83. KTB, 16 Army, 7–8 December 1941, T312/544/815123–24; Order 73, XXXVIII Corps, 7 December 1941, T315/1350/1126–27;

DOPS, CI, December 1941, DEV 28/34/3/4, pp. 51–52; DIV, DOPS, December 1941, DEV 28/34/3/3, pp. 29–30; DOPS, 269, December 1941, DEV 28/34/1, pp. 19–20; Martínez Esparza, *División Azul*, pp. 343–44.

CHAPTER 7.   *"Nailed to the Ground"*

1. Martínez Esparza, *División Azul*, p. 346.
2. DOPS, CI, December 1941, DEV 28/34/3/4, pp. 51–52; DOPS, 269, December 1941, DEV 28/34/3/4, pp. 69–70.
3. KTB, XXXVIII Corps, 8 December 1941, T312/898/806–7.
4. Supplement to AOK 16 Report, Conversation of General of XXXVIII Corps with Commander of 250 Division, T312/548/8156802–4.
5. Ibid., 8156804.
6. KTB, Halder, 23 November 1941, 3: 306.
7. Ibid., 6 December 1941, 3: 329.
8. Trevor-Roper, *Hitler's War Directives*, p. 107.
9. KTB, Nord, 9 December 1941, T311/54/7066530.
10. Ibid., 10 December 1941, T311/54/7066536.
11. DOPS, CI, December 1941, DEV 28/34/3/4, pp. 52–53; Martínez Esparza, *División Azul*, pp. 344–46.
12. KTB, Nord, 10–11 December 1941, T311/54/7066538–50.
13. Ibid., 15 December 1941, T311/54/7066566–67.
14. Ibid., 13–17 December 1941, T311/54/706657–80, 25 December 1941, 706616; KTB, Halder, 15–20 December 1941, 3: 348–61; XXXVIII Corps, POW Interrogation Reports, 23–26 December 1941, T314/900/1055–61; 126 Division, POW Interrogation Reports, 29 December 1941, T314/900/1051–52.
15. KTB, Nord, 19–20 December 1941, T311/54/7066589–94.
16. Ibid., 21 December 1941, T311/54/7066598.
17. Errando Vilar, *Campaña*, pp. 108–9; Ruíz Ayucar, *La Rusia*, pp. 110–16.
18. Ruíz Ayucar, *La Rusia*, p. 131.
19. Ibid., p. 132.
20. Ibid., p. 135.
21. XXXVIII Corps, POW Interrogation Reports, 26 December 1941, T314/900/1053–54.
22. GS, 2d Section, POW Interrogation Reports, 24–31 December 1941, DEV 28/28/9/1, pp. 30–43.
23. Gómez Tello, *Canción*, pp. 142–43; *Informaciones*, 11 July 1942, p. 3; *Vieja Guardia* interview, December 1971.
24. Martínez Esparza, *División Azul*, p. 347, and see Gómez Tello, *Canción*, p. 143.
25. XXXVIII Corps, Daily Reports, December 1941, T314/898/1233–43; DIV, DOPS, December 1941, DEV 28/34/3/3, pp. 35–36; DOPS, CI, December 1941, DEV 28/34/3/4, pp. 54–55.

26. XXXVIII Corps, Order 76, 20 December 1941, T315/1350/1130–32; DOPS, CI, December 1941, DEV 28/14/3/4, pp. 54–55.

27. Martínez Esparza, *División Azul*, p. 30; Errando Vilar, *Campaña*, p. 126; DOPS, 269, December 1941, DEV 28/34/3/1, p. 21.

28. Martínez Esparza, *División Azul*, p. 354.

29. Blanco, *Rusia*, p. 41.

30. Martínez Esparza, *División Azul*, p. 355.

31. KTB, XXXVIII Corps, December 1941, T314/898/844.

32. Blanco, *Rusia*, pp. 42–43.

33. Martínez Esparza, *División Azul*, p. 356; *Informaciones*, 5 January 1942, p. 1.

34. XXXVIII Corps, Daily Reports, 27 December 1941, T314/898/1213; DOPS, 269, December 1941, DEV 28/34/3/1, p. 21.

35. DOPS, CI, December 1941, DEV 28/34/34, pp. 54–55; DOPS, 269, December 1941, DEV 28/34/3/1, p. 21; *Informaciones*, 19 January 1942, p. 3.

36. DIV, DOPS, December 1941, DEV 28/34/3/3, pp. 36–37.

37. Errando Vilar, *Campaña*, pp. 123–24.

38. *Informaciones*, 2 January 1942, p. 1; ibid., 5 January 1942, p. 1.

Chapter 8.   *Vlasov and the Volkhov Pocket*

1. Adolf Hitler, *Hitler's Secret Conversations, 1941–1944*, trans. Norman Cameron and R. H. Stevens (New York: New American Library, Signet, 1961), pp. 188–89.

2. DIV, DOPS, December 1941, DEV 28/34/3/3, pp. 48–49; GS, 3d Section, DGO, 6 January 1942, DEV 28/3/7/1, p. 7; Martínez Esparza, *División Azul*, pp. 460–65.

3. High General Staff, Madrid, 1st Section, January 1942, DEV 29/43/8/2, p. 25; AOK 16 to Nord, 27 January 1942, T311/72/7093787; GS, 4th Section, Report on Rations, 10 January 1942, DEV 29/44/15/1, pp. 5–10; *Vieja Guardia* interview, December 1971.

4. KTB, Nord, 8–12 January 1942, T311/54/7066688–704; 16 Army, Situation Reports, T312/564/8178141–60.

5. Werner Haupt, "Blaue Division am Ilmensee," *Soldatengeschichten Nr. 99* (Munich: Moewig, 1959), p. 5.

6. DOPS, Recon 250, January 1942, DEV 28/34/5/1, pp. 40–42.

7. "Una gesta heroica," *Hoja de Campaña*, 17 February 1942, p. 2.

8. Gómez Tello, *Canción*, p. 146.

9. Haupt, "Ilmensee," pp. 16–19; *Informaciones*, 27 March 1942, p. 6.

10. García Pérez, *Héroes*, pp. 18–24.

11. Haupt, "Ilmensee," p. 12.

12. Ibid., p. 15.

13. 250 Division, Ski Company Report, T315/1726/40.

14. Haupt, "Ilmensee," pp. 23–24.

15. DOPS, Recon 250, January 1942, DEV 28/34/5/1, pp. 40–42;

KTB Liaison Staff, 14 January 1942, T315/1726/121; Blanco, *Rusia*, pp. 45–46; *Informaciones*, 18 March 1942, pp. 1, 3.

16. CI, Relation of Ski Patrol, 9–25 January 1942, 11 February 1942, DEV 28/34/5/2, pp. 22–23; DIV, DOPS, January 1942, 28/34/5/1, pp. 3–9; Military Attache, Berlin, Report 79, 1 February 1942, DEV 29/52/7, pp. 55–63.

17. KTB, Liaison Staff, 17, 20 January 1942, T315/1726/123,124.

18. G. Zhukov, *The Memoirs of Marshal Zhukov*, trans. A. P. N. (New York: Delacorte, 1971), p. 352; John Erickson, *The Road to Stalingrad* (New York: Harper & Row, 1975), p. 292; K. Meretskov, "Na Volkhovskikh rubezhakh," *Voenno-isotoricheskii zhurnal* 1 (1965): 54–56.

19. Nord, Campaign Report, 1942, T311/136/7181610.

20. Walter Schelm and Dr. Hans Mehrle, *Erinnerungsbuch—Von den Kampfen der 215. wurttembergisch-badischen Infanterie-Division* (N.p.: Traditionsverband, n.d.), p. 78; Lohse, *126. ID*, p. 90.

21. KTB, Nord, 12 January 1942, T311/54/7066704.

22. Ibid., 7066710.

23. KTB, Nord, 13 January 1942, T311/54/7066715; Meretskov, "Na Volkhovskikh rubezhakh," pp. 60–61; KTB, XXXVIII Corps, 13 January 1942, T314/898/873–76; XXXVIII Corps, Evening Report, 14 January 1942, T314/901/1121; 126 Division, Evening Report, 13 January 1942, T315/1357/171; XXXVIII Corps, Ic, Synthesis of POW Interrogation Reports from Second Shock Army, n.d., DEV 28/29/6/1, pp. 1–3.

24. 126 Division, Daily Report, 13 January 1942, T315/1357/171; DIV, DOPS, January 1942, DEV 28/34/5/1, p. 4.

25. KTB, Nord, 14 January 1942, T311/54/7066781; KTB, 18 Army, 14 January 1942, T312/808/8464503; Eugen Kreidler, *Die Eisenbahnen im Machtbereich der Achsenmächte während des Zweiten Weltkrieges* (Frankfurt: Musterschmidt, 1975), pp. 135–38.

26. DOPS, Second of 269, January 1942, DEV 29/38/2/4, p. 34; 126 Division, Midday Report, 14 January 1942, T315/1357/147; DIV, DOPS, January 1942, DEV 28/34/5/1, p. 4; 424 Regiment, Daily Report, 15 January 1942, T315/1357/117–18; DIV, DOPS, January 1942, DEV 28/34/5/1, pp. 4–5; CI, January 1942, DEV 28/34/5/2, pp. 20–21.

27. Lohse, *126.ID*, p. 95; Nord, Volkhov Report, T311/136/7181655; KTB, XXXVIII Corps, T314/898/879914; GS, 2d Section, January 1942, DEV 28/28/11/1, pp. 10–12; KTB, Nord, 15–23 January 1942, T311/54/7066720–80.

28. GS, 2d Section, Information Bulletin 36, January 1942, DEV 28/28/11/1, p. 9.

29. 18 Army, Report on Tours of Inspection of Commander, 3 April 1942, T312/825/8486678; High General Staff, Madrid, Summary of Attaché Reports, January–February 1942, DEV 29/52/6/4, p. 65; Roca de Togores to Madrid, 26 January 1942, DEV 29/52/6/4, p. 66.

30. Army General Staff, Asensio Memorandum, Madrid, 9 February 1942, DEV 28/28/14/1, pp. 4–6.

31. Krappe Memorandum, Madrid, 21 May 1942, T311/99/7130681.

32. Friese to Luther, SD Memorandum, Berlin, 2 February 1942, 342816; Ritter to Jodl, Berlin, 24 February 1942, E285579–82; Weizsäcker to Ribbentrop, Berlin, 5 February 1942, Political Archives of Foreign Ministry Archives of the Federal Republic of Germany, Bonn, E285586–88; Siegfried Memorandum, Berlin, 23 December 1941, T120/95/107228; Likus Memorandum, Berlin, 13 December 1941, T120/82/62780–88; Note, Madrid, 14 November 1941, T120/82/62782.

33. Payne, *Politics*, p. 379.

34. Stohrer to Berlin, 2 January 1942, T120/295/234812; Weizsäcker Memorandum, Berlin, 10 January 1942, T120/95/107264–65.

35. GS, 1st Section, List of 390 Replacements, Hof, 19 January 1942, DEV 28/3/8/2, pp. 14–20; Army General Staff, Asensio Memorandum, Madrid, 9 February 1942, DEV 28/28/14/1, pp. 4–6; Army General Staff, 2d Section, Note on Difficulties of Liaison with the Division, Madrid, 4 February 1942, DEV 28/28/14/1, pp. 1–2; GS, 2d Section, Ruíz de la Serna to Fidel de la Cuerda, 9 February 1942, DEV 28/28/14/2, pp. 10–11.

36. Krappe to Asensio, Madrid, 30 January 1942, DEV 28/3/8/2, p. 2; Weizsäcker Memorandum, Berlin, 19 February 1942, T120/95/107425; Weizsäcker to Ribbentrop, Berlin, 13 February 1942, T120/95/107404; Weizsäcker to Ribbentrop, Berlin, 5 February 1942, E285586; Collatz Memorandum, 12 March 1942, T312/954/9144084–87.

37. Weizsäcker to Ribbentrop, Berlin, 5 February 1942, E285586–87; Roca de Togores to Madrid, Report 81, Berlin, 24 February 1942, DEV 29/52/7, pp. 79–82.

38. Doussinague, *España*, p. 116.

39. *Informaciones*, 16 February 1942, p. 1.

40. Weizsäcker Memoranda, Berlin, 13, 16, 21, 26 February 1942, E285597, E285585, E285590–93, T120/95/107444–45; Roca de Togores to Madrid, Report 81, Berlin, 24 February 1942, DEV 29/52/7, pp. 79–81; Roca de Togores to Madrid, Telegram 151, 26 February 1942, DEV 29/52/7, p. 88.

41. Stohrer to Berlin, Madrid, 26 February 1942, T120/295/234831–32.

42. Ritter to Weizsäcker, "Westfalen," 4 March 1942, T120/95/107465–67; Beaulac to Secretary of State, Madrid, 10 March 1942, USNA, 740.0011/20468.

43. Ritter to Stohrer, Berlin, 22 March 1942, T120/295/234840; Roca de Togores to Asensio, Berlin, 11 February 1942, DEV 29/52/2, pp. 52, 54; Brig. W. W. Torr to Foreign Office, Madrid, PRO, FO/371/31235/809, pp. 1–3.

44. KTB, Liaison Staff, 15, 22 March 1942, T315/1726/137,139; *Führerhauptquartier DNB Release*, Muñoz Grandes, 13 March 1942; GS, 1st Section, Comparative State of Forces, 14 March 1942, DEV 28/4/1/1, p. 1; Handwritten note by Muñoz Grandes to Army General Staff, 1st Section, Asensio to Muñoz Grandes, 17 February 1942, Madrid, DEV 28/4/6/3, p. 80; Collatz Memorandum, 12 March 1942, T312/954/9144084–87.

45. Esteban Infantes, *Azul*, pp. 104–5; Wilhelmi to Berlin, 23 March 1942, Madrid, T120/295/234841–42.

46. Erickson, *Stalingrad*, p. 319.

47. KTB, XXXVIII Corps, 9 February 1942, T314/898/959.

48. DIV, DOPS, January 1942, DEV 28/34/5/1, pp. 6–9; 269, GO 36, 21 February 1942, DEV 28/3/16/2, p. 38; Ruíz Ayucar, *La Rusia*, pp. 151–59; *Vieja Guardia* interview, December 1971; KTB, XXXVIII Corps, 20 February 1942, T314/898/943–44; DOPS, Second Artillery Group, February 1942, DEV 28/34/3/2, p. 22; von Chappuis Memorandum, 1 February 1942, T315/1359/1209; S. P. Pozharskaia, "Golubaia divizia," *Voprosy istorii* 8 (1969): 112.

49. Esteban Infantes, *Azul*, pp. 113–14; 269, Order 29, 9 February 1942, DEV 28/3/16/2, pp. 25–26; Errando Vilar, *Campaña*, pp. 215–20; 426 Regiment State of Forces 14 January 1942, T315/1358/164; DOPS, 269, February 1942, DEV 28/34/8/2, pp. 16–18; García Pérez, *Héroes*, pp. 24–26; DOPS, Second of 269, February 1942, DEV 29/38/2/4, p. 37; GS, 3d Section, DGO, 15 February 1942, DEV 28/3/12/2, pp. 7, 9; KTB, XXXVIII Corps, 11–13 February 1942, T314/898/961–68; 426 Regiment, Reports, 11–13 February 1942, T315/1357/220–178.

50. Errando Vilar, *Campaña*, p. 220; DOPS, Second of 269, February 1942, DEV 29/38/2/4, p. 37; 269, Order, 19 January 1942, DEV 28/2/17/2, pp. 41–42; 126 Division, Daily Report, 14 February 1942, T315/1358/161; 426 Regiment, Daily Report, 15 February 1942, T315/1358/130; KTB, XXXVIII Corps, 15 February 1942, T314/898/971–74.

51. Nord, Report of MP Chief, 24 July 1942, T311/99/7130705; Gómez Tello, *Canción*, pp. 24–29; Nord, Military Police Report, 1 January 1942, T311/72/7093783–85; Abwehr Report, 24 January 1942, T311/99/7130665–66.

52. Lindemann to XXXVIII Corps, 24 February 1942, T314/898/991; Lindemann-von Chappuis Conference, Raglizy, 24 February 1942, T312/808/8464372.

53. KTB, Nord, 3 March 1942, T311/54/706748–49; KTB, Halder, 2 March 1942, 3:408; 18 Army, Lindemann Memorandum, 2 March 1942, T312/805/8461212.

54. GS, 2d Section, Information Bulletin 70, 5 March 1942, DEV 28/28/15/1, p. 3; Nord, Volkhov Report, 1942, T311/136/7181657–58; Erickson, *Stalingrad*, pp. 321–22.

55. KTB, XXXVIII Corps, 7 March 1942, T314/898/1017–19.

56. Sven Steenberg, *Vlasov* (New York: Knopf, 1970), p. 23; 18 Army, Lindemann Conference, 8 March 1942, T312/808/8464387–91; KTB, 126 Division, 15 March 1942, T315/1356/1020; XXXVIII Corps, Order 86, 6 March 1942, T315/1357/72–76; GS, 3d Section, DGO, 5 March 1942, DEV 28/4/2/4, p. 7.

57. DOPS, 269, March 1942, DEV 28/34/10/3, p. 17; Roca de Togores to Madrid, Report 81, Berlin, 15 February 1942, DEV 29/52/7, p. 77; DIV, DOPS, March 1942, DEV 28/34/10/2, p. 5.

58. *Informaciones*, 26 February 1942, pp. 1, 3; ibid., 27 February 1942, p. 1.

59. Errando Vilar, *Campaña*, pp. 237–39; *Vieja Guardia* interview, December 1971.

60. DIV, DOPS, March 1942, DEV 28/34/10/2, p. 5; DOPS, Second of 269, March 1942, DEV 29/38/2/4, p. 1; 126 Division, Table of Effectives, 11 March 1942, T315/1359/1086.

61. Lindemann-von Chappuis Conversation, 14 March 1942, T312/808/8464628.

62. DOPS, Second of 269, March 1942, DEV 29/38/2/4, p. 39; DIV, DOPS, March 1942, DEV 28/34/10/2, p. 7; 424 Regiment, Daily Report, 16 March 1942, T315/1358/777; KTB, 126 Division, 15–16 March 1942, T315/1356/1019–21.

63. 18 Army, Lindemann-von Chappuis Conversation, 17 March 1942, T312/808/8464638.

64. Friedrich Husemann, *Die guten Glaubens waren: Geschichte der SS-Polizei-Division* (Osnabrück: Munin, 1971), 1: 238–65; KTB, XXXVIII Corps, 19 March 1942, T314/898/1050.

65. DOPS, Second of 269, March 1942, DEV 29/38/2, pp. 31–32; Gómez Tello, *Canción*, pp. 63–64.

66. Steenberg, *Vlasov*, p. 24; Carell, *Hitler*, pp. 401, 409; 18 Army, Reports, 27 March 1942, T312/808/8464656; Nord, Volkhov Report, 1942, T311/136/7181657; Werner Haupt, *Heeresgruppe Nord, 1941–1945* (Bad Nauheim: Podzun, 1966), p. 128.

67. 18 Army, Lindemann-von Chappuis Conversation, 25 March 1942, T312/808/8464653.

68. DIV, DOPS, March 1942, DEV 28/34/15/3, pp. 3–4; KTB, XXXVIII Corps, von Chappuis-Muñoz Grandes Conference, 26 March 1942, T314/898/1068; KTB, XXXVIII Corps, 29 March 1942, T314/898/1078; KTB, Nord, 29 March 1942, T311/54/7067545–46.

69. "Ni La Muerte . . ." by Tomás Salvador, *Hoja de Campaña*, 5 August 1942, p. 5; García Pérez, *Héroes*, p. 39.

70. GS, 1st Section, von Graffen to Muñoz Grandes, 13 April 1942, DEV 28/4/8/4, p. 6; DOPS, Second of 269, April 1942, DEV 29/38/2/4, p. 40; KTB, Liaison Staff, 2 April 1942, T315/1726/141; KTB, Nord, 2 April 1942, T311/54/7067601; DOPS, 269, April 1942, DEV 28/34/13/2, pp. 17–18; DIV, DOPS, April 1942, DEV 28/34/13/1, p. 2; 424 Regiment, Daily Report, 2 April 1942, T315/1358/1091; Personal Communication of Maj. Werner Bruch to the authors, June 1975; KTB, XXXVIII Corps, 2 April 1942, T314/902/308; Lohse, *126.ID*, p. 98.

71. "Jueves y Viernes Santos en la División Azul," *Hoja de Campaña*, 4 May 1942, p. 4.

72. 18 Army, Lindemann-Muñoz Grandes Conversation, 3 April 1942, T312/825/8486679–80.

73. DIV, DOPS, April 1942, DEV 28/34/13/1, pp. 2–3; DOPS, Second of 269, April 1942, DEV 29/38/2/4, pp. 40–41.

74. Army General Staff, Asensio Memorandum, Madrid, 9 February 1942, DEV 28/28/14/1, p. 406; Krappe to Asensio, Madrid, 30 January 1942, DEV 28/3/8/2, p. 2; High General Staff, Information Recruiting from Militia, DEV 29/43/8/2, p. 30.

75. Esteban Infantes, *Azul*, pp. 104–5; Nord, Replacement Reports, 20–23 February 1942, T311/72/7093797–801; Nord, Rotation Reports, 23–29 April 1942, T311/72/7093823.

76. DIV, DOPS, March 1942, DEV 28/34/10/2, p. 11.

77. Errando Vilar, *Campaña*, pp. 271–89; *Informaciones*, 22, 23 April 1942, pp. 1–2, 1–6.

78. DOPS, Recon 250, March–April 1942, DEV 29/38/11/2, p. 16; *Völkischer Beobachter*, 8 April 1942, p. 1.

79. Gerardo Oroquieta Arbiol, *De Leningrado a Odesa* (Barcelona: Ed. AHR, n.d.), p. 22.

80. Ibid.

81. GS, 1st Section, Nominal List of 4th March Battalion, 17 April 1942, DEV 28/4/11/1, pp. 12–19.

82. DOPS, Recon 250, April 1942, DEV 29/38/11/2, pp. 16–18; GS, 1st Section, 9–30 April 1942, DEV 28/4/13/1, pp. 23–47.

83. Max Domarus, ed., *Hitler: Reden 1932 bis 1945* (Munich: Süddeutscher Verlag, 1965), 4: 1873.

84. DOPS, Recon 250, April–May 1942, DEV 29/38/11/2, pp. 18–19.

85. Salvador, *250*, pp. 219–23.

86. Guijarro interview, December 1971.

87. GS, DGO, Muñoz Grandes to Repatriated Volunteers, 12 May 1942, DEV 28/5/4/1, p. 12.

88. GS, 2d Section, Bulletin of Information 122, 27 April 1942, DEV 28/28/16/1, p. 13; *Informaciones*, 23 May 1942, p. 1; GS, 1st Section, Regulations for Arriving March Battalions, Hof, 30 May 1942, DEV 28/4/13/4.

89. *Informaciones*, 26 May 1942, p. 1.

90. KTB, Nord, Summary of Conversation at *Führerhauptquartier*, 13 April 1942, T311/54/7067710–13.

91. OKH Order, 2 May 1942, T314/902/360.

92. Salisbury, *900 Days*, p. 529.

93. Meretskov, *Na sluzhbe narodu*, pp. 276–82; Fediuninskii, *Podniatye po trevoge*, p. 107.

94. Nord, Volkhov Report, T311/136/7181659–60; Haupt, *Nord*, pp. 128–31.

95. KTB, Liaison Staff, 27 May 1942, T315/1726/152; *Informaciones*, 12 June 1942, p. 1, 17 June 1942, pp. 1, 3, 18 June 1942, p. 1; GS, 1st Section, 16 May 1942, DEV 28/5/4/1, p. 12; Oroquieta Arbiol, *De Leningrado*, pp. 24–25; DOPS, 269, May 1942, DEV 28/35/1/2, pp. 23–24; DIV, DOPS, May 1942, DEV 28/35/1/1, pp. 15–20.

96. GS, XXXVIII Corps, Ia, 1957/42, 31 May 1942, DEV 28/35/6/4, p. 136; DIV, DOPS, June 1942, DEV 28/35/7/1, p. 13; DOPS, Recon 250, May–June 1942, DEV 29/38/11/2, pp. 19–20; DOPS, Sap-

pers 250, June 1942, DEV 28/35/7/3, p. 41; DOPS, Second Company Sappers 250, June 1942, DEV 28/35/7/3, p. 48.

97. KTB, Liaison Staff, 1–4 June 1942, T315/1726/154; DIV, DOPS, June 1942, DEV 28/35/7/1, p. 13.

98. Meretskov, "Na Volkhovskikh rubezhakh," p. 68.

99. 18 Army, Daily Report, 10 June 1942, T312/1588/824–32; Meretskov, Na sluzhbe narodu, p. 292; DOPS, Recon 250, June 1942, DEV 29/38/11/2, p. 21.

100. XXXVIII Corps, Telegraphic Order 2330, 24 June 1942, T315/1359/903; Esteban Infantes, Azul, pp. 118–19; DOPS, Recon 250, June 1942, DEV 29/38/11/2, p. 23.

101. Meretskov, Na sluzhbe narodu, pp. 232–34.

102. Salisbury, 900 Days, p. 531; Meretskov, Na sluzhbe narodu, p. 294; DIV, DOPS, June 1942, DEV 28/35/7/1, pp. 19–20.

103. 18 Army, Lindemann Proclamation, 28 June 1942, T314/902/1230–31; OKW, Report on Volkhov, 29 June 1942, T314/902/1234.

Chapter 9. *Conspiracy, Change of Front, and the Palace of Catherine the Great*

1. Hoffmann to Likus, Berlin, 30 May 1942, T120/82/62748.

2. Hitler, *Hitler's Secret Conversations*, 7 June 1942, p. 488.

3. Likus to Muñoz Grandes, Novgorod, T120/82/62732; von Ungern-Sternberg to Ribbentrop, 22 June 1942, T120/82/62728; Brissaud, *Canaris*, pp. 263–332; Weizsäcker to Ribbentrop, Berlin, 22 June 1942, T120/2522/E285605; Stohrer to Ribbentrop, Madrid, 25 June 1942, T120/2522/E285606.

4. Sonnleithner to Ritter, 8 July 1942, T120/82/62738; Likus to Ribbentrop, 2 July 1942, T120/82/62739.

5. Hoffmann Memorandum, T120/82/62759.

6. Ibid.

7. Ibid., 62762.

8. Ibid., 62763.

9. Ibid., 62759.

10. "Wenn ihr einmarschiert, schiessen wir," *Der Spiegel* 17/18 (1 May 1963): 71–80.

11. Likus Memorandum, Berlin, 2 July 1942, T120/82/62739.

12. Ibid., 62741–42.

13. Ibid.

14. Ibid., 62743.

15. Likus Memorandum, Berlin, 24 August 1942, T120/82/62735–36.

16. Hitler, *Hitler's Secret Conversations*, 7 July 1942, pp. 532–33.

17. Ibid., 7 June 1942, p. 488.

18. Likus Memorandum, 13 July 1942, T120/82/62745.

19. Monteys report of visit of Muñoz Grandes to Führer Headquarters,

Supplement 1 to Embassy report 4353, Madrid, 31 August 1942, T120/82/62661.

20. Ibid.

21. Ibid.

22. "Wenn ihr einmarschiert," p. 79.

23. Likus Memorandum, 13 July 1942, T120/82/62745–47; Monteys report, 56879–89; von Küchler to Schmundt, 10 July 1942, T311/72/7093828.

24. Stohrer to Berlin, Madrid, 16 July 1942, Wöhrmann to Stohrer, Berlin, 25 July 1942, T120/95/234870–71; "Wenn ihr einmarschiert," p. 79.

25. Carleton J. H. Hayes, *Wartime Mission in Spain, 1942–45* (New York: Macmillan, 1946), pp. 7–16; Charles R. Halstead, "Historians in Politics: Carleton J. Hayes as American Ambassador to Spain, 1942–45," *Journal of Contemporary History* 10, No. 4 (July 1975): 383–405.

26. Hayes, *Wartime Mission*, p. 54.

27. Trevor-Roper, *Hitler's War Directives*, p. 131.

28. *Geschichte des Grossen Vaterländischen Krieges der Sowjetunion* (Berlin: Deutscher Militärverlag, 1964), 3:165.

29. *Informaciones*, 19 June 1942, p. 1; DOPS, 269, June 1942, DEV 28/35/7/3, pp. 37–38; DOPS, Second of 269, July 1942, DEV 29/38/2/4, p. 46; GS, 1st Section, 2 July 1942, DEV 28/6/7/1, p. 1.

30. Esteban Infantes, *Azul*, p. 119; Steenberg, *Vlasov*, pp. 26–27; DIV, DOPS, July 1942, DEV 28/35/10/1, pp. 2–9.

31. *Informaciones*, 26 August 1942, p. 3.

32. Oroquieta Arbiol, *De Leningrado*, p. 25.

33. KTB, XXXVIII Corps, 15 August 1942, T314/902/541–42; KTB, Nord, 30 July 1942, T311/55/7068422.

34. KTB, Nord, 5 August 1942, T311/55/7068465.

35. Guijarro interview, December 1971.

36. DOPS, Recon 250, August 1942, DEV 29/38/11/2, pp. 27–28; KTB, XXXVIII Corps, 8–13 August 1942, T314/902/533–39; XXXVIII Corps, Orders Received, 6–15 August 1942, T314/903/404–16; DIV, DOPS, August 1942, DEV 28/35/12/1, pp. 3–4; KTB, XXXVIII Corps, 21, 27 August 1942, T314/902/549/557.

37. KTB, Nord, 10 August 1942, T311/55/7068508; OKH to Nord, 20 May 1942, T311/99/7130675; AOK 18 to Nord, 12 June 1942, T311/99/7130688; *Vieja Guardia* Interview, December 1971; Guijarro interview, December 1971; personal interview of the authors with *Rittmeister* Dr. Edwin Haxel, Madrid, June 1974; personal communication to authors by Col. H. Nolte (GS) Ret., 20 February 1975.

38. Emmet J. Hughes, *Report from Spain* (New York: Henry Holt, 1947), pp. 92–93; Foltz, *Masquerade*, pp. 172–74; Francisco J. Marinas, *General Varela* (Barcelona: Ed. AHR, 1956), pp. 242–43; Hoare, *Ambassador on Special Mission*, pp. 165–66; Hayes, *Wartime Mission*, p. 57; Payne, *Falange*, pp. 234–35.

39. Payne, *Politics*, p. 431.

40. AA Report, 3 September 1942, T311/99/713–30; Yencken to Eden, 291, Madrid, 28 August 1942, PRO, FO 371/31236/8085, pp. 64–65.

41. Von Küchler to Keitel, 18 August 1942, T312/1610/54–56.

42. Hansen to Lindemann, 8 December 1942, T312/1610/33.

43. GS, 1st Section, Air Ministry, Madrid, 13 June 1942, DEV 29/45/14/1, p. 1; Chief of Rear Service, Berlin, 2 July 1942, DEV 29/45/19/1, p. 1.

44. Hasse to AOK 18, 18 August 1942, T312/1610/59–60.

45. Hoffmann Summary of Muñoz Grandes Conversation, Canaris Report 2, September 1942, T311/99/7130731–33.

46. Personal letter to the authors from Ramón Serrano Suñer, 19 September 1977 and see AA report, 3 September 1942, T311/99/7130730; Ramón Serrano Suñer, *Entre el silencio y la propoganda, la historia como fue: Memorias* (Barcelona: Ed. Planeta, 1977), pp. 370–72.

47. Meyer-Döhner to OKM, 5 September 1942, T77/889/5640380; Payne, *Falange*, p. 236; Payne, *Politics*, pp. 430–32; *Informaciones*, 3 September 1942, p. 1; Hayes, *Wartime Mission*, pp. 57–58; Serrano Suñer, *Entre el silencio*, pp. 370–73.

48. Canaris to Keitel, 8 September 1942, T311/99/7130733.

49. Likus to Ribbentrop, 5 September 1942, T120/82/62605–6.

50. Likus Memorandum, 5 September 1942, T120/82/62618–19.

51. Likus Memorandum, 6 September 1942, T120/82/62615.

52. Ibid., 62614.

53. Serrano Suñer interview, December 1971; Hayes to Hull, 204, Madrid, 11 August 1942, USNA, State 352.20/187.

54. Doussinague, *España*, pp. 62–63.

55. Hayes to Hull, No. 1929, Madrid, 21 January 1944, USNA, State 852.00/10935, p. 3.

56. Ibid.

57. Hayes, *Wartime Mission*, p. 59.

58. Doussinague, *España*, p. 63.

59. Burdick, *Germany's Military Strategy*, p. 164.

60. Hayes, *Wartime Mission*, p. 71.

61. Ibid.

62. Ibid.

63. Ibid., pp. 71–72; Eden to Hoare, C10410/175/41, London, 30 October 1942, PRO, FO 371/31230/8034, p. 159.

64. DIV, DOPS, August 1942, DEV 28/35/12/1, pp. 7–10; GS, 3d Section, General Instruction 1076, 27 August 1942, DEV 28/35/15/3, pp. 27–28; General Orders, 269, August 1942, DEV 28/7/4/1, pp. 44, 58–59; DOPS, Second of 269, August 1942, DEV 29/38/2/4, pp. 47–48.

65. Manstein, *Lost Victories*, p. 260.

66. KTB, 11 Army, 21 August 1942, T312/1696/6; KTB, Nord, 8, 21 August 1942, T311/55/7068482–91, 7068575; KTB, Nord, Operation Northern Light, 12 August 1942, T311/55/7068515–16; Manstein, *Lost Victories*, p. 263; KTB, Nord, 22 August 1942, T311/55/706854.

67. Manstein, *Lost Victories*, pp. 262–64.

68. AOK 11, Disposition Map, 30 September 1942, T312/1697/1111–12.

69. KTB, Nord, 28 August 1942, T311/55/706834; Manstein, *Lost Victories*, p. 264.

70. Manstein, *Lost Victories*, pp. 262–63.

71. Esteban Infantes, *Azul*, pp. 125–26; DIV, DOPS, August 1942, DEV 28/35/12/1, p. 10.

72. AOK 11, Case George, 31 August 1942, T78/337/6293548; Esteban Infantes, *Azul*, pp. 125–26; KTB, LIV Corps, 24 and 31 August 1942, T314/1351/435.

73. AOK 11, Case George, Artillery Order 1, 31 August 1942, T78/337/6293553.

74. Ibid.

75. Ibid., 6293551–57; Andreas Hillgruber, "Nordlicht—Die deutschen Pläne zur Eroberung Leningrads im Jahre 1942," in Peter Classen, ed., *Festschrift Percy Ernst Schramm zu seinem siebzigsten Geburtstag von Schülern und Freunden Gewidmet*, 2 vols (Wiesbaden: S. Steiner, 1964), 2: 269–87.

76. Meretskov, *Na sluzhbe narodu*, pp. 299–307.

77. Ibid., pp. 308–9; Manstein, *Lost Victories*, pp. 264–65.

78. AOK 18 to 250 Division, 31 August 1942, T312/1696/1016; DIV, DOPS, September 1942, DEV 29/36/1/2, p. 10; L Corps, March Orders for 250 Division, 1 September 1942, T314/1237/518.

79. Gómez Tello, *Canción*, p. 188; *Hoja de Campaña*, 3 October 1943, p. 3; DOPS, 269, September 1942, DEV 29/36/1/3, p. 23.

80. DOPS, 269, September 1942, DEV 29/36/1/3, p. 23; AOK 18, 250 Division Assembly Area, 3 September 1942, T312/1696/986–88; DIV, DOPS, September 1942, DEV 29/36/1/2, pp. 11–12; Manstein, *Lost Victories*, pp. 264–66; *Informaciones*, 9 September 1942, p. 3; KTB, L Corps, 2–4 September 1942, T314/1235/378–90; Husemann, *SS Polizei*, 2: 373–79.

81. AOK 11, Order of the Day, 4 September 1942, T312/1696/954.

82. Ibid., 954–55; AOK 11 to LIV Corps, 4 September 1942, T312/1696/977; 121 Division, Relief Order, 5 September 1942, T314/1352/273–83.

83. Esteban Infantes, *Azul*, pp. 128–29; Personal observation of the authors, June 1974.

84. 121 Division, Relief Order, 5 September 1942, T314/1352/275.

85. *Informaciones*, 12 September 1942, p. 3.

86. DIV, DOPS, September 1942, DEV 29/36/1/2, p. 11; DOPS, Third of 263, September 1942, DEV 29/36/12/1, pp. 27–28; DOPS, 269, September 1942, DEV 29/36/1/3, pp. 23–24; DOPS, Second Artillery, September 1942, DEV 29/36/1/3, pp. 25–26.

87. LIV Corps to 250 Division, 5 September 1942, T314/1352/269; Liaison Staff to LIV Corps, 11 September 1942, T314/1352/419; DIV, DOPS, September 1942, DEV 29/36/1/2, pp. 12–13.

88. DOPS, Sappers 250, September 1942, DEV 29/36/1/3, p. 34; DOPS, Recon 250, September 1942, DEV 29/38/11/2, pp. 28–29; LIV Corps to 250 Division, 17 September 1942, T314/1352/423.

89. DOPS, Third of 263, September 1942, DEV 29/36/12/1, pp. 37–38; DOPS, Second Artillery, September 1942, DEV 29/36/1/3, p. 25.

90. Oroquieta Arbiol, *De Leningrado*, p. 26.

91. Ibid., pp. 25–27; Esteban Infantes, *Azul*, p. 131; GS, 2d Section, L Corps, Enemy Situation at St. Petersburg, 25 August 1942, DEV 28/29/2/3, pp. 22–30; AOK 11, Enemy Disposition Map, 5 September 1942, T312/1698/816; 250 Division, Intelligence Report, Enemy Dispositions, 21 September 1942, T314/1355/328–34; LIV Corps, Enemy Disposition Map, 5 September 1942, T314/1355/350; Erickson, *Stalingrad*, pp. 371–75.

92. GS, 2d Section, L Corps, Enemy Situation at St. Petersburg, 25 August 1942, DEV 28/29/2/3, pp. 24–27; AOK 11, Artillery Summation, 9 September 1942, T314/1352/315.

93. DOPS, Second of 269, DEV 29/38/2/4, pp. 49–50; *Informaciones*, 17 September 1942, p. 3; DOPS, Sappers 250, September 1942, DEV 29/36/1/3, pp. 34–37.

94. *Informaciones*, 26 December 1942, p. 3; *Hoja de Campaña*, 4 January 1943, p. 3, 19 December 1943, p. 4; 263 Regiment, Sagrado Report, 19 September 1942, DEV 29/36/4/1, pp. 1–3; GS, 3d Section, Bulletin, 14 September 1942, DEV 29/36/4/1, p. 14; KTB, LIV Corps, 14 September 1942, T314/1352/95.

95. Muñoz Grandes to Hansen, 26 September 1942, T314/1352/528–29; KTB, LIV Corps, 28 September 1942, T314/1352/197–98; Hoffmann Conversation with Muñoz Grandes of 20 September 1942, Berlin, 27 September 1942, T120/82/62574.

96. Manstein, *Lost Victories*, p. 267; Manstein to Halder, 30 September 1942, T78/431/6402714.

97. KTB, LIV Corps, 12 October 1942, T314/1352/88–90; DIV, DOPS, October 1942, DEV 29/36/6/2, p. 26; *Informaciones*, 13 October 1942, p. 1, 26 December 1942, p. 3; *Hoja de Campaña*, 4 November 1942, p. 1, 4 January 1943, p. 3, 19 September 1942, p. 4.

98. GS, 1st Section, DGO, 30 September 1942, DEV 28/7/12/2, p. 34.

99. KTB, 11 Army, 13 October 1942, T312/1696/212; Esteban Infantes, *Azul*, pp. 132, 136.

100. Arko 138 to LIV Corps, 10 October 1942, T314/1353/321; LIV Corps, Divisional Armament Status, 15 October 1942, T314/1353/384–85; AOK 11, Operational Order 2, 28 October 1942, T314/1240/300–307; AOK 11, Status Report, 29 October 1942, T312/902/9081140; GS, 1st Section, TO & E, 28 October 1942, DEV 28/8/5/1, p. 2.

101. Hayes, *Wartime Mission*, p. 89.

102. Ibid., pp. 87–89.

103. Abwehr Report, 7 November 1942, T77/889/5639979.

104. Likus Memorandum, 6 November 1942, T120/115/116981–83.

105. Hoffmann Memorandum, Madrid, 17 October 1942, T120/82/62709–10.

106. Likus Memorandum, 1 November 1942, T120/82/62686–91.

107. Likus Memorandum, 4 November 1942, T120/82/62683–85; Likus Memorandum, November 1942, T120/82/62504–9; *Informaciones*, 12 November 1942, p. 1.

108. Department of State, Memorandum of Conversation, 18 November 1942, USNA, State 852.20/70 PS/HCW; Doussinague, *España*, pp. 102–3.

109. Burdick, *Germany's Military Strategy*, p. 169; Abwehr Report on Mobilization, 16 November 1942, T77/889/564016.

110. Abwehr Report, Madrid, 23 November 1942, T77/889/564022.

111. Hoare to FO, Madrid, 17 December 1942, PRO, FO 371/31239/8043.

112. Andreas Hillgruber, ed., *Staatsmänner und Diplomaten bei Hitler* (Frankfurt: Bernard & Graefe, 1970), 2: 148.

113. Doussinague, *España*, p. 265.

114. Serrano Suñer interview, December 1971.

115. Moltke to Berlin, Madrid, 27 February 1942, T77/885/5635119; Burdick, *Germany's Military Strategy*, pp. 25, 48, 67, 77; Brissaud, *Canaris*, p. 412; Karl Heinz Abshagen, *Canaris*, trans. Alan Houghton Broderick (London: Hutchinson, 1956), p. 214.

116. Brissaud, *Canaris*, p. 413.

117. Ibid., p. 414; Abshagen, *Canaris*, pp. 214–15.

118. Brissaud, *Canaris*, p. 414.

119. Ibid.

120. Esteban Infantes, *Azul*, p. 138; Nord to OKH, 12 December 1942, T311/99/7130765; KTB, LIV Corps, 13 December 1942, T314/1353/442.

121. Hansen to OKW via Nord, 9 December 1942, T312/1610/33.

122. Collatz interview, August 1971.

123. Interview of Mrs. Gertrude Schuback with Prince Metternich, Schloss Metternich, July 1975; and see Esteban Infantes, *Azul*, p. 201.

124. Hasse to Lindemann, 19 August 1942, T312/1610/59–60.

125. Nord to OKH, 1942, T311/99/7130765; Summary of Hitler-Muñoz Grandes Conversation, 13 December 1942, Hillgruber, *Staatsmänner*, 2: 152.

126. Hillgruber, *Staatsmänner*, 2: 154.

127. Ibid., pp. 152–59; Jodl to Ritter, 14 December 1942, T77/885/5635162–63; *Informaciones*, 14 December 1942, p. 1.

128. Likus Memorandum, 13 December 1942, T120/116/116945–46.

129. Summary of Muñoz Grandes-Ribbentrop Conversation, 15 December 1942, T120/116/116950–51.

130. Ibid., 116953–54.

131. Ibid.

132. Ibid.

133. Likus Memorandum, 15 December 1942, T120/116/116894–95.

134. Tugay to Ankara, Madrid, 19 December 1942, T77/885/5634853; Menzell to OKM, Madrid, 9 January 1943, T77/885/5634836.

135. Likus Memorandum, 7 January 1943, T120/116/116856; *Informaciones*, 19 December 1942, p. 1.

136. FO Memorandum, 20 December 1942, PRO, FO, 371/31239/8043, p. 59; Doussinague, *España*, pp. 117–26; Churchill to Eden, Whitehall, 27 November and 3 December 1942, PRO, FO 371/3120/8034, pp. 204, 207–10.

137. *Informaciones*, 21 December 1942, pp. 1, 3, 15 August 1942, p. 6, 29 August 1942, p. 1, 23 December 1942, p. 1.

138. Ibid., 26 December 1942, p. 3.

139. Likus Memorandum, 7 January 1943, T120/116/116859–63.

140. Brissaud, *Canaris*, p. 417.

141. Doussinague, *España*, p. 205.

142. Likus Memorandum, 7 January 1943, T120/116/116863–64.

143. Ibid., 116871–72.

CHAPTER 10. *The Krasni Bor Crucible*

1. Gardemann-Valdés Conversation, Madrid, 5 April 1943, T120/116/116834–37; Hoare, *Ambassador on Special Mission*, p. 185.

2. Doussinague, *España*, pp. 143–44.

3. *Informaciones*, 5 January 1943, p. 1.

4. Bürkner to AA, 1 January 1943, T120/85/63125–26.

5. Von Moltke to Ribbentrop, Madrid, 13 January 1943, T120/85/63146–48; Likus Memorandum, 13 January 1943, T120/116/11683.

6. Dörnberg to Ribbentrop, 15 January 1943, T120/85/63162–67.

7. Lohmann text of Franco Letter, 25 January 1943, T120/85/63207–9.

8. Ribbentrop to von Moltke, 25 January 1943, T120/85/13202; Zhukov, *Memoirs*, p. 425.

9. GS, 3d Section, DGO, 2 November 1942, DEV 28/8/10/11, p. 1; DIV, DOPS, December 1942, DEV 29/37/6/2, pp. 9–24; *Hoja de Campaña*, 1 January 1943, p. 3; *Informaciones*, 5 January 1943, p. 8.

10. GS, 1st Section, 4th Expedition, 17 April 1942, DEV 28/4/11/1, p. 15; DOPS, Second of 269, November–December 1942, DEV 29/38/2/4, pp. 51–54; Orders, 269, December 1942, DEV 28/9/1/2, pp. 33, 46; DOPS, 269, December 1942, DEV 29/37/6/3, p. 43; Torcuato Luca de Tena, *Embajador en el infierno: Memorias del capitán Palacios* (Barcelona: Planeta, 1955), pp. 16–17; *Hoja de Campaña*, January 1943, p. 4; *Informaciones*, 1 January 1943, p. 8.

11. KTB, LIV Corps, 8 December 1942, T314/1354/384–86.

12. KTB, LIV Corps, 11 December 1942, T314/1354/422.

13. GS, 3d Section, Destruction of Advanced Fieldworks, 29 December 1942, DEV 29/37/8/3, pp. 48–51; *Hoja de Campaña*, 14 November 1943, p. 3.

14. DIV, DOPS, 29 December 1942, DEV 29/37/6/2, p. 22.

15. Group Robles, After Action Report, 31 December 1942, DEV 29/37/11/1, pp. 5–8; DOPS, Sappers 250, December 1942, DEV 29/37/6/3, pp. 65–66; GS, 3d Section, Attack Plan, 29 December 1942, DEV 29/37/8/3, pp. 48–50; GS, Daily Reports, 29, 30 December 1942, DEV 29/37/10, pp. 139–40; *Hoja de Campaña*, January 1943, pp. 1, 3; *Informaciones*, 9 January 1943, p. 1, 11 January 1943, p. 1; AOK 18 to Nord, 31 December 1942, T311/99/771–72.

16. KTB, LIV Corps, Lindemann-Hansen Conversation, 31 December 1942, T314/1354/124–26.

17. Biography supplied by Bundesarchiv-Militärarchiv, Freiburg, 1975.

18. Meretskov, *Na sluzhbe narodu*, pp. 318–22; Fediuninskii, *Podniatye po trevoge*, pp. 129–33; Chaney, *Zhukov*, pp. 247–49.

19. *Geschichte des Grossen Vaterländischen Krieges der Sowjetunion*, 3:154–56; XXVI Corps, Ic, Interrogation Report to AOK 18, 2 January 1943, T314/763/87.

20. Meretskov, *Na Sluzhbe narodu*, pp. 121–25; I. V. Shikin and I. Ia. Fomichenko, [A historic triumph], *Voprosy istorii* 1 (January 1973): 108–24; Fediuninskii, *Podniatye po trevoge*, pp. 174–81; Salisbury, *900 Days*, pp. 547–49; Paul Carell, *Scorched Earth* (London: Harrap, 1970), pp. 214–31; AOK 18, Ladoga-Kolpino Report, 14 April 1943, T312/866/9037688–90.

21. KTB, 18 Army, 15 January 1943, T312/856/9024326.

22. KTB, LIV Corps, 16 January 1943, T314/1355/842; KTB, 250 Division, January 1943, T315/1726/414–15.

23. DOPS, 269, December 1942, DEV 29/37/6/3, pp. 43–50; DOPS, 269, January 1943, DEV 29/38/2/3, pp. 19–22.

24. *Hoja de Campaña*, 20 June 1943, p. 8, 12 January 1943, p. 2.

25. KTB, LIV Corps, 17 January 1943, T314/1355/848.

26. LIV Corps to 250 Division 16 January 1943, T314/1355/1128.

27. Salisbury, *900 Days*, pp. 548–49.

28. Zhukov, *Memoirs*, p. 425; Group Hilpert to XXVI Corps, 23 January 1943, T314/1355/1225; LIV Corps to Second of 269, 21 January 1943, T314/1355/1195.

29. KTB, 250 Division, Supplement for Second of 269, 21–30 January 1943, T315/1726/426.

30. DOPS, Second of 269, January 1943, DEV 29/38/2/4, p. 55; Battle of Lake Ladoga, January 1943, DEV 29/38/2/1, p. 1.

31. Battle of Lake Ladoga, January 1943, DEV 29/38/2/1, p. 1; Annex to Operations, 269, January 1943, DEV 29/38/2/1, p. 3.

32. Battle of Lake Ladoga, January 1943, DEV 29/38/2/1, pp. 1–2; Annex to Operations, 269, January 1943, DEV 29/38/2/1, pp. 3–4; GS, DGO, Testimony on Massip, 10 April 1943, DEV 28/12/13/1, pp. 11–12.

33. GS, DGO, Testimony on Massip, 10 April 1943, DEV 28/12/13/1, pp. 11–12.

34. Ibid.

35. Ibid.; Battle of Lake Ladoga, January 1943, DEV 29/38/2/1, pp. 1–2; Annex to Operations, 269, DEV 29/38/2/1, pp. 3–4.

36. DOPS, 269, January 1943, DEV 29/33/2/3, pp. 21–23; Battle of Lake Ladoga, January 1943, DEV 29/33/2/1, pp. 1–2; Annex to Operations, 269, January 1943, DEV 29/33/2/1, pp. 3–4; Esteban Infantes, *Azul*, pp. 150–51; Hartwig Pohlmann, *Wolchow: 900 Tage Kampf um Leningrad, 1941–1944* (Bad Nauheim: Podzun, 1962), p. 85.

37. L Corps to AOK 18, 24 January 1943, T314/1238/771.

38. L Corps Inspection Report, 25 January 1943, T314/1238/767–68; and 2 February 1943, T314/1238/320.

39. GS, 3d Section, Particular Order 574, 26 January 1943, DEV 29/38/6/2, pp. 8–9.

40. KTB, L Corps, 29 January 1943, T314/1235/605–6.

41. L Corps, Inspection Report, 2 February 1943, T314/1239/320; KTB, L Corps, 3–4 February 1943, T314/1235/613–17; L Corps to 250 Division, 3 February 1943, T314/1239/311.

42. Esteban Infantes, *Azul*, p. 155; KTB, Nord, 1 February 1943, T311/56/7069455; KTB, L Corps, 1 February 1943, T314/1235/619–21; GS, 3d Section, DGO 29, 1 February 1943, DEV 28/10/11/1, p. 6.

43. L Corps, Order to 250 Division, 1 February 1943, T314/1239/275; GS, 3d Section, Particular Order to Sector Chiefs, 1 February 1943, DEV 29/38/14/1, p. 1.

44. KTB, L Corps, 7–8 February 1943, T314/1235/623–25; L Corps, Reports, 7–8 February 1943, T314/1239/265–52; Husemann, *SS Polizei*, 2: 136.

45. GS, 3d Section, Daily Reports, 4–7 February 1943, DEV 29/38/11/2, pp. 5–8; KTB, 250 Division, February 1943, T315/1726/431.

46. GS, 2d Section, POW Interrogation Reports, 28 January 1943, DEV 28/29/11/1, pp. 33–34; and 2 February 1943, DEV 28/29/14/1, pp. 1–2; GS, 2d Section, Daily Intelligence Reports, January 1943, DEV 28/29/12/3, pp. 39–41.

47. Salisbury, *900 Days*, pp. 550–51; AOK 18, Ladoga-Kolpino Battle Report, 14 April 1943, T312/866/9037692–93.

48. K. A. Meretskov, "V Boiakh pod Leningradom," *Voprosy istorii* 3 (March 1968): 119–20; Meretskov, *Na sluzhbe narodu*, pp. 330–35; Carell, *Scorched Earth*, pp. 245–46; AOK 18, Ladoga-Kolpino Battle Report, 14 April 1943, T312/866/9037692–94; GS, 2d Section, Krasni Bor Report, 20 February 1943, DEV 28/29/14/2, pp. 24–25.

49. GS, 2d Section, POW Interrogation Reports, 8 February 1943, DEV 28/29/14/1, p. 3.

50. Ibid.

51. GS, 2d Section, POW Interrogation Reports, 10 February 1943, DEV 28/29/14/1, pp. 8–9; GS, 2d Section, February Intelligence Summary, 1 March 1943, DEV 28/29/14/5, pp. 45–46.

52. Personal observation of the authors, June 1974; KTB, 250 Division February 1943, T315/1726/431.

53. Esteban Infantes, *Azul*, pp. 151–57; GS, 2d Section, Krasni Bor Report, 20 February 1943, DEV 28/29/14/2, pp. 24–25.

54. L Corps, Artillery TO & E, 14 February 1943, T314/1235/870; KTB, 250 Division, February 1943, T314/1726/426–32; GS, 3d Section, Daily Reports, February 1943, DEV 29/32/11/2, p. 41; DOPS, 3 Company Sappers, February 1943, DEV 29/43/3/2, pp. 105–6.

55. Esteban Infantes, *Azul*, p. 154; Yencken to FO, 2 October 1943, PRO, FO 371/34814/8060.

56. Esteban Infantes, *Azul*, pp. 155–56; DOPS, 3 Company, First of 263, February 1943, DEV 29/43/5, p. 21; GS, 3d Section, Daily Report, 9 February 1943, DEV 29/38/14/12, p. 10; KTB, 250 Division, February 1943, T315/1726/431.

57. GS, 3d Section, Daily Report, 9 February 1943, DEV 29/38/14/1, p. 10.

58. GS, 2d Section, Monthly Intelligence Summary, February 1943, DEV 28/29/14/5, p. 46; L Corps, Midday Report, 9 February 1943, T314/1239/223.

59. Oroquieta Arbiol, *De Leningrado*, pp. 35–36.

60. GS, 2d Section, Interrogation Report, 9 February 1943, DEV 28/29/14/1, p. 4.

61. Oroquieta Arbiol, *De Leningrado*, pp. 34–35.

62. Ibid., p. 35; GS, 2d Section, Monthly Intelligence Summary, February 1943, DEV 28/29/14/5, p. 46.

63. GS, 3d Section, Daily Report, 9–10 February 1943, DEV 29/38/14/2, p. 1.

64. Oroquieta Arbiol, *De Leningrado*, pp. 31–33.

65. Ibid., pp. 32–34; KTB, 250 Division, February 1943, T314/1726/435.

66. Oroquieta Arbiol, *De Leningrado*, p. 36.

67. Luca de Tena, *Embajador*, p. 15.

68. Ibid., p. 16.

69. Ibid., pp. 17–20; *Hoja de Campaña*, 12 January 1944, p. 12.

70. Luca de Tena, *Embajador*, p. 20.

71. Juan Negro Castro, *Españoles en la U.R.S.S.* (Madrid: Escelicer, 1959), p. 9.

72. *Ibid.*, pp. 9–10.

73. Ibid.

74. Esteban Infantes, *Azul*, p. 157.

75. Kleffel to all Units, 9 February 1943, T314/1239/235.

76. KTB, L Corps, 9 February 1943, T314/1235/623, 627.

77. Liaison Staff, Excerpt of Krasni Bor Investigation, 10 April 1943, T312/859/9028069; GS, 2d Section, Daily Report, 10 February 1943, DEV 29/38/14/1, p. 11.

78. Oroquieta Arbiol, *De Leningrado*, pp. 36–37.

79. 1 Ind. Armored Battalion, Popov Manuscript and Translation, February 1943, T314/1240/19.

80. Ibid., 18–23; GS, 2d Section, DEV 28/29/14/2, pp. 24–25; AOK

18, Enemy Disposition Maps, 9–11 February 1943, T312/872/9044780–96; L Corps, Intelligence Report, 14 February 1943, T314/1239/1021; KTB, 250 Division, February 1943, T315/1726/432–33.

81. Luca de Tena, *Embajador*, pp. 19–20.

82. Negro Castro, *Españoles*, pp. 11–13.

83. Ibid.; GS, 2d Section, DGO 32, Huidobro Testimony, 11 August 1943, DEV 28/16/7/1, p. 20; KTB, 250 Division, February 1943, T315/1726/434.

84. Negro Castro, *Españoles*, p. 12.

85. *Ibid.*; KTB, 250 Division, February 1943, T315/1726/434; L Corps, Orders, Reports, 10 February 1943, T314/1239/105–6.

86. Theodore Plievier, *Stalingrad* (New York: Berkeley Medallion Editions, 1964), pp. 19–20; GS, 2d Section, Krasni Bor Report, 20 February 1943, DEV 28/29/14/3, p. 24; KTB, 250 Division, February 1943, T315/1726/433; Carell, *Scorched Earth*, pp. 246–47; *Vieja Guardia* interview, December 1971.

87. Oroquieta Arbiol, *De Leningrado*, pp. 38–39.

88. Luca de Tena, *Embajador*, pp. 22–23.

89. Plievier, *Stalingrad*, p. 19.

90. Negro Castro, *Españoles*, pp. 13–15; GS, 2d Section, DGO 32, Huidobro Testimony, 11 August 1943, DEV 28/16/7/1, pp. 20–21.

91. KTB, 250 Division, February 1943, T315/1726/436; Esteban Infantes, *Azul*, pp. 159–60; KTB, L Corps, 10 February 1943, T314/1235/631.

92. Huidobro Testimony, DEV 28/17/7/1, pp. 19–21.

93. DOPS, 269, February 1943, DEV 29/38/11/1, p. 11.

94. Esteban Infantes, *Azul*, p. 157.

95. Ibid., p. 158.

96. KTB, L Corps, 10 February 1943, T314/1235/631; KTB, 18 Army, 10 February 1943, T312/856/9024894–96; Arko 138, Daily Report, 10 February 1943, T314/1239/201; *Vieja Guardia* interview, December 1971.

97. GS, 2d Section, POW Interrogation Report, 10 February 1943, DEV 28/29/14/1, p. 5.

98. Luca de Tena, *Embajador*, p. 22.

99. Ibid., pp. 22–23.

100. Negro Castro, *Españoles*, p. 15; KTB, 250 Division, February 1943, T315/1726/433.

101. Huidobro Testimony, 11 August 1943, DEV 28/16/7/1, p. 19.

102. Negro Castro, *Españoles*, pp. 14–16.

103. SS Police, Daily Report, 10 February 1943, T314/1239/201; KTB, 250 Division, February 1943, T315/1726/433–34; L Corps, Intelligence Report, 14 February 1943, T314/1239/1021.

104. KTB, 250 Division, February 1943, T315/1726/434.

105. Ibid.

106. Ibid.

107. Huidobro Testimony, 11 August 1943, DEV 28/16/7/1, p. 19.

108. Luca de Tena, *Embajador*, pp. 23–43.

109. KTB, 250 Division, February 1943, T315/1726/435; *Hoja de Campaña*, 19 March 1943, p. 1; GS, 2d Section, Krasni Bor Report, 20 February 1943, DEV 28/29/14/3, p. 24; FLAK Regiment 164 (Motorized), Daily Report, 10 February 1943, T312/862/9031994.

110. *Hoja de Campaña*, 21 November 1943, p. 3; L Corps, Intelligence Report, 14 February 1943, T314/1239/1021; KTB, 250 Division, February 1943, T315/1726/436–38.

111. Oroquieta Arbiol, *De Leningrado*, pp. 45–46.

112. Ibid.; GS, 2d Section, POW Interrogations, 11 February 1943, DEV 28/29/14/1, pp. 7–11; GS, 2d Section, Krasni Bor Report, 20 February 1943, DEV 28/29/14/2, pp. 24–25.

113. GS, 2d Section, POW Interrogation, 11 February 1943, DEV 28/29/14/1, pp. 8–9; GS, 2d Section, Krasni Bor Report, 20 February 1943, DEV 28/29/14/2, pp. 24–25.

114. Esteban Infantes, *Azul*, p. 158.

115. DOPS, 3 Company, First of 263, February 1943, DEV 29/43/5, p. 21.

116. Esteban Infantes, *Azul*, pp. 158–59.

117. L Corps, Intelligence Report, 14 February 1943, T314/1239/1020–22.

118. KTB, 250 Division, February 1943, T315/1726/435–36; Esteban Infantes, *Azul*, pp. 159–60.

119. KTB, 18 Army, 10 February 1943, T312/856/9024898–91; KTB, L Corps, 10 February 1943, T314/1235/631.

120. KTB, 250 Division, February 1943, T315/1726/436; DOPS, Sappers 250, February 1943, DEV 29/38/11/4, p. 47; L Corps, Krasni Bor Intelligence Summary, 14 February 1943, T314/1239/1020–24; KTB, L Corps, 10 February 1943, T314/1235/631; KTB, 18 Army, 10 February 1943, T312/856/9024901.

121. Esteban Infantes, *Azul*, p. 163.

122. Privately reported to the authors.

123. *Hoja de Campaña*, 30 May 1943, p. 4.

124. DOPS, Recon 250, February 1943, DEV 29/32/11/3, p. 41.

125. KTB, 250 Division, February 1943, T315/1726/436.

126. Esteban Infantes, *Azul*, p. 160.

127. DOPS, Sappers 250, February 1943, DEV 29/38/11/4, pp. 47–49; DOPS, Recon 250, February 1943, DEV 29/32/11/3, pp. 41–42; GS, 2d Section, Krasni Bor Report, 20 February 1943, DEV 28/29/14/3, p. 25; KTB, 250 Division, February 1943, T315/1726/436; KTB, L Corps, 10 February 1943, T314/1235/631.

128. AOK 18, Excerpt of Spanish Krasni Bor Investigation, T312/859/9028071; KTB, 250 Division, February 1943, T314/1726/436; Esteban Infantes, *Azul*, p. 165; L Corps, Artillery TO&E, 27 January 1943, T314/1235/900.

129. DOPS, Sappers 250, February 1943, DEV 29/38/11/4, pp. 47–

49; KTB, 250 Division, February 1943, T315/1726/436; Arko 138, Daily Report, 10 February 1943, T314/1239/201.

130. DOPS, Sappers 250, February 1943, DEV 29/38/11/4, pp. 47–48; *Hoja de Campaña*, 23 November 1943, p. 3.

131. Oroquieta Arbiol, *De Leningrado*, p. 42.

132. DOPS, Sappers 250, February 1943, DEV 29/38/11/4, pp. 48–49; *Hoja de Campaña*, 2 January 1944, p. 2; KTB, L Corps, 10 February 1943, T314/1235/631.

133. Oroquieta Arbiol, *De Leningrado*, p. 43.

134. Estado Mayor Central del Ejército, *Galería Militar, Medalla Militar, 1933–1969* (Madrid: 1970), 2: 534–35.

135. Oroquieta Arbiol, *De Leningrado*, pp. 44–47.

136. Luca de Tena, *Embajador*, pp. 25–26.

137. Negro Castro, *Españoles*, pp. 14–17.

138. Esteban Infantes, *Azul*, p. 160.

139. *Galería Militar*, 2: 71–72; Esteban Infantes, *Azul*, pp. 160–61.

140. Esteban Infantes, *Azul*, p. 161.

141. Ibid.; Private Interviews, Madrid, June 1974; GS, 1st Section, 3 March 1943, DEV 28/11/6/2, p. 10; Fernando Ramos, "Entre Calé y Calé," in *División Azul, Temas Españoles*, no. 25 (Madrid: Publicaciones Españolas, 1953), p. 4.

142. Esteban Infantes, *Azul*, p. 161.

143. KTB, 18 Army, 10 February 1943, T312/856/9024916.

144. Esteban Infantes, *Azul*, pp. 37–48; Díaz de Villegas, *Línea*, pp. 80–88.

145. Husemann, *SS Polizei*, 2: 139–41.

146. Liaison Staff, Excerpts of Krasni Bor Investigation, T312/859/9028069–70.

147. KTB, 250 Division, February 1943, T315/1726/435; KTB, 18 Army, 10 February 1943, T312/846/9024921.

148. Oroquieta Arbiol, *De Leningrado*, p. 47.

149. Ibid., pp. 47–48; *Galería Militar*, 2: 535.

150. Luca de Tena, *Embajador*, p. 25.

151. Esteban Infantes, *Azul*, p. 164.

152. José García Luna, *Las Cartas del Sargento Basilio* (Barcelona: Ed. Pentágono, 1959), pp. 160–61; Cano Report, 1 March 1943, DEV 28/38/11/1, p. 3; DOPS, Second of 269, February 1943, DEV 29/40/14/1, pp. 37–38.

153. Cano Report, 1 March 1943, DEV 28/38/11/1, p. 3.

154. Blanco, *Rusia*, p. 48; Cano Report, 1 March 1943, DEV 29/38/11/1, pp. 2–3; DOPS, 269, February 1943, DEV 29/38/11/1, pp. 12–13.

155. Blanco, *Rusia*, pp. 48–49.

156. Ibid., p. 49.

157. Ibid.

158. Ibid.

159. Ibid., pp. 49–50.

160. Oroquieta Arbiol, *De Leningrado*, pp. 48–49.

161. Luca de Tena, *Embajador*, pp. 25–27.

162. Negro Castro, *Españoles*, pp. 17–18.

163. Ibid., p. 19.

164. Oroquieta Arbiol, *De Leningrado*, pp. 49–51.

165. DOPS, Sappers 250, February 1943, DEV 29/38/11/4, pp. 47–48.

166. KTB, 18 Army, 10 February 1943, T312/846/9024942.

167. Ibid., 9024918–42; Husemann, *SS Polizei*, 2: 141.

168. AOK 18, Excerpt of Spanish Krasni Bor Investigation, T312/859/9028071; DOPS, Intendency 250, February 1943, DEV 29/38/11/5, p. 56; Esteban Infantes, *Azul*, pp. 165–66.

169. AOK 18, Excerpt of Spanish Krasni Bor Investigation, T312/859/9028072.

170. Ibid.

171. Schelm and Mehrle, *215*, p. 167.

172. AOK 18, Excerpt of Spanish Krasni Bor Investigation, T312/859/9028072; Esteban Infantes, *Azul*, pp. 162–63, 167.

173. AOK 18, Excerpt of Spanish Krasni Bor Investigation, T312/859/9028073; Personal communication of the authors with Dr. Walter Speer, former adjutant, 390 Grenadier Regiment, May 1976.

174. KTB, 18 Army, 10 February 1943, T312/856/9024918–52; KTB, 18 Army, 10 February 1943, T312/856/9024916.

175. Esteban Infantes, *Azul*, pp. 166–68; *Informaciones*, 2 April 1943, p. 3; García Luna, *Cartas*, p. 161; KTB, 250 Division, February 1943, T315/1726/437.

176. DOPS, 269, February 1943, DEV 28/38/11/1, p. 2; Esteban Infantes, *Azul*, pp. 167–68.

177. Cano Report, 1 March 1943, DEV 28/38/11/1, pp. 2–3; Ramos, *Temas Españoles*, no. 25, p. 3.

178. Cano Report, 1 March 1943, DEV 28/38/11/1, p. 3.

179. Ibid., pp. 2–3; DOPS, 3 Company, Second of 263, February 1943, DEV 29/54/5/1, pp. 21–23.

180. Blanco, *Rusia*, pp. 49–50.

181. Ibid., p. 51.

182. Ibid., pp. 51–52.

183. Negro Castro, *Españoles*, pp. 20–21; *Vieja Guardia* interview, December 1971.

184. Negro Castro, *Españoles*, p. 20.

185. Ibid., pp. 21–22.

186. Isidoro Paloma Yagüe, in *Vieja Guardia* interview, December 1971.

187. GS, 3d Section, DGO, Ponte Testimony, 2 May 1943, DEV 29/13/13/1, pp. 1–2; DEV 28/13/7/2, pp. 39–41; GS, 2d Section, List of Interpreters, 28 June 1941, DEV 28/28/3/1, p. 22; DOPS, Sappers 250, February 1943, DEV 29/38/11/4, pp. 47–49.

188. GS, 3d Section, DGO, 14 February 1943, DEV 28/10/12/1, p.

18; Liaison Staff, Excerpt of Spanish Krasni Bor Investigation, T312/859/ 9028072.

189. KTB, 18 Army, 10 February 1943, T312/856/9024946; DOPS, Sappers 250, February 1943, DEV 29/38/11/4, pp. 47–48.

190. Liaison Staff, Excerpt of Jobst Report of Krasni Bor Battle, T312/ 859/9028070; DOPS, Recon 250, February 1943, DEV 29/32/11/3, pp. 41–42; DOPS, Sappers 250, February 1943, DEV 29/38/11/4, p. 48; KTB, 18 Army, 10 February 1943, T312/856/9024950; DOPS, Recon 250, February 1943, DEV 29/54/3/2, p. 106.

191. DOPS, Intendency 250, February 1943, DEV 29/38/11/5, p. 56.

192. Ramos, *Temas Españoles*, no. 25, pp. 3–4.

193. KTB, 18 Army, 10 February 1943, T312/856/9024957.

194. Ramos, *Temas Españoles*, no. 25, p. 4.

195. Luca de Tena, *Embajador*, p. 33.

196. Ibid.

197. Ibid.

198. Ibid., pp. 33–34.

199. Ibid., p. 34.

200. Ibid.

201. Ibid., p. 35.

202. Liaison Staff, Excerpt of Spanish Krasni Bor Investigation, T312/ 859/9028073.

203. Ibid.

204. KTB, 250 Division, February 1943, T315/1726/437; KTB, 18 Army, 10, 11 February 1943, T312/856/9024966 and 1924977; KTB, L Corps, 10 February 1943, T314/1235/635.

205. Ramos, *Temas Españoles*, no. 25, p. 3; *Vieja Guardia* interview, December, 1971.

206. *Galería Militar*, 2: 523–24; KTB, 250 Division, February 1943, T315/1726/437; GS, 3d Section, DGO, 14 February 1943, DEV 28/10/ 12/1, p. 18; Esteban Infantes, *Azul*, p. 165.

207. DOPS, Sappers 250, February 1943, DEV 29/38/11/4, pp. 47– 48.

208. Ibid.

CHAPTER 11.   Sin Novedad *and Neutrality*

1. GS, 2d Section, POW Interrogation Reports, 11 February 1943, DEV 28/29/14/1, pp. 6–7.

2. Military Attaché, Berlin, Report, 18 February 1943, DEV 29/52/7, p. 70.

3. Ibid., pp. 70–71; GS, 2d Section, 20 March Battalion, 25 February 1943, DEV 28/10/12/1, p. 27.

4. Hoare to FO 358, Madrid, 20 February 1943, PRO, FO 371/34813/ 8096, p. 48.

5. Díaz de Villegas, *Línea*, pp. 71–72; Payne, *Politics*, pp. 432–36.

6. Doussinague, *España*, pp. 131–32; Hayes, *Wartime Mission*, pp. 99–101.

7. Doussinague, *España*, p. 132; Mohr to AA, Tangiers, 29 January 1943, T120/85/63233–34.

8. Doussinague, *España*, p. 132.

9. Ibid., pp. 133–34.

10. Von Moltke to AA, Madrid, 23 January 1943, T120/85/63188–89.

11. Ibid., 63193–95.

12. Doussinague, *España*, p. 206.

13. Von Moltke to AA, Madrid, 20 January 1943, T120/85/63239.

14. Doussinague, *España*, pp. 134–38; Foltz, *Masquerade*, pp. 147–50.

15. Von Moltke to OKH, Madrid, 9 February 1943, T77/885/5635141.

16. Burdick, *Germany's Military Strategy*, p. 179.

17. OKW, WFst to OKH, GS, Army, 9 February 1943, T78/319/6273460.

18. Serrano Suñer interview, June 1974; Abwehr, Bürkner Report, Berlin, 16 February 1943, T77/885/5635124; von Moltke to OKW, Madrid, 27 February 1943, T77/885/5635119.

19. Abwehr, Krahmer Report, Madrid, 8 March 1943, T77/885/5635075.

20. Von Moltke to AA, Madrid, 27 February 1943, T77/885/5635898; Abwehr, Krahmer Report, Madrid, 8 March 1943, T77/885/5635075.

21. Joseph Goebbels, *The Goebbels Diaries*, trans. and ed. Louis P. Lochner (London: Hamish Hamilton, 1948), p. 233.

22. Hitler-Martínez Campos Interview, Minutes, 18 March 1943, T77/885/5634986–93; *Informaciones*, 22 March 1943, p. 1; Canaris to OKW, Berlin, 26 March 1943, T77/885/563008; OKH Attaché Section to OKW, Berlin, April 1943, T77/885/5634981–82.

23. *Informaciones*, 22, 23, and 25 March 1943, p. 1.

24. Hencke to AA, Madrid, 23 March 1943, T120/85/63466, and enclosures, 63467–71.

25. Gardemann to Ribbentrop, Madrid, 3 April 1943, T120/116/116817.

26. Gardemann to Ribbentrop, Valdés Conversation, Madrid, 5 April 1943, T120/116/116836.

27. *Informaciones*, 16, 17 March 1943, p. 1; Hoffmann Memorandum, 28 March 1943, T120/116/116832–33; Gardemann Memorandum, 5 April 1943, T120/116/116836–37.

28. Serrano Suñer interview, June 1974.

29. Canaris to OKW, Berlin, 28 March 1943, T77/885/563508; OKH, Attaché Section to OKW, Madrid, 16 April 1943, T77/885/5634963.

30. Díaz de Villegas, *Línea*, p. 8.

31. DOPS, 262, March 1943, DEV 29/39/2/1, p. 4.

32. Cano Report, 1 March 1943, DEV 28/38/11/1, pp. 3–4; GS, *Partes*, 11 February 1943, DEV 29/38/14/2, p. 12.

33. Cano Report, 1 March 1943, DEV 28/38/11/1, pp. 2–7; KTB,

250 Division, February 1943, T315/1726/431–56; L Corps, Effectives, 14 February 1943, T312/862/9032277; L Corps, Liaison Staff Report, 12 February 1943, T314/1239/173; DOPS, Recon 250, February 1943, DEV 29/43/3/2, p. 106; DOPS, 3 Company, First of 263; February 1943, DEV 29/43/5, pp. 21–22; L Corps, Order, 12 February 1943, T314/1239/175; Personal communication to the authors of Dr. Walter Speer, former adjutant, 390 Grenadier Regiment, June 1976.

34. Esteban Infantes, *Azul*, p. 168.

35. KTB, 18 Army, 12 February 1943, T312/856/9025013.

36. Esteban Infantes, *Azul*, pp. 167–68; GS, 2d Section, DGO, 14 February 1943, DEV 28/10/12/1, p. 18.

37. KTB Nord, 1 March 1943, T311/56/7069618; KTB, L Corps, 2, 3 March 1943, T314/1235/823 and 831.

38. Military Attaché, Berlin, 20 February 1943, DEV 28/10/7/2, pp. 7–8.

39. GS, 2d Section, Krasni Bor Report, 20 February 1943, DEV 28/29/14/2, pp. 24–25; KTB, 250 Division, February 1943, T315/1726/438–44.

40. Von Küchler to Lindemann, 14 March 1943, T312/918/9102740–41.

41. *Hoja de Campaña*, 21 March 1943, p. 1.

42. Lindemann-Esteban Infantes Conversation, 16 March 1943, T312/859/9028219–20.

43. DOPS, 262, March 1943, DEV 29/39/2/1, pp. 4–6; DOPS, 13 Company of 262, 19 March 1943, DEV 29/39/2/1, pp. 10–13; DOPS, 14 Company of 262, 19 March 1943, DEV 29/39/2/1, pp. 15–17; KTB, 250 Division, March 1943, T315/1726/471–72; KTB, L Corps, 19 March 1943, T314/1240/477–89; Ramos, *Temas Españoles*, no. 25, pp. 19–24.

44. Díaz de Villegas, *Línea*, pp. 29–35.

45. Ibid., p. 45.

46. Ibid., pp. 45–46.

47. DIV, DOPS, April 1943, DEV 29/39/11/1, p. 8; GS, 1st Section, TO & E, 1 April 1943, DEV 28/11/12/1, p. 2; GS, 1st Section, DGO, 10 April 1943, DEV 28/12/8/1, p. 8; L Corps, TO & E, March, April 1943, T314/1240/864–957.

48. Hoare, *Ambassador on Special Mission*, p. 193.

49. FO Minutes, 2 April 1943, PRO, FO 371/34811/8041, p. 12.

50. Eden to Hoare, 8 April 1943, PRO, FO 371/34811/8041, p. 24.

51. Burdick, *Germany's Military Strategy*, p. 183.

52. M. I. 3a to FO, Matthew to Williams, London, 21 April 1943, PRO, FO 371/34811/8041, p. 61.

53. Doussinague, *España*, p. 188.

54. Hoare to FO, Madrid, 7 May 1943, PRO, FO 371/35811/8041, p. 72.

55. Doussinague, *España*, pp. 207–8; José María Cordero Torres, *Relaciones exteriores de España* (Madrid: Ed. del Movimiento, 1954), pp. 186–88.

56. GS, DGO, 28 April 1943, DEV 28/12/8/1, p. 12.

57. Díaz de Villegas, *Línea*, p. 222.

58. B. H. Liddell-Hart, *History of the Second World War* (New York: Putnam, 1970), p. 488.

59. Esteban Infantes, *Azul*, p. 175; DIV, DOPS, May 1943, DEV 29/40/8/1, pp. 2–22; 18 Army, Overlays, May 1943, T312/902/9081599–600; L Corps, Order Reorganizing Sectors, 9 May 1943, T315/1533/69–73; DIV, DOPS, April 1943, DEV 29/39/11/1, p. 13; Esteban Infantes to Kleffel, 30 April 1943, T314/1242/203–4; Knüppel to Kleffel, 4 May 1943, T314/1242/211; GS, 1st Section, 23 March Battalion, Hof, 6, 11, 15 May 1943, DEV 28/13/9/1, pp. 1–15, 18, 30–83.

60. KTB, Nord, 2 June 1943, T311/56/7069894; von Küchler to Lindemann, 2 June 1943, T312/918/9102689–90; Lindemann Memorandum, 27 May 1943, T312/918/9102700–710; GS, 1st Section, DGO 26, 14 June 1943, DEV 28/14/7/1, p. 9.

61. DIV, DOPS, June 1942, DEV 29/41/1/3, p. 14; Esteban Infantes, *Azul*, p. 184; Summary of Raids, January to June 1943, DEV 29/41/9/2, p. 35.

62. GS, 3d Section, Daily Reports, 1–2 July 1943, DEV 29/41/13/2, pp. 7–8; Díaz de Villegas, *Línea*, pp. 65–67.

63. Seaton, *Russo-German War*, pp. 356–58; Domarus, *Hitler: Reden, 1933 bis 1945*, 2: 2021; Martin Caidin, *The Tigers Are Burning* (New York: Hawthorn, 1974), pp. 83–84.

64. Esteban Infantes, *Azul*, pp. 189–93; Díaz de Villegas, *Línea*, pp. 100–103; *Hoja de Campaña*, 18 July 1943, p. 1, and 12 January 1944, p. 2.

65. Military Attaché to Madrid, Telegram, Berlin, 11 August 1943, DEV 28/15/9/1, p. 79.

66. L Corps, Special Order, 20 July 1943, T314/1242/466–67.

67. Hayes to Hull, Memorandum of Beaulac-Doussinague Conversation 1929, 12 January 1944, Madrid, 21 January 1944, USNA, State, 852.00/10935, p. 3; Dieckhoff to AA, Madrid, 16 June 1943, T120/85/63964–65; *Informaciones*, 6, 8, 26 July 1943, p. 1.

68. Dieckhoff to AA, Madrid, 16 June 1943, T77/889/5639664.

69. Ibid.

70. Hayes, *Wartime Mission*, pp. 157–64.

71. *Hoja de Campaña*, 5 September 1943, p. 8.

72. Hayes, *Wartime Mission*, p. 165.

73. Hayes to Hull, Doussinague-Beaulac Conversation, 21 January 1944, USNA, State, 852.00/10935, p. 1.

74. Hoare, *Ambassador on Special Mission*, pp. 221–22; Hayes, *Wartime Mission*, p. 166; Hayes to Hull, Telegram, Madrid, 30 September 1943, USNA, State, 852.20/198, pp. 1–6.

75. Hayes, *Wartime Mission*, pp. 166–67.

76. Von Leeb, Generalfeldmarschall Wilhelm, *Tagebuchaufzeichnungen und Lagebeurteilungen aus zwei Weltkriegen*, ed. Georg Meyer (Stuttgart: Deutsche Verlags-Anstalt, 1976), 23 August 1943, p. 75, n. 182.

77. DOPS, 262, September 1943, DEV 29/42/6/3, p. 18; KTB, L

Corps, 9 September 1943, T314/1240/817; G-2, 262, Daily Intelligence Report, 9, 11 September 1943, DEV 28/31/12/1, pp. 11–14.

78. DOPS, 262, September 1943, DEV 29/42/6/3, pp. 17–19; GS, 1st Section, 14 Return Battalion, Hof, 23 September 1943, DEV 28/17/11/1, p. 83.

79. Speth to OKH, 28 September 1943, T311/99/7130828–29.

80. José Luis de Arrese, *Escritos y discursos* (Madrid: Vicesecretaría de Educación Popular, 1943), p. 219.

81. Ibid.

82. Torr to War Office, Madrid, 30 September 1943, PRO, FO 371/34814/8060, p. 11.

83. Ibid., p. 10; Yencken to FO, Telegram 1672, Madrid, 29 September 1943, PRO, FO 371/34813/8005, p. 107.

84. Dieckhoff to AA, Madrid, 27 September 1943, T77/885/5634793.

85. OKW to WFst, Berlin, 3 October 1943, T77/885/5634788.

86. Dieckhoff to AA, Madrid, 2 October 1943, T77/885/5634781.

87. Ibid.

88. Ibid.

89. Helmut Heiber, ed., *Hitlers Lagebesprechungen: Die Protokollfragmente seine militärischen Konferenzen 1942–1945* (Stuttgart: Deutsche Verlags-Anstalt, 1962), pp. 385–86.

90. Ibid.

91. Hayes, *Wartime Mission*, pp. 175–76; *Informaciones*, 1 October 1943, pp. 1, 3, 16.

92. Knuppel to OKH, 11 October 1943, T312/1610/10.

93. Speth to OKH, 28 September 1943, T311/99/7130828–29.

94. KTB, 18 Army, 4 October 1943, T312/903/9082751.

95. GS, 1st Section, 26 March Battalion, Hof, 9 September 1943, DEV 28/17/12/5, p. 27; 269, Order 620, 5 October 1943, DEV 28/18/9/1, p. 55; 269, Order 614, 29 September 1943, DEV 28/17/11/1, p. 54.

96. 269, Cano Report, 5 October 1943, DEV 29/38/11/1, pp. 9–10; GS, 3d Section, Daily Report, 5 October 1943, DEV 29/42/17/1, pp. 9–10; *Hoja de Campaña*, 31 October 1943, p. 1; GS, 2d Section, Daily Intelligence Report, 5 October 1943, DEV 28/31/14/1, p. 8; Díaz de Villegas, *Línea*, p. 230.

97. Esteban Infantes, *Azul*, pp. 229–30.

98. GS, 3d Section, Order of Operations 5, 9 October 1943, DEV 29/42/17/1, p. 19.

99. *Hoja de Campaña*, 7 October 1943, p. 1; Esteban Infantes, *Azul*, pp. 231–32; Personal communication of the authors with Lt. Col. Konrad Zeller, Ret., president, Veterans Association of 215 Division, 20 May 1976.

100. L Corps, Visits, 13 October 1943, T314/1244/237; AOK 18, Lindemann-Esteban Infantes Conversation, 13 October 1943, T314/920/9104003; KTB, 18 Army, 13 October 1943, T314/903/9082901–15.

101. GS, 3d Section, DGO, 17 October 1943, DEV 28/18/9/1, p. 11.

102. 263, Orders, 17 October 1943, DEV 28/18/15/1, p. 1; GS, 1st Section, 8–9 March Battalions, 25, 27 October 1943, DEV 28/18/15/1, pp.

14, 16; GS, 1st Section, Legion Recruitment, 22 October 1943, DEV 28/ 18/15/2, pp. 20–21; Sappers 250, Report on Volunteers, 29 October 1943, DEV 28/18/15/2, p. 22; OKW Report, 15 October 1943, T77/885/ 5634775.

103. Hoare to FO, 1858, 27 October 1943, PRO, FO 371/34814/ 8060, p. 57; also Serrano Suñer interviews, December 1971 and June 1974.

104. Hoare to FO, 1805, 16 October 1943, PRO, FO 371/34814/ 8060, p. 36.

105. Abwehr, Schuchardt Report, Berlin, 1 November 1943, T77/885/ 5634766; OKH, Attaché Section, 3 November 1943, T77/885/5634765; Yencken to FO, 1714, 4 October 1943, PRO, FO 371/34814/8060, pp. 6–9.

106. GS, 3d Section, Report, 2 November 1943, DEV 28/18/5/2, p. 14.

107. Díaz de Villegas, Línea, pp. 106–9.

108. Hoare to FO, 1858, 27 October 1943, PRO, FO 371/34814/ 8060, p. 57; Yencken to Eden, 566, 28 October 1943, PRO, FO 371/ 34814/8010, p. 59; Díaz de Villegas, Línea, pp. 108–9; Esteban Infantes, Azul, p. 242.

109. Bürkner Memorandum, 6 November 1943, T77/885/563754; Esteban Infantes, Azul, pp. 243, 247; Esteban Infantes telephone conversation, Monitor Report, 7 November 1943, T77/885/56472.

110. Esteban Infantes, Azul, p. 250.

111. Ibid.

112. Ibid., pp. 248–51.

113. Ibid.; GS, 2d Section, DGO, 8 November 1943, DEV 28/18/15/2, p. 18.

114. Hayes to Hull, Madrid, 22 October 1943, USNA, State, 852.20/ 203, pp. 1–3; Hayes to Hull, Madrid, 9 November 1943, USNA, State, 852.20/205, p. 1; Hayes to Hull, Madrid, 852.20/207, p. 1.

115. GS, DGO 69, 17 November 1943, DEV 28/18/5/2, p. 30; Nord, Legion TO&E, 20 November 1943, T311/72/7093872; Esteban Infantes, Azul, pp. 252–54.

116. KTB, 18 Army, 29 November 1943, T314/903/9083443; KTB, 18 Army, 5 January 1943, T312/928/9112451.

117. Military Attaché to Army Chief of Staff, Telegram 813, Berlin, 19 November 1943, DEV 29/53/11, p. 16.

118. GS, Order to Concentrate Division, 6 December 1943, DEV 29/ 43/5/4, pp. 50–51; Haupt, Nord, p. 16; Walter Görlitz, Model: Strategie der Defensive (Wiesbaden: Limes, 1975), pp. 161–63; KTB, Nord, 21 January 1944, T311/58/7072233; Díaz de Villegas, Línea, pp. 108–9, 155–56, 232–33.

119. Hayes to Hull, Telegram, Madrid, 21 December 1943, USNA, State 852.20/213.

120. Dieckhoff to AA, Madrid, 30 December 1943, T77/885/5634745– 46; Air Attaché to Abwehr, Madrid, 2 January 1944, T77/885/5634744; Informaciones, 20 December 1943, p. 8.

121. *Informaciones*, 22, 23 November 1943, pp. 1, 8.

122. Ibid., 20 December 1943, pp. 1, 3.

123. Hayes to Hull, 1929, Report of 12 January 1944, Madrid, 21 January 1944, USNA, State, 852.00/10935, p. 3.

124. GS, Legión Española de Voluntarios (LEV), 27 November 1943, DEV 28/18/5/2, p. 33; DOPS, II *Bandera*, November 1943, DEV 29/13/1/2, p. 11.

125. OKH, Attaché Section, 27 November 1943, T77/885/5634751; OKH, Legion Formation, 21 December 1943, T311/72/7093875-78; AOK 18, Report on LEV, 5 January 1944, T311/72/7093882-83; Hoare to FO, Recruiting for Blue Division, 361, Madrid, 13 August 1943, PRO, FO 371/34813/8096, p. 96; Babbitt to M.I.D.W.G.S., Recruiting for Blue Division, 6610, Tangier, 30 August 1943, USNA, 340/MID/322.13, pp. 1-3; J. Rives Childs to Hull, 3724, Tangier, 6 October 1943, USNA, State 852.20/201, pp. 1-2.

126. AOK 18, Report to LEV, 5 January 1944, T311/72/7093882-83.

127. LEV, Report to Chief of Staff, Spain, 10 January 1944, DEV 28/21/4/2, pp. 2-31.

128. Haxel interview, 1974.

129. Salisbury, *900 Days*, pp. 560-68; Seaton, *Russo-German War*, pp. 408-11; Liddell-Hart, *Second World War*, pp. 576-77; Haupt, *Nord*, pp. 177-82; KTB, Nord, 15-20 January 1944, T311/58/7071907-2223; KTB, 18 Army, 15-20 January 1944, T312/928/9112601-827.

130. KTB, XXVI Corps, 1-2 February 1944, T314/763/449-55.

131. Haxel to XXVI Corps, 1 February 1944, T314/763/783-84; LEV, Report to Chief of Staff, Spain, 14 February 1944, DEV 29/43/6/1, pp. 1-9; Esteban Infantes, *Azul*, pp. 258-65.

132. Görlitz, *Model*, pp. 161-68; AOK 18 to Nord, 29 January 1944, T311/72/7093893.

133. Haxel interview, June 1974.

134. Dieckhoff to AA, Madrid, 11 February 1944, T120/86/102418-22; Doussinague, *España*, pp. 290, 301-8.

135. Harriman to Hull, Moscow, 6 January 1944, USNA, State, 852.20/214, p. 2.

136. Model to OKH, 5 March 1944, T311/72/7093903; Zeitzler to Nord, 8 March 1944, T311/72/7093904; OKH to Op, 26 February 1944, T77/885/5634693; Keitel to AA, 21 February 1944, T77/885/5634699; AA to Dieckhoff, Berlin, 26 February 1944, T77/885/5634697.

137. DOPS, II *Bandera*, March 1944, DEV 29/43/6/4, p. 32; DOPS, 2 Company, I *Bandera*, March 1944, 29/43/6/2, p. 14; DOPS, 1 Company, I *Bandera*, March 1944, DEV 29/43/6/3, p. 22; LEV, GO 547, 5 March 1944, DEV 28/21/8/1, p. 8.

138. García Navarro Speech, Haxel to von Küchler, 16 March 1944, T311/99/7130843-47.

CHAPTER 12. *Tattoo*

1. Albert P. Ebright to M.I.D.W.G.S., Report 8973, 13 April 1944, USNA, State, 475 MID 322.13.

2. Hayes to Hull, Telegram, 27 January 1944, USNA, State, 852.20/218.

3. Interview of the authors with Capt. Karl Taegert, Ret., Hamburg, June 1974; Rotfelder Memorandum, 16 December 1944, T77/885/634561; SD, Schellenberg Report, 2 June 1944, T77/885/5634585–606; Sonderstab F, 5 August 1944, T77/885/563485–86.

4. Miguel Ezquerra Sánchez, *Lutei até ao fim* (Lisbon: Astória, 1947), pp. 255–81; Moisés Puente, *Yo, muerto en Rusia: Memorias del Alférez Ocañas* (Madrid: Ed. del Movimiento, 1954), pp. 21–25; George H. Stein, *The Waffen-SS* (Ithaca, N.Y.: Cornell University Press, 1966), p. 246.

5. Díaz de Villegas, *Línea*, p. 193; Esteban Infantes, *Azul*, pp. 300–301.

6. Esteban Infantes, *Azul*, pp. 300–301.

7. *Informaciones*, 27 April 1944, p. 10.

SELECTED BIBLIOGRAPHY

Unpublished Documents

SPAIN:
Estado Mayor Central del Ejército, Servicio Histórico Militar, Madrid. *Archivo de la Guerra de Liberación, División Española de Voluntarios. División Azul*, Armario 28, Legajos 1–58.

GERMANY:
United States National Archives Collection of Captured German Records: Microcopies T-77, T-78, T-120, T-311, T-312, T-314, T-315, containing documents of the German Foreign Ministry, the German Embassy in Madrid, German security and intelligence services, OKW (Armed Forces High Command), OKH (Army High Command), Army Group North, 16th and 18th Armies, Group von Roques, I, XXVI, XXVIII, XXXVIII, XXXIX, L, and LIV Army Corps, 18 Motorized, 81, 126, 170, 215, and 250 Divisions, the German Liaison Staff with 250 Division, and numerous other units.
Political Archives of Foreign Ministry Archives of the Federal Republic of Germany. Bonn: Documents of German Embassy, Madrid.
Bundesarchiv-Militärarchiv. Freiburg: Biographical, organizational, technical material.

GREAT BRITAIN:
Public Record Office. London: Records of British Embassy, Madrid, Military Intelligence, the Foreign Office.

UNITED STATES:
United States National Archives. Washington, D.C.: Records of United States Embassy, Madrid, Military Intelligence, Department of State.
Mueller-Hillebrand, Burkhart. *Der Feldzug gegen die Sowjetunion im Nordabschnitt der Ostfront 1941–1945.* Historical Division, Headquarters, United States Army Europe, USNA, MS No. P-114m, 1954.

Published Documents

Arrese, José Luis de. *Escritos y discursos.* Madrid: Vicesecretaría de Educación Popular, 1943.

405

Ciano, Galeazzo. *Ciano Diaries.* Ed. H. Gibson. New York: Doubleday, 1946.

———. *Ciano's Diplomatic Papers.* Trans. Stuart Wood, ed. Malcolm Muggeridge. London: Odhams, 1948.

Díaz Plaja, Fernando, ed. *La posguerra española en sus documentos.* Barcelona: Plaza & Janés, 1970.

Documents on German Foreign Policy 1918–1945. Series D, Vol. 13. Washington, D.C.: Department of State, 1964.

Domarus, Max, ed. *Hitler: Reden 1932 bis 1945.* 4 vols. Munich: Süddeutscher Verlag, 1965.

Estado Mayor Central del Ejército, Servicio Historico Militar. *Galeria Militar, Medalla Militar, 1933–1969.* Madrid, 1970.

Goebbels, Joseph. *The Goebbels Diaries.* Trans. and ed. Louis P. Lochner. London: Hamish Hamilton, 1948.

Greiner, Helmuth and Percy Ernst Schramm, eds. *Kriegstagebuch des Oberkommandos der Wehrmacht.* 4 vols. in 7. Frankfurt: Bernard & Graefe, 1961–65.

Handbook on German Military Forces, TM-E-451. Washington, D.C.: War Department, 1945.

Heiber, Helmut, ed. *Hitlers Lagebesprechungen: Die Protokollfragmente seine militärischen Konferenzen 1942–1945.* Stuttgart: Deutsche Verlags-Anstalt, 1962.

Hillgruber, Andreas, ed. *Staatsmänner und Diplomaten bei Hitler.* 2 vols. Frankfurt: Bernard & Graefe, 1970.

Hitler, Adolf. *Hitler's Secret Conversations, 1941–1944.* Trans. Norman Cameron and R. H. Stevens. New York: New American Library, Signet. 1961.

Jacobsen, Hans-Adolf, ed. *Generaloberst Halder: Kriegstagebuch.* 3 vols. Stuttgart: W. Kohlhammer, 1962–64.

Trevor-Roper, H. R., ed. *Hitler's War Directives.* London: Sidgwick and Jackson, 1964.

Memoirs

Abshagen, Karl Heinz. *Canaris.* Trans. Alan Houghton Brodrick. London: Hutchinson, 1956.
Personal biography by one of Canaris's associates, reveals the admiral's partiality for Spain and indicates his efforts to keep Iberia out of the war. Little specifically on the Blue Division.
Alvarez Esteban, José. *Agonia de Europa.* Madrid, 1947.
An observant and sensitive account of Germany, Austria and occupied France after the German defeats at Stalingrad and Kursk which portrays the feeling of impending doom as the Red Army advanced in 1943 and 1944.
Beaulac, Willard L. *Career Ambassador.* New York: Macmillan, 1951.
A restrained memoir by the counselor of the United States Embassy in

Madrid. Serving under two ambassadors, Beaulac, since he spoke fluent Spanish and was a Foreign Service officer, often was more informed than his superiors. But though he knows, he doesn't tell. Useful for background.

Blanco, Juan Eugenio. *Rusia no es cuestión de un día*. Madrid: Publicaciones Españolas, 1954.
A series of vivid vignettes by a volunteer who served in 2 Company of Divisional Antitanks from June 1941 until late 1942. Since many students, intellectuals, and Falangist leaders served in this unit, it gives an intimate, if somewhat favorable, view of their activities.

Díaz de Villegas, José. *La División Azul en línea*. Barcelona: Ed. Acervo, 1967.
Written by an educated and observant general staff officer with a rare sense of humor. This book, though overloaded with statistics, presents an intimate view of the static front before Leningrad from April to December 1943. Trusted even by Franco, Villegas presided over the dismantling of the division as chief of staff.

Doussinague, José M. *España tenía razón*. Madrid: Espasa-Calpe, 1949.
The author served a chief of the Technical Cabinet of the Foreign Office under both Serrano Suñer and Count Jordana. Since Doussinague was a professional diplomat he couches his narrative in cryptic terms. Unless the reader is familiar with the personalities and events as well as the relevant archival material this work can be misleading.

Eizaguirre, Ramón P. *El abismo rojo*. Madrid: n.p., 1955.
Primarily a relation of the author's years as a Soviet POW, this work is enlightening in that it gives one *guripa*'s view of the battle of Krasni Bor, 10 February 1943.

Errando Vilar, Enrique. *Campaña de invierno*. Madrid: Rehyma, 1943.
Covers the period from 12 October 1941 to 22 April 1942 when the writer returned to Madrid. Flashbacks piece together the months of recruitment, training, and the long march to the front. As an officer in charge of a motorized ambulance section Errando Vilar traveled constantly behind the front. As a medical officer he was welcomed by the regulars and as an ardent Falangist by the students, intellectuals, and political leaders. An encompassing intriguing memoir.

Esteban Infantes, Emilio. *La División Azul*. Barcelona: Ed. AHR, 1956.
A self-serving autobiographical account by the second commander of the Blue Division which reveals perhaps more than the author intended. He tends to supress parts of the Krasni Bor battle while magnifying later local actions. His statistics are basically sound and based on documentation and personal observation. Moreover, his encounters with Hitler and other high Nazi officials are frank, detailed, and personal.

Ezquerra Sánchez, Miguel. *Lutei até ao fim*. Lisbon: Astória, 1947.
Too controversial to be published in post–World War II Spain since Franco was seeking rehabilitation with the victorious Allies this detailed story by one of the diehards was brought out in Portugal. Ezquerra Sánchez served first as an officer in the Blue Division and later as a

Special Forces operator in France against the British and Americans. He commanded the Spanish SS units defending the Chancellery in Berlin in April and May 1945.

Fediuninskii, I. A. *Podniatye po trevoge*, 2d rev. ed. Moscow: Voennoe izd-vo Min-va Oborony SSR, 1964.
Military memoirs of the Volkhov, Volkhovstroi, and Leningrad campaign with important assessments of Army Group North.

Foltz, Charles. *Masquerade in Spain*. New York: Houghton Mifflin, 1948.
An inside, anti-Franco work written by a press officer in the United States Embassy during World War II. Foltz is not always accurate, but he is gifted with keen insight and has a journalist's ear for interesting gossip, rumor, and character.

García Luna, José. *Las cartas del sargento Basilio*. Barcelona: Ed. Pentágono, 1959.
A collection of letters from the front dating from 1942 and 1943. Not a combat diary, but more a reflection of rear area views, relations with Russian civilians and German comrades.

Gómez Tello, J. L. *Canción del invierno en el este*. Barcelona: Caralt, 1945.
A series of scenes ranging through France, Germany, Poland, Latvia, Estonia, and Russia running from August 1941 to October 1942. The author has a clear eye for detail, and his descriptions are colorful and absorbing. As a radio operator Gómez Tello came into contact with the higher echelons of the divisional command and was able to form his own appreciation of the officers and the combat situation.

Hayes, Carleton J. H. *Wartime Mission in Spain, 1942–1945*. New York: Macmillan, 1946.
A personal account of the author's ambassadorship from May 1942 to January 1945. Touching only incidentally on Spanish internal affairs, the author focuses on United States-Spanish relations and the Allied effort to woo Franco from the Axis. Details his efforts to get the Blue Division withdrawn.

Hoare, Sir Samuel, Viscount Templewood. *Ambassador on Special Mission*. London: Collins, 1946.
———. *Complacent Dictator*. New York: Knopf, 1947.
These two works are essentially the same. Written immediately after the cessation of hostilities when the author still had hopes for continuing his political career and in an effort to prove antifascist credentials after being associated with the appeasement policies of the 1930s as a cabinet minister in various posts from 1931 to 1940, these memoirs are somewhat less than reliable. Nevertheless, since Hoare served as British ambassador from May 1940 to August 1944 and had numerous visits with leading personalities, the presentation has some value.

Hughes, Emmet J. *Report from Spain*. New York: Henry Holt, 1947.
Written by the United States press attaché in Madrid from August 1942 to May 1946, this memoir was one of the many anti-Franco tracts which

appeared immediately after World War II. Although slanted and often inaccurate this work does provide insights into both American and Spanish attitudes.

Jiménez y Malo de Molina, Victor José. *De España a Rusia*. Madrid: Imp. de Madrid, 1943.
Essentially a diary of the raising, training, and marching of the Blue Division from June 24 to October 12, 1941. Since the author was the interpreter of Second Artillery Group and served as liaison and billeting officer he traveled more extensively than most volunteers and had more contact with senior commanders. Certainly one of the most romantic and tragic stories of the campaign.

Kemp, Peter. *Mine Were of Trouble*. London: Cassell, 1957.
Recollections by a British volunteer who fought with the Nationalist forces as a legionnaire during the Spanish Civil War. Twice wounded, the author served under Muñoz Grandes and had the opportunity to observe the general firsthand. Breveted a lieutenant, he had a lengthy interview with Franco after recovering from a near-fatal wound.

Luca de Tena, Torcuato. *Embajador en el infierno: Memorias del capitán Palacios*. Barcelona: Planeta, 1955.
An excellent account by 5 Company's commander of the battle of Krasni Bor. While the initial chapters are sound, much of the material relating to the pirsoner of war years is colored by the imagination of the co-author.

Mannerheim, Carl Gustav. *The Memoirs of Marshal Mannerheim*, Trans. Eric Lewenhaupt. New York: Dutton, 1954.
Revealing autobiography of the Finnish patriot who refused to threaten Leningrad. No mention of the Blue Division, but useful for descriptions of cooperation with Army Group North and assessment of Russians.

Manstein, Erich von. *Lost Victories*. Trans. and ed. Anthony G. Powell. Chicago: Henry Regnery, 1958.
Abridged version of his autobiography. Descriptive of the field marshal's views concerning Operation Northern Light, the Soviet attempts to break the siege in 1942, and the condition of Army Group North and its opposing forces.

Martínez Esparza, José. *Con la División Azul en Rusia*. Madrid: Ed. Ejército, 1943.
A detailed, day-to-day record from June 1941 to January 1942 by the colonel commanding the 269 Infantry Regiment. As a trained, observant combat leader who at one time had over half the division under his orders this memoir is of particular importance. Moreover, Esparza knew his officers from previous campaigns and was close to Muñoz Grandes. Thus, his comments and criticisms are particularly valuable.

Meretskov, Kiril A. *Na sluzhbe narodu*. Moscow: Izd-vo polit. lit.-ry, 1970.
Memoir of the Soviet commander revealing the independence of thought which lost him favor.

Negro Castro, Juan. *Españoles en la U.R.S.S.* Madrid: Escelicer, 1959.

A story of the Krasni Bor battle and his subsequent captivity by a *guripa* in 1 Company of 262 Regiment. Provides the GI's limited but intimate view of combat, which in European armies is sometimes difficult to find.

Oroquieta Arbiol, Gerardo. *De Leningrado a Odesa.* Barcelona: Ed. AHR, n.d.

As a member of one of the first march battalions this young legionnaire lieutenant arrived in the summer of 1942 and served on the Volkhov as a captain. He commanded 3 Company of Mobile Reserve 250 at Krasni Bor. Captured, he spent the next eleven years in Soviet captivity. Another company-level account which cross-checks with the documents.

Pavlov, Dimitri. *Leningrad 1941: The Blockade, Trans.* J. C. Adams. Chicago: University of Chicago Press, 1965.

Slim Russian survey of the siege. Useful for variety of details.

Plenn, Abel. *Wind in the Olive Trees.* New York: Boni and Gaer, 1946.

Arriving late in 1944 as the United States Embassy's chief of propaganda analysis, the author has little to offer about the Blue Division except gossip and rumor, mostly uninformed and inaccurate.

Puente, Moisés. *Yo muerto en Rusia: Memorias del Alférez Ocañas.* Madrid: Ed. del Movimiento, 1954.

Dwells mostly on the prisoner of war years and, hence, of limited value.

Ramos, Fernando. *División Azul. Temas Españoles,* no. 25. Madrid: Publicaciones Españolas, 1953.

A series of short snapshots of behind the line scenes and front actions. Excellent in that it portrays a collage both critical and complementary.

Reginato, Enrique. *Operacion Tifus.* Madrid: Ed. Taurus, n.d.

An Italian medical officer's story of his captivity in the Soviet Union. Useful as a cross-check on Spanish POW accounts and for gaining another impression of the Spanish officers captured at Krasni Bor.

Ridruejo, Dionisio. *En once años: Poesias completas de juventud.* Madrid: Ed. Nacional, 1950.

A collection of poems written when the author was still an ardent Falangist and the poet of the movement. Useful because they display the romanticism and youthful fervor of the intellectual wing of Spanish fascism. As a volunteer this poet while writing of the courage of his comrades on the Volkhov also became disillusioned with both the crusade and the manipulation of the movement by Franco.

Riudavets de Montes, Luis. *Estampas de la vieja Rusia.* Madrid, 1960.

A memoir by a keen and sensitive member of the First Division which concentrates mostly on behind the front scenes, relations with civilians, and the moral destruction wrought on the Russian people by the Stalin regime.

Ruíz Ayucar, Angel. *La Rusia que conocí.* Madrid: Ed. del Movimiento, 1954.

Commander of a machine gun section of 263 Regiment from the forming of the unit until early 1942 this officer concentrates on the human dimension—the suffering and heroism of both his own men and the Russian soldiers and civilians. A keen and thoughtful observer, he sensed, perhaps with some hindsight, the colossal drama of the Eastern Front.

Serrano Suñer, Ramón. *Entre el silencio y la propoganda, la historia como fue: Memorias.* Barcelona: Ed. Planeta, 1977.
A post-Franco publication dealing primarily with the Civil War, Franco's seizure of power, Hendaya, and the co-opting of the Falange by the Caudillo. Little on the Blue Division.

———. *Entre Hendaya y Gibraltar.* Madrid: Ediciones y Publicaciones Españolas, 1947.
Dismissed upon publication by many as an apologia, this work, though certainly self-serving and cryptic on many points, is increasingly substantiated by documentation. The author is more guilty of omission than commission. His main point that he was a nationalist first and a fascist second when it came to what he believed his country's best interest is most probably correct.

———. *Entre Hendaya y Gibraltar.* Rev. ed. Barcelona: Ed. Nauta, 1973.
Although this revised edition is adorned with photographs and explanatory notes the text remains essentially the same. The notes, while couched in smooth, restrained tones, pointedly indicate the clash between Muñoz Grandes and the foreign minister who raised and dispatched the Blue Division to Russia. Also evident is Serrano Suñer's poor opinion of his successor, Count Jordana. All in all a very personal document.

Warlimont, Walter. *Inside Hitler's Headquarters, 1939–1945.* Trans. R. H. Barry. New York: Praeger, 1964.
Formidable memoir with relatively little material about Army Group North.

Zhukov, G. *The Memoirs of Marshal Zhukov.* Trans. A. P. N. New York: Delacorte, 1971.
Stalin's great commander uses a broad sweep to describe his exploits.

Books

Bialer, Seweryn, ed. *Stalin and His Generals.* New York: Pegasus, 1969.
Brissaud, Andre. *Canaris: la guerra española y la II guerra mundial,* 2d ed. Barcelona: Ed Nóguer, 1972.
Burdick, Charles B. *Germany's Military Strategy in Spain During World War II.* Syracuse: Syracuse University Press, 1968.
Buxa, Werner. *Weg und Schicksal der 11. Infanterie-Division.* Bad Nauheim: Podzun, 1963.
Caidin, Martin. *The Tigers Are Burning.* New York: Hawthorn, 1974.
Carell, Paul. *Hitler Moves East.* Trans. Evald Osers. Boston: Little, Brown, 1964.
———. *Scorched Earth.* London: Harrap, 1970.
Chaney, Otto P., Jr. *Zhukov.* Norman: University of Oklahoma Press, 1971.

Cordero Torres, José María. *Relaciones exteriores de España.* Madrid: Ed. del Movimiento, 1954.

Dankelmann, Otfried. *Franco zwischen Hitler und den Westmächten.* Berlin: VEB Deutscher Verlag der Wissenschaften, 1970.

Detwiler, Donald S. *Hitler, Franco und Gibraltar.* Wiesbaden: Franz Steiner, 1962.

Doyle, William L., Jr. "El Cuñadísimo: A Political Biography of Serrano Suñer." Master's thesis, Creighton University, 1967.

En once años: 1935–1945. Madrid: Ed. Nacional, 1950.

Erickson, John. *The Road to Stalingrad.* New York: Harper & Row, 1975.

Feis, Herbert. *Churchill, Roosevelt, Stalin.* Princeton: Princeton University Press, 1957.

———. *The Spanish Story.* New York: Norton, 1966.

García Pérez, A. *Héroes de España en campos de Rusia, 1941–1942.* Madrid: Camarasa, 1942.

Geschichte des Grossen Vaterländischen Krieges der Sowjetunion. 6 vols. Berlin: Deutscher Militärverlag, 1964.

González, Sancho. *Diez años de historia difícil: Indice de la neutralidad de España.* Madrid: Graficas Espejo, 1947.

Görlitz, Walter. *Model: Strategie der Defensive.* Wiesbaden: Limes, 1975.

Gouré, Leon. *The Siege of Leningrad.* Stanford: Stanford University Press, 1962.

Great Britain, Naval Intelligence Division. *Spain & Portugal.* Vol. 3, *Spain.* Oxford: Prepared by the Oxford Sub Centre, 1941–45.

Hamilton, Thomas J. *Appeasement's Child: The Franco Regime in Spain.* New York: Knopf, 1943.

Haupt, Werner. *Heeresgruppe Nord: 1941–1945.* Bad Nauheim: Podzun, 1966.

Hayes, Carleton J. H. *The United States and Spain.* New York: Sheed and Ward, 1951.

Hillgruber, Andreas. *Hitler's Strategie: Politik und Kriegführung, 1940–1941.* Frankfurt: Bernard & Graefe, 1965.

Hills, George. *Franco.* New York: Macmillan, 1967.

Hodgson, Robert. *Spain Resurgent.* London, 1953.

Husemann, Friedrich. *Die guten Glaubens waren: Geschichte der SS-Polizei-Division.* 2 vols. Osnabrück: Munin, 1971.

Kreidler, Eugen. *Die Eisenbahnen im Machtbereich der Achsenmächte während des Zweiten Weltkrieges.* Frankfurt: Musterschmidt, 1975.

Leverkuehn, Paul. *German Military Intelligence.* Trans. R. H. Stevens and Constantine Fitzgibbon. London: Weidenfeld and Nicolson, 1954.

Liddell-Hart, B. H. *History of the Second World War.* New York: Putnam, 1970.

Lohse, Gerhart. *Geschichte der rheinisch-westphälischen 126. Infanterie-Division, 1940–1945.* Bad Nauheim: Podzun, 1957.

Loveday, Arthur. *Spain: 1923–1948.* London, 1939.

Lukacs, John. *The Last European War: September 1939–December 1941.* Garden City, New York: Doubleday, Anchor, 1976.

Marinas, Francisco J. *General Varela*. Barcelona: Ed. AHR, 1956.

Martínez Friera, J. *Las batallas de España en el mundo*. Madrid: Ed. Gran Capitán, 1950.

Matthews, Herbert. *The Yoke and the Arrows: A Report on Spain*, rev. ed. New York: George Braziller, 1961.

Mirandet, François. *L'Espagne de Franco*. Paris: Hachette, 1948.

Payne, Stanley G. *Falange: A History of Spanish Fascism*. Stanford: Stanford University Press, 1961.

————. *Politics and the Military in Modern Spain*. Stanford: Stanford University Press, 1967.

Philippi, Alfred, and Ferdinand Heim. *Der Feldzug gegen Sowjetrussland, 1941–1945*. Stuttgart: W. Kohlhammer, 1962.

Plievier, Theodore. *Stalingrad*. Trans. Richard and Clara Winston. New York: Berkeley Medallion Editions, 1964.

Plocher, Hermann. *The German Air Force versus Russia, 1941*. New York: Arno, 1965.

Pohlmann, Hartwig. *Wolchow: 900 Tage Kampf um Leningrad, 1941–1944*. Bad Nauheim: Podzun, 1962.

Prego, Adolfo. *Héroes Españoles en Rusia*. Temas Españolas, no. 85. Madrid: Publicaciones Españolas, 1954.

Proctor, Raymond L. *Agony of a Neutral: La División Azul*. Moscow: Idaho Research Foundation, 1974.

Puzzo, Dante A. *Spain and the Great Powers*. New York: Columbia University Press, 1962.

Roig, Pedro V. *Spanish Soldiers in Russia*. Miami: Ediciones Universal, 1976.

Salisbury, Harrison E. *The 900 Days: The Siege of Leningrad*. New York: Harper & Row, 1969.

Schelm, Walter, and Dr. Hans Mehrle. *Erinnerungsbuch—Von den Kämpfen der 215. württembergisch-badischen Infanterie-Division*. N.p.: Traditionsverband, n.d.

Seaton, Albert. *The Russo-German War, 1941–1945*. London: Arthur Barker, 1971.

————. *Stalin as Military Commander*. New York: Praeger, 1976.

Skomorovsky, Boris, and E. G. Morris. *The Siege of Leningrad*. New York: Books, Inc., 1944.

Steenberg, Sven. *Vlasov*. New York: Knopf, 1970.

Stevenson, William. *A Man Called Intrepid*. New York: Harcourt Brace Jovanovich, 1976.

Vagts, Alfred. *Hitler's Second Army*. Washington: Infantry Journal–Penguin Books, 1943.

Vicesecretaría de Educación Popular. *Ier Cuaderno, Division Azul*. Madrid, 1942.

Wegner, Carl. *Moskau 1941*. Bad Nauheim: Podzun, 1966.

Zhilin, P. A., ed. *Vazhneishie operatsii Velikoi Otechestvennoi voiny, 1941–1945*. Moscow: Voennoe izd-vo Ministerstva Oborony Soiuza SSR, 1956.

Zimmermann, Erich, and Hans-Adolf Jacobsen. *Germans Against Hitler*, Third Edition. Bonn: Press and Information Office, 1969.

Articles

Dankelmann, Otfried. "Zur Spanischen "Nichtkriegführung" im Zweiten Weltkrieg." *Zeitschrift für Militärgeschichte* 9, no. 6 (1970): 683–92.

Detwiler, Donald S. "Spain and the Axis During World War II." *Review of Politics* 33, no. 1 (1971): 36–53.

Filippov, Boris. "An Old Country Estate." *Novoe Russkoe Slovo*, 30 March 1975, p. 7.

Galey, John H. "Bridegrooms of Death: A Profile Study of the Spanish Foreign Legion." *Journal of Contemporary History* 4, no. 2 (April 1969): 47–64.

Halstead, Charles R. "Historians in Politics: Carleton J. Hayes as American Ambassador to Spain, 1942–45." *Journal of Contemporary History* 10, no. 4 (July 1975): 383–405.

Haupt, Werner. "Blaue Division am Ilmensee." *Soldatengeschichten Nr. 99.* Munich: Moewig, 1959.

Hillgruber, Andreas. "Nordlicht—Die deutschen Pläne zur Eroberung Leningrads im Jahre 1942." In Peter Classen, ed., *Festschrift Percy Ernst Schramm zu seinem siebzigsten Geburtstag von Schülern und Freunden Gewidmet*, vol. 2, pp. 269–87. Wiesbaden: S. Steiner, 1964.

Kleinfeld, Gerald R., and Lewis A. Tambs. "North to Russia: The Spanish Blue Division in World War II." *Military Affairs* 37, no. 1 (February 1973): 8–13.

———. "The Spanish Blue Division in Russia." *History Today* (London) 27, no. 8 (August 1977): 520–25, 551.

Krammer, Arnold. "Spanish Volunteers Against Bolshevism: The Blue Division." *The Russian Review* 32, no. 4 (October 1973): 388–401.

"La Guardia Civil en la División Azul." *Revista de Estudios Historicos de la Guardia Civil* 3, no. 6 (1970): 23–36.

Meretskov, K. A. "Dorogami Srazhenii." *Voprosy Istorii* 10 (1965): 107–18.

———. "Na Volkhovskikh rubezakh." *Voenno-istoricheskii zhurnal* 1 (1965): 54–70.

———. "V Boiakh pod Leningradom," *Voprosy istorii* 3 (March 1968): 118–29.

Miller, Jesse W., Jr. "Forest Fighting on the Eastern Front in World War II." *Geographical Review* 62 (April 1972): 186–202.

O'Balance, Edgar. "The Spanish Blue Division in the Second World War." *The Royal United Service Institution Journal* 109, no. 635 (August 1964): 240–45.

Pozharskaia, S. P. "Golubaia divizia," *Voprosy istorii* 8 (1969): 107–26.

Shikin, I. V., and I. Ia. Fomichenko. [A historic triumph.] *Voprosy istorii* 1 (January 1973): 108–24.

Vadillo, Fernando. "Así fue la campaña de la División Azul." *La Actualidad Española* (Madrid) 21, no. 1105 (8 March 1973): 169–77.

"Wenn ihr einmarschiert, schiessen wir." *Der Spiegel* 17/18 (1 May 1963): 71–80.

Newspapers

Hoja de Campaña (Riga-Reval)
Informaciones (Madrid)
Neue Zürcher Zeitung (Zürich)
The New York Times (New York)
Völkischer Beobachter (Berlin)

Most worthy of mention in addition to the works cited above are the realistic novels of Tomás Salvador, *División 250* (Barcelona: Ed. Destino, 1954), and Fernando Vadillo, *Orillas del Voljov, Arrabales de Leningrado*, and *Y lucharon en Krasny Bor* (Barcelona: Ed. Marte, 1967, 1971 and 1975). Both of the authors served in the Blue Division and have incorporated their own observations, as well as other testimonies, diaries, and records into their accounts.

INDEX